# International Series in Operations Research & Management Science

Volume 313

The book series *International Series in Operations Research and Management Science* encompasses the various areas of operations research and management science. Both theoretical and applied books are included. It describes current advances anywhere in the world that are at the cutting edge of the field. The series is aimed especially at researchers, doctoral students, and sophisticated practitioners.

The series features three types of books:

- *Advanced expository books* that extend and unify our understanding of particular areas.
- *Research monographs* that make substantial contributions to knowledge.
- *Handbooks* that define the new state of the art in particular areas. They will be entitled *Recent Advances in (name of the area)*. Each handbook will be edited by a leading authority in the area who will organize a team of experts on various aspects of the topic to write individual chapters. A handbook may emphasize expository surveys or completely new advances (either research or applications) or a combination of both.

The series emphasizes the following four areas:

*Mathematical Programming:* Including linear programming, integer programming, nonlinear programming, interior point methods, game theory, network optimization models, combinatorics, equilibrium programming, complementarity theory, multiobjective optimization, dynamic programming, stochastic programming, complexity theory, etc.

*Applied Probability:* Including queuing theory, simulation, renewal theory, Brownian motion and diffusion processes, decision analysis, Markov decision processes, reliability theory, forecasting, other stochastic processes motivated by applications, etc.

*Production and Operations Management:* Including inventory theory, production scheduling, capacity planning, facility location, supply chain management, distribution systems, materials requirements planning, just-in-time systems, flexible manufacturing systems, design of production lines, logistical planning, strategic issues, etc.

*Applications of Operations Research and Management Science:* Including telecommunications, health care, capital budgeting and finance, marketing, public policy, military operations research, service operations, transportation systems, etc.

More information about this series at http://www.springer.com/series/6161

Xu Andy Sun • Antonio J. Conejo

# Robust Optimization in Electric Energy Systems

Springer

Xu Andy Sun
Operations Research and Statistics
Sloan School of Management
Massachusetts Institute of Technology
Cambridge, MA, USA

Antonio J. Conejo
Department of Integrated Systems Engineering
The Ohio State University
Columbus, OH, USA

ISSN 0884-8289 ISSN 2214-7934 (electronic)
International Series in Operations Research & Management Science
ISBN 978-3-030-85127-9 ISBN 978-3-030-85128-6 (eBook)
https://doi.org/10.1007/978-3-030-85128-6



This Springer imprint is published by the registered company Springer Nature Switzerland AG
The registered company address is: Gewerbestrasse 11, 6330 Cham, Switzerland

# Preface

Robust optimization (RO) has been increasingly applied to address electric power system problems in the past decade. Applications range from real-time operation and day-ahead unit commitment to maintenance and long-term transmission and generation expansion planning. As the electric power system undergoes fundamental changes and different energy systems become increasingly interdependent, robust optimization provides an appealing framework for ensuring that these systems remain reliable and resilient.

Most results in RO are only available in the form of research articles. Moreover, the methodology of RO is still, to a large degree, only taught in advanced courses in operations research, applied mathematics, or related fields. Existing book-length treatments of RO, although important in the theoretical development of the field, are not easily accessible to application-oriented engineering communities. In this sense, there is a notable mismatch between the "supply" of easily accessible RO and its growing demand in engineering, in particular electric power engineering. This book aims to fill this gap.

It is our belief that the connection between theory and applications of RO is not a one-way street. Indeed, many fundamental developments of the RO methodology have been motivated by new applications and would not otherwise be pursued. On the other hand, in order to find innovative and creative applications of RO, it is important that the users of RO are equipped with sufficient understanding of the basic ingredients of the methodology. Although the optimization theory behind RO may be quite foreign to the traditional curriculum of electrical engineering, we believe that it can be effectively learned by students with basic background in optimization, if aided with sufficient motivation and illustration.

The approach that we took in writing this book is to develop a detailed and comprehensive exposition of the basic methodologies of RO and provide numerous applications of RO in power systems. The book is roughly divided into two parts. Chapter 1 gives an overview of basic RO models and their applications in the field of electric power engineering. Then, Chaps. 2, 3, and 4 form the first part that covers the basic methodologies of RO. In particular, Chap. 2 introduces static robust optimization, starting from the most basic robust linear optimization and discussing both exact reformulations and approximations of robust second-order conic optimization and robust semidefinite optimization. Chapter 3 provides a comprehensive discussion of adaptive robust optimization, focusing on the structural properties of two-stage and multistage robust linear and conic optimization and the development of efficient algorithms. Chapter 4 gives an up-to-date treatment of distributionally robust optimization, introducing major classes of uncertainty models such as moment-based, $\phi$-divergence-based, and Wasserstein distance-based ambiguity sets, their reformulations to deterministic optimization problems, and adaptive and distributionally robust chance constrained programs.

The second part of the book includes Chaps. 5, 6, 7, and 8, which focus on the applications of the RO methodologies, introduced in the previous chapters, to power engineering applications. In particular, Chap. 5 introduces hybrid adaptive robust optimization models and their applications in transmission expansion planning. Formulation and decomposition methods are discussed and a detailed computational example is given for illustration. Chapter 6 applies adaptive two-stage and multistage robust optimization to short-term power system operation problems, including some of the first application of RO to power systems, namely the unit commitment problem, the economic dispatch problem, and the AC optimal power flow problem. Chapter 7 studies the applications of RO to medium-term planning problems, including the grid maintenance scheduling problem, the fuel procurement problem, hydro scheduling, selling electricity via contracts, and consumer electricity procurement. Chapter 8 concludes the book with a detailed discussion of RO in power system long-term planning, including generation and transmission expansion and long-term hydroelectric scheduling.

Atlanta, GA, USA Xu Andy Sun

Columbus, OH, USA Antonio J. Conejo

# Contents

# Chapter 1
# Decision Making Under Uncertainty in the Power Sector

This introductory chapter provides an overview of the main approaches available to address optimization problems under uncertainty, namely, stochastic programming and robust optimization. It then points out the advantages of robust optimization approaches for a large class of decision-making problems under uncertainty. Selected examples from the power sector are briefly discussed throughout the chapter. The chapter concludes by providing a number of references for further study.

## 1.1 Introduction

Both the operation and the planning of electric energy systems require making decisions on a continuous basis. At the operation level (one week to real-time), decisions include the scheduling (commitment) and dispatch of production facilities to supply the demand for electricity. At the operation-planning level (several months to one week), decisions include the procurement of fuel (nuclear, coal, natural gas, biomass and others) for the production of electricity and the preventive maintenance of the system components (lines, transformers, and production facilities). At the planning level (years), decisions include the reinforcement and expansion of the grid (both transmission and distribution) and the building of new production facilities.

Almost always, these decisions have to be made under great uncertainty. This is particularly so with the increasing integration of weather-dependent (wind- and solar-based) production facilities, which makes the available production capacity uncertain. Moreover, distributed energy resources close to individual consumptions (e.g., rooftop solar units) that are being increasingly adopted greatly increase the load uncertainty from the viewpoint of the system operator. Thus, future electric energy systems involve great uncertainty at both the production and the consumption sides.

 
X. A. Sun, A. J. Conejo, *Robust Optimization in Electric Energy Systems*,
International Series in Operations Research & Management Science 313,
https://doi.org/10.1007/978-3-030-85128-6_1

Therefore, it is very important to accurately represent the uncertainty involved in decision-making models for the power sector. Two main methodologies allow representing uncertain parameters in an effective way. Stochastic Programming (SP) does so by considering a large enough, but finite number of realizations of the uncertain parameters, which are called scenarios [1]. SP includes single-stage SP, two-stage SP that involves decisions before (first-stage or here-and-now decisions) and after (second-stage or wait-and-see decisions) the uncertainty realization, and multi-stage SP that involves decisions before the uncertainty realization and at every time that the uncertainty partially realizes. Robust Optimization (RO) uses sets or distribution bounds to characterize the range of variability of the uncertain parameters [2]. RO includes single-stage RO, Adaptive Robust Optimization (ARO) that allows for recourse, and Adaptive Distributionally Robust Optimization (ADRO) that characterizes the uncertain parameters by establishing bounds over their unknown probability distributions and allows for recourse.

Within the power sector, it is critical to distinguish among different types of uncertainty, particularly, long- and short-term uncertainty. Long-term uncertainty refers to uncertain parameters that change over long periods of time, e.g., the addition of new production facilities to the existing generation mix or the growth of the electricity peak demand, which may change significantly from year to year, but not within a day. Short-term uncertainty refers to uncertain parameters that change over a short period of time, e.g., the electricity demand hourly value at a particular node within one day, or the production of a wind plant throughout the hours of a given day. It is relevant to note that modeling accurately these two uncertainties generally requires different representation techniques.

It is important to realize that the objective function of an optimization problem that includes uncertain parameters needs to be a real-valued function (as the objective function of any other optimization problem), and not a random variable. For instance, if we intend to maximize the profit of operating a production facility subject to its operation constraints, but its actual production depends on a random parameter, e.g., the wind speed where the plant in located, the resulting profit is generally a random variable that cannot be maximized. However, its expected value can. Therefore, the expected value is often used in optimization problems under uncertainty to achieve a real-valued objective function. We note that other metrics can also be used, such as the Conditional Value at Risk (CVaR) that focuses on the tail of the distribution of the objective to be achieved [3], or the buffered probability of exceedance [4] that focuses also on the tail of the distribution.

We note that modeling the uncertainty in a particular decision-making problem generally allows materializing the tradeoff security vs. cost. Not representing the uncertainty may result in an overly conservative outcome that uses much more resources that those needed, being therefore costly. Conversely, not representing uncertainty may result in a risky outcome that is cheap, but that may entail an operation breakdown.

A final note on the importance of representing uncertainty follows. A possible way to overcome the complexities pertaining to representing uncertainty would be to substitute all uncertain parameters by their corresponding expected values, and solve the resulting deterministic problem. This will save us of a significant number of complications, but is it a good idea? Would it provide the best solutions? Would the solutions obtained be feasible? Would these solutions be robust with respect to different uncertainty realizations? The reader is encouraged to consider these questions, which are at the core of uncertainty representation for decision making. The answers are provided throughout this book.

## 1.2 Stochastic Programming

A number of stochastic programming models are considered below and analyzed in detail in [1]. We describe them as a complement to robust optimization models, and because we analyze hybrid models that involve both robust and stochastic representations.

### *1.2.1 Single-Stage Stochastic Programming*

A single-stage stochastic programming problem has the generic form:

$$\min_{\mathbf{x}\in\mathscr{X}(\boldsymbol{\xi})} \quad \mathbb{E}_{\boldsymbol{\xi}}\{f(\mathbf{x},\boldsymbol{\xi})\}, \tag{1.2.1}$$

where $\mathbf{x}\in\mathscr{X}(\boldsymbol{\xi})$ is the vector of optimization variables within the feasibility set $\mathscr{X}(\boldsymbol{\xi})$, which may or may not depend on $\boldsymbol{\xi}$. $\boldsymbol{\xi}$ is the vector of uncertain parameters, $f(\mathbf{x},\boldsymbol{\xi})$ is the targeted objective, which is a scalar random variable because it depends on the vector of uncertain parameters $\boldsymbol{\xi}$, and $\mathbb{E}_{\boldsymbol{\xi}}$ is the expectation operator over the uncertain parameter vector $\boldsymbol{\xi}$, which renders the objective function, $\mathbb{E}_{\boldsymbol{\xi}}\{f(\mathbf{x},\boldsymbol{\xi})\}$, real-valued.

Instead of using the expectation operator, the CVaR can be used to focus on one of the tails of the distribution of $f(\mathbf{x},\xi)$ [3, 5]. In this case, the stochastic programming problem has the generic form:

$$\min_{\mathbf{x}\in\mathscr{X}(\boldsymbol{\xi})} \quad \mathrm{CVaR}_{\boldsymbol{\xi}}\{f(\mathbf{x},\boldsymbol{\xi})\}, \tag{1.2.2}$$

where $\mathrm{CVaR}_{\boldsymbol{\xi}}$ is the CVaR of $f(\mathbf{x},\boldsymbol{\xi})$ over the uncertain parameter vector $\boldsymbol{\xi}$.

We note that the single-stage stochastic programming problem can also be a maximization problem, namely:

$$\max_{\mathbf{x}\in\mathscr{X}(\boldsymbol{\xi})} \quad \mathbb{E}_{\boldsymbol{\xi}}\{f(\mathbf{x},\boldsymbol{\xi})\}. \tag{1.2.3}$$

The example below provides the formulation and solution of a simple stochastic programming problem.

**Illustrative Example 1.1 (Simple stochastic programming example.)** *Consider an electricity producer that offers its production $x$ to an electricity pool. For technical reason, its production level needs to be either 3 or 10, and its per unit production cost is 5. Once the production offer is submitted to the pool, the clearing price to be paid to the producer is revealed. We assume that this price $u$ is either 4 or 7 with equal probability, $\frac{1}{2}$. To derive a stochastic optimization offer $x$, the producer needs to solve the problem below:*

$$\max_{x \in \{3,10\}} \quad z = \frac{1}{2}\left[x(4-5)\right] + \frac{1}{2}\left[x(7-5)\right].$$

*The first term of the objective function corresponds to the realization of a clearing price $u = 4$. This is the first scenario that happens with probability $\frac{1}{2}$. Likewise, the second term of the objective function corresponds to the realization of a clearing price of $u = 7$, which corresponds to the second scenario that also happens with probability $\frac{1}{2}$. Therefore, this objective function corresponds to the expected value of the profit of the producer.*

*The problem above is equivalent to:*

$$\max_{x \in \{3,10\}} \quad z = \frac{1}{2}x,$$

*whose solution is $x = 10$.*

*Thus the optimal stochastic solution is $x^{\text{stochastic}} = 10$, with an objective function value of $z = 5$. We denote this solution as risk neutral since the objective function used is the expected value of the profit.*

□

Besides the simple model above, two specific stochastic programming methodologies have particular relevance in practice, namely, two-stage stochastic programming and multi-stage stochastic programming. These methodologies are succinctly described below.

### *1.2.2 Two-Stage Stochastic Programming*

A two-stage stochastic programming problem has the form below [1, 3]:

$$\min_{\mathbf{x}^1 \in \mathscr{X}^1} \quad f^1(\mathbf{x}^1) + \mathbb{E}_{\xi^1}\left\{z^1_{\xi^1}\right\}, \text{ where: } z^1_{\xi^1} = \left\{\min_{\mathbf{x}^2_{\xi^1} \in \mathscr{X}^2(\xi^1)} \quad f^2(\mathbf{x}^1, \mathbf{x}^2_{\xi^1})\right\}, \tag{1.2.4}$$

where $\mathbf{x}^1 \in \mathscr{X}^1$ is the vector of first-stage optimization variables within the feasible set $\mathscr{X}^1$, $f^1(\mathbf{x}^1)$ is the part of the objective function related to the vector of first-stage optimization variables, $\mathbf{x}^2_{\boldsymbol{\xi}^1}$ is the vector of second-stage optimization variables within the feasible set $\mathscr{X}^2(\boldsymbol{\xi}^1)$, which take optimal values once the uncertain parameters have taken specific values (and the uncertainty has thus vanished), $f^2(\mathbf{x}^1, \mathbf{x}^2_{\boldsymbol{\xi}^1})$ is the part of the objective function related to the vector of second-stage optimization variables, and $\mathbb{E}_{\boldsymbol{\xi}^1}\left\{z^1_{\boldsymbol{\xi}^1}\right\}$ is the expected value of the part of the objective function specifically related to the vector of second-stage optimization variables.

A generic power system example follows. A two-stage stochastic programming problem can be used to model a daily production scheduling problem of generating units, considering that the hourly electricity demand to be supplied is the uncertain parameter.

The first stage represents the scheduling (commitment) decisions at the beginning of the day that involve the starting-up and/or shutting-down of the generating units. Note that starting-up units is generally costly, and thus these decisions need to be made carefully. The first stage is therefore represented by:

$$\min_{\mathbf{x}^1 \in \mathscr{X}^1} \quad f^1(\mathbf{x}^1).$$

The second stage represents all possible operating conditions (scenarios) related to the actual realization of the electricity demand (uncertain parameter) throughout the hours of the day. Each scenario of the second stage is represented by:

$$z^1_{\boldsymbol{\xi}^1} = \left\{ \min_{\mathbf{x}^2_{\boldsymbol{\xi}^1} \in \mathscr{X}^2(\boldsymbol{\xi}^1)} \quad f^2(\mathbf{x}^1, \mathbf{x}^2_{\boldsymbol{\xi}^1}) \right\}.$$

The effect of all scenarios on average are added to the objective function through the term $\mathbb{E}_{\boldsymbol{\xi}^1}\left\{z^1_{\boldsymbol{\xi}^1}\right\}$, rendering:

$$\min_{\mathbf{x}^1 \in \mathscr{X}^1} \quad f^1(\mathbf{x}^1) + \mathbb{E}_{\boldsymbol{\xi}^1}\left\{z^1_{\boldsymbol{\xi}^1}\right\}.$$

Finally, we note that the objective is to minimize the scheduling cost (first stage) plus the expected operation cost (second stage).

A different simple example is considered below. This simple two-stage stochastic programming example pertains to a transmission planner and is formulated and solved below.

**Illustrative Example 1.2 (Simple two-stage stochastic programming example.)** *Consider a transmission planner that has the option of building just one of two alternative transmission lines of capacity either* 2 *or* 4 *to connect electrical nodes 1 and 2, as represented in Fig.* 1.1. *The per unit building cost for the line is* 1.

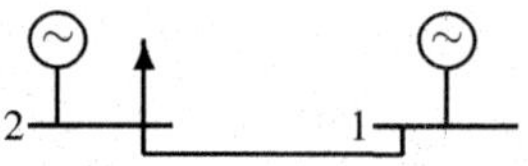


**Fig. 1.1** Simple 2-stage SP example: Transmission planner

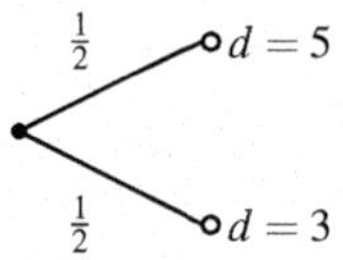


**Fig. 1.2** Simple two-stage SP example: Scenario tree

*At node 1, a generator of unlimited capacity and per unit production cost of* 5 *is available, while at node 2 another generator also of unlimited capacity and per unit production cost of* 10 *is available.*

*The demand is located at node 2 and can take only two values, either* 3 *or* 5*, with equal probability,* $\frac{1}{2}$*. We note that the demand uncertainty is conveniently visualized using a scenario tree, as shown in Fig.* 1.2*.*

*A two-stage SP model for the transmission planner to decide which transmission line to build is:*

$$\begin{aligned}
\min_{x \in \{2,4\}} \; 1x + \min_{y_1, y_2 \geq 0} \quad & \tfrac{1}{2}\left(5y_1^{(1)} + 10y_2^{(1)}\right) + \tfrac{1}{2}\left(5y_1^{(2)} + 10y_2^{(2)}\right) \\
\text{s.t.} \quad & y_1^{(1)} + y_2^{(1)} = 3 \\
& y_1^{(1)} \leq x \\
& y_1^{(2)} + y_2^{(2)} = 5 \\
& y_1^{(2)} \leq x,
\end{aligned}$$

*where $x$ represents the capacity of the transmission line to be built, $y_1^{(1)}$ and $y_2^{(1)}$ the production of the units at nodes 1 and 2, respectively, if the demand is $d = 3$ (scenario 1 identified by superscript* (1)*), and $y_1^{(2)}$ and $y_2^{(2)}$ the production of the units at nodes 1 and 2, respectively, if the demand is $d = 5$ (scenario 2 identified by superscript* (2)*).*

*The first minimization term of the problem above corresponds to the investment cost in the transmission facility, while the second one corresponds to the expected operation cost over the two possible scenarios, each one involving a weight of* $\frac{1}{2}$.

*Constraints pertain to the actual operation of the power system in both scenarios, and include energy balance and transmission limit.*

*The problem above is equivalent to:*

$$\begin{aligned}
\min_{x \in \{2,4\};\, y_1, y_2 \geq 0} \quad & z = 1x + \tfrac{1}{2}\left(5y_1^{(1)} + 10y_2^{(2)}\right) + \tfrac{1}{2}\left(5y_1^{(1)} + 10y_2^{(2)}\right) \\
\text{s.t.} \quad & y_1^{(1)} + y_2^{(1)} = 3 \\
& y_1^{(1)} \leq x \\
& y_1^{(2)} + y_2^{(2)} = 5 \\
& y_1^{(2)} \leq x.
\end{aligned}$$

*Given the small size and simplicity of this problem, it can be solved by enumeration. This is done below.*

1. *We first consider that the planner builds the line of capacity 2, i.e.,* $x = 2$*. Then, the problem to be solved is:*

$$\begin{aligned} \min_{y_1, y_2 \geq 0} \quad & z = 2 + \tfrac{1}{2}\left(5y_1^{(1)} + 10y_2^{(1)}\right) + \tfrac{1}{2}\left(5y_1^{(2)} + 10y_2^{(2)}\right) \\ \text{s.t.} \quad & y_1^{(1)} + y_2^{(1)} = 3 \\ & y_1^{(1)} \leq 2 \\ & y_1^{(2)} + y_2^{(2)} = 5 \\ & y_1^{(2)} \leq 2, \end{aligned}$$

*whose solution can be easily obtained and is* $y_1^{(1)} = 2$*,* $y_2^{(1)} = 1$*,* $y_1^{(2)} = 2$*,* $y_2^{(2)} = 3$*, and* $z = 32$*.*

2. *We then consider that the planner builds the line of capacity 4, i.e.,* $x = 4$*. Then, the problem to be solved is:*

$$\begin{aligned} \min_{y_1, y_2 \geq 0} \quad & z = 4 + \tfrac{1}{2}(5y_1^{(1)} + 10y_2^{(1)}) + \tfrac{1}{2}(5y_1^{(2)} + 10y_2^{(2)}) \\ \text{s.t.} \quad & y_1^{(1)} + y_2^{(1)} = 3 \\ & y_1^{(1)} \leq 4 \\ & y_1^{(2)} + y_2^{(2)} = 5 \\ & y_1^{(2)} \leq 4, \end{aligned}$$

*whose solution is* $y_1^{(1)} = 3$*,* $y_2^{(1)} = 0$*,* $y_1^{(2)} = 4$*,* $y_2^{(2)} = 1$*, and* $z = 26.5$*.*

*Finally, considering the two alternatives for investment* $x = 2$ *and* $x = 4$*, and the fact that the planner seeks minimum total cost (investment cost plus expected operation cost), the solution is* $x = 4$*,* $y_1^{(1)} = 3$*,* $y_2^{(1)} = 0$*,* $y_1^{(2)} = 4$*,* $y_2^{(2)} = 1$*, and* $z = 26.5$*.*

*The planner builds the larger line (*$x = 4$*) because this is best on average.*

□

On the computational side, we note that two-stage stochastic programming problems are generally tractable if they are continuous or mixed-integer linear. For continuous nonlinear instances, it is important to keep the size of the problem small enough (thousands of variables and constraints). For mixed-integer linear instances, it is important the avoid integer variables in the second stage, so that the number of such variables does not grow with the number of scenarios. Mixed-Integer Linear Programming (MILP) problems with millions of real variables and constraints, and thousands of integer variables are generally tractable. Nonlinear instances including integer variables are generally intractable, and no of-the-shelf algorithm is available to attack such problems. They generally require decomposition or special-purpose algorithms [3, 6].

### 1.2.3 Multi-stage Stochastic Programming

A multi-stage stochastic programming problem generalizes the two-stage stochastic programming problem in Sect. 1.2.2 and has the general form [3]:

$$\min_{\mathbf{x}^1 \in \mathscr{X}^1} \quad f^1(\mathbf{x}^1) + \mathbb{E}_{\xi^1}\{z^1_{\xi^1}\}, \text{ where} \tag{1.2.5a}$$

$$z^1_{\xi^1} = \left\{ \min_{\mathbf{x}^2_{\xi^1} \in \mathscr{X}^2(\xi^1)} \quad f^2(\mathbf{x}^1, \mathbf{x}^2_{\xi^1}) + \mathbb{E}_{\xi^2}\{z^2_{\xi^2}\} \right\}, \text{ where} \tag{1.2.5b}$$

$$z^2_{\xi^2} = \left\{ \min_{\mathbf{x}^3_{\xi^2} \in \mathscr{X}^3(\xi^2)} \quad f^3(\mathbf{x}^1, \mathbf{x}^2_{\xi^1}, \mathbf{x}^3_{\xi^2}) + \mathbb{E}_{\xi^3}\{z^3_{\xi^3}\} \right\}, \text{ where} \tag{1.2.5c}$$

$$\vdots$$

$$z^{r-1}_{\xi^{r-1}} = \left\{ \min_{\mathbf{x}^r_{\xi^{r-1}} \in \mathscr{X}^r(\xi^{r-1})} \quad f^r(\mathbf{x}^1, \mathbf{x}^2_{\xi^1}, \ldots, \mathbf{x}^r_{\xi^{r-1}}) \right\}. \tag{1.2.5d}$$

The decision variables at stage $i$ are represented by vector $\mathbf{x}^i_{\xi^{i-1}} \in \mathscr{X}^i(\xi^{i-1})$. The objective function of the subproblem at stage $i$, $z^{i-1}_{\xi^{i-1}}$, includes the actual cost incurred in stage $i$, which is $f^i(\mathbf{x}^1, \mathbf{x}^2_{\xi^1}, \ldots, \mathbf{x}^i_{\xi^{i-1}})$, and the expected cost in future stages, which is $\mathbb{E}_{\xi^i}\{z^i_{\xi^i}\}$.

A generic power system example follows. A multi-stage stochastic programming problem can be used to model the weekly production scheduling of the generating facilities of an electric energy system. Such problem has seven stages corresponding to the seven days of the week.

Just before Sunday (the first day of the week), we represent the scheduling of the production units to supply the hourly demand throughout the week, knowing that such scheduling decisions can be *adjusted* just before each day of the remaining days of the week (Monday to Saturday). Sunday operation is then represented considering the hourly demand as an uncertain parameter. This corresponds to stage one:

$$\min_{\mathbf{x}^1 \in \mathscr{X}^1} \quad f^1(\mathbf{x}^1) + \mathbb{E}_{\xi^1}\{z^1_{\xi^1}\}.$$

Just before Monday and knowing the hourly demand realization throughout Sunday, we represent scheduling re-adjustments to supply the hourly demand throughout the remaining days of the week, knowing that the resulting scheduling decisions can be re-adjusted just before each day of the remaining days of the week

(Tuesday to Saturday). Monday operation is then represented considering the hourly demand as an uncertain parameter. This corresponds to stage two:

$$z^1_{\xi^1} = \left\{ \min_{\mathbf{x}^2_{\xi^1} \in \mathscr{X}^2(\xi^1)} f^2(\mathbf{x}^1, \mathbf{x}^2_{\xi^1}) + \mathbb{E}_{\xi^2}\{z^2_{\xi^2}\} \right\}.$$

The process above for Monday is repeated for Tuesday, Wednesday, Thursday and Friday.

Finally, before Saturday and knowing the hourly demand realization from Sunday to Friday, we represent scheduling adjustments to supply the hourly demand throughout Saturday. Saturday operation is then represented considering the hourly demand as an uncertain parameter. This corresponds to stage seven:

$$z^6_{\xi^6} = \left\{ \min_{\mathbf{x}^7_{\xi^6} \in \mathscr{X}^7(\xi^6)} f^7(\mathbf{x}^1, \mathbf{x}^2_{\xi^1}, \dots, \mathbf{x}^7_{\xi^6}) \right\}.$$

The objective is to minimize the scheduling cost (Sunday) plus the adjustment cost of re-scheduling (Monday to Saturday) plus the expected operation costs of serving the uncertain load throughout the week (Sunday to Saturday).

A different example is considered below This simple example provides the formulation and solution of a three-stage stochastic programming problem pertaining the generation expansion planning.

It is relevant to note that two- or multi-stage formulations represent the decision sequence in one single optimization problem. However, only first-stage decisions are implemented. Subsequent decisions depend on the realization of the random variables, which might or might not be equal to the realizations represented in the problem via scenarios. Once first-stage decisions are implemented and the values of some uncertain parameters realize, a new stochastic optimization problem generally arises.

**Illustrative Example 1.3 (Simple three-stage stochastic programming example.)** *Consider a generation capacity planner that at the beginning of the first planning period has the option of building one of two alternative solar units of capacity either* 2 *or* 3 *to supply a demand, which in this first period can take only two values, either* 3 *or* 5*, with equal probability,* $\frac{1}{2}$.

*At the beginning of the second planning period, the planner has the option of building again one of two alternative solar units of capacity either* 2 *or* 3*. Additionally, we know that if the demand in the initial planning period is* 3*, it will increase by* 2 *with probability* 1 *in the second period; and if it is* 5*, it will increase by* 3 *with probability* 1 *in the second period.*

*The demand uncertainty is conveniently visualized using the scenario tree shown in Fig. 1.3. Black circles in the scenario tree indicate investment decision points.*

*The per unit building cost of the solar unit is* 1 *and its per unit operating cost is* 0 *in both planning periods. We note that this solar unit (concentrated solar power plant) is capable or producing at full capacity when needed.*

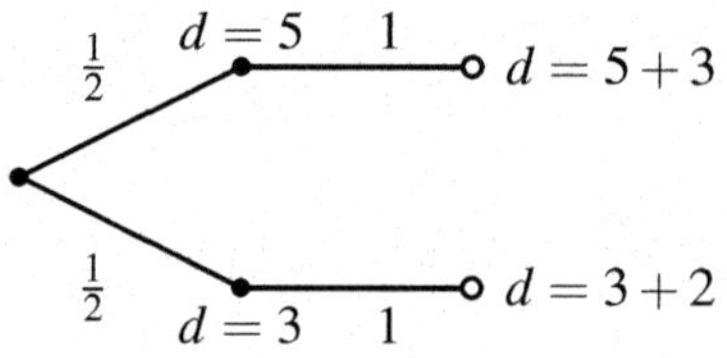


**Fig. 1.3** Simple three-stage SP example: Scenario tree

*In addition, a costly generation unit of unlimited capacity and operating cost of* 10 *per unit is available.*

*A three-stage stochastic programming model to address the problem above has the form:*

$$
\min_{x_1 \in \{2,3\}} \quad 1x_1 \quad + \min_{\substack{y_1^{(1)},\, y_2^{(1)} \ge 0 \\ y_1^{(2)},\, y_2^{(2)} \ge 0}} \quad \tfrac{1}{2}\left(10y_2^{(1)}\right) + \tfrac{1}{2}\left(10y_2^{(2)}\right) \quad +
$$

$$
\begin{aligned}
\text{s.t.} \quad & y_1^{(1)} + y_2^{(1)} = 3 \\
& y_1^{(1)} \le x_1 \\
& y_1^{(2)} + y_2^{(2)} = 5 \\
& y_1^{(2)} \le x_1
\end{aligned}
$$

$$
\min_{\substack{x_2^{(1)} \in \{2,3\} \\ x_2^{(2)} \in \{2,3\}}} \quad \tfrac{1}{2}\left(1x_2^{(1)}\right) + \tfrac{1}{2}\left(1x_2^{(2)}\right) \quad + \min_{\substack{y_3^{(1)},\, y_4^{(1)} \ge 0 \\ y_3^{(2)},\, y_4^{(2)} \ge 0}} \quad \tfrac{1}{2}\cdot 1\left(10y_4^{(1)}\right) + \tfrac{1}{2}\cdot 1\left(10y_4^{(2)}\right)
$$

$$
\begin{aligned}
\text{s.t.} \quad & y_3^{(1)} + y_4^{(1)} = 3 + 2 \\
& y_3^{(1)} \le x_1 + x_2^{(1)} \\
& y_3^{(2)} + y_4^{(2)} = 5 + 3 \\
& y_3^{(2)} \le x_1 + x_2^{(2)},
\end{aligned}
$$

*where $x_1$ is the capacity of the solar plant to be built at the beginning of the first period of the planning horizon, $y_1^{(1)}$ is the production of the solar unit during the first operating period if the demand is 3 (scenario 1), $y_2^{(1)}$ is the production of the expensive unit during the first operating period if the demand is 3 (scenario 1), $y_1^{(2)}$ is the production of the solar unit during the first operating period if the demand is 5 (scenario 2), $y_2^{(2)}$ is the production of the expensive unit during the first operating period if the demand is 5 (scenario 2), $x_2^{(1)}$ is the capacity of the solar plant to be built at the beginning of the second period of the planning horizon if the demand in the first period was 3 (scenario 1), $x_2^{(2)}$ is the capacity of the solar plant to be built at the beginning of the second period of the planning horizon if the demand in the first period was 5 (scenario 2), $y_3^{(1)}$ is the production of the solar unit during the second operating period if the demand in period 2 is* $3 + 2$ *(scenario 1), $y_4^{(1)}$ is the* *production of the expensive unit during the second operating period if the demand in period 2 is* $3+2$ *(scenario 1),* $y_3^{(2)}$ *is the production of the solar unit during the second operating period if the demand in period 2 is* $5+3$ *(scenario 2),* $y_4^{(2)}$ *is the production of the expensive unit during the second operating period if the demand in period 2 is* $5+3$ *(scenario 2).*

*The first minimization term of the problem above represents the investment decision of the planner at the beginning of the first period of the planning horizon. The second minimization term represents operating decisions regarding the production plants during the the first period of the planning horizon. Constraints include energy balance and the production limit of the solar unit. The third minimization term represents the decision investment of the planner at the beginning of the second period of the planning horizon. The fourth minimization term represents operating decisions regarding the production plants during the the second period of the planning horizon. Constraints include energy balance and the production limit of the solar units.*

*This problem is equivalent to:*

$$
\begin{aligned}
\min_{\Xi}\ & 1x_1 + \tfrac{1}{2}\cdot 10y_2^{(1)} + \tfrac{1}{2}\cdot 10y_2^{(2)} + \tfrac{1}{2}\cdot 1x_2^{(1)} + \tfrac{1}{2}\cdot 1x_2^{(2)} + \tfrac{1}{2}\cdot 1\cdot 10y_4^{(1)} + \tfrac{1}{2}\cdot 1\cdot 10y_4^{(2)} \\
\text{s.t.}\ & x_1 \in \{2, 3\} \\
& y_1^{(1)} + y_2^{(1)} = 3 \\
& y_1^{(1)} \le x_1 \\
& y_1^{(2)} + y_2^{(2)} = 5 \\
& y_1^{(2)} \le x_1 \\
& x_2^{(1)} \in \{2, 3\} \\
& x_2^{(2)} \in \{2, 3\} \\
& y_3^{(1)} + y_4^{(1)} = 3 + 2 \\
& y_3^{(1)} \le x_1 + x_2^{(1)} \\
& y_3^{(2)} + y_4^{(2)} = 5 + 3 \\
& y_3^{(2)} \le x_1 + x_2^{(2)}
\end{aligned}
$$

*where*

$$
\Xi = \{x_1; y_1^{(1)}, y_2^{(1)}, y_1^{(2)}, y_2^{(2)}; x_2^{(1)}, x_2^{(2)}; y_3^{(1)}, y_4^{(1)}, y_3^{(2)}, y_4^{(2)}\}
$$

*The optimal solution of the above mixed-integer linear programming problem can be easily obtained using an appropriate solver, e.g. GUROBI [7] under GAMS [8]. A GAMS code to solve this problem is provided at the end of this chapter, in Sect. 1.9.*

*The optimal solution requires that the planner builds at the beginning of the first period of the planning horizon a solar plant of capacity* $x_1 = 3$*, and at the beginning of the second period of the planning horizon a solar plant of capacity* $x_2^{(1)} = 2$ *if* *the demand in the first period is* 3*, and a solar plant of capacity* $x_2^{(2)} = 2$ *as well if the demand in the second period is* 5*.*

*We clarify next the stages of this problem. The first stage corresponds to the investment decisions prior to the beginning of the planning horizon. The second stage corresponds to the actual operation during the first period of the planning horizon. The third stage corresponds to the investment decision prior to the beginning of the second period of the planning horizon and the operating decisions during that second period.*

□

The same computational observations made at the end of Sect. 1.2.2 for two-stage problems are applicable to multi-stage problems, with an additional layer of complexity due to the multi-stage structure. Particularly, if integer variables are required in stages other than the first one, tractability is at risk due to the growth of the number of such variables with the number of scenarios [1, 3].

## 1.3 Robust Optimization

A number of robust optimization models are introduced in the following [2], including single-stage robust optimization, adaptive robust optimization, adaptive robust stochastic optimization, and adaptive distributionally robust optimization.

### *1.3.1 Single-Stage Robust Optimization*

A single-stage robust optimization problem has the form [2, 9]:

$$\min_{\mathbf{x}\in\mathscr{X}} \quad \max_{\mathbf{u}\in\mathscr{U}} \quad f(\mathbf{x},\mathbf{u}), \tag{1.3.1}$$

where the decision variables are represented by vector $\mathbf{x} \in \mathscr{X}$, and the uncertain parameters are represented by vector $\mathbf{u} \in \mathscr{U}$.

Using a preventive view, we desire to be *protected* against the worst realization of the uncertain parameters $\mathbf{u} \in \mathscr{U}$, hence the inner maximization operator. For the worst uncertainty realization, we seek to minimize the objective function $f(\mathbf{x},\mathbf{u})$ to get the optimal decision variable vector $\mathbf{x}^* \in \mathscr{X}$.

We emphasize that this model materializes a preventive view: it provides ex-ante protection against the worst uncertainty realization, within the uncertainty set.

Finally, we note that a single-stage robust optimization problem can also be formulated as a max-min problem, namely:

$$\max_{\mathbf{x}\in\mathscr{X}} \quad \min_{\mathbf{u}\in\mathscr{U}} \quad f(\mathbf{x},\mathbf{u}).$$

A generic power system example follows. A robust optimization problem can be used to model the offering strategy of an electricity producer in an electricity market.

In such a market, the producer submits a step-wise offering curve (set of quantities and corresponding prices) to the market, and then the market operator uses a clearing algorithm to identify the quantity to be produced by each producer and the corresponding price per hour. The offer strategy to be indentified is represented by $\mathbf{x} \in \mathscr{X}$. Clearing prices are thus uncertain parameters described by $\mathbf{u} \in \mathscr{U}$.

The producer generally desires that its offering strategy does not lead to a loss, i.e., the producer desires to be protected against market clearing prices that result in a negative profit for it.

Thus, the producer seeks to maximize its profit anticipating the worst price outcome that leads to a minimum profit. Therefore, a max-min problem is in order:

$$\max_{\mathbf{x} \in \mathscr{X}} \quad \min_{\mathbf{u} \in \mathscr{U}} \quad f(\mathbf{x}, \mathbf{u}).$$

We consider that the worst price outcome is bounded within an uncertainty set, $\mathbf{u} \in \mathscr{U}$.

The example below provides the formulation and solution of a simple robust optimization problem also pertaining to market offering.

**Illustrative Example 1.4 (Simple robust optimization example.)** *We consider the same problem analyzed in Illustrative Example* 1.1. *That is, an electricity producer that offers its production* $x$ *to an electricity pool. We recall that for technical reasons, its production level needs to be either* 3 *or* 10, *and its per unit production cost is* 5. *Once the production offer is submitted, the clearing price to be paid to the producer is obtained. We assume that this price* $u$ *is either* 4 *or* 7. *To derive a robust optimization offer* $x$, *the producer needs to solve the problem below:*

$$\max_{x \in \{3,10\}} \quad \min_{u \in \{4,7\}} \quad z = x(u - 5),$$

*where* $z$ *represents the profit of the producer (the objective function value).*

*Given the discrete and simple nature of this problem, it can be solved by enumeration. This is done below.*

*If the producer decides to produce* $x = 3$, *the resulting problem is:*

$$\min_{u \in \{4,7\}} \quad z = 3(u - 5),$$

*whose solution is* $u = 4$ *leading to an objective function value* $z = -3$.

*If, on the other hand, the producer decides to produce* $x = 10$, *the resulting problem is:*

$$\min_{u \in \{4,7\}} \quad z = 10(u - 5),$$

*whose solution is* $u = 4$ *leading to an objective function value* $z = -10$.

*Considering the outcomes above ($z = -3$ and $z = -10$) and the fact that the producer seeks to maximize its profit, the optimal robust solution is $x^{\text{robust}} = 3$, with an objective function value of $z = -3$.*

*Next, we recall the risk-neutral stochastic model described in Illustrative* Example 1.1. *The corresponding problem to be solved is:*

$$\max_{x \in \{3,10\}} \quad z = \frac{1}{2}x(4-5) + \frac{1}{2}x(7-5),$$

*whose solution is $x = 10$.*

*Thus the optimal (risk-neutral) stochastic solution is $x^{\text{stochastic}} = 10$, with an objective function value of $z = 5$.*

*Finally, we perform a scenario analysis to characterize both solutions, the stochastic and the robust one.*

*We consider first the robust solution $x^{\text{robust}} = 3$. If the price turns out to be $u = 4$, the producer profit becomes $z = 3(4-5) = -3$. If, on the other hand, the price is $u = 7$, the producer profit becomes $z = 3(7-5) = 6$.*

*We consider next the stochastic solution $x^{\text{stochastic}} = 10$. If the price turns out to be $u = 4$, the producer profit becomes $z = 10(4-5) = -10$. If, on the other hand, the price is $u = 7$, the producer profit becomes $z = 10(7-5) = 20$.*

*We conclude that the robust solution ($x^{\text{robust}} = 3$) protects the producer against a big loss ($z = -10$), but prevents it to achieve a big gain ($z = +20$). On the other hand, the stochastic solution ($x^{\text{stochastic}} = 10$) allows the producer to achieve a big gain ($z = +20$), but does not prevent it to incur a big loss ($z = -10$).*

*On average, the stochastic solution is a better choice ($\frac{1}{2}(20-10) = 5$) than the robust one ($\frac{1}{2}(-3+6) = \frac{3}{2}$), but it does not protect the producer from a potential big loss ($-10$), while the robust solution does (maximum loss $-3$).*

□

Generally, the RO form of a linear/nonlinear/MILP problem is itself linear/nonlinear/MILP problem, but of a larger size. Therefore, if the deterministic version of the problem under consideration is tractable, its RO version is generally tractable as well [10].

RO models are exhaustively analyzed in Chap. 2.

### *1.3.2 Adaptive Robust Optimization*

More often than not, once the uncertainty realizes, it is possible to react to mitigate the potentially pernicious effect of the uncertainty. This is embodied in the adaptive robust optimization model below.

A generic adaptive robust optimization problem has the form [2]:

$$\min_{\mathbf{x}\in\mathcal{X}} \quad \max_{\mathbf{u}\in\mathcal{U}} \quad \min_{\mathbf{y}\in\mathcal{Y}(\mathbf{x},\mathbf{u})} \quad f(\mathbf{x},\mathbf{y},\mathbf{u}). \tag{1.3.2}$$

An ARO problem comprises three levels. The first-level represents a *planning* strategy prior to the uncertainty realization and seeks to minimize the objective function value. Decision variables are represented by vector $\mathbf{x} \in \mathcal{X}$.

The second-level represents the uncertainty realization in the worst possible manner within an uncertainty set, and thus it seeks to maximize the objective function value. The variables describing uncertain parameters are represented by vector $\mathbf{u} \in \mathcal{U}$.

The third-level represents the *operation* actions to mitigate the pernicious effects of the uncertainty, once it realizes. It therefore seeks to minimize the objective function value. Decision variables at this level are represented by vector $\mathbf{y} \in \mathcal{Y}(\mathbf{x},\mathbf{u})$. Note that $\mathcal{Y}$ generally depends on both $\mathbf{x}$ and $\mathbf{u}$.

The overall objective is to minimize the objective function value under the worst uncertainty realization within the robust set $\mathcal{U}$.

It is important to note that model (1.3.2) provides both a preventive and a corrective view: planning, then uncertainty realization, then mitigation. Therefore, it provides both ex-ante protection (planning decisions) and ex-post correction (operation decisions).

In expanded form, considering equality and inequality constraints, problem (1.3.2) becomes:

$$\begin{aligned}
\min_{\mathbf{x}} \quad & \max_{\mathbf{u}\in\mathcal{U}} \quad \min_{\mathbf{y}} \quad f(\mathbf{x},\mathbf{u},\mathbf{y}) \\
& \qquad\qquad \text{s.t.} \quad \mathbf{h}^{\mathrm{Y}}(\mathbf{x},\mathbf{u},\mathbf{y}) = \mathbf{0} \\
& \qquad\qquad \text{s.t.} \quad \mathbf{g}^{\mathrm{Y}}(\mathbf{x},\mathbf{u},\mathbf{y}) \le \mathbf{0} \\
\text{s.t.} \quad & \mathbf{h}^{\mathrm{X}}(\mathbf{x}) = \mathbf{0} \\
\text{s.t.} \quad & \mathbf{g}^{\mathrm{X}}(\mathbf{x}) \le \mathbf{0}.
\end{aligned} \tag{1.3.3}$$

A generic power system example follows. An ARO problem can be used to model a transmission investment problem under demand uncertainty.

First, the planner makes investment decisions regarding the reinforcement and expansion of the transmission system seeking minimum total cost (investment cost plus operation cost) to supply the future electricity demand. This is represented by the decision vector $\mathbf{x} \in \mathcal{X}$.

In turn, the uncertain demand realizes in the worst possible manner within a pre-specified uncertainty set *seeking* maximum total cost. This is represented by $\mathbf{u} \in \mathcal{U}$.

Finally, the operator reacts in the best possible manner to supply the demand at minimum cost, which is represented by $\mathbf{y} \in \mathcal{Y}(\mathbf{x},\mathbf{u})$.

The overall objective is to minimize investment plus operation cost under the worst demand realization, and the problem has a min-max-min format:

$$\min_{\mathbf{x}\in\mathscr{X}} \quad \max_{\mathbf{u}\in\mathscr{U}} \quad \min_{\mathbf{y}\in\mathscr{Y}(\mathbf{x},\mathbf{u})} \quad f(\mathbf{x},\mathbf{y},u).$$

The simple example below provides the formulation and the solution of a simple ARO problem pertaining also to transmission expansion planning.

**Illustrative Example 1.5 (Simple adaptive robust optimization example.)** *We recall the transmission expansion planner in Illustrative Example* 1.2 *that has the option of building just one of two alternatives transmission lines of capacity either* 2 *or* 4 *to connect electrical nodes 1 and 2 (see Fig.* 1.1*). The per unit building cost for the transmission lines is* 1.

*At node 1, a generator of unlimited capacity and per unit production cost of* 5 *is available, while in node 2 another generator of unlimited capacity and per unit production cost of* 10 *is available.*

*The demand is located at node 2 and can take solely two values, either* 3 *or* 5.

*A robust model for the transmission planner to decide which transmission line to build is:*

$$\begin{aligned}\min_{x\in\{2,4\}}\ \max_{d\in\{3,5\}}\ \min_{y_1,y_2\geq 0}\quad & z = 1x + 5y_1 + 10y_2\\ \text{s.t.}\quad & y_1 + y_2 = d\\ & y_1 \leq x\end{aligned}$$

*where $x$ represents the capacity of the transmission line to be built, $d$ the unknown demand, and $y_1$ and $y_2$, the production of the units at nodes 1 and 2, respectively.*

*Given the small size and simplicity of this problem, it can be solved by enumeration. This is done below.*

1. *We first consider that the planner builds the line of capacity* 2*, i.e., $x = 2$. Then, the problem to be solved is:*

$$\begin{aligned}\max_{d\in\{3,5\}}\ \min_{y_1,y_2\geq 0}\quad & z = 2 + 5y_1 + 10y_2\\ \text{s.t.}\quad & y_1 + y_2 = d\\ & y_1 \leq 2.\end{aligned}$$

*To solve this problem we consider the two alternatives for $d$,* 3 *and* 5.

1.1 *If the demand is $d = 3$, the problem to be solved becomes:*

$$\begin{aligned}\min_{y_1,y_2\geq 0}\quad & z = 2 + 5y_1 + 10y_2\\ \text{s.t.}\quad & y_1 + y_2 = 3\\ & y_1 \leq 2,\end{aligned}$$

*whose solution is $y_1 = 2$, $y_2 = 1$ and $z = 22$.*

1.2 *On the other hand, if the demand is* $d = 5$*, the problem to be solved becomes:*

$$\begin{aligned}\min_{y_1, y_2 \geq 0} \quad & z = 2 + 5y_1 + 10y_2 \\ \text{s.t.} \quad & y_1 + y_2 = 5 \\ & y_1 \leq 2,\end{aligned}$$

*whose solution is* $y_1 = 2$, $y_2 = 3$ *and* $z = 42$.

*Considering the above results and the fact that maximum cost is pursued at this level (uncertainty realization), the solution in case* $x = 2$ *is* $d = 5$ *and* $z = 42$.

2. *We then consider that the planner builds the line of capacity 4, i.e.,* $x = 4$*. Then, the problem to be solved is:*

$$\begin{aligned}\max_{d \in \{3,5\}} \min_{y_1, y_2 \geq 0} \quad & z = 4 + 5y_1 + 10y_2 \\ \text{s.t.} \quad & y_1 + y_2 = d \\ & y_1 \leq 4.\end{aligned}$$

*To solve this problem we consider the two alternatives for* $d$*, 3 and 5.*

2.1 *If the demand is* $d = 3$*, the problem to be solved becomes:*

$$\begin{aligned}\min_{y_1, y_2 \geq 0} \quad & z = 4 + 5y_1 + 10y_2 \\ \text{s.t.} \quad & y_1 + y_2 = 3 \\ & y_1 \leq 4,\end{aligned}$$

*whose solution is* $y_1 = 3$, $y_2 = 0$ *and* $z = 19$.

2.2 *On the other hand, if the demand is* $d = 5$*, the problem to be solved becomes:*

$$\begin{aligned}\min_{y_1, y_2 \geq 0} \quad & z = 4 + 5y_1 + 10y_2 \\ \text{s.t.} \quad & y_1 + y_2 = 5 \\ & y_1 \leq 4,\end{aligned}$$

*whose solution is* $y_1 = 4$, $y_2 = 1$ *and* $z = 34$.

*Considering the above results and the fact that maximum cost is pursued at this level (uncertainty realization), the solution in case* $x = 4$ *is* $d = 5$ *and* $z = 34$.

*Finally, considering the two alternatives for investment* $x = 2$ *and* $x = 4$*, and that the planner seeks minimum cost, the solution is* $x = 4$, $d = 5$, $y_1 = 4$, $y_2 = 1$ *and* $z = 34$.

*We conclude that the planner builds the larger transmission line to be protected against the high cost of the generator at node 2.*

□

On the computational side, we note that tri-level problem (1.3.2) requires a specific solution algorithm that generally relies on merging the second- and third-level problems using duality theory and decomposing the resulting bi-level problem through a column-and-constraint generation algorithm [11, 12].

ARO models are exhaustively analyzed in Chap. 3.

### *1.3.3 Adaptive Robust Stochastic Optimization*

ARSO models combine robust protection and scenario modeling. A generic adaptive robust stochastic optimization (ARSO) problem has the form [13]:

$$\min_{\mathbf{x}\in\mathscr{X}} \quad \max_{\mathbf{u}\in\mathscr{U}} \quad \min_{\mathbf{y}\in\mathscr{Y}(\mathbf{x},\mathbf{u},\boldsymbol{\xi})} \quad \mathbb{E}_{\boldsymbol{\xi}} f(\mathbf{x}, \mathbf{u}, \mathbf{y}, \boldsymbol{\xi}). \tag{1.3.4}$$

As in the ARO case, this problem involves three levels.

The first level represents a *planning* strategy prior to the uncertainty realization and seeks to minimize the objective function. Decision variables are represented by vector $\mathbf{x} \in \mathscr{X}$.

The second level represents *long-term* uncertainty realization in the worst possible manner within an uncertainty set, and thus it seeks to maximize the objective function. The variables describing long-term uncertain parameters are represented by vector $\mathbf{u} \in \mathscr{U}$.

The third level represents the mitigation actions once the long-term uncertainty realizes and involves a number of *short-term* uncertain operating conditions represented by the uncertain parameter vector $\boldsymbol{\xi}$. Therefore, the third level seeks to minimize the objective function. Decision variables at this level are represented by vector $\mathbf{y} \in \mathscr{Y}(\mathbf{x}, \mathbf{u}, \boldsymbol{\xi})$.

The overall objective function to be minimized is the expected value of the objective over the short-term uncertainty parameters in vector $\boldsymbol{\xi}$ under the worst long-term uncertainty realization $\mathbf{u}$ within the robust set $\mathscr{U}$.

As ARO problems, ARSO problems involve both ex-ante protection (planning decisions) and ex-post correction (operation decisions tailored per scenario).

A generic power system example is provided below. Considering a power system with a high penetration of renewable sources (wind- and solar-powered units), its transmission expansion planning can be modeled using an ARSO problem.

The long-term uncertainty pertains to the peak load in the target year (e.g., 10 years into the future), while short-term uncertainty pertains to the daily evolution of the net load (actual load minus the uncertain renewable production).

At the first level, the planner models investment decisions on transmission lines, represented by $\mathbf{x} \in \mathscr{X}$, anticipating the worst long-term uncertainty realization (peak load) and the subsequent best reactions of the operator for different operating conditions.

The second level represents the worst peak demand realization (long-term uncertainty) by $\mathbf{u} \in \mathscr{U}$.

The third level describes the operator reactions with respect to all possible realization of the daily evolution of the net load (short-term uncertainty) represented by the uncertain parameter vector $\boldsymbol{\xi}$.

The model is then a min-max-min problem with an objective function that represents for the worst long-term uncertainty realization the investment cost plus the expected operation cost over the operating conditions dictated by the short-term uncertainty.

A different example is considered below. This illustrative example provides the formulation and solution of a simple ARSO problem pertaining to generation expansion planning.

**Illustrative Example 1.6 (Simple adaptive robust stochastic optimization example.)** *Consider a generation capacity planner that has the option of building just one of two alternative wind units of capacity either* 2 *or* 4 *to supply a demand that can take only two values, either* 3 *or* 5*. The per unit building cost of the wind unit is* 1 *and its per unit operating cost is* 0*. In addition, a costly generation unit of unlimited capacity and operating cost of* 10 *per unit is available. Whichever wind unit is built, it will operate under two conditions (scenarios), either at* $\frac{3}{4}$ *of capacity or at* $\frac{1}{4}$ *of capacity, with equal probability,* $\frac{1}{2}$*.*

*An ARSO model for the generation capacity planner to decide which wind unit to build is:*

$$
\begin{aligned}
\min_{x\in\{2,4\}} \ \max_{d\in\{3,5\}} \ \min_{y^{(1)},y^{(2)}\geq 0} \quad & \tfrac{1}{2}\left(10y^{(1)}\right) + \tfrac{1}{2}\left(10y^{(2)}\right) \\
\text{s.t.} \quad & y^{(1)} + \tfrac{3}{4}x = d \\
& y^{(2)} + \tfrac{1}{4}x = d,
\end{aligned}
$$

*where $x$ represents the capacity of the wind unit to be built, $d$ the unknown demand, and $y^{(1)}$ and $y^{(2)}$, the production of the expensive unit if the demand is $d = 3$ (scenario* 1*) and if the demand is $d = 5$ (scenario* 2*), respectively.*

*Given the small size and simplicity of this problem, it can be solved by enumeration. This is done below.*

1. *We first consider that the planner builds a wind unit of capacity 2, i.e., $x = 2$. Then, the problem to be solved is:*

$$
\begin{aligned}
\max_{d\in\{3,5\}} \ \min_{y^{(1)},y^{(2)}\geq 0} \quad & \tfrac{1}{2}\left(10y^{(1)}\right) + \tfrac{1}{2}\left(10y^{(2)}\right) \\
\text{s.t.} \quad & y^{(1)} + \tfrac{3}{2} = d \\
& y^{(2)} + \tfrac{1}{2} = d.
\end{aligned}
$$

*To solve this problem we consider the two alternatives for $d$, 3 and 5.*

1.1 *If the demand is $d = 3$, the problem to be solved becomes:*

$$\begin{aligned} \min_{y^{(1)},y^{(2)}\geq 0} \quad & \tfrac{1}{2}\left(10y^{(1)}\right) + \tfrac{1}{2}\left(10y^{(2)}\right) \\ \text{s.t.} \quad & y^{(1)} + \tfrac{3}{2} = 3 \\ & y^{(2)} + \tfrac{1}{2} = 3, \end{aligned}$$

*whose solution is $y^{(1)} = \frac{3}{2}$, $y^{(2)} = \frac{5}{2}$ and $z = 20$.*

1.2 *On the other hand, if the demand is $d = 5$, the problem to be solved becomes:*

$$\begin{aligned} \min_{y^{(1)},y^{(2)}\geq 0} \quad & \tfrac{1}{2}\left(10y^{(1)}\right) + \tfrac{1}{2}\left(10y^{(2)}\right) \\ \text{s.t.} \quad & y^{(1)} + \tfrac{3}{2} = 5 \\ & y^{(2)} + \tfrac{1}{2} = 5, \end{aligned}$$

*whose solution is $y^{(1)} = \frac{7}{2}$, $y^{(2)} = \frac{9}{2}$ and $z = 40$.*

*Considering the above results and the fact that maximum cost is pursued at this level (uncertainty realization), the solution in case $x = 2$ is $d = 5$ and $z = 40$.*

2. *We then consider that the planner builds a line of capacity 4, i.e., $x = 4$. In this case the problem to be solved is:*

$$\begin{aligned} \max_{d\in\{3,5\}} \min_{y^{(1)},y^{(2)}\geq 0} \quad & \tfrac{1}{2}\left(10y^{(1)}\right) + \tfrac{1}{2}\left(10y^{(2)}\right) \\ \text{s.t.} \quad & y^{(1)} + 3 = d \\ & y^{(2)} + 1 = d. \end{aligned}$$

*To solve this problem we consider the two alternatives for $d$, 3 and 5.*

2.1 *If the demand is $d = 3$, the problem to be solved becomes:*

$$\begin{aligned} \min_{y^{(1)},y^{(2)}\geq 0} \quad & \tfrac{1}{2}\left(10y^{(1)}\right) + \tfrac{1}{2}\left(10y^{(2)}\right) \\ \text{s.t.} \quad & y^{(1)} + 3 = 3 \\ & y^{(2)} + 1 = 3, \end{aligned}$$

*whose solution is $y^{(1)} = 0$, $y^{(2)} = 2$ and $z = 10$.*

2.2 *On the other hand, if the demand is* $d = 5$, *the problem to be solved becomes:*

$$\begin{aligned} \min_{y^{(1)}, y^{(2)} \geq 0} \quad & \tfrac{1}{2}\left(10y^{(1)}\right) + \tfrac{1}{2}\left(10y^{(2)}\right) \\ \text{s.t.} \quad & y^{(1)} + 3 = 5 \\ & y^{(2)} + 1 = 5, \end{aligned}$$

*whose solution is* $y^{(1)} = 2$, $y^{(2)} = 4$ *and* $z = 30$.

*Considering the above results and the fact that maximum cost is pursued at this level (uncertainty realization), the solution in case* $x = 4$ *is* $d = 5$ *and* $z = 30$.

*Finally, considering the two alternatives for investment* $x = 2$ *and* $x = 4$, *and that the planner seeks minimum cost, the solution is* $x = 4$, $d = 5$, $y^{(1)} = 2$, $y^{(2)} = 4$ *and* $z = 30$.

*The planner builds a wind unit of capacity* 4 *to be protected against the high cost of the costly generator.*

□

As ARO problems, ARSO problems generally require a specific solution algorithm that generally relies on merging the second-level and the multi-scenario third-level problems using duality theory, and decomposing the resulting bi-level problem through a column-and-constraint generation algorithm [11, 12].

ARSO models are exhaustively analyzed in Chap. 4.

### *1.3.4 Adaptive Distributionally Robust Optimization*

Adaptive distributionally robust optimization assumes that each uncertain parameter follows an unknown but bounded distribution. Therefore, each uncertain parameter is not described by a variable that belongs to a robust set. This model has the form [14, 15]:

$$\min_{\mathbf{x} \in \mathscr{X}} \quad \max_{\mathscr{F} \in \mathscr{D}} \quad \min_{\mathbf{y} \in \mathscr{Y}(\mathbf{x}, \boldsymbol{\xi}_{\mathscr{F}})} \quad \mathbb{E}_{\boldsymbol{\xi}_{\mathscr{F}}} \left\{ f(\mathbf{x}, \mathbf{y}, \boldsymbol{\xi}_{\mathscr{F}}) \right\}, \tag{1.3.5}$$

where the first-stage decision variables are represented by vector $\mathbf{x} \in \mathscr{X}$, and the uncertain parameters are represented by vector $\boldsymbol{\xi}_{\mathscr{F}}$. Each element in vector $\boldsymbol{\xi}_{\mathscr{F}}$ has an unknown, but bounded distribution, as indicated by $\mathscr{F} \in \mathscr{D}$. Second stage decision variables are represented by vector $\mathbf{y} \in \mathscr{Y}(\mathbf{x}, \boldsymbol{\xi}_{\mathscr{F}})$. The objective function is the expectation over the uncertain vector $\boldsymbol{\xi}_{\mathscr{F}}$ of the objective targeted. Alternative metrics, such as CVaR, can also be used.

As ARO models, we note that model (1.3.5) provides both a preventive and a corrective view: planning, then worst uncertainty realization, then mitigation. Therefore, it provides both ex-ante protection (planning decisions) and ex-post correction (operation decisions).

Using scenarios to describe the uncertain parameter vector $\boldsymbol{\xi}_{\mathscr{F}}$, model (1.3.5) becomes:

$$\begin{array}{llll} \min\limits_{\mathbf{x}\in\mathscr{X}} & \max\limits_{\sigma_1,\ldots,\sigma_n\geq 0} & \min\limits_{\mathbf{y}^{(\omega)}\in\mathscr{Y}_\omega,\forall\omega} & \sum\limits_{\omega=1}^{n}\sigma_\omega f^{(\omega)}\left(\mathbf{x},\mathbf{y}^{(\omega)}\right) \\ & \text{s.t.} & \text{s.t.} & \\ & \sum\limits_{\omega=1}^{n}\sigma_\omega = 1 & \mathbf{h}^{(\omega)}\left(\mathbf{x},\mathbf{y}^{(\omega)}\right) = 0, \forall\omega & \\ & \sum\limits_{\omega=1}^{n}|\sigma_\omega - \hat{\sigma}_\omega| \leq \alpha & \mathbf{g}^{(\omega)}\left(\mathbf{x},\mathbf{y}^{(\omega)}\right) \leq 0, \forall\omega, & \end{array} \tag{1.3.6}$$

where $\hat{\sigma}_\omega$ is the data-derived probability of scenario $\omega$ (known), and $\sigma_\omega$ is a variable representing the weight of scenario $\omega$, whose optimal value is to be derived so that the worst scenario weights are identified. Parameter $\alpha$ bounds the deviation of the worst set of scenario weights from the data-derived scenario weights, $\hat{\sigma}_\omega$, $\forall\omega$.

A generic power system example follows. An adaptive distributionally robust optimization problem can be used to model a daily production scheduling problem of electricity production facilities similar to the one explained in Sect. 1.2.2. In this case, the distribution of the hourly electricity demand to be supplied is unknown, but characterized by a histogram based on historical data.

A different simple example is considered below. This example provides the formulation and characterization of a distributionally robust optimization problem that pertains to transmission expansion planning.

**Illustrative Example 1.7 (Simple Distributionally Robust Optimization Example.)** *We recall the transmission planner of Illustrative Example* 1.2. *This planner has the option of building just one of two alternative transmission lines of capacity either* 2 *or* 4 *to connect electrical nodes 1 and 2, as represented in Fig.* 1.1. *The per unit building cost for the line is* 1.

*At node 1, a generator of unlimited capacity and per unit production cost of* 5 *is available, while at node 2 another generator also of unlimited capacity and per unit production cost of* 10 *is available.*

*The demand is located at node 2 and is described by a data-derived distribution that includes two demand values,* 3 *and* 5, *with probabilities,* $\frac{1}{2}$ *and* $\frac{1}{2}$, *respectively.*

*An ADRO model for the transmission planner to decide which transmission line to build is:*

$$\begin{array}{llll} \min\limits_{x\in\{2,4\}} & \max\limits_{\sigma_1,\sigma_2\geq 0} & \min\limits_{y_1,y_2\geq 0} & 1x+\sigma_1\left(5y_1^{(1)}+10y_2^{(1)}\right)+ \\ & & & \sigma_2\left(5y_1^{(2)}+10y_2^{(2)}\right) \\ & \text{s.t.} & \text{s.t.} & \\ & \sigma_1+\sigma_2=1 & y_1^{(1)}+y_2^{(1)}=3 & \\ & |\sigma_1-\frac{1}{2}|+ & y_1^{(1)}\leq x & \\ & |\sigma_2-\frac{1}{2}|\leq 0.1 & y_1^{(2)}+y_2^{(2)}=5 & \\ & & y_1^{(2)}\leq x, & \end{array}$$

*where $x$ represents the capacity of the transmission line to be built, $y_1^{(1)}$ and $y_2^{(1)}$ the production of the units at nodes 1 and 2 if the demand is $d=3$ (scenario 1 identified by superscript (1)), and $y_1^{(2)}$ and $y_2^{(2)}$ the production of the units at nodes 1 and 2 is the demand is $d=5$ (scenario 2 identified by superscript (2)). Variables $\sigma_1$ and $\sigma_2$ are scenario weights pertaining to the second-level problem.*

*The first minimization problem of the tri-level problem above corresponds to the investment cost in the transmission line, the second one selects the scenario weights in the worst possible manner within a 0.1 total deviation, and the third one corresponds to the expected operation cost over the two possible scenarios, with weights $\sigma_1$ and $\sigma_2$ .*

*Constraints pertain to the actual operation of the power system in both scenarios, and include energy balance and transmission limit.*

*The problem above is equivalent to the problem below with linear constraints:*

$$\begin{array}{llll} \min\limits_{x\in\{2,4\}} & \max\limits_{\sigma_1,\sigma_2\geq 0;\kappa_1,\kappa_2} & \min\limits_{y_1,y_2\geq 0} & 1x+\sigma_1\left(5y_1^{(1)}+10y_2^{(1)}\right)+ \\ & & & \sigma_2\left(5y_1^{(2)}+10y_2^{(2)}\right) \\ & \text{s.t.} & \text{s.t.} & \\ & \kappa_1+\kappa_2\leq 0.1 & y_1^{(1)}+y_2^{(1)}=3 & \\ & \sigma_1-\frac{1}{2}\leq\kappa_1 & y_1^{(1)}\leq x & \\ & \sigma_1-\frac{1}{2}\geq-\kappa_1 & y_1^{(2)}+y_2^{(2)}=5 & \\ & \sigma_2-\frac{1}{2}\leq\kappa_2 & y_1^{(2)}\leq x & \\ & \sigma_2-\frac{1}{2}\geq-\kappa_2, & & \end{array}$$

*where $\kappa_1$ and $\kappa_2$ are auxiliary variables used for linearization purposes.*

*Since the second-level problem of the problem above is continuous, it cannot be solved by enumeration. Moreover, the objective function is bi-linear. Solving this problem requires the use of one of the techniques described in Chap. 4.*

□

The computational complexity of a ADRO problem is similar to that of an ARO problem. Solution techniques generally rely on merging the second- and third-level problem via duality, and solving the resulting bilevel problem using decomposition techniques [11, 12, 16].

ADRO models are analyzed in detail in Chap. 4.

## 1.4 Uncertainty Modeling

Uncertainty is generally modeled using scenarios in stochastic programming and using either robust sets or distribution bounds in robust optimization.

### *1.4.1 Scenarios*

A scenario is a given realization of the uncertain parameter vector $\mathbf{u}$ that is represented by $\mathbf{u}^{(\omega)}$, with an occurrence probability of $p^{(\omega)}$. Scenarios should describe all possible uncertainty realizations and thus $\sum_{\omega} p^{(\omega)} = 1$.

The simple example below describes how to represent uncertainty using scenarios.

**Illustrative Example 1.8 (Uncertainty description via scenarios.)** *We recall Illustrative Example* 1.1. *The uncertainty in price is described using just 2 scenarios:*

$$\textit{price } u : \begin{cases} u^{(1)} = 4, & \text{with probability} = p^{(1)} = \frac{1}{2} \\ u^{(2)} = 7, & \text{with probability} = p^{(2)} = \frac{1}{2}. \end{cases}$$

*Observe that the above definition constitutes a full description of the probability distribution of the price u. Scenarios are conveniently arranged in a scenario tree, as in Fig.* 1.2.

□

If continuous uncertainty parameters need to be represented, the above discretization constitutes an approximation. We note that a detailed uncertainty description via scenarios may require a large number of these scenarios to be accurate, which may have pernicious computational consequences.

### 1.4.2 *Robust Sets*

Robust sets are generally based on boxes or polyhedral constraints. A typical box-based robust set is defined below.

We consider that every uncertain parameter $u_i \in \mathbb{R}$ in vector $\mathbf{u} \in \mathscr{U}$ may deviate from a *reference* value $u_i^{\text{ref}}$ by at most $\pm u_i^{\Delta}$. Thus:

$$u_i \in \left[ u_i^{\text{ref}} - u_i^{\Delta} \quad u_i^{\text{ref}} + u_i^{\Delta} \right], \quad \forall i. \tag{1.4.1}$$

Note that, if appropriate, this "box" constraint can be replaced by a more general polyhedral constraint consisting of linear combinations of the elements of $\mathbf{u}$.

While constructing robust sets, it is important to model the linkage (correlation) of these sets across time and space. For instance, if the wind speed in a particular location at minute $m$ can vary within the interval $[a, b]$, its variation interval at minute $m + 1$ is highly correlated with the variation interval $[a, b]$ at minute $m$. This correlation generally needs to be represented at the time of defining robust sets.

The simple example below describes a robust set.

**Illustrative Example 1.9 (Uncertainty description via a robust set.)** *We recall Illustrative Example* 1.4. *In this example, the uncertainty in price is described by a robust set:*

$$\textit{price:} \quad u \in \{4, 7\}$$

*Observe the above definition entails no assumption on the probability distribution of the price $u$.*

□

### 1.4.3 *Uncertainty Budget*

Considering robust set (1.4.1), an *uncertainty budget* can be imposed by the constraint [2]:

$$\sum_{i=1}^{n} \frac{|u_i - u_i^{\text{ref}}|}{u_i^{\Delta}} \leq \Gamma, \tag{1.4.2}$$

where $\Gamma$ varies between 0 and $n$.

We note that $\Gamma = 0$ implies no uncertainty since each uncertain parameter equals its reference value, while $\Gamma = n$ implies maximum uncertainty, as each uncertain parameter deviates the maximum from its reference value. Intermediate values of $\Gamma$ represent different levels of uncertainty.

The simple example below illustrates the concept of uncertainty budget.

**Illustrative Example 1.10 (Uncertainty budget.)** *Consider two random parameters, $u_1$ and $u_2$, characterized, respectively, by the two robust sets:*

$$u_1 \in [4-1, 4+1] = [3, 5]$$
$$u_2 \in [6-1, 6+1] = [5, 7],$$

*where the reference values for uncertain parameters $u_1$ and $u_2$ are 4 and 6, respectively. An uncertainty budget $\Gamma = 1$:*

$$\frac{|u_1-4|}{1} + \frac{|u_2-6|}{1} \leq 1$$

*allows one of the two random parameters to take one of its two extreme values.*

*On the other hand, an uncertainty budget $\Gamma = 2$:*

$$\frac{|u_1-4|}{1} + \frac{|u_2-6|}{1} \leq 2$$

*allows the two random parameters to take one of its two extreme values.*

*Finally, an uncertainty budget $\Gamma = 0$:*

$$\frac{|u_1-4|}{1} + \frac{|u_2-6|}{1} \leq 0$$

*allows none of the two random parameters to take one of its two extreme values. Their values are fixed to their respective reference values.*

□

Robust sets and uncertainty budgets are exhaustively analyzed in Chap. 2.

## 1.5 Why Robust Optimization?

Robust optimization is particularly appropriate to identify optimal decisions under uncertainty if these decisions are *important*. That is, if these decisions entail important consequences and thus, protection against bad decisions is a must. Important decisions are, for example, investment decisions in electrical infrastructure because these decisions are generally costly and difficult to modify at a future time.

Robust optimization allows for robustness (risk) control, making it possible to adapt the decisions to be made to the desired (or required) level of robustness (protection). Stochastic programming allows for risk control as well, but risk-based formulations (e.g., those based on CVaR) are generally computationally complex.

Robust optimization problems are generally tractable since their sizes do not generally depend on the accuracy of the uncertainty description. This is not the case with stochastic programming problems since the size of a stochastic problem depends on the number of considered scenarios.

## 1.6 Concluding Remarks

This chapter introduces two families of optimization methodologies under uncertainty, namely, stochastic programming and robust optimization. Different instances of these two families are intuitively introduced in this chapter. A number of clarifying examples are provided to ensure the comprehension of the models described. Some observations on the computational tractability of these models are provided as well. Both stochastic programming models and robust optimization ones are most useful to represent real-world decision-making problems under uncertainty. Robust optimization is particularly suited for problem involving *important* decisions, i.e., decisions that are costly and/or difficult to alter in the future.

The reader interested in stochastic programming is referred, for example, to the classical monograph by Birge and Louveaux [1]. Robust optimization is introduced in the tutorial paper by Bertsimas et al. [2], while an extensive but hard-to-read monograph on the topic is [17]. Hybrid models considering both stochastic programming and robust optimization are described and used, for instance, in [18] and [13]. Decomposition techniques to computationally address ARO and ARSO models are described in [11] and [12].

Relevant applications, among others, include offering strategies for producers [19], generation dispatch [20], generation scheduling [11, 21], hydrothermal coordination [22], transmission expansion planning [23, 14], generation and transmission expansion planning [24], and generation expansion planning [25].

## 1.7 End-of-Chapter Exercises

**1.1** Which are the advantages of robust optimization with respect to stochastic programming?

**1.2** If the deterministic counterpart of a robust optimization problem is mixed-integer linear, which is the nature of the original robust optimization problem?

**1.3** Which is the main difference between a RO and an ARO model?

**1.4** Which is the main difference between an ARO and an ARSO model?

**1.5** Under which circumstances is an ARSO model advisable?

**1.6** Does an ARO model provide either preventive or corrective protection? And a RO model?

**1.7** What is the uncertainty budget? Use an example to explain its meaning.

**1.8** Formulate, solve and discuss the result of a problem similar to that in Illustrative Example 1.4.

**1.9** Formulate, solve and discuss the result of a problem similar to that in Illustrative Example 1.5.

**1.10** Formulate, solve and discuss the result of a problem similar to that in Illustrative Example 1.6.

## 1.8 Appendix: Acronyms

ADRO: Adaptive distributionally robust optimization.
ARO: Adaptive robust optimization.
ARSO: Adaptive robust stochastic optimization.
RO: Robust optimization.
SP: Stochastic programming.

## 1.9 Appendix: GAMS Code

An input GAMS [8] file to solve the problem in Illustrative Example 1.3 is provided below.

```
variable z
integer variables x1,x21,x22;
positive variables y11, y21, y12, y22;
positive variables y31, y41, y32, y42;
equations of;
equations b1, b2, b3, b4, b5, b6;
equations o1, o2, o3, o4, o5, o6, o7, o8;
of.. z =e= x1+5*y21+5*y22+.5*x21+.5*x22+5*y41+5*422;
b1.. x1 =l= 3;
b2.. x1 =g= 2;
b3.. x21 =l= 3;
b4.. x21 =g= 2;
b5.. x22 =l= 3;
b6.. x22 =g= 2;
o1.. y11+y21 =e= 3;
o2.. y11 =l= x1;
o3.. y12+y22 =e= 5;
o4.. y12 =l= x1;
o5.. y31+y41 =e= 5;
```

```
o6.. y31 =l= x1;
o7.. y32+y42 =e= 8;
o8.. y32 =l= x1;
model sSP /all/;
solve sSP using MIP minimizing z;
```

Note that this GAMS code reproduces almost verbatim the mathematical formulation of the problem in Illustrative Example 1.3.

The part of the GAMS output file that provides the optimal solution is given below:

```
                        LOWER      LEVEL      UPPER     MARGINAL
---- VAR z              -INF    2135.000      +INF        .
---- VAR x1               .        3.000    100.000    -14.000
---- VAR x21              .        2.000    100.000      0.500
---- VAR x22              .        2.000    100.000      0.500
---- VAR y11              .        3.000      +INF        .
---- VAR y21              .          .        +INF        .
---- VAR y12              .        3.000      +INF        .
---- VAR y22              .        2.000      +INF        .
---- VAR y31              .        3.000      +INF        .
---- VAR y41              .        2.000      +INF        .
---- VAR y32              .          .        +INF       EPS
---- VAR y42              .        8.000      +INF        .
```

Note that this output file is self-explanatory.

## References


1. Birge, J. R., & Louveaux, F. (2011). *Introduction to Stochastic programming* (2nd ed.). New York: Springer.
2. Bertsimas, D., Brown, D. B., & Caramanis, C. (2011). Theory and applications of robust optimization. *SIAM Review, 53*(3), 464–501.
3. Conejo, A. J., Carrión, M., & Morales, J. M. (2010). *Decision making under uncertainty in electricity markets*. New York: Springer.
4. Shang, D,, Kuzmenko, V., & Uryasev, S. (2018). Cash flow matching with risks controlled by buffered probability of exceedance and conditional value-at-risk. *Annals of Operations Research, 260*(1), 501–514.
5. Rockafellar, R. T., & Uryasev, S. (2002). Conditional value-at-risk for general loss distributions. *Journal of Banking & Finance, 26*(7), 1443–1471.
6. Floudas, C. A. (1995). *Nonlinear and mixed-integer optimization: Fundamentals and applications*. Cary, NC: Oxford University Press.
7. Gurobi Optimization, Inc. (2017). Gurobi optimizer reference manual. http://www.gurobi.com.
8. GAMS Development Corporation. (2017). GAMS — A user's guide. http://www.gams.com.
9. Soyster, A. L. (1973). Convex programming with set-inclusive constraints and applications to inexact linear programming. *Operations Research, 21*(5), 1154–1157.
10. Bertsimas, D., & Sim, M. (2011). The price of robustness. *Operations Research, 52*(1), 35–53.

11. Bertsimas, D., Litvinov, E., Sun, X. A., Zhao, J., & Zheng, T. (2013). Adaptive robust optimization for the security constrained unit commitment problem. *IEEE Transactions on Power Systems, 28*(1), 52–63.
12. Zeng, B., & Zhao, L. (2013). Solving two-stage robust optimization problems using a column-and-constraint generation method. *Operations Research Letters, 41*(5), 457–461.
13. Zhang, X., & Conejo, A. J. (2017). Robust transmission expansion planning representing long- and short-term uncertainty. *IEEE Transactions on Power Systems,.33*(2), 1329–1338.
14. Bagheri, A., Wang, J., & Zhao C. (2017). Data-driven stochastic transmission expansion planning. *IEEE Transactions on Power Systems, 32*(5), 3461–3470.
15. Delage, E., & Ye, Y. (2010). Distributionally robust optimization under moment uncertainty with application to data-driven problems. *Operations Research, 58*(3), 595–612.
16. Conejo, A. J., Castillo, E., Minguez, R., & Garcia-Bertrand, R. (2006). *Decomposition techniques in mathematical programming. Engineering and science applications*. Heidelberg: Springer.
17. Ben-Tal, A., El Ghaoui, L., & Nemirovski, A. (2009). *Robust optimization*. Princeton, NJ: Princeton University Press.
18. Shapiro, A., Tekaya, W., Pereira Soares, M., & Paulo da Costa, J. Worst-case-expectation approach to optimization under uncertainty. *Operations Research, 61*(6), 1435–1449 (2013)
19. Baringo, L., & Conejo, A. J. (2011). Offering strategy via robust optimization. *IEEE Transactions on Power Systems, 26*(3), 1418–1425.
20. Zugno, M., & Conejo, A. J. (2015). A robust optimization approach to energy and reserve dispatch in electricity markets. *European Journal of Operational Research, 247*(2), 659–671.
21. Lorca, A., & Sun, X. A. (2017). Multistage robust unit commitment with dynamic uncertainty sets and energy storage. *IEEE Transactions on Power Systems, 32*(3), 1678–1688.
22. Dashti, H., Conejo, A. J., Jiang, R., & Wang, J. (2016). Weekly two-stage robust generation scheduling for hydrothermal power systems. *IEEE Transactions on Power Systems, 31*(6), 4554–4564.
23. Ruiz, C., & Conejo, A. J. Robust transmission expansion planning. *European Journal of Operational Research, 242*(2) (2015), 390–401.
24. Li, J., Li, Z., Liu, F., Ye, H., Zhang, X., Mei, S., & Chang, N. (2017). Robust coordinated transmission and generation expansion planning considering ramping requirements and construction periods. *IEEE Transactions on Power Systems, 33*(1), 268–280.
25. Dehghan, S., Amjady, N., & Kazemi, A. (2014). Two-stage robust generation expansion planning: A mixed-integer linear programming model. *IEEE Transactions on Power Systems, 29*(2), 584–597.

# Chapter 2
# Static Robust Optimization

## 2.1 Introduction

### *2.1.1 Preliminary*

Robust optimization is a rich and powerful modeling paradigm for decision making under uncertainty (See Chap. 1). The basic philosophy of robust decision making is to seek a decision that is feasible against all realizations of uncertain parameters in a bounded set, the so-called uncertainty set. For instance, in a linear constraint

$$\boldsymbol{a}^\top \boldsymbol{x} \leq b, \tag{2.1.1}$$

the coefficient $\boldsymbol{a} \in \mathbb{R}^n$ may not be known exactly. For example, we may only know that every coefficient $a_i$ of $\boldsymbol{a}$ is in a range, $a_i \in [\bar{a}_i - \Delta_i,\ \bar{a}_i + \Delta_i]$, centered around the nominal value $\bar{a}_i$ with some deviation $\Delta_i \geq 0$ for each $i$. In this case, we want to make a decision $\boldsymbol{x}$ that is feasible for all realizations of $\boldsymbol{a}$ in the hypercube $\mathscr{U}$ around $\bar{\boldsymbol{a}} = (\bar{a}_1, \bar{a}_2, \ldots, \bar{a}_n)^\top$, that is, we seek a *robust feasible* solution to the following problem

$$\boldsymbol{a}^\top \boldsymbol{x} \leq b, \quad \forall \boldsymbol{a} \in \mathscr{U}. \tag{2.1.2}$$

If $\mathscr{U}$ is an infinite set, like a hypercube, then (2.1.2) contains an infinite number of deterministic linear constraints (2.1.1), each for a realization of $\boldsymbol{a}$ taken from $\mathscr{U}$. Such a robust constraint is called a *static* robust linear constraint with a *deterministic* uncertainty set. It is called static, because, the solution $\boldsymbol{x}$ does not depend on any specific realization of $\boldsymbol{a}$, i.e. $\boldsymbol{x}$ does not change with respect to $\boldsymbol{a}$. The set $\mathscr{U}$ is called a deterministic uncertainty set, because the uncertainty in parameter $\boldsymbol{a}$ is modeled as an unknown deterministic quantity taking value in a bounded set. Both terms, "static" decision and "deterministic uncertainty", will be generalized in later



X. A. Sun, A. J. Conejo, *Robust Optimization in Electric Energy Systems*, International Series in Operations Research & Management Science 313, https://doi.org/10.1007/978-3-030-85128-6_2

chapters respectively to include "adaptive" decisions (Chap. 3) and "probabilistic uncertainty" or " uncertainty over probability distributions" (Chap. 4).

In this chapter, we will focus on static robust convex constraints with deterministic uncertainty sets of the following form

$$f(\boldsymbol{x}, \boldsymbol{\xi}) \leq 0, \quad \forall \boldsymbol{\xi} \in \mathscr{U}, \tag{2.1.3}$$

where $\boldsymbol{x}$ is the decision variable and $\boldsymbol{\xi}$ is the uncertainty parameter with uncertainty set $\mathscr{U}$. We assume $f(\boldsymbol{x}, \boldsymbol{\xi})$ is a convex function in $\boldsymbol{x}$ for any $\boldsymbol{\xi}$ and $\mathscr{U}$ is a convex, compact set. The choice of $f(\boldsymbol{x}, \boldsymbol{\xi})$ is usually dictated by the deterministic version of the problem. For example, in a unit commitment problem, if the power flow model uses DC approximation and the uncertainty is in the net load, then a robust transmission constraint can be modeled as a robust linear constraint. If the power flow model instead uses the full AC representation, then the robust transmission constraint becomes a nonconvex one. The choice of uncertainty set is usually made by considering how to best capture statistical characteristics of uncertain parameters, such as spatial and temporal correlations of wind power production among several geographically close wind farms over a day, how to trade off between robustness and conservativeness of the decision, and how to ensure some guarantees of feasibility of the robust solution when the uncertain parameter value is outside of the uncertainty set. In Chap. 4, Sect. 4.2.4, we will introduce a systematic way of using statistical hypothesis testing to construct uncertainty sets.

In this chapter, our main focus is on the *computationally tractable* reformulations of the robust constraint (2.1.3) (for a discussion on computability of convex optimization, see [1, Chapter 4]). As we have already observed, the robust constraint (2.1.3) could involve an infinite number of deterministic constraints, each for a realization of $\boldsymbol{\xi}$, and a finite number of variables, such a problem is called a *semi-infinite program* [2] and is in general computationally hard. In order for the robust convex optimization methodology to enjoy as much computational tractability as their deterministic counterparts, the robust constraints (2.1.3) should be reformulated to a *finite* set of deterministic convex constraints. We will use the model of convex conic constraints as the canonical model for convex constraints, which unifies linear programming, second-order cone programming (SOCP), and semidefinite programming (SDP). See [1] for a thorough treatment of convex conic optimization. We will see that the robust linear, SOCP, and SDP constraints have drastically different reformulation properties, which heavily depend on the structures of the uncertainty sets. We present many types of uncertainty sets which allow an *exact* reformulation of the robust convex conic constraints. It turns out that exact reformulation of robust convex conic constraints is a "rare commodity" – the majority of robust conic constraints are in fact computationally intractable [3]. For these difficult ones, we will present a broad class of uncertainty sets, for which robust SOCP and robust SDP constraints can be *safely approximated* by tractable deterministic convex constraints [16]. For some of these safe approximations, we can even characterize the approximation quality.

### 2.1.2 Summary and Organization

The main results of this chapter can be summarized in Fig. 2.1. As Fig. 2.1 indicates, robust linear optimization is tractable for any tractable conic uncertainty set, and can be reformulated as a convex conic optimization problem, where the complexity of the reformulation is determined by the complexity of the convex cone. In contrast, the tractability of a robust SOCP, convex quadratic, and SDP constraints is very much limited and is only achievable for some simple uncertainty sets such as an ellipsoidal uncertainty set or some class of unstructured uncertainty sets, which we call the "rank-2" ellipsoid. The main tools that are very useful for reformulation of robust conic constraints are conic duality, which is an extension of LP duality in the elegant framework of convex conic optimization, S-lemma, which gives an important strong duality result for nonconvex quadratic programs, and Schur complement, a very useful matrix technique (all these topics are thoroughly discussed in [1]).

In contrast, when the uncertainty set has more structures than an ellipsoid, such as a product of ellipsoids and hypercubes or as the intersection of multiple ellipsoids, the robust SOCP, convex quadratic, and SDP constraints are in general intractable, but safe approximations using deterministic SDP constraints can be derived quite easily for all of them. The more difficult task is to characterize how good the approximations are. This requires some important technical results, such

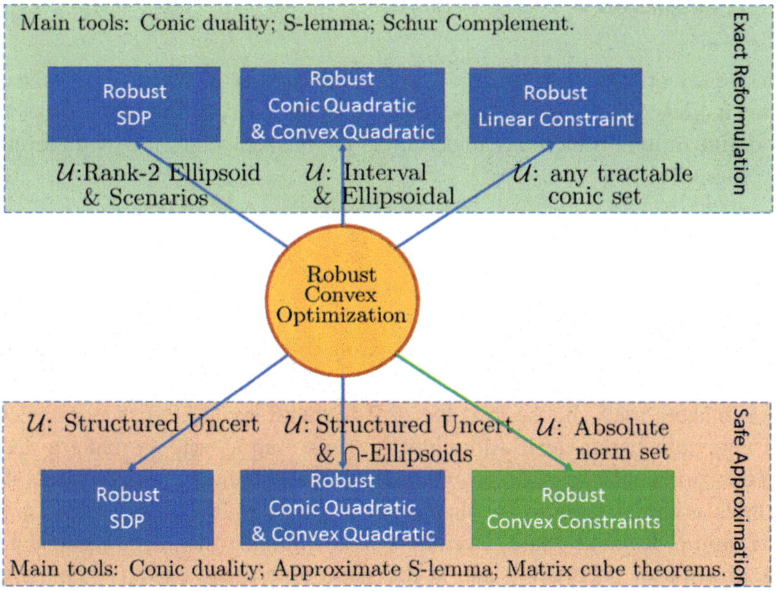


**Fig. 2.1** Summary of exact reformulations and safe approximations of robust convex conic optimization and uncertainty sets

as the approximate S-lemma [4, 6, 5] and matrix cube theorems [7, 8], which in turn rely on some probabilistic methods and deep results in probability theory, especially measure concentration inequalities. If we could exempt ourselves from explicit performance guarantees, then there is an alternative approach to derive safe approximations for robust conic problems and the advantage of this approach is that the robust constraints and their deterministic approximations have the same complexity. This chapter is based on the classic works on robust optimization e.g. [9, 10, 11, 12, 13, 14, 4, 7, 15, 16, 3].

The chapter is organized as follows. In Sect. 2.2, we introduce one of the most fundamental robust models, the robust linear optimization problems, and present exact reformulations for various uncertainty sets. Section 2.3 presents robust convex conic models with exact reformulations. Section 2.4 discusses the cases where exact reformulation of a robust constraint is not possible. The concept of safe approximations of robust convex conic constraints is introduced. Then, we work on robust SOCP and robust SDP constraints with some structured uncertainty sets and present safe approximations with performance guarantees. Finally, we introduce a disciplined way to construct safe approximations for a wide range of robust convex constraints.

## 2.2 Robust Linear Optimization

### *2.2.1 Preliminary*

The first study of robust optimization can be traced back to static linear robust optimization models, where the coefficients of the objective function and constraints of a linear optimization problem are uncertain [9]. Consider the following deterministic linear program (LP)

$$\min \ \boldsymbol{c}^\top \boldsymbol{x} \tag{2.2.1a}$$

$$\text{s.t.} \ \ \boldsymbol{A}\boldsymbol{x} \le \boldsymbol{b}. \tag{2.2.1b}$$

Now, $\boldsymbol{c}$, $\boldsymbol{A}$, and $\boldsymbol{b}$ are uncertain and can take any value in an uncertainty set. There is no unique way to make decision in this situation. The deterministically minded decision makers may choose to solve (2.2.1a) with some kind of nominal values of the uncertain parameters. Although this is a simple way to make a decision, such a decision could be quite problematic, when the uncertain parameters deviate from their nominal values, as illustrated in Chap. 1. The philosophy of robust optimization is to make “safe” decisions that minimize the cost against the worst case realization of uncertainty and at the same time always satisfy constraints for all uncertainty realizations. This modeling philosophy leads to the following robust linear optimization model

$$\min_{x} \max_{c \in \mathscr{C}} \boldsymbol{c}^\top \boldsymbol{x} \tag{2.2.2a}$$

$$\text{s.t. } \boldsymbol{A}\boldsymbol{x} \le \boldsymbol{b}, \quad \forall (\boldsymbol{A}, \boldsymbol{b}) \in \mathscr{U}, \tag{2.2.2b}$$

where $\mathscr{C}$ and $\mathscr{U}$ are uncertainty sets for $\boldsymbol{c}$ and $(\boldsymbol{A}, \boldsymbol{b})$, respectively. The objective function in (2.2.2a) is to minimize the worst-case cost, which is given by the maximization of $\boldsymbol{c}^\top \boldsymbol{x}$ over the uncertainty set $\mathscr{C}$. This worst-case objective can be moved to the constraints by introducing a new variable $t$ as

$$\min_{x,\, t} \quad t \tag{2.2.3a}$$

$$\text{s.t.} \quad \max_{c \in \mathscr{C}} \boldsymbol{c}^\top \boldsymbol{x} \le t, \tag{2.2.3b}$$

$$\boldsymbol{A}\boldsymbol{x} \le \boldsymbol{b}, \quad \forall (\boldsymbol{A}, \boldsymbol{b}) \in \mathscr{U}.$$

Notice that (2.2.3b) is equivalent to a robust feasibility constraint

$$\boldsymbol{c}^\top \boldsymbol{x} \le t, \quad \forall \boldsymbol{c} \in \mathscr{C}. \tag{2.2.4}$$

With this reformulation, it becomes clear that any static robust linear program can be modeled by a deterministic objective and robust constraints. In other words, it does not lose any generality if a static robust model has uncertainty only in the constraints. This is the reason that from now on we will focus on robust constraints in the form of (2.2.2b).

Suppose $\boldsymbol{A}$ is an $m$-by-$n$ matrix. Then we can look at each robust linear constraint corresponding to a row $i$ of $\boldsymbol{A}$ and rewrite (2.2.2b) as

$$\boldsymbol{a}_i^\top \boldsymbol{x} \le b_i, \quad \forall (\boldsymbol{A}, \boldsymbol{b}) \in \mathscr{U}, \ \forall i = 1, 2, \ldots, m. \tag{2.2.5}$$

For each $i$, the $i$-th robust linear constraint in (2.2.5) only involves uncertainty in $(\boldsymbol{a}_i, b_i)$. Therefore, we can form the uncertainty set $\mathscr{U}_i$ for $(\boldsymbol{a}_i, b_i)$ out of $\mathscr{U}$ as

$$\mathscr{U}_i := \Big\{ (\boldsymbol{a}_i, b_i) \in \mathbb{R}^{n+1} : \exists (\boldsymbol{a}_j, b_j) \in \mathbb{R}^{n+1} \text{ for } j \ne i, j = 1, 2, \ldots, m, \text{ s.t.}$$
$$([\boldsymbol{a}_1^\top; \ldots; a_m^\top], [b_1; \ldots; b_m]) \in \mathscr{U} \Big\}. \tag{2.2.6}$$

In other words, the uncertainty set $\mathscr{U}_i$ of $(\boldsymbol{a}_i, b_i)$ is the *projection* of the uncertainty $\mathscr{U}$ onto the space of $(\boldsymbol{a}_i, b_i)$. With these projected uncertainty sets $\mathscr{U}_i$, the robust linear constraints (2.2.5) are equivalent to

$$\boldsymbol{a}_i^\top \boldsymbol{x} \le b_i, \quad \forall (\boldsymbol{a}_i, b_i) \in \mathscr{U}_i, \ \forall i = 1, 2, \ldots, m. \tag{2.2.7}$$

If we put all the individual robust linear constraints in (2.2.7) back together, we get the following one

$$\boldsymbol{Ax} \leq \boldsymbol{b}, \quad \forall (\boldsymbol{A}, \boldsymbol{b}) \in \mathscr{U}_1 \times \mathscr{U}_2 \times \cdots \times \mathscr{U}_m, \tag{2.2.8}$$

which is equivalent to the original robust constraint (2.2.2b). But note that the new uncertainty set $\mathscr{U}_1 \times \mathscr{U}_2 \times \cdots \times \mathscr{U}_m$ in (2.2.8) is the Cartesian product of $\mathscr{U}_i$, which, intuitively speaking, is the smallest hypercube that contains the original $\mathscr{U}$. It is instructional to realize that, from the perspective of robust constraints, it does not make a difference whether we consider the uncertainty set $\mathscr{U}$, which may have couplings of $(\boldsymbol{a}_i, b_i)$ between different $i$, or the uncertainty set $\mathscr{U}_1 \times \cdots \times \mathscr{U}_m$, where $(\boldsymbol{a}_i, b_i)$ of different $i$ are completely independent of each other. However, from the perspective of uncertainty modeling, it is indeed meaningful to set up a joint uncertainty set $\mathscr{U}$ first in order to model correlations and dependencies of the uncertainty parameters and then to derive the projections $\mathscr{U}_i$ to each constraint.

Before we proceed to general reformulations of robust linear constraints, let us look at some simple examples to get some intuition of robust constraints.

**Illustrative Example 2.1** *Let us first look at a simple example of a robust constraint in* $\mathbb{R}^2$.

$$a_1x_1 + a_2x_2 \leq 1, \quad \forall a_i \in [-1, 1], \ i = 1, 2, \tag{2.2.9}$$

*where each coefficient of* $\boldsymbol{a}$ *can take any value in the interval* $[-1, 1]$, *i.e. the uncertain coefficient* $\boldsymbol{a} = (a_1, a_2)$ *takes value in a two-dimensional box. This robust linear constraint contains an uncountably infinite number of deterministic linear constraints as*

$$\begin{aligned}
&-x_1 - x_2 \leq 1,\\
&-x_1 - 0.8x_2 \leq 1,\\
&-x_1 - 0.7x_2 \leq 1,\\
&\ldots\ldots\ldots\\
&x_1 + x_2 \leq 1.
\end{aligned}$$

*The feasible region of* $\boldsymbol{x} = (x_1, x_2)^\top$ *defined by the robust constraint* (2.2.9) *is the intersection of all of the above halfspaces. From Fig.* 2.2, *we can see that the intersection of the infinitely many linear inequalities defines a feasible region for* $\boldsymbol{x}$ *that actually looks like a simple polyhedron with four inequalities, which will be identified using the duality reformulation technique discussed in the next section. See Exercise* 2.1.

□

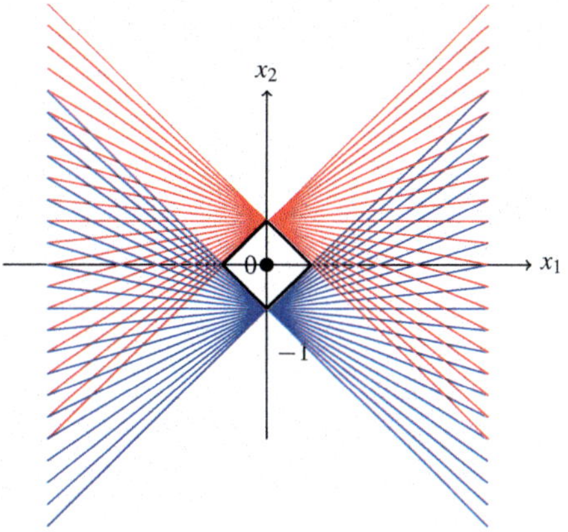


**Fig. 2.2** The diamond shape area around 0 outlined by black lines is the feasible region of robust constraint $a_1x_1 + a_2x_2 \leq 1$ for all $(a_1, a_2) \in [-1, 1]^2$

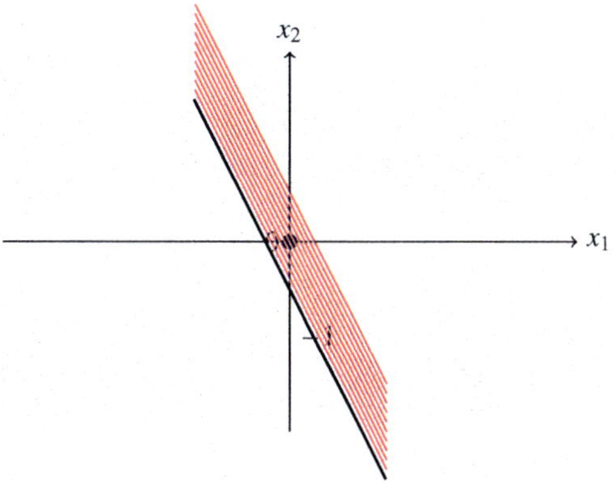


**Fig. 2.3** The space below the black line is the feasible region of the robust linear constraint $2x_1 + x_2 \leq b$ for all $b \in [-1, 1]$

**Illustrative Example 2.2** *Here is another simple robust linear constraint, whose coefficients are deterministic but the right-hand side is uncertain:*

$$2x_1 + x_2 \leq b, \quad \forall b \in [-1, 1].$$

*It is easy to see that the above robust linear constraint contains an infinite number of deterministic linear constraints in the form* $2x_1 + x_2 \leq -1, 2x_1 + x_2 \leq -0.99, \ldots, 2x_1 + x_2 \leq 1$. *Since the linear function part is fixed, only the right-hand side is changing. Then it is easy to see that feasible region of the robust constraint is defined by only one inequality:* $2x_1 + x_2 \leq \min_{b\in[-1,1]} b = -1$. *Figure* 2.3 *shows the feasible region.*

□

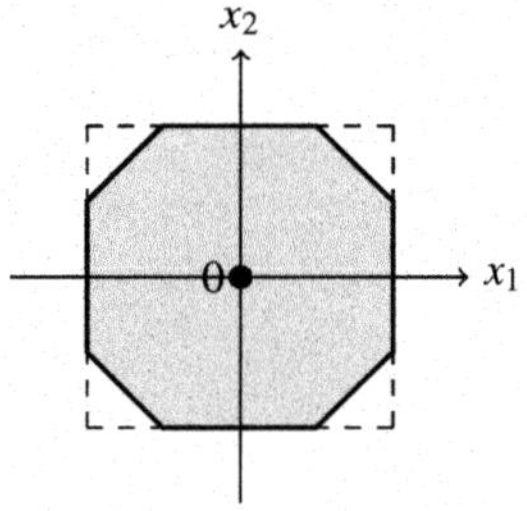


**Fig. 2.4** The budgeted uncertainty set $\{(a_1, a_2) : |a_1| + |a_2| \leq 1.5,\ a_i \in [-1, 1],\ i = 1, 2\}$

**Illustrative Example 2.3** *Here is the third example of a robust linear constraint with a more complicated uncertainty set:*

$$a_1x_1 + a_2x_2 \leq 1, \quad \forall (a_1, a_2) : |a_1| + |a_2| \leq 1.5,\ a_i \in [-1, 1],\ i = 1, 2. \tag{2.2.10}$$

*The uncertain parameters* $a_1, a_2$ *are contained in the box* $[-1, 1]^2$ *and are further restricted so that the total absolute deviation of* $(a_1, a_2)$ *from the origin is less than or equal to* 1.5*. Let us first draw this uncertainty set in Fig.* 2.4*. Exercise* 2.2 *asks the reader to plot the feasible region defined by the robust constraint* (2.2.10).

□

## *2.2.2 Reformulations*

### 2.2.2.1 Polyhedral Uncertainty Sets

Consider a robust linear constraint with a polyhedral uncertainty set $\mathcal{U}$ as

$$\boldsymbol{a}^\top \boldsymbol{x} \leq b, \quad \forall \boldsymbol{a} \in \mathcal{U} := \{\boldsymbol{a} \in \mathbb{R}^n : \boldsymbol{B}\boldsymbol{a} = \boldsymbol{d},\ \boldsymbol{a} \geq \boldsymbol{0}\}. \tag{2.2.11}$$

The following reformulation of (2.2.11) exploits linear programming duality. In particular, we have

A robust linear constraint (2.2.11) with a polyhedral uncertainty set can be reformulated as

$$\boldsymbol{a}^\top \boldsymbol{x} \leq b, \quad \forall \boldsymbol{a} \in \mathcal{U} := \{\boldsymbol{a} \in \mathbb{R}^n : \boldsymbol{B}\boldsymbol{a} = \boldsymbol{d}, \boldsymbol{a} \geq \boldsymbol{0}\},$$

$$\iff \max_{\boldsymbol{a}:\boldsymbol{B}\boldsymbol{a}=\boldsymbol{d},\boldsymbol{a}\geq\boldsymbol{0}} \boldsymbol{a}^\top \boldsymbol{x} \leq b, \tag{2.2.12a}$$

(continued)

$$\iff \min_{y:B^\top y \geq x} d^\top y \leq b, \tag{2.2.12b}$$

$$\iff \begin{cases} d^\top y \leq b, \\ B^\top y \geq x. \end{cases} \tag{2.2.12c}$$

Equation (2.2.12a) follows from the fact that if a real number ($b$ here) is greater than or equal to a set of real numbers ($a^\top x$ for each $a \in \mathscr{U}$), then $b$ should satisfy $b \geq \sup_{a \in \mathscr{U}} a^\top x$; moreover, the supremum is achieved by some particular $a$ in $\mathscr{U}$ because we always assume $\mathscr{U}$ is a compact set. So we can replace sup with max and get (2.2.12a). Equation (2.2.12b) holds because the uncertainty set $\mathscr{U}$ is a nonempty polytope, so the maximum in (2.2.12a) for any $x$ is finite, therefore, LP strong duality holds between the primal maximization problem and the dual problem in (2.2.12b). Finally, since the minimum in (2.2.12b) exists for any $x$ and is less than or equal to $b$, then there must exist some $y$ in the dual polyhedron so that the objective value of the dual problem is less than $b$.

From the above discussion, we can see that if the uncertainty set is a polyhedron, then a robust linear constraint is equivalent to a finite set of deterministic linear constraints. Now let us work out some important class of polyhedral uncertainty sets.

1. **Box uncertainty set:** If each uncertain coefficient $a_i$ takes value in an interval around a nominal value $\bar{a}_i$ with width $\Delta_i$, i.e. $a_i \in [\bar{a}_i - \Delta_i, \bar{a}_i + \Delta_i]$ for $i = 1, 2, \ldots, n$, then the uncertain vector $a$ is in a box uncertainty set $\mathscr{U}$

$$\mathscr{U}_{\text{box}} = \left\{ a \in \mathbb{R}^n : \exists \xi \text{ s.t. } a = \bar{a} + \Delta\xi, \ \|\xi\|_\infty \leq 1 \right\}, \tag{2.2.13}$$

where $\bar{a}$ is the vector of nominal value $a_i$'s and $\Delta$ is a diagonal matrix with $\Delta_i$'s on the diagonal. The $\ell_\infty$ norm $\|\xi\|_\infty := \max_{i=1,2,\ldots,n} |\xi_i|$.

The linear constraint over a box uncertainty set (2.2.13) can be reformulated as

$$a^\top x \leq b, \quad \forall a \in \mathscr{U}_{\text{box}},$$

$$\iff \max_{\|\xi\|_\infty \leq 1} \left\{ \bar{a}^\top x + \xi^\top (\Delta x) \right\} \leq b, \tag{2.2.14a}$$

$$\iff \bar{a}^\top x + \|\Delta x\|_1 \leq b, \tag{2.2.14b}$$

(continued)

$$\iff \quad \bar{a}^\top x + \sum_{i=1}^{n} |\Delta_i x_i| \le b, \tag{2.2.14c}$$

$$\iff \quad \begin{cases} \bar{a}^\top x + \sum_{i=1}^{n} t_i \le b, \\ -t_i \le \Delta_i x_i \le t_i, \quad \forall i = 1, 2, \ldots, n, \end{cases} \tag{2.2.14d}$$

where (2.2.14b) comes from the fact that the $\ell_\infty$ norm and the $\ell_1$ norm are dual to each other (see [1] for more discussions). Constraint (2.2.14d) replaces the absolute value function in (2.2.14c) using additional variables $t_i$'s. Notice that the $\boldsymbol{\xi}$ that achieves the maximum in (2.2.14a), i.e., the worst case scenario $\boldsymbol{\xi}$, has the form $\xi_i = \pm 1$ for each $i$. In other words, the worst-case scenario takes the largest deviation from the nominal value. If the reader is not familiar with LP duality, it is beneficial to verify the steps in (2.2.14d) (see Exercise 2.3).

We can go back to the earlier example (2.2.9), where the uncertainty set is a standard box $[-1, 1]^2$. So, the diagonal matrix $\boldsymbol{\Delta}$ is the identity matrix and the nominal value $\bar{a}_i = 0$ for $i = 1, 2$. The deterministic reformulation is directly given by (2.2.14c) as

$$|x_1| + |x_2| \le 1,$$

which can be rewritten by four linear constraints as

$$x_1 + x_2 \le 1, \quad x_1 - x_2 \le 1, \quad -x_1 + x_2 \le 1, \quad -x_1 - x_2 \le 1.$$

The feasible region defined by these four inequalities are exactly the diamond shape outlined in Fig. 2.2.

2. **Budget uncertainty set:** The box uncertainty set $\mathscr{U}_{\text{box}}$ contains the entire range of the extreme deviations of the uncertainty parameters from $\bar{a}_i - \Delta_i$ to $\bar{a}_i + \Delta_i$ for each $i$. In order to control the size of the uncertainty set and restrict the amount of uncertainty considered, we can impose a constraint that the total deviation from the nominal value is bounded as

$$\mathscr{U}_{\text{budget}} = \left\{ \boldsymbol{a} \in \mathbb{R}^n : \exists \boldsymbol{\xi} \text{ s.t. } \boldsymbol{a} = \bar{\boldsymbol{a}} + \boldsymbol{\Delta}\boldsymbol{\xi},\ \|\boldsymbol{\xi}\|_\infty \le 1,\ \sum_{i=1}^{n} |\xi_i| \le r \right\}, \tag{2.2.15}$$

where $\theta$ controls the conservative level of the robust constraint. If $r = 0$, then $\xi_i = 0$ for all $i$ and the uncertainty set is a singleton of the nominal value $\mathscr{U}_{\text{budget}} = \{\bar{\boldsymbol{a}}\}$. If $r = n$, then $\mathscr{U}_{\text{budget}} = \mathscr{U}_{\text{box}}$. Note that $\sum_{i=1}^{n} |\xi_i| \le r$ can be also written as $\|\boldsymbol{\xi}\|_1 \leq r$. So the budget uncertainty set is an intersection of the unit $\ell_\infty$ ball and an $\ell_1$ ball with radius $r$.

The robust linear constraint with a budget uncertainty set is given as

$$\begin{aligned}
& \boldsymbol{a}^\top \boldsymbol{x} \leq b, \quad \forall \boldsymbol{a} \in \mathcal{U}_{\text{budget}}, \\
\iff \quad & \bar{\boldsymbol{a}}^\top \boldsymbol{x} + \max_{\substack{\|\boldsymbol{\xi}\|_\infty \leq 1 \\ \|\boldsymbol{\xi}\|_1 \leq r}} \left\{ \boldsymbol{\xi}^\top (\boldsymbol{\Delta x}) \right\} \leq b. \qquad (2.2.16a)
\end{aligned}$$

So we only need to reformulate the maximization problem over $\boldsymbol{\xi}$ in the intersection of two balls.

$$\begin{aligned}
& \max_{\boldsymbol{\xi}} \left\{ \boldsymbol{c}^\top \boldsymbol{\xi} : \|\boldsymbol{\xi}\|_\infty \leq 1, \ \|\boldsymbol{\xi}\|_1 \leq r \right\} \\
= & \max_{\boldsymbol{\xi}, \boldsymbol{t}} \left\{ \boldsymbol{c}^\top \boldsymbol{\xi} : \sum_{i=1}^n t_i \leq r, \ \xi_i \leq 1, \ -\xi_i \leq 1, \ \xi_i \leq t_i, \ -\xi_i \leq t_i, \ \forall i = 1, 2, \ldots, n \right\} \\
= & \min_{\boldsymbol{y}^\pm, \boldsymbol{z}^\pm, \theta} \quad r\theta + \sum_{i=1}^n (y_i^+ + y_i^-) \\
& \text{s.t.} \quad y_i^+ - y_i^- + z_i^+ - z_i^- = c_i, \quad \forall i = 1, 2, \ldots, n, \qquad (2.2.17a) \\
& \qquad \theta - z_i^+ - z_i^- = 0, \quad \forall i = 1, 2, \ldots, n, \qquad (2.2.17b) \\
& \qquad \theta \geq 0, \ y_i^\pm \geq 0, \ z_i^\pm \geq 0, \quad \forall i = 1, 2, \ldots, n. \qquad (2.2.17c)
\end{aligned}$$

Now substituting $\boldsymbol{c} = \boldsymbol{\Delta x}$ into (2.2.17a), we have the formulation reformulation result.

The robust linear constraint over a budget uncertainty set (2.2.15) can be reformulated as

$$\begin{aligned}
& \boldsymbol{a}^\top \boldsymbol{x} \leq b, \quad \forall \boldsymbol{a} \in \mathcal{U}_{\text{budget}}, \\
\iff \quad & \begin{cases}
\bar{\boldsymbol{a}}^\top \boldsymbol{x} + r\theta + \sum_{i=1}^n (y_i^+ + y_i^-) \leq b, \\
y_i^+ - y_i^- + z_i^+ - z_i^- = \Delta_i x_i, \quad \forall i = 1, 2, \ldots, n, \\
\theta - z_i^+ - z_i^- = 0, \quad \forall i = 1, 2, \ldots, n, \\
\theta \geq 0, \ y_i^\pm \geq 0, \ z_i^\pm \geq 0, \quad \forall i = 1, 2, \ldots, n.
\end{cases}
\end{aligned}$$

Going back to the example in (2.2.10), we can reformulate this robust constraint with a budget uncertainty set as

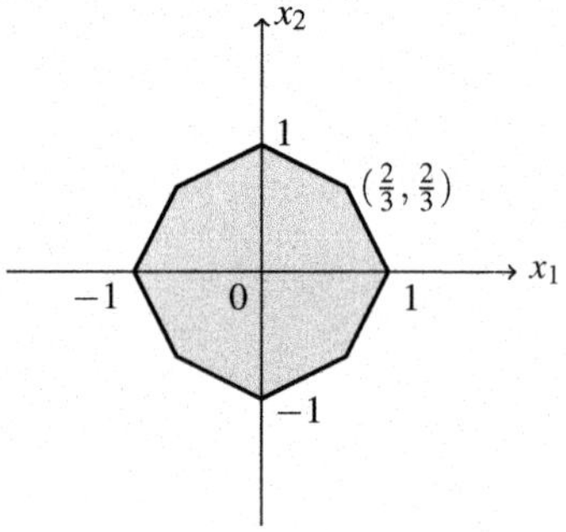


**Fig. 2.5** Feasible region of the robust constraint $a_1x_1 + a_2x_2 \leq 1, \forall |a_1| + |a_2| \leq 1.5, -1 \leq a_i \leq 1, i = 1, 2$

$$
\begin{aligned}
&\max_{a_1,a_2} \left\{ a_1x_1 + a_2x_2 : |a_1| + |a_2| \leq 1.5, -1 \leq a_1, a_2 \leq 1 \right\} \leq 1 \\
\Longleftrightarrow\ &\max_{a_1,a_2} \left\{ a_1x_1 + a_2x_2 : t_1 + t_2 \leq 1.5, a_i \leq 1, -a_i \leq 1, a_i - t_i \leq 0, -a_i - t_i \leq 0, i=1,2 \right\} \leq 1 \\
\Longleftrightarrow\ &\min \Big\{ 1.5\theta + y_1^+ + y_1^- + y_2^+ + y_2^- : y_i^+ - y_i^- + z_i^+ - z_i^- = x_i, \theta - z_i^+ - z_i^- = 0, \\
&\qquad \theta \geq 0, y_i^\pm \geq 0, z_i^\pm \geq 0, i = 1, 2 \Big\} \leq 1
\end{aligned}
$$

$$
\begin{aligned}
\Longleftrightarrow\ & 1.5\theta + y_1^+ + y_1^- + y_2^+ + y_2^- \leq 1, && \text{(2.2.18a)} \\
& y_i^+ - y_i^- + z_i^+ - z_i^- = x_i, \quad \forall i = 1, 2, && \text{(2.2.18b)} \\
& \theta - z_i^+ - z_i^- = 0, \quad \forall i = 1, 2, && \text{(2.2.18c)} \\
& \theta \geq 0, y_i^\pm \geq 0, z_i^\pm \geq 0, \quad \forall i = 1, 2. && \text{(2.2.18d)}
\end{aligned}
$$

Notice that the original robust constraint is about $x_1, x_2$, while the reformulation (2.2.18) involves $x_1, x_2$ and nine additional variables $\theta$, $y_1^\pm$, $y_2^\pm$, $z_1^\pm$, $z_2^\pm$. In other words, the feasible region of the robust constraint is lifted from $\mathbb{R}^2$ to $\mathbb{R}^{11}$. To illustrate what the robust feasible region looks like in the original space $\mathbb{R}^2$, we can use the Fourier-Motzkin elimination [17], the feasible region of the robust constraint in $\mathbb{R}^2$ can be found as

$$|x_1| + 2|x_2| \leq 2, \ \ 2|x_1| + |x_2| \leq 2, \tag{2.2.19}$$

which is plotted in Fig. 2.5. Also see Exercise 2.4.

#### 2.2.2.2 Linear Conic Uncertainty Sets

As we see from the previous subsection that a polyhedral uncertainty set can be written in the form of

$$\mathscr{U} := \{\boldsymbol{a} \in \mathbb{R}^n : \boldsymbol{B}\boldsymbol{a} = \boldsymbol{d}, \boldsymbol{a} \geq \boldsymbol{0}\}, \tag{2.2.20}$$

then a natural question is whether we could also express a nonlinear uncertainty set in a similar form. Surprisingly, the answer is yes. This comes from a beautiful insight offered by the modern convex optimization theory, in particular, the theory of linear conic optimization. For a comprehensive study of this topic, interested reader should refer to the textbook [1].

In a nutshell, an elegant way to extend a system of linear constraints as (2.2.20) to a system of nonlinear convex constraints is to extend the nonnegative constraint $\boldsymbol{a} \geq 0$ to a nonlinear one. The idea is the following. The nonnegative constraint $\boldsymbol{a} \geq \boldsymbol{0}$ can be interpreted as saying $\boldsymbol{a}$ is in the nonnegative orthant $\mathbb{R}^n_+$, which is a special example of a *convex cone*. A cone $K$ is a set such that if $\boldsymbol{x} \in K$ then the entire ray starting from the origin and pointing toward the direction of $\boldsymbol{x}$ is also contained in $K$, i.e. $\lambda \boldsymbol{x} \in K$ for any $\lambda \geq 0$. A cone is a convex cone if the cone is a convex set.

In addition to the nonnegative orthant cone $\mathbb{R}^n_+$, another important convex cone is the second-order cone (SOC) $\mathbb{L}^n$ defined as

$$\mathbb{L}^n = \left\{(x_1, \ldots, x_n) : \sqrt{x_1^2 + \cdots + x_n^2} \leq x_n\right\}. \tag{2.2.21}$$

Figure 2.6 plots these two convex cones $\mathbb{R}^3_+$ and $\mathbb{L}^3$. Now, we can view the nonnegativity constraints $\boldsymbol{a} \geq \boldsymbol{0}$ as the geometric constraint that $\boldsymbol{a}$ is contained in the convex cone $\mathbb{R}^n_+$, i.e., $\boldsymbol{a} \in \mathbb{R}^n_+$. This geometric view inspires us to consider $\boldsymbol{a} \in K$ for other convex cones $K$, such as the second-order cone $\mathbb{L}^n$. Then, coming back to the algebraic view, we can write $\boldsymbol{a} \in K$ as an inequality $\boldsymbol{a} \succeq_K \boldsymbol{0}$. Here $\succeq_K$ defines a (partial) order such that $\boldsymbol{a} \succeq_K \boldsymbol{b}$ if and only if $\boldsymbol{a} - \boldsymbol{b} \in K$. It is called a partial order, because we can only compare two vectors when their difference is in the cone $K$. Just like in the case of $K = \mathbb{R}^n_+$, we can only compare two vectors $\boldsymbol{a}, \boldsymbol{b}$ if $a_i - b_i \geq 0$ for each component $i$.

The constraint $\boldsymbol{a} \succeq_K \boldsymbol{0}$ is called a *linear conic inequality* – the left-hand side is still linear in $\boldsymbol{a}$ and the ordering $\succeq_K$ is defined by a convex cone $K$. Since the convex cone $K$ may not be linear (think about the SOC cone), the conic constraint $\boldsymbol{a} \succeq_K \boldsymbol{0}$ may not be a linear constraint in $\boldsymbol{a}$. Using linear conic constraint, we can define a robust linear conic constraint as

$$\boldsymbol{a}^\top \boldsymbol{x} \leq b, \quad \forall \boldsymbol{a} \in \mathscr{U} := \left\{\boldsymbol{a} \in \mathbb{R}^n : \boldsymbol{B}\boldsymbol{a} = \boldsymbol{d},\ \boldsymbol{a} \succeq_K \boldsymbol{0}\right\}. \tag{2.2.22}$$

The reformulation of (2.2.22) follows exactly the format of the reformulation of a linear robust constraint over a polyhedral uncertainty set. The only difference is that the LP duality is generalized to the linear conic duality, where the nonnegative orthant is replaced by a proper convex cone and its *dual cone*. The book [1] gives an excellent introduction of conic duality theory.

Applying conic duality, we have the following result.

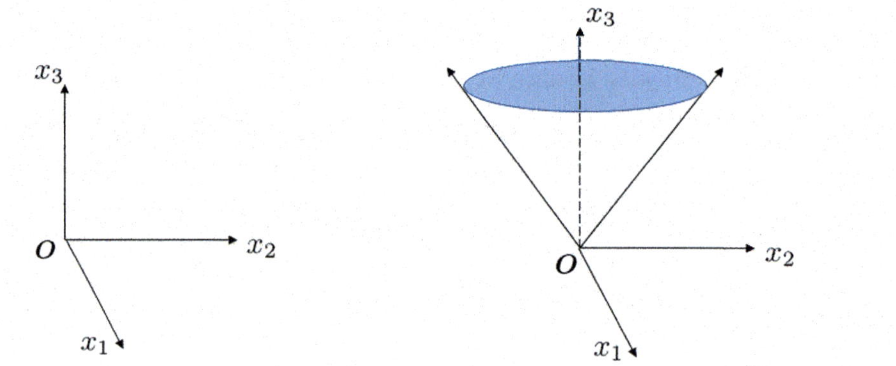


Nonnegative orthant $\mathbb{R}^n_+$

Second-order Cone: $\mathbb{L}^n$
$\mathbb{L}^n = \{(x_1, x_2, \ldots, x_n) : \|(x_1, \ldots, x_{n-1})\|_2 \le x_n\}$

**Fig. 2.6** Examples of convex cones: Nonnegative orthant $\mathbb{R}^n_+$ and a second-order cone $\mathbb{L}^n$

The robust linear constraint over a linear conic uncertainty set

$$\boldsymbol{a}^\top \boldsymbol{x} \le b, \quad \forall \boldsymbol{a} \in \mathscr{U} := \{\boldsymbol{a} \in \mathbb{R}^n : \boldsymbol{B}\boldsymbol{a} = \boldsymbol{d},\ \boldsymbol{a} \succeq_K \boldsymbol{0}\}, \tag{2.2.23}$$

can be equivalently reformulated as

$$\max_{\boldsymbol{B}\boldsymbol{a}=\boldsymbol{d},\ \boldsymbol{a}\succeq_K \boldsymbol{0}} \quad \boldsymbol{a}^\top \boldsymbol{x} \le b, \tag{2.2.24a}$$

$$\Longleftrightarrow \quad \min_{\boldsymbol{B}^\top \boldsymbol{y} \succeq_{K^*} \boldsymbol{x}} \quad \boldsymbol{d}^\top \boldsymbol{y} \le b, \tag{2.2.24b}$$

$$\Longleftrightarrow \quad \begin{cases} \boldsymbol{d}^\top \boldsymbol{y} \le b, \\ \boldsymbol{B}^\top \boldsymbol{y} \succeq_{K^*} \boldsymbol{x}. \end{cases} \tag{2.2.24c}$$

Here, the set $K^*$ is the dual cone of $K$, defined as $K^* = \{\boldsymbol{x} \in \mathbb{R}^n : \boldsymbol{x}^\top \boldsymbol{y} \ge 0,\ \forall \boldsymbol{y} \in K\}$. For example, the dual cones of $\mathbb{R}^n_+$ and $\mathbb{L}^n$ are themselves. That is, these two cones are *self-dual*. As soon as we know the dual cone of a cone $K$, then we can use the above reformulation (2.2.24c) for a robust linear constraint.

**Ellipsoidal uncertainty set:** A widely used nonlinear uncertainty set is the ellipsoidal set. An ellipsoid centered at $\boldsymbol{0}$ in $\mathbb{R}^n$ can be expressed as

$$\mathscr{U}_{\text{ellip}} = \{\boldsymbol{a} : \boldsymbol{a}^\top \boldsymbol{Q} \boldsymbol{a} \le 1\}, \tag{2.2.25}$$

where $Q$ is a symmetric positive definite matrix. The shape of the ellipsoid is determined by $Q$. If $Q$ is the identity matrix, then the ellipsoid is the standard Euclidean ball with radius 1. More generally, let $Q = V\Lambda V^\top$ be an eigendecomposition of $Q$, where $V$ contains a set of orthonormal eigenvectors of $Q$ in its columns and $\Lambda = \text{diag}(\lambda_1, \ldots, \lambda_n)$ is a diagonal matrix with positive eigenvalues of $Q$. Then $a^\top Q a = (a^\top V \Lambda^{1/2})(\Lambda^{1/2} V^\top a)$. If we let $u = \Lambda^{1/2} V^\top a$, then $a \in \mathcal{U}_{\text{ellip}} \Leftrightarrow u^\top u \leq 1$. This derivation tells us that the ellipsoid $\mathcal{U}_{\text{ellip}}$ in the space of $a$ can be obtained from a standard Euclidean ball in the space of $u$ by a linear transformation $R = V\Lambda^{-1/2}$. The axes of $\mathcal{U}_{\text{ellip}}$ can be obtained by applying $R$ to the standard bases of $\mathbb{R}^n$, and immediately we see that the $j$-th axis of $\mathcal{U}_{\text{ellip}}$ is the $j$-th column of $V$ with length $1/\sqrt{\lambda_j}$. It is sometimes more convenient to use this linear transformation to represent the ellipsoid $\mathcal{U}_{\text{ellip}}$ as

$$\mathcal{U}_{\text{ellip}} = \{a : a = Ru,\ \|u\|_2 \leq 1\}. \tag{2.2.26}$$

**Illustrative Example 2.4** *Let us see an example of a 2-dimensional ellipsoid, centered at the origin with the axes given by directions* $[1, 1]^\top, [-1, 1]^\top$ *with lengths* 1 *and* 2 *respectively. See Fig.* 2.7.

*The matrices* $V$, $\Lambda$, *and* $Q$ *are given as*

$$V = \frac{1}{\sqrt{2}}\begin{bmatrix} 1 & -1 \\ 1 & 1 \end{bmatrix}, \quad \Lambda = \begin{bmatrix} 1 & \\ & 1/4 \end{bmatrix},$$

$$Q = V\Lambda V^\top = \frac{1}{2}\begin{bmatrix} 1 & -1 \\ 1 & 1 \end{bmatrix}\begin{bmatrix} 1 & \\ & 1/4 \end{bmatrix}\begin{bmatrix} 1 & 1 \\ -1 & 1 \end{bmatrix} = \begin{bmatrix} \frac{5}{8} & \frac{3}{8} \\ \frac{3}{8} & \frac{5}{8} \end{bmatrix}.$$

*Matrix* $R$ *can be computed as*

$$R = V\Lambda^{-1/2} = \frac{1}{\sqrt{2}}\begin{bmatrix} 1 & -1 \\ 1 & 1 \end{bmatrix}\begin{bmatrix} 1 & \\ & 2 \end{bmatrix} = \frac{1}{\sqrt{2}}\begin{bmatrix} 1 & -2 \\ 1 & 2 \end{bmatrix}.$$

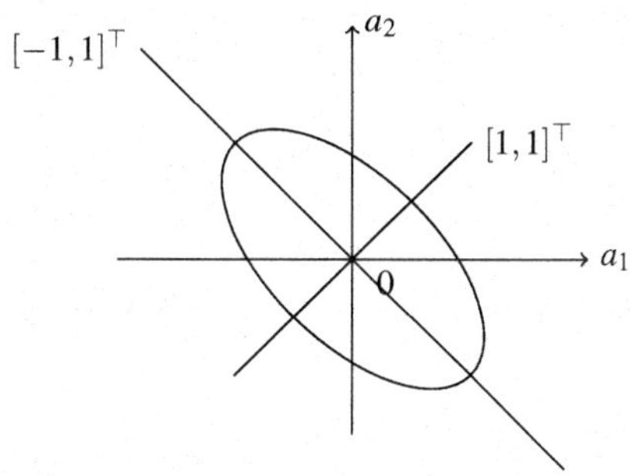


**Fig. 2.7** An ellipsoid centered at 0 with axes directions $[1, 1]^\top$ and $[-1, 1]$ and length 1, 2 respectively

*So the ellipsoid can be represented as*

$$\mathscr{U}_{ellip} = \left\{(a_1, a_2) : \begin{bmatrix} a_1 \\ a_2 \end{bmatrix}^\top \begin{bmatrix} \frac{5}{8} & \frac{3}{8} \\ \frac{3}{8} & \frac{5}{8} \end{bmatrix} \begin{bmatrix} a_1 \\ a_2 \end{bmatrix} \le 1 \right\}$$
$$= \left\{(a_1, a_2) : \begin{bmatrix} a_1 \\ a_2 \end{bmatrix} = \frac{1}{\sqrt{2}} \begin{bmatrix} 1 & -2 \\ 1 & 2 \end{bmatrix} \begin{bmatrix} u_1 \\ u_2 \end{bmatrix}, \ \|\boldsymbol{u}\|_2 \le 1 \right\}. \tag{2.2.27}$$

□

More generally, an ellipsoidal uncertainty set $\mathscr{U}_{\text{ellip}}$ can be centered at a nominal vector $\bar{\boldsymbol{a}}$ as

$$\mathscr{U}_{\text{ellip}} = \left\{\boldsymbol{a} \in \mathbb{R}^n : (\boldsymbol{a} - \bar{\boldsymbol{a}})^\top \boldsymbol{Q}(\boldsymbol{a} - \bar{\boldsymbol{a}}) \le 1\right\} \tag{2.2.28}$$
$$= \left\{\boldsymbol{a} \in \mathbb{R}^n : \boldsymbol{a} = \bar{\boldsymbol{a}} + \boldsymbol{R}\boldsymbol{u}, \ \|\boldsymbol{u}\|_2 \le 1\right\}. \tag{2.2.29}$$

The robust linear constraint over this ellipsoidal uncertainty set can be reformulated as

$$\boldsymbol{a}^\top \boldsymbol{x} \le b, \quad \forall \boldsymbol{a} \in \mathscr{U}_{\text{ellip}},$$
$$\Longleftrightarrow \bar{\boldsymbol{a}}^\top \boldsymbol{x} + \max_{\|\boldsymbol{u}\|_2 \le 1} \{\boldsymbol{u}^\top \boldsymbol{R}^\top \boldsymbol{x}\} \le b,$$
$$\Longleftrightarrow \bar{\boldsymbol{a}}^\top \boldsymbol{x} + \|\boldsymbol{R}^\top \boldsymbol{x}\|_2 \le b, \tag{2.2.30a}$$
$$\Longleftrightarrow \bar{\boldsymbol{a}}^\top \boldsymbol{x} + \sqrt{\boldsymbol{x}^\top \boldsymbol{Q}\boldsymbol{x}} \le b. \tag{2.2.30b}$$

We can apply the reformulation (2.2.30b) to the 2-dimensional example: $a_1x_1 + a_2x_2 \le 1$ for all $(a_1, a_2) \in \mathscr{U}_{\text{ellip}}$ defined by (2.2.27). Then according to (2.2.30a), the feasible region of the robust constraint is given by

$$\left\{(x_1, x_2) : \begin{bmatrix} x_1 \\ x_2 \end{bmatrix}^\top \begin{bmatrix} \frac{5}{8} & \frac{3}{8} \\ \frac{3}{8} & \frac{5}{8} \end{bmatrix} \begin{bmatrix} x_1 \\ x_2 \end{bmatrix} \le 1 \right\},$$

which actually coincides with the ellipsoid of the uncertainty set. See Exercise 2.5.

We can also directly apply the reformulation for a linear conic uncertainty set. We first need to write the ellipsoidal uncertainty set in the linear conic form

$$\mathscr{U}_{\text{ellip}} = \{\boldsymbol{a} \in \mathbb{R}^n : \boldsymbol{a} = \bar{\boldsymbol{a}} + \boldsymbol{R}\boldsymbol{u}, \ \|\boldsymbol{u}\|_2 \le 1\},$$
$$\Longleftrightarrow \mathscr{U}_{\text{ellip}} = \{\boldsymbol{a} \in \mathbb{R}^n : \boldsymbol{a} = \bar{\boldsymbol{a}} + \boldsymbol{R}\boldsymbol{u}, \ [\boldsymbol{u}; v] \in \mathbb{L}^{n+1}, \ v = 1\}, \tag{2.2.31a}$$
$$\Longleftrightarrow \mathscr{U}_{\text{ellip}} = \{\boldsymbol{a} \in \mathbb{R}^n : \boldsymbol{a} = \bar{\boldsymbol{a}} + \tilde{\boldsymbol{R}}\tilde{\boldsymbol{u}}, \ \boldsymbol{e}_{n+1}^\top \tilde{\boldsymbol{u}} = 1, \ \tilde{\boldsymbol{u}} \in \mathbb{L}^{n+1}\}, \tag{2.2.31b}$$

where $\tilde{\boldsymbol{u}} = [\boldsymbol{u}^\top, v]^\top$ and $\tilde{\boldsymbol{R}}$ is the matrix formed by appending a new column of zeros to $\boldsymbol{R}$, and $\boldsymbol{e}_{n+1} = [0, \ldots, 0, 1]^\top \in \mathbb{R}^{n+1}$. Recall that the dual cone of $\mathbb{L}^{n+1}$ is itself. Then, the robust linear constraint can be reformulated as

$$\boldsymbol{a}^\top \boldsymbol{x} \leq b, \quad \forall \boldsymbol{a} \in \mathscr{U}_{\text{ellip}},$$

$$\iff \bar{\boldsymbol{a}}^\top \boldsymbol{x} + \max_{\substack{\tilde{\boldsymbol{u}} \in \mathbb{L}^{n+1} \\ \boldsymbol{e}_{n+1}^\top \tilde{\boldsymbol{u}} = 1}} \{\tilde{\boldsymbol{u}}^\top \tilde{\boldsymbol{R}}^\top \boldsymbol{x}\} \leq b, \tag{2.2.32a}$$

$$\iff \bar{\boldsymbol{a}}^\top \boldsymbol{x} + \left\{ \min_{\boldsymbol{e}_{n+1} t \succeq_{K^*} \tilde{\boldsymbol{R}}^\top \boldsymbol{x}} t \right\} \leq b, \quad (K^* = \mathbb{L}^{n+1}) \tag{2.2.32b}$$

$$\iff \begin{cases} \bar{\boldsymbol{a}}^\top \boldsymbol{x} + t \leq b, \\ \boldsymbol{e}_{n+1} t \succeq_{K^*} \tilde{\boldsymbol{R}}^\top \boldsymbol{x}. \end{cases} \tag{2.2.32c}$$

It would be a good exercise to further reformulate (2.2.32c) to obtain (2.2.30a). See Exercise 2.6.

Once the reader gets used to the formalism of conic optimization, the derivation shown above would become very natural. It provides a unified approach that includes linear programming as a special case. In the general linear conic setting, there are more subtle questions about the strong duality of the reformulation. However, the process of taking the dual of robust linear constraints over a conic uncertainty set is as simple as taking the dual of a linear program. The resulting deterministic linear conic constraints can be readily implemented and solved in modern convex optimization solvers such as MOSEK [18].

## 2.3 Robust Convex Conic Optimization

The last section gives a detailed discussion on robust linear constraints over polyhedral uncertainty sets and over the more general convex conic uncertainty sets. The conclusion is that robust linear constraints are in general tractable. In particular, as long as we can describe the convex cones involved in the uncertainty set in a tractable way, the reformulation of the robust linear constraint is a finite set of convex conic constraints, which can be handled efficiently by modern convex optimization solvers.

The situation becomes much more complicated when we have robust nonlinear constraints. The reformulation of a robust nonlinear constraint may not be a convex constraint anymore, therefore, may become computationally difficult to solve, i.e. may fall into the category of NP-hard problems. Facing this situation, there are two directions moving forward. One is to identify classes of robust nonlinear constraints and associated uncertainty sets that lead to computationally tractable reformulations. The other one is to develop methods to approximate intractable robust constraints.

In this section, we will discuss both directions. An excellent reference for the optimization techniques involved in this section is [1].

### 2.3.1 Preliminary

Recall the general robust convex constraint (2.1.3), restated here for convenience,

$$f(\boldsymbol{x}, \boldsymbol{\xi}) \leq 0, \quad \forall \boldsymbol{\xi} \in \mathcal{U}. \tag{2.3.1}$$

We assume that $f(\boldsymbol{x}, \boldsymbol{\xi})$ is a convex-concave function, i.e. $f(\boldsymbol{x}, \boldsymbol{\xi})$ is convex in $\boldsymbol{x}$ for any $\boldsymbol{\xi}$ and concave in $\boldsymbol{\xi}$ for any $\boldsymbol{x}$. While a robust linear constraint is represented by a bilinear function $f(\boldsymbol{x}, \boldsymbol{\xi}) = \boldsymbol{\xi}^\top \boldsymbol{x}$, which has a well defined structure, there is no universal way to express an arbitrary nonlinear convex function for a robust nonlinear constraint. A central theme in modern convex optimization is to study some core convex structures that can be used to represent a wide range of convex problems and lead to tractable models for computation. The key idea is already shown in the previous section, namely, in order to generalize linear constraints to nonlinear constraints for uncertainty sets, we generalized the polyhedral cone, the nonnegative orthant $\mathbb{R}^n$, to nonlinear convex cones, in particular, the second-order cone $\mathbb{L}^n$. Later we will see that another very important convex cone is the cone of symmetric positive semidefinite $n$-by-$n$ matrices, the so-called positive semidefinite (PSD) cone denoted as $\mathbb{S}_+^n$. In particular, we study the following two classes of convex constraints.

1. **Second-order cone constraints:** Consider the following constraints

$$\|\boldsymbol{A}\boldsymbol{x} - \boldsymbol{b}\|_2 \leq \boldsymbol{c}^\top \boldsymbol{x} + d, \tag{2.3.2}$$

with $\boldsymbol{A} \in \mathbb{R}^{m \times n}$, which can be represented as

$$\begin{bmatrix} \boldsymbol{A}\boldsymbol{x} - \boldsymbol{b} \\ \boldsymbol{c}^\top \boldsymbol{x} + d \end{bmatrix} \in \mathbb{L}^{m+1}. \tag{2.3.3}$$

We say that (2.3.2) is second-order cone (SOC) representable and (2.3.2) is called an SOC constraint.

Readers familiar with quadratic constraints may wonder whether a convex quadratic constraint is SOC representable. The answer is yes. The following simple derivation shows that a convex quadratic constraint is a special case of an SOC constraint.

$$\boldsymbol{x}^\top \boldsymbol{Q}\boldsymbol{x} + 2\boldsymbol{c}^\top \boldsymbol{x} + g \leq 0, \quad (\boldsymbol{Q} = \boldsymbol{A}^2 \succ \boldsymbol{0}), \tag{2.3.4a}$$

$$\Longleftrightarrow (\boldsymbol{A}\boldsymbol{x} + \boldsymbol{b})^\top (\boldsymbol{A}\boldsymbol{x} + \boldsymbol{b}) \leq \boldsymbol{b}^\top \boldsymbol{Q}^{-1} \boldsymbol{b} - g, \quad (\boldsymbol{b} = \boldsymbol{A}^{-1}\boldsymbol{c}), \tag{2.3.4b}$$

$$\iff \|\boldsymbol{A}\boldsymbol{x} + \boldsymbol{b}\|_2 \leq \boldsymbol{0}^\top \boldsymbol{x} + d := \sqrt{\boldsymbol{b}^\top \boldsymbol{Q}^{-1}\boldsymbol{b} - g}. \tag{2.3.4c}$$

As an example, we can write the 2-dimensional ellipsoid (2.2.27) as an SOC constraint

$$\mathscr{U}_{\text{ellip}} = \left\{(a_1, a_2) : \begin{bmatrix} a_1 \\ a_2 \end{bmatrix}^\top \begin{bmatrix} \frac{5}{8} & \frac{3}{8} \\ \frac{3}{8} & \frac{5}{8} \end{bmatrix} \begin{bmatrix} a_1 \\ a_2 \end{bmatrix} \leq 1 \right\} = \left\{(a_1, a_2) : \left\| \begin{bmatrix} \frac{3}{4} & \frac{1}{4} \\ \frac{1}{4} & \frac{3}{4} \end{bmatrix} \begin{bmatrix} a_1 \\ a_2 \end{bmatrix} \right\|_2 \leq 1 \right\}.$$

2. **Semidefinite constraints:** A linear PSD constraint is expressed as

$$\boldsymbol{A}_1 x_1 + \boldsymbol{A}_2 x_2 + \cdots + \boldsymbol{A}_m x_m \succeq \boldsymbol{B}, \tag{2.3.5}$$

where $\boldsymbol{A} \succeq \boldsymbol{B}$ means $\boldsymbol{A} - \boldsymbol{B} \succeq \boldsymbol{0}$, i.e., $(\boldsymbol{A} - \boldsymbol{B}) \in \mathbb{S}_+^n$. So the PSD constraint can also be given by

$$\boldsymbol{A}_1 x_1 + \boldsymbol{A}_2 x_2 + \cdots + \boldsymbol{A}_m x_m - \boldsymbol{B} \in \mathbb{S}_+^n. \tag{2.3.6}$$

Note that the left-hand side of (2.3.5) is a linear function in $\boldsymbol{x}$, sometimes expressed as $\mathscr{A}(\boldsymbol{x})$.

**Illustrative Example 2.5** *Let us consider the following PSD constraint*

$$Q(\boldsymbol{x}) = \begin{bmatrix} x_1 + x_2 & -2x_1 - x_2 + 1 \\ -2x_1 - x_2 + 1 & x_1 - 2x_2 \end{bmatrix} \succeq 0. \tag{2.3.7}$$

*Note that the matrix is symmetric and the entries are linear in $x_1, x_2$. It is clear that this linear PSD constraint can be written in the form of* (2.3.5) *as*

$$\underbrace{\begin{bmatrix} 1 & -2 \\ -2 & 1 \end{bmatrix}}_{\boldsymbol{A}_1} x_1 + \underbrace{\begin{bmatrix} 1 & -1 \\ -1 & -2 \end{bmatrix}}_{\boldsymbol{A}_2} x_2 \succeq \underbrace{\begin{bmatrix} 0 & -1 \\ -1 & 0 \end{bmatrix}}_{\boldsymbol{B}}.$$

*The coefficient matrices $\boldsymbol{A}_1, \boldsymbol{A}_2$ and the right-hand side matrix $\boldsymbol{B}$ are symmetric but do not need to be positive semidefinite. The reader may also realize that this PSD constraint* (2.3.7) *is equivalent to the constraints that the diagonal elements of $Q(\boldsymbol{x})$ and the determinant of $Q(\boldsymbol{x})$ are nonnegative, which are given by*

$$x_1 + x_2 \geq 0, \; x_1 - 2x_2 \geq 0, \tag{2.3.8a}$$

$$(-2x_1 - x_2 + 1)^2 \leq (x_1 + x_2)(x_1 - 2x_2), \tag{2.3.8b}$$

*The second inequality* (2.3.8b) *can be reformulated using the identity* $2ab = (a+b)^2 - (a-b)^2$ *as*

$$\sqrt{(-2x_1 - x_2 + 1)^2 + \frac{1}{2}(3x_2)^2} \leq \frac{1}{\sqrt{2}}(2x_1 - x_2),$$

*where we also use the two linear constraints to derive* $2x_1 - x_2 \geq 0$*. This is an SOC constraint according to the definition of the second-order cone. This indicates that SOC constraints can be represented as PSD constraints. We will show shortly that this is true in general that PSD constraints are more general and include SOC constraints as a special case.*

□

Readers may wonder why we only focus on the nonnegative orthant, SOC, and PSD cones. The reason is quite deep. In fact, in a well-defined sense, these three classes of convex cones almost exhaust all possible types of the so-called convex homogeneous cones that enjoy some special properties, such as symmetry, self-dual, and homogeneity. These properties are very important for computational tractability of this class of cones. Furthermore, the PSD cone is the most versatile among the three. The nonnegative orthants and SOC cones can be obtained as the intersection of a PSD cone with a linear subspace. In particular, we can get $\mathbb{R}^n_+$ from $\mathbb{S}^n_+$ by imposing linear constraints on off-diagonal elements as

$$\{\boldsymbol{X} \in \mathbb{S}^n_+ : X_{ij} = 0, \quad \forall i \neq j\}. \tag{2.3.9}$$

That is $\mathbb{R}^n_+$ can be formed by intersecting $\mathbb{S}^n_+$ with a linear subspace defined by the linear equalities in (2.3.9), because the diagonal elements of an PSD matrix are nonnegative. To get the second-order cone from the PSD cone, we have

$$\begin{bmatrix} \boldsymbol{x} \\ v \end{bmatrix} \in \mathbb{L}^n \iff \boldsymbol{x}^\top \boldsymbol{x} \leq v^2, \tag{2.3.10}$$

$$\iff \quad X = \begin{bmatrix} v & \boldsymbol{x}^\top \\ \boldsymbol{x} & v\boldsymbol{I} \end{bmatrix} \succeq \boldsymbol{0}, \tag{2.3.11}$$

$$\iff \quad \begin{cases} X_{ii} = v, & \forall i = 1, 2, \ldots, n, \\ X_{1i} = x_{i-1}, & \forall i = 2, 3, \ldots, n, \\ \boldsymbol{X} \in \mathbb{S}^n_+. \end{cases} \tag{2.3.12}$$

Here (2.3.11) uses the Schur complement [1]. This shows that the SOC cone can be obtained from intersecting $\mathbb{S}^n_+$ with an affine subspace defined by the linear equalities in (2.3.12). Although both $\mathbb{R}^n_+$ and $\mathbb{L}^n_+$ can be obtained from $\mathbb{S}^n_+$, it is usually more convenient to directly work with $\mathbb{R}^n_+$ and $\mathbb{L}^n_+$ rather than converting them to a subset of a PSD cone.

Now we introduce two key techniques frequently used in the reformulation of robust conic constraints.

1. **S-Lemma:** This lemma originated from control theory and it can be shown to be equivalent to the strong duality of a nonconvex quadratic optimization problem with a single nonconvex quadratic constraint. The S-lemma states that for any two symmetric matrices $\boldsymbol{A}$ and $\boldsymbol{B}$, not necessarily PSD, the following implication holds

$$\boldsymbol{y}^\top \boldsymbol{A}\boldsymbol{y} \geq 0 \quad \Rightarrow \quad \boldsymbol{y}^\top \boldsymbol{B}\boldsymbol{y} \geq 0, \tag{2.3.13}$$

if and only if there exists a $\lambda \geq 0$ such that

$$\boldsymbol{B} - \lambda \boldsymbol{A} \succeq \boldsymbol{0}, \tag{2.3.14}$$

that is, $\boldsymbol{B} - \lambda \boldsymbol{A}$ is positive semidefinite.

Note that the condition (2.3.13) has a geometric meaning, namely the sets $S_A := \{\boldsymbol{y} : \boldsymbol{y}^\top \boldsymbol{A}\boldsymbol{y} \geq 0\}$ and $S_B := \{\boldsymbol{y} : \boldsymbol{y}^\top \boldsymbol{B}\boldsymbol{y} \geq 0\}$ satisfy $S_A \subseteq S_B$.

**Illustrative Example 2.6** *As an example, consider the following two matrices*

$$\boldsymbol{A} = \begin{bmatrix} 1 & 2 \\ 2 & 1 \end{bmatrix}, \quad \boldsymbol{B} = \begin{bmatrix} \frac{3}{8} & \frac{5}{8} \\ \frac{5}{8} & \frac{3}{8} \end{bmatrix}.$$

*To test if they satisfy* (2.3.13), *we only need to prove or disprove whether there exists some* $\lambda \geq 0$ *such that* (2.3.14) *holds, which can be verified by hand for this simple 2-by-2 case. We have*

$$\boldsymbol{B} - \lambda \boldsymbol{A} = \begin{bmatrix} \frac{3}{8} - \lambda & \frac{5}{8} - 2\lambda \\ \frac{5}{8} - 2\lambda & \frac{3}{8} - \lambda \end{bmatrix} \succeq \boldsymbol{0} \Longleftrightarrow \left(\frac{3}{8} - \lambda\right)^2 - \left(\frac{5}{8} - 2\lambda\right)^2 \geq 0, \ \frac{3}{8} - \lambda \geq 0,$$

*which is reduced to* $\frac{1}{4} \leq \lambda \leq \frac{3}{8}$. *This shows that* (2.3.14) *is indeed satisfied.*

*We can also verify* (2.3.13) *using its geometric meaning. It turns out the sets* $S_A$ *and* $S_B$ *defined by the quadratic inequalities in* (2.3.13) *are unions of polyhedral cones:*

$$S_A = \left\{(x, y) \in \mathbb{R}^2 : \sqrt{3}|x + y| \geq |x - y|\right\},$$

$$S_B = \left\{(x, y) \in \mathbb{R}^2 : 2|x + y| \geq |x - y|\right\}. \tag{2.3.15}$$

*From* (2.3.15), *It is easy to see that* $S_A \subseteq S_B$. *We can also plot the two sets as in Fig.* 2.8.

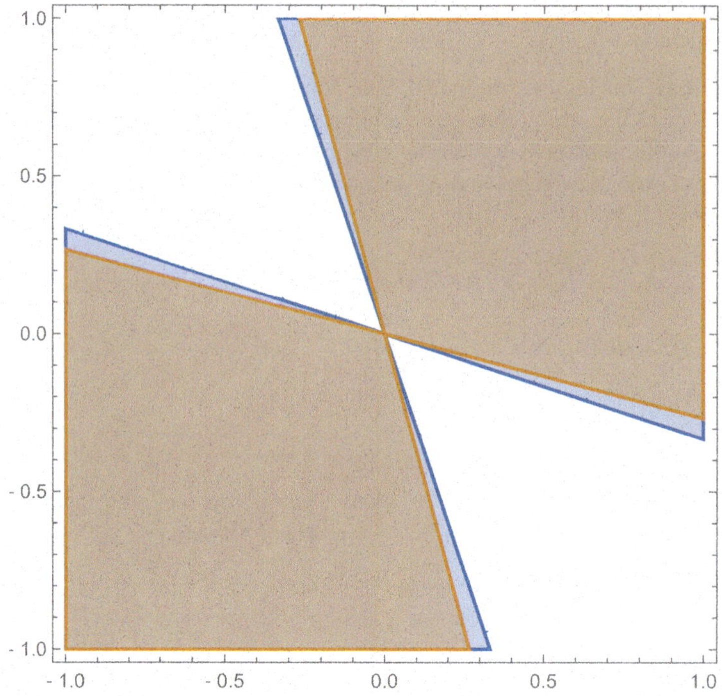


**Fig. 2.8** Plot of $S_A$ (brown region) and $S_B$ (blue region) in Example 2.6

□

The implication (2.3.13) can also be written as

$$\min\{\boldsymbol{y}^\top \boldsymbol{B}\boldsymbol{y} : \boldsymbol{y}^\top \boldsymbol{A}\boldsymbol{y} \geq 0\} \geq 0. \tag{2.3.16}$$

This is a quadratically constrained quadratic program (QCQP). The matrices $\boldsymbol{A}$, $\boldsymbol{B}$ may not be PSD, therefore, this QCQP may not be convex. However, the constraint (2.3.14) is a PSD constraint, therefore, it is a convex constraint. The S-lemma essentially reveals the equivalence between a nonconvex QCQP with one quadratic constraint and a linear PSD constraint. Also, this reformulation (2.3.16) look very much like some kind of robust constraint. This is exactly how the S-lemma is connected to robust optimization and we will make this connection precise in the next subsection.

2. **Schur Complement Property:** This is another important property related to PSD matrices. Suppose $\boldsymbol{M}$ is a square block matrix

$$\boldsymbol{M} = \begin{bmatrix} \boldsymbol{A} & \boldsymbol{B} \\ \boldsymbol{C} & \boldsymbol{D} \end{bmatrix}, \tag{2.3.17}$$

where $\boldsymbol{A} \in \mathbb{R}^{n\times n}$, $\boldsymbol{B} \in \mathbb{R}^{n\times m}$, $\boldsymbol{C} \in \mathbb{R}^{m\times n}$, and $\boldsymbol{D} \in \mathbb{R}^{m\times m}$. Furthermore, suppose $\boldsymbol{D}$ is invertible. Then the Schur complement of $\boldsymbol{M}$ with respect to $\boldsymbol{D}$ is defined as

$$\boldsymbol{M}/\boldsymbol{D} := \boldsymbol{A} - \boldsymbol{B}\boldsymbol{D}^{-1}\boldsymbol{C}. \tag{2.3.18}$$

The Schur complement property states that

- $\boldsymbol{M}$ is positive definite if and only if both $\boldsymbol{D}$ and $\boldsymbol{M}/\boldsymbol{D}$ are positive definite:

$$\boldsymbol{M} \succ \boldsymbol{0} \iff \boldsymbol{D} \succ \boldsymbol{0},\ \boldsymbol{M}/\boldsymbol{D} = \boldsymbol{A} - \boldsymbol{B}\boldsymbol{D}^{-1}\boldsymbol{C} \succ \boldsymbol{0}. \tag{2.3.19}$$

- If $\boldsymbol{D}$ is positive definite, then $\boldsymbol{M}$ is positive semidefinite if and only if $\boldsymbol{M}/\boldsymbol{D}$ is positive semidefinite:

$$\text{If } \boldsymbol{D} \succ \boldsymbol{0},\ \text{then } \boldsymbol{M} \succeq \boldsymbol{0} \iff \boldsymbol{M}/\boldsymbol{D} = \boldsymbol{A} - \boldsymbol{B}\boldsymbol{D}^{-1}\boldsymbol{C} \succeq \boldsymbol{0}. \tag{2.3.20}$$

As an example, consider a block matrix $\boldsymbol{M}$ defined as in (2.3.17) with blocks

$$\boldsymbol{A} = \begin{bmatrix} 8 & 2 \\ 2 & 8 \end{bmatrix}, \quad \boldsymbol{B} = \boldsymbol{C}^\top = \begin{bmatrix} 1 & 2 \\ 2 & 1 \end{bmatrix}, \quad \boldsymbol{D} = \begin{bmatrix} 1 & \\ & 1 \end{bmatrix}.$$

Then, $\boldsymbol{D} \succ \boldsymbol{0}$ and

$$\boldsymbol{M}/\boldsymbol{D} = \boldsymbol{A} - \boldsymbol{B}\boldsymbol{B}^\top = \begin{bmatrix} 3 & -2 \\ -2 & 3 \end{bmatrix} \succ \boldsymbol{0}.$$

Therefore, $\boldsymbol{M} \succ \boldsymbol{0}$. We can also directly verify this by computing the smallest eigenvalue of $\boldsymbol{M}$, which is $0.0917 > 0$.

## 2.3.2 *Robust Second-Order Conic Constraints*

With the above setup, we can introduce robust counterparts of the SOC and PSD constraints. A robust version of the SOC constraint (2.3.2) with uncertain data can be naturally represented as

$$\|\boldsymbol{A}\boldsymbol{x} - \boldsymbol{b}\|_2 \leq \boldsymbol{c}^\top\boldsymbol{x} + d, \quad \forall(\boldsymbol{A}, \boldsymbol{b}, \boldsymbol{c}, d) \in \mathcal{U}, \tag{2.3.21a}$$

$$\iff \begin{bmatrix} \boldsymbol{A}\boldsymbol{x} - \boldsymbol{b} \\ \boldsymbol{c}^\top\boldsymbol{x} + d \end{bmatrix} \in \mathbb{L}^{m+1}, \quad \forall(\boldsymbol{A}, \boldsymbol{b}, \boldsymbol{c}, d) \in \mathcal{U}. \tag{2.3.21b}$$

Clearly, the reformulation of a robust SOC constraint depends on the structure of the uncertainty set. In the following, we consider four types of uncertainty sets, which lead to computationally tractable reformulations.

#### 2.3.2.1 Convex Hull Uncertainty Set

The simplest uncertainty set is perhaps the one directly constructed as the convex hull of a set of scenarios of the uncertain data:

$$\mathcal{U}_{\text{hull}} = \text{conv}\left\{(\boldsymbol{A}^1, \boldsymbol{b}^1, \boldsymbol{c}^1, d^1), (\boldsymbol{A}^2, \boldsymbol{b}^2, \boldsymbol{c}^2, d^2), \ldots, (\boldsymbol{A}^N, \boldsymbol{b}^N, \boldsymbol{c}^N, d^N)\right\}. \tag{2.3.22}$$

Then, we have the following result.

The robust SOC constraint over $\mathcal{U}_{\text{hull}}$ can be readily reformulated as

$$\begin{bmatrix} \boldsymbol{A}\boldsymbol{x} - \boldsymbol{b} \\ \boldsymbol{c}^\top \boldsymbol{x} + d \end{bmatrix} \in \mathbb{L}^{m+1}, \quad \forall (\boldsymbol{A}, \boldsymbol{b}, \boldsymbol{c}, d) \in \mathcal{U}_{\text{hull}} \tag{2.3.23a}$$

$$\Longleftrightarrow \begin{bmatrix} \boldsymbol{A}^i \boldsymbol{x} - \boldsymbol{b}^i \\ (\boldsymbol{c}^i)^\top \boldsymbol{x} + d^i \end{bmatrix} \in \mathbb{L}^{m+1}, \quad \forall i = 1, 2, \ldots, N. \tag{2.3.23b}$$

This reformulation can be easily verified. Clearly, (2.3.23a) implies (2.3.23b). To show the other direction, suppose $\boldsymbol{x}$ satisfies (2.3.23b). Take any uncertain data realization $\boldsymbol{\xi} = (\boldsymbol{A}, \boldsymbol{b}, \boldsymbol{c}, d)$ from the uncertainty set $\mathcal{U}_{\text{hull}}$. Due to the convex hull structure (2.3.22), there exists a finite set of $k$ extreme points $\boldsymbol{\xi}^{i_1}, \boldsymbol{\xi}^{i_2}, \ldots, \boldsymbol{\xi}^{i_k} \in \mathcal{U}_{\text{hull}}$, and nonnegative weights $\lambda^1, \lambda^2, \ldots, \lambda^k$ that sum to one, so that

$$\boldsymbol{\xi} = \sum_{j=1}^{k} \lambda^j \boldsymbol{\xi}^{i_j}.$$

Then,

$$\begin{bmatrix} \boldsymbol{A}\boldsymbol{x} - \boldsymbol{b} \\ \boldsymbol{c}^\top \boldsymbol{x} + d \end{bmatrix} = \sum_{i=1}^{k} \lambda^j \begin{bmatrix} \boldsymbol{A}^{i_j} \boldsymbol{x} - \boldsymbol{b}^{i_j} \\ (\boldsymbol{c}^{i_j})^\top \boldsymbol{x} + d^{i_j} \end{bmatrix}. \tag{2.3.24}$$

Since $\boldsymbol{x}$ satisfies (2.3.23b), hence

$$\begin{bmatrix} A^{i_j}x - b^{i_j} \\ (c^{i_j})^\top x + d^{i_j} \end{bmatrix} \in \mathbb{L}^{m+1}, \quad \forall j = 1, 2, \ldots, k. \tag{2.3.25}$$

Since $\mathbb{L}^{m+1}$ is a convex set, the the convex combination on the right-hand side of (2.3.24) is also in $\mathbb{L}^{m+1}$. This shows $x$ satisfies (2.3.23b).

The convex hull uncertainty set is related to the robust mathematical programming methodology proposed in [19].

#### 2.3.2.2 Interval Uncertainty Set

The interval uncertainty set is defined as below

$$\mathcal{U}_{\text{interval}} = \mathcal{U}_{\text{interval}}^{A,b} \times \mathcal{U}^{c,d}, \tag{2.3.26}$$

where $A \in\in \mathbb{R}^{m\times n}$, $b \in \mathbb{R}^n$, and

$$\mathcal{U}_{\text{interval}}^{A,b} = \left\{(A, b) : A_{ij} \in [\bar{A}_{ij} - \Delta A_{ij}, \bar{A}_{ij} + \Delta A_{ij}],\ b_i \in [\bar{b}_i - \Delta b_i, \bar{b}_i + \Delta b_i],\ \forall i, j\right\}, \tag{2.3.27}$$

and the uncertainty set $\mathcal{U}^{c,d}$ of $(c, d)$ can be any conic representable set as discussed in the previous section. This uncertainty set $\mathcal{U}_{\text{interval}}$ is a Cartesian product of two uncertainty sets of the right-hand side and the left-hand side uncertainty. Under such a side-wise uncertainty set, the robust SOC constraint (2.3.21a) can be treated side-wise as

$$\max_{(A,b)\in\mathcal{U}_{\text{interval}}^{A,b}} \|Ax - b\|_2 \le \min_{(c,d)\in\mathcal{U}^{c,d}} c^\top x + d, \tag{2.3.28}$$

$$\iff \begin{cases} \max_{(A,b)\in\mathcal{U}_{\text{interval}}^{A,b}} \|Ax - b\|_2 \le \tau, \\ \min_{(c,d)\in\mathcal{U}^{c,d}} c^\top x + d \ge \tau. \end{cases} \tag{2.3.29}$$

The second constraint in (2.3.29) is a robust linear constraint, which has been thoroughly discussed in the previous section. We only need to deal with the first robust SOC constraint for the left-hand side uncertainty. We can see that the interval uncertainty set $\mathcal{U}_{\text{interval}}^{A,b}$ of the uncertain data $(A, b)$ is defined constraint-wise, i.e. each row $i$ of $(A, b)$ has an interval uncertainty set $\mathcal{U}_{\text{interval}}^{a_i,b_i}$ as

$$\mathcal{U}_{\text{interval}}^{a_i,b_i} = \left\{(a_i, b_i) \in \mathbb{R}^{n+1} : a_i = \bar{a}_i + \Delta_i\xi,\ \|\xi\|_\infty \le 1,\ b_i = \bar{b}_i + \Delta b_i\eta,\ |\eta| \le 1\right\}, \tag{2.3.30}$$

where $\bar{\boldsymbol{a}}_i = [\bar{A}_{i1}, \ldots, \bar{A}_{in}]^\top$ and $\boldsymbol{\Delta}_i$ is the diagonal matrix with diagonals being $\Delta A_{ij}$ for all $j = 1, 2, \ldots, n$. Now we can reformulate the first robust SOC constraint in (2.3.29) as

$$\max_{(\boldsymbol{A},\boldsymbol{b})\in\mathscr{U}^{\boldsymbol{A},\boldsymbol{b}}_{\text{interval}}} \|\boldsymbol{A}\boldsymbol{x} - \boldsymbol{b}\|_2 \le \tau \tag{2.3.31a}$$

$$\Longleftrightarrow \sum_{i=1}^{m} \left( \max_{\forall i, (\boldsymbol{a}_i, b_i)\in\mathscr{U}^{\boldsymbol{a}_i,b_i}_{\text{interval}}} |\boldsymbol{a}_i^\top \boldsymbol{x} - b_i|^2 \right) \le \tau^2 \tag{2.3.31b}$$

$$\Longleftrightarrow \begin{cases} z_1^2 + z_2^2 + \cdots + z_m^2 \le \tau^2 \\ \max_{(\boldsymbol{a}_i, b_i)\in\mathscr{U}^{\boldsymbol{a}_i,b_i}_{\text{interval}}} |\boldsymbol{a}_i^\top \boldsymbol{x} - b_i| \le z_i, \quad \forall i = 1, 2, \ldots, m, \end{cases} \tag{2.3.31c}$$

where the second constraint in (2.3.31c) can be further reformulated as

$$\max_{(\boldsymbol{a}_i, b_i)\in\mathscr{U}^{\boldsymbol{a}_i,b_i}_{\text{interval}}} \max\{\boldsymbol{a}_i^\top \boldsymbol{x} - b_i, -\boldsymbol{a}_i^\top \boldsymbol{x} + b_i\} \le z_i \tag{2.3.32a}$$

$$\Longleftrightarrow \max\left\{ \max_{(\boldsymbol{a}_i, b_i)\in\mathscr{U}^{\boldsymbol{a}_i,b_i}_{\text{interval}}} \{\boldsymbol{a}_i^\top \boldsymbol{x} - b_i\}, \max_{(\boldsymbol{a}_i, b_i)\in\mathscr{U}^{\boldsymbol{a}_i,b_i}_{\text{interval}}} \{-\boldsymbol{a}_i^\top \boldsymbol{x} + b_i\} \right\} \le z_i \tag{2.3.32b}$$

$$\Longleftrightarrow \max\left\{ \max_{\substack{\|\boldsymbol{\xi}\|_\infty \le 1 \\ |\eta|\le 1}} \{\underbrace{(\bar{\boldsymbol{a}}_i^\top \boldsymbol{x} - \bar{b}_i)}_{=:\bar{\alpha}_i} + \boldsymbol{\xi}^\top \boldsymbol{\Delta}_i \boldsymbol{x} - \Delta b_i \eta\}, \max_{\substack{\|\boldsymbol{\xi}\|_\infty \le 1 \\ |\eta|\le 1}} \{-\bar{\alpha}_i - \boldsymbol{\xi}^\top \boldsymbol{\Delta}_i \boldsymbol{x} + \Delta b_i \eta\} \right\} \le z_i \tag{2.3.32c}$$

$$\Longleftrightarrow \max\left\{ \bar{\alpha}_i + \max_{\substack{\|\boldsymbol{\xi}\|_\infty \le 1 \\ |\eta|\le 1}} \{\boldsymbol{\xi}^\top \boldsymbol{\Delta}_i \boldsymbol{x} - \Delta b_i \eta\}, -\bar{\alpha}_i + \max_{\substack{\|\boldsymbol{\xi}\|_\infty \le 1 \\ |\eta|\le 1}} \{-\boldsymbol{\xi}^\top \boldsymbol{\Delta}_i \boldsymbol{x} + \Delta b_i \eta\} \right\} \le z_i \tag{2.3.32d}$$

$$\Longleftrightarrow \max\left\{ \bar{\alpha}_i + \|\boldsymbol{\Delta}_i \boldsymbol{x}\|_1 + \Delta b_i, -\bar{\alpha}_i + \|\boldsymbol{\Delta}_i \boldsymbol{x}\|_1 + \Delta b_i \right\} \le z_i \tag{2.3.32e}$$

$$\Longleftrightarrow |\bar{\alpha}_i| + \|\boldsymbol{\Delta}_i \boldsymbol{x}\|_1 + \Delta b_i \le z_i \tag{2.3.32f}$$

$$\Longleftrightarrow \left|\bar{\boldsymbol{a}}_i^\top \boldsymbol{x} - \bar{b}_i\right| + \sum_{j=1}^{n} \left|\Delta A_{ij} x_j\right| + \Delta b_i \le z_i. \tag{2.3.32g}$$

Putting everything together, we have the following result.

The robust SOC constraint with an interval uncertainty set can be reformulated as a simple quadratic constraint and a set of linear constraints involving the $\ell_1$ norm as

$$\max_{(\boldsymbol{A},\boldsymbol{b})\in\mathscr{U}^{\boldsymbol{A},\boldsymbol{b}}_{\text{interval}}} \|\boldsymbol{A}\boldsymbol{x} - \boldsymbol{b}\|_2 \le \tau, \tag{2.3.33a}$$

(continued)

$$\Longleftrightarrow \begin{cases} z_1^2 + z_2^2 + \cdots + z_m^2 \le \tau^2, \\ \left|\bar{\boldsymbol{a}}_i^\top \boldsymbol{x} - \bar{b}_i\right| + \sum_{j=1}^n \left|\Delta A_{ij} x_j\right| + \Delta b_i \le z_i, \quad \forall i = 1, 2, \ldots, m. \end{cases} \tag{2.3.33b}$$

The above reformulation (2.3.33b) makes intuitive sense. Basically, since the uncertainty set $\mathcal{U}_{\text{interval}}$ is completely separable for each row of $\boldsymbol{A}, \boldsymbol{b}$, the robust constraint seeks to find the worst case realization of each $A_{ij}$ and $b_i$ to be on one of the two end points of their intervals for a selected decision $\boldsymbol{x}$ such that the left-hand side $\ell_2$ norm of $\boldsymbol{Ax} - \boldsymbol{b}$ is maximized componentwise.

**Illustrative Example 2.7** *Let us look at a simple case where* $\boldsymbol{Ax} - \boldsymbol{b}$ *has only one row, i.e.* $\boldsymbol{Ax} - \boldsymbol{b} = \boldsymbol{a}^\top \boldsymbol{x} - b$, *and* $(\boldsymbol{a}, b) \in \mathcal{U}_{interval}^{\boldsymbol{a},b} = \{(\boldsymbol{a}, b) : -\boldsymbol{\Delta} \le \boldsymbol{a} - \bar{\boldsymbol{a}} \le \boldsymbol{\Delta}, -\Delta b \le b - \bar{b} \le \Delta b\}$. *Then the robust SOC constraint becomes*

$$\max\{|\boldsymbol{a}^\top \boldsymbol{x} - b| : -\boldsymbol{\Delta} \le \boldsymbol{a} - \bar{\boldsymbol{a}} \le \boldsymbol{\Delta}, -\Delta b \le b - \bar{b} \le \Delta b\} \le \tau,$$

*which can be reformulated as*

$$|\bar{\boldsymbol{a}}^\top \boldsymbol{x} - \bar{b}| + \sum_{j=1}^n \Delta_j |x_j| + \Delta b \le \tau. \tag{2.3.34}$$

*Let us further plug in some numbers to the above example. Suppose* $\bar{\boldsymbol{a}}^\top \boldsymbol{x} + \bar{b} = x_1 + x_2$, $\tau = 1$, $\Delta_j = 1$ *for all* $j$, *and* $\Delta b = 1$, *i.e. the nominal constraint is* $|x_1 + x_2| \le 1$ *and the uncertainty set* $\mathcal{U}_{interval}^{\boldsymbol{a},b}$ *is* $a_j \in [0, 2]$ *for all* $j$ *and* $b \in [-1, 1]$. *The reformulation of the robust constraint* (2.3.34) *becomes*

$$|x_1 + x_2| + |x_1| + |x_2| \le 1. \tag{2.3.35}$$

*The following figure plots the feasible regions of the nominal versus the robust constraints (Fig. 2.9).*

□

#### 2.3.2.3 Simple Ellipsoidal Uncertainty Set

In an interval uncertainty set, each row of $\boldsymbol{A}$ and $\boldsymbol{b}$ has independent uncertainty. This makes it easy to reformulate a robust SOCP constraint over an interval uncertainty set. However, the interval uncertainty set could be also very conservative as it allows the worst-case realization of uncertainty to simultaneously take the end-points of the

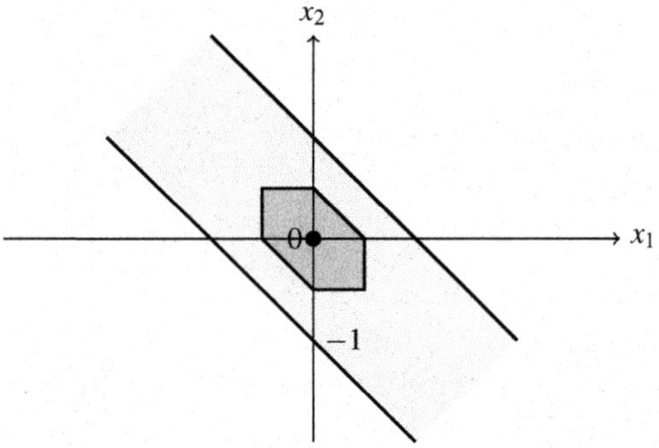


**Fig. 2.9** The light gray region between the two outer parallel lines is the feasible region of the nominal constraint $|x_1 + x_2| \leq 1$. The gray polytope is the feasible region of the robust constraint $\max_{a_j \in [0,2], b \in [-1,1]} |a_1 x_1 + a_2 x_2 + b| \leq 1$ reformulated as (2.3.35)

uncertainty intervals. To reduce the conservativeness of robust constraints, we need to allow uncertainty of constraints to be coupled. An ellipsoid uncertainty set can be used to model the correlations between uncertain data. Again, we consider a side-wise uncertainty set, because in general a joint uncertainty set of the right- and left-hand side uncertain data leads to intractable robust conic constraints. We will show an example later. Similar to the ellipsoidal uncertainty set (2.2.26) discussion in Sect. 2.2, we can define an ellipsoidal uncertainty set for the uncertain data $(\boldsymbol{A}, \boldsymbol{b})$ as

$$\mathscr{U}_{\text{ellip}}^{\boldsymbol{A},\boldsymbol{b}} = \left\{ (\boldsymbol{A}, \boldsymbol{b}) : \boldsymbol{A} = \bar{\boldsymbol{A}} + \sum_{i=1}^{k} \boldsymbol{A}_i \xi_i, \ \boldsymbol{b} = \bar{\boldsymbol{b}} + \sum_{i=1}^{k} \boldsymbol{b}_i \xi_i, \ \|\boldsymbol{\xi}\|_2 \leq 1 \right\}, \tag{2.3.36}$$

where $\bar{\boldsymbol{A}}$ and $\bar{\boldsymbol{b}}$ are nominal values of $\boldsymbol{A}$, $\boldsymbol{b}$, and $\boldsymbol{A}_i$, $\boldsymbol{b}_i$ can be viewed as scenarios or deviations from the nominal values. Note that $\boldsymbol{A}$ and $\boldsymbol{b}$ are controlled by the same underlying uncertain factor $\boldsymbol{\xi}$. Later we will show that if $\boldsymbol{A}$ and $\boldsymbol{b}$ are controlled by two independent uncertain factors, then the robust constraint becomes intractable.

**Illustrative Example 2.8** *Now let us look at an example with the following robust SOCP constraint:*

$$\sqrt{(a_1x_1 - b_1)^2 + (a_2x_2 - b_2)^2} \leq 1, \quad \forall (a_1, a_2, b_1, b_2) : a_i = b_i = \xi_i, i = 1, 2, \sum_{i=1}^{2} \xi_i^2 \leq 1. \tag{2.3.37}$$

*We can put this robust constraint in the form of robust conic constraints* (2.3.21a) *and the ellipsoidal uncertainty set* (2.3.36)*, where we have*

$$\boldsymbol{A} = \begin{bmatrix} a_1 & 0 \\ 0 & a_2 \end{bmatrix}, \boldsymbol{b} = \begin{bmatrix} b_1 \\ b_2 \end{bmatrix}, \bar{\boldsymbol{A}} = \boldsymbol{0}, \bar{\boldsymbol{b}} = \boldsymbol{0}, \boldsymbol{A}_1 = \begin{bmatrix} 1 & 0 \\ 0 & 0 \end{bmatrix}, \boldsymbol{A}_2 = \begin{bmatrix} 0 & 0 \\ 0 & 1 \end{bmatrix}, \boldsymbol{b}_1 = \begin{bmatrix} 1 \\ 0 \end{bmatrix}, \boldsymbol{b}_2 = \begin{bmatrix} 0 \\ 1 \end{bmatrix}.$$

*In other words, the robust SOCP constraint can be reformulated as the following*

$$\left\| \begin{bmatrix} (x_1-1)\xi_1 \\ (x_2-1)\xi_2 \end{bmatrix} \right\|_2 = \sqrt{(x_1-1)^2\xi_1^2 + (x_2-1)^2\xi_2^2} \le 1, \quad \forall \|\boldsymbol{\xi}\|_2 \le 1. \tag{2.3.38}$$

□

Note that the robust constraint (2.3.38) involves maximizing a quadratic function (after squaring both sides of the robust inequality) over a quadratic constraint (the unit ball). This should immediately remind the reader that such a problem is connected to the S-lemma. Indeed, the reformulation below heavily relies on the S-lemma, and another useful technique called homogenization. Such a reformulation can be applied to many situations. To emphasize the intuition, we also provide an alternative reformulation that looks more systematic than the first one.

**Reformulation Using Homogenization and S-Lemma**

The left-hand side robust conic constraint over $\mathscr{U}_{\text{ellip}}$ is now given as

$$\max_{(\boldsymbol{A},\boldsymbol{b})\in\mathscr{U}_{\text{ellip}}^{\boldsymbol{A},\boldsymbol{b}}} \|\boldsymbol{A}\boldsymbol{x}-\boldsymbol{b}\|_2 \le \tau, \tag{2.3.39}$$

$$\iff \max_{\|\boldsymbol{\xi}\|_2\le 1} \left\| (\bar{\boldsymbol{A}}\boldsymbol{x}-\bar{\boldsymbol{b}}) + \sum_{i=1}^{k} (\boldsymbol{A}_i\boldsymbol{x}-\boldsymbol{b}_i)\xi_i \right\|_2 \le \tau. \tag{2.3.40}$$

In order to make notation simple, we first consider the following problem

$$\max_{\|\boldsymbol{\xi}\|_2\le 1} \left\| \bar{\boldsymbol{c}} + \sum_{i=1}^{k} \boldsymbol{c}_i\xi_i \right\|_2 \le \tau \quad \iff \quad \max_{\|\boldsymbol{\xi}\|_2\le 1} \left\| \bar{\boldsymbol{c}} + \boldsymbol{C}\boldsymbol{\xi} \right\|_2 \le \tau, \tag{2.3.41}$$

which can be reformulated as

$$(\bar{\boldsymbol{c}}+\boldsymbol{C}\boldsymbol{\xi})^\top(\bar{\boldsymbol{c}}+\boldsymbol{C}\boldsymbol{\xi}) \le \tau^2, \quad \forall \boldsymbol{\xi} : \|\boldsymbol{\xi}\|_2 \le 1, \tag{2.3.42a}$$

$$\iff \begin{bmatrix} \tau & (\bar{\boldsymbol{c}}+\boldsymbol{C}\boldsymbol{\xi})^\top \\ \bar{\boldsymbol{c}}+\boldsymbol{C}\boldsymbol{\xi} & \tau\boldsymbol{I} \end{bmatrix} \succeq \boldsymbol{0}, \quad \forall \boldsymbol{\xi} : \|\boldsymbol{\xi}\|_2 \le 1, \tag{2.3.42b}$$

$$\iff \begin{bmatrix} u \\ \boldsymbol{v} \end{bmatrix}^\top \begin{bmatrix} \tau & (\bar{\boldsymbol{c}}+\boldsymbol{C}\boldsymbol{\xi})^\top \\ \bar{\boldsymbol{c}}+\boldsymbol{C}\boldsymbol{\xi} & \tau\boldsymbol{I} \end{bmatrix} \begin{bmatrix} u \\ \boldsymbol{v} \end{bmatrix} \ge 0, \quad \forall \boldsymbol{\xi} : \|\boldsymbol{\xi}\|_2 \le 1,\ \forall (u,\boldsymbol{v}) \in \mathbb{R}^{m+1}, \tag{2.3.42c}$$

$$\iff \tau u^2 + 2u(\bar{\boldsymbol{c}}+\boldsymbol{C}\boldsymbol{\xi})^\top\boldsymbol{v} + \tau\boldsymbol{v}^\top\boldsymbol{v} \ge 0, \quad \forall \boldsymbol{\xi} : \|\boldsymbol{\xi}\|_2 \le 1,\ \forall (u,\boldsymbol{v}) \in \mathbb{R}^{m+1}, \tag{2.3.42d}$$

$$\iff \tau u^2 + 2u\bar{\boldsymbol{c}}^\top\boldsymbol{v} + \tau\boldsymbol{v}^\top\boldsymbol{v} + 2u\boldsymbol{\xi}^\top\boldsymbol{C}^\top\boldsymbol{v} \ge 0, \quad \forall \boldsymbol{\xi} : \|\boldsymbol{\xi}\|_2 \le 1,\ \forall (u,\boldsymbol{v}) \in \mathbb{R}^{m+1}, \tag{2.3.42e}$$

$$\iff \tau u^2 + 2u\bar{\boldsymbol{c}}^\top\boldsymbol{v} + \tau\boldsymbol{v}^\top\boldsymbol{v} + \min_{\|\boldsymbol{\xi}\|_2\le 1} 2u\boldsymbol{\xi}^\top\boldsymbol{C}^\top\boldsymbol{v} \ge 0, \quad \forall (u,\boldsymbol{v}) \in \mathbb{R}^{m+1}, \tag{2.3.42f}$$

$$\iff \tau u^2 + 2u\bar{\boldsymbol{c}}^\top\boldsymbol{v} + \tau\boldsymbol{v}^\top\boldsymbol{v} - \|2u\boldsymbol{C}^\top\boldsymbol{v}\|_2 \ge 0, \quad \forall (u,\boldsymbol{v}) \in \mathbb{R}^{m+1}, \tag{2.3.42g}$$

$$\iff \tau u^2 + 2u\bar{\boldsymbol{c}}^\top\boldsymbol{v} + \tau\boldsymbol{v}^\top\boldsymbol{v} + \min_{\boldsymbol{\xi}^\top\boldsymbol{\xi}\le u^2} 2\boldsymbol{\xi}^\top\boldsymbol{C}^\top\boldsymbol{v} \ge 0, \quad \forall (u,\boldsymbol{v}) \in \mathbb{R}^{m+1}, \tag{2.3.42h}$$

$$\iff \quad \tau u^2 + 2u\bar{c}^\top v + \tau v^\top v + 2\xi^\top C^\top v \geq 0, \quad \forall (u, v, \xi) \in \mathbb{R}^{m+k+1} : \xi^\top \xi \leq u^2, \tag{2.3.42i}$$

$$\iff \begin{bmatrix} u \\ v \\ \xi \end{bmatrix}^\top \begin{bmatrix} \tau & \bar{c}^\top & \mathbf{0}^\top \\ \bar{c} & \tau I & C \\ \mathbf{0} & C^\top & \mathbf{0} \end{bmatrix} \begin{bmatrix} u \\ v \\ \xi \end{bmatrix} \geq 0, \quad \forall (u, v, \xi) \in \mathbb{R}^{m+k+1} : \begin{bmatrix} u \\ v \\ \xi \end{bmatrix}^\top \begin{bmatrix} 1 & & \\ & \mathbf{0} & \\ & & -I \end{bmatrix} \begin{bmatrix} u \\ v \\ \xi \end{bmatrix} \geq 0, \tag{2.3.42j}$$

$$\iff \begin{bmatrix} u \\ v \\ \xi \end{bmatrix}^\top \begin{bmatrix} 1 & & \\ & \mathbf{0} & \\ & & -I \end{bmatrix} \begin{bmatrix} u \\ v \\ \xi \end{bmatrix} \geq 0 \Rightarrow \begin{bmatrix} u \\ v \\ \xi \end{bmatrix}^\top \begin{bmatrix} \tau & \bar{c}^\top & \mathbf{0}^\top \\ \bar{c} & \tau I & C \\ \mathbf{0} & C^\top & \mathbf{0} \end{bmatrix} \begin{bmatrix} u \\ v \\ \xi \end{bmatrix} \geq 0, \quad \forall (u, v, \xi) \in \mathbb{R}^{m+k+1}, \tag{2.3.42k}$$

$$\iff \begin{bmatrix} \tau & \bar{c}^\top & \mathbf{0}^\top \\ \bar{c} & \tau I & C \\ \mathbf{0} & C^\top & \mathbf{0} \end{bmatrix} - \lambda \begin{bmatrix} 1 & & \\ & \mathbf{0} & \\ & & -I \end{bmatrix} \succeq \mathbf{0}, \ \lambda \geq 0, \tag{2.3.42l}$$

$$\iff \begin{bmatrix} \tau - \lambda & \bar{c}^\top & \mathbf{0}^\top \\ \bar{c} & \tau I & C \\ \mathbf{0} & C^\top & \lambda I \end{bmatrix} \succeq \mathbf{0}, \ \lambda \geq 0. \tag{2.3.42m}$$

The second last step uses the well-known S-lemma. Here we can summarize the reformulation of a robust conic constraint over an ellipsoid.

The robust conic constraint (2.3.40) over an ellipsoid can be reformulated as the following PSD constraint

$$\max_{(A,b)\in\mathscr{U}_{\text{ellip}}^{A,b}} \|Ax - b\|_2 \leq \tau \iff \begin{bmatrix} \tau - \lambda & (\bar{A}x - \bar{b})^\top & \mathbf{0}^\top \\ \bar{A}x - \bar{b} & \tau I & C \\ \mathbf{0} & C^\top & \lambda I \end{bmatrix} \succeq \mathbf{0}, \ \lambda \geq 0, \tag{2.3.43}$$

where the $i$-th column of $C$ is equal to $A_i x - b_i$ for each $i = 1, 2, \ldots, k$.

The above derivation follows the steps in [11] and it seems like magic. However, we can summarize two key techniques at work. The first one is "homogenization", i.e. lifting the quadratic constraint in (2.3.42a) from the $\xi$ space to a higher dimensional space of $(u, v, \xi)$ so that the resulting quadratic functions in (2.3.42j) are homogeneous (i.e. the constant term is zero) and an important byproduct is that these quadratic functions are linear in $\tau, \bar{c}, C$. The second technique is the application of the S-lemma in (2.3.42l), which also implies a strong duality property of QCQP with a single quadratic constraint. In particular, the last three steps in (2.3.42) can also be viewed as applying strong duality to the lifted QCQP

$$Z_p := \min_{u,v,\xi} \begin{bmatrix} u \\ v \\ \xi \end{bmatrix}^\top \begin{bmatrix} \tau & \bar{c}^\top & \mathbf{0}^\top \\ \bar{c} & \tau I & C \\ \mathbf{0} & C^\top & \mathbf{0} \end{bmatrix} \begin{bmatrix} u \\ v \\ \xi \end{bmatrix} \tag{2.3.44}$$

$$\text{s.t.} \quad \begin{bmatrix} u \\ v \\ \xi \end{bmatrix}^\top \begin{bmatrix} 1 & & \\ & \mathbf{0} & \\ & & -I \end{bmatrix} \begin{bmatrix} u \\ v \\ \xi \end{bmatrix} \geq 0, \tag{2.3.45}$$

whose dual is

$$Z_d := \max \quad 0 \tag{2.3.46}$$

$$\text{s.t.} \quad \lambda \begin{bmatrix} 1 & & \\ & \mathbf{0} & \\ & & -I \end{bmatrix} \preceq \begin{bmatrix} \tau & \bar{c}^\top & \mathbf{0}^\top \\ \bar{c} & \tau I & C \\ \mathbf{0} & C^\top & \mathbf{0} \end{bmatrix}, \tag{2.3.47}$$

$$\lambda \geq 0. \tag{2.3.48}$$

Step (2.3.42j) is equivalent to requiring $Z_p \geq 0$, i.e. the primal problem is bounded from below. So strong duality holds between the primal QCQP and dual SDP, which implies that the dual is feasible and $Z_d = 0$. Then, (2.3.42j) is equivalent to requiring the dual constraint is feasible, which exactly gives the final PSD constraint (2.3.42m).

**Another Reformulation Using QCQP**

Since the reformulation of (2.3.40) embodies some important optimization techniques. Let us give an alternative way of derivation. For readers familiar with quadratic programming, it is easy to recognize that the problem in (2.3.42a) can be modeled as a quadratic constrained quadratic program (QCQP)

$$\max_{\xi^\top \xi \leq 1} \; \xi^\top C^\top C \xi + 2\bar{c}^\top C \xi + \bar{c}^\top \bar{c} \leq \tau^2. \tag{2.3.49}$$

The first step is to homogenize the above constraint. The idea is to realize that for any $r \neq 0$ the above constraint is equivalent to

$$\max_{(\xi/r)^\top (\xi/r) \leq 1} \quad (\xi/r)^\top C^\top C (\xi/r) + 2\bar{c}^\top C (\xi/r) + \bar{c}^\top \bar{c} \leq \tau^2, \tag{2.3.50a}$$

$$\Longleftrightarrow \max_{\xi^\top \xi \leq r^2} \; \xi^\top C^\top C \xi + 2r\bar{c}^\top C \xi + \bar{c}^\top \bar{c} r^2 \leq \tau^2 r^2, \tag{2.3.50b}$$

$$\Longleftrightarrow \max_{\xi^\top \xi \leq r^2} \; \xi^\top (\frac{1}{\tau} C^\top C) \xi + 2r(\frac{1}{\tau}\bar{c}^\top C)\xi + \frac{1}{\tau}\bar{c}^\top \bar{c} r^2 \leq \tau r^2, \tag{2.3.50c}$$

$$\Longleftrightarrow \max_{\xi^\top \xi \leq r^2} \; \xi^\top (\frac{1}{\tau} C^\top C) \xi + 2r(\frac{1}{\tau}\bar{c}^\top C)\xi + (\frac{1}{\tau}\bar{c}^\top \bar{c} - \tau) r^2 \leq 0. \tag{2.3.50d}$$

Now notice that we have a homogeneous quadratic objective function and an homogeneous quadratic constraint in $(r, \boldsymbol{\xi})$. The alert reader would recognize an opportunity to apply the homogeneous S-lemma now. In particular, the last constraint is equivalent to saying the following implication

$$\begin{bmatrix} r \\ \boldsymbol{\xi} \end{bmatrix}^\top \begin{bmatrix} 1 & \\ & -\boldsymbol{I} \end{bmatrix} \begin{bmatrix} r \\ \boldsymbol{\xi} \end{bmatrix} \geq 0 \quad \Rightarrow \quad \begin{bmatrix} r \\ \boldsymbol{\xi} \end{bmatrix}^\top \begin{bmatrix} \tau - \frac{1}{\tau}\bar{\boldsymbol{c}}^\top \bar{\boldsymbol{c}} & -\frac{1}{\tau}\bar{\boldsymbol{c}}^\top \boldsymbol{C} \\ -\frac{1}{\tau}\boldsymbol{C}^\top \bar{\boldsymbol{c}} & -\frac{1}{\tau}\boldsymbol{C}^\top \boldsymbol{C} \end{bmatrix} \begin{bmatrix} r \\ \boldsymbol{\xi} \end{bmatrix} \geq 0, \tag{2.3.51}$$

therefore, by the S-lemma, there exists $\lambda \geq 0$ such that

$$\begin{bmatrix} \tau - \frac{1}{\tau}\bar{\boldsymbol{c}}^\top \bar{\boldsymbol{c}} & -\frac{1}{\tau}\bar{\boldsymbol{c}}^\top \boldsymbol{C} \\ -\frac{1}{\tau}\boldsymbol{C}^\top \bar{\boldsymbol{c}} & -\frac{1}{\tau}\boldsymbol{C}^\top \boldsymbol{C} \end{bmatrix} - \lambda \begin{bmatrix} 1 & \\ & -\boldsymbol{I} \end{bmatrix} \succeq \boldsymbol{0}. \tag{2.3.52}$$

The work is not done yet, because the first matrix has product terms of $\bar{\boldsymbol{c}}$ and $\boldsymbol{C}$, which are linear in $\boldsymbol{x}$, therefore, the product terms are quadratic in $\boldsymbol{x}$. So the above constraint is not a convex constraint. We need one more key technique. The key idea is to realize the product terms can be written as the following product

$$\begin{bmatrix} \tau - \lambda & \\ & \lambda \boldsymbol{I} \end{bmatrix} - \frac{1}{\tau} \begin{bmatrix} \bar{\boldsymbol{c}}^\top \\ \boldsymbol{C}^\top \end{bmatrix} \begin{bmatrix} \bar{\boldsymbol{c}}^\top \\ \boldsymbol{C}^\top \end{bmatrix}^\top \succeq \boldsymbol{0}. \tag{2.3.53}$$

Now, we can use the Schur complement and conclude the above inequality is equivalent to

$$\begin{bmatrix} \tau - \lambda & & \bar{\boldsymbol{c}}^\top \\ & \lambda \boldsymbol{I} & \boldsymbol{C}^\top \\ \bar{\boldsymbol{c}} & \boldsymbol{C} & \tau \boldsymbol{I} \end{bmatrix} \succeq \boldsymbol{0}, \tag{2.3.54}$$

which is equivalent to the reformulation (2.3.42m). Note that in (2.3.50c) we divided $\tau$ on both sides. If we did not divide, the resulting PSD constraint would contain a $\tau^2$ term, which destroys convexity.

**Illustrative Example 2.9** *Now let us apply the reformulation to the example* (2.3.37)–(2.3.38). *We get the following equivalent reformulation*

$$\begin{bmatrix} 1-\lambda & & & & \\ & 1 & & x_1 - 1 & \\ & & 1 & & x_2 - 1 \\ & x_1 - 1 & & \lambda & \\ & & x_2 - 1 & & \lambda \end{bmatrix} \succeq \boldsymbol{0}, \ \lambda \geq 0, \tag{2.3.55}$$

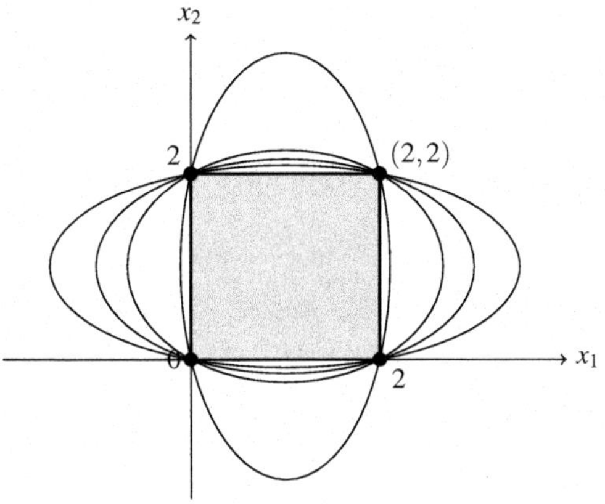


**Fig. 2.10** The gray area is the feasible region of the robust constraint (2.3.37) by intersecting ellipsoids (2.3.38) centered at (1, 1) with principal axes of lengths $1/\xi_1$ and $1/\xi_2$ for all $\|\boldsymbol{\xi}\|_2 \leq 1$

*which can be further simplified using the Schur complement as*

$$\begin{bmatrix} \lambda - (x_1 - 1)^2 & \\ & \lambda - (x_2 - 1)^2 \end{bmatrix} \succeq \mathbf{0}, \quad 0 \leq \lambda \leq 1,$$

*which has a very simple form* $|x_1 - 1| \leq 1$ *and* $|x_2 - 1| \leq 1$, *that is* $0 \leq x_i \leq 2$ *for* $i = 1, 2$ *(Fig. 2.10).*

□

#### 2.3.2.4 Ellipsoidal Uncertainty Set for Robust Quadratic Constraints

As shown earlier in (2.3.4), any convex quadratic constraint can be written as an SOC constraint. We have seen robust SOC constraints over ellipsoidal uncertainty sets can be reformulated as SDPs. It would be natural to think that robust quadratic constraints over ellipsoidal uncertainty sets could be similarly formulated as SDPs. However, we need to be more careful here. The key issue is the representation of the uncertainty. In particular, a robust quadratic constraint could be represented as

$$\text{Type-1:} \quad \boldsymbol{x}^\top \boldsymbol{Q}\boldsymbol{x} + 2\boldsymbol{b}^\top \boldsymbol{x} + c \leq 0, \quad \forall (\boldsymbol{Q}, \boldsymbol{b}, c) \in \mathcal{U}_{\text{ellip}}^{\boldsymbol{Q},\boldsymbol{b},c}, \tag{2.3.56}$$

where the uncertainty parameters $\boldsymbol{Q}$, $\boldsymbol{b}$, and $c$ are in an ellipsoidal uncertainty set

$$\mathcal{U}_{\text{ellip}}^{\boldsymbol{Q},\boldsymbol{b},c} = \left\{ (\boldsymbol{Q}, \boldsymbol{b}, c) : \boldsymbol{Q} = \bar{\boldsymbol{Q}} + \sum_{i=1}^{k} \boldsymbol{Q}_i \xi_i, \boldsymbol{b} = \bar{\boldsymbol{b}} + \sum_{i=1}^{k} \boldsymbol{b}_i \xi_i, c = \bar{c} + \sum_{i=1}^{k} c_i \xi_i, \ \|\boldsymbol{\xi}\|_2 \leq 1 \right\}. \tag{2.3.57}$$

Alternatively, a robust quadratic constraint could also be represented as

$$\text{Type-2:}\quad \boldsymbol{x}^\top \boldsymbol{A}^\top \boldsymbol{A}\boldsymbol{x} + 2\boldsymbol{b}^\top \boldsymbol{x} + c \le 0, \quad \forall (\boldsymbol{A}, \boldsymbol{b}, c) \in \mathcal{U}_{\text{ellip}}^{\boldsymbol{A},\boldsymbol{b},c}, \tag{2.3.58}$$

where the uncertain parameters are $\boldsymbol{A}$, $\boldsymbol{b}$, $c$ in an ellipsoidal uncertainty set given as

$$\mathcal{U}_{\text{ellip}}^{\boldsymbol{A},\boldsymbol{b},c} = \left\{ (\boldsymbol{A}, \boldsymbol{b}, c) : \boldsymbol{A} = \bar{\boldsymbol{A}} + \sum_{i=1}^{k} \boldsymbol{A}_i \xi_i,\ \boldsymbol{b} = \bar{\boldsymbol{b}} + \sum_{i=1}^{k} \boldsymbol{b}_i \xi_i,\ c = \bar{c} + \sum_{i=1}^{k} c_i \xi_i,\ \|\boldsymbol{\xi}\|_2 \le 1 \right\}. \tag{2.3.59}$$

The key difference between the two types of robust quadratic constraints comes from the uncertainty being in the matrices $\boldsymbol{Q}$ or $\boldsymbol{A}$. Since we can take $\boldsymbol{Q} = \boldsymbol{A}^\top \boldsymbol{A}$, if $\boldsymbol{A}$ is an affine function of the uncertain factor $\boldsymbol{\xi}$, $\boldsymbol{Q}$ would be a quadratic function of $\boldsymbol{\xi}$. Vice versa, if $\boldsymbol{Q}$ is an affine function of $\boldsymbol{\xi}$, then $\boldsymbol{A}$ is a "square root" function of $\boldsymbol{\xi}$. So we can see that even though deterministic quadratic constraints can be represented in either form, robust quadratic constraints of the two types may be very different. Indeed this is the case. In the following we will show that (1) the Type-2 robust constraints in the form of (2.3.58)–(2.3.59) can always be reformulated as SDPs. (2) In contrast, the Type-1 robust constraints in the form of (2.3.56)–(2.3.57) can be formulated as SOCPs when only $\boldsymbol{Q}$ is uncertain, but in general are computationally intractable. Let us illustrate (2) first by examples, and then derive the general SDP reformulation for (1).

Consider the first type of robust constraint (2.3.56)–(2.3.57) where only $\boldsymbol{Q}$ is uncertain but $\boldsymbol{b}$ and $c$ are deterministic. In particular, we have

$$\boldsymbol{x}^\top \boldsymbol{Q}\boldsymbol{x} \le -\boldsymbol{b}^\top \boldsymbol{x} - c, \quad \forall \boldsymbol{Q} \in \mathcal{U}_{\text{ellip}}^{\boldsymbol{Q}} := \left\{ \boldsymbol{Q} : \boldsymbol{Q} = \bar{\boldsymbol{Q}} + \sum_{i=1}^{k} \boldsymbol{Q}_i \xi_i,\ \|\boldsymbol{\xi}\|_2 \le 1 \right\}, \tag{2.3.60}$$

$$\iff \quad \max_{\|\boldsymbol{\xi}\|_2 \le 1} \sum_{i=1}^{k} (\boldsymbol{x}^\top \boldsymbol{Q}_i \boldsymbol{x})\xi_i + \boldsymbol{x}^\top \bar{\boldsymbol{Q}}\boldsymbol{x} \le -\boldsymbol{b}^\top \boldsymbol{x} - c,$$

$$\iff \quad \left\| [\boldsymbol{x}^\top \boldsymbol{Q}_1 \boldsymbol{x}, \ldots, \boldsymbol{x}^\top \boldsymbol{Q}_k \boldsymbol{x}] \right\|_2 + \boldsymbol{x}^\top \bar{\boldsymbol{Q}}\boldsymbol{x} \le -\boldsymbol{b}^\top \boldsymbol{x} - c, \tag{2.3.61}$$

$$\iff \quad \sqrt{(\boldsymbol{x}^\top \boldsymbol{Q}_1 \boldsymbol{x})^2 + \cdots + (\boldsymbol{x}^\top \boldsymbol{Q}_k \boldsymbol{x})^2} + \boldsymbol{x}^\top \bar{\boldsymbol{Q}}\boldsymbol{x} \le -\boldsymbol{b}^\top \boldsymbol{x} - c, \tag{2.3.62}$$

where (2.3.61) uses the dual norm. Let $f(\boldsymbol{x}) = \sqrt{(\boldsymbol{x}^\top \boldsymbol{Q}_1 \boldsymbol{x})^2 + \cdots + (\boldsymbol{x}^\top \boldsymbol{Q}_k \boldsymbol{x})^2}$. If $\boldsymbol{Q}_i$'s are PSD matrices, then each $\boldsymbol{x}^\top \boldsymbol{Q}_i \boldsymbol{x} \ge 0$ for all $\boldsymbol{x}$. In this case, it turns out that $f(\boldsymbol{x})$ is a convex function in $\boldsymbol{x}$. In Exercise 2.8, the reader is asked to prove a more general result that for any $\ell_p$ norm for $p \ge 1$, a composite function $f(\boldsymbol{x}) = \|[g_1(\boldsymbol{x}), \ldots, g_k(\boldsymbol{x})]\|_p$ is convex as long as $g_i(\boldsymbol{x}) \ge 0$ for all $\boldsymbol{x}$. For the above $\ell_2$ norm case, we can further reformulate (2.3.62) as SOCP constraints

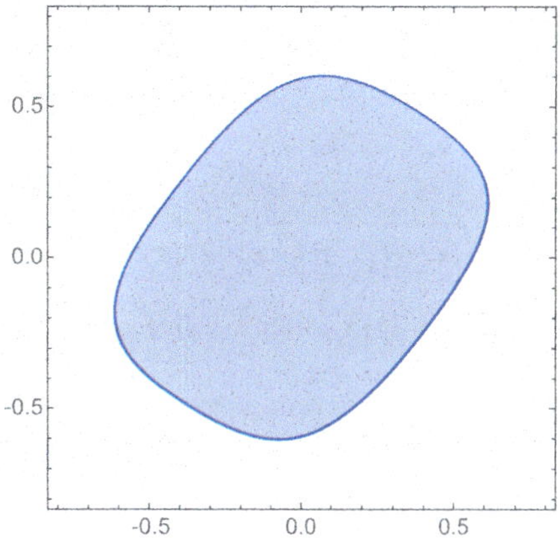


**Fig. 2.11** The feasible region of the robust constraint (2.3.63)

$$(2.3.62) \quad \Longleftrightarrow \quad \begin{cases} t + \boldsymbol{x}^\top \bar{\boldsymbol{Q}} \boldsymbol{x} \leq -\boldsymbol{b}^\top \boldsymbol{x} - c, \\ \boldsymbol{x}^\top \boldsymbol{Q}_i \boldsymbol{x} \leq z_i, \quad \forall i = 1, 2, \ldots, k, \\ \|z\|_2 \leq t. \end{cases}$$

**Illustrative Example 2.10** *Let us see a concrete example. The robust quadratic constraint is given by*

$$\boldsymbol{x}^\top \boldsymbol{Q} \boldsymbol{x} \leq 1, \quad \forall\ \boldsymbol{Q} = \underbrace{\begin{bmatrix} 1 & 1 \\ 1 & 2 \end{bmatrix}}_{\boldsymbol{Q}_1} \xi_1 + \underbrace{\begin{bmatrix} 3 & -2 \\ -2 & 2 \end{bmatrix}}_{\boldsymbol{Q}_2} \xi_2, \ \|\boldsymbol{\xi}\|_2 \leq 1, \tag{2.3.63}$$

$$\Longleftrightarrow \sqrt{(\boldsymbol{x}^\top \boldsymbol{Q}_1 \boldsymbol{x})^2 + (\boldsymbol{x}^\top \boldsymbol{Q}_2 \boldsymbol{x})^2} \leq 1, \tag{2.3.64}$$

$$\Longleftrightarrow (x_1^2 + 2x_1x_2 + 2x_2^2)^2 + (3x_1^2 - 4x_1x_2 + 2x_2^2)^2 \leq 1, \tag{2.3.65}$$

*where the last inequality involves a quartic (degree-4) polynomial (*Fig. 2.11*). We can graph it and see it is indeed convex. Note that since* $\xi_1, \xi_2$ *can be negative in the uncertainty set,* $\boldsymbol{x}^\top(\boldsymbol{Q}_1\xi_1 + \boldsymbol{Q}_2\xi_2)\boldsymbol{x}$ *may not be a convex quadratic function for all* $\boldsymbol{\xi}$ *in the ball* $\|\boldsymbol{\xi}\|_2 \leq 1$.

□

**Illustrative Example 2.11** *Now we give an example of the Type-1 robust quadratic constraint that ends up having a nonconvex feasible region. To do this, we only need to add uncertainty in* $\boldsymbol{b}$*. Let us modify the above example* (2.3.63) *as follows.*

$$\boldsymbol{x}^\top \boldsymbol{Q}\boldsymbol{x} + \boldsymbol{b}^\top \boldsymbol{x} \le 1, \quad \forall\, \boldsymbol{Q} = \underbrace{\begin{bmatrix} 1 & 1 \\ 1 & 2 \end{bmatrix}}_{\boldsymbol{Q}_1}\xi_1 + \underbrace{\begin{bmatrix} 3 & -2 \\ -2 & 2 \end{bmatrix}}_{\boldsymbol{Q}_2}\xi_2,\ \boldsymbol{b} = \underbrace{\begin{bmatrix} -1 \\ \alpha \end{bmatrix}}_{\boldsymbol{b}_1}\xi_1,\ \|\boldsymbol{\xi}\|_2 \le 1, \tag{2.3.66}$$

$$\Leftrightarrow \quad \sqrt{(\boldsymbol{x}^\top \boldsymbol{Q}_1\boldsymbol{x} + \boldsymbol{b}_1^\top \boldsymbol{x})^2 + (\boldsymbol{x}^\top \boldsymbol{Q}_2\boldsymbol{x})^2} \le 1, \tag{2.3.67}$$

$$\Leftrightarrow \quad (x_1^2 + 2x_1x_2 + 2x_2^2 - x_1 + \alpha x_2)^2 + (3x_1^2 - 4x_1x_2 + 2x_2^2)^2 \le 1. \tag{2.3.68}$$

*The feasible region of* (2.3.68) *depends on the value of* $\alpha$. *the following figure plots for* $\alpha = -3, -4$. *We can see that the feasible region of the robust constraint* (2.3.66) *not only can be nonconvex, but also disconnected. The reason that the robust constraint* (2.3.66) *has a nonconvex feasible region is because* $x_1^2 + 2x_1x_2 + 2x_2^2 - x_1 + \alpha x_2$ *can be strictly negative. The fact that the feasible region of this example is nonconvex demonstrates that in general there is no way to reformulate the Type-1 robust quadratic constraint in the form of* (2.3.56)–(2.3.57) *as a convex optimization problem. This implies that this type of robust constraints is in general difficult for computation (Fig.* 2.12*).*

□

Now let us turn to the Type-2 robust quadratic constraints with ellipsoidal uncertainty sets (2.3.58)–(2.3.59). The reader may wonder whether we could directly transform this type of robust quadratic constraints into robust SOC constraints and use the reformulation for the latter we derived in the previous subsection. We can indeed rewrite a Type-2 robust quadratic constraint as

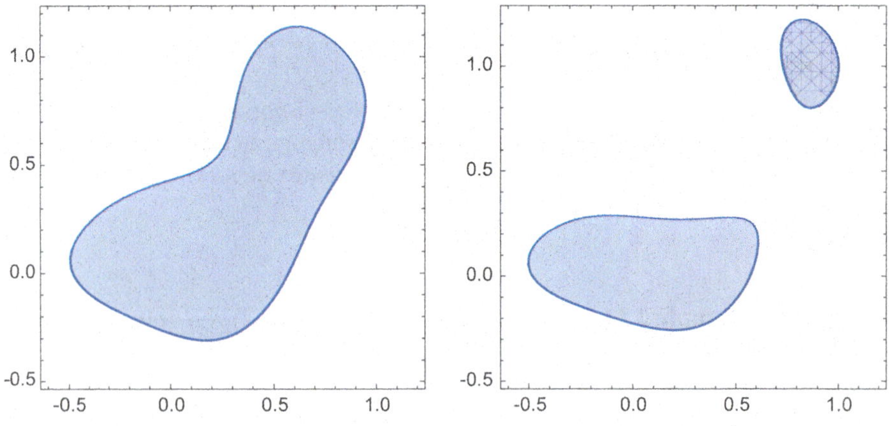


**Fig. 2.12** The feasible region of robust constraint (2.3.66) with $\alpha = -3$ (left) and $\alpha = -4$ (right)

$$x^\top A^\top A x + 2b^\top x + c \le 0 \iff \|Ax + A^{-\top} b\|_2 \le \sqrt{b^\top A^{-1} A^{-\top} b - c}.$$

However, when $A, b, c$ are affine functions of the uncertain factor $\xi$, the dependence of $A^{-\top}b$ and $\sqrt{b^\top A^{-1} A^{-\top} b - c}$ on $\xi$ can be quite complicated. Therefore, it would not be easy to exploit robust SOC constraints. Instead, we do the following transformation.

$$x^\top(\bar{A} + \sum_i A_i \xi_i)^\top(\bar{A} + \sum_i A_i \xi_i)x + 2(\bar{b} + \sum_i b_i \xi_i)^\top x + \bar{c} + \sum_i c_i \xi_i \le 0, \quad \forall \xi : \|\xi\|_2 \le 1, \tag{2.3.69}$$

which has bi-quadratic and bilinear terms in $x$ and $\xi$, so we can rewrite it as

$$\xi^\top L(x)^\top L(x)\xi + 2\beta(x)^\top \xi + \alpha(x) \le 0, \quad \forall \xi : \|\xi\|_2 \le 1, \tag{2.3.70}$$

where the $i$-th column of $L(x)$ is $A_i x$, the $i$-th entry of $\beta(x)$ is $x^\top \bar{A}^\top A_i x + b_i^\top x + c_i/2$, and $\alpha(x) = x^\top \bar{A}^\top \bar{A} x + 2\bar{b}^\top x + \bar{c}$.

The three key techniques, homogenization, S-lemma, and Schur complement, are needed to reformulate (2.3.70). In particular, for any $\tau \neq 0$, (2.3.70) is equivalent to

$$(\xi/\tau)^\top L(x)^\top L(x)(\xi/\tau) + 2\beta(x)^\top(\xi/\tau) + \alpha(x) \le 0, \quad \forall \xi, \tau \neq 0 : \|\xi/\tau\|_2 \le 1, \tag{2.3.71}$$

by multiplying $\tau^2$ on both sides and realizing $\tau = 0$ is also feasible, we get

$$\xi^\top L(x)^\top L(x)\xi + 2\beta(x)^\top \xi\tau + \alpha(x)\tau^2 \le 0, \quad \forall \xi, \tau : \xi^\top \xi \le \tau^2. \tag{2.3.72}$$

Now applying the homogeneous S-lemma, we have that there exists a $\lambda \ge 0$, such that

$$\begin{bmatrix} -\alpha(x) & -\beta(x)^\top \\ -\beta(x) & -L(x)^\top L(x) \end{bmatrix} - \lambda \begin{bmatrix} 1 & \\ & -I \end{bmatrix} \succeq \mathbf{0}, \tag{2.3.73}$$

$$\iff \begin{bmatrix} -\alpha(x) - \lambda & -\beta(x)^\top \\ -\beta(x) & \lambda I \end{bmatrix} - \begin{bmatrix} \mathbf{0}^\top \\ L(x)^\top \end{bmatrix} \begin{bmatrix} \mathbf{0}^\top \\ L(x)^\top \end{bmatrix}^\top \succeq \mathbf{0}, \tag{2.3.74}$$

$$\iff \begin{bmatrix} -\alpha(x) - \lambda & -\beta(x)^\top & \mathbf{0}^\top \\ -\beta(x) & \lambda I & L(x)^\top \\ \mathbf{0} & L(x) & I \end{bmatrix} \succeq \mathbf{0}. \tag{2.3.75}$$

The last step uses the Schur complement argument. To summarize, we have the following result.

The robust convex quadratic constraint over a joint ellipsoidal uncertainty set (2.3.59) can be reformulated as an SDP constraint,

$$x^\top A^\top A x + 2b^\top x + c \le 0, \quad \forall (A, b, c) \in \mathcal{U}^{A,b,c}_{\text{ellip}}, \tag{2.3.76}$$

$$\Leftrightarrow \begin{bmatrix} -\alpha(x) - \lambda & -x^\top \bar{A}^\top A_1 x - b_1^\top x - c_1/2 & \cdots & x^\top \bar{A}^\top A_k x - b_k^\top x - c_k/2 & 0^\top \\ -x^\top \bar{A}^\top A_1 x - b_1^\top x - c_1/2 & \lambda & & & x^\top A_1^\top \\ \vdots & & \ddots & & \vdots \\ -x^\top \bar{A}^\top A_k x - b_k^\top x - c_k/2 & & & \lambda & x^\top A_k^\top \\ 0 & A_1^\top x & \cdots & A_k^\top x & I \end{bmatrix} \succeq 0$$

$$\lambda \ge 0. \tag{2.3.77}$$

**Illustrative Example 2.12** *Again, let us see a simple example*

$$\bar{A} = 0, \bar{b} = \begin{bmatrix} 1 \\ 1 \end{bmatrix}, \bar{c} = 0, A_1 = \begin{bmatrix} 1 & 0 \\ 0 & 0 \end{bmatrix}, A_2 = \begin{bmatrix} 0 & 0 \\ 0 & 1 \end{bmatrix}, b_1 = \begin{bmatrix} 1 \\ 0 \end{bmatrix}, b_2 = \begin{bmatrix} 0 \\ 1 \end{bmatrix}, c_1 = 2, c_2 = -2.$$

*So the robust quadratic constraint can be written as*

$$\xi_1^2 x_1^2 + \xi_2^2 x_2^2 + 2\xi_1 x_1 + 2\xi_2 x_2 + 2x_1 + 2x_2 + 2\xi_1 - 2\xi_2 \le 0, \quad \forall \|\xi\|_2 \le 1,$$

$$\Leftrightarrow \begin{bmatrix} \xi_1 \\ \xi_2 \end{bmatrix}^\top \begin{bmatrix} x_1^2 & 0 \\ 0 & x_2^2 \end{bmatrix} \begin{bmatrix} \xi_1 \\ \xi_2 \end{bmatrix} + 2 \begin{bmatrix} x_1 + 1 \\ x_2 - 1 \end{bmatrix}^\top \begin{bmatrix} \xi_1 \\ \xi_2 \end{bmatrix} + 2(x_1 + x_2) \le 0, \quad \forall \|\xi\|_2 \le 1,$$

$$\Leftrightarrow \begin{bmatrix} \xi_1 \\ \xi_2 \end{bmatrix}^\top \begin{bmatrix} x_1 & 0 \\ 0 & x_2 \end{bmatrix} \begin{bmatrix} x_1 & 0 \\ 0 & x_2 \end{bmatrix} \begin{bmatrix} \xi_1 \\ \xi_2 \end{bmatrix} + 2 \begin{bmatrix} x_1 + 1 \\ x_2 - 1 \end{bmatrix}^\top \begin{bmatrix} \xi_1 \\ \xi_2 \end{bmatrix} + 2(x_1 + x_2) \le 0, \quad \forall \|\xi\|_2 \le 1,$$

$$\Leftrightarrow \begin{bmatrix} \xi_1 \\ \xi_2 \end{bmatrix}^\top \begin{bmatrix} x_1 & 0 \\ 0 & x_2 \end{bmatrix} \begin{bmatrix} x_1 & 0 \\ 0 & x_2 \end{bmatrix} \begin{bmatrix} \xi_1 \\ \xi_2 \end{bmatrix} + 2 \begin{bmatrix} x_1 + 1 \\ x_2 - 1 \end{bmatrix}^\top \begin{bmatrix} \xi_1 \\ \xi_2 \end{bmatrix} \tau + 2(x_1 + x_2)\tau^2 \le 0,$$

$$\forall \|\xi\|_2 \le \tau, \ \textit{(homogenization)}$$

$$\Leftrightarrow \begin{bmatrix} \tau \\ \xi_1 \\ \xi_2 \end{bmatrix}^\top \begin{bmatrix} 2(x_1 + x_2) & x_1 + 1 & x_2 - 1 \\ x_1 + 1 & x_1 & 0 \\ x_2 - 1 & 0 & x_2 \end{bmatrix} \begin{bmatrix} \tau \\ \xi_1 \\ \xi_2 \end{bmatrix} \le 0, \quad \forall \|\xi\|_2 \le \tau,$$

$$\Leftrightarrow \exists \lambda \ge 0, \begin{bmatrix} 2(x_1 + x_2) & x_1 + 1 & x_2 - 1 \\ x_1 + 1 & x_1 & 0 \\ x_2 - 1 & 0 & x_2 \end{bmatrix} - \lambda \begin{bmatrix} -1 & & \\ & 1 & \\ & & 1 \end{bmatrix} \preceq 0, \ \textit{(S-lemma)}$$

$$\Leftrightarrow \exists \lambda \ge 0, \begin{bmatrix} 2(x_1 + x_2) + \lambda & x_1 + 1 & x_2 - 1 \\ x_1 + 1 & x_1 - \lambda & 0 \\ x_2 - 1 & 0 & x_2 - \lambda \end{bmatrix} \preceq 0.$$

□

### 2.3.3 *Robust Semidefinite Constraints*

A robust SDP constraint is naturally defined as

$$\boldsymbol{A}_1 x_1 + \boldsymbol{A}_2 x_2 + \cdots + \boldsymbol{A}_m x_m \succeq \boldsymbol{B}, \quad \forall (\boldsymbol{A}_1, \ldots, \boldsymbol{A}_m, \boldsymbol{B}) \in \mathcal{U}, \tag{2.3.78a}$$

$$\Leftrightarrow \quad \boldsymbol{A}_1 x_1 + \boldsymbol{A}_2 x_2 + \cdots + \boldsymbol{A}_m x_m - \boldsymbol{B} \in \mathbb{S}^n_+, \quad \forall (\boldsymbol{A}_1, \ldots, \boldsymbol{A}_m, \boldsymbol{B}) \in \mathcal{U}. \tag{2.3.78b}$$

The classes of uncertainty sets for which the robust SDP constraint admits a tractable reformulation are much more restricted than the robust SOC constraints. In particular, there are only two classes of uncertainty sets that we know are tractable: the convex hull of scenarios and a class of rank-2 ellipsoidal uncertainty sets. Let us describe them now.

#### 2.3.3.1 Convex Hull Uncertainty Set

The case of convex hull uncertainty set is simple. We have the following result.

If the uncertainty set is described as

$$\mathcal{U}_{\text{hull}} = \text{conv}\{(\boldsymbol{A}_1^1, \ldots, \boldsymbol{A}_m^1, \boldsymbol{B}^1), \ldots, (\boldsymbol{A}_1^k, \ldots, \boldsymbol{A}_m^k, \boldsymbol{B}^k)\}, \tag{2.3.79}$$

then the robust SDP constraint (2.3.78) can be reformulated as a set of deterministic SDP constraints, each for a scenario in $\mathcal{U}_{\text{hull}}$ as

$$\boldsymbol{A}_1^i x_1 + \boldsymbol{A}_2^i x_2 + \cdots + \boldsymbol{A}_m^i x_m \succeq \boldsymbol{B}^i, \quad \forall i = 1, 2, \ldots, k. \tag{2.3.80}$$

The reason is the same as the case of robust SOC constraints over the convex hull uncertainty set.

**Illustrative Example 2.13** *Let us see a concrete example continued from* (2.3.7), *which is a deterministic SDP constraint reproduced below*

$$\begin{bmatrix} 1 & -2 \\ -2 & 1 \end{bmatrix} x_1 + \begin{bmatrix} 1 & -1 \\ -1 & -2 \end{bmatrix} x_2 \succeq \begin{bmatrix} 0 & -1 \\ -1 & 0 \end{bmatrix}. \tag{2.3.81}$$

*Recall that the feasible region of* $(x_1, x_2)$ *defined by this SDP constraint is an ellipsoid.*

*Now imagine the matrices* $\boldsymbol{A}_1, \boldsymbol{A}_2, \boldsymbol{B}$ *are uncertain in a convex hull uncertainty set*

$$\mathcal{U}_{hull} = conv\left\{\Big(\underbrace{\begin{bmatrix} 0.5 & -2.5 \\ -2.5 & 0.5 \end{bmatrix}}_{\boldsymbol{A}_1^1}, \underbrace{\begin{bmatrix} 0.5 & -1.5 \\ -1.5 & -2.5 \end{bmatrix}}_{\boldsymbol{A}_2^1}, \underbrace{\begin{bmatrix} -0.5 & -1.5 \\ -1.5 & -0.5 \end{bmatrix}}_{\boldsymbol{B}^1}\Big), \Big(\underbrace{\begin{bmatrix} 1.5 & -1.5 \\ -1.5 & 1.5 \end{bmatrix}}_{\boldsymbol{A}_1^2}, \underbrace{\begin{bmatrix} 1.5 & -0.5 \\ -0.5 & -1.5 \end{bmatrix}}_{\boldsymbol{A}_2^2}, \underbrace{\begin{bmatrix} 0.5 & -0.5 \\ -0.5 & 0.5 \end{bmatrix}}_{\boldsymbol{B}^2}\Big)\right\},$$

*which contains the original deterministic matrices in* (2.3.82). *The robust version of* (2.3.82) *is given as*

$$\boldsymbol{A}_1 x_1 + \boldsymbol{A}_2 x_2 \succeq \boldsymbol{B}, \quad \forall (\boldsymbol{A}_1, \boldsymbol{A}_2, \boldsymbol{B}) \in \mathcal{U}_{hull}. \tag{2.3.82}$$

*Then, according to the above reformulation, this robust SDP constraint is equivalent to the following two deterministic SDP constraints*

$$\begin{bmatrix} 0.5 & -2.5 \\ -2.5 & 0.5 \end{bmatrix} x_1 + \begin{bmatrix} 0.5 & -1.5 \\ -1.5 & -2.5 \end{bmatrix} x_2 \succeq \begin{bmatrix} -0.5 & -1.5 \\ -1.5 & -0.5 \end{bmatrix} \Leftrightarrow \begin{bmatrix} x_1 + x_2 + 1 & -5x_1 - 3x_2 + 3 \\ -5x_1 - 3x_2 + 3 & x_1 - 5x_2 + 1 \end{bmatrix} \succeq \boldsymbol{0}, \tag{2.3.83a}$$

$$\begin{bmatrix} 1.5 & -1.5 \\ -1.5 & 1.5 \end{bmatrix} x_1 + \begin{bmatrix} 1.5 & -0.5 \\ -0.5 & -1.5 \end{bmatrix} x_2 \succeq \begin{bmatrix} 0.5 & -0.5 \\ -0.5 & 0.5 \end{bmatrix} \Leftrightarrow \begin{bmatrix} 3x_1 + 3x_2 - 1 & -3x_1 - x_2 + 1 \\ -3x_1 - x_2 + 1 & 3x_1 - 3x_2 - 1 \end{bmatrix} \succeq \boldsymbol{0}. \tag{2.3.83b}$$

*The feasible region of this robust SDP constraint is depicted in Fig.* 2.13.

□

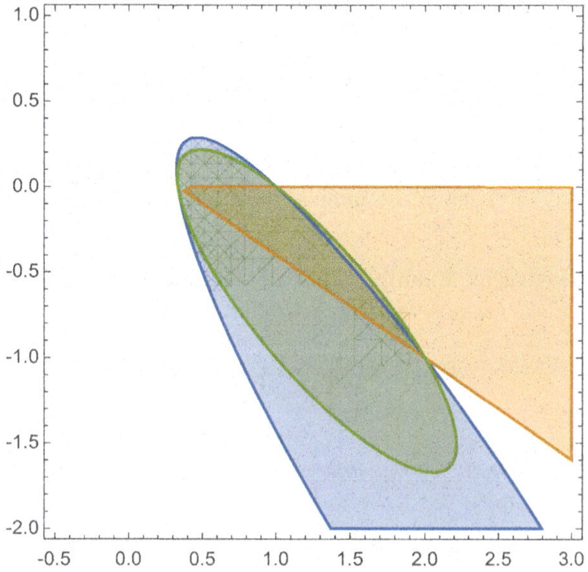


**Fig. 2.13** The green ellipse is the feasible region of the deterministic SDP (2.3.81). The blue is that of (2.3.83a) and the orange is for (2.3.83b). The intersection of the latter two is the feasible region of the robust SDP (2.3.82)

#### 2.3.3.2 Rank-2 Ellipsoidal Uncertainty Set

It is natural to consider an ellipsoidal uncertainty set for robust SDP constraints similar to what we have done for the robust SOC constraints in Sect. 2.3.2.3, namely

$$\mathcal{U} = \Bigg\{(\boldsymbol{A}_1, \ldots, \boldsymbol{A}_m, \boldsymbol{B}) : \boldsymbol{A}_i = \bar{\boldsymbol{A}}_i + \sum_{j=1}^{k} \Delta \boldsymbol{A}_{ij}\xi_j,$$

$$\boldsymbol{B} = \bar{\boldsymbol{B}} + \sum_{j=1}^{k} \Delta \boldsymbol{B}_j \xi_j,\ \forall\, i = 1, \ldots, m,\ \forall \boldsymbol{\xi} : \|\boldsymbol{\xi}\|_2 \le 1\Bigg\}. \tag{2.3.84}$$

Then the robust SDP constraint (2.3.78) with the above ellipsoidal uncertainty set (2.3.84) looks like

$$\left(\sum_{i=1}^{m} \bar{\boldsymbol{A}}_i x_i - \bar{\boldsymbol{B}}\right) + \sum_{j=1}^{k}\left(\sum_{i=1}^{m} \Delta \boldsymbol{A}_{ij} x_i - \Delta \boldsymbol{B}_j\right)\xi_j \succeq \boldsymbol{0}, \quad \forall \boldsymbol{\xi} : \|\boldsymbol{\xi}\|_2 \le 1. \tag{2.3.85}$$

**Illustrative Example 2.14** *Let us look at a simple example to get a sense of how the above uncertainty set affects the matrices in an SDP constraint. Let us take* (2.3.81) *as the example and add some ellipsoidal uncertainty to all the components of the* $\boldsymbol{A}_1, \boldsymbol{A}_2, \boldsymbol{B}$ *matrices as*

$$\begin{bmatrix} 1+\xi_1 & -2+\xi_2 \\ -2+\xi_3 & 1+\xi_4 \end{bmatrix} x_1 + \begin{bmatrix} 1+\xi_1 & -1+\xi_2 \\ -1+\xi_3 & -2+\xi_4 \end{bmatrix} x_2 \succeq \begin{bmatrix} \xi_1 & -1+\xi_2 \\ -1+\xi_3 & \xi_4 \end{bmatrix}, \quad \forall \boldsymbol{\xi} : \|\boldsymbol{\xi}\|_2 \le \alpha. \tag{2.3.86}$$

*In this case, the nominal values of* $\boldsymbol{A}_1, \boldsymbol{A}_2, \boldsymbol{B}$ *are given in the deterministic constraint* (2.3.81). *The perturbation matrices are given by*

$$\Delta_1 = \begin{bmatrix} \alpha & 0 \\ 0 & 0 \end{bmatrix},\ \Delta_2 = \begin{bmatrix} 0 & \alpha \\ 0 & 0 \end{bmatrix},\ \Delta_3 = \begin{bmatrix} 0 & 0 \\ \alpha & 0 \end{bmatrix},\ \Delta_4 = \begin{bmatrix} 0 & 0 \\ 0 & \alpha \end{bmatrix}.$$

*Then the* $\Delta \boldsymbol{A}_{ij}$ *and* $\Delta \boldsymbol{B}_j$ *matrices in* (2.3.85) *can be defined as*

$$\Delta \boldsymbol{A}_{ij} = \Delta \boldsymbol{B}_j = \Delta_j, \quad \forall i = 1, 2,\ j = 1, 2, 3, 4.$$

*We can also rearrange the above robust constraint as*

$$\left(\begin{bmatrix} 1 & -2 \\ -2 & 1 \end{bmatrix} x_1 + \begin{bmatrix} 1 & -1 \\ -1 & -2 \end{bmatrix} x_2 - \begin{bmatrix} 0 & -1 \\ -1 & 0 \end{bmatrix}\right) + \sum_{j=1}^{4} \Delta_j (x_1 + x_2 - 1)\xi_j \succeq \boldsymbol{0},\ \forall \boldsymbol{\xi} : \|\boldsymbol{\xi}\|_2 \le 1.$$

□

Unfortunately, robust constraints with ellipsoidal uncertainty sets in general are difficult to compute. Consider the following rather peculiar situation where the uncertainty set is given by

$$\bar{\boldsymbol{A}}_i = \Delta \boldsymbol{A}_{ij} = \boldsymbol{0}, \ \bar{\boldsymbol{B}} = -\boldsymbol{I}, \qquad \forall i = 1, \ldots, m, \forall j = 1, \ldots, k.$$

The robust SDP constraint becomes

$$\sum_{i=1}^{k} \Delta \boldsymbol{B}_i \xi_i \preceq \boldsymbol{I}, \quad \forall \boldsymbol{\xi} : \|\boldsymbol{\xi}\|_2 \leq 1, \tag{2.3.87}$$

which does not even involve $\boldsymbol{x}$. In other words, the robust SDP constraint (2.3.85) is only about verifying whether (2.3.87) is feasible or not. Then, we have

$$(2.3.87) \iff \sum_{j=1}^{k} (\boldsymbol{y}^\top \Delta \boldsymbol{B}_j \boldsymbol{y}) \xi_j \leq \boldsymbol{y}^\top \boldsymbol{y}, \quad \forall \boldsymbol{y}, \boldsymbol{\xi} : \|\boldsymbol{\xi}\|_2 \leq 1, \tag{2.3.88a}$$

$$\iff \max_{\|\boldsymbol{\xi}\|_2 \leq 1} \sum_{j=1}^{k} (\boldsymbol{y}^\top \Delta \boldsymbol{B}_j \boldsymbol{y}) \xi_j \leq \boldsymbol{y}^\top \boldsymbol{y}, \quad \forall \boldsymbol{y} \tag{2.3.88b}$$

$$\iff \sum_{j=1}^{k} (\boldsymbol{y}^\top \Delta \boldsymbol{B}_j \boldsymbol{y})^2 \leq (\boldsymbol{y}^\top \boldsymbol{y})^2, \quad \forall \boldsymbol{y} \tag{2.3.88c}$$

$$\iff \max_{\boldsymbol{y}^\top \boldsymbol{y} = 1} \sum_{j=1}^{k} (\boldsymbol{y}^\top \Delta \boldsymbol{B}_j \boldsymbol{y})^2 \leq 1, \tag{2.3.88d}$$

where the last maximization problem is an NP-hard problem for general $\Delta \boldsymbol{B}_j$ [3]. Roughly speaking, as the dimension of $\Delta \boldsymbol{B}_i$ increases, verifying (2.3.87) becomes very difficult.

If we look at the ellipsoidal uncertainty set (2.3.84) more carefully, we will see that each uncertain matrix $\boldsymbol{A}_i$ and $\boldsymbol{B}$ can be perturbed in all its entries with an arbitrary linear function in $\boldsymbol{\xi}$. In other words, the perturbation $\sum_{j=1}^{k} \Delta \boldsymbol{B}_j \xi_j$ may be full rank. As shown by the above example, such a perturbation turns out to be too arbitrary, or too strong, for a tractable reformulation to exist. Instead of a full rank perturbation, we have to restrict to essentially the simplest perturbation to a symmetric matrix, namely rank-2 perturbations. Let us discuss an example. Suppose the uncertain matrix $\boldsymbol{A}$ is perturbed in its first row and first column by linear functions in $\boldsymbol{\xi}$ as

$$\sum_{i=1}^{m} \boldsymbol{A}_i x_i = \sum_{i=1}^{m} \bar{\boldsymbol{A}}_i x_i + \begin{bmatrix} 0 & \boldsymbol{\xi}^\top L(\boldsymbol{x}) \\ L(\boldsymbol{x})^\top \boldsymbol{\xi} & \boldsymbol{0} \end{bmatrix}, \tag{2.3.88e}$$

where $L(\boldsymbol{x})$ is a matrix of linear functions of $\boldsymbol{x}$. The perturbation part can be expressed as

$$\begin{bmatrix} 0 & \boldsymbol{\xi}^\top L(\boldsymbol{x}) \\ L(\boldsymbol{x})^\top \boldsymbol{\xi} & \mathbf{0} \end{bmatrix} = \begin{bmatrix} \mathbf{0}^\top \\ L(\boldsymbol{x})^\top \end{bmatrix} \boldsymbol{\xi} \begin{bmatrix} 1 & \mathbf{0}^\top \end{bmatrix} + \begin{bmatrix} 1 \\ \mathbf{0} \end{bmatrix} \boldsymbol{\xi} \begin{bmatrix} \mathbf{0} & L(\boldsymbol{x}) \end{bmatrix} \tag{2.3.88f}$$

$$= \sum_{j=1}^{k} \left( \begin{bmatrix} 0 \\ l_j(\boldsymbol{x}) \end{bmatrix} \begin{bmatrix} 1 & \mathbf{0}^\top \end{bmatrix} + \begin{bmatrix} 1 \\ \mathbf{0} \end{bmatrix} \begin{bmatrix} 0 & l_j(\boldsymbol{x})^\top \end{bmatrix} \right) \xi_j, \tag{2.3.88g}$$

where $l_j(\boldsymbol{x})^\top$ is the $j$-th row of $L(\boldsymbol{x})$. If we compare the right-hand side of (2.3.88g) with the general perturbation (2.3.85), we can see that the perturbation matrix for each $\xi_i$ is a rank-2 matrix, whereas the perturbation matrix $\sum_{i=1}^{m} \Delta \boldsymbol{A}_{ij} x_i - \Delta \boldsymbol{B}_j$ for $\xi_i$ in (2.3.85) can have an arbitrary rank.

We can generalize the particular rank-2 example to a general rank-2 perturbation as

$$\sum_{i=1}^{m} \boldsymbol{A}_i x_i - \boldsymbol{B} = \sum_{i=1}^{m} (\bar{\boldsymbol{A}}_i x_i - \bar{\boldsymbol{B}}) + \sum_{j=1}^{k} \left( l_j(\boldsymbol{x}) \boldsymbol{r}^\top + \boldsymbol{r} l_j(\boldsymbol{x})^\top \right) \xi_j \succeq \mathbf{0}, \quad \forall \boldsymbol{\xi} : \|\boldsymbol{\xi}\|_2 \le 1. \tag{2.3.88h}$$

Let $\boldsymbol{C}(\boldsymbol{x}) = \sum_{i=1}^{m} (\bar{\boldsymbol{A}}_i x_i - \bar{B})$. This robust constraint now can be reformulated exactly as shown below.

$$\text{(2.3.88h)} \iff \boldsymbol{y}^\top \boldsymbol{C}(\boldsymbol{x}) \boldsymbol{y} + 2 \sum_{j=1}^{k} \boldsymbol{y}^\top l_j(\boldsymbol{x}) \boldsymbol{r}^\top \boldsymbol{y} \xi_j \ge 0, \quad \forall \boldsymbol{y}, \boldsymbol{\xi} : \|\boldsymbol{\xi}\|_2 \le 1, \tag{2.3.89a}$$

$$\iff \boldsymbol{y}^\top \boldsymbol{C}(\boldsymbol{x}) \boldsymbol{y} + \min_{\|\boldsymbol{\xi}\|_2 \le 1} 2 \sum_{j=1}^{k} (\boldsymbol{y}^\top l_j(\boldsymbol{x}))(\boldsymbol{r}^\top \boldsymbol{y}) \xi_j \ge 0, \quad \forall \boldsymbol{y}, \tag{2.3.89b}$$

$$\iff \boldsymbol{y}^\top \boldsymbol{C}(\boldsymbol{x}) \boldsymbol{y} + \min_{\|\boldsymbol{\xi}\|_2 \le 1} 2(\boldsymbol{r}^\top \boldsymbol{y}) \boldsymbol{y}^\top L(\boldsymbol{x}) \boldsymbol{\xi} \ge 0, \quad \forall \boldsymbol{y}, \tag{2.3.89c}$$

$$\iff \boldsymbol{y}^\top \boldsymbol{C}(\boldsymbol{x}) \boldsymbol{y} - 2|\boldsymbol{r}^\top \boldsymbol{y}| \|\boldsymbol{y}^\top L(\boldsymbol{x})\|_2 \ge 0, \quad \forall \boldsymbol{y}, \tag{2.3.89d}$$

$$\iff \boldsymbol{y}^\top \boldsymbol{C}(\boldsymbol{x}) \boldsymbol{y} + 2 \min_{\boldsymbol{\xi}^\top \boldsymbol{\xi} \le \boldsymbol{y}^\top \boldsymbol{r} \boldsymbol{r}^\top \boldsymbol{y}} \boldsymbol{y}^\top L(\boldsymbol{x}) \boldsymbol{\xi} \ge 0, \quad \forall \boldsymbol{y}, \tag{2.3.89e}$$

$$\iff \boldsymbol{y}^\top \boldsymbol{C}(\boldsymbol{x}) \boldsymbol{y} + 2 \boldsymbol{y}^\top L(\boldsymbol{x}) \boldsymbol{\xi} \ge 0, \quad \forall \boldsymbol{y}, \boldsymbol{\xi} : \boldsymbol{\xi}^\top \boldsymbol{\xi} \le \boldsymbol{y}^\top \boldsymbol{r} \boldsymbol{r}^\top \boldsymbol{y}, \tag{2.3.89f}$$

$$\iff \begin{bmatrix} \boldsymbol{r}\boldsymbol{r}^\top & \\ & -\boldsymbol{I} \end{bmatrix} \succeq \boldsymbol{0} \;\Rightarrow\; \begin{bmatrix} C(\boldsymbol{x}) & L(\boldsymbol{x}) \\ L(\boldsymbol{x})^\top & \boldsymbol{0} \end{bmatrix} \succeq \boldsymbol{0}, \tag{2.3.89g}$$

$$\iff \begin{bmatrix} C(\boldsymbol{x}) - \lambda \boldsymbol{r}\boldsymbol{r}^\top & L(\boldsymbol{x}) \\ L(\boldsymbol{x})^\top & \lambda \boldsymbol{I} \end{bmatrix} \succeq \boldsymbol{0}, \quad \lambda \geq 0. \tag{2.3.89h}$$

Looking deeper into the above derivation, we can see that the reason that it goes through critically depends on the structure of the perturbation. In particular, in (2.3.89b), the perturbation has the structure $\sum_{j=1}^{k} \boldsymbol{y}^\top E_j(\boldsymbol{x})\boldsymbol{y}\xi_j$ and $E_j(\boldsymbol{x}) = l_j(\boldsymbol{x})\boldsymbol{r}^\top$, i.e. $E_j(\boldsymbol{x})$ is a rank-one matrix. This allows the product term to be broken into two terms $\boldsymbol{y}^\top l_j(\boldsymbol{x})$ and $\boldsymbol{r}^\top \boldsymbol{y}$, each one being a linear function of $\boldsymbol{y}$. Now, imagine that $E_j(\boldsymbol{x})$ is a general linear matrix of $\boldsymbol{x}$, not necessarily rank one. Then, $\sum_{j=1}^{k} \boldsymbol{y}^\top E_j(\boldsymbol{x})\boldsymbol{y}\xi_j$ is not decomposable anymore and it indeed leads to intractable reformulation. This case exactly corresponds to the general ellipsoid uncertainty set (2.3.84).

**Illustrative Example 2.15** *Let us see an example. Consider the following robust SOCP constraint with an ellipsoidal uncertainty set*

$$\left\| \begin{bmatrix} 1+\xi_1 & \xi_2 \\ \xi_2 & 1+\xi_1 \end{bmatrix} \begin{bmatrix} x_1 \\ x_2 \end{bmatrix} + \begin{bmatrix} \xi_3 \\ \xi_4 \end{bmatrix} \right\|_2 \leq 1, \quad \forall \|(\xi_1, \xi_2, \xi_3, \xi_4)\|_2 \leq \alpha. \tag{2.3.90}$$

*The deterministic constraint $\|(x_1, x_2)\|_2 \leq 1$ is a unit disk. This robust SOCP constraint can be reformulated as a robust SDP constraint that, for all $\|(\xi_1, \xi_2, \xi_3, \xi_4)\|_2 \leq \alpha$, it holds*

$$\begin{bmatrix} 1 & (1+\xi_1)x_1 + \xi_2 x_2 + \xi_3 & \xi_2 x_1 + (1+\xi_1)x_2 + \xi_4 \\ (1+\xi_1)x_1 + \xi_2 x_2 + \xi_3 & 1 & 0 \\ \xi_2 x_1 + (1+\xi_1)x_2 + \xi_4 & 0 & 1 \end{bmatrix} \succeq \boldsymbol{0}, \tag{2.3.91}$$

$$\iff \begin{bmatrix} 1 & x_1 & x_2 \\ x_1 & 1 & 0 \\ x_2 & 0 & 1 \end{bmatrix} + \begin{bmatrix} 0 & x_1\xi_1 + x_2\xi_2 + \xi_3 & x_2\xi_1 + x_1\xi_2 + \xi_4 \\ x_1\xi_1 + x_2\xi_2 + \xi_3 & 0 & 0 \\ x_2\xi_1 + x_1\xi_2 + \xi_4 & 0 & 0 \end{bmatrix} \succeq \boldsymbol{0}, \tag{2.3.92}$$

$$\iff C(\boldsymbol{x}) + \begin{bmatrix} 0 & x_1 & x_2 \\ x_1 & 0 & 0 \\ x_2 & 0 & 0 \end{bmatrix}\xi_1 + \begin{bmatrix} 0 & x_2 & x_1 \\ x_2 & 0 & 0 \\ x_1 & 0 & 0 \end{bmatrix}\xi_2 + \begin{bmatrix} 0 & 1 & 0 \\ 1 & 0 & 0 \\ 0 & 0 & 0 \end{bmatrix}\xi_3 + \begin{bmatrix} 0 & 0 & 1 \\ 0 & 0 & 0 \\ 1 & 0 & 0 \end{bmatrix}\xi_4 \succeq \boldsymbol{0}, \tag{2.3.93}$$

$$\iff C(\boldsymbol{x}) + \left( \begin{bmatrix} 0 \\ x_1 \\ x_2 \end{bmatrix} \begin{bmatrix} 1 \\ 0 \\ 0 \end{bmatrix}^\top + \begin{bmatrix} 1 \\ 0 \\ 0 \end{bmatrix} \begin{bmatrix} 0 \\ x_1 \\ x_2 \end{bmatrix}^\top \right)\xi_1 + \left( \begin{bmatrix} 0 \\ x_2 \\ x_1 \end{bmatrix} \begin{bmatrix} 1 \\ 0 \\ 0 \end{bmatrix}^\top + \begin{bmatrix} 1 \\ 0 \\ 0 \end{bmatrix} \begin{bmatrix} 0 \\ x_2 \\ x_1 \end{bmatrix}^\top \right)\xi_2 \tag{2.3.94}$$

$$+\left(\begin{bmatrix}0\\1\\0\end{bmatrix}\begin{bmatrix}1\\0\\0\end{bmatrix}^{\top}+\begin{bmatrix}1\\0\\0\end{bmatrix}\begin{bmatrix}0\\1\\0\end{bmatrix}^{\top}\right)\xi_3+\left(\begin{bmatrix}0\\0\\1\end{bmatrix}\begin{bmatrix}1\\0\\0\end{bmatrix}^{\top}+\begin{bmatrix}1\\0\\0\end{bmatrix}\begin{bmatrix}0\\0\\1\end{bmatrix}^{\top}\right)\xi_4\succeq \mathbf{0}, \tag{2.3.95}$$

*where $C(\boldsymbol{x})$ is the first 3-by-3 matrix in the left-hand-side of the second inequality. Now form the $L(\boldsymbol{x})$ matrix as*

$$L(\boldsymbol{x})=\begin{bmatrix}0&0&0&0\\x_1&x_2&1&0\\x_2&x_1&0&1\end{bmatrix}. \tag{2.3.96}$$

*The SDP reformulation then is given by* (2.3.89h) *as*

$$\begin{bmatrix}1-\lambda&x_1&x_2&0&0&0&0\\x_1&1&0&x_1&x_2&1&0\\x_2&0&1&x_2&x_1&0&1\\0&x_1&x_2&\lambda&0&0&0\\0&x_2&x_1&0&\lambda&0&0\\0&1&0&0&0&\lambda&0\\0&0&1&0&0&0&\lambda\end{bmatrix}\succeq \mathbf{0},\ \ \lambda\geq 0. \tag{2.3.97}$$

□

## 2.4 Approximations of Robust Convex Constraints

The reformulations that we have introduced so far could be summarized as follows. Robust linear optimization is usually tractable; robust conic optimization is tractable for the following uncertainty sets: convex hull of scenarios, simple interval sets, simple ellipsoidal uncertainty set of the left-hand side, and joint ellipsoidal uncertainty set for robust quadratic optimization, and otherwise in general not tractable for other uncertainty sets; robust SDP optimization is tractable for an even smaller class of uncertainty sets: convex hull of scenarios and a rank-2 type ellipsoidal uncertainty set, and is otherwise not tractable. For example, robust SDP is not tractable for the general ellipsoidal uncertainty set, nor for the general polyhedral uncertainty sets.

In this section, we will discuss how to deal with a robust convex constraint and an associated uncertainty set that cannot be exactly reformulated as tractable deterministic constraints. The key idea is to find another tractable reformulation, whose feasible solutions are guaranteed to satisfy the intractable robust constraint. In other words, if we denote the set of feasible solutions of the robust constraint as $\mathscr{D}$, then we want to find a tractable reformulation whose feasible region $\mathscr{D}'$ is contained in $\mathscr{D}$, i.e. $\mathscr{D}'\subseteq\mathscr{D}$. Why is such a tractable reformulation a desirable replacement for the robust constraint? First, because the approximation leads to a convex reformulation, which is computationally tractable. Second, and more importantly, because such a reformulation provides a *safe approximation* to the robust one, as every solution to the reformulation is also robust feasible. Moreover, for some classes of problems, we can characterize how good the safe approximation is compared to the true robust constraint. To characterize this, we want to find an $\alpha > 1$ such that

$$\mathcal{D}' \subseteq \mathcal{D} \subseteq \alpha\mathcal{D}'. \tag{2.4.1}$$

We call $\mathcal{D}'$ an $\alpha$-approximation of $\mathcal{D}$. Here $\alpha$ may depend on the dimension of $\mathcal{D}$ or other features of the robust constraint, such as the rank of the matrices involved in the uncertainty sets, but as long as $\alpha$ is not too much larger than 1, or $\alpha$ does not grow too fast with respect to the dimension of the robust constraint, then we deem the $\alpha$-approximation a good approximation.

## 2.4.1 *Safe Approximations of Robust Second-Order Conic Optimization*

In Sects. 2.3.2.2 and 2.3.2.3, we see that a robust SOC constraint with an interval uncertainty set or an ellipsoidal uncertainty set for the left-hand side parameters has an exact reformulation. However, if the uncertainty set has some finer structures as discussed below, the robust SOC constraint may no longer be tractable.

### 2.4.1.1 The Concept of Structured Uncertainty

Uncertain parameters may have some finer structures in the sense that some uncertain parameters are confined in an interval uncertainty set, while other uncertain parameters may be in an ellipsoidal uncertainty set, that is, the overall uncertainty set is a *Cartesian product* of an interval and an ellipsoidal uncertainty set, as described below

$$\mathcal{U}_{\text{box}\times\text{ellip}} = \{\boldsymbol{\xi} = (\boldsymbol{\xi}_1, \boldsymbol{\xi}_2) \in \mathbb{R}^{m_1+m_2} : \|\boldsymbol{\xi}_1\|_\infty \le 1,\ \|\boldsymbol{\xi}_2\|_2 \le 1\}. \tag{2.4.2}$$

Or more generally, the overall uncertainty set could be a cartesian product of a hyberbox and several ellipsoidal uncertainty sets as

$$\mathcal{U}_{\text{str}} = \{\boldsymbol{\xi} = (\boldsymbol{\xi}_1, \boldsymbol{\xi}_2, \ldots, \boldsymbol{\xi}_N) \in \mathbb{R}^{m_1+\cdots+m_N} : \|\boldsymbol{\xi}_1\|_\infty \le 1,$$

$$\|\boldsymbol{\xi}_i\|_2 \le 1,\ \forall i = 2, 3, \ldots, N\}, \tag{2.4.3a}$$

$$= \mathcal{U}_1 \times \mathcal{U}_2 \times \cdots \times \mathcal{U}_N. \tag{2.4.3b}$$

Such an uncertainty set is called a *structured* norm-bounded uncertainty set. Here, the term "structured" is meant to contrast with the simpler uncertainty set of an ellipsoid or a box. The latter are called *unstructured* norm-bounded uncertainty set, because all the parameters are confined in one set without further structures. These terminologies come from the robust control literature [20]. Note that the product of two $\ell_\infty$ balls is another $\ell_\infty$ ball in higher dimension, therefore, it is without loss of generality to have only one $\ell_\infty$ ball in $\mathscr{U}_{\text{str}}$. However, the product of two $\ell_2$ balls is not an $\ell_2$ ball in higher dimension. So having multiple ellipsoids in $\mathscr{U}_{\text{str}}$ is meaningful. In fact, it will be more convenient if we treat the $\ell_\infty$ ball as the product of one dimensional intervals. So from now on, we denote $\boldsymbol{\xi}_1 = (\xi_{11}, \ldots, \xi_{1m_1})^\top$ and define $\mathscr{U}_{1j} = \{\xi_{1j} : |\xi_{1j}| \le 1\}$, so $\mathscr{U}_1 = \mathscr{U}_{11} \times \cdots \times \mathscr{U}_{1m_1}$.

#### 2.4.1.2 Safe Approximation of Robust SOC with $\mathscr{U}_{\text{str}}$

We consider a robust least square constraint

$$\|\boldsymbol{A}(\boldsymbol{\xi})\boldsymbol{x} - \boldsymbol{b}(\boldsymbol{\xi})\|_2 \le \tau, \quad \forall \boldsymbol{\xi} \in \mathscr{U}_{\text{str}}, \tag{2.4.4}$$

where the uncertain parameters $\boldsymbol{A}(\boldsymbol{\xi})$ and $\boldsymbol{b}(\boldsymbol{\xi})$ are affinely parametrized by $\boldsymbol{\xi}$ as

$$\boldsymbol{A}(\boldsymbol{\xi}) = \bar{\boldsymbol{A}} + \sum_{i=1}^{N}\sum_{j=1}^{m_i} \boldsymbol{A}_{ij}\xi_{ij}, \ \boldsymbol{b}(\boldsymbol{\xi}) = \bar{\boldsymbol{b}} + \sum_{i=1}^{N}\sum_{j=1}^{m_i} \boldsymbol{b}_{ij}\xi_{ij}. \tag{2.4.5}$$

So the linear expression in the norm in (2.4.4) can be written as

$$\boldsymbol{A}(\boldsymbol{\xi})\boldsymbol{x} - \boldsymbol{b}(\boldsymbol{\xi}) = (\bar{\boldsymbol{A}}\boldsymbol{x} - \bar{\boldsymbol{b}}) + \sum_{i=1}^{N}\Big(\sum_{j=1}^{m_i}(\boldsymbol{A}_{ij}\boldsymbol{x} - \boldsymbol{b}_{ij})\xi_{ij}\Big), \tag{2.4.6}$$

$$= \boldsymbol{B}_0(\boldsymbol{x}) + \sum_{i=1}^{N} \boldsymbol{B}_i(\boldsymbol{x}, \boldsymbol{\xi}_i), \tag{2.4.7}$$

where $\boldsymbol{B}_0(\boldsymbol{x}) = \bar{\boldsymbol{A}}\boldsymbol{x} - \bar{\boldsymbol{b}}$ and $\boldsymbol{B}_i(\boldsymbol{x}, \boldsymbol{\xi}_i) = \sum_{j=1}^{m_i}(\boldsymbol{A}_{ij}\boldsymbol{x} - \boldsymbol{b}_{ij})\xi_{ij}$ for each $i$. Now let us derive a safe approximation for (2.4.4)–(2.4.5).

Observe that the robust least square constraint (2.4.4) is also a robust SDP constraint. Using the same observation as in (2.3.42b) in Sect. 2.3.2.3, we can rewrite (2.4.4) as a robust SDP constraint

$$\|\boldsymbol{A}(\boldsymbol{\xi})\boldsymbol{x} - \boldsymbol{b}(\boldsymbol{\xi})\|_2 \le \tau, \quad \forall \boldsymbol{\xi} \in \mathscr{U}_{\text{str}}, \tag{2.4.8a}$$

$$\Leftrightarrow \begin{bmatrix} \tau & (\boldsymbol{A}(\boldsymbol{\xi})\boldsymbol{x} - \boldsymbol{b}(\boldsymbol{\xi}))^\top \\ \boldsymbol{A}(\boldsymbol{\xi})\boldsymbol{x} - \boldsymbol{b}(\boldsymbol{\xi}) & \tau\boldsymbol{I} \end{bmatrix} \succeq \boldsymbol{0}, \quad \forall \boldsymbol{\xi} \in \mathscr{U}_{\text{str}}, \tag{2.4.8b}$$

$$\Leftrightarrow \begin{bmatrix} \tau & (\boldsymbol{B}_0(\boldsymbol{x}) + \sum_{i=1}^{N} \boldsymbol{B}_i(\boldsymbol{x}, \boldsymbol{\xi}_i))^\top \\ \boldsymbol{B}_0(\boldsymbol{x}) + \sum_{i=1}^{N} \boldsymbol{B}_i(\boldsymbol{x}, \boldsymbol{\xi}_i) & \tau\boldsymbol{I} \end{bmatrix} \succeq \boldsymbol{0}, \quad \forall \boldsymbol{\xi} \in \mathscr{U}_{\text{str}}, \tag{2.4.8c}$$

$$\Leftrightarrow \begin{bmatrix} \tau & \boldsymbol{B}_0(\boldsymbol{x})^\top \\ \boldsymbol{B}_0(\boldsymbol{x}) & \tau\boldsymbol{I} \end{bmatrix} + \sum_{i=1}^{N} \begin{bmatrix} 0 & \boldsymbol{B}_i(\boldsymbol{x}, \boldsymbol{\xi}_i)^\top \\ \boldsymbol{B}_i(\boldsymbol{x}, \boldsymbol{\xi}_i) & \boldsymbol{0} \end{bmatrix} \succeq \boldsymbol{0}, \quad \forall \boldsymbol{\xi} \in \mathscr{U}_{\text{str}}, \tag{2.4.8d}$$

$$\Leftrightarrow \begin{bmatrix} \tau & \boldsymbol{B}_0(\boldsymbol{x})^\top \\ \boldsymbol{B}_0(\boldsymbol{x}) & \tau \boldsymbol{I} \end{bmatrix} + \sum_{j=1}^{m_1} \begin{bmatrix} 0 & \boldsymbol{B}_{1j}(\boldsymbol{x}, \xi_{1j})^\top \\ \boldsymbol{B}_{1j}(\boldsymbol{x}, \xi_{1j}) & \boldsymbol{0} \end{bmatrix} + \sum_{i=2}^{N} \begin{bmatrix} 0 & \boldsymbol{B}_i(\boldsymbol{x}, \boldsymbol{\xi}_i)^\top \\ \boldsymbol{B}_i(\boldsymbol{x}, \boldsymbol{\xi}_i) & \boldsymbol{0} \end{bmatrix} \succeq \boldsymbol{0},$$

$$\forall \boldsymbol{\xi} \in \mathcal{U}_{11} \times \cdots \times \mathcal{U}_{1m_1} \times \mathcal{U}_2 \times \cdots \times \mathcal{U}_N. \tag{2.4.8e}$$

Now we come to a conjuncture that it is impossible to go further with the chain of "if and only if" implications, as we already know that even when there is only one box uncertainty set and no ellipsoidal uncertainty set, (2.4.8e) can be NP-hard to certify. Instead, we have a simple observation that (2.4.8e) is *implied* by the following conditions:

$$\begin{cases} \begin{bmatrix} \tau & \boldsymbol{B}_0(\boldsymbol{x})^\top \\ \boldsymbol{B}_0(\boldsymbol{x}) & \tau \boldsymbol{I} \end{bmatrix} - \sum_{j=1}^{m_j} Y_{1j} - \sum_{i=2}^{N} Y_i \succeq \boldsymbol{0}, \\ Y_{1j} \succeq \begin{bmatrix} 0 & \boldsymbol{B}_{1j}(\boldsymbol{x}, \xi_{1j})^\top \\ \boldsymbol{B}_{1j}(\boldsymbol{x}, \xi_{1j}) & \boldsymbol{0} \end{bmatrix}, \quad \forall \xi_{1j} : |\xi_{1j}| \le 1, \ \forall j = 1, \ldots, m_1, \\ Y_i \succeq \begin{bmatrix} 0 & \boldsymbol{B}_i(\boldsymbol{x}, \boldsymbol{\xi}_i)^\top \\ \boldsymbol{B}_i(\boldsymbol{x}, \boldsymbol{\xi}_i) & \boldsymbol{0} \end{bmatrix}, \quad \forall \boldsymbol{\xi}_i : \|\boldsymbol{\xi}_i\|_2 \le 1, \ \forall i = 2, \ldots, N. \end{cases} \tag{2.4.9}$$

The first condition in (2.4.9) is already a deterministic SDP constraint. The second condition in (2.4.9) takes the form, for each $j = 1, \ldots, m_1$,

$$Y_{1j} \succeq \begin{bmatrix} 0 & \boldsymbol{B}_{1j}(\boldsymbol{x}, \xi_{1j})^\top \\ \boldsymbol{B}_{1j}(\boldsymbol{x}, \xi_{1j}) & \boldsymbol{0} \end{bmatrix} = \begin{bmatrix} 0 & \xi_{1j}(\boldsymbol{A}_{1j}\boldsymbol{x} - \boldsymbol{b}_{1j})^\top \\ \xi_{1j}(\boldsymbol{A}_{1j}\boldsymbol{x} - \boldsymbol{b}_{1j}) & \boldsymbol{0} \end{bmatrix}, \ \forall \xi_{1j} : |\xi_{1j}| \le 1. \tag{2.4.10}$$

Clearly, (2.4.10) should hold for both $\xi_{1j} = 1$ and $\xi_{1j} = -1$, i.e. (2.4.10) implies that

$$Y_{1j} \succeq \pm \begin{bmatrix} 0 & (\boldsymbol{A}_{1j}\boldsymbol{x} - \boldsymbol{b}_{1j})^\top \\ (\boldsymbol{A}_{1j}\boldsymbol{x} - \boldsymbol{b}_{1j}) & \boldsymbol{0} \end{bmatrix}. \tag{2.4.11}$$

Conversely, if (2.4.11) holds, then for any $\lambda \in [0, 1]$, we have

$$\lambda Y_{1j} \succeq \lambda \begin{bmatrix} 0 & (\boldsymbol{A}_{1j}\boldsymbol{x} - \boldsymbol{b}_{1j})^\top \\ (\boldsymbol{A}_{1j}\boldsymbol{x} - \boldsymbol{b}_{1j}) & \boldsymbol{0} \end{bmatrix}, \text{ and}$$

$$(1-\lambda) Y_{1j} \succeq -(1-\lambda) \begin{bmatrix} 0 & (\boldsymbol{A}_{1j}\boldsymbol{x} - \boldsymbol{b}_{1j})^\top \\ (\boldsymbol{A}_{1j}\boldsymbol{x} - \boldsymbol{b}_{1j}) & \boldsymbol{0} \end{bmatrix}. \tag{2.4.12}$$

Summing the above two inequalities, we recover (2.4.10), because $\lambda - (1 - \lambda)$ takes all values in $[-1, 1]$. Therefore, we see that the second condition in (2.4.9), which itself is a robust constraint, is equivalent to the two simple deterministic SDP constraint in (2.4.11).

The third condition in (2.4.9) is a robust SDP constraint with an ellipsoidal uncertainty set. The structure of the matrix on the right-hand side of the second condition has a special structure, namely, its rank is at most two. This is exactly the structure that we have encountered in (2.3.88e), which we already know how to obtain an exact reformulation. Let us first write the third condition in an explicit form as in (2.3.88e).

$$Y_i + \begin{bmatrix} 0 & (L_i(\boldsymbol{x})\boldsymbol{\xi}_i)^\top \\ L_i(\boldsymbol{x})\boldsymbol{\xi}_i & \mathbf{0} \end{bmatrix} \succeq \mathbf{0}, \quad \forall \boldsymbol{\xi}_i : \|\boldsymbol{\xi}_i\|_2 \le 1, \tag{2.4.13}$$

where $L_i(\boldsymbol{x})\boldsymbol{\xi}_i = -\boldsymbol{B}_i(\boldsymbol{x}, \boldsymbol{\xi}_i)$ and $-L_i(\boldsymbol{x})$ is a matrix with columns $[\boldsymbol{A}_{i1}\boldsymbol{x} - \boldsymbol{b}_{i1}, \ldots, \boldsymbol{A}_{im_i}\boldsymbol{x} - \boldsymbol{b}_{im_i}]$. Directly applying the reformulation result of (2.3.89h), we get

$$\begin{bmatrix} Y_i - \lambda_i \boldsymbol{r}\boldsymbol{r}^\top & L_i(\boldsymbol{x})^\top \\ L_i(\boldsymbol{x}) & \lambda_i \boldsymbol{I} \end{bmatrix} \succeq \mathbf{0}, \quad \lambda_i \ge 0, \tag{2.4.14}$$

where $\boldsymbol{r} = [1, \mathbf{0}^\top]^\top$. Now, putting things together, we get the following result.

The following set of deterministic SDP constraints

$$\begin{cases} \begin{bmatrix} \tau & \boldsymbol{B}_0(\boldsymbol{x})^\top \\ \boldsymbol{B}_0(\boldsymbol{x}) & \tau \boldsymbol{I} \end{bmatrix} - \sum_{j=1}^{m_j} Y_{1j} - \sum_{i=2}^{N} Y_i \succeq \mathbf{0}, \\ Y_{1j} \succeq \pm \begin{bmatrix} 0 & (\boldsymbol{A}_{1j}\boldsymbol{x} - \boldsymbol{b}_{1j})^\top \\ (\boldsymbol{A}_{1j}\boldsymbol{x} - \boldsymbol{b}_{1j}) & \mathbf{0} \end{bmatrix}, \quad \forall j = 1, \ldots, m_1, \\ \begin{bmatrix} Y_i - \lambda_i \boldsymbol{r}\boldsymbol{r}^\top & L_i(\boldsymbol{x})^\top \\ L_i(\boldsymbol{x}) & \lambda_i \boldsymbol{I} \end{bmatrix} \succeq \mathbf{0}, \quad \lambda_i \ge 0, \quad \forall i = 2, \ldots, N, \end{cases} \tag{2.4.15}$$

is a safe approximation of the robust least square constraint (2.4.4) with the structured norm-bounded uncertainty set (2.4.3).

**Illustrative Example 2.16** *Let us see a concrete example. Consider the following robust SOCP constraint with two ellipsoidal uncertainty sets*

$$\left\| \begin{bmatrix} 1+\xi_1 & \xi_2 \\ \xi_2 & 1+\xi_1 \end{bmatrix} \begin{bmatrix} x_1 \\ x_2 \end{bmatrix} + \begin{bmatrix} \xi_3 \\ \xi_4 \end{bmatrix} \right\|_2 \le 1, \quad \forall \|(\xi_1, \xi_2)\|_2 \le \alpha, \ \|(\xi_3, \xi_4)\|_2 \le \alpha. \tag{2.4.16}$$

*It is similar to the example* (2.3.90)*, except that the uncertainty parameters $\xi_i$'s belong to two ellipsoidal uncertainty sets rather than one. The deterministic constraint $\|(x_1, x_2)\|_2 \le 1$ is still a unit disk. The robust SOCP constraint* (2.4.16) *can be transformed to a robust SDP constraint as*

$$
\begin{aligned}
&\begin{bmatrix} 1 & (1+\xi_1)x_1 + \xi_2 x_2 + \xi_3 & \xi_2 x_1 + (1+\xi_1)x_2 + \xi_4 \\ (1+\xi_1)x_1 + \xi_2 x_2 + \xi_3 & 1 & 0 \\ \xi_2 x_1 + (1+\xi_1)x_2 + \xi_4 & 0 & 1 \end{bmatrix} \succeq \mathbf{0}, \\
\iff &\begin{bmatrix} 1 & x_1 & x_2 \\ x_1 & 1 & 0 \\ x_2 & 0 & 1 \end{bmatrix} + \begin{bmatrix} 0 & x_1 & x_2 \\ x_1 & 0 & 0 \\ x_2 & 0 & 0 \end{bmatrix}\xi_1 + \begin{bmatrix} 0 & x_2 & x_1 \\ x_2 & 0 & 0 \\ x_1 & 0 & 0 \end{bmatrix}\xi_2 + \begin{bmatrix} 0 & 1 & 0 \\ 1 & 0 & 0 \\ 0 & 0 & 0 \end{bmatrix}\xi_3 + \begin{bmatrix} 0 & 0 & 1 \\ 0 & 0 & 0 \\ 1 & 0 & 0 \end{bmatrix}\xi_4 \succeq \mathbf{0}, \\
\Leftarrow &\begin{cases} \begin{bmatrix} 1 & x_1 & x_2 \\ x_1 & 1 & 0 \\ x_2 & 0 & 1 \end{bmatrix} - Y - Z \succeq \mathbf{0}, \\ Y \succeq \begin{bmatrix} 0 & x_1 & x_2 \\ x_1 & 0 & 0 \\ x_2 & 0 & 0 \end{bmatrix}\xi_1 + \begin{bmatrix} 0 & x_2 & x_1 \\ x_2 & 0 & 0 \\ x_1 & 0 & 0 \end{bmatrix}\xi_2, \quad \forall\, (\xi_1, \xi_2) : \|(\xi_1, \xi_2)\|_2 \le \alpha, \\ Z \succeq \begin{bmatrix} 0 & 1 & 0 \\ 1 & 0 & 0 \\ 0 & 0 & 0 \end{bmatrix}\xi_3 + \begin{bmatrix} 0 & 0 & 1 \\ 0 & 0 & 0 \\ 1 & 0 & 0 \end{bmatrix}\xi_4, \quad \forall\, (\xi_3, \xi_4) : \|(\xi_3, \xi_4)\|_2 \le \alpha, \end{cases} \\
\Leftarrow &\begin{cases} \begin{bmatrix} 1 & x_1 & x_2 \\ x_1 & 1 & 0 \\ x_2 & 0 & 1 \end{bmatrix} - Y - Z \succeq \mathbf{0}, \\ \begin{bmatrix} y_{11} - \lambda_1 & y_{12} & y_{13} & 0 & 0 \\ y_{12} & y_{22} & y_{23} & x_1 & x_2 \\ y_{13} & y_{23} & y_{33} & x_2 & x_1 \\ 0 & x_1 & x_2 & \lambda_1 & 0 \\ 0 & x_2 & x_1 & 0 & \lambda_1 \end{bmatrix} \succeq \mathbf{0}, \quad \begin{bmatrix} z_{11} - \lambda_2 & z_{12} & z_{13} & 0 & 0 \\ z_{12} & z_{22} & z_{23} & 1 & 0 \\ z_{13} & z_{23} & z_{33} & 0 & 1 \\ 0 & 1 & 0 & \lambda_2 & 0 \\ 0 & 0 & 1 & 0 & \lambda_2 \end{bmatrix} \succeq \mathbf{0}, \\ \lambda_1 \ge 0, \ \lambda_2 \ge 0. \end{cases}
\end{aligned}
$$

□

This result itself is not particularly deep. As we have seen, all we need is a simple realization that (2.4.8e) can be guaranteed by ensuring each term in the sum is robustly dominated by a fixed matrix plus the old tricks that we used in the previous section, primarily the S-lemma. However, what indeed is deep is the following result about the quality of the safe approximation of (2.4.1.2). We will simply state it without giving a proof.

The tightness factor $\alpha$ of the safe approximation (2.4.1.2) of the robust least square constraint (2.4.4) with the structured norm-bounded uncertainty set (2.4.3) satisfies $\alpha \le \pi/2 \approx 1.57$ and equals 1 if the uncertainty set $\mathscr{U}_{\text{str}}$ is an ellipsoidal set.

The proof of this result relies on a deep theorem called the real matrix cube theorem [7, 8]. The same ideas used in the above derivation can be applied to find a safe approximations of robust convex quadratic constraints with the structured uncertainty set $\mathscr{U}_{\text{str}}$. The same tightness factor of $\pi/2$ applies. Moreover, the robust least square constraint with an uncertainty set given by the intersection of ellipsoids, defined as

$$\mathscr{U}_{\cap\text{-ellip}} = \{\boldsymbol{\xi} : \boldsymbol{\xi}^\top Q_i \boldsymbol{\xi} \le 1,\ \forall i = 1, 2, \ldots, J\}, \tag{2.4.17}$$

also has a safe approximation. The derivation uses the same techniques as above, therefore, is left as an exercise. To characterize the tightness factor of this approximation is, however, different from the above two cases, and requires a different technique called the approximate S-lemma. The resulting tightness factor is shown to be upper bounded by $9.19\sqrt{\ln(J)}$, where $J$ is the number of ellipsoids in the uncertainty set and $J \ge 2$, and for $J = 1$ the safe approximation is the same as the exact reformulation derived in Sect. 2.3.2.3.

## 2.4.2 Safe Approximation of Robust SDP Constraints

In general, robust SDP constraints are more challenging to reformulate and handle than robust SOCP constraints. Exactly because of this challenge, there is not much room we can maneuver in the space of robust SDPs. In particular, the only known nontrivial case with a safe approximation and tightness factor characterization for robust SDP is the case of the structured uncertainty set with rank-2 perturbations, i.e. a generalization of the rank-2 ellipsoidal uncertainty set (2.3.88h) from one ellipsoid to a product of multiple ellipsoids.

$$\begin{aligned}\boldsymbol{A}(\boldsymbol{\xi})(\boldsymbol{x}) - \boldsymbol{B}(\boldsymbol{\xi}) &= \sum_{i=1}^{m} (\bar{\boldsymbol{A}}_i x_i - \bar{B}) \\ &+ \sum_{i=1}^{N} \sum_{j=1}^{m_i} \left( L_i(\boldsymbol{x}) \boldsymbol{R}_i^\top + \boldsymbol{R}_i L_i(\boldsymbol{x})^\top \right) \xi_{ij} \succeq \boldsymbol{0}, \quad \forall \boldsymbol{\xi} \in \mathscr{U}_{\text{str}}.\end{aligned} \tag{2.4.18}$$

The method to derive a safe approximation follows exactly the same steps as that of the robust least square constraint with the structured norm-bounded uncertainty set.

### 2.4.3 A Quick Summary

Before we go on to introduce a general method for deriving safe approximations of robust conic constraints, let us give a quick summary of the results we obtained so far.

1. A robust linear constraint can be reformulated in a closed form as a deterministic convex conic optimization problem if the uncertainty set can be expressed as a set of linear constraints over a convex cone, e.g. the nonnegative orthant, the SOC cone, and the SDP cone.
2. A robust constraint with a convex hull uncertainty set can usually be reformulated as a set of deterministic constraints of the same type.
3. A robust conic constraint with row-wise independent interval uncertainty sets can be reformulated exactly as SOCP constraints.
4. A robust conic constraint with an ellipsoidal uncertainty can be reformulated exactly as an SDP constraint.
5. A robust conic constraint with more than one ellipsoidal uncertainty sets cannot be reformulated exactly but can be safely approximated by SDP constraints with a performance guarantee.
6. A robust quadratic constraint of type-1 with an ellipsoidal uncertainty set on the matrix of the quadratic term alone can be reformulated exactly as SOCP constraints. If both the matrix and the linear term of the robust quadratic constraint are uncertainty, then it may not be possible to reformulate as a convex constraint.
7. A robust quadratic constraint of type-2 with an ellipsoidal uncertainty set on all parameters can be reformulated exactly as an SDP constraint.
8. A robust SDP constraint with rank-2 type uncertainty matrices and an ellipsoidal uncertainty set can be reformulated as SDP constraints.
9. A robust SDP constraint with rank-2 type uncertainty matrices and more than one ellipsoidal uncertainty sets cannot be reformulated exactly as SDPs, but can be safely approximated by SDP constraints with a performance guarantee.
10. A robust SDP constraint with general uncertainty matrices and one or multiple ellipsoidal uncertainty sets cannot be exactly reformulated as SDP constraints and it is not known if any safe approximation with performance guarantee exists.

From this list we can see that, although exact reformulation and safe approximation with performance guarantee are very desired commodity, they seem to be quite rare. Beyond the simple rank-2 type matrix perturbations and ellipsoidal uncertainty sets, it is not known how to approximate general robust SDP constraints with performance guarantee. In this context, it is quite amazing to see in the next subsection that a general methodology can be developed to derive safe approximations to a wide range of robust linear, conic, quadratic, and SDP constraints that go well beyond the above listed classes of problems. However, the general methodology comes with a price that in general we do not have an a priori bound on how well the approximations are.

## 2.4.4 A General Principle for Deriving Safe Approximation

The above two subsections give safe approximations of three classes of robust conic constraints with structured uncertainty set, namely robust least square, robust convex quadratic, and robust SDP constraints and robust least square constraints with the uncertainty set of intersection of ellipsoids. The type of the robust constraints and uncertainty sets covered is quite restrictive. However, one can argue that the strength of the result is the fact that the tightness factor of the approximation is characterized. In the following, we introduce an alternative method to generate safe approximations to the same classes of robust conic constraints and potentially much more, with an additional advantage that the complexity of the safe approximation is in general at the same level as the deterministic counterparts, and the problem size of the approximation is quite small. This section follows the development in [16].

### 2.4.4.1 Basic Model and Assumption

Let us consider the following general robust constraint

$$f(\boldsymbol{x}, \boldsymbol{D}) \leq 0, \quad \forall \boldsymbol{D} \in \mathcal{U}, \tag{2.4.19}$$

where $\boldsymbol{D}$ is the uncertain data and the uncertainty set $\mathcal{U}$ is defined as

$$\mathcal{U} = \left\{\boldsymbol{D} : \boldsymbol{D} = \bar{\boldsymbol{D}} + \sum_{j=1}^{m} \Delta \boldsymbol{D}_j \xi_j, \; \|\boldsymbol{\xi}\| \leq 1\right\}. \tag{2.4.20}$$

For example, in a robust linear constraint $f(\boldsymbol{x}, \boldsymbol{D}) = \boldsymbol{a}^\top \boldsymbol{x} - b \leq 0$, the uncertain data can be $\boldsymbol{D} = (\boldsymbol{a}, b)$. The uncertainty set (2.4.20) looks like the ellipsoidal uncertainty set in (2.2.32c) or (2.3.36), except that the norm $\|\cdot\|$ now is a generalization of the Euclidean norm used in the previous ellipsoidal uncertainty sets. In particular, we only require that $\|\cdot\|$ is a norm and satisfies the following condition

$$\|\boldsymbol{\xi}\| = \||\boldsymbol{\xi}|\|, \tag{2.4.21}$$

where $|\boldsymbol{\xi}| = (|\xi_1|, \ldots, |\xi_m|)^\top$. Such a norm is called an *absolute norm*. For example, $\ell_1$-, $\ell_2$-, $\ell_\infty$-norms are all absolute norms. Furthermore, the intersection

**Table 2.1** Robust linear, SOCP, QCQP, and SDP constraints $f(\boldsymbol{x}, \boldsymbol{D}) \le 0$

| Type | Constraint | $\boldsymbol{D}$ | $f(\boldsymbol{x}, \boldsymbol{D})$ |
|---|---|---|---|
| LP | $\boldsymbol{a}^\top \boldsymbol{x} \le b$ | $(\boldsymbol{a}, b)$ | $\boldsymbol{a}^\top \boldsymbol{x} - b$ |
| SOCP | $\\|\boldsymbol{A}\boldsymbol{x} - \boldsymbol{b}\\|_2 \le \boldsymbol{c}^\top \boldsymbol{x} + d$ | $(\boldsymbol{A}, \boldsymbol{b}, \boldsymbol{c}, d)$ | $\\|\boldsymbol{A}\boldsymbol{x} - \boldsymbol{b}\\|_2 - \boldsymbol{c}^\top \boldsymbol{x} - d$ |
| QCQP | $\boldsymbol{x}^\top \boldsymbol{A}^\top \boldsymbol{A}\boldsymbol{x} + 2\boldsymbol{b}^\top \boldsymbol{x} + c \le 0$ | $(\boldsymbol{A}, \boldsymbol{b}, c)$ | $\boldsymbol{x}^\top \boldsymbol{A}^\top \boldsymbol{A}\boldsymbol{x} + 2\boldsymbol{b}^\top \boldsymbol{x} + c$ |
| SDP | $\sum_{i=1}^m \boldsymbol{A}_i x_i \succeq \boldsymbol{B}$ | $(\boldsymbol{A}_1, \ldots, \boldsymbol{A}_k, \boldsymbol{B})$ | $\lambda_{\max}(\boldsymbol{B} - \sum_{i=1}^m \boldsymbol{A}_i x_i)$ |

of $\ell_p$ norms is also an absolute norm. For example, the intersection of $\ell_2 \cap \ell_\infty$ is defined as $\max\{\|\boldsymbol{\xi}\|_2, \|\boldsymbol{\xi}\|_\infty\}$.

Let us first make the following assumption on the class of functions $f(\boldsymbol{x}, \boldsymbol{D})$.

**Assumption 1** *Assume the function $f(\boldsymbol{x}, \boldsymbol{D})$ satisfies the following assumptions:*

1. *The function $f(\boldsymbol{x}, \boldsymbol{D})$ is convex in $\boldsymbol{D}$ for all $\boldsymbol{x} \in \mathbb{R}^n$;*
2. *The function $f(\boldsymbol{x}, \boldsymbol{D})$ is positive homogeneous of degree one in $\boldsymbol{D}$ for all $x$, i.e.*

$$f(\boldsymbol{x}, k\boldsymbol{D}) = kf(\boldsymbol{x}, \boldsymbol{D}), \quad \forall k \ge 0. \tag{2.4.22}$$

All the constraint functions that we have encountered so far satisfy these properties. See Table 2.1. In particular, notice that for the case of QCQP, the function $f$ can be written as

$$f(\boldsymbol{x}, \boldsymbol{D}) = \boldsymbol{x}^\top \boldsymbol{A}^\top \boldsymbol{A}\boldsymbol{x} + 2\boldsymbol{b}^\top \boldsymbol{x} + c = \|\boldsymbol{A}\boldsymbol{x}\|_2^2 + 2\boldsymbol{b}^\top \boldsymbol{x} + c, \tag{2.4.23}$$

where the term $\|\boldsymbol{A}\boldsymbol{x}\|_2^2$ is a convex quadratic function in $\boldsymbol{A}$ for all $\boldsymbol{x}$, so $f(\boldsymbol{x}, \boldsymbol{D})$ is convex in $\boldsymbol{D}$. Also note that in the SDP case, the function $f(\boldsymbol{x}, \boldsymbol{D}) = \lambda_{\max}(\boldsymbol{B} - \sum_{i=1}^k \boldsymbol{A}_i x_i)$ is the maximum eigenvalue of the constraint matrix, which is well-known to be a convex function.

### 2.4.4.2 Safe Approximation

Now we can state the following main result on safe approximation of robust constraint (2.4.19).

Suppose the norm $\|\cdot\|$ in the uncertainty set (2.4.20) is an absolute norm and the function satisfies the properties in Assumption 1. The following robust constraint

$$\max_{(\boldsymbol{u},\boldsymbol{v})\in\mathcal{V}} \left\{ f(\boldsymbol{x}, \bar{\boldsymbol{D}}) + \sum_{j=1}^{k} \left( f(\boldsymbol{x}, \Delta\boldsymbol{D}_j)u_j + f(\boldsymbol{x}, -\Delta\boldsymbol{D}_j)v_j \right) \right\} \le 0, \tag{2.4.24}$$

(continued)

with the uncertainty set

$$\mathcal{V} = \{(\boldsymbol{u}, \boldsymbol{v}) \in \mathbb{R}^k \times \mathbb{R}^k : \|\boldsymbol{u} + \boldsymbol{v}\| \le 1,\ \boldsymbol{u} \ge \boldsymbol{0}, \boldsymbol{v} \ge \boldsymbol{0}\}, \tag{2.4.25}$$

is a safe approximation to the robust constraint (2.4.19) with the uncertainty set (2.4.20).

Let us see why (2.4.24)–(2.4.25) gives a safe approximation to the original robust constraint. The reasoning is quite simple. Assume $\boldsymbol{x}$ satisfies (2.4.24)–(2.4.25), that is

$$f(\boldsymbol{x}, \bar{\boldsymbol{D}}) + \sum_{j=1}^{k} \big(f(\boldsymbol{x}, \Delta \boldsymbol{D}_j) u_j + f(\boldsymbol{x}, -\Delta \boldsymbol{D}_j) v_j\big) \le 0, \quad \forall (\boldsymbol{u}, \boldsymbol{v}) \in \mathcal{V}, \tag{2.4.26a}$$

$$\Leftrightarrow \quad f(\boldsymbol{x}, \bar{\boldsymbol{D}}) + \sum_{j=1}^{k} \big(f(\boldsymbol{x}, \Delta \boldsymbol{D}_j u_j) + f(\boldsymbol{x}, -\Delta \boldsymbol{D}_j v_j)\big) \le 0, \quad \forall (\boldsymbol{u}, \boldsymbol{v}) \in \mathcal{V}, \tag{2.4.26b}$$

$$\Rightarrow \quad f\left(\boldsymbol{x}, \bar{\boldsymbol{D}} + \sum_{j=1}^{k} \Delta \boldsymbol{D}_j (u_j - v_j)\right) \le 0, \quad \forall (\boldsymbol{u}, \boldsymbol{v}) : \|\boldsymbol{u} + \boldsymbol{v}\| \le 1, \boldsymbol{u} \ge \boldsymbol{0}, \boldsymbol{v} \ge \boldsymbol{0}, \tag{2.4.26c}$$

$$\Leftrightarrow \quad f\left(\boldsymbol{x}, \bar{\boldsymbol{D}} + \sum_{j=1}^{k} \Delta \boldsymbol{D}_j \xi_j\right) \le 0, \quad \forall \boldsymbol{\xi} : \|\boldsymbol{\xi}\| \le 1, \tag{2.4.26d}$$

$$\Leftrightarrow \quad f(\boldsymbol{x}, \boldsymbol{D}) \le 0, \quad \forall \boldsymbol{D} \in \mathcal{U}. \tag{2.4.26e}$$

The key steps are (2.4.26c) and (2.4.26d). Step (2.4.26c) uses the properties in Assumption 1. In particular, we have

$$f(\boldsymbol{x}, \boldsymbol{A} + \boldsymbol{B}) = f\big(\boldsymbol{x}, \frac{1}{2}(2\boldsymbol{A}) + \frac{1}{2}(2\boldsymbol{B})\big) \le \frac{1}{2} f(\boldsymbol{x}, 2\boldsymbol{A}) + \frac{1}{2} f(\boldsymbol{x}, 2\boldsymbol{B}) = f(\boldsymbol{x}, \boldsymbol{A}) + f(\boldsymbol{x}, \boldsymbol{B}), \tag{2.4.27}$$

where the inequality uses convexity of $f(\boldsymbol{x}, \boldsymbol{D})$ in $\boldsymbol{D}$ and the last equality uses the positive homogeneity of $f(\boldsymbol{x}, \boldsymbol{D})$ in $\boldsymbol{D}$. Step (2.4.26c) exactly follows from (2.4.27).

Step (2.4.26d) uses a common trick in optimization. Suppose $\boldsymbol{x}$ satisfies (2.4.26c), then take any $\boldsymbol{\xi}$ in $\|\boldsymbol{\xi}\| \le 1$, we can always let $u_j = \xi_j, v_j = 0$ if $\xi_j \ge 0$, and $u_j = 0, v_j = -\xi_j$ if $\xi_j < 0$. Then $\boldsymbol{\xi} = \boldsymbol{u} - \boldsymbol{v}$ and $u_j + v_j = |\xi_j|$, so $\boldsymbol{x}$ satisfies (2.4.26d). Now suppose $\boldsymbol{x}$ satisfies (2.4.26d), then for any $\boldsymbol{u}, \boldsymbol{v} \in \mathcal{V}$, let $\boldsymbol{\xi} = \boldsymbol{u} - \boldsymbol{v}$. We see that $\|\boldsymbol{\xi}\| = \|\boldsymbol{u} - \boldsymbol{v}\| \le \|\boldsymbol{u} + \boldsymbol{v}\| \le 1$, because $\boldsymbol{u}, \boldsymbol{v} \ge 0$. So $\boldsymbol{x}$ satisfies (2.4.26c).

#### 2.4.4.3 Reformulation

Under the simple Assumption 1 of the constraint function $f$, the robust constraint (2.4.19) with the uncertainty set (2.4.20) has a safe approximation (2.4.24), which is again a robust constraint with the uncertainty set (2.4.25). It turns out that the safe approximation can be reformulated to tractable deterministic constraints for a wide range of robust conic optimization problems.

The safe approximation (2.4.24)–(2.4.25) is equivalent to

$$f(\boldsymbol{x}, \bar{\boldsymbol{D}}) + \|\boldsymbol{s}\|_* \leq 0, \tag{2.4.28a}$$

where $\|\cdot\|_*$ is the dual norm of $\|\cdot\|$, $\boldsymbol{s} = (s_1, \ldots, s_k)^\top$, and each $s_j$ is given by

$$s_j = \max\{f(\boldsymbol{x}, \Delta \boldsymbol{D}_j), f(\boldsymbol{x}, -\Delta \boldsymbol{D}_j)\}, \quad \forall j = 1, 2, \ldots, k, \tag{2.4.28b}$$

which can be further written as

$$\begin{cases} f(\boldsymbol{x}, \bar{\boldsymbol{D}}) + t \leq 0, \\ \|\boldsymbol{s}\|_* \leq t, \\ s_j \geq f(\boldsymbol{x}, \Delta \boldsymbol{D}_j), \quad \forall j = 1, 2, \ldots, k, \\ s_j \geq f(\boldsymbol{x}, -\Delta \boldsymbol{D}_j), \quad \forall j = 1, 2, \ldots, k. \end{cases} \tag{2.4.28c}$$

The reformulation (2.4.28c) follows easily from (2.4.28a)–(2.4.28b). So we only focus on deriving (2.4.28a). To see (2.4.28a), we can work on the following problem to simplify notation.

$$\max_{\boldsymbol{u}, \boldsymbol{v}} \quad \sum_{j=1}^{k} (a_j u_j + b_j v_j) \tag{2.4.29a}$$

$$\text{s.t.} \quad \|\boldsymbol{u} + \boldsymbol{v}\| \leq 1, \ \boldsymbol{u} \geq \boldsymbol{0}, \ \boldsymbol{v} \geq \boldsymbol{0}. \tag{2.4.29b}$$

We can use a similar technique in the previous subsection to do a proprocessing of (2.4.29). For each term $j$, we discuss two cases. If both $a_j \leq 0, b_j \leq 0$, then since $\boldsymbol{u}, \boldsymbol{v}$ are nonnegative, an optimal solution of (2.4.29) would have $u_j = v_j = 0$ in order to maximize the objective. If $a_j \geq 0$ or $b_j \geq 0$, then an optimal solution would put all the weight on the maximum of $a_j$ and $b_j$, i.e. $u_j = 0$ or $v_j = 0$. So in both cases, the optimal objective value of the $i$-th term takes the form $\max\{a_j, b_j, 0\}y_j$, where $y_j$ is equal to either $u_j$ or $v_j$. So (2.4.29) is equivalent to the following problem

$$Z = \max_{\boldsymbol{y}} \sum_{j=1}^{k} \max\{a_j, b_j, 0\} y_j \tag{2.4.30a}$$

$$\text{s.t. } \|\boldsymbol{y}\| \leq 1. \tag{2.4.30b}$$

The optimal value of this problem can be obtained by the dual norm as

$$Z = \|\boldsymbol{s}\|_*, \quad s_j = \max\{a_j, b_j, 0\}, \ \forall j = 1, 2, \dots, k. \tag{2.4.31}$$

This exactly gives the reformulation (2.4.28a).

#### 2.4.4.4 Applications

Now let us apply the safe approximation to the robust linear, SOCP, QP, and SDP constraints.

1. **Robust linear constraints with ellipsoidal uncertainty set:** For a robust linear constraint

$$\boldsymbol{a}^\top \boldsymbol{x} \leq b, \quad \forall (\boldsymbol{a}, b) \in \mathscr{U}_{\text{ellip}}^{\boldsymbol{a},b}, \tag{2.4.32}$$

   with the following ellipsoidal uncertainty set

$$\mathscr{U}_{\text{ellip}}^{\boldsymbol{a},b} = \left\{ (\boldsymbol{a}, b) \in \mathbb{R}^{n+1} : (\boldsymbol{a}, b) = (\bar{\boldsymbol{a}}, \bar{b}) + \sum_{j=1}^{k} (\boldsymbol{a}_j, b_j)\xi_j, \ \|\boldsymbol{\xi}\|_2 \leq 1 \right\}. \tag{2.4.33}$$

   Then, $f(\boldsymbol{x}, \boldsymbol{D}) = \boldsymbol{a}^\top \boldsymbol{x} - b$, and the safe approximation takes the following form

$$\bar{\boldsymbol{a}}^\top \boldsymbol{x} - \bar{b} + \left( \sum_{j=1}^{k} |\max\{\boldsymbol{a}_j^\top \boldsymbol{x} - b_j, -(\boldsymbol{a}_j^\top \boldsymbol{x} - b_j)\}|^2 \right)^{1/2} \leq 0, \tag{2.4.34}$$

$$\Leftrightarrow \quad \bar{\boldsymbol{a}}^\top \boldsymbol{x} + \left( \sum_{j=1}^{k} |\boldsymbol{a}_j^\top \boldsymbol{x} - b_j|^2 \right)^{1/2} \leq \bar{b}, \tag{2.4.35}$$

which is equivalent to the exact reformulation of the robust linear constraint (compare with (2.2.30a)). This means the safe approximation is exact for robust linear constraints with an ellipsoidal uncertainty set. In fact, it is not difficult to show that if the constraint function $f(\boldsymbol{x}, \boldsymbol{D})$ satisfies Assumption 1 and is linear in $\boldsymbol{D}$, then the safe approximation is exact. This is an exercise.

2. **Robust SOC constraints with ellipsoidal uncertainty set:** For a robust SOCP constraint

$$\|\boldsymbol{Ax} - \boldsymbol{b}\|_2 \le \boldsymbol{c}^\top \boldsymbol{x} + d, \quad \forall (\boldsymbol{A}, \boldsymbol{b}, \boldsymbol{c}, d) \in \mathcal{U}_{\text{ellip}}^{\boldsymbol{A},\boldsymbol{b},\boldsymbol{c},d}, \tag{2.4.36}$$

with an ellipsoidal uncertainty set

$$\mathcal{U}_{\text{ellip}}^{\boldsymbol{A},\boldsymbol{b},\boldsymbol{c},d} = \left\{ (\boldsymbol{A}, \boldsymbol{b}, \boldsymbol{c}, d) : (\boldsymbol{A}, \boldsymbol{b}, \boldsymbol{c}, d) = (\bar{\boldsymbol{A}}, \bar{\boldsymbol{b}}, \bar{c}, \bar{d}) + \sum_{j=1}^{k} (\boldsymbol{A}_j, \boldsymbol{b}_j, \boldsymbol{c}_j, d_j)\xi_j, \ \|\boldsymbol{\xi}\|_2 \le 1 \right\}. \tag{2.4.37}$$

hen $f(\boldsymbol{x}, \boldsymbol{D}) = \|\boldsymbol{Ax} - \boldsymbol{b}\|_2 - \boldsymbol{c}^\top \boldsymbol{x} - d$. The safe approximation takes the form

$$\|\bar{\boldsymbol{A}}\boldsymbol{x} - \bar{\boldsymbol{b}}\|_2 + \left( \sum_{j=1}^{k} |\max\{\|\boldsymbol{A}_j \boldsymbol{x} - \boldsymbol{b}_j\|_2 - \boldsymbol{c}_j^\top \boldsymbol{x} - d_j, \|\boldsymbol{A}_j \boldsymbol{x} - \boldsymbol{b}_j\|_2 + \boldsymbol{c}_j^\top \boldsymbol{x} + d_j\}|^2 \right)^{1/2} \le \bar{\boldsymbol{c}}^\top \boldsymbol{x} + \bar{d}. \tag{2.4.38}$$

With further simplification, we have the following result.

A robust SOCP constraint with a joint ellipsoidal uncertainty set $\mathcal{U}_{\text{ellip}}^{\boldsymbol{A},\boldsymbol{b},\boldsymbol{c},d}$ (2.4.37) can be reformulated as

$$\|\boldsymbol{Ax} - \boldsymbol{b}\|_2 \le \boldsymbol{c}^\top \boldsymbol{x} + d, \quad \forall (\boldsymbol{A}, \boldsymbol{b}, \boldsymbol{c}, d) \in \mathcal{U}_{\text{ellip}}^{\boldsymbol{A},\boldsymbol{b},\boldsymbol{c},d}, \tag{2.4.39a}$$

$$\Leftrightarrow \quad \|\bar{\boldsymbol{A}}\boldsymbol{x} - \bar{\boldsymbol{b}}\|_2 + \left( \sum_{j=1}^{k} (\|\boldsymbol{A}_j \boldsymbol{x} - \boldsymbol{b}_j\|_2 + |\boldsymbol{c}_j^\top \boldsymbol{x} + d_j|)^2 \right)^{1/2} \le \bar{\boldsymbol{c}}^\top \boldsymbol{x} + \bar{d}. \tag{2.4.39b}$$

A robust SOCP constraint with an ellipsoidal uncertainty set of $(\boldsymbol{A}, \boldsymbol{b})$, i.e. $\boldsymbol{c}_j = \boldsymbol{0}, b_j = 0$ for all $j$, can be reformulated as

$$\|\boldsymbol{Ax} - \boldsymbol{b}\|_2 \le \boldsymbol{c}^\top \boldsymbol{x} + d, \quad \forall (\boldsymbol{A}, \boldsymbol{b}) \in \mathcal{U}_{\text{ellip}}^{\boldsymbol{A},\boldsymbol{b}}, \tag{2.4.39c}$$

(continued)

$$\Leftrightarrow \quad \|\bar{A}x - \bar{b}\|_2 + \left(\sum_{j=1}^{k} \|A_j x - b_j\|_2^2\right)^{1/2} \leq \bar{c}^\top x + \bar{d}. \tag{2.4.39d}$$

It is worth comparing the deterministic reformulations obtained from safe approximation, (2.4.37) and (2.4.39d), with the exact reformulation obtained in the last subsection. In particular, the robust SOCP constraint with a joint ellipsoidal uncertainty set is not computational tractable. However, (2.4.39b) gives a safe, tractable approximation. Meanwhile, as shown in Sect. 2.3.2.3, a robust SOCP constraint with an ellipsoidal uncertainty set only of the left-hand side data can be reformulated exactly as an SDP in (2.3.43).

3. **Robust quadratic constraints with ellipsoidal uncertainty set:** For a robust quadratic constraint with a joint ellipsoidal uncertainty set, we have

The robust quadratic constraint with a joint ellipsoidal uncertainty set

$$x^\top A^\top A x + 2b^\top x + c \leq 0, \quad \forall (A, b, c) \in \mathscr{U}_{\text{ellip}}^{A,b,c}, \tag{2.4.40a}$$

$$\Leftrightarrow \quad x^\top \bar{A}^\top \bar{A} x + 2\bar{b}^\top x + \bar{c} + \left(\sum_{j=1}^{k} (x^\top A_j^\top A_j x + |2b_j^\top x + c_j|)^2\right)^{1/2} \leq 0. \tag{2.4.40b}$$

It is interesting to compare the safe approximation (2.4.40b) with the exact reformulation (2.3.77).

4. **Robust SDP with a joint ellipsoidal uncertainty set:** Now we consider a robust SDP constraint with a joint ellipsoidal uncertainty set

$$A_1 x_1 + A_2 x_2 + \cdots + A_m x_m \succeq B, \quad \forall (A_1, \ldots, A_m, B) \in \mathscr{U}_{\text{ellip}}^{A_1,\ldots,A_m,B},$$

where $\mathscr{U}_{\text{ellip}}^{A_1,\ldots,A_m,B}$ is given in (2.3.84). We repeat the robust SDP constraint here for reader's convenience,

$$\left(\sum_{i=1}^{m} \bar{A}_i x_i - \bar{B}\right) + \sum_{j=1}^{k} \left(\sum_{i=1}^{m} \Delta A_{ij} x_i - \Delta B_j\right) \xi_j \succeq \mathbf{0}, \quad \forall \boldsymbol{\xi} : \|\boldsymbol{\xi}\|_2 \leq 1. \tag{2.4.41}$$

From Sect. 2.3.3.2, we know that this robust constraint is computationally intractable. Now applying the safe approximation developed in this section, we can get a tractable inner approximation.

A safe approximation to the robust SDP constraint with a joint ellipsoidal uncertainty set can be reformulated as

$$\boldsymbol{A}_1 x_1 + \boldsymbol{A}_2 x_2 + \cdots + \boldsymbol{A}_m x_m \succeq \boldsymbol{B}, \quad \forall (\boldsymbol{A}_1, \ldots, \boldsymbol{A}_m, \boldsymbol{B}) \in \mathscr{U}_{\text{ellip}}^{\boldsymbol{A}_1,\ldots,\boldsymbol{A}_m,\boldsymbol{B}}, \tag{2.4.42a}$$

$$\Leftrightarrow \quad \lambda_{\max}\Big(\sum_{i=1}^{m} \bar{\boldsymbol{B}} - \bar{\boldsymbol{A}}_i x_i\Big) + \Big(\sum_{j=1}^{k} \rho\big(\Delta \boldsymbol{B}_j - \sum_{i=1}^{m} \Delta \boldsymbol{A}_{ij} x_i\big)^2\Big)^{1/2} \leq 0, \tag{2.4.42b}$$

where $\rho(\boldsymbol{A}) := \max\{|\lambda| : \lambda \text{ is an eigenvalue of } A\}$, i.e. the spectral radius of $\boldsymbol{A}$.

The derivation of (2.4.42b) follows from the fact that $\rho(\boldsymbol{A}) = \max\{\lambda_{\max}(\boldsymbol{A}), -\lambda_{\min}(\boldsymbol{A})\}$ for a real symmetric matrix $\boldsymbol{A}$. Also note that $\lambda_{\max}(\boldsymbol{A})$ is a convex function of $\boldsymbol{A}$ and $-\lambda_{\min}(\boldsymbol{A})$ is also convex, therefore, $\rho(\boldsymbol{A})$ is a convex function, so we can confirm (2.4.42b) is convex.

**Illustrative Example 2.17** *As a concrete example, let us consider the following robust SDP constraint*

$$\begin{bmatrix} 1+\xi_1 & -2+\xi_2 \\ -2+\xi_2 & 1+\xi_3 \end{bmatrix} x_1 + \begin{bmatrix} 1+\xi_1 & -1+\xi_2 \\ -1+\xi_2 & -2+\xi_3 \end{bmatrix} x_2 \succeq \begin{bmatrix} \xi_1 & -1+\xi_2 \\ -1+\xi_2 & \xi_3 \end{bmatrix}, \quad \forall \boldsymbol{\xi} : \|\boldsymbol{\xi}\|_2 \leq \alpha, \tag{2.4.43}$$

*which can be rewritten as*

$$\begin{bmatrix} x_1+x_2 & -2x_1-x_2+1 \\ -2x_1-x_2+1 & x_1-2x_2 \end{bmatrix} + \begin{bmatrix} x_1+x_2-1 & 0 \\ 0 & 0 \end{bmatrix} \xi_1 + \begin{bmatrix} 0 & x_1+x_2-1 \\ x_1+x_2-1 & 0 \end{bmatrix} \xi_2$$
$$+ \begin{bmatrix} 0 & 0 \\ 0 & x_1+x_2-1 \end{bmatrix} \xi_3 \succeq \boldsymbol{0}, \quad \forall \boldsymbol{\xi} : \|\boldsymbol{\xi}\|_2 \leq \alpha, \tag{2.4.44}$$

$$\Leftrightarrow \lambda_{max}\left(\begin{bmatrix} -x_1-x_2 & 2x_1+x_2-1 \\ 2x_1+x_2-1 & -x_1+2x_2 \end{bmatrix}\right) + \alpha\sqrt{3}|x_1+x_2-1| \leq 0, \tag{2.4.45}$$

$$\Leftrightarrow \frac{1}{2}\left[-2x_1+x_2+\sqrt{(3x_2)^2+4(2x_1+x_2-1)^2}\right] + \alpha\sqrt{3}|x_1+x_2-1| \leq 0. \tag{2.4.46}$$

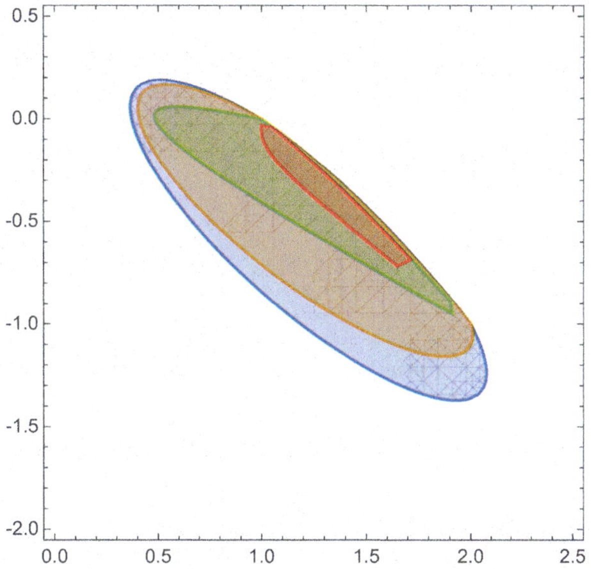


**Fig. 2.14** The feasible regions of robust constraint (2.4.43) for $\alpha = 0.1$ (blue), 0.2 (brown), 0.5 (green), and 0.8 (red)

*The robust feasible region is plotted in Fig. 2.14 for* $\alpha = 0.1, 0.2, 0.5, 0.8$. *We can see that as* $\alpha$ *increases, the size of the uncertainty set increases, and the feasible region of the robust constraint shrinks. It becomes infeasible for* $\alpha \geq 1.2$.

□

## 2.5 End-of-Chapter Exercises

**2.1** Consider the following robust linear constraint

$$a_1x_1 + a_2x_2 \leq 1, \quad \forall a_1 \in [-2, 1],\ a_2 \in [1, -2]. \tag{2.5.1}$$

Write down the infinite number of linear constraints associated with this robust constraint. Plot several of these linear constraints until the feasible region of the robust constraint is clearly visible.

**2.2** Plot the feasible region of the following robust constraint by plotting many linear constraints associated with the robust constraint

$$a_1x_1 + a_2x_2 \leq 1, \quad \forall (a_1, a_2) : |a_1| + |a_2| \leq 1.5,\ a_i \in [-1, 1],\ i = 1, 2. \tag{2.5.2}$$

**2.3** Derive the steps in (2.2.14d).

**2.4** Verify the robust linear constraint over the budgted uncertainty set can indeed be projected to the feasible region (2.2.19). Also check if your plot in Exercise 2.2 is the same as Fig. 2.5.

**2.5** Consider the following ellipsoidal uncertainty set

$$\mathscr{U}_{\text{ellip}} = \left\{ (a_1, a_2) : \begin{bmatrix} a_1 \\ a_2 \end{bmatrix}^\top \begin{bmatrix} \frac{3}{4} & \frac{1}{8} \\ \frac{1}{8} & \frac{1}{2} \end{bmatrix} \begin{bmatrix} a_1 \\ a_2 \end{bmatrix} \leq 1 \right\}. \tag{2.5.3}$$

Derive the reformulation of the robust linear constraint $a_1x_1 + a_2x_2 \leq 1$ over $(a_1, a_2) \in \mathscr{U}_{\text{ellip}}$.

**2.6** Continue to reformulate (2.2.32c) until you obtain (2.2.30a).

**2.7** Verify the steps in (2.3.32). These steps contain some reformulation techniques that are frequently used.

**2.8** Prove that for any $\ell_p$ norm for $p \geq 1$, a composite function $f(\boldsymbol{x}) = \|[g_1(\boldsymbol{x}), \ldots, g_k(\boldsymbol{x})]\|_p$ is convex as long as $g_i(\boldsymbol{x}) \geq 0$ for all $\boldsymbol{x}$.

**2.9** Verify the $f(\boldsymbol{x}, \boldsymbol{D})$ functions in Table 2.1.

# References


1. Ben-Tal, A., & Nemirovski, A. (2001). *Lectures on modern convex optimization: Analysis, algorithms and engineering applications*. Philadelphia: SIAM.
2. Goberna, M. A., & López, M. A. (1998). *Linear semi-infinite optimization*. Chichester/New York: Wiley.
3. Ben-Tal, A., El Ghaoui, L., & Nemirovski, A. (2009). *Robust optimization*. Princeton, NJ: Princeton University Press.
4. Ben-Tal, A., Nemirovski, A., & Roos, C. (2002). Robust solutions of uncertain quadratic and conic-quadratic problems. *SIAM Journal on Optimization, 13*, 535–560.
5. Derinkuyu, K., & Pinar, M. (2006). On the S-procedure and some variants. *Mathematical Methods of Operations Research, 64*, 55–77. https://doi.org/10.1007/s00186-006-0070-8.
6. Pólik, I., & Terlaky, T. (2007). A survey of the S-lemma. *SIAM Review, 49*(3), 371–418.
7. Ben-Tal, A., & Nemirovski, A. (2002). On tractable approximations of uncertain linear matrix inequalities affected by interval uncertainty. *SIAM Journal on Optimization, 12*, 811–833.
8. Ben-Tal, A., Nemirovski, A., & Roos, C. (2003). Extended matrix cube theorems with applications to $\mu$-theory in control. *Mathematics of Operations Research, 28*(3), 497–523.
9. Soyster, A. L. (1973). Convex programming with set-inclusive constraints and applications to inexact linear programming. *Operations Research, 21*, 1154–1157.
10. El Ghaoui, L., & Lebret, H. (1997). Robust solution to least-squares problems with uncertain data. *SIAM Journal of Matrix Analysis and Applications, 18*, 1035–1064.
11. Ben-Tal, A., & Nemirovski, A. (1998). Robust convex optimization. *Mathematics of Operations Research, 23*(4), 769–805.
12. El Ghaoui, L., & Lebret, H. (1998). Robust solutions to uncertain semidefinite programs. *SIAM Journal on Optimization, 9*, 33–52.

13. Ben-Tal, A., & Nemirovski, A. (1999). Robust solutions of uncertain linear programs. *Operations Research Letters, 25*, 1–13.
14. Ben-Tal, A., El Ghaoui, L., & Nemirovski, A. (2000). Robust semidefinite programming. In R. Saigal, H. Wolkowitcz, & L. Vandenberghe (Eds.), *Handbook on semidefinite programming* (pp. 139–162). Boston: Kluwer Academic Publishers.
15. Bertsimas, D., & Sim, M. (2011). The price of robustness. *Operations Research, 52*(1), 35–53.
16. Bertsimas, D., & Sim, M. (2006). Tractable approximations to robust conic optimization problems. *Mathematical Programming Series B, 107*(1–2), 5–36.
17. Bertsimas, D., & Tsitsiklis, J. (1997). *Introduction to linear optimization.* Belmont: Athena Scientific.
18. Andersen, E. D., & Andersen, K. D. (2000). The MOSEK interior point optimizer for linear programming: An implementation of the homogeneous algorithm. In H. Frenk, K. Roos, T. Terlaky, & S. Zhang (Eds.), *High performance optimization* (pp. 197–232). US: Springer.
19. Mulvey, J. M., Vanderbei, R., & Zenios, S. (1995). Robust optimization of large-scale systems. *Operations Research, 43*(2), 264–281.
20. Toivonen, H. Robust control methods. http://users.abo.fi/htoivone/courses/robust/rob1.pdf.

# Chapter 3
# Adaptive Robust Optimization

## 3.1 Introduction

In Chap. 2, we have studied static robust optimization with the following robust inequality constraint

$$f(\boldsymbol{x}, \boldsymbol{\xi}) \leq 0, \quad \forall \boldsymbol{\xi} \in \mathcal{U}, \tag{3.1.1}$$

where $\mathcal{U}$ is an uncertainty set, $\boldsymbol{\xi}$ is the uncertain parameter taking values in $\mathcal{U}$, and $\boldsymbol{x}$ is the decision. This robust model seeks *one* robust decision $\boldsymbol{x}$ that is feasible for *all* uncertainty realizations in $\mathcal{U}$. This embodies the canonical meaning of "robustness" in decision making. We call such a robust decision a *static policy*. However, in many situations, static policy may not be the best choice. More specifically, (1) we may need to deal with *equality* constraints involving uncertain parameters, or (2) the uncertainty may have some dynamic structures that call for the decisions to adapt accordingly. Both situations can be illustrated by examples from electric power systems. For the first situation, we know that the electricity supply must be equal to the electricity demand all the time. In other words, there is an equality constraint between supply and demand. As the electricity demand, viewed as an uncertain parameter, fluctuates between peaks and troughs everyday, the generation decision must also follow the demand, i.e., must be a function of the demand. A static policy for electricity generation in this case would amount to a fixed supply for all varying levels of demand, which clearly would lead to violation of the balance between generation and consumption.

The second situation is more subtle and will be the focus of this chapter. Consider the day-ahead electricity market. The system operator needs to decide which generators to turn on or off for the next 24 h, before knowing the exact demand in the next day. This is called the unit commitment (UC) decision. This binary decision has to be made today according to market rules. However, there



X. A. Sun, A. J. Conejo, *Robust Optimization in Electric Energy Systems*,
International Series in Operations Research & Management Science 313,
https://doi.org/10.1007/978-3-030-85128-6_3

**Fig. 3.1** Illustration of the decision structure of a two-stage decision making problem

is another type of decision, namely how much electricity to generate in each hour of the next day by those generators that are to be turned on. This is a continuous decision, and its specific value does not have to be fixed today, because after all the true electricity demand for tomorrow is not known today. As the next day comes, the electricity demand of each hour will be observed, so that the electricity generation can be determined immediately after observing the electricity demand. Therefore, in the decision problem of the day-ahead market, the generation plan for the next day should not be a fixed value, i.e., should not be a static policy, but rather should be made a *function* of the demand.

What we have just described is called a *two-stage* decision-making problem. The decision and uncertainty structure can be illustrated by Fig. 3.1. Here, $\boldsymbol{x}_0$ is the vector of the turn-on/off decisions of generators for the next day. $\boldsymbol{\xi}$ is the vector of demand in the next 24 h, which is an uncertain parameter in the day-ahead decision making problem. $\boldsymbol{x}(\boldsymbol{\xi})$ is the vector of the generation decisions for the next 24 h. Notice that $\boldsymbol{x}_0$ does not depend on $\boldsymbol{\xi}$, but $\boldsymbol{x}(\cdot)$ is a function of $\boldsymbol{\xi}$. This reflects the basic causality relation. Namely, since the UC decision $\boldsymbol{x}_0$ is made *before* knowing the demand $\boldsymbol{\xi}$, then $\boldsymbol{x}_0$ is not allowed to depend on $\boldsymbol{\xi}$, while $\boldsymbol{x}$ is made in the next day *after* the demand $\boldsymbol{\xi}$ is realized, so $\boldsymbol{x}(\boldsymbol{\xi})$ is a function of $\boldsymbol{\xi}$.

Readers may raise a question at this point. In the above two-stage decision model, if we write out the decision $\boldsymbol{x}(\boldsymbol{\xi})$ explicitly, we will have $\boldsymbol{x}(\boldsymbol{\xi}) = (\boldsymbol{x}_1(\boldsymbol{\xi}), \boldsymbol{x}_2(\boldsymbol{\xi}), \ldots, \boldsymbol{x}_{24}(\boldsymbol{\xi}))$, where each component $\boldsymbol{x}_t(\boldsymbol{\xi})$ is the generation plan for hour $t$ in the next day. Notice that $\boldsymbol{x}_t(\boldsymbol{\xi})$ for $t < 24$ assumes a function form of $\boldsymbol{\xi}$, which is the vector of demand of the *entire day*, including hours *after* $t$. "Doesn't it violate the causality law we just invoked?" The answer is "yes, it does." The two-stage model only partially obeys the causality law. It correctly distinguishes the day-ahead decision $\boldsymbol{x}_0$, which cannot depend on $\boldsymbol{\xi}$, from the real-time decision $\boldsymbol{x}$, which can depend on the demand realized in each hour. However, it violates the causality law within the real-time decision $\boldsymbol{x}(\boldsymbol{\xi})$ by allowing $\boldsymbol{x}_t(\boldsymbol{\xi})$ to depend on the demand realized after $t$.

Can we construct a decision-making model that *fully* obeys the causality law? The answer is yes. It is not difficult to guess what we should do here. Let us write out the components of the 24-h demand vector as $\boldsymbol{\xi} = (\boldsymbol{\xi}_1, \boldsymbol{\xi}_2, \ldots, \boldsymbol{\xi}_{24})$, where each $\boldsymbol{\xi}_t$ is the demand at hour $t$, which itself is a vector of demand at different locations of the power network. Then, the generation decision $\boldsymbol{x}_t$ at time $t$ should only depend on the subvector $\boldsymbol{\xi}_{[t]} := (\boldsymbol{\xi}_1, \ldots, \boldsymbol{\xi}_t)$ of demand from time 1 to $t$. That is, we have $\boldsymbol{x}_t(\boldsymbol{\xi}_{[t]})$ for each $t$. This decision structure is called *multistage* decision making. See Fig. 3.2 for an illustration.

Two-stage and multistage decision making are called sequential decision making under uncertainty or adaptive decision making. In this chapter, we will study adaptive decision making under the framework of robust optimization. The philosophy

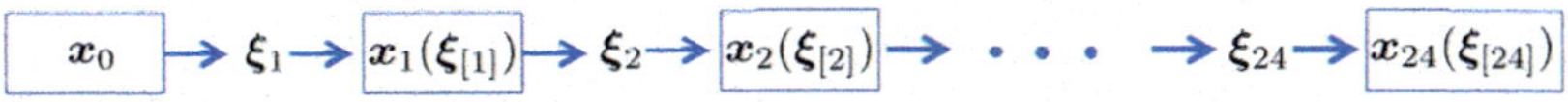


**Fig. 3.2** Illustration of decision structure of a multistage decision making problem

of robust optimization will the way we construct the uncertainty model and the objective function in an adaptive decision making problem. We first delve deep into the two-stage robust optimization in Sect. 3.2. We will study the formulation of a two-stage robust linear optimization model, and then will discuss solution methods. Section 3.3 will extend our model to multistage robust optimization. Multistage decision making is significantly more difficult than the two-stage one, both in model formulation and in computation methods. We will introduce exact algorithms as well as approximation heuristics.

## 3.2 Two-Stage Robust Optimization

In this section, we first formulate a two-stage robust linear optimization (2S-RLO) model. Then, we will study in depth an important class of 2S-RLO, where the uncertain parameter is in the right-hand side of the robust linear constraints. Many problems can be modeled by this class of 2S-RLO. Then, we will introduce two-stage robust conic optimization (2S-RCO) problems. Finally, we will introduce two algorithmic frameworks for solving 2S-RLO and 2S-RCO with right-hand side uncertainty.

### *3.2.1 Two-Stage Robust Linear Optimization Formulations*

In the following, we discuss two ways of formulating a 2S-RLO model.

#### 3.2.1.1 Functional Formulation of 2S-RLO

In order to implement a two-stage robust model, we need to decide how to model the objective function, the uncertainty set, and the robust constraints. The basic principle of robust optimization is to minimize the worst-case objective cost over the uncertain parameter. The same principle can be applied to 2S-RLO. Suppose that both the first-stage decision $\boldsymbol{x}_0$ and the second-stage decision $\boldsymbol{x}(\boldsymbol{\xi})$ incur linear costs as $\boldsymbol{c}^\top \boldsymbol{x}_0$ and $\boldsymbol{g}^\top \boldsymbol{x}(\boldsymbol{\xi})$, respectively. Then, the total cost $\boldsymbol{c}^\top \boldsymbol{x}_0 + \boldsymbol{g}^\top \boldsymbol{x}(\boldsymbol{\xi})$ is a function of $\boldsymbol{\xi}$. Therefore, the worst-case total cost is given by the maximum total cost over all the uncertain parameters $\boldsymbol{\xi}$ in an uncertainty set $\mathscr{U}$, i.e., $\max_{\boldsymbol{\xi} \in \mathscr{U}} \left\{\boldsymbol{c}^\top \boldsymbol{x}_0 + \boldsymbol{g}^\top \boldsymbol{x}(\boldsymbol{\xi})\right\} = \boldsymbol{c}^\top \boldsymbol{x}_0 + \max_{\boldsymbol{\xi} \in \mathscr{U}} \left\{\boldsymbol{g}^\top \boldsymbol{x}(\boldsymbol{\xi})\right\}$.

Now let us specify the constraints on $\boldsymbol{x}_0$ and $\boldsymbol{x}(\cdot)$. The constraints on the first-stage decision $\boldsymbol{x}_0$ are not different from constraints in a deterministic optimization problem. We only need to be careful that the first-stage constraints on $\boldsymbol{x}_0$ should not involve any uncertain parameter $\boldsymbol{\xi}$ to respect the causality law, and hence, the first-stage constraints should not involve the second-stage decision $\boldsymbol{x}(\cdot)$. Since we are considering robust linear programs, the first-stage constraints on $\boldsymbol{x}_0$ can be simply written as $\boldsymbol{x} \in X_0$, where $X_0$ is a polyhedron. More specifically, $X_0 = \{\boldsymbol{x}_0 \in \mathbb{R}^{n_0} : \boldsymbol{A}_0\boldsymbol{x}_0 \leq \boldsymbol{b}_0\}$, where the matrix $\boldsymbol{A}_0 \in \mathbb{R}^{m_0 \times n_0}$ and the vector $\boldsymbol{b}_0 \in \mathbb{R}^{m_0}$ have the appropriate dimensions and are deterministic quantities. The constraints on the second-stage decision $\boldsymbol{x}(\cdot)$ need more consideration. First, they are constraints on the function $\boldsymbol{x}(\cdot)$. Second, the constraints on $\boldsymbol{x}(\cdot)$ may involve the first-stage decision $\boldsymbol{x}_0$. For example, the generation level of a generator in time $t$ can be nonzero only if this generator is turned on in the first-stage decision. In general, we can write the second-stage constraints as $\boldsymbol{x}(\cdot) \in X(\boldsymbol{x}_0)$, where $X(\boldsymbol{x}_0)$ is defined as

$$X(\boldsymbol{x}_0) := \left\{\boldsymbol{x}(\cdot) : \mathcal{U} \to \mathbb{R}^n : \boldsymbol{A}(\boldsymbol{\xi})\boldsymbol{x}_0 + \boldsymbol{B}(\boldsymbol{\xi})\boldsymbol{x}(\boldsymbol{\xi}) \geq \boldsymbol{d}(\boldsymbol{\xi}),\ \forall \boldsymbol{\xi} \in \mathcal{U}\right\}. \tag{3.2.1}$$

Notice that we have allowed both the matrices $\boldsymbol{A}(\boldsymbol{\xi}) \in \mathbb{R}^{m \times n_0}$ and $\boldsymbol{B}(\boldsymbol{\xi}) \in \mathbb{R}^{m \times n}$ and the right-hand side vector $\boldsymbol{d}(\boldsymbol{\xi}) \in \mathbb{R}^m$ to be affected by the uncertainty $\boldsymbol{\xi}$. An important special case we will focus on is that the uncertainty only affects the right-hand side, i.e., $\boldsymbol{A}(\boldsymbol{\xi}) = \boldsymbol{A}$ and $\boldsymbol{B}(\boldsymbol{\xi}) = \boldsymbol{B}$, the two coefficient matrices are deterministic, and $\boldsymbol{d}(\boldsymbol{\xi}) = \boldsymbol{D}\boldsymbol{\xi} + \boldsymbol{h}$, where both $\boldsymbol{D}$ and $\boldsymbol{h}$ are deterministic. Note that we have already assumed the cost coefficients $\boldsymbol{c}$ and $\boldsymbol{g}$ are deterministic in the objective function.

Putting everything together, we have the following 2S-RLO model,

$$\min_{\boldsymbol{x}_0, \boldsymbol{x}(\cdot)} \left\{\boldsymbol{c}^\top \boldsymbol{x}_0 + \max_{\boldsymbol{\xi} \in \mathcal{U}} \boldsymbol{g}^\top \boldsymbol{x}(\boldsymbol{\xi})\right\}, \tag{3.2.2a}$$

$$\text{s.t.} \quad \boldsymbol{x}_0 \in X_0, \tag{3.2.2b}$$

$$\boldsymbol{A}\boldsymbol{x}_0 + \boldsymbol{B}\boldsymbol{x}(\boldsymbol{\xi}) \geq \boldsymbol{D}\boldsymbol{\xi} + \boldsymbol{h}, \quad \forall \boldsymbol{\xi} \in \mathcal{U}. \tag{3.2.2c}$$

We call (3.2.2) a *functional formulation* of 2S-RLO, because the second-stage decision variable is modeled as a function of $\boldsymbol{\xi}$.

#### 3.2.1.2 Nested Formulation for 2S-RLO

The functional formulation (3.2.2) implements the two-stage decision structure of Fig. 3.1 in a way that is conceptually clear. However, it is completely impractical for the computational purpose, because the functional decision $\boldsymbol{x}(\cdot)$ may be infinite dimensional. As we will see later that, for 2S-RLO with right-hand side uncertainty, the adaptive policy $\boldsymbol{x}(\cdot)$ can in fact be restricted to be a finite dimensional vector. However, this important observation is made only after we transform the functional formulation to an equivalent formulation that is both computationally more tractable and also easier to analyze. Let us carry out this transformation now.

The key observation is that the two-stage decision structure in Fig. 3.1 can be implemented in a *nested* model. In particular, the second-stage decision problem is itself an optimization problem that determines a best action $\boldsymbol{x}$ for each specific value of $\boldsymbol{\xi} \in \mathscr{U}$. In other words, for each fixed realization of $\boldsymbol{\xi}$ in the uncertainty set $\mathscr{U}$, the decision maker needs to solve a second-stage problem that minimizes the second-stage cost $\boldsymbol{g}^\top \boldsymbol{x}$ while satisfying the constraints in (3.2.2c) for this specific value of $\boldsymbol{\xi}$. The optimal solution thus obtained is a finite dimensional vector, which can be viewed as the value of the optimal policy $\boldsymbol{x}(\cdot)$ at $\boldsymbol{\xi}$. Let us write down the second-stage decision problem when the uncertainty parameter takes the value $\boldsymbol{\xi} \in \mathscr{U}$.

$$\min_{\boldsymbol{x}} \quad \boldsymbol{g}^\top \boldsymbol{x} \tag{3.2.3}$$

$$\text{s.t.} \quad \boldsymbol{B}\boldsymbol{x} \geq \boldsymbol{D}\boldsymbol{\xi} + \boldsymbol{h} - \boldsymbol{A}\boldsymbol{x}_0. \tag{3.2.4}$$

The decision $\boldsymbol{x}$ in the above problem is a vector in $\mathbb{R}^n$. The optimal objective value of the above second-stage decision problem is apparently a function of $\boldsymbol{\xi}$. Different uncertainty realization $\boldsymbol{\xi}$ would lead to different second-stage optimal cost. The worst-case such cost is given by

$$V(\boldsymbol{x}_0) = \max_{\boldsymbol{\xi} \in \mathscr{U}} \min_{\boldsymbol{x}} \quad \boldsymbol{g}^\top \boldsymbol{x} \tag{3.2.5a}$$

$$\text{s.t.} \quad \boldsymbol{B}\boldsymbol{x} \geq \boldsymbol{D}\boldsymbol{\xi} + \boldsymbol{h} - \boldsymbol{A}\boldsymbol{x}_0. \tag{3.2.5b}$$

The worst-case second-stage cost $V(\boldsymbol{x}_0)$ of the above max-min problem is a function of $\boldsymbol{x}_0$ alone, because $\boldsymbol{\xi}$ is already maximized over. Finally, the overall 2S-RLO minimizes the total cost $\boldsymbol{c}^\top \boldsymbol{x}_0 + V(\boldsymbol{x}_0)$.

Putting everything together, we have a new reformulation of 2S-RLO,

$$\min_{\boldsymbol{x}_0 \in X_0} \left\{ \boldsymbol{c}^\top \boldsymbol{x}_0 + \max_{\boldsymbol{\xi} \in \mathscr{U}} \min_{\boldsymbol{x} \in W(\boldsymbol{x}_0, \boldsymbol{\xi})} \boldsymbol{g}^\top \boldsymbol{x} \right\}, \tag{3.2.6}$$

where the constraint set $W(\boldsymbol{x}_0, \boldsymbol{\xi})$ for the second-stage decision $\boldsymbol{x}$ is given by

$$W(\boldsymbol{x}_0, \boldsymbol{\xi}) = \left\{ \boldsymbol{x} \in \mathbb{R}^n : \boldsymbol{B}\boldsymbol{x} \geq \boldsymbol{D}\boldsymbol{\xi} + \boldsymbol{h} - \boldsymbol{A}\boldsymbol{x}_0 \right\}. \tag{3.2.7}$$

The reformulation (3.2.6)–(3.2.7) is called a *nested* formulation of 2S-RLO, because the min-max-min is written in a nested from the first, outside most min to the last, inner most min.

The functional formulation (3.2.2) and the nested formulation (3.2.6) are equivalent. The nested formulation has some advantages over the functional one, especially for understanding properties of the two-stage RLO and developing algorithms to solve a two-stage RLO. In the following, we will focus on the nested formulation.

#### 3.2.1.3 Value-Function Formulation of 2S-RLO

The nested two-stage RLO model (3.2.6) can be rewritten in the following way,

$$\min_{\boldsymbol{x}_0} \quad \boldsymbol{c}^\top \boldsymbol{x}_0 + V(\boldsymbol{x}_0) \tag{3.2.8a}$$

$$\text{s.t.} \quad \boldsymbol{x}_0 \in X_0, \tag{3.2.8b}$$

where $V(\boldsymbol{x}_0)$ is the second-stage optimal cost function defined in (3.2.5). $V(\cdot)$ is also called the *value function* of the two-stage robust problem. Later we will see that the nested formulation and the notion of value function can be readily extended to multistage robust models. We call (3.2.8) the *value-function formulation* of 2S-RLO. In this form, 2S-RLO becomes a problem of the first-stage decision $\boldsymbol{x}_0$ alone. This nicely reflects the view that the only decision that needs to be implemented today before the uncertainty is realized is the first-stage decision, which once made cannot change, but the second-stage decision $\boldsymbol{x}(\boldsymbol{\xi})$ can wait to be implemented until after seeing the uncertainty. For this reason, $\boldsymbol{x}_0$ is also called the *right-now* decision, while the second-stage decision $\boldsymbol{x}(\boldsymbol{\xi})$ is called the *wait-and-see* decision. The value-function formulation (3.2.8) clearly indicates that the properties of the value function $V(\cdot)$ are critical for understanding the two-stage RLO. The most important properties of $V(\cdot)$, including convexity and piecewise linear structure of $V(\cdot)$, are discussed below.

### *3.2.2 Structural Properties of Two-Stage Robust Linear Optimization*

#### 3.2.2.1 Properties of the Cost-to-Go Function

To facilitate the discussion, let us rewrite the formulation of $V(\cdot)$ in (3.2.5) in the following form. For $\boldsymbol{x}_0 \in X_0$,

$$V(\boldsymbol{x}_0) = \max_{\boldsymbol{\xi} \in \mathscr{U}} V(\boldsymbol{\xi}, \boldsymbol{x}_0), \tag{3.2.9}$$

where $V(\boldsymbol{\xi}, \boldsymbol{x}_0)$ is the so-called *cost-to-go function*, given as

$$V(\boldsymbol{\xi}, \boldsymbol{x}_0) = \min_{\boldsymbol{x}} \quad \boldsymbol{g}^\top \boldsymbol{x} \tag{3.2.10a}$$

$$\text{s.t.} \quad \boldsymbol{B}\boldsymbol{x} \geq \boldsymbol{D}\boldsymbol{\xi} + \boldsymbol{h} - \boldsymbol{A}\boldsymbol{x}_0. \tag{3.2.10b}$$

To simplify discussion, we assume that the second-stage problem has *relatively complete recourse*, i.e., the minimization problem in (3.2.10) is always feasible for all $\boldsymbol{\xi} \in \mathscr{U}$ and $\boldsymbol{x}_0 \in X_0$. Under this assumption, we know that strong duality holds for (3.2.10) and we have

$$V(\boldsymbol{\xi}, \boldsymbol{x}_0) = \max_{\boldsymbol{y}} \quad (\boldsymbol{D}\boldsymbol{\xi} + \boldsymbol{h} - \boldsymbol{A}\boldsymbol{x}_0)^\top \boldsymbol{y} \tag{3.2.11a}$$

$$\text{s.t.} \quad \boldsymbol{B}^\top \boldsymbol{y} = \boldsymbol{g}, \tag{3.2.11b}$$

$$\boldsymbol{y} \geq \boldsymbol{0}. \tag{3.2.11c}$$

An important observation is that the feasible region of the above dual problem defined as $Y := \{\boldsymbol{y} \in \mathbb{R}^m : (3.2.11\text{b}) - (3.2.11\text{c})\}$ is independent of $\boldsymbol{\xi}$ and $\boldsymbol{x}_0$. Only the coefficients of the objective function (3.2.11a) depend linearly on $\boldsymbol{\xi}$ and $\boldsymbol{x}_0$. If $Y$ is a nonempty polyhedron, then by strong duality and the relatively complete recourse assumption we know that (3.2.11) must have a finite maximum for all $\boldsymbol{\xi} \in \mathscr{U}$ and $\boldsymbol{x}_0 \in X_0$ (see Exercise 3.1). Since $Y$ is a standard form LP, and we know that any feasible standard form LP has at least one extreme point [1]. Therefore, we only need to look at the extreme points of $Y$, denoted as $\{\boldsymbol{y}^1, \ldots, \boldsymbol{y}^K\}$. In this case, (3.2.11) is equivalent to maximizing the linear objective function (3.2.11a) over the extreme points of $Y$.

That is, we can rewrite the cost-to-go function $V(\boldsymbol{\xi}, \boldsymbol{x}_0)$ as

$$V(\boldsymbol{\xi}, \boldsymbol{x}_0) = \max_{\boldsymbol{y}} \quad (\boldsymbol{D}\boldsymbol{\xi} + \boldsymbol{h} - \boldsymbol{A}\boldsymbol{x}_0)^\top \boldsymbol{y}$$

$$\text{s.t.} \quad \boldsymbol{y} \in \text{conv}\{\boldsymbol{y}^1, \ldots, \boldsymbol{y}^K\}, \tag{3.2.12}$$

$$= \max_{i=1,2,\ldots,K} \quad (\boldsymbol{y}^i)^\top (\boldsymbol{D}\boldsymbol{\xi} + \boldsymbol{h} - \boldsymbol{A}\boldsymbol{x}_0). \tag{3.2.13}$$

The last equality (3.2.13) clearly shows that $V(\boldsymbol{\xi}, \boldsymbol{x}_0)$ *is a convex piecewise linear function in* $(\boldsymbol{\xi}, \boldsymbol{x}_0)$.

#### 3.2.2.2 Properties of the Value Function

Now let us look at the value function $V(\cdot)$. The value-function formulation (3.2.9) and the dual maximization (3.2.11) show that the value function $V(\boldsymbol{x}_0)$ involves two maximization problems, one in $\boldsymbol{\xi}$ and one in $\boldsymbol{y}$, as $V(\boldsymbol{x}_0) =$

$\max_{\boldsymbol{\xi}\in\mathcal{U}} \max_{\boldsymbol{y}\in Y} l(\boldsymbol{\xi}, \boldsymbol{x}_0, \boldsymbol{y})$, where $l(\boldsymbol{\xi}, \boldsymbol{x}_0, \boldsymbol{y})$ is the objective function (3.2.11a), which is a bilinear function in $(\boldsymbol{\xi}, \boldsymbol{x}_0)$ and $\boldsymbol{y}$. Since the two maximization operators can be swapped, we get

$$V(\boldsymbol{x}_0) = \max_{\boldsymbol{y}\in Y} \max_{\boldsymbol{\xi}\in\mathcal{U}} \ \boldsymbol{y}^\top \boldsymbol{D}\boldsymbol{\xi} + (\boldsymbol{h} - \boldsymbol{A}\boldsymbol{x}_0)^\top \boldsymbol{y}. \tag{3.2.14}$$

The uncertainty set $\mathcal{U}$ is assumed to be a polytope, which is the convex hull of a finite number of extreme points $\mathcal{U} = \text{conv}\{\boldsymbol{\xi}^1, \boldsymbol{\xi}^2, \ldots, \boldsymbol{\xi}^M\}$. Since the inner maximization problem in (3.2.14) is a linear optimization problem over the variable $\boldsymbol{\xi}$, the maximum is achieved at an extreme point of $\mathcal{U}$. In other words, both the maximum over $\boldsymbol{\xi}$ and the maximum of $\boldsymbol{y}$ are achieved at an extreme point of the respective feasible region.

Hence, we can rewrite the value function as

$$\begin{aligned} V(\boldsymbol{x}_0) &= \max_{i=1,\ldots,M} \max_{j=1,\ldots,K} l(\boldsymbol{\xi}^i, \boldsymbol{x}_0, \boldsymbol{y}^j) \\ &= \max_{i=1,\ldots,M} \max_{j=1,\ldots,K} -(\boldsymbol{y}^j)^\top \boldsymbol{A}^\top \boldsymbol{x}_0 + (\boldsymbol{D}\boldsymbol{\xi}^i + \boldsymbol{h})^\top \boldsymbol{y}^j. \end{aligned} \tag{3.2.15}$$

Clearly (3.2.15) shows that *the value function $V(\boldsymbol{x}_0)$ is a convex piecewise linear function of $\boldsymbol{x}_0$*.

#### 3.2.2.3 Properties of the 2S-RLO

An important implication of the structural property of the value function in (3.2.15) is:

The 2S-RLO problem with right-hand side uncertainty is in fact a *convex optimization problem with a convex piecewise linear objective function and a polyhedral feasible region*, as shown below

$$\text{(2S-RLO)} \quad \min_{\boldsymbol{x}_0\in X_0} \left\{ \boldsymbol{c}^\top \boldsymbol{x}_0 + \max_{i=1,\ldots,M} \max_{j=1,\ldots,K} -(\boldsymbol{y}^j)^\top \boldsymbol{A}^\top \boldsymbol{x}_0 + (\boldsymbol{D}\boldsymbol{\xi}^i + \boldsymbol{h})^\top \boldsymbol{y}^j \right\}, \tag{3.2.16}$$

which can be further reformulated as a deterministic linear program as

$$\text{(2S-RLO)} \quad \min_{\boldsymbol{x}_0, z} \ \boldsymbol{c}^\top \boldsymbol{x}_0 + z \tag{3.2.17a}$$

(continued)

$$\text{s.t. } z + (\boldsymbol{y}^j)^\top \boldsymbol{A}^\top \boldsymbol{x}_0 \geq (\boldsymbol{D}\boldsymbol{\xi}^i + \boldsymbol{h})^\top \boldsymbol{y}^j \quad \forall i = 1, 2, \ldots, M,\ j = 1, 2, \ldots, K, \tag{3.2.17b}$$

$$\boldsymbol{x}_0 \in X_0. \tag{3.2.17c}$$

The final linear programming reformulation (3.2.17) of 2S-RLO looks quite different from the functional form (3.2.2) and the nested form (3.2.6) that we started with. However, it is better than the other two in revealing the structure of a 2S-RLO with right-hand-side uncertainty. The insights obtained from (3.2.17) are important for designing algorithms. Before we get into algorithms, we will first study the computational properties of 2S-RLO. In particular, we want to characterize the computational complexity of 2S-RLO, which will set up a limit on how much we can expect from any algorithm for solving 2S-RLO.

### 3.2.3 *Computational Complexity of Two-Stage Robust Linear Optimization*

While the functional formulation (3.2.2) is not computable, as it involves infinite dimensional decision variables, the nested formulation (3.2.8) and its linear programming reformulation (3.2.17) do provide optimization problems in finite dimensional spaces. Let us discuss the complexity of solving these two representations.

1. We may aim at solving the linear programming reformulation (3.2.17). However, the linear pieces in $V(\boldsymbol{x}_0)$, namely $-(\boldsymbol{y}^j)^\top \boldsymbol{A}^\top \boldsymbol{x}_0 + (\boldsymbol{D}\boldsymbol{\xi}^i + \boldsymbol{h})^\top \boldsymbol{y}^j$ for each $i, j$ given in (3.2.14), are not known beforehand. In particular, the extreme points $\boldsymbol{y}^j$ of $Y$ and $\boldsymbol{\xi}^i$ of $\mathcal{U}$ are not known. Instead, the given data are the linear constraints in the uncertainty set $\mathcal{U}$ and the feasible region $Y$ of the dual maximization problem. Finding all the extreme points of a polytope from its linear constraints is a computationally difficult problem. For example, determining the total number of extreme points of a polytope is *strongly NP-hard* [2]. An implication of a problem being strongly NP-hard is that it is unlikely to find a polynomial time algorithm for even finding an $\epsilon$-approximate solution.

   A manifestation of this difficulty for finding extreme points of a polytope is that the number of extreme points can be an exponential function of the number of linear constraints. Just think about the $n$-dimensional hypercube $[0, 1]^n$, which has $2^n$ extreme points. So, directly formulating the linear program (3.2.17) is computationally hard, unless the numbers of extreme points of $\mathcal{U}$ and $Y$ are small, for example, when the uncertainty set $\mathcal{U}$ has low dimension.

2. We may also try to directly solve the nested reformulation (3.2.8), which is a minimization problem of a convex piecewise linear function $\boldsymbol{c}^\top \boldsymbol{x}_0 + V(\boldsymbol{x}_0)$ subject to linear constraints on $\boldsymbol{x}_0$. In order to solve this problem, we need to at least be able to evaluate the value function $V(\boldsymbol{x}_0)$ at any $\boldsymbol{x}_0 \in X_0$. This task is equivalent to solving problem (3.2.14). The objective function of (3.2.14) is a bilinear function of $\boldsymbol{\xi}$ and $\boldsymbol{y}$, i.e., linear in one variable as the other is fixed. The feasible region of (3.2.14) consists of linear constraints on $\boldsymbol{\xi}$ and $\boldsymbol{y}$ separately. Such a problem is called a *bilinear program*. It is well known that solving bilinear programs is strongly NP-hard [3]. Moreover, we can see that any bilinear program can be reduced to a 2S-RLO problem as follows,

$$\max_{\boldsymbol{\xi}\in\mathcal{U},\boldsymbol{B}^\top \boldsymbol{y}=\boldsymbol{g},\boldsymbol{y}\geq\boldsymbol{0}} \boldsymbol{y}^\top \boldsymbol{D}\boldsymbol{\xi} + \boldsymbol{a}^\top \boldsymbol{y} + \boldsymbol{b}^\top \boldsymbol{\xi} = \min_{\boldsymbol{x}_0=\boldsymbol{0}} \left\{ 0 + \max_{\boldsymbol{\xi}\in\mathcal{U}} \min_{\boldsymbol{x}:\boldsymbol{B}\boldsymbol{x}\geq\boldsymbol{D}\boldsymbol{\xi}+\boldsymbol{a}} \boldsymbol{b}^\top \boldsymbol{\xi} + \boldsymbol{g}^\top \boldsymbol{x} \right\}. \tag{3.3.18}$$

Therefore, solving 2S-RLO is strongly NP-hard. So it is unlikely any polynomial time approximation algorithm exists that can obtain $\epsilon$-optimal solutions for *all* 2S-RLO problems.

The reader, however, should not give up the hope of developing good algorithms that may work for *many* 2S-RLO problems. The situation is similar for other NP-hard problems, e.g., integer optimization, for which effective algorithms have been developed and can routinely solve quite large integer programs. Seemingly impossible problems have been subjected to increasingly effective algorithms, and progress over a few decades can be astonishing. Interested reader can refer to the fascinating account of the revolution of integer programming solvers in [4].

### 3.2.4 The Concepts of Oracles and Oracle-Based Algorithms

By now we have a pretty clear picture of the structural properties and the source of computational difficulties of 2S-RLO, it is time to use our ingenuity to device algorithms for its solution. A recurring theme in studying 2S-RLO is that the value function is the central object. In the following, we develop two algorithmic frameworks that exploit the properties of the value function of 2S-RLO. Since this is the first time we discuss algorithms for solving optimization problems in this book, we will introduce some basic notions in numerical optimization, in particular, the notions of *oracles* and oracle-based algorithms. See [5] for a comprehensive treatment of complexity theory of convex optimization.

The value function formulation (3.2.8) of 2S-RLO is very revealing. It shows that 2S-RLO is nothing but a problem of minimizing $\boldsymbol{c}^\top \boldsymbol{x}_0 + V(\boldsymbol{x}_0)$ over $\boldsymbol{x}_0 \in X_0$. The values of the linear function's coefficient $\boldsymbol{c}$ and the linear constraints that describe the set $X_0$ are explicitly given as data of the problem. We also know the structure of the value function $V(\cdot)$, namely it is a convex piecewise linear function on $X_0$. However, the tricky thing is that we do not know the values of the coefficients of those linear pieces. This kind of information is crucial for solving 2S-RLO, but it is not directly given to us as in the case of $\boldsymbol{c}$ and $X_0$. Instead, this information needs to be found out in the process of solving a 2S-RLO. In other words, an algorithm for solving a 2S-RLO problem gathers information about $V(\cdot)$ and processes this information in a proper way to finally arrive at an optimal solution of the original problem 2S-RLO or declare no such optimal solution exists. The way to find information about $V(\cdot)$ is to ask an *oracle*, which is a device that when queried with the right data will output precious information about the object being queried about. In the following, we will try to be more precise about these concepts, but without being overburdened with notations.

A basic realization about designing algorithms is that an algorithm is designed not to solve one specific instance of a problem, but rather to solve a family of problems sharing the same structure. In the current context, we can define the *family of 2S-RLO* as the set of problems sharing the structural properties that we have uncovered in Sect. 3.2.2. In particular, we have the following definition.

The family of 2S-RLO problems, denoted as $\mathscr{F}_{\text{2S-RLO}}$, is the set of problems having the form of the value-function formulation defined in (3.2.8) and (3.2.5) with the data $(X_0, \mathscr{U}, \boldsymbol{c}, \boldsymbol{g}, \boldsymbol{h}, \boldsymbol{A}, \boldsymbol{B}, \boldsymbol{D})$, where the sets $X_0$ and $\mathscr{U}$ are nonempty polytopes described by linear inequalities.

Note that the first-stage feasible region $X_0$ and the uncertainty set $\mathscr{U}$ are part of the data. As shown in Sect. 3.2.3, the computational complexity of 2S-RLO is affected by the representation of $\mathscr{U}$. If $\mathscr{U}$ is given by the convex hull of a small number of extreme points, then 2S-RLO is easy to solve by enumerating over the extreme points of $\mathscr{U}$. But if $\mathscr{U}$ is represented by linear constraints, then 2S-RLO is difficult to solve. In our definition, we assume that $X_0$ and $\mathscr{U}$ are nonempty polytopes described by linear inequalities and the coefficients of the linear inequalities are given as data.

The oracle $\mathscr{O}$ for the family of 2S-RLO is defined to be a function that takes the following data $(\mathscr{U}, \boldsymbol{g}, \boldsymbol{h}, \boldsymbol{A}, \boldsymbol{B}, \boldsymbol{D}, \boldsymbol{x}_0)$ as input, and outputs the function value of $V(\cdot)$ at $\boldsymbol{x}_0$ and a subgradient $\partial V(\boldsymbol{x}_0)$ of $V(\cdot)$ at $\boldsymbol{x}_0$. The value $V(\boldsymbol{x}_0)$ is the exact optimal cost of (3.2.5) and $\partial V(\boldsymbol{x}_0)$ is the exact subgradient in the form of a linear function in (3.2.15).

We call such an oracle $\mathscr{O}$ an *exact first-order* oracle, because it provides exact information about the function value, which is the zeroth-order information about

$V(\cdot)$, and the subgradient, which is the first-order information about $V(\cdot)$. In a more general setting, an oracle's output may not provide exact information, e.g., the output may be corrupted by noise or systematically biased due to suboptimality of solutions.

An algorithm for solving problems in the family of 2S-RLO using the oracle $\mathcal{O}$ is a set of rules that produces a sequence of points $\{\boldsymbol{x}_0^1, \boldsymbol{x}_0^2, \ldots, \}$ for each problem $P \in \mathcal{F}_{\text{2S-RLO}}$ in a way that at any point $\boldsymbol{x}_0^k$ the algorithm uses all the information obtained from the oracle up to step $k$ and produces a new point $\boldsymbol{x}_0^{k+1}$, i.e., $\boldsymbol{x}_0^{k+1}(\boldsymbol{x}_0^1, \mathcal{O}(\boldsymbol{x}_0^1); \cdots; \boldsymbol{x}_0^k, \mathcal{O}(\boldsymbol{x}_0^k))$, and in a finite number of steps, the algorithm terminates with a point that is feasible and $\epsilon$-optimal to $P$.

The $\epsilon$-optimality means the objective value of the solution is within $\epsilon$ of the true optimum. The number of calls of the oracle is the complexity of the algorithm on the specific problem $P$. The *worst-case* complexity of the algorithm over all problems in $\mathcal{F}_{\text{2S-RLO}}$ is called the *oracle complexity* of the algorithm on the family of 2S-RLO.

### 3.2.5 Benders Decomposition

In this section, we introduce a fundamental algorithm, called the Benders decomposition. It was first proposed in the 1960s for solving mixed-integer linear programs and stochastic programs [6, 7]. We will apply it to solve 2S-RLO with an exact first-order oracle that provides the value and a subgradient of the value function.

In the above Benders decomposition algorithm, we assume that we know a lower bound $L$ to the second-stage problem's objective value for any $\boldsymbol{x}_0 \in X_0$. This lower bound exists, because we always assume that the second-stage problem has relatively complete recourse and $X_0, \mathcal{U}, Y$ are all nonempty and compact. We can also start the algorithm by solving the first-stage problem alone $\min_{\boldsymbol{x}_0 \in X_0} \boldsymbol{c}^\top \boldsymbol{x}_0$. Denote an optimal solution as $\boldsymbol{x}_0^{-1}$. Then, evaluate the oracle $\mathcal{O}(\boldsymbol{x}_0^{-1})$ to find a valid inequality in the form (3.2.19b) and update the upper bound. Then, we can start the while-loop as in Algorithm 1.

The optimization problem (3.2.19) approximates the value function $V(\cdot)$ from below by a convex piecewise linear function in (3.2.19b). We call these linear inequalities *valid inequalities* or *Benders cuts* for approximating $V(\cdot)$. We call (3.2.19) the *forward problem*, and call the problem solved by the oracle the *backward problem*. Solving (3.2.19) provides a solution $\boldsymbol{x}_0^i$, which is a candidate for the optimal first-stage solution. The algorithm then queries the oracle by solving the backward problem $\mathcal{O}(\boldsymbol{x}_0^i)$ at $\boldsymbol{x}_0^i$ to obtain a new valid inequality with new extreme points $\boldsymbol{\xi}^{i+1} \in \mathcal{U}$, $\boldsymbol{y}^{i+1} \in Y$. This new valid inequality lower approximates $V(\cdot)$ and is added to the forward problem in the next iteration. The oracle also produces the

**Algorithm 1** Benders decomposition for 2S-RLO

**Require:** An initial lower bound $L$ on value function
**Ensure:** An $\epsilon$-optimal solution $\boldsymbol{x}_0$ for 2S-RLO (3.2.8)

Initialize: $i \leftarrow -1$
Set LowerBound $\leftarrow -\infty$, UpperBound $\leftarrow +\infty$
**while** UpperBound $-$ LowerBound $> \epsilon$ **do**
  Solve the forward problem

$$v^i = \min_{\boldsymbol{x}_0 \in X_0, z \geq L} \quad \boldsymbol{c}^\top \boldsymbol{x}_0 + z \tag{3.2.19a}$$

$$\text{s.t.} \quad z + (\boldsymbol{y}^j)^\top \boldsymbol{A}^\top \boldsymbol{x}_0 \geq (\boldsymbol{D}\boldsymbol{\xi}^j + \boldsymbol{h})^\top \boldsymbol{y}^j, \quad j = 0, 1, \ldots, i \tag{3.2.19b}$$

  Denote an optimal solution as $\boldsymbol{x}_0^i$ and the optimal objective value $v^i$.
  Query the Oracle: Evaluate $(V^{i+1}, \boldsymbol{\xi}^{i+1}, \boldsymbol{y}^{i+1}) \leftarrow \mathscr{O}(\boldsymbol{x}_0^i)$
  Update LowerBound $\leftarrow v^i$
  Update UpperBound $\leftarrow \boldsymbol{c}^\top \boldsymbol{x}_0^i + V^{i+1}$
  Update $i \leftarrow i + 1$
**end while**
Output $\boldsymbol{x}_0^i$.

**Algorithm 2** Exact first-order Oracle $\mathscr{O}(\boldsymbol{x}_0)$

**Require:** A first-stage decision $\boldsymbol{x}_0 \in X_0$
**Ensure:** The optimal cost $\overline{V}$ of the second-stage problem (3.2.5) and a valid inequality in the form of (3.2.19b).

Solve the backward problem

$$\overline{V} = \max_{\boldsymbol{\xi}, \boldsymbol{y}} \quad (\boldsymbol{D}\boldsymbol{\xi} + \boldsymbol{h} - \boldsymbol{A}\boldsymbol{x}_0)^\top \boldsymbol{y} \tag{3.2.20a}$$

$$\text{s.t.} \quad \boldsymbol{B}^\top \boldsymbol{y} = \boldsymbol{g}, \tag{3.2.20b}$$

$$\boldsymbol{y} \geq \boldsymbol{0}, \tag{3.2.20c}$$

$$\boldsymbol{\xi} \in \mathscr{U}. \tag{3.2.20d}$$

  Denote an optimal solution $\boldsymbol{\xi}^*, \boldsymbol{y}^*$.
Generate a linear valid cut for $V(\cdot)$ as $z \geq (\boldsymbol{D}\boldsymbol{\xi}^* + \boldsymbol{h} - \boldsymbol{A}\boldsymbol{x}_0)^\top \boldsymbol{y}^*$.
Output $(\overline{V}, \boldsymbol{\xi}^*, \boldsymbol{y}^*)$

optimal value $V^{i+1}$ of the second-stage cost-to-go function evaluated at $\boldsymbol{x}_0^i$, which, combining with the first-stage cost $\boldsymbol{c}^\top \boldsymbol{x}_0^i$, gives an upper bound on the optimal cost of the overall 2S-RLO problem.

The oracle solves the second-stage problem at a given first-stage decision. Algorithm 2 gives some details of the oracle problem.

The Benders decomposition algorithm with the exact oracle always terminates in a finite number of iterations. This can be argued as follows. Suppose the optimal solutions $\boldsymbol{\xi}^*, \boldsymbol{y}^*$ returned by the oracle $\mathscr{O}$ are always the extreme points of $\mathscr{U}$ and $Y$, respectively, then since both $\mathscr{U}$ and $Y$ are polytopes with a finite number of extreme points, the algorithm would eventually enumerate all the extreme points. So the Benders algorithm would always terminate in a finite number of steps.

**Algorithm 3** Inexact Oracle $\mathscr{O}_{\mathrm{ADM}}(\boldsymbol{x}_0)$ using an alternating direction method

**Require:** A first-stage solution $\boldsymbol{x}_0 \in X_0$, and an initial extreme point $\boldsymbol{\xi}^0 \in \mathscr{U}$.
**Ensure:** Return a local optimal solution of the second-stage problem (3.2.5) and a lower linear approximation of $V(\cdot)$.
1: Initialize: $i \leftarrow 0$, $V_y^0 \leftarrow -\infty$, $V_\xi^0 \leftarrow \infty$
2: **while** $V_\xi^i - V_y^i > \epsilon$ **do**
3: Solve $\max_y \left\{(\boldsymbol{D}\boldsymbol{\xi}^i + \boldsymbol{h} - \boldsymbol{A}\boldsymbol{x}_0)^\top \boldsymbol{y} : \boldsymbol{B}^\top \boldsymbol{y} = \boldsymbol{g},\ \boldsymbol{y} \geq \boldsymbol{0}\right\}$
Obtain the optimal cost $V_y^{i+1}$ and an optimal solution $\boldsymbol{y}^{i+1}$.
4: Solve $\max_{\boldsymbol{\xi} \in \mathscr{U}} (\boldsymbol{D}\boldsymbol{\xi} + \boldsymbol{h} - \boldsymbol{A}\boldsymbol{x}_0)^\top \boldsymbol{y}^i$
Obtain the optimal cost $V_\xi^{i+1}$ and an optimal solution $\boldsymbol{\xi}^{i+1}$.
5: $i \leftarrow i + 1$
6: **end while**
7: Return $\boldsymbol{\xi}^i$, $V_\xi^i$, and a linear under-estimator $z \geq (\boldsymbol{D}\boldsymbol{\xi}^i + \boldsymbol{h} - \boldsymbol{A}\boldsymbol{x}_0)^\top \boldsymbol{y}^i$.

The alert reader may wonder what would happen if the oracle is not exact. After all, as we discussed in Sect. 3.2.3, evaluating the value function $V(\boldsymbol{x}_0)$ is an NP-hard problem. So it may be too much to ask the oracle to always return a global optimum for the second-stage problem. Indeed, it makes sense to consider an inexact oracle that solves the second-stage problem to a suboptimal solution. Algorithm 3 provides such an alternative.

In each iteration of the alternating direction method (ADM), one variable is fixed, while the other variable is maximized over. Since the objective function is bilinear, fixing one variable makes the objective linear in the other variable. So each iteration of ADM solves a linear optimization problem, which is a much easier problem to solve than the bilinear program. Moreover, the ADM produces a sequence of nondecreasing values $V_y^i \leq V_\xi^i \leq V_y^{i+1} \leq V_\xi^{i+1} \leq \cdots$. Therefore, given that the second-stage problem (3.2.5) always admits an optimal solution for any $\boldsymbol{x}_0$, the alternating direction method always terminates. At termination, a pair $(\boldsymbol{y}^i, \boldsymbol{\xi}^i)$ is found, and each is an extreme point of the corresponding polytope. It is possible that $(\boldsymbol{y}^i, \boldsymbol{\xi}^i)$ is only a local maximum, not a global maximum, of the second-stage problem, i.e., $V_\xi^i \leq V(\boldsymbol{x}_0)$. The generated cut is always valid for $V(\cdot)$.

We can replace the exact oracle $\mathscr{O}$ in Algorithm 1 by the inexact oracle $\mathscr{O}_{\mathrm{ADM}}$. Following a similar argument about enumerating the extreme points of $\mathscr{U}$ and $Y$, the Benders algorithm would still terminate. But the obtained solution $\boldsymbol{x}_0$ may be a strictly suboptimal solution.

### *3.2.6 Column-and-Constraint Generation*

Every iteration of the Benders algorithm generates one Benders cuts for the value function $V(\cdot)$. Now we introduce a new algorithm that essentially generates many Benders cuts in each iteration. So it can be considered as an acceleration of the

Benders algorithm. The idea is very simple, and again it is motivated by the nested formulation (3.2.6) and the value function form in (3.2.9). We can reformulate the two-stage RLO as follows.

$$\min_{x_0 \in X_0} \left\{ c^\top x_0 + \max_{\xi \in \mathcal{U}} V(\xi, x_0) \right\}$$

$$= \min_{x_0 \in X_0, z} \quad c^\top x_0 + z \tag{3.2.21a}$$

$$\text{s.t.} \quad z \geq \max_{\xi \in \mathcal{U}} V(\xi, x_0) \tag{3.2.21b}$$

$$= \min_{x_0 \in X_0, z} \quad c^\top x_0 + z$$

$$\text{s.t.} \quad z \geq V(\xi, x_0), \quad \forall \xi \in \mathcal{U}, \tag{3.2.21c}$$

$$= \min_{x_0 \in X_0, z} \quad c^\top x_0 + z$$

$$\text{s.t.} \quad z \geq \min_{x} \left\{ g^\top x : Bx \geq D\xi + h - Ax_0 \right\}, \quad \forall \xi \in \mathcal{U}, \tag{3.2.21d}$$

$$= \min_{x_0 \in X_0, z, x^1, \ldots, x^M} \quad c^\top x_0 + z \tag{3.2.21e}$$

$$\text{s.t.} \quad z \geq g^\top x^j, \quad \forall j = 1, 2, \ldots, M, \tag{3.2.21f}$$

$$Bx^i \geq D\xi^j + h - Ax_0, \quad \forall j = 1, 2, \ldots, M. \tag{3.2.21g}$$

Let us go through this derivation line by line. Equation (3.2.21a)–(3.2.21b) just applies the epigraph reformulation that we introduced in Chap. 2. Equation (3.2.21c) holds because if $z$ is greater than or equal to the maximum of $V(\xi, x_0)$ over $\xi \in \mathcal{U}$, then $z \geq V(\xi, x_0)$ for every $\xi \in \mathcal{U}$. Equation (3.2.21d) is just replacing $V(\xi, x_0)$ with its explicit form from (3.2.10). Equation (3.2.21f)–(3.2.21g) uses the same trick as we did in Chap. 2 for reformulating static robust constraints, where $\{\xi^1, \cdots, \xi^M\}$ are the extreme points of $\mathcal{U}$, and $x^j$'s are the new variables associated with $\xi^j$'s.

Equation (3.2.21e)–(3.2.21g) gives a new reformulation of 2S-RLO. It is instructive to compare it with the other deterministic linear programming reformulation (3.2.17). First, (3.2.17) only involves $x_0$ and $z$, while the new reformulation (3.2.21e)–(3.2.21g) involves additional $M$ variables $x^j$, which are the second-stage variables for each scenario $\xi^j$ of the uncertain parameter. Second, the original reformulation (3.2.17) involves the extreme points $y^j$ of the polytope $Y$, which is the dual of the second-stage inner minimization problem, while the new reformulation only involves primal variables $x^j$ of the inner minimization problem. Third, the number of linear constraints representing the value function in (3.2.17b) is $K \cdot M$, where $K$ is the number of extreme points in polytope $K$, while the number of linear constraints in (3.2.21f)–(3.2.21g) is $(m + 1)M$, where $m$ the number of rows in the matrix $B$. Usually $m$ is much smaller than $K$.

**Algorithm 4** Column-and-constraint generation for 2S-RLO

**Require:** An initial lower bound $L$ on value function
**Ensure:** An $\epsilon$-optimal solution $\boldsymbol{x}_0$ for 2S-RLO (3.2.8)
1: Initialize: $i \leftarrow 0$
2: Set LOWERBOUND $\leftarrow -\infty$, UPPERBOUND $\leftarrow +\infty$
3: **while** UPPERBOUND $-$ LOWERBOUND $> \epsilon$ **do**
4: Solve the forward problem

$$v^i = \min_{\boldsymbol{x}_0 \in X_0, z \geq L, \boldsymbol{x}^1, \ldots, \boldsymbol{x}^i} \quad \boldsymbol{c}^\top \boldsymbol{x}_0 + z \tag{3.2.22a}$$

$$\text{s.t.} \quad z \geq \boldsymbol{g}^\top \boldsymbol{x}^j, \quad \forall j = 1, 2, \ldots, i, \tag{3.2.22b}$$

$$\boldsymbol{B}\boldsymbol{x}^j \geq \boldsymbol{D}\boldsymbol{\xi}^j + \boldsymbol{h} - \boldsymbol{A}\boldsymbol{x}_0, \quad \forall j = 1, 2, \ldots, i. \tag{3.2.22c}$$

Denote an optimal solution as $\boldsymbol{x}_0^i$ and the optimal objective value $v^i$.
5: Query the Oracle: Evaluate $(V^{i+1}, \boldsymbol{\xi}^{i+1}, \boldsymbol{x}^{i+1}) \leftarrow \mathscr{O}(\boldsymbol{x}_0^i)$
6: Update LOWERBOUND $\leftarrow v^i$
7: Update UPPERBOUND $\leftarrow \boldsymbol{c}^\top \boldsymbol{x}_0^i + V^{i+1}$
8: Update $i \leftarrow i + 1$
9: **end while**
10: Output $\boldsymbol{x}_0^i$.

From the above comparison we can see that the new reformulation (3.2.21e)–(3.2.21g) has much more variables and much fewer constraints than the original reformulation (3.2.17). Since the new reformulation uses much fewer constraints to represent the value function, we may expect that each pair of constraints in (3.2.21f)–(3.2.21g) is much stronger than a single Benders cut. This is indeed the case. Let us first introduce the new algorithm that exploits the new reformulation, and then discuss the strength of the new reformulation.

Similar to the Benders decomposition, the new algorithm has a constraint generation framework. For a candidate first-stage solution $\boldsymbol{x}_0$, it identifies a worst-case scenario $\boldsymbol{\xi}^j \in \mathscr{U}$ for the second-stage problem and generates a set of new constraints in the form (3.2.21f)–(3.2.21f) for $\boldsymbol{\xi}^j$. Note the new constraints are nothing but the primal constraints of the second-stage inner minimization problem. In order to do this, the new algorithm deviates from the pure constraint generation framework of the Benders decomposition, and adds both new constraints and the associated new variables $\boldsymbol{x}^j$. Therefore, it is termed the *column-and-constraint generation* (CCG) algorithm. The form of CCG algorithm was proposed in [8] as a way to significantly speed-up Benders decomposition for solving the two-stage robust unit commitment problem, and is also proposed and analyzed in [9].

The only thing we need to mention is that in Step 5 of Algorithm 4, the oracle $\mathscr{O}$ is still the exact first-order oracle that gives the value $V(\boldsymbol{x}_0)$ and an optimal dual variable $\boldsymbol{\xi}^i$. The only difference from the exact oracle (Algorithm 2) used in the Benders decomposition is that the oracle now should also return a primal optimal solution of the inner minimization problem (3.2.10). The inexact oracle Algorithm 3 can also be used. Also see [10] for some discussions on how to use mixed-integer reformulation for solving the bilinear program of the second-stage problem.

Suppose the second-stage solutions $\boldsymbol{x}^i$ are extreme point solutions of the inner minimization problem (3.2.10), then since there are only a finite number of such extreme point solutions, the CCG algorithm will terminate in a finite number of steps. Extensive numerical experiments demonstrate that the CCG algorithm is usually much more efficient than the Benders decomposition algorithm. Let us analyze why this should be the case. For a fixed $\boldsymbol{x}_0$, Benders decomposition generates one cut in the form

$$z \geq (\boldsymbol{D}\boldsymbol{\xi}^i + \boldsymbol{h} - \boldsymbol{A}\boldsymbol{x}_0)^\top \boldsymbol{y}^i,$$

by solving the second-stage problem (3.2.5) and obtaining optimal extreme points $\boldsymbol{\xi}^i \in \mathcal{U}$ and $\boldsymbol{y}^i \in Y$. The CCG algorithm solves the same second-stage problem with the same $\boldsymbol{x}_0$. So let us suppose CCG finds the same optimal extreme point $\boldsymbol{\xi}^i \in \mathcal{U}$ as the Benders does. But instead of a dual cut, CCG generates primal constraints (3.2.21f)–(3.2.21g) for $\boldsymbol{\xi}^i$. Reversing back to (3.2.21d), we know that $z \geq \boldsymbol{g}^\top \boldsymbol{x}^i = V(\boldsymbol{\xi}^i, \boldsymbol{x}_0)$, but the cost-to-go value satisfies

$$\begin{aligned} V(\boldsymbol{\xi}^i, \boldsymbol{x}_0) &= \max_{y \in Y} (\boldsymbol{D}\boldsymbol{\xi}^i + \boldsymbol{h} - \boldsymbol{A}\boldsymbol{x}_0)^\top \boldsymbol{y} \\ &= \max_{j=1,\ldots,K} (\boldsymbol{D}\boldsymbol{\xi}^i + \boldsymbol{h} - \boldsymbol{A}\boldsymbol{x}_0)^\top \boldsymbol{y}^j && (3.2.23) \\ &\geq (\boldsymbol{D}\boldsymbol{\xi}^i + \boldsymbol{h} - \boldsymbol{A}\boldsymbol{x}_0)^\top \boldsymbol{y}^i. && (3.2.24) \end{aligned}$$

That is, the cut generated by CCG, $z \geq \boldsymbol{g}^\top \boldsymbol{x}^i$, is at least as strong as the single cut generated by the Benders, because the CCG cut is the maximum over all Benders-type cuts for all the extreme points in $Y$, while the cut (3.2.24) generated by Benders is just one of these many cuts in (3.2.23).

## 3.3 Multistage Robust Optimization

Now we are ready to introduce multistage robust optimization. We will discuss both the similarities in the properties of 2S-RLO and MS-RLO and the great differences in computation. We will first generalize the functional, nested, and value-function formulations of 2S-RLO to MS-RLO. The key ingredient in the generalization is again the concept of value function. Rather than having one value function as in 2S-RLO, a $(T + 1)$-stage RLO has $T$ value functions, one for each stage from stage $1, \ldots$, stage $T$. The value functions in two consecutive stages are connected by the well-known *dynamic programming (DP) recursion*, also known as the *Bellman equation*. We will see that the structural properties of the 2S-RLO, especially the convex piecewise linearity of the value function, still holds for all the value functions in an MS-RLO.

To effectively reduce the complexity of MS-RLO, we introduce the concept of approximate decision rules and an important class, namely the linear decision rules in Sect. 3.3.4. We will also introduce an effective cutting-plane algorithm for solving the resulting large-scale robust problem.

## *3.3.1 Multistage Robust Linear Optimization Formulations*

We have illustrated the sequential decision structure of MS-RLO in Fig. 3.2. Now let us implement this structure in multistage robust optimization. In particular, we will generalize the functional formulation and nested formulation from 2S-RLO to the multistage setting. Then, we will introduce the value-function formulation, which is an embodiment of the DP recursion.

### 3.3.1.1 A Functional Formulation of MS-RLO

Let us return to the example of electricity day-ahead market scheduling problem. The decision $\boldsymbol{x}_t$ is generators' production level at time $t$ in the next day after seeing the demand up to time $t$. So the best decision of $\boldsymbol{x}_t$ should be a function of the realized demand up to time $t$, written as $\boldsymbol{x}_t(\boldsymbol{\xi}_{[t]})$. Recall that $\boldsymbol{\xi}_{[t]}$ denotes the vector of demand up to time $t$, i.e., $\boldsymbol{\xi}_{[t]} = (\boldsymbol{\xi}_1, \ldots, \boldsymbol{\xi}_t)$. In a multistage robust day-ahead scheduling problem, the decision maker needs to determine the day-ahead unit commitment decision $\boldsymbol{x}_0$ as well as the functional forms of all the generation decisions $\boldsymbol{x}_1(\cdot), \ldots, \boldsymbol{x}_T(\cdot)$ in the next day, in order to minimize the worst-case total production cost. So we come to the following functional formulation of a $(T+1)$-stage RLO problem.

$$\min_{\boldsymbol{x}_0, \boldsymbol{x}_1(\cdot), \ldots, \boldsymbol{x}_T(\cdot)} \max_{(\boldsymbol{\xi}_1, \ldots, \boldsymbol{\xi}_T) \in \mathscr{U}} \left\{ \boldsymbol{c}^\top \boldsymbol{x}_0 + \boldsymbol{g}_1^\top \boldsymbol{x}_1(\boldsymbol{\xi}_{[1]}) + \cdots + \boldsymbol{g}_T^\top \boldsymbol{x}_T(\boldsymbol{\xi}_{[T]}) \right\} \tag{3.3.1a}$$

$$\text{s.t.} \quad \boldsymbol{A}_0 \boldsymbol{x}_0 \geq \boldsymbol{b}_0, \tag{3.3.1b}$$

$$\boldsymbol{B}_{1,0} \boldsymbol{x}_0 + \boldsymbol{B}_{1,1} \boldsymbol{x}_1(\boldsymbol{\xi}_{[1]}) \geq \boldsymbol{D}_1 \boldsymbol{\xi}_1 + \boldsymbol{h}_1, \ \forall \boldsymbol{\xi}_1 \in \mathscr{U}_1 \tag{3.3.1c}$$

$$\boldsymbol{B}_{2,1} \boldsymbol{x}_1(\boldsymbol{\xi}_{[1]}) + \boldsymbol{B}_{2,2} \boldsymbol{x}_2(\boldsymbol{\xi}_{[2]}) \geq \boldsymbol{D}_2 \boldsymbol{\xi}_{[2]} + \boldsymbol{h}_2, \ \forall \boldsymbol{\xi}_{[2]} \in \mathscr{U}_2 \tag{3.3.1d}$$

$$\cdots\cdots\cdots$$

$$\boldsymbol{B}_{T,T-1} \boldsymbol{x}_{T-1}(\boldsymbol{\xi}_{[T-1]}) + \boldsymbol{B}_{T,T} \boldsymbol{x}_T(\boldsymbol{\xi}_{[T]}) \geq \boldsymbol{D}_T \boldsymbol{\xi}_{[T]} + \boldsymbol{h}_T, \ \forall \boldsymbol{\xi}_{[T]} \in \mathscr{U}_T. \tag{3.3.1e}$$

Let us interpret this formulation. The overall objective (3.3.1a) is to minimize the worst-case total cost, which is given by the inner maximization problem that maximizes the total sum of the first-stage commitment cost and all the subsequent stages' production cost over all the uncertain demand realizable in the uncertainty set $\mathscr{U}$.

The constraints include the first-stage constraint (3.3.1b) on $\boldsymbol{x}_0$, and then the second-stage constraint (3.3.1c) on $\boldsymbol{x}_1(\cdot)$, which couples $\boldsymbol{x}_1(\cdot)$ with the first-stage decision $\boldsymbol{x}_0$. For example, there could be a constraint like $0 \le x_1^i(\boldsymbol{\xi}_1) \le \overline{P}^i x_0^i$, which says that the generator $i$ can produce up to the maximum production level $\overline{P}^i$ at time $t = 1$, if it is committed, i.e., $x_0^i = 1$, otherwise, if $x_0^i = 0$, then generator $i$ cannot produce any electricity at time $t = 1$. Since the variable $x_1^i(\boldsymbol{\xi}_1)$ is a function of $\boldsymbol{\xi}_1$, the above production constraint needs to hold for all $\boldsymbol{\xi}_1$ in the uncertainty set for $\boldsymbol{\xi}_1$. So, we should enforce $0 \le x_1^i(\boldsymbol{\xi}_1) \le \overline{P}^i x_0^i$ for all $\boldsymbol{\xi}_1 \in \mathscr{U}_1$, which can be written in the general form of (3.3.1c). Each constraint in stage $(t+1)$ for $1 \le t \le T-1$ is expressed as a linear constraint that couples two consecutive stages $\boldsymbol{x}_{t-1}(\cdot), \boldsymbol{x}_t(\cdot)$, and each constraint in stage $(t+1)$ should hold for all uncertainty $\boldsymbol{\xi}_{[t]}$ in the uncertainty $\mathscr{U}_t$ to be robust.

The uncertainty set $\mathscr{U}_t$ can be viewed as the projection of the uncertainty set $\mathscr{U}$ of all time periods $(\boldsymbol{\xi}_1, \ldots, \boldsymbol{\xi}_T)$ to the uncertainty $(\boldsymbol{\xi}_1, \ldots, \boldsymbol{\xi}_t)$. For example, if the overall uncertainty set $\mathscr{U}$ is the budgeted uncertainty set

$$\mathscr{U} = \left\{ (\xi_1, \ldots, \xi_T) : \sum_{t=1}^{T} \frac{|\xi_t - \bar{\xi}_t|}{\Delta_t} \le \Gamma, \bar{\xi}_t - \Delta_t \le \xi_t \le \bar{\xi}_t + \Delta_t, \forall t = 1, 2, \ldots, T \right\},$$

which we introduced in Chap. 2 (see Eq. (2.2.15)). Then, the corresponding uncertainty set of $\xi_t$ is the projection of $\mathscr{U}$ to $\xi_t$ as

$$\mathscr{U}_t = \left\{ \xi_{[t]} = (\xi_1, \ldots, \xi_t) : \exists\, \xi_{t+1}, \ldots, \xi_T, \text{ s.t. } (\xi_{[t]}, \xi_{t+1}, \ldots, \xi_T) \in \mathscr{U} \right\}. \tag{3.3.2}$$

More generally, we may allow the constraints at each stage $(t+1)$ to couple $\boldsymbol{x}_t(\cdot)$ with all the previous stages' decision policies $\boldsymbol{x}_0, \boldsymbol{x}_1(\cdot), \ldots, \boldsymbol{x}_{t-1}(\cdot)$ as

$$\boldsymbol{B}_{t,0}\boldsymbol{x}_0 + \boldsymbol{B}_{t,1}\boldsymbol{x}_1(\boldsymbol{\xi}_{[1]}) + \cdots + \boldsymbol{B}_{t,t}\boldsymbol{x}_t(\boldsymbol{\xi}_{[t]}) \ge \boldsymbol{D}_t\boldsymbol{\xi}_{[t]} + \boldsymbol{h}_t, \quad \forall \boldsymbol{\xi}_{[t]} \in \mathscr{U}_t. \tag{3.3.3}$$

The constraints (3.3.1c)–(3.3.1e) are a special case of (3.3.3) with $B_{t,0} = \boldsymbol{0}, \ldots, B_{t,t-2} = \boldsymbol{0}$. To save notations and better illustrate the key ideas, we will stick with the model (3.3.1). All the following development also applies to the general constraint (3.3.3). In fact, (3.3.3) with couplings between two consecutive stages is a very practical model with many applications. Also note that we allow the constraint in each stage $(t+1)$ to depend on all previous uncertainty $\boldsymbol{\xi}_{[t]}$. This is already more general than the usual setup of MS-RLO, which always assumes the constraint in stage $(t+1)$ only depends on the uncertainty $\boldsymbol{\xi}_t$. With this more general dependency on the uncertainty, the nested decomposition algorithm that we develop in Sect. 3.3.3 is also a generalization of the usual nested decomposition algorithms [11, 7].

A major benefit of writing MS-RLO in the functional form (3.3.1) is its conceptual appeal. It clearly shows the central role of *decision policies* $\boldsymbol{x}_1(\cdot), \ldots, \boldsymbol{x}_T(\cdot)$ in MS-RLO. Later when we develop approximation algorithms for solving MS-RLO, it would be natural to start from the functional formulation and consider policies that approximate the true optimal policies $\boldsymbol{x}_1(\cdot), \ldots, \boldsymbol{x}_T(\cdot)$.

### 3.3.1.2 Nested Formulation of MS-RLO

The sequential decision process in Fig. 3.2 and the worst-case oriented objective leads to the following nested formulation of MS-RLO.

$$\min_{\boldsymbol{x}_0 \in X_0} \left\{ \boldsymbol{c}^\top \boldsymbol{x}_0 + \max_{\boldsymbol{\xi}_{[1]} \in \mathscr{U}_1} \min_{\boldsymbol{x}_1 \in X_1(\boldsymbol{x}_0, \boldsymbol{\xi}_{[1]})} \left\{ \boldsymbol{g}_1^\top \boldsymbol{x}_1 + \max_{\boldsymbol{\xi}_2 \in \mathscr{U}_2(\boldsymbol{\xi}_{[1]})} \min_{\boldsymbol{x}_2 \in X_2(\boldsymbol{x}_1, \boldsymbol{\xi}_{[2]})} \left\{ \boldsymbol{g}_2^\top \boldsymbol{x}_2 + \cdots \right.\right.\right.$$
$$\left.\left.\left. + \max_{\boldsymbol{\xi}_T \in \mathscr{U}_T(\boldsymbol{\xi}_{[T-1]})} \min_{\boldsymbol{x}_T \in X_T(\boldsymbol{x}_{T-1}, \boldsymbol{\xi}_{[T]})} \boldsymbol{g}_T^\top \boldsymbol{x}_T \right\}\right\}\right\}. \tag{3.3.4}$$

The nested max-min formulation looks quite complicated. But it is a straightforward generalization of the transformation of 2S-RLO from the functional formulation (3.2.2) to the nested formulation (3.2.6).

In each stage $(t+1)$ of the nested formulation (3.3.4), we have a max-min problem, where the maximization is to find a worst-case uncertain parameter $\boldsymbol{\xi}_t \in \mathscr{U}_t(\boldsymbol{\xi}_{[t-1]})$ that maximizes the minimum production cost over $\boldsymbol{x}_t$ and the future cost, where the future cost is again a max-min problem, etc. Here the uncertainty set $\mathscr{U}_t(\boldsymbol{\xi}_{[t-1]})$ is understood as follows. In stage $(t+1)$, the uncertain parameters $\boldsymbol{\xi}_{[t-1]}$ in all previous stages are already observed, so the maximization is only over $\boldsymbol{\xi}_t$ in the uncertainty set $\mathscr{U}_t$ with $\boldsymbol{\xi}_{[t-1]}$ fixed at the value revealed in the previous stages.

The decision $\boldsymbol{x}_t$ is made after observing $\boldsymbol{\xi}_{[t]}$ and $\boldsymbol{x}_{t-1}$, so the feasible region for $\boldsymbol{x}_t$ is parametrized by $\boldsymbol{x}_{t-1}$ and $\boldsymbol{\xi}_{[t]}$ as $X_t(\boldsymbol{x}_{t-1}, \boldsymbol{\xi}_{[t]})$. The internal constraints for $X_t(\boldsymbol{x}_{t-1}, \boldsymbol{\xi}_{[t]})$ are formed by directly translating the constraints in the functional form (3.3.1c)–(3.3.1e) as

$$\boldsymbol{x}_t \in X_t(\boldsymbol{x}_{t-1}, \boldsymbol{\xi}_{[t]}) \iff \boldsymbol{B}_{t,t-1}\boldsymbol{x}_{t-1} + \boldsymbol{B}_{t,t}\boldsymbol{x}_t \geq \boldsymbol{D}_t\boldsymbol{\xi}_{[t]} + \boldsymbol{h}_t, \quad \forall t = 1, 2, \ldots, T. \tag{3.3.5}$$

Unlike the functional formulation (3.3.1), which is an optimization problem in infinite dimensional spaces of policy functions, the nested formulation (3.3.4)–(3.3.5) brings us back to finite dimensional spaces. It also leads us to a general principle, the so-called dynamic programming recursion, which we develop next.

#### 3.3.1.3 Value-Function Formulation of MS-RLO and DP Recursion

In the nested formulation (3.2.6) of 2S-RLO, the entire second-stage max-min problem can be represented by the value function $V(\boldsymbol{x}_0)$ as in (3.2.5). In this way, the nested formulation is transformed to the compact value-function formulation (3.2.8). The same idea can be used to transform the nested formulation (3.3.4) to a recursive form. Starting from stage 1 with $t = 0$, we can define a *cost-to-go function* $V_0(\boldsymbol{\xi}_{[1]}, \boldsymbol{x}_0)$ to be the minimum total cost of future stages starting from stage 2 with $t = 1$, when the stage 1 decision is fixed at $\boldsymbol{x}_0$ and the uncertainty is realized as $\boldsymbol{\xi}_{[1]}$. In particular, we have

$$V_0(\boldsymbol{\xi}_{[1]}, \boldsymbol{x}_0) = \min_{\boldsymbol{x}_1 \in X_1(\boldsymbol{x}_0, \boldsymbol{\xi}_{[1]})} \Bigg\{ \boldsymbol{g}_1^\top \boldsymbol{x}_1 + \max_{\boldsymbol{\xi}_2 \in \mathscr{U}_2(\boldsymbol{\xi}_{[1]})} \min_{\boldsymbol{x}_2 \in X_2(\boldsymbol{x}_1, \boldsymbol{\xi}_{[2]})} \Bigg\{ \boldsymbol{g}_2^\top \boldsymbol{x}_2 + \cdots + \max_{\boldsymbol{\xi}_T \in \mathscr{U}_T(\boldsymbol{\xi}_{[T-1]})} \min_{\boldsymbol{x}_T \in X_T(\boldsymbol{x}_{T-1}, \boldsymbol{\xi}_{[T]})} \boldsymbol{g}_T^\top \boldsymbol{x}_T \Bigg\}\Bigg\}. \tag{3.3.6}$$

Using the cost-to-go function $V_0(\boldsymbol{\xi}_{[1]}, \boldsymbol{x}_0)$, the entire nested MS-RLO formulation (3.3.4) can be formulated as

$$\min_{\boldsymbol{x}_0 \in X_0} \left\{ \boldsymbol{c}^\top \boldsymbol{x} + \max_{\boldsymbol{\xi}_{[1]} \in \mathscr{U}_1} V_0(\boldsymbol{\xi}_{[1]}, \boldsymbol{x}_0) \right\} = \min_{\boldsymbol{x}_0 \in X_0} \left\{ \boldsymbol{c}^\top \boldsymbol{x} + \mathscr{V}_0(\boldsymbol{x}_0) \right\}, \tag{3.3.7}$$

where $\mathscr{V}_0(\boldsymbol{x}_0)$ is the worst-case *value function* at stage 1, that is

$$\mathscr{V}_0(\boldsymbol{x}_0) = \max_{\boldsymbol{\xi}_{[1]} \in \mathscr{U}_1} V_0(\boldsymbol{\xi}_{[1]}, \boldsymbol{x}_0). \tag{3.3.8}$$

Now let's look into the cost-to-go function $V_0(\boldsymbol{\xi}_{[1]}, \boldsymbol{x}_0)$. From the right-hand side of its formulation (3.3.6), it is easy to see that we can define a new cost-to-go function $V_1(\boldsymbol{\xi}_{[2]}, \boldsymbol{x}_1)$ at stage 2 after observing uncertainty $\boldsymbol{\xi}_{[2]} = (\boldsymbol{\xi}_1, \boldsymbol{\xi}_2)$ and the second-stage decision $\boldsymbol{x}_1$, which is the nested problem starting from the minimization over $\boldsymbol{x}_2$ as

$$V_1(\boldsymbol{\xi}_{[2]}, \boldsymbol{x}_1) = \min_{\boldsymbol{x}_2 \in X_2(\boldsymbol{x}_1, \boldsymbol{\xi}_{[2]})} \left\{ \boldsymbol{g}_2^\top \boldsymbol{x}_2 + \cdots + \max_{\boldsymbol{\xi}_T \in \mathscr{U}_T(\boldsymbol{\xi}_{[T-1]})} \min_{\boldsymbol{x}_T \in X_T(\boldsymbol{x}_{T-1}, \boldsymbol{\xi}_{[T]})} \boldsymbol{g}_T^\top \boldsymbol{x}_T \right\}. \tag{3.3.9}$$

Then, Eq. (3.3.6) can be written as

$$\begin{aligned} V_0(\boldsymbol{\xi}_{[1]}, \boldsymbol{x}_0) &= \min_{\boldsymbol{x}_1 \in X_1(\boldsymbol{x}_0, \boldsymbol{\xi}_{[1]})} \left\{ \boldsymbol{g}_1^\top \boldsymbol{x}_1 + \max_{\boldsymbol{\xi}_2 \in \mathscr{U}_2(\boldsymbol{\xi}_{[1]})} V_1(\boldsymbol{\xi}_{[2]}, \boldsymbol{x}_1) \right\} \\ &= \min_{\boldsymbol{x}_1 \in X_1(\boldsymbol{x}_0, \boldsymbol{\xi}_{[1]})} \left\{ \boldsymbol{g}_1^\top \boldsymbol{x}_1 + \mathscr{V}_1(\boldsymbol{\xi}_{[1]}, \boldsymbol{x}_1) \right\}, \end{aligned}$$

where the maximization term defines the worst-case value function $\mathcal{V}_1(\boldsymbol{\xi}_{[1]}, \boldsymbol{x}_1)$. Notice that $\mathcal{V}_1(\boldsymbol{\xi}_{[1]}, \boldsymbol{x}_1)$ is not only a function of the stage variable $\boldsymbol{x}_1$, but also a function of the uncertainty of the previous stage $\boldsymbol{\xi}_{[1]}$.

Carrying out this procedure until the last stage, we get the *dynamic programming (DP) recursion*.

The cost-to-go functions $V_{t-1}(\boldsymbol{\xi}_{[t]}, \boldsymbol{x}_{t-1})$ and $V_t(\boldsymbol{\xi}_{[t+1]}, \boldsymbol{x}_t)$ of two consecutive stages $t$ and $(t+1)$ satisfy the following recursion, for $t = 1, 2 \ldots, T-1$:

$$V_{t-1}(\boldsymbol{\xi}_{[t]}, \boldsymbol{x}_{t-1}) = \min_{\boldsymbol{x}_t \in X_t(\boldsymbol{x}_{t-1}, \boldsymbol{\xi}_{[t]})} \left\{ \boldsymbol{g}_t^\top \boldsymbol{x}_t + \max_{\boldsymbol{\xi}_{t+1} \in \mathcal{U}_{t+1}(\boldsymbol{\xi}_{[t]})} V_t(\boldsymbol{\xi}_{[t+1]}, \boldsymbol{x}_t) \right\}, \tag{3.3.10}$$

$$= \min_{\boldsymbol{x}_t \in X_t(\boldsymbol{x}_{t-1}, \boldsymbol{\xi}_{[t]})} \left\{ \boldsymbol{g}_t^\top \boldsymbol{x}_t + \mathcal{V}_t(\boldsymbol{\xi}_{[t]}, \boldsymbol{x}_t) \right\}, \tag{3.3.11}$$

where $\boldsymbol{\xi}_{[0]}$ only takes a deterministic value and the value function $\mathcal{V}_t(\boldsymbol{\xi}_{[t]}, \boldsymbol{x}_t)$ is defined as

$$\mathcal{V}_t(\boldsymbol{\xi}_{[t]}, \boldsymbol{x}_t) = \max_{\boldsymbol{\xi}_{t+1} \in \mathcal{U}_{t+1}(\boldsymbol{\xi}_{[t]})} V_t(\boldsymbol{\xi}_{[t+1]}, \boldsymbol{x}_t), \tag{3.3.12}$$

and at $t = T - 1$,

$$V_{T-1}(\boldsymbol{\xi}_{[T]}, \boldsymbol{x}_{T-1}) = \min_{\boldsymbol{x}_T \in X_T(\boldsymbol{x}_{T-1}, \boldsymbol{\xi}_{[T]})} \boldsymbol{g}_T^\top \boldsymbol{x}_T, \tag{3.3.13}$$

where the last stage $(T+1)$'s value function $\mathcal{V}_T \equiv 0$.

### 3.3.2 *Structural Properties of Multistage Robust Linear Optimization*

The DP recursion (3.3.10)–(3.3.13) provides a very appealing reformulation of the complicated nested formulation (3.3.4). From this recursive formulation, we can derive key structural properties of the cost-to-go functions $V_t(\boldsymbol{\xi}_{[t+1]}, \boldsymbol{x}_t)$ and value functions $\mathcal{V}_t(\boldsymbol{\xi}_{[t]}, \boldsymbol{x}_t)$, which will be exploited for developing solution methods. In particular, recall in the two-stage setting, the most important property of the cost-to-go function $V_0(\boldsymbol{\xi}, \boldsymbol{x}_0)$ is that it is a convex piecewise linear function in $\boldsymbol{\xi}$ and $\boldsymbol{x}_0$. It is this joint convexity structure of $V_0(\boldsymbol{\xi}, \boldsymbol{x}_0)$ that makes it possible to develop the Benders decomposition and the column-and-constraint generation algorithm.

#### 3.3.2.1 Uncertainty Sets with Stagewise Independence

Unfortunately, this key convex property of value functions in general does *not* carry over to multistage robust optimization. In fact, the cost-to-go functions in MS-RLO can have rather complicated nonconvex structure. The culprit for this disaster turns out to be the uncertainty set $\mathcal{U}$. If the uncertainty parameters in different stages are coupled together in $\mathcal{U}$, then the value functions in MS-RLO will in general have nonconvex structures. But if the uncertainty in different stages are *independent*, then convexity of value functions still holds in MS-RLO. In the remaining of this subsection, we will make the following important assumption on the uncertainty set $\mathcal{U}$.

**Assumption 2 (Stagewise Independent Uncertainty)** *The uncertainty set $\mathcal{U}$ for the uncertainty parameters $(\boldsymbol{\xi}_1, \ldots, \boldsymbol{\xi}_T)$ in a $(T+1)$-stage RLO satisfies a product structure, namely*

$$\mathcal{U} = \mathcal{U}_1 \times \mathcal{U}_2 \times \cdots \times \mathcal{U}_T, \tag{3.3.14}$$

*where $\mathcal{U}_t$ is the uncertainty set of $\boldsymbol{\xi}_t$ for $t = 1, \ldots, T$.*

This assumption exactly ensures that $\boldsymbol{\xi}_t$ is not coupled to uncertainty in any other stage. That is,

$$(\boldsymbol{\xi}_1, \ldots, \boldsymbol{\xi}_T) \in \mathcal{U} \iff \boldsymbol{\xi}_t \in \mathcal{U}_t, \quad \forall t = 1, \ldots, T.$$

With this assumption, the parametrized uncertainty sets $\mathcal{U}_t(\boldsymbol{\xi}_{[t-1]})$ in the DP recursion (3.3.10) is independent of $\boldsymbol{\xi}_{[t-1]}$, therefore, it can be denoted as $\mathcal{U}_t$. We call such uncertainty $\mathcal{U}$ a *stagewise independent* uncertainty set. As we will show below, this assumption is consequential.

#### 3.3.2.2 Convexity with Stagewise Independent Uncertainty

In order to derive the structure of the cost-to-go functions, we will start from the end of the horizon and work backward. This follows the principle of backward induction. Let's start from stage $(T+1)$ and write out (3.3.13) and take its dual as

$$\begin{aligned} V_{T-1}(\boldsymbol{\xi}_{[T]}, \boldsymbol{x}_{T-1}) = \min_{\boldsymbol{x}_T} \quad & \boldsymbol{g}_T^\top \boldsymbol{x}_T \\ \text{s.t.} \quad & \boldsymbol{B}_{T,T-1}\boldsymbol{x}_{T-1} + \boldsymbol{B}_{TT}\boldsymbol{x}_T \geq \boldsymbol{D}_T\boldsymbol{\xi}_{[T]} + \boldsymbol{h}_T, \end{aligned}$$

$$
\begin{aligned}
&= \max_{\boldsymbol{y}_T} \quad \boldsymbol{y}_T^\top \big(\boldsymbol{D}_T \boldsymbol{\xi}_{[T]} + \boldsymbol{h}_T - \boldsymbol{B}_{T,T-1}\boldsymbol{x}_{T-1}\big) &\text{(3.3.15a)}\\
&\quad \text{s.t.} \quad \boldsymbol{B}_{TT}\boldsymbol{y}_T = \boldsymbol{g}_T, \ \boldsymbol{y}_T \ge \boldsymbol{0}, &\text{(3.3.15b)}\\
&= \max_{i=1,\dots,K_T} \quad (\boldsymbol{y}_T^i)^\top \big(\boldsymbol{D}_T \boldsymbol{\xi}_{[T]} + \boldsymbol{h}_T - \boldsymbol{B}_{T,T-1}\boldsymbol{x}_{T-1}\big), &\text{(3.3.15c)}
\end{aligned}
$$

where the first equality (3.3.15a) takes the dual and assumes that both the primal and dual problems have a finite optimum for all $\boldsymbol{\xi}_{[T]}$ and $\boldsymbol{x}_{T-1}$; the last equality (3.3.15c) is just enumerating over the extreme points $\boldsymbol{y}_T^i$ of the polyhedron for $\boldsymbol{y}_T$ defined in the constraint (3.3.15b), because the objective function in (3.3.15a) is linear in $\boldsymbol{y}_T$. Then, from (3.3.15c) we can see that the cost-to-go function $V_{T-1}(\boldsymbol{\xi}_{[T]}, \boldsymbol{x}_{T-1})$ is a convex piecewise linear function of $(\boldsymbol{\xi}_{[T]}, \boldsymbol{x}_{T-1})$.

Now in order to see this pattern persists in all stages, let's go back to stage $T$. We have

$$
\begin{aligned}
V_{T-2}(\boldsymbol{\xi}_{[T-1]}, \boldsymbol{x}_{T-2}) = &\min_{\boldsymbol{x}_{T-1} \in X_{T-1}(\boldsymbol{x}_{T-2}, \boldsymbol{\xi}_{[T-1]})} \left\{ \boldsymbol{g}_{T-1}^\top \boldsymbol{x}_{T-1} + \mathscr{V}_{T-1}(\boldsymbol{\xi}_{[T-1]}, \boldsymbol{x}_{T-1}) \right\} &\text{(3.3.16)}\\
&\text{s.t.} \quad \boldsymbol{B}_{T-1,T-2}\boldsymbol{x}_{T-2} + \boldsymbol{B}_{T-1,T-1}\boldsymbol{x}_{T-1} \ge \boldsymbol{D}_{T-1}\boldsymbol{\xi}_{[T-1]} + \boldsymbol{h}_{T-1},
\end{aligned}
$$

where value function $\mathscr{V}_{T-1}(\boldsymbol{\xi}_{[T-1]}, \boldsymbol{x}_{T-1})$ can be written out as

$$
\begin{aligned}
\mathscr{V}_{T-1}(\boldsymbol{\xi}_{[T-1]}, \boldsymbol{x}_{T-1}) &= \max_{\boldsymbol{\xi}_T \in \mathscr{U}_T} \ V_{T-1}(\boldsymbol{\xi}_{[T]}, \boldsymbol{x}_{T-1}), &\text{(3.3.17a)}\\
&= \max_{\boldsymbol{y}_T \in Y_T} \max_{\boldsymbol{\xi}_T \in \mathscr{U}_T} \ \boldsymbol{y}_T^\top \big(\boldsymbol{D}_T \boldsymbol{\xi}_{[T]} + \boldsymbol{h}_T - \boldsymbol{B}_{T,T-1}\boldsymbol{x}_{T-1}\big), &\text{(3.3.17b)}\\
&= \max_{\boldsymbol{y}_T^i \in Y_T} \max_{\boldsymbol{\xi}_T^j \in \mathscr{U}_T} \ (\boldsymbol{y}_T^i)^\top \big(\boldsymbol{D}_T' \boldsymbol{\xi}_T^j + \boldsymbol{D}_{T-1}' \boldsymbol{\xi}_{[T-1]} + \boldsymbol{h}_T - \boldsymbol{B}_{T,T-1}\boldsymbol{x}_{T-1}\big), &\text{(3.3.17c)}
\end{aligned}
$$

where $Y_T$ in (3.3.17b) is the polyhedral constraint set for $\boldsymbol{y}_T$ defined in (3.3.15b), $\boldsymbol{y}_T^i$ are all the extreme points of $Y_T$ and $\boldsymbol{\xi}_T^j$ are all the extreme points of $\mathscr{U}_T$, and $\boldsymbol{D}_T = [\boldsymbol{D}_T', \boldsymbol{D}_{T-1}']$ with block matrices $\boldsymbol{D}_T'$ and $\boldsymbol{D}_{T-1}'$ corresponding to $\boldsymbol{\xi}_T$ and $\boldsymbol{\xi}_{[T-1]}$, respectively.

Keep in mind that $\mathscr{U}_T$ is independent of $\boldsymbol{\xi}_{[T-1]}$. Since $Y_T$ and $\mathscr{U}_T$ are polyhedra, they have a finite number of extreme points. Now, from (3.3.17c) we can see that the value function $\mathscr{V}_{T-1}(\boldsymbol{\xi}_{[T-1]}, \boldsymbol{x}_{T-1})$ is a convex piecewise linear function of $(\boldsymbol{\xi}_{[T-1]}, \boldsymbol{x}_{T-1})$. To emphasize this important structure, we can write the above value function as

$$
\mathscr{V}_{T-1}(\boldsymbol{\xi}_{[T-1]}, \boldsymbol{x}_{T-1}) = \max_{k=1,\dots,N_{T-1}} \left\{ (\boldsymbol{\alpha}_{T-1}^k)^\top \boldsymbol{\xi}_{[T-1]} + (\boldsymbol{\beta}_{T-1}^k)^\top \boldsymbol{x}_{T-1} + \gamma_{T-1}^k \right\}, \tag{3.3.18}
$$

where $\alpha^k_{T-1}, \beta^k_{T-1}, \gamma^k_{T-1}$ are the proper parameters formed from (3.3.17c) and $N_{T-1}$ is the total number of distinct linear pieces in (3.3.17c).

Plugging $\mathscr{V}_{T-1}(\xi_{[T-1]}, x_{T-1})$ back to the cost-to-go function problem (3.3.16) and reformulating it as a linear program, we have

$$V_{T-2}(\xi_{[T-1]}, x_{T-2}) = \min_{x_{T-1}, z_{T-1}} \; g^\top_{T-1} x_{T-1} + z_{T-1}$$

$$\text{s.t.} \quad B_{T-1,T-1} x_{T-1} \geq D_{T-1} \xi_{[T-1]} + h_{T-1} - B_{T-1,T-2} x_{T-2},$$

$$z_{T-1} - (\beta^k_{T-1})^\top x_{T-1} \geq (\alpha^k_{T-1})^\top \xi_{[T-1]} + \gamma^k_{T-1}, \; \forall k = 1, \ldots, N_{T-1}.$$

We can see that $\xi_{[T-1]}$ and $x_{T-2}$ are parameters on the right-hand side of the linear constraints. Therefore, $V_{T-2}(\xi_{[T-1]}, x_{T-2})$ is again a convex piecewise linear function of $(\xi_{[T-1]}, x_{T-2})$.

The same arguments of convexity can be carried out backward until the first stage. The reader is encouraged to do a few more backward steps to be fully convinced that the cost-to-go functions and the value functions in all stages are convex piecewise linear functions of the associated uncertainty and stage variables.

#### 3.3.2.3 What Could Go Wrong Without Stagewise Independence

The curious reader may wonder what could go wrong if we do not impose Assumption 2 of the stagewise independent structure on $\mathscr{U}$. So suppose $\mathscr{U}$ does not have stagewise independence, then the uncertainty set $\mathscr{U}_t$ of stage $(t+1)$ would depend on the uncertainty realization before stage $(t + 1)$, i.e., we need to use $\mathscr{U}_t(\xi_{[t-1]})$ to describe the uncertainty set of $\xi_t$ in stage $(t + 1)$ after $\xi_{[t-1]}$ has been realized in previous stages. Now the problem starts with the value function $\mathscr{V}_{T-1}(\xi_{[T-1]}, x_{T-1})$ in (3.3.17) of stage $T$. In particular, we need to replace $\mathscr{U}_T$ in (3.3.17a)–(3.3.17c) with $\mathscr{U}_T(\xi_{[T-1]})$ as follows

$$\mathscr{V}_{T-1}(\xi_{[T-1]}, x_{T-1}) = \max_{\xi_T \in \mathscr{U}_T(\xi_{[T-1]})} V_{T-1}(\xi_{[T]}, x_{T-1}), \tag{3.3.19a}$$

$$= \max_{y^i_T \in Y_T} \max_{\xi_T \in \mathscr{U}_T(\xi_{[T-1]})} (y^i_T)^\top \big(D'_T \xi_T + D'_{T-1} \xi_{[T-1]} + h_T - B_{T,T-1} x_{T-1}\big). \tag{3.3.19b}$$

Note that the inner maximization problem over $\xi_T$ involves $\xi_{[T-1]}$ in the constraints in $\mathscr{U}_T(\xi_{[T-1]})$. In the simplest case, assume that $\xi_{[T-1]}$ appears in the right-hand side of the linear constraints in $\mathscr{U}_T(\xi_{[T-1]})$ as follows

$$\xi_T \in \mathscr{U}_T(\xi_{[T-1]}) \iff U_{T,T-1} \xi_{[T-1]} + U_{T,T} \xi_T \leq u_T. \tag{3.3.20}$$

Dualizing the inner maximization problem in (3.3.19b) with (3.3.20), we get

$$\phi_T^i(\boldsymbol{\xi}_{[T-1]}, \boldsymbol{x}_{T-1}) := \min_{\boldsymbol{\rho}_T^i} \quad (\boldsymbol{\rho}_T^i)^\top (\boldsymbol{u}_T - \boldsymbol{U}_{T,T-1}\boldsymbol{\xi}_{[T-1]}) + (\boldsymbol{y}_T^i)^\top (\boldsymbol{D}'_{T-1}\boldsymbol{\xi}_{[T-1]} + \boldsymbol{h}_T - \boldsymbol{B}_{T,T-1}\boldsymbol{x}_{T-1}) \tag{3.3.21a}$$

$$\text{s.t.} \quad (\boldsymbol{\rho}_T^i)^\top \boldsymbol{U}_{T,T} = (\boldsymbol{y}_T^i)^\top \boldsymbol{D}'_T, \quad \boldsymbol{\rho}_T^i \geq \boldsymbol{0}. \tag{3.3.21b}$$

Due to the minimization in (3.3.21), we know that $\phi_T^i(\boldsymbol{\xi}_{[T-1]}, \boldsymbol{x}_{T-1})$ is a *concave* piecewise linear function in $(\boldsymbol{\xi}_{[T-1]}, \boldsymbol{x}_{T-1})$. Therefore, the cost-to-go function $\mathcal{V}_{T-1}(\boldsymbol{\xi}_{[T-1]}, \boldsymbol{x}_{T-1}) = \max_{\boldsymbol{y}_T^i \in Y_T} \phi_T^i(\boldsymbol{\xi}_{[T-1]}, \boldsymbol{x}_{T-1})$ is a pointwise maximum of a finite number of concave piecewise linear functions, which itself is *not* a concave nor convex function in general. This shows that the stagewise dependent uncertainty set $\mathcal{U}_T(\boldsymbol{\xi}_{[T-1]})$ in (3.3.20) destroys the convex structure of the cost-to-go function and value functions.

To be more precise, we can see from (3.3.21) that $\phi_T^i(\boldsymbol{\xi}_{[T-1]}, \boldsymbol{x}_{T-1})$ is the sum of a concave piecewise linear function in $\boldsymbol{\xi}_{[T-1]}$ and a *linear* function in $\boldsymbol{x}_{T-1}$. So, the cost-to-go function $\mathcal{V}_{T-1}(\boldsymbol{\xi}_{[T-1]}, \boldsymbol{x}_{T-1})$ is a convex piecewise linear function in $\boldsymbol{x}_{T-1}$, but not convex nor concave in $\boldsymbol{\xi}_{[T-1]}$. By an induction argument, this structure holds for all stages, i.e., value functions $V_t(\boldsymbol{\xi}_{[t+1]}, \boldsymbol{x}_t)$ are always convex piecewise linear in $\boldsymbol{x}_t$ but nonconvex in $\boldsymbol{\xi}_{[t+1]}$. This structure makes the Benders decomposition inapplicable.

### 3.3.3 Nested Benders Decomposition

From the above discussion, it should become clear that an MS-RLO problem with general uncertainty sets is pretty "hopeless" to solve. However, we should also recognize that problems in practice usually come with special structures. For example, uncertainty may be independent or Markovian. It is a modeler's job to create optimization models that best approximate the problems at hand and are also amenable for numerical solution. In this subsection, we will discuss generalization of Benders decomposition to MS-RLO, which exploits the stagewise independence assumption.

Let's first recall Benders decomposition for 2S-RLO. The key idea is to solve an approximation problem of 2S-RLO, which is built upon a sequence of convex piecewise linear functions that underestimate the value function $V_0(\boldsymbol{x}_0)$ better and better until a sufficiently good first-stage solution is obtained. Such a method can work because the value function is convex. For MS-RLO with stagewise independent uncertainty, we know the value functions are also convex. Therefore, the basic idea of Benders decomposition can be applied to MS-RLO, although there are some key differences.

1. In 2S-RLO, the value function $V_0(\boldsymbol{x}_0)$ in (3.2.5) is only a function of the stage decision $\boldsymbol{x}_0$. But in MS-RLO, the value function $\mathscr{V}_t(\boldsymbol{\xi}_{[t]}, \boldsymbol{x}_t)$ in (3.3.12) is a function of both $\boldsymbol{\xi}_{[t]}$ and $\boldsymbol{x}_t$. So to approximate the value function $\mathscr{V}_t(\boldsymbol{\xi}_{[t]}, \boldsymbol{x}_t)$, we need to generate valid inequalities in both $\boldsymbol{\xi}_{[t]}$ and $\boldsymbol{x}_t$ at each stage $t$.
2. In 2S-RLO, the value function can be directly evaluated by solving a bilinear program (3.2.14). In MS-RLO, the value functions, except the zero value function of the last stage, are simply not known. Furthermore, stage $t$'s value function depends on stage $(t + 1)$'s value function via the DP recursion (3.3.10). So in order to have a good approximation of the value function at stage $t$, we need to build sufficiently good approximations of the value function in stage $(t + 1)$, which in turn requires a good approximation of the value function in stage $(t+2)$, etc. This recursive relation makes the approximation of value functions in MS-RLO much more challenging than the case of 2S-RLO.
3. Since the true value functions are not known beforehand and all we know is some lower estimates of the value functions, there is no easy way to generate an upper bound on the optimal objective value of the overall problem. Some practical termination criterion can be used that stops the algorithm when the incremental improvement on the overall problem is small.

Despite these differences, the convexity structure of the value functions in MS-RLO with stagewise independent uncertainty is the key that allows us to develop a Nested Benders decomposition (NBD) algorithm for MS-RLO, which generalizes the Benders decomposition for 2S-RLO. The procedure of NBD follows the nested structure of MS-RLO. It starts with some initial estimation of the value functions at all stages. Each iteration of NBD consists of a forward sweep and a backward sweep. In the forward sweep of iteration $i$, the algorithm starts from stage $(t + 1)$ with $t = 0$ and solves the stage problem (3.3.10) using the current approximate cost-to-go function $\tilde{V}_t^i((\boldsymbol{\xi}_{[t-1]}^i, \boldsymbol{\xi}_t), \boldsymbol{x}_t)$ in place of the true but unknown cost-to-go function $V_t((\boldsymbol{\xi}_{[t-1]}^i, \boldsymbol{\xi}_t), \boldsymbol{x}_t)$ at the worst-case uncertainty vector $\boldsymbol{\xi}_{[t-1]}^i$ and the stage solution $\boldsymbol{x}_{t-1}^i$ obtained from the previous stages. Solving this approximate stage problem leads to a new worst-case uncertainty $\boldsymbol{\xi}_t^i$ and a stage solution $\boldsymbol{x}_t^i$ in stage $(t + 1)$. Repeating this procedure, we obtain a sequence of stage solutions $(\boldsymbol{x}_0^i, \boldsymbol{x}_1^i, \ldots, \boldsymbol{x}_T^i)$ and worst-case uncertainty $(\boldsymbol{\xi}_1^i, \ldots, \boldsymbol{\xi}_T^i)$. This forward sweep generalizes the forward step 4 in the Benders decomposition Algorithm 1.

When the forward sweep reaches the last stage $(T + 1)$, the algorithm starts the backward sweep, which generates new valid inequalities to update cost-to-go and value functions. At each stage $(t + 1)$ in the backward sweep, NBD solves (3.3.10) with a new cost-to-go function $\tilde{V}_t^{i+1}((\boldsymbol{\xi}_{[t-1]}^i, \boldsymbol{\xi}_t), \boldsymbol{x}_t)$, which is just updated from stage $(t + 2)$, and generates a new valid inequality to update the approximate cost-to-go function $\tilde{V}_{t-1}^{i+1}(\boldsymbol{\xi}_{[t]}, \boldsymbol{x}_{t-1})$ at the stage solution $\boldsymbol{x}_{t-1}^i$ and the worst-case uncertainty scenario $\boldsymbol{\xi}_{[t]}^i$. Then the backward sweep goes to stage $t$ and repeats this procedure until it reaches back to the first stage.

The NBD algorithm is presented in Algorithm 5. One thing we would like to comment is the termination criterion. As we pointed out in the comparison to Benders decomposition for 2S-RLO, since all we have is lower estimates of the value functions and the true value functions are not known, then it is not possible to generate an upper bound on the objective value of the iterates. There are some methods to create statistical upper estimates of value functions. However, for practical purposes, the algorithm can be terminated when the incremental improvement on the objective value is small enough. So the termination criterion given in Algorithm 5 is reasonable.

We can also write Algorithm 5 using the language of oracles. A forward oracle can be defined to solve Step (3.3.22) and a backward oracle for solving (3.3.24). Both (3.3.22) and (3.3.24) can be formulated as linear programs. So both oracles essentially solve LPs. The backward oracle at stage $(t+1)$ needs to output dual variables associated with constraints that contain $\boldsymbol{\xi}_{[t]}$ and $\boldsymbol{x}_{t-1}$ as parameters. This can be easily done by any off-the-shelf LP solvers. A new cut $(\boldsymbol{\alpha}_{t-1}^{i+1})^\top \boldsymbol{\xi}_{[t]} + (\boldsymbol{\beta}_{t-1}^{i+1})^\top \boldsymbol{x}_{t-1} + \gamma_{t-1}^{i+1}$ is generated from these dual variables as we described in (3.3.18).

A little history: Nested decomposition methods have been studied extensively for multistage stochastic programming, going back to [12, 13, 14]. The literature is too extensive to do any justice to. See e.g., [7, 11, 15, 16]. Nested decomposition and its variants have been proposed to solve multistage robust and distributionally robust programs [17, 18, 19]. The iteration complexity is studied in [20].

### *3.3.4 Linear Decision Rules and a Cutting Plane Method*

At this point, we can step back and recount what we have achieved so far. The structural analysis of the value functions under the stagewise independence assumption in Sect. 3.3.2 leads to the development of the nested Benders decomposition. It is a rather sophisticated algorithm, albeit based on simple ideas. The outcome of NBD, besides a near-optimal first-stage decision $\boldsymbol{x}_0$, is the cost-to-go functions recursively constructed in the process of the algorithm. These functions $\tilde{V}_t^i(\boldsymbol{\xi}_{[t+1]}, \boldsymbol{x}_t)$ provide a *fully adaptive*, *near-optimal* policy. Full adaptability means they are defined for any realization of uncertainty $\boldsymbol{\xi}_{[t+1]}$ in the uncertainty set and any stage variable $\boldsymbol{x}_t$ for any stage $t$. This is quite an accomplishment—we are essentially solving a problem whose decision variables are functions. However, NBD comes with significant computational cost.

In this subsection, we will introduce a different philosophy for solving MS-RLO. Rather than seeking a set of near-optimal fully adaptive policies, we will be content with a policy that is much easier to compute and hopefully still provide good performance. This is the idea of an *approximate policy*. In this subsection, we will relax the requirement on the optimality of the obtained policy and introduce a family of approximation policies with a particularly simple structure, namely *affine policies*, i.e., policies that are affine functions of the uncertainty. Such policies are also called *linear decision rules*.

**Algorithm 5** Nested benders decomposition (NBD) for MS-RLO

**Require:** Initial lower estimates $(\tilde{V}_1^0, \ldots, \tilde{V}_{T-1}^0)$ of the cost-to-go functions
Initialize: $i \leftarrow -1$
Set $v_0^{-1} \leftarrow -\infty$
**repeat**
  Update $i \leftarrow i + 1$
  **for** $t = 0, \ldots, T-1$ **do** ▷ Forward sweep
    **if** $t = 0$ **then**
      $g_0 = c$ ▷ Keep notation consistent
    **end if**
    Solve

$$v_t^i = \min_{x_t \in X_t(x_{t-1}^i, \xi_{[t]}^i)} \left\{ g_t^\top x_t + \max_{\xi_{t+1} \in \mathscr{U}_{t+1}} \tilde{V}_t^i((\xi_{[t]}^i, \xi_{t+1}), x_t) \right\} \quad (3.3.22a)$$

    Denote a pair of optimal solution as $(x_t^i, \xi_{t+1}^i)$
  **end for**
  **for** $t = T, \ldots, 1$ **do** ▷ Backward sweep
    **if** $t = T$ **then**
      Solve

$$\min_{x_T \in X_T(x_{T-1}^i, \xi_{[T]}^i)} g_T^\top x_T \quad (3.3.23a)$$

    **else**
      Solve

$$\min_{x_t \in X_t(x_{t-1}^i, \xi_{[t]}^i)} \left\{ g_t^\top x_t + \max_{\xi_{t+1} \in \mathscr{U}_{t+1}} \tilde{V}_t^{i+1}((\xi_{[t]}^i, \xi_{t+1}), x_t) \right\} \quad (3.3.24a)$$

    **end if**
    Generate coefficients $(\alpha_{t-1}^{i+1}, \beta_{t-1}^{i+1}, \gamma_{t-1}^{i+1})$ from dual variables of (3.3.24)
    Update $\tilde{V}_{t-1}^{i+1}(\xi_{[t]}, x_{t-1}) \leftarrow \max \left\{ \tilde{V}_{t-1}^i(\xi_{[t]}, x_{t-1}), \ (\alpha_{t-1}^{i+1})^\top \xi_{[t]} + (\beta_{t-1}^{i+1})^\top x_{t-1} + \gamma_{t-1}^{i+1} \right\}$
  **end for**
**until** $v_0^i - v_0^{i-1} \le \epsilon$

#### 3.3.4.1 Linear Decision Rules in Functional Form MS-RLO

To introduce linear decision rules, let us return to the functional formulation of MS-RLO (3.3.1) with a slight simplification, as given below.

$$\begin{aligned}
\min_{x_0, x_1(\cdot), \ldots, x_T(\cdot)} \ \max_{(\xi_1, \ldots, \xi_T) \in \mathscr{U}} \ & \left\{ c^\top x_0 + g_1^\top x_1(\xi_1) + \cdots + g_T^\top x_T(\xi_T) \right\} \\
\text{s.t.} \ & A_0 x_0 \ge b_0, \\
& B_{10} x_0 + B_{11} x_1(\xi_1) \ge D_1 \xi_1 + h_1, \quad \forall \xi_1 \in \mathscr{U}_1, \\
& B_{21} x_1(\xi_1) + B_{22} x_2(\xi_2) \ge D_2 \xi_{[2]} + h_2, \quad \forall \xi_{[2]} \in \mathscr{U}_2, \\
& \cdots\cdots\cdots
\end{aligned}$$

$$\boldsymbol{B}_{T,T-1}\boldsymbol{x}_{T-1}(\boldsymbol{\xi}_{T-1})+\boldsymbol{B}_{TT}\boldsymbol{x}_T(\boldsymbol{\xi}_T) \geq \boldsymbol{D}_T\boldsymbol{\xi}_{[T]}+\boldsymbol{h}_T, \quad \forall \boldsymbol{\xi}_{[T]} \in \mathcal{U}_T.$$

The simplification from the original (3.3.1) is that each $\boldsymbol{x}_t(\xi_t)$ only depends on the uncertainty $\xi_t$ at time $t$, rather than on the uncertainty $\boldsymbol{\xi}_{[t]}$ of all previous periods. This is mainly for illustration purpose. The methods developed below also apply to the original more general case.

Now instead of optimizing over all possible forms for policies $\boldsymbol{x}_t(\cdot)$, we will restrict ourselves to consider some special classes of policies. A natural choice is to consider policies that are affine functions of the uncertainty as

$$\boldsymbol{x}_t(\boldsymbol{\xi}_t) = \boldsymbol{X}_t\boldsymbol{\xi}_t + \boldsymbol{q}_t, \quad \forall t = 1, \ldots, T. \tag{3.3.26}$$

With this linear decision rule, the coefficients $\{(\boldsymbol{X}_t, \boldsymbol{q}_t)\}_{t=1}^T$ become the decision variables in place of the functional variables $\boldsymbol{x}_t(\cdot)$. Thus, the functional formulation of MS-RLO takes the following form with affine polices.

$$\min_{\boldsymbol{x}_0,\boldsymbol{X}_1,\boldsymbol{q}_1,\ldots,\boldsymbol{X}_T,\boldsymbol{q}_T} \max_{(\boldsymbol{\xi}_1,\ldots,\boldsymbol{\xi}_T)\in\mathcal{U}} \left\{\boldsymbol{c}^\top \boldsymbol{x}_0 + \boldsymbol{g}_1^\top(\boldsymbol{X}_1\boldsymbol{\xi}_1 + \boldsymbol{q}_1) + \cdots + \boldsymbol{g}_T^\top(\boldsymbol{X}_T\boldsymbol{\xi}_T + \boldsymbol{q}_T)\right\} \tag{3.3.27a}$$

$$\text{s.t.} \quad \boldsymbol{A}_0\boldsymbol{x}_0 \geq \boldsymbol{b}_0, \tag{3.3.27b}$$

$$\boldsymbol{B}_{10}\boldsymbol{x}_0 + \boldsymbol{B}_{11}(\boldsymbol{X}_1\boldsymbol{\xi}_1 + \boldsymbol{q}_1) \geq \boldsymbol{D}_1\boldsymbol{\xi}_1 + \boldsymbol{h}_1, \quad \forall \boldsymbol{\xi}_1 \in \mathcal{U}_1, \tag{3.3.27c}$$

$$\boldsymbol{B}_{21}(\boldsymbol{X}_1\boldsymbol{\xi}_1 + \boldsymbol{q}_1) + \boldsymbol{B}_{22}(\boldsymbol{X}_2\boldsymbol{\xi}_2 + \boldsymbol{q}_2) \geq \boldsymbol{D}_2\boldsymbol{\xi}_{[2]} + \boldsymbol{h}_2, \quad \forall \boldsymbol{\xi}_{[2]} \in \mathcal{U}_2, \tag{3.3.27d}$$

.........

$$\boldsymbol{B}_{T,T-1}(\boldsymbol{X}_{T-1}\boldsymbol{\xi}_{T-1} + \boldsymbol{q}_{T-1}) + \boldsymbol{B}_{TT}(\boldsymbol{X}_T\boldsymbol{\xi}_T + \boldsymbol{q}_T) \geq \boldsymbol{D}_T\boldsymbol{\xi}_{[T]} + \boldsymbol{h}_T, \ \forall \boldsymbol{\xi}_{[T]} \in \mathcal{U}_T. \tag{3.3.27e}$$

Next, we will study how to reformulate and solve (3.3.27) in two different ways, dualization and a cutting plane method.

#### 3.3.4.2 Reformulation by Dualization

Attentive reader would immediately notice that the above MS-RLO formulation is nothing but a static robust linear optimization model that we have discussed in length in Chap. 2. We can apply the dualization techniques we learned in that chapter to get the deterministic LP counterpart of this robust program. For example, let us look at (3.3.27d) for stage 2. Each row of (3.3.27d) corresponds to a robust linear constraint. The total number of robust linear constraints in stage 2 is equal to the number of rows in $\boldsymbol{B}_{21}$, $\boldsymbol{B}_{22}$, $\boldsymbol{D}_2$, $\boldsymbol{h}_2$. Assume the uncertainty set $\mathcal{U}_2$ has the following linear form $\mathscr{U}_2 = \{\boldsymbol{\xi}_{[2]} = (\boldsymbol{\xi}_1, \boldsymbol{\xi}_2) : \boldsymbol{U}_1\boldsymbol{\xi}_1 + \boldsymbol{U}_2\boldsymbol{\xi}_2 \le \boldsymbol{e}_2\}$. Then, the robust linear constraint in the $i$-th row of (3.3.27d) can be reformulated as follows.

$$(\boldsymbol{b}_{21}^i)^\top(\boldsymbol{X}_1\boldsymbol{\xi}_1+\boldsymbol{q}_1) + (\boldsymbol{b}_{22}^i)^\top(\boldsymbol{X}_2\boldsymbol{\xi}_2+\boldsymbol{q}_2) \ge (\boldsymbol{d}_2^i)^\top\boldsymbol{\xi}_{[2]} + h_2^i, \quad \forall(\boldsymbol{\xi}_1,\boldsymbol{\xi}_2) : \boldsymbol{U}_1\boldsymbol{\xi}_1+\boldsymbol{U}_2\boldsymbol{\xi}_2 \le \boldsymbol{e}_2 \tag{3.3.28a}$$

$$\Longleftrightarrow \min_{(\boldsymbol{\xi}_1,\boldsymbol{\xi}_2):\boldsymbol{U}_1\boldsymbol{\xi}_1+\boldsymbol{U}_2\boldsymbol{\xi}_2\le\boldsymbol{e}_2} (\boldsymbol{b}_{21}^i)^\top\boldsymbol{X}_1\boldsymbol{\xi}_1 + (\boldsymbol{b}_{22}^i)^\top\boldsymbol{X}_2\boldsymbol{\xi}_2 - (\boldsymbol{d}_2^i)^\top\boldsymbol{\xi}_{[2]} \ge h_2^i - (\boldsymbol{b}_{21}^i)^\top\boldsymbol{q}_1 - (\boldsymbol{b}_{22}^i)^\top\boldsymbol{q}_2 \tag{3.3.28b}$$

$$\Longleftrightarrow \begin{cases} \boldsymbol{e}_2^\top\boldsymbol{\lambda}_2^i \ge h_2^i - (\boldsymbol{b}_{21}^i)^\top\boldsymbol{q}_1 - (\boldsymbol{b}_{22}^i)^\top\boldsymbol{q}_2, \\ (\boldsymbol{\lambda}_2^i)^\top\boldsymbol{U}_1 = (\boldsymbol{b}_{21}^i)^\top\boldsymbol{X}_1 - (\boldsymbol{d}_{21}^i)^\top, \\ (\boldsymbol{\lambda}_2^i)^\top\boldsymbol{U}_2 = (\boldsymbol{b}_{22}^i)^\top\boldsymbol{X}_2 - (\boldsymbol{d}_{22}^i)^\top, \\ \boldsymbol{\lambda}_2^i \le \boldsymbol{0}, \end{cases} \tag{3.3.28c}$$

where we partitioned vector $\boldsymbol{d}_2^i$ as $(\boldsymbol{d}_{21}^i; \boldsymbol{d}_{22}^i)$ such that $(\boldsymbol{d}_2^i)^\top\boldsymbol{\xi}_{[2]} = (\boldsymbol{d}_{21}^i)^\top\boldsymbol{\xi}_1 + (\boldsymbol{d}_{22}^i)^\top\boldsymbol{\xi}_2$.

By this dualization procedure, each robust linear constraint (3.3.28a) is transformed to a set of deterministic linear constraints in (3.3.28c) jointly in the variables $\boldsymbol{X}_1, \boldsymbol{X}_2, \boldsymbol{q}_1, \boldsymbol{q}_2$ and the new dual variable $\boldsymbol{\lambda}_2^i$. In this way, the MS-RLO with affine polices can be transformed to a deterministic LP. If the resulting LP is not too large, it can be certainly solved by some off-the-shelf solver.

However, for practical large-scale MS-RLO problems, dualizing every robust linear constraint in (3.3.27) and the objective will lead to a deterministic linear program with a significantly larger size than the robust model, thus, causing scalability issues. A simple calculation will illustrate this. Let us find the number of dualized linear constraints in (3.3.28c). Suppose the dimension of $\boldsymbol{\xi}_j$ is $k_j$ and the number of linear constraints in the uncertainty set $\mathscr{U}_2$ is $N_{\mathscr{U}_2}$. Then, the dimension of dual variable $\boldsymbol{\lambda}_2^i$ is $N_{\mathscr{U}_2}$ and the number of linear constraints in (3.3.28c) is $k_1+k_2+1$ (not counting the nonpositivity constraint $\boldsymbol{\lambda}_2^i \le \boldsymbol{0}$). So, if stage 2 has $m_2$ robust linear constraints in (3.3.1c) (i.e., $\boldsymbol{B}_{21}$ has $m_2$ rows), then dualization will introduce $m_2 \cdot (k_1+k_2+1)$ new linear constraints and $m_2 \cdot N_{\mathscr{U}_2}$ new variables. This causes a big increase in problem size. Later in Chap. 6, Sect. 6.3, we will show an application of linear decision rules to the multistage robust unit commitment problem. There, we will see that even the simplest form of linear decision rules could lead to an MS-RLO whose deterministic LP reformulation is too large to solve for practical use.

#### 3.3.4.3 A Constraint Generation Method

We come to the question of how to handle the MS-RLO problem (3.3.27) with affine policies, when its dualized reformulation is too large to be directly solved. The solution method we will describe is motivated by an alternative perspective on robust constraints like (3.3.1c). Instead of going to the dual, the "primal view" of the robust constraint

$$(\boldsymbol{b}_{21}^i)^\top(\boldsymbol{X}_1\boldsymbol{\xi}_1+\boldsymbol{q}_1)+(\boldsymbol{b}_{22}^i)^\top(\boldsymbol{X}_2\boldsymbol{\xi}_2+\boldsymbol{q}_2)\geq(\boldsymbol{d}_2^i)^\top\boldsymbol{\xi}_{[2]}+h_2^i,\quad\forall\,\boldsymbol{\xi}_{[2]}\in\mathcal{U}_2, \tag{3.3.29}$$

is that (3.3.29) is simply a list of deterministic linear constraints parametrized by $\boldsymbol{\xi}_{[2]}$ for each value $\boldsymbol{\xi}_{[2]}$ in $\mathcal{U}_2$. This is exactly the interpretation of robust constraints we discussed in Chap. 2. Moreover, the robust linear constraints in (3.3.29) achieve the worst-case scenarios at extreme points of $\mathcal{U}_2$. Since we assumed that the uncertainty set $\mathcal{U}_2$ is a polytope, then the robust constraint (3.3.29) entails a *finite number* of deterministic linear constraints. Therefore, the original MS-RLO model with affine policies (3.3.27) has a finite number of deterministic linear constraints.

With this primal viewpoint, the MS-RLO formulation (3.3.27) is already a deterministic linear program with potentially a lot of linear constraints in the set of primal variables $(\boldsymbol{x}_0, \boldsymbol{X}_1, \boldsymbol{q}_1, \ldots, \boldsymbol{X}_T, \boldsymbol{q}_T)$. To solve a large-scale optimization problem with many constraints, a standard technique is *constraint generation*. The basic procedure is the follows. Start from a small subset of the constraints in the original problem, and call it a restricted problem. Solve the restricted problem, which should be amenable to direct solution, and then test whether the solution of the restricted problem satisfies all the constraints in the original problem. If it does, then we have found the optimal solution to the original problem. Otherwise, we identify the violated constraints, add them to the restricted problem, and repeat this process until an optimal solution is found. If the original problem has a finite number of constraints, then this constraint generation process will terminate in a finite number of steps, because the worst case is all the constraints in the original problem are added.

Many constraints in the original problem may be redundant constraints, so they would never be violated in the constraint generation process. This is why the constraint generation algorithm may work well. It is reasonable to expect so for the robust problem we have at hand, because for each robust constraint, there is a worst-case uncertainty scenario, while all other scenarios are not essential. In the following, we will describe the constraint generation algorithm for a general robust optimization problem in the following form.

$$\min_{\boldsymbol{x}} \quad \boldsymbol{c}^\top\boldsymbol{x} \tag{3.3.30a}$$

$$\text{s.t.} \quad f_i(\boldsymbol{x},\boldsymbol{\xi})\leq 0,\quad \forall\boldsymbol{\xi}\in\mathcal{U},\ i=1,2,\ldots,M. \tag{3.3.30b}$$

$$\boldsymbol{x}\in X. \tag{3.3.30c}$$

It is easy to see the correspondence between the MS-RLO problem (3.3.27) and the above abstract model (3.3.30). In particular, the robust objective in (3.3.30) can be moved to the constraints. So we can focus on a problem with only robust constraints, which are modeled by Eq. (3.3.30b). $M$ is the total number of robust constraints. The

**Algorithm 6** Constraint generation for MS-RLO with linear decision rule

Initialization: A subset of scenarios for all robust constraints, $\tilde{\mathscr{U}}_1, \tilde{\mathscr{U}}_2, \ldots, \tilde{U}_M \subseteq \mathscr{U}$

$k \leftarrow 1$

**repeat**

  Solve the restricted problem

$$\min_{x \in X} \; c^\top x \tag{3.3.31a}$$

$$\text{s.t.} \quad f_i(x, \xi^{ij}) \le 0, \quad \forall \xi^{ij} \in \tilde{\mathscr{U}}_i, \; i = 1, 2, \ldots, M. \tag{3.3.31b}$$

  Obtain an optimal solution $x^k$.

  **for** $i = 1, \ldots, M$ **do** ▷ Find violated constraints

    Solve the pricing problem

$$v_i = \max_{\xi \in \mathscr{U}} f_i(x^k, \xi) \tag{3.3.32}$$

    Obtain an optimal solution $\xi^{ik}$.

    **if** $v_i > 0$ **then** ▷ $x^k$ violates robust constraint $i$

      $\tilde{U}_i \leftarrow \tilde{U}_i \cup \{\xi^{ik}\}$ ▷ Update $\tilde{\mathscr{U}}_i$

    **end if**

  **end for**

  $k \leftarrow k + 1$

**until** No constraint violation is found

polytopal uncertainty set $\mathscr{U}$ can be represented by the set of $N_{\mathscr{U}}$ extreme points as $\mathscr{U} = \text{conv}\{\xi^1, \xi^2, \ldots, \xi^{N_{\mathscr{U}}}\}$.

The constraint generation algorithm will be applied to multistage robust unit commitment problem in Chap. 6, where its performance, speed-up heuristics, and scalability will be studied in detail. The above algorithm and its application to multistage robust unit commitment is proposed in [21]. Constraint-generation based algorithms have also been proposed for the much more general model of multistage robust mixed-integer programming, where the decision variables $x_t$ are mixed-integer variables. An important class of approximate policy, called finitely adaptive policy, together with a constraint-generation algorithm is proposed in [22].

## 3.4 End-of-Chapter Exercises

**3.1** Suppose that the primal problem (3.2.9) satisfies the relatively complete recourse and the dual problem (3.2.11) is feasible. Then, use duality theory to argue that the dual maximization problem (3.2.11) must have a finite maximum for all $\xi \in \mathscr{U}$ and $x_0 \in X_0$, therefore, the primal minimization problem (3.2.9) must also have a finite minimum for all $\xi \in \mathscr{U}$ and $x_0 \in X_0$.

**3.2** Consider the following 2S-RLO.

$$\min_{x_1, x_2} \left\{ 100x_1 + 150x_2 + \max_{(d_1, d_2) \in B} \; \min_{(y_1, y_2) \in W(x, d)} -24y_1 - 28y_2 \right\}, \tag{3.4.1a}$$

$$\text{s.t.} \quad x_1 + x_2 \leq 120, \tag{3.4.1b}$$

$$x_1 \geq 40, \tag{3.4.1c}$$

$$x_2 \geq 20, \tag{3.4.1d}$$

where the uncertainty set

$$B = \{(d_1, d_2) \in \mathbb{R}^2 : 300 \leq d_1 \leq 500,\ 100 \leq d_2 \leq 300,\ d_1 + d_2 \leq 600\} \tag{3.4.1e}$$

and the set $W(\boldsymbol{x}, \boldsymbol{d})$ is defined by the following linear inequalities

$$6y_1 + 10y_2 \leq 60x_1, \tag{3.4.1f}$$

$$8y_1 + 5y_2 \leq 80x_2, \tag{3.4.1g}$$

$$0 \leq y_1 \leq d_1, \tag{3.4.1h}$$

$$0 \leq y_2 \leq d_2. \tag{3.4.1i}$$

Use the Benders decomposition algorithm to solve the above 2S-RLO. write down the iterations. How can you solve the second-stage problem to global optimality in each iterate of the Benders algorithm?

**3.3** Solve (3.4.1) by Column-and-Constraint generation. Write down the iterates of the algorithm.

**3.4** In the nested formulation of a multistage robust linear optimization problem (3.3.4), suppose that the constraint in each stage $(t+1)$ only involves the uncertainty parameter $\boldsymbol{\xi}_t$ rather than $\boldsymbol{\xi}_{[t]}$ as in (3.3.5). That is, the constraint in stage $(t+1)$ is in the following form

$$\boldsymbol{B}_{t,t-1}\boldsymbol{x}_{t-1} + \boldsymbol{B}_{t,t}\boldsymbol{x}_t \geq \boldsymbol{D}_t\boldsymbol{\xi}_t + \boldsymbol{h}_t. \tag{3.4.2}$$

Adapt the nested decomposition algorithm to this problem. For example, think about how the cuts in Algorithm 5 would be generated in the backward sweep.

## References

1. Bertsimas, D., & Tsitsiklis, J. (1997). *Introduction to linear optimization*. Athena Scientific.
2. Dyer, M. E. (1983). The complexity of vertex enumeration methods. *Mathematics of Operations Research*, *8*(3), 381–402.
3. Hansen, P., Jaumard, B., & Savard, G. (1992). New branch-and-bound rules for linear bilevel programming. *SIAM Journal on Scientific and Statistical Computing* , *13*(5), 1194–1217.
4. Bixby, R. (2012). A brief history of linear and mixed-integer programming computation. *Documenta Mathematica, Extra Volume ISMP*, 107–121.
5. Nemirovski, A. S., & Yudin, D. B. (1983). *Problem complexity and method efficiency in optimization*. Wiley.

6. Benders, J. F. (1962). Partitioning procedures for solving mixed-variables programming problems. *Numerische Mathematik, 4*, 238–252.
7. Birge, J. R., & Louveaux, F. (2011). *Introduction to stochastic programming* (2nd ed.). Springer.
8. Bertsimas, D., Litvinov, E., Sun, X. A., Zhao, J., & Zheng, T. (2013). Adaptive robust optimization for the security constrained unit commitment problem. *IEEE Transactions on Power Systems, 28*(1), 52–63.
9. Zeng, B., & Zhao, L. (2013). Solving two-stage robust optimization problems using a column-and-constraint generation method. *Operations Research Letters, 41*(5), 457–461.
10. Ayoub J., & Poss, M. (2016). Decomposition for adjustable robust linear optimizationsubject to uncertainty polytope. *Computational Management Science, 13*, 219–239.
11. Shapiro, A., Dentcheva, D., & Ruszczyński, A. (2009). *Lectures on stochastic programming: modeling and theory.* SIAM.
12. Glassey, C. R. (1973). Nested decomposition and multistage linear programs. *Management Science, 20*, 282–292.
13. Ho, J. K., & Manne, A. S. (1974). Nested decomposition for dynamic models. *Mathematical Programming, 6*, 121–140.
14. Birge, J. (1985). Decomposition and partitioning methods for multi-stage stochastic linear programs. *Operations Research, 33*, 989–1007.
15. Shapiro, A. (2011). Analysis of stochastic dual dynamic programming method. *European Journal of Operations Research, 209*, 63–72.
16. Philpott, A., de Matos, V., & Finardi, E. (2013). On solving multistage stochastic programs with coherent risk measures. *Operations Research, 61*(4), 957–970 (2013)
17. Georghiou, A., Tsoukalas, A., & Wiesemann, W. (2019). Robust dual dynamic programming. *Operations Research, 67*(3), 813–830.
18. Philpott, A., de Matos, V. L., & Kapalevich, L. (2018). Distributionally robust SDDP. *Computational Management Science, 15*, 431–454.
19. Duque, D., & Morton, D. (2020). Distributionally robust stochastic dual dynamic programming. *SIAM Journal on Optimization, 30*(4), 2841–2865.
20. Zhang, S., & Sun, X. A. (2020). On distributionally robust multistage convex optimization: new algorithms and complexity analysis. https://arxiv.org/pdf/2010.06759.pdf
21. Lorca, A., Sun, X. A., Litvinov, E., & Zheng, T. (2016). Multistage adaptive robust optimization for the unit commitment problem. *Operations Research, 64*(1), 32–51.
22. Bertsimas, D., & Dunning, I. (2016). Multistage robust mixed-integer optimization with adaptive partitions. *Operations Research, 64*(4), 980–998.

# Chapter 4
# Distributionally Robust Optimization

## 4.1 Introduction

The robust optimization methodology that we have introduced so far is built on a fundamental modeling approach, that is based on set-theoretic, deterministic uncertainty models. In particular, we have the following typical min–max robust optimization problem

$$\min_{\boldsymbol{x} \in X} \max_{\boldsymbol{\xi} \in \mathscr{U}} f(\boldsymbol{x}, \boldsymbol{\xi}), \tag{4.1.1}$$

where $\boldsymbol{x}$ is the decision variable, $\boldsymbol{\xi}$ is the uncertain parameter taking values in the uncertainty set $\mathscr{U}$, and $f(\boldsymbol{x}, \boldsymbol{\xi})$ has some favorable structures for computation.

Stochastic optimization, another major modeling framework for decision making under uncertainty, offers a different approach. Instead of deterministic uncertainty sets and worst-case performance, stochastic programs are built upon fully known probability distributions and average performance criteria. In particular, a typical stochastic program can be formulated as

$$\min_{\boldsymbol{x} \in X} \mathbb{E}_{\mathbb{P}_0}[f(\boldsymbol{x}, \boldsymbol{\xi})], \tag{4.1.2}$$

where $\mathbb{P}_0$ is a known probability distribution for the random element $\boldsymbol{\xi}$.

These two methodologies, robust versus stochastic, offer almost two diametrically opposite approaches, one completely freed from any probability distribution and the other fully embraces one fixed probability distribution. Despite their successes, both approaches also suffer limitations from their very modeling premises. We can see at least three types of limitations. Firstly, robust optimization could be overly conservative if it ignores valuable probabilistic information, while stochastic optimization may be requiring too much information about the probability distribu-



X. A. Sun, A. J. Conejo, *Robust Optimization in Electric Energy Systems*,
International Series in Operations Research & Management Science 313,
https://doi.org/10.1007/978-3-030-85128-6_4

tion that may not be available to the modeler. Secondly, the solutions obtained from robust or stochastic optimization models may perform badly on out-of-sample tests, or may have intrinsic bias that would not be removable by simply increasing the size of the sampled data. Thirdly, as we have already seen in previous chapters, robust models could be computationally challenging to solve, especially for adaptive robust optimization problems. And stochastic programs may involve high-dimensional integration, which is also intractable in general.

In this chapter, we introduce an important generalization of robust and stochastic optimization, which provides a very powerful modeling framework and resolves some of the above mentioned limitations of both robust and stochastic optimization. The idea is very simple. Instead of being fixated on a specific probability distribution, which may be difficult to observe in practice, we allow to have some ambiguity about the probability distribution. For example, instead of assuming the probability distribution of the random element is a standard Gaussian distribution with mean 0 and variance 1, we may consider all Gaussian distributions with the same mean but different variances, or we may even allow to consider all distributions with mean close to 0 and variance close to 1. This ambiguity about probability distributions can be modeled by specifying a set $\mathscr{P}$, whose elements are all the probability distributions that we may consider. This set is called the *ambiguity set*.

The stochastic optimization model (4.1.2) can be viewed as having an ambiguity set that only has one element, namely $\mathscr{P} = \{\text{the nominal distribution } \mathbb{P}_0\}$. Once $\mathscr{P}$ has more than one element, the objective of minimizing the average cost in (4.1.2) becomes ambiguous—which distribution's average cost do we consider? Here, the robust optimization's philosophy of worst-case performance offers a natural choice. We will minimize the worst-case average cost over all distributions considered in the ambiguity set. So, we come to the following optimization model

$$\min_{\boldsymbol{x}\in X} \max_{\mathbb{P}\in\mathscr{P}} \mathbb{E}_{\mathbb{P}}[f(\boldsymbol{x}, \boldsymbol{\xi})]. \tag{4.1.3}$$

This is called a *distributionally robust optimization* (DRO) model.

Notice that if the ambiguity set $\mathscr{P}$ contains only one distribution, then the DRO model (4.1.3) reduces to a stochastic program (4.1.2), as we already know. On the contrary, if $\mathscr{P}$ contains all distributions on a fixed support $\mathscr{U}$, then DRO model (4.1.3) reduces to a robust optimization problem (4.1.1), where $\mathscr{U}$ is the deterministic uncertainty set. Therefore, DRO offers a unified framework, in which robust and stochastic optimization are two extreme cases. The DRO framework turns out to be extremely rich in its modeling power and has many deep implications on its two opposing special cases.

In this chapter, we will discuss how to construct ambiguity sets, which is a central question in DRO, how to formulate static and adaptive DRO models, and how to solve DRO models with various ambiguity sets through reformulation. We will also discuss in detail a special class of DRO models, called the *distributionally robust chance constraints* (DRCC), which model soft constraints that can be violated in a probabilistic sense.

## 4.2 Static Distributionally Robust Convex Optimization

In this section, we study the following two questions: (i) how to construct an ambiguity set; and (ii) how to solve the resulting static DRO problem. Although answering these two questions involves different techniques, a satisfactory solution of these two questions need to go hand-in-hand, because the structure of an ambiguity set directly determines the tractability of the resulting DRO, and without computational tractability (which, in the broadest sense, also includes approximability), a DRO is essentially useless.

In the literature, two broad classes of ambiguity sets have been extensively studied, namely the moment based ambiguity sets and the distance based ambiguity sets. The moment based ambiguity sets are defined using information on the moments of the underlying distributions, e.g. the mean and the covariance, while the distance based ambiguity sets are defined by some "distance" between a nominal distribution, usually obtained through data-driven methods such as sampling, and another close-by probability distribution. Sometimes, the distance used is not a true distance, i.e. not a metric in the space of probability distributions. But nevertheless, some kind of difference between distributions is captured. In the following, we will present some widely used examples from each class. For each ambiguity set, we will derive a reformulation of the associated DRO problem.

### *4.2.1 Moment-Based Ambiguity Sets and Reformulations*

#### 4.2.1.1 Motivation

Very often in practice, the modeler does not know the true distribution of the underlying random element, but rather only has information about its moments, e.g. the mean, the variance, or covariance. How can we get these moment information? For example, in a data-driven modeling framework, independently and identically distributed (iid) samples from the unknown distribution may be drawn, from which we can estimate these moments. Why do we care about moment information? Intuitively, mean and variance offer some basic characterization of a random variable. Mathematically, we can ask the following question. Suppose for a random variable $\xi$ with probability distribution $\mathbb{P}$, all the moments, $m^k := \mathbb{E}_{\mathbb{P}}[\xi^k]$, for $k = 1, 2, \ldots,$ are finite and known. Then, is $\mathbb{P}$ uniquely determined by the sequence of moments $\{m^k\}_{k=1}^{\infty}$? This type of question is called the *moment problem*. It is a classic topic in mathematics, dating back to the late nineteenth century.

If the answer to the moment problem for a particular distribution $\mathbb{P}$ is yes, then we call the distribution $\mathbb{P}$ *moment determinate* or *M-det* for short. In this case, $\mathbb{P}$ is fully characterized by the moment sequence. Then, we would expect that if two moment sequences (or a finite truncation of them) are close to each other in some sense, then their corresponding distributions should also be close in some sense. Indeed, this intuition is supported by a classical result, the Fréchet-Shohat Theorem [1]. The theorem says the following. Suppose we have a sequence of real-valued random variables $\xi_n$ with distributions $\mathbb{P}_n$ for $n = 1, 2, \ldots,$ and each $\mathbb{P}_n$ has finite moments $\{m_n^k = \mathbb{E}_{\mathbb{P}_n}[\xi_n^k]\}_{k=1}^{\infty}$. If the moment sequences converge, i.e. $\lim_{n\to\infty} m_n^k = m^k < \infty$ for each $k$, then the limit $\{m^k\}_{k=1}^{\infty}$ is again a moment sequence, i.e. there exists a probability distribution $\mathbb{P}$ such that $m^k = \mathbb{E}_{\mathbb{P}}[\xi^k]$ for all $k = 1, 2, \ldots, \infty$. Furthermore, if this $\mathbb{P}$ is M-det (then by definition $\mathbb{P}$ is uniquely determined by this limit moment sequence), then $\mathbb{P}_n$ weakly converges to $\mathbb{P}$ as $n \to \infty$.

#### 4.2.1.2 The Principle of Reformulation Through a Simple Example

The above intuition and the mathematical statement inspire the construction of ambiguity sets using moment information. Let us look at a very simple example.

$$\mathscr{P}(\mathscr{U}, \boldsymbol{\mu}^+, \boldsymbol{\mu}^-) := \Big\{ \mathbb{P} \in \mathscr{M}_+(\mathbb{R}^l) : \mathbb{P}(\boldsymbol{\xi} \in \mathscr{U}) = 1, \tag{4.2.1a}$$

$$\boldsymbol{\mu}^- \le \mathbb{E}_{\mathbb{P}}[\boldsymbol{\xi}] \le \boldsymbol{\mu}^+ \Big\}. \tag{4.2.1b}$$

Here, $\mathscr{U} \subseteq \mathbb{R}^l$ is the common support of all distributions $\mathbb{P}$ in this ambiguity set. $\mathscr{M}_+(\mathbb{R}^l)$ is the set of nonnegative measures on $\mathbb{R}^l$, i.e. $\mu \in \mathscr{M}_+(\mathbb{R}^l)$, if $\mu(A) \ge 0$ for all Borel measurable set $A \subseteq \mathbb{R}^l$. The second constraint restricts the mean of each $\mathbb{P}$ to be in the box defined by the upper and lower bounds $\boldsymbol{\mu}^{\pm}$. More sophisticated ambiguity sets with moment constraints will be discussed later. We will mainly use this simple example to illustrate the principle of reformulation of a DRO model using convex optimization duality.

The DRO problem (4.1.3) with this ambiguity set has the following inner maximization problem over the worst-case probability distribution

$$\max_{\mathbb{P}} \quad \mathbb{E}_{\mathbb{P}}[f(\boldsymbol{x}, \boldsymbol{\xi})] \tag{4.2.2a}$$

$$\text{s.t.} \quad \mathbb{P} \in \mathscr{M}_+(\mathbb{R}^l), \tag{4.2.2b}$$

$$\mathbb{P}(\boldsymbol{\xi} \in \mathscr{U}) = 1, \tag{4.2.2c}$$

$$\boldsymbol{\mu}^- \le \mathbb{E}_{\mathbb{P}}[\boldsymbol{\xi}] \le \boldsymbol{\mu}^+. \tag{4.2.2d}$$

This problem looks quite different from other problems that we have seen so far, mainly because the variable now is a probability distribution, which in general are *infinite* dimensional objects. Therefore, this inner maximization problem (4.2.2) in general is an optimization problem with an infinite number of variables and a finite number of constraints. It is instructive to compare with robust optimization problems, e.g. the static robust linear constraint (2.2.11) in Chap. 2, which has an infinite number of constraints and a finite number of decision variables. In the case of static robust optimization, the convex duality theory in finite dimensional spaces can be applied to take the dual of the robust constraint. See the derivation in (2.2.12a)–(2.2.12c). The result is a standard linear program with a finite number of constraints and a finite number of variables.

Before we tackle the infinite dimensional problem (4.2.2), let us look at an important special case, where the probability distributions in the ambiguity set are restricted discrete distributions on a fixed, finite support. That is, the support of the distributions is the set $\mathcal{U} = \{\boldsymbol{\xi}_1, \boldsymbol{\xi}_2, \ldots, \boldsymbol{\xi}_m\}$ with $m$ fixed scenarios. Any probability measure on $\mathcal{U}$ can be represented by a vector $\boldsymbol{p} = (p_1, p_2, \ldots, p_m)^\top \in \mathbb{R}^m$. In this case, problem (4.2.2) takes on the following form

$$\max_{\boldsymbol{p}=(p_1,\ldots,p_m)^\top} \quad \sum_{i=1}^m p_i f(\boldsymbol{x}, \boldsymbol{\xi}_i) \tag{4.2.3a}$$

$$\text{s.t.} \quad \sum_{i=1}^m p_i = 1, \tag{4.2.3b}$$

$$\boldsymbol{p} \geq \boldsymbol{0}, \tag{4.2.3c}$$

$$\boldsymbol{\mu}^- \leq \sum_{i=1}^m \boldsymbol{\xi}_i p_i \leq \boldsymbol{\mu}^+. \tag{4.2.3d}$$

This is a finite dimensional optimization problem. It is important to notice that the objective function is a *linear function* in $\boldsymbol{p}$, because the expectation operation $\mathbb{E}_{\mathbb{P}}[\cdot]$ is a linear function of the probability measure $\mathbb{P}$. So (4.2.3) is a linear program in $\mathbb{P}$. This key feature is preserved in the infinite dimensional problem (4.2.2), even when the measure $\mathbb{P}$ has a continuous support.

Let us write down the inner maximization problem with general probability distributions.

$$\max_{\mu} \quad \int_{\mathcal{U}} f(\boldsymbol{x}, \boldsymbol{\xi}) d\mu(\boldsymbol{\xi}) \tag{4.2.4a}$$

$$\text{s.t.} \quad \mu \in \mathcal{M}_+(\mathbb{R}^l), \tag{4.2.4b}$$

$$\int_{\mathcal{U}} d\mu(\boldsymbol{\xi}) = 1, \tag{4.2.4c}$$

$$\int_{\mathcal{U}} \boldsymbol{\xi} d\mu(\boldsymbol{\xi}) \leq \boldsymbol{\mu}^+, \tag{4.2.4d}$$

$$\int_{\mathcal{U}} -\boldsymbol{\xi} d\mu(\boldsymbol{\xi}) \leq -\boldsymbol{\mu}^-. \tag{4.2.4e}$$

The linearity of the integrals with respect to $\mu$ implies that (4.2.4) is a *linear program* in an infinite dimensional space. Now let us formulate the dual program of (4.2.4). To do this, we follow the same procedure as we formulate the dual of a finite dimensional optimization problem. First, we form the Lagrangian function

$$\begin{aligned} L(\mu, \lambda, \boldsymbol{\beta}, \boldsymbol{\gamma}) = & \int_{\mathscr{U}} f(\boldsymbol{x}, \boldsymbol{\xi}) d\mu(\boldsymbol{\xi}) + \lambda\Big(1 - \int_{\mathscr{U}} d\mu(\boldsymbol{\xi})\Big) \\ & + \boldsymbol{\beta}^\top\Big(\boldsymbol{\mu}^+ - \int_{\mathscr{U}} \boldsymbol{\xi} d\mu(\boldsymbol{\xi})\Big) + \boldsymbol{\gamma}^\top\Big(-\boldsymbol{\mu}^- + \int_{\mathscr{U}} \boldsymbol{\xi} d\mu(\boldsymbol{\xi})\Big) \end{aligned} \tag{4.2.5a}$$

$$= \lambda + \boldsymbol{\beta}^\top \boldsymbol{\mu}^+ - \boldsymbol{\gamma}^\top \boldsymbol{\mu}^- + \int_{\mathscr{U}} \Big(f(\boldsymbol{x}, \boldsymbol{\xi}) - \lambda + (\boldsymbol{\gamma} - \boldsymbol{\beta})^\top \boldsymbol{\xi}\Big) d\mu(\boldsymbol{\xi}). \tag{4.2.5b}$$

Note that we relaxed the constraint $\int_{\mathscr{U}} d\mu(\boldsymbol{\xi}) = 1$.

The Lagrangian dual of (4.2.4) is given by

$$\min_{\lambda, \boldsymbol{\beta} \geq \mathbf{0}, \boldsymbol{\gamma} \geq \mathbf{0}} \max_{\mu \in \mathscr{M}_+(\mathbb{R}^l)} \Big\{\lambda + \boldsymbol{\beta}^\top \boldsymbol{\mu}^+ - \boldsymbol{\gamma}^\top \boldsymbol{\mu}^- + \int_{\mathscr{U}} \Big(f(\boldsymbol{x}, \boldsymbol{\xi}) - \lambda + (\boldsymbol{\gamma} - \boldsymbol{\beta})^\top \boldsymbol{\xi}\Big) d\mu(\boldsymbol{\xi})\Big\} \tag{4.2.6a}$$

$$= \min_{\lambda, \boldsymbol{\beta} \geq \mathbf{0}, \boldsymbol{\gamma} \geq \mathbf{0}} \Big\{\lambda + \boldsymbol{\beta}^\top \boldsymbol{\mu}^+ - \boldsymbol{\gamma}^\top \boldsymbol{\mu}^- + \max_{\mu \in \mathscr{M}_+(\mathbb{R}^l)} \int_{\mathscr{U}} \Big(f(\boldsymbol{x}, \boldsymbol{\xi}) - \lambda + (\boldsymbol{\gamma} - \boldsymbol{\beta})^\top \boldsymbol{\xi}\Big) d\mu(\boldsymbol{\xi})\Big\} \tag{4.2.6b}$$

$$= \min_{\lambda, \boldsymbol{\beta} \geq \mathbf{0}, \boldsymbol{\gamma} \geq \mathbf{0}} \lambda + \boldsymbol{\beta}^\top \boldsymbol{\mu}^+ - \boldsymbol{\gamma}^\top \boldsymbol{\mu}^- \tag{4.2.6c}$$

$$\text{s.t. } f(\boldsymbol{x}, \boldsymbol{\xi}) - \lambda + (\boldsymbol{\gamma} - \boldsymbol{\beta})^\top \boldsymbol{\xi} \leq 0, \quad \forall \boldsymbol{\xi} \in \mathscr{U}. \tag{4.2.6d}$$

After relaxing the constraint that $\mu(\mathscr{U}) = 1$, the only constraint left for $\mu$ to be a probability measure is the nonnegativity of $\mu$. The dual constraint (4.2.6d) is obtained to guarantee the integral in (4.2.6b) is bounded, therefore, must be zero. Problems (4.2.4) and (4.2.6c)–(4.2.6d) are a primal-dual pair. If $\mathscr{U}$ is a finite set, then (4.2.6c)–(4.2.6d) exactly recovers the dual linear program of (4.2.3) (See Exercise 4.1).

Notice that the dual constraint (4.2.6d) is a static robust constraint with uncertain parameter $\boldsymbol{\xi}$ and uncertainty set $\mathscr{U}$. Depending on the structure of $f(\boldsymbol{x}, \boldsymbol{\xi})$ and $\mathscr{U}$, we can use the techniques from Chap. 2 to further reformulate the robust constraint to a deterministic constraint. Assuming strong duality holds between the inner maximization (4.2.2) and its dual (4.2.6c)–(4.2.6d), we can replace the maximization with its dual in the DRO problem (4.1.3). Then, we get the following static robust optimization problem

$$\min_{x,\lambda,\beta,\gamma} \quad \lambda + \beta^\top \mu^+ - \gamma^\top \mu^- \tag{4.2.7a}$$

$$\text{s.t.} \quad f(x,\xi) - \lambda + (\gamma - \beta)^\top \xi \leq 0, \quad \forall \xi \in \mathcal{U}, \tag{4.2.7b}$$

$$x \in X. \tag{4.2.7c}$$

It is worthwhile keeping in mind this intrinsic connection between DRO and the classic robust optimization. Whenever a DRO problem can be reformulated through dualization, be ready to look for an equivalent classic robust optimization problem.

The above procedure of forming the Lagrangian dual of the inner DRO problem is purely formal and can be applied to a broad class of DRO problems. In particular, it only requires paired vector spaces, and linear functionals and bilinear functions on the vector spaces. In our case, the set of probability measures on $\mathbb{R}^l$ is a real vector space of infinite dimension, which is paired with the space of functions that are measurable under every probability measure on $\mathbb{R}^l$. Then, the linear functionals from this vector space to $\mathbb{R}$ are all the integrals expressing the expectations. These integrals are also linear in the integrand when the measure is fixed. So they are bilinear functions of the measure $\mu$ and the integrand function. This is all we need to formulate the dual problem. The way that the Lagrangian relaxation is done automatically guarantees that weak duality always holds, i.e. if both the primal and dual problems are feasible, then the optimal objective value of the primal maximization problem is upper bounded by that of the dual minimization problem. All of these results do not require any topological properties of the underlying spaces.

However, to study sufficient conditions that guarantee strong duality between (4.2.2) and its dual (4.2.6c)–(4.2.6d), we do need to endow topologies on the vector spaces and make them into topological vector spaces. Details go beyond the scope of this book, but the readers can be assured that there is a mature body of theory that characterizes various conditions under which strong duality of primal-dual pairs holds for locally convex topological vector spaces. The conditions for strong duality take a similar form as constraint qualification conditions in finite dimensional optimization, such as the Slater type conditions. Interested readers can consult [2, 3, 4].

#### 4.2.1.3 A More Sophisticated Example with Cross Moments

Now let us see a more sophisticated example on how to incorporate cross second moment information to an ambiguity set and how to reformulate the resulting DRO.

$$\mathscr{P}(\mathscr{U}, \boldsymbol{\mu}_0, \boldsymbol{\Sigma}_0, \gamma) := \Big\{ \mathbb{P} \in \mathscr{M}_+(\mathbb{R}^l) : \mathbb{P}(\boldsymbol{\xi} \in \mathscr{U}) = 1, \tag{4.2.8a}$$

$$\mathbb{E}_{\mathbb{P}}[\boldsymbol{\xi}] = \boldsymbol{\mu}_0, \tag{4.2.8b}$$

$$\mathbb{E}_{\mathbb{P}}[(\boldsymbol{\xi} - \boldsymbol{\mu}_0)(\boldsymbol{\xi} - \boldsymbol{\mu}_0)^\top] \preceq \gamma \boldsymbol{\Sigma}_0 \Big\}. \tag{4.2.8c}$$

This ambiguity set, also called the Chebyshev ambiguity set [5, 6, 7, 8], contains all the probability measures that have the same mean $\boldsymbol{\mu}_0$. The third constraint is a positive semidefinite constraint, which we have encountered in Chap. 2. It says that the covariance matrix of $\mathbb{P}$ should be close to the known covariance matrix $\boldsymbol{\Sigma}_0$ and $\gamma$ is a scaling parameter that controls the size of the ambiguity set.

Now let us directly go to the difficult case of continuous distributions and formulate the dual of the following maximization problem

$$\max_{\mu} \quad \int_{\mathscr{U}} f(\boldsymbol{x}, \boldsymbol{\xi}) d\mu(\boldsymbol{\xi}) \tag{4.2.9a}$$

$$\text{s.t.} \quad \mu \in \mathscr{P}(\mathbb{R}^l), \tag{4.2.9b}$$

$$\int_{\mathscr{U}} \boldsymbol{\xi} d\mu(\boldsymbol{\xi}) = \boldsymbol{\xi}_0, \tag{4.2.9c}$$

$$\int_{\mathscr{U}} (\boldsymbol{\xi} - \boldsymbol{\xi}_0)(\boldsymbol{\xi} - \boldsymbol{\xi}_0)^\top d\mu(\boldsymbol{\xi}) \preceq \gamma \boldsymbol{\Sigma}_0. \tag{4.2.9d}$$

First, form the Lagrangian function as

$$L(\mu, \lambda, \boldsymbol{\beta}, \boldsymbol{Q}) = \lambda + \boldsymbol{\xi}_0^\top \boldsymbol{\beta} + \gamma \boldsymbol{\Sigma}_0 \bullet \boldsymbol{Q} + \int_{\mathscr{U}} \Big( f(\boldsymbol{x}, \boldsymbol{\xi}) - \lambda - \boldsymbol{\xi}^\top \boldsymbol{\beta} - (\boldsymbol{\xi} - \boldsymbol{\xi}_0)^\top \boldsymbol{Q} (\boldsymbol{\xi} - \boldsymbol{\xi}_0) \Big) d\mu(\boldsymbol{\xi}), \tag{4.2.10}$$

where $\boldsymbol{Q}$ is a positive semidefinite matrix of the same size as $\boldsymbol{\Sigma}_0$ and $\boldsymbol{\Sigma}_0 \bullet \boldsymbol{Q}$ is the Frobenius inner product of the two matrices defined as the sum of componentwise products $\boldsymbol{\Sigma}_0 \bullet \boldsymbol{Q} := \sum_{i,j} (\boldsymbol{\Sigma}_0)_{ij} Q_{ij}$. The dual can now be formulated as

$$\min_{\lambda, \boldsymbol{\beta}, \boldsymbol{Q} \succeq \boldsymbol{0}} \Big\{ \lambda + \boldsymbol{\xi}_0^\top \boldsymbol{\beta} + \gamma \boldsymbol{\Sigma}_0 \bullet \boldsymbol{Q} + \max_{\mu \in \mathscr{M}_+(\mathbb{R}^l)} \int_{\mathscr{U}} \Big( f(\boldsymbol{x}, \boldsymbol{\xi}) - \lambda - \boldsymbol{\xi}^\top \boldsymbol{\beta} - (\boldsymbol{\xi} - \boldsymbol{\xi}_0)^\top \boldsymbol{Q} (\boldsymbol{\xi} - \boldsymbol{\xi}_0) \Big) d\mu(\boldsymbol{\xi}) \Big\}$$

$$= \min_{\lambda, \boldsymbol{\beta}, \boldsymbol{Q} \succeq \boldsymbol{0}} \quad \lambda + \boldsymbol{\xi}_0^\top \boldsymbol{\beta} + \gamma \boldsymbol{\Sigma}_0 \bullet \boldsymbol{Q} \tag{4.2.11a}$$

$$\text{s.t.} \quad f(\boldsymbol{x}, \boldsymbol{\xi}) - \lambda - \boldsymbol{\xi}^\top \boldsymbol{\beta} - (\boldsymbol{\xi} - \boldsymbol{\xi}_0)^\top \boldsymbol{Q} (\boldsymbol{\xi} - \boldsymbol{\xi}_0) \le 0, \quad \forall \boldsymbol{\xi} \in \mathscr{U}. \tag{4.2.11b}$$

Again, the dual problem involves a static robust constraint. And it can be shown that strong duality holds for this pair of primal and dual problems [2, 6, 8].

Let us work out a concrete example. Suppose that $f(\boldsymbol{x}, \boldsymbol{\xi})$ is a convex piecewise linear function in $(\boldsymbol{x}, \boldsymbol{\xi})$ given by $f(\boldsymbol{x}, \boldsymbol{\xi}) = \max_{1 \le k \le K} \{\boldsymbol{y}_k^\top \boldsymbol{\xi} + \ell_k(\boldsymbol{x})\}$, where $\ell_k(\boldsymbol{x})$ is an affine function of $\boldsymbol{x}$. Furthermore, suppose that $\mathscr{U}$ is an ellipsoid centered at

$\boldsymbol{\xi}_0$ as $\mathscr{U} = \{\boldsymbol{\xi} \in \mathbb{R}^l : (\boldsymbol{\xi} - \boldsymbol{\xi}_0)^\top \boldsymbol{\Lambda}(\boldsymbol{\xi} - \boldsymbol{\xi}_0) \leq 1\}$, where $\boldsymbol{\Lambda}$ is a symmetric positive definite matrix. The reformulation of this problem can be worked out as follows.

$$
\begin{aligned}
&\min_{\lambda,\boldsymbol{\beta},\boldsymbol{Q}\succeq\mathbf{0}} \quad \lambda + \boldsymbol{\xi}_0^\top\boldsymbol{\beta} + \gamma\boldsymbol{\Sigma}_0 \bullet \boldsymbol{Q} \\
&\qquad \text{s.t.} \quad \max_{1\leq k\leq K}\left\{\boldsymbol{y}_k^\top\boldsymbol{\xi} + \ell_k(\boldsymbol{x})\right\} - \lambda - \boldsymbol{\xi}^\top\boldsymbol{\beta} - (\boldsymbol{\xi}-\boldsymbol{\xi}_0)^\top\boldsymbol{Q}(\boldsymbol{\xi}-\boldsymbol{\xi}_0) \leq 0, \quad \forall\boldsymbol{\xi}\in\mathscr{U}, \\
= &\min_{\lambda,\boldsymbol{\beta},\boldsymbol{Q}\succeq\mathbf{0}} \quad \lambda + \boldsymbol{\xi}_0^\top\boldsymbol{\beta} + \gamma\boldsymbol{\Sigma}_0 \bullet \boldsymbol{Q} \\
&\qquad \text{s.t.} \quad \boldsymbol{y}_k^\top\boldsymbol{\xi} + \ell_k(\boldsymbol{x}) - \lambda - \boldsymbol{\xi}^\top\boldsymbol{\beta} - (\boldsymbol{\xi}-\boldsymbol{\xi}_0)^\top\boldsymbol{Q}(\boldsymbol{\xi}-\boldsymbol{\xi}_0) \leq 0, \quad \forall k\in[K],\ \forall\boldsymbol{\xi}\in\mathscr{U}, \\
= &\min_{\lambda,\boldsymbol{\beta},\boldsymbol{Q}\succeq\mathbf{0}} \quad \lambda + \boldsymbol{\xi}_0^\top\boldsymbol{\beta} + \gamma\boldsymbol{\Sigma}_0 \bullet \boldsymbol{Q} \\
&\qquad \text{s.t.} \quad \min_{\boldsymbol{\xi}:(\boldsymbol{\xi}-\boldsymbol{\xi}_0)^\top\boldsymbol{\Lambda}(\boldsymbol{\xi}-\boldsymbol{\xi}_0)\leq 1}\left\{(\boldsymbol{\xi}-\boldsymbol{\xi}_0)^\top\boldsymbol{Q}(\boldsymbol{\xi}-\boldsymbol{\xi}_0) + (\boldsymbol{\beta}-\boldsymbol{y}_k)^\top\boldsymbol{\xi}\right\} \geq \ell_k(\boldsymbol{x}) - \lambda, \quad \forall k\in[K],
\end{aligned} \tag{4.2.12a}
$$

$$
\begin{aligned}
= &\min_{\lambda,\boldsymbol{\beta},\boldsymbol{\alpha},\boldsymbol{\mu},\boldsymbol{Q}} \quad \lambda + \boldsymbol{\xi}_0^\top\boldsymbol{\beta} + \gamma\boldsymbol{\Sigma}_0 \bullet \boldsymbol{Q} \\
&\qquad \text{s.t.} \quad (\boldsymbol{\beta}-\boldsymbol{y}_k)^\top\boldsymbol{\xi}_0 - \alpha_k - \eta_k - \ell_k(\boldsymbol{x}) + \lambda \geq 0, \quad \forall k\in[K], &(4.2.12b)\\
&\qquad\qquad \begin{bmatrix} \eta_k & \frac{1}{2}(\boldsymbol{\beta}-\boldsymbol{y}_k)^\top \\ \frac{1}{2}(\boldsymbol{\beta}-\boldsymbol{y}_k) & \boldsymbol{Q}+\alpha_k\boldsymbol{\Lambda} \end{bmatrix} \succeq \mathbf{0}, \quad \forall k\in[K], &(4.2.12c)\\
&\qquad\qquad \alpha_k \geq 0,\ \eta_k \geq 0,\ \boldsymbol{Q}\succeq\mathbf{0}, \quad \forall k\in[K]. &(4.2.12d)
\end{aligned}
$$

Notice that the reformulation involves an SDP constraint (See Exercise 4.2.)

## 4.2.2 *ϕ-Divergence Based Ambiguity Sets and Reformulations*

### 4.2.2.1 Motivation

Moment-based ambiguity sets contain probability distributions that admit some common characterizations on moments. This type of ambiguity sets does not have a specific distribution that stands out as special. For example, there is no easy way to define a nominal distribution or an empirical distribution in a moment-base ambiguity set purely using moments. However, it is usually the case that a modeler has access to some empirical distribution obtained from sampling the true distribution. Then, it becomes natural to study an ambiguity set of distributions that are "close" to this specific empirical distribution, and expect that if the ambiguity set is chosen properly, it should contain the true, unknown distribution, at least in a statistical sense. This is exactly the motivation to study *distance-based* ambiguity set. The key question is how to measure closeness between probability distributions. Just as the classic problem of moment lying behind the moment-based ambiguity set, measuring distances between probability distributions is another classical problem in statistics. Many measures for this purpose have been proposed.

In this subsection, we focus on the so-called *$\phi$-divergence* functions. In the next subsection, we will introduce a different class of metrics, called the *Wasserstein metrics* or more broadly *optimal transport metrics*.

#### 4.2.2.2 Kullback-Leibler Divergence

Kullback-Leibler (KL) divergence is probably the most well-known example of a $\phi$-divergence, studied by Kullback and Leibler [9]. To introduce the KL divergence, let us first define the following function $\phi_{KL} : \mathbb{R}_+ \to \mathbb{R}$ as

$$\phi_{KL}(t) = t\log(t) - t + 1, \quad t \geq 0. \tag{4.2.13}$$

It is easy to verify that $\phi_{KL}(t)$ is a convex function on $t \geq 0$ (See Exercise 4.3), and also $\phi_{KL}(1) = 0$. Then we use $\phi_{KL}(t)$ to define the following

$$D_{\phi_{KL}}(\mathbb{P}, \mathbb{Q}) := \sum_{i=1}^{m} q_i \cdot \phi_{KL}\left(\frac{p_i}{q_i}\right), \tag{4.2.14}$$

where $\mathbb{P}$ and $\mathbb{Q}$ are two discrete probability distributions defined on the same finite support $\mathscr{U}$, where $\mathscr{U} = \{\boldsymbol{\xi}_1, \boldsymbol{\xi}_2, \ldots, \boldsymbol{\xi}_m\} \subseteq \mathbb{R}^l$ has $m$ scenarios and $\mathbb{P}$ and $\mathbb{Q}$ are represented by two vectors $\mathbb{P} = (p_1, p_2, \ldots, p_m)^\top$ and $\mathbb{Q} = (q_1, q_2, \ldots, q_m)^\top$ of probabilities on these scenarios. The quantity $D_{\phi_{KL}}(\mathbb{P}, \mathbb{Q})$ is called the KL divergence of $\mathbb{P}$ with respect to $\mathbb{Q}$. If we substitute (4.2.13) into (4.2.14), we get

$$\begin{aligned} D_{\phi_{KL}}(\mathbb{P}, \mathbb{Q}) &= \sum_{i=1}^{m} q_i \left(\frac{p_i}{q_i}\log\left(\frac{p_i}{q_i}\right) - \frac{p_i}{q_i} + 1\right) \\ &= \sum_{i=1}^{m} p_i \log\left(\frac{p_i}{q_i}\right) \\ &= \mathbb{E}_{\mathbb{P}}\left[\log\left(\frac{\mathbb{P}(\boldsymbol{\xi})}{\mathbb{Q}(\boldsymbol{\xi})}\right)\right]. \end{aligned}$$

KL divergence is closely related to Shannon's entropy function $H(\mathbb{P}) = -\mathbb{E}_{\mathbb{P}}[\log(\mathbb{P}(\boldsymbol{\xi}))]$ and the cross entropy function $H(\mathbb{P}, \mathbb{Q}) = -\mathbb{E}_{\mathbb{P}}[\log(\mathbb{Q}(\boldsymbol{\xi}))]$. It is easy to see that $D_{\phi_{KL}}(\mathbb{P}, \mathbb{Q}) = H(\mathbb{P}, \mathbb{Q}) - H(\mathbb{P})$. The cross entropy $H(\mathbb{P}, \mathbb{Q})$ can be viewed as a measure of distance from $\mathbb{P}$ to $\mathbb{Q}$. However, its defect is that $H(\mathbb{P}, \mathbb{P}) = H(\mathbb{P}) \neq 0$. So we subtract $H(\mathbb{P})$ from $H(\mathbb{P}, \mathbb{Q})$ to define the KL divergence. In information theory, the KL divergence $D_{\phi_{KL}}(\mathbb{P} \mid \mathbb{Q})$ is also called the relative entropy of $\mathbb{P}$ with respect to $\mathbb{Q}$.

If for some index $i \in [m] := \{1, 2, \ldots, m\}$, $q_i = 0$ but $p_i > 0$, then the KL divergence has a term $p_i \log(p_i/0) = \infty$. If both $p_i = 0$ and $q_i = 0$, then we define the term $0\log(0/0)$ to be equal to 0. So to have a finite KL divergence, we need to have $p_i = 0$ whenever $q_i = 0$ for all $i \in [m]$. When $\mathbb{P}$ and $\mathbb{Q}$ satisfy this property, we say that $\mathbb{P}$ is *absolutely continuous* with respect to $\mathbb{Q}$, also called that $\mathbb{P}$ is dominated by $\mathbb{Q}$. In this case, the ratio $p_i/q_i$ is finite for all scenarios $i$ where $q_i \neq 0$. This ratio is called the density of $\mathbb{P}$ wrt $\mathbb{Q}$. KL divergence has the following elementary properties (see Exercise 4.4):

1. $D_{\phi_{KL}}(\mathbb{P}, \mathbb{Q}) \geq 0$ for all probability distributions $\mathbb{P}, \mathbb{Q}$ on $\mathscr{U}$.
2. $D_{\phi_{KL}}(\mathbb{P}, \mathbb{Q}) = 0$ if and only if $\mathbb{P} = \mathbb{Q}$.
3. KL divergence is directional, namely in general $D_{\phi_{KL}}(\mathbb{P}, \mathbb{Q}) \neq D_{\phi_{KL}}(\mathbb{Q}, \mathbb{P})$, if $\mathbb{P} \neq \mathbb{Q}$.
4. KL divergence does not satisfy the triangle inequality $D_{\phi_{KL}}(\mathbb{P}_1, \mathbb{P}_3) \leq D_{\phi_{KL}}(\mathbb{P}_1, \mathbb{P}_2) + D_{\phi_{KL}}(\mathbb{P}_2, \mathbb{P}_3)$.

Let us compare the KL divergence to a metric. A function $d : X \times X \rightarrow \mathbb{R}_+$ on a space $X$ is called a *metric* function or a *distance* function if the following properties hold

1. Identity of indiscernibles: $d(x, y) = 0$ if and only if $x = y$.
2. Symmetry: $d(x, y) = d(y, x)$ for all $x, y \in X$.
3. Triangle inequality: $d(x, z) \leq d(x, y) + d(y, z)$ for all $x, y, z \in X$.

For example, $d(\boldsymbol{x}, \boldsymbol{y}) = \|\boldsymbol{x} - \boldsymbol{y}\|_2$ using the $\ell_2$-norm is a metric on any finite dimensional Euclidean space. But KL divergence is not a metric—it satisfies the identity of indiscernibles, but is not symmetric and does not satisfy the triangle inequality. Most of the other $\phi$-divergence functions that we will see are also not metrics. But KL divergence, like other $\phi$-divergence, does provide a measure of divergence between distributions.

#### 4.2.2.3 General Definition of $\phi$-Divergence and Examples

Now we introduce the general definition of $\phi$-divergence in the same setting of a finite probability space with probability measures $\mathbb{P}$ absolutely continuous with respect to $\mathbb{Q}$. The $\phi$-divergence $D_\phi(\mathbb{P}, \mathbb{Q})$ from $\mathbb{P}$ to $\mathbb{Q}$ is defined as

$$D_\phi(\mathbb{P}, \mathbb{Q}) = \mathbb{E}_{\mathbb{Q}}\left[\phi\left(\frac{\mathbb{P}(\boldsymbol{\xi})}{\mathbb{Q}(\boldsymbol{\xi})}\right)\right] = \sum_{i=1}^{m} q_i \cdot \phi\left(\frac{p_i}{q_i}\right), \tag{4.2.15}$$

where $\phi : \mathbb{R}_+ \rightarrow \mathbb{R}$ is a convex function such that

1. $\phi(1) = 0$,
2. $0 \cdot \phi(t/0) := \begin{cases} t \lim_{p \to +\infty} \phi(p)/p & \text{if } t > 0, \\ 0 & \text{if } t = 0. \end{cases}$

Any function $\phi$ that satisfies the above conditions induces a $\phi$-divergence. The following table lists some widely used examples of $\phi$-divergence.

**Table 4.1** Some $\phi$-divergence examples

| Divergence | $\phi(t)$ | $\phi^*(s)$ | $D_\phi(\mathbb{P},\mathbb{Q})$ |
|---|---|---|---|
| Kullback-Leibler ($\phi_{KL}$) | $t\log(t)-t+1$ | $e^s-1$ | $\sum_i p_i \log\left(\frac{p_i}{q_i}\right)$ |
| Burg Entropy ($\phi_B$) | $-\log(t)+t-1$ | $-\log(1-s),\ s<1$ | $\sum_i q_i \log\left(\frac{q_i}{p_i}\right)$ |
| Hellinger divergence ($\phi_H$) | $(\sqrt{t}-1)^2$ | $\frac{s}{1-s},\ s<1$ | $\sum_i(\sqrt{p_i}-\sqrt{q_i})^2$ |
| $\chi$-divergence of order 2 ($\phi_\chi$) | $(t-1)^2$ | $\begin{cases} s^2/4+s & s\geq -2 \\ -1 & s\leq -2 \end{cases}$ | $\sum_i \frac{(p_i-q_i)^2}{q_i}$ |
| Variation distance ($\phi_V$) | $\lvert t-1\rvert$ | $\begin{cases} \max\{s,-1\} & s\leq 1 \\ +\infty & s>1 \end{cases}$ | $\sum_i \lvert p_i-q_i\rvert$ |

In the third column of Table 4.1, $\phi^*:\mathbb{R}\to\mathbb{R}\cup\{\infty\}$ is the conjugate function of $\phi$ defined as

$$\phi^*(s)=\sup_{t\geq 0}\{st-\phi(t)\}, \tag{4.2.16}$$

which will play an important role in the reformulation of DRO with ambiguity sets built from $\phi$-divergence. In particular, $\phi^*$ has the following properties: (1) $\phi^*$ is a convex function. (2) $\phi^*$ is a nondecreasing function. 3) $\phi^*(x)\geq x$ for all $x\in\mathbb{R}$. (see Exercise 4.5.)

Among all the $\phi$-divergence in Table 4.1, only the variation distance, $\phi_V$, induces a metric on $\mathbb{P},\mathbb{Q}$, which is equivalent to the $\ell_1$-norm. Note that the Hellinger divergence $D_{\phi_H}$ is not a metric, but its square root $\sqrt{D_{\phi_H}}=\sqrt{\sum_i(\sqrt{p_i}-\sqrt{q_i})^2}$ is indeed a metric, which is easy to see using $\ell_2$-norm. This distance $\sqrt{D_{\phi_H}}$ is called the Hellinger distance. $\sqrt{D_{\phi_\chi}}$ is not a distance, as it is not symmetric.

There are some nice order relations between the Hellinger divergence, $\chi$-divergence of order 2, and the variation distance. For example, we know that

$$D_{\phi_H}(\mathbb{P},\mathbb{Q})\leq D_{\phi_V}(\mathbb{P},\mathbb{Q})\leq 2\sqrt{D_{\phi_H}(\mathbb{P},\mathbb{Q})}, \tag{4.2.17}$$

and

$$D_{\phi_H}(\mathbb{P},\mathbb{Q})\leq \sqrt{D_{\phi_{KL}}(\mathbb{P},\mathbb{Q})}\leq \sqrt{D_{\phi_\chi}(\mathbb{P},\mathbb{Q})}. \tag{4.2.18}$$

See [10, Lemma 1] for details of a proof.

#### 4.2.2.4 Equivalent Reformulation of General Form

Now we can use the $\phi$-divergence to build ambiguity sets. Let $\mathbb{Q}_0$ be an estimation of the true probability distribution of the underlying random parameters in a decision making problem. Then, we define the following ambiguity set using $\phi$-divergence

$$\mathscr{P}_\phi(\mathbb{Q}_0, d) = \left\{ \mathbb{P} \in \mathbb{R}^m_+ : \mathbb{P}(\boldsymbol{\xi} \in \mathscr{U}) = 1,\ D_\phi(\mathbb{P}, \mathbb{Q}_0) \le d \right\}. \tag{4.2.19}$$

We still assume discrete probability measures $\mathbb{P}$ on a finite support $\mathscr{U}$ with $m$ elements. Here $d$ is a positive parameter that controls the size of the ambiguity set. The choice of the $\phi$-divergence and $d$ is up to the modeler and reflects the modeler's risk aversion preference. We will discuss how to make these choices in the next subsection. Right now, let us study how to equivalently reformulate a DRO problem (4.1.3) with the above ambiguity set (4.2.19). The key step is to dualize the inner maximization problem in (4.1.3), which is given below.

$$\max_{\mathbb{P}} \quad \sum_{i=1}^m p_i f(\boldsymbol{x}, \boldsymbol{\xi}_i) \tag{4.2.20a}$$

$$\text{s.t.} \quad \sum_{i=1}^m p_i = 1, \tag{4.2.20b}$$

$$p_i \ge 0, \quad \forall i = 1, 2, \ldots, m, \tag{4.2.20c}$$

$$\sum_{i=1}^m q_i \cdot \phi\left(\frac{p_i}{q_i}\right) \le d, \tag{4.2.20d}$$

where $\mathbb{Q}_0 = (q_1, q_2, \ldots, q_m)^\top$. It is reasonable to assume $q_i > 0$ for all $i \in [m]$.

We first form the Lagrangian function of the above primal problem (4.2.20).

$$L(\mathbb{P}, \lambda, \alpha) = \lambda + d \cdot \alpha + \sum_{i=1}^m p_i \big(f(\boldsymbol{x}, \boldsymbol{\xi}_i) - \lambda\big) - \sum_{i=1}^m q_i \alpha \phi\left(\frac{p_i}{q_i}\right). \tag{4.2.21}$$

The dual problem is then given by

$$\min_{\lambda, \alpha \ge 0} \left\{ \lambda + d \cdot \alpha + \max_{\mathbb{P} \ge \mathbf{0}} \sum_{i=1}^m \left\{ p_i \big(f(\boldsymbol{x}, \boldsymbol{\xi}_i) - \lambda\big) - q_i \alpha \phi\left(\frac{p_i}{q_i}\right) \right\} \right\}. \tag{4.2.22}$$

Note that the inner maximization problem is completely separable over $p_i$. Therefore, we only need to look at the maximization problem over each $p_i$ separately. We will denote $h_i := f(\boldsymbol{x}, \boldsymbol{\xi}_i) - \lambda$, and suppress the index $i$ to save notation. So, we can write down the subproblem for each $p_i$ as

$$\max_{p \ge 0} \quad \left\{ h \cdot p - q \cdot \alpha \phi(p/q) \right\} \tag{4.2.23a}$$

$$= q \cdot \max_{\tilde{p} \ge 0} \quad \left\{ h \cdot \tilde{p} - \alpha \phi(\tilde{p}) \right\} \tag{4.2.23b}$$

$$= q \cdot (\alpha \phi)^*(h). \tag{4.2.23c}$$

In (4.2.23b), we defined a new variable $\tilde{p} = p/q$. Remember that we assume $q_i > 0$ for all $i \in [m]$. In (4.2.23c), we used the definition of conjugate function in (4.2.16). Table 4.1 has the form of $\phi^*$ for some most commonly used $\phi$-divergence. Recall that $\phi(t)$ is defined for $t \geq 0$. The relation between $\phi^*$ and $(\alpha\phi)^*$ for $\alpha \geq 0$ is the following.

If $\alpha = 0$, then

$$(0\phi)^*(s) = \sup_{t\geq 0} \{st - 0 \cdot \phi(t)\} = \begin{cases} 0 & \text{if } s \leq 0, \\ +\infty & \text{if } s > 0. \end{cases} \tag{4.2.24}$$

If $\alpha > 0$, then

$$(\alpha\phi)^*(s) = \sup_{t\geq 0} \{st - \alpha \cdot \phi(t)\} = \alpha \cdot \sup_{t\geq 0} \{(s/\alpha) \cdot t - \phi(t)\} = \alpha \cdot \phi^*(s/\alpha). \tag{4.2.25}$$

To unify the two cases (4.2.24) and (4.2.25), we define $0\phi^*(s/0) := (0\phi)^*(s)$. Now we can substitute (4.2.23c) back to (4.2.22), which leads to the dual reformulation

$$\min_{\lambda,\alpha\geq 0} \left\{ \lambda + d \cdot \alpha + \alpha \sum_{i=1}^{m} q_i \phi^* \left( \frac{f(\boldsymbol{x}, \boldsymbol{\xi}_i) - \lambda}{\alpha} \right) \right\}. \tag{4.2.26}$$

Since $\phi(\cdot)$ is a convex function, strong duality holds between the primal-dual pair (4.2.20) and (4.2.26) if the Slater condition for the primal problem is satisfied, which is always the case because we can choose $\mathbb{P} = \mathbb{Q}_0$ and every $q_i$ is assumed positive.

Incorporating the outer minimization over $\boldsymbol{x}$, we have the following equivalent reformulation of the DRO problem (4.1.3) with a $\phi$-divergence ambiguity set.

A DRO problem with the $\phi$-divergence ambiguity set $\mathscr{P}_\phi(\mathbb{Q}_0, d)$ given in (4.2.19)

$$v_1 = \min_{\boldsymbol{x}\in X} \max_{\mathbb{P}\in\mathscr{P}_\phi(\mathbb{Q}_0,d)} f(\boldsymbol{x}, \boldsymbol{\xi}) \tag{4.2.27}$$

and the following deterministic optimization problem

$$v_2 = \min_{\boldsymbol{x}\in X,\lambda,\alpha\geq 0} \left\{ \lambda + d \cdot \alpha + \alpha \sum_{i=1}^{m} q_i \phi^* \left( \frac{f(\boldsymbol{x}, \boldsymbol{\xi}_i) - \lambda}{\alpha} \right) \right\}, \tag{4.2.28}$$

are equivalent in the sense that they have the same optimal objective cost, i.e. $v_1 = v_2$, and the same optimal solution in $\boldsymbol{x}$. Furthermore, the reformulation (4.2.28) is a convex optimization problem if $f(\boldsymbol{x}, \boldsymbol{\xi})$ is a convex function in $\boldsymbol{x}$ for every $\boldsymbol{\xi}$.

As we know, the conjugate function $(\alpha\phi)^*$ is always a closed convex function for any nonnegative $\alpha$, because it is the pointwise maximum of linear functions in $(s, \alpha)$ as shown in (4.2.25). Therefore, it is easy to show that the composite function $(\alpha\phi)^*(f(\boldsymbol{x}, \boldsymbol{\xi}_i) - \lambda)$ is a convex function *jointly* in $(\boldsymbol{x}, \lambda, \alpha)$ for $\alpha \geq 0$ (see Exercise 4.6.) Therefore, (4.2.28) is a convex optimization problem in $(\boldsymbol{x}, \lambda, \alpha)$.

#### 4.2.2.5 Examples of Equivalent Reformulation

Now Let us go back to the examples of the $\phi$-divergence listed in Table 4.1. We will work out the equivalent reformulations of DROs with ambiguity set using these $\phi$-divergence. In the following, we assume that $f(\boldsymbol{x}, \boldsymbol{\xi})$ is a linear function in $\boldsymbol{x}$ for every fixed $\boldsymbol{\xi}$, i.e. $f(\boldsymbol{x}, \boldsymbol{\xi}) = \boldsymbol{c}(\boldsymbol{\xi})^\top \boldsymbol{x} + g(\boldsymbol{\xi})$, where $\boldsymbol{c}(\boldsymbol{\xi})$ is a vector function of $\boldsymbol{\xi}$ and $g(\boldsymbol{\xi})$ is a scalar function of $\boldsymbol{\xi}$.

1. **KL divergence**: The conjugate of the KL divergence is $\phi_{KL}^*(s) = e^s - 1$. Substituting to (4.2.28), the equivalent reformulation of the DRO problem (4.2.27) takes the following form

$$\min_{\boldsymbol{x} \in X, \lambda, \alpha \geq 0} \left\{ \lambda + (d-1) \cdot \alpha + \alpha \sum_{i=1}^{m} q_i \exp\left( \frac{\boldsymbol{c}(\boldsymbol{\xi}_i)^\top \boldsymbol{x} + g(\boldsymbol{\xi}_i) - \lambda}{\alpha} \right) \right\}. \tag{4.2.29}$$

   The reformulation (4.2.29) can be efficiently solved by interior point methods, when $X$ has some nice structure, e.g. $X$ is a polyhedron or a conic representable set. See the discussion in [11] on the existence of a self-concordant barrier function for a reformulation of (4.2.29).
2. **Hellinger divergence**: For the Hellinger divergence $\phi_H$, we have $\phi_H(t) = (\sqrt{t} - 1)^2$ and its conjugate $\phi_H^*(s) = s/(1-s)$ for $s < 1$ and $+\infty$ for $s \geq 1$. We will show that the DRO problem with $\phi_H$-divergence set can be reformulated as a second-order conic (SOC) program. In particular, the equivalent reformulation of DRO (4.2.27) takes the following form

$$\begin{aligned} \min_{\boldsymbol{x}, \lambda, \alpha} \quad & \left\{ \lambda + d \cdot \alpha + \alpha \sum_{i=1}^{m} q_i \frac{\boldsymbol{c}(\boldsymbol{\xi}_i)^\top \boldsymbol{x} + g(\boldsymbol{\xi}_i) - \lambda}{\alpha + \lambda - \boldsymbol{c}(\boldsymbol{\xi}_i)^\top \boldsymbol{x} - g(\boldsymbol{\xi}_i)} \right\} \\ \text{s.t.} \quad & \boldsymbol{c}(\boldsymbol{\xi}_i)^\top \boldsymbol{x} + g(\boldsymbol{\xi}_i) - \lambda \leq \alpha, \quad \forall i \in [m], \\ & \boldsymbol{x} \in X, \\ & \alpha \geq 0. \end{aligned}$$

   The rational function in the objective can be further reformulated to SOC constraints. To do this, introduce an auxiliary variable $z_i$ to replace each rational function in the objective and have the following in the constraints, for each $i \in [m]$,

$$\alpha \frac{c(\boldsymbol{\xi}_i)^\top \boldsymbol{x} + g(\boldsymbol{\xi}_i) - \lambda}{\alpha + \lambda - c(\boldsymbol{\xi}_i)^\top \boldsymbol{x} - g(\boldsymbol{\xi}_i)} \le z_i. \tag{4.2.30}$$

To save notation, let us denote $l_i := c(\boldsymbol{\xi}_i)^\top \boldsymbol{x} + g(\boldsymbol{\xi}_i) - \lambda$. Note that the denominator $\alpha - l_i \ge 0$. Multiplying the denominator on both sides of (4.2.30), we have

$$\begin{aligned}
\alpha \cdot l_i \le z_i \cdot (\alpha - l_i) &\Longleftrightarrow \alpha \cdot (\alpha - (\alpha - l_i)) \le z_i \cdot (\alpha - l_i) \\
&\Longleftrightarrow \alpha^2 \le (z_i + \alpha)(\alpha - l_i) \\
&\Longleftrightarrow \alpha^2 + \frac{1}{4}(z_i + l_i)^2 \le \frac{1}{4}(z_i + 2\alpha - l_i)^2 \\
&\Longleftrightarrow \sqrt{\alpha^2 + \frac{1}{4}(z_i + l_i)^2} \le \frac{1}{2}(z_i + 2\alpha - l_i), \quad (z_i + 2\alpha - l_i \ge 0).
\end{aligned}$$

Here we used the standard trick that $a^2 \le bc$ and $b + c \ge 0 \Longleftrightarrow \sqrt{a^2 + (b - c)^2/4} \le (b + c)/2$. (Why do we have $z_i + 2\alpha - l_i \ge 0$? See Exercise 4.7.) Finally, putting everything together, we have a convex program involving SOC constraints

$$\min_{\boldsymbol{x},\lambda,\alpha,\boldsymbol{z}} \quad \lambda + d \cdot \alpha + \alpha \sum_{i=1}^m q_i z_i \tag{4.2.31a}$$

$$\text{s.t.} \quad \sqrt{\alpha^2 + \frac{1}{4}(z_i + c(\boldsymbol{\xi}_i)^\top \boldsymbol{x} + g(\boldsymbol{\xi}_i) - \lambda)^2} \le \frac{1}{2}\big(z_i + 2\alpha - c(\boldsymbol{\xi}_i)^\top \boldsymbol{x} - g(\boldsymbol{\xi}_i) + \lambda\big), \quad \forall i \in [m], \tag{4.2.31b}$$

$$c(\boldsymbol{\xi}_i)^\top \boldsymbol{x} + g(\boldsymbol{\xi}_i) - \lambda \le \alpha, \quad \forall i \in [m], \tag{4.2.31c}$$

$$\boldsymbol{x} \in X, \tag{4.2.31d}$$

$$\alpha \ge 0. \tag{4.2.31e}$$

3. **Variation distance**: The variation distance $\phi_V(t) = |t - 1|$ and its conjugate takes the form $\phi_V^*(s) = \max\{s, -1\}$ for $s \le 1$. The equivalent reformulation of DRO with variation distance based ambiguity set turns out to be a *linear program* (assuming $X$ is a polyhedron).

$$\begin{aligned}
&\min_{x \in X, \lambda, \alpha \ge 0} \left\{ \lambda + d \cdot \alpha + \alpha \sum_{i=1}^m q_i \max\left\{ \frac{c(\boldsymbol{\xi}_i)^\top \boldsymbol{x} + g(\boldsymbol{\xi}_i) - \lambda}{\alpha}, -1 \right\} \right\} \\
\Longleftrightarrow \quad &\min_{x \in X, \lambda, \alpha \ge 0} \left\{ \lambda + d \cdot \alpha + \sum_{i=1}^m q_i \max\left\{ c(\boldsymbol{\xi}_i)^\top \boldsymbol{x} + g(\boldsymbol{\xi}_i) - \lambda, -\alpha \right\} \right\}
\end{aligned}$$

$$
\begin{aligned}
\Longleftrightarrow \min_{x,z,\lambda,\alpha} \quad & \lambda + d \cdot \alpha + \sum_{i=1}^{m} q_i z_i \\
\text{s.t.} \quad & z_i - c(\xi_i)^\top x - g(\xi_i) + \lambda \geq 0, \quad \forall i \in [m], \\
& z_i + \alpha \geq 0, \quad \forall i \in [m], \\
& \alpha \geq 0, \\
& x \in X.
\end{aligned}
$$

Note that if the DRO's objective function $f(x, \xi)$ is a nonlinear convex function in $x$, the above reformulation is still convex. This nice property does not hold for the equivalent reformulations of DRO with KL divergence and Hellinger divergence based ambiguity sets.

### *4.2.3 Wasserstein-Distance Based Ambiguity Sets and Reforulations*

In this section, we introduce another important class of ambiguity sets, which are built from a class of metrics on probability measures. By contrast, $\phi$-divergence is usually not a metric as we discussed in the previous section. We will study equivalent reformulations of DRO problems with the new ambiguity sets. The origin of the ideas for this new class of metrics on probability measures goes back more than two hundred years to 1781, when French mathematician Gaspard Monge published a classic paper on the problem of optimal transportation. See [12] for some history. We will start from discussing this problem.

#### 4.2.3.1 The Optimal Transportation Problem and Wasserstein Distance

Suppose there are $m$ suppliers and $n$ customers of a good. Supplier $i$ has $p_i$ units of the good to supply, and consumer $j$ has $q_j$ units of demand of the good. It costs $c_{ij}$ to transport one unit of the good from supplier $i$ to consumer $j$ for each pair of $i \in [m] = \{1, \ldots, m\}$, $j \in [n] = \{1, \ldots, n\}$. We want to find a transportation schedule to send all the supply from the suppliers to meet all the demand from the customers with a minimum transportation cost. This problem is called an *optimal transportation problem*. Let $\pi_{ij}$ be the amount of goods sent from supplier $i$ to consumer $j$. Then, the optimal transportation problem can be formulated as the following linear program.

$$d^P(\boldsymbol{p},\boldsymbol{q}) = \min_{\boldsymbol{\pi}} \quad \sum_{i=1}^{m}\sum_{j=1}^{n} c_{ij}\pi_{ij} \tag{4.2.32a}$$

$$\text{s.t.} \quad \sum_{j=1}^{n} \pi_{ij} = p_i, \quad i \in [m], \quad \text{[all supply at } i \text{ needs to be shipped]} \tag{4.2.32b}$$

$$\sum_{i=1}^{m} \pi_{ij} = q_j, \quad j \in [n], \quad \text{[all demand at } j \text{ need to be met]} \tag{4.2.32c}$$

$$\pi_{ij} \geq 0, \quad i \in [m], \ j \in [n]. \tag{4.2.32d}$$

The dual problem is also easy to construct.

$$d^D(\boldsymbol{p},\boldsymbol{q}) = \max_{\boldsymbol{u},\boldsymbol{v}} \quad \sum_{i=1}^{m} p_i u_i + \sum_{j=1}^{n} q_j v_j \tag{4.2.33a}$$

$$\text{s.t.} \quad u_i + v_j \leq c_{ij}, \quad \forall i \in [m], \ j \in [n]. \tag{4.2.33b}$$

Strong duality holds $d^P(\boldsymbol{p},\boldsymbol{q}) = d^D(\boldsymbol{p},\boldsymbol{q})$ if either the primal problem (4.2.32) and the dual problem (4.2.33) has a finite optimum.

Now suppose the supply $\boldsymbol{p}$ and the demand $\boldsymbol{q}$ in the optimal transportation problem are probability measures. More specifically, on a sample space $\Omega$ in $\mathbb{R}^l$, the supply $\boldsymbol{p} = (p_1, p_2, \ldots, p_m)^\top$ is a probability mass function over $m$ support points $\{\boldsymbol{\xi}_1, \ldots, \boldsymbol{\xi}_m\}$ in $\Omega$, and similarly the target $\boldsymbol{q} = (q_1, q_2, \ldots, q_n)^\top$ is another probability mass function over $n$ support points $\{\boldsymbol{\zeta}_1, \ldots, \boldsymbol{\zeta}_n\}$ in $\Omega$. From constraints (4.2.32b) and (4.2.32c), we can see that $\sum_{i\in[m]}\sum_{j\in[n]}\pi_{ij} = 1$. And $\pi_{ij} \geq 0$ by (4.2.32d). Therefore, $\boldsymbol{\pi}$ is a joint probability distribution on the product $\{\boldsymbol{\xi}_1, \ldots, \boldsymbol{\xi}_m\} \times \{\boldsymbol{\zeta}_1, \ldots, \boldsymbol{\zeta}_n\}$. Then, constraints (4.2.32b) and (4.2.32c) can be interpreted as saying that the marginal distributions of $\boldsymbol{\pi}$ are $\boldsymbol{p}$ and $\boldsymbol{q}$. The unit transportation cost $c_{ij}$ from $i$ to $j$ usually depends on how far away the two locations $i$ and $j$ are. This can be characterized by some distance between the two vectors $\boldsymbol{\xi}_i$ and $\boldsymbol{\zeta}_j$ in $\mathbb{R}^l$, e.g. we can define $c_{ij} = \|\boldsymbol{\xi}_i - \boldsymbol{\zeta}_j\|^p$, where $\|\cdot\|$ is any norm on $\mathbb{R}^l$ and $p \in [1, +\infty)$. Finally, the primal optimal transportation problem (4.2.32) can be viewed as finding a joint probability distribution $\boldsymbol{\pi}$, whose marginal distributions are $\boldsymbol{p}$ and $\boldsymbol{q}$, such that the probability measure $\boldsymbol{p}$ supported on $\{\boldsymbol{\xi}_1, \ldots, \boldsymbol{\xi}_m\}$ can be transported via $\boldsymbol{\pi}$ to the probability measure $\boldsymbol{q}$ supported on $\{\boldsymbol{\zeta}_1, \ldots, \boldsymbol{\zeta}_n\}$ in the most cost effective way. The $1/p$-th power of the optimal cost $(d^P(\boldsymbol{p},\boldsymbol{q}))^{1/p}$ with $c_{ij} = \|\boldsymbol{\xi}_i - \boldsymbol{\zeta}_j\|^p$ is called the *Wasserstein distance* of order $p$ between $\boldsymbol{p}$ and $\boldsymbol{q}$.

The Wasserstein distance can be defined for general probability measures $\mathbb{P}$ and $\mathbb{Q}$ in $\mathscr{P}(\mathscr{U})$, not necessarily discrete distributions on a finite support, where $\mathscr{U}$ is a closed subset of $\mathbb{R}^l$. In particular, we define the $p$-th order Wasserstein distance between $\mathbb{P}$ and $\mathbb{Q}$ as

$$(W_p(\mathbb{P}, \mathbb{Q}))^p = \inf_{\pi \in \mathscr{P}(\mathscr{U} \times \mathscr{U})} \int_{\mathscr{U} \times \mathscr{U}} \|\xi - \zeta\|^p d\pi(\xi, \zeta) \tag{4.2.34a}$$

$$\text{s.t.} \int_{\{\xi\} \times \mathscr{U}} d\pi(\xi, \zeta) = \mathbb{P}(\xi), \quad \forall \xi \in \mathscr{U}, \tag{4.2.34b}$$

$$\int_{\mathscr{U} \times \{\zeta\}} d\pi(\xi, \zeta) = \mathbb{Q}(\zeta), \quad \forall \zeta \in \mathscr{U}. \tag{4.2.34c}$$

Using Kantorovich's duality theory, the above Wasserstein distance has a dual representation as

$$(W_p(\mathbb{P}, \mathbb{Q}))^p = \sup_{u \in L^1(\mathbb{P}), v \in L^1(\mathbb{Q})} \int_{\mathscr{U}} u(\xi) d\mathbb{P}(\xi) + \int_{\mathscr{U}} v(\zeta) d\mathbb{Q}(\zeta) \tag{4.2.35a}$$

$$\text{s.t. } u(\xi) + v(\zeta) \leq \|\xi - \zeta\|^p, \quad \forall \xi, \zeta \in \mathscr{U}, \tag{4.2.35b}$$

where $L^1(\mathbb{P})$ is the $L^1$ space of $\mathbb{P}$-measurable functions. We can recognize that this pair of primal and dual problems (4.2.34)–(4.2.35) is the extension of the primal-dual pair (4.2.32)–(4.2.33) from finite dimensional space to infinite dimension spaces of functions and probability measures. It can be verified that $W_p(\mathbb{P}, \mathbb{Q})$ is indeed a distance function (i.e. a metric) in the space of probability measures, i.e. it satisfies the three conditions, identity of indiscernibles, symmetry, and the triangle inequality, of a distance function (see Sect. 4.2.2.2.)

#### 4.2.3.2 Comparison of Wasserstein Distance and $\phi$-Divergence

Let us do a comparison of Wasserstein distance and $\phi$-divergence. In particular, we will show that $\phi$-divergence has two kinds of undesirable behaviors that Wasserstein distance does not have. In short, the advantage of the Wasserstein distance comes from the fact that it is a true distance function, i.e. a metric, on probability measures, whereas $\phi$-divergence is not.

1. In a $\phi$-divergence ambiguity set $\mathscr{P}_\phi(\mathbb{Q}_0, d)$, if the nominal distribution $\mathbb{Q}_0$ is a discrete measure with a finite support, then any probability measure $\mathbb{P}$ in the ambiguity set $\mathscr{P}_\phi(\mathbb{Q}_0, d)$ satisfies

$$\sum_{i=1}^{m} q_i \cdot \phi(p_i/q_i) \leq d. \tag{4.2.36}$$

If some $q_i = 0$, then $p_i$ must be zero, otherwise $0 \cdot \phi(p_i/0)$ may be infinity for $p_i > 0$. For example, except the variation distance $\phi_V$, all other $\phi$-divergence in Table 4.1 has $0 \cdot \phi(t/0) = \infty$ for $t > 0$. So, all the distributions in such a $\phi$-divergence ambiguity set must be *absolutely continuous* with respect to $\mathbb{Q}_0$, e.g. no continuous distribution can be contained in such a ambiguity set, and no discrete distribution with positive probability at a point that is not in the support of $\mathbb{Q}_0$ can be obtained either. Such an ambiguity set is quite restrictive. In comparison, the Wasserstein-distance based ambiguity set does not have this issue. Even when $\mathbb{Q}_0$ is a discrete distribution, the Wasserstein ball can still contain continuous distributions.

2. Since $\phi$-divergence is in general not a distance function, e.g. only the variation distance in Table 4.1 is a true distance, the $\phi$-divergence ambiguity set may have some counter-intuitive behavior. See [13, Example 1] for an illuminating example and discussion.

#### 4.2.3.3 Equivalent Reformulations of DRO with Wasserstein-Distance Ambiguity Sets

We can now use Wasserstein distance to define an ambiguity set around a nominal distribution.

$$\mathscr{P}_W(\mathbb{Q}_0, d) := \{\mathbb{P} \in \mathscr{P}_0(\mathscr{U}) : W_p(\mathbb{P}, \mathbb{Q}_0) \le d\}, \tag{4.2.37}$$

where $\mathbb{Q}_0$ is the nominal distribution, e.g. an empirical distribution. Consider the following DRO problem.

$$\min_{\boldsymbol{x} \in X} \max_{\mathbb{P} \in \mathscr{P}_W(\mathbb{Q}_0, d)} \mathbb{E}_{\mathbb{P}}[f(\boldsymbol{x}, \boldsymbol{\xi})]. \tag{4.2.38}$$

The task is to find an equivalent reformulation of the inner maximization problem using convex optimization duality theory. Let us first study the simplest case, where both $\mathbb{P}$ and $\mathbb{Q}_0$ are restricted to be discrete distributions on finite supports, i.e. $\mathbb{P} = \sum_{i=1}^m p_i \delta_{\boldsymbol{\xi}_i}$ and $\mathbb{Q}_0 = \sum_{j=}^n q_j \delta_{\boldsymbol{\zeta}_j}$, where $\delta_{\boldsymbol{x}}$ is the Dirac measure that is 1 at $\boldsymbol{x}$ and 0 elsewhere. In this case, the Wasserstein distance is given by the linear programs (4.2.32)–(4.2.33). The reformulation of the inner maximization of the DRP problem (4.2.38) is given below.

$$\max_{\mathbb{P} \in \mathscr{P}(\mathscr{U})} \sum_{i=1}^m p_i f(\boldsymbol{x}, \boldsymbol{\xi}_i) \tag{4.2.39a}$$

$$\text{s.t. } W_p(\mathbb{P}, \mathbb{Q}_0) \le d, \tag{4.2.39b}$$

$$\Longleftrightarrow \max_{\mathbb{P} \in \mathscr{P}(\mathscr{U})} \sum_{i=1}^m p_i f(\boldsymbol{x}, \boldsymbol{\xi}_i) \tag{4.2.39c}$$

$$\text{s.t.} \quad \min_{\boldsymbol{\pi}} \left\{ \sum_{i=1}^{m} \sum_{j=1}^{n} \|\boldsymbol{\xi}_i - \boldsymbol{\zeta}_j\|^p \cdot \pi_{ij} : \text{(4.2.32b)–(4.2.32d)} \right\} \leq d^p, \tag{4.2.39d}$$

$$\iff \max_{\mathbb{P},\boldsymbol{\pi}} \quad \sum_{i=1}^{m} p_i f(\boldsymbol{x}, \boldsymbol{\xi}_i) \tag{4.2.39e}$$

$$\text{s.t.} \quad \sum_{i=1}^{m} \sum_{j=1}^{n} \|\boldsymbol{\xi}_i - \boldsymbol{\zeta}_j\|^p \cdot \pi_{ij} \leq d^p, \tag{4.2.39f}$$

$$\sum_{j=1}^{n} \pi_{ij} - p_i = 0, \quad \forall i \in [m], \tag{4.2.39g}$$

$$\sum_{i=1}^{m} \pi_{ij} = q_j, \quad \forall j \in [n], \tag{4.2.39h}$$

$$\sum_{i=1}^{m} p_i = 1, \tag{4.2.39i}$$

$$p_i \geq 0, \quad \forall i \in [m], \tag{4.2.39j}$$

$$\pi_{ij} \geq 0, \quad \forall i \in [m], \; j \in [n], \tag{4.2.39k}$$

$$\iff \min_{\alpha,\lambda,\boldsymbol{u},\boldsymbol{v}} \quad \lambda + d^p \cdot \alpha + \sum_{j=1}^{n} q_j v_j \tag{4.2.39l}$$

$$\text{s.t.} \quad \lambda - u_i \geq f(\boldsymbol{x}, \boldsymbol{\xi}_i), \quad \forall i \in [m], \tag{4.2.39m}$$

$$\|\boldsymbol{\xi}_i - \boldsymbol{\zeta}_j\|^p \cdot \alpha + u_i + v_j \geq 0, \quad \forall i \in [m], \; j \in [n], \tag{4.2.39n}$$

$$\alpha \geq 0. \tag{4.2.39o}$$

Note that we removed the minimization operator in (4.2.39d) using the elementary trick for reformulating robust constraints introduced in Chap. 2. The resulting problem (4.2.39l)–(4.2.39o) is a linear program in $(\alpha, \lambda, \boldsymbol{u}, \boldsymbol{v})$. Since all the programs in the derivation process are linear, strong duality holds throughout as long as the primal problem (4.2.39a)–(4.2.39b) is feasible.

There is another equivalent way to reformulating (4.2.39a)–(4.2.39b) that is easier to generalize to the infinite dimensional case of continuous probability distributions. We derive this reformulation below. Again, we assume strong duality holds for all the linear programs involved.

$$\max_{\mathbb{P}\in\mathscr{P}(\mathscr{U})} \sum_{i=1}^{m} p_i f(\boldsymbol{x}, \boldsymbol{\xi}_i)$$

$$\text{s.t. } W_p(\mathbb{P}, \mathbb{Q}_0) \le d,$$

$$= \min_{\alpha\ge 0} \max_{\mathbb{P}\in\mathscr{P}(\mathscr{U})} \left\{ \sum_{i=1}^{m} p_i f(\boldsymbol{x}, \boldsymbol{\xi}_i) + d^p \cdot \alpha - \alpha \cdot W_p^p(\mathbb{P}, \mathbb{Q}_0) \right\}, \tag{4.2.40a}$$

$$= \min_{\alpha\ge 0} \left\{ d^p \cdot \alpha - \min_{\mathbb{P}\in\mathscr{P}(\mathscr{U})} \left\{ \alpha W_p^p(\mathbb{P}, \mathbb{Q}_0) - \sum_{i=1}^{m} p_i f(\boldsymbol{x}, \boldsymbol{\xi}_i) \right\} \right\},$$

$$= \min_{\alpha\ge 0} \left\{ d^p \cdot \alpha - \min_{\substack{\mathbb{P}\in\mathscr{P}(\mathscr{U}) \\ \boldsymbol{\pi}:(4.2.32\text{b})\text{–}(4.2.32\text{d})}} \left\{ \sum_{i=1}^{m}\sum_{j=1}^{n} \alpha \|\boldsymbol{\xi}_i - \boldsymbol{\zeta}_j\|^p \pi_{ij} - \sum_{i=1}^{m} p_i f(\boldsymbol{x}, \boldsymbol{\xi}_i) \right\} \right\},$$

$$= \min_{\alpha\ge 0} \left\{ d^p \cdot \alpha - \min_{\boldsymbol{\pi}:(4.2.32\text{c})\text{–}(4.2.32\text{d})} \sum_{i=1}^{m}\sum_{j=1}^{n} \left( \alpha \|\boldsymbol{\xi}_i - \boldsymbol{\zeta}_j\|^p - f(\boldsymbol{x}, \boldsymbol{\xi}_i) \right) \pi_{ij} \right\}. \tag{4.2.40b}$$

In (4.2.40a), we directly relaxed the Wasserstein distance constraint and formed the Lagrangian dual. In the last step (4.2.40b), we eliminated the $\mathbb{P}$ variable using constraint $\sum_j \pi_{ij} = p_i$ for all $i \in [m]$. We now derive a closed form for the inner minimization problem in (4.2.40b).

$$\min_{\boldsymbol{\pi}} \sum_{i=1}^{m}\sum_{j=1}^{n} \left( \alpha \|\boldsymbol{\xi}_i - \boldsymbol{\zeta}_j\|^p - f(\boldsymbol{x}, \boldsymbol{\xi}_i) \right) \pi_{ij}$$

$$\text{s.t. } \sum_{i=1}^{m} p_{ij} = q_j, \quad \forall j \in [n],$$

$$\boldsymbol{\pi} \ge \mathbf{0},$$

$$= \max_{\boldsymbol{v}} \min_{\boldsymbol{\pi}\ge \mathbf{0}} \sum_{i=1}^{m}\sum_{j=1}^{n} \left( \alpha \|\boldsymbol{\xi}_i - \boldsymbol{\zeta}_j\|^p - f(\boldsymbol{x}, \boldsymbol{\xi}_i) \right) \pi_{ij} + \sum_{j=1}^{n} \left( q_j - \sum_{i=1}^{m} \pi_{ij} \right) v_j, \tag{4.2.41a}$$

$$= \max_{\boldsymbol{v}} \left\{ \boldsymbol{q}^\top \boldsymbol{v} + \min_{\boldsymbol{\pi}\ge \mathbf{0}} \sum_{i=1}^{m}\sum_{j=1}^{n} \left( \alpha \|\boldsymbol{\xi}_i - \boldsymbol{\zeta}_j\|^p - f(\boldsymbol{x}, \boldsymbol{\xi}_i) - v_j \right) \pi_{ij} \right\}, \tag{4.2.41b}$$

$$= \max_{\boldsymbol{v}} \ \boldsymbol{q}^\top \boldsymbol{v} \tag{4.2.41c}$$

$$\text{s.t. } \alpha \|\boldsymbol{\xi}_i - \boldsymbol{\zeta}_j\|^p - f(\boldsymbol{x}, \boldsymbol{\xi}_i) - v_j \ge 0, \quad \forall i \in [m], \ j \in [n], \tag{4.2.41d}$$

$$= \max_{\boldsymbol{v}} \ \boldsymbol{q}^\top \boldsymbol{v} \tag{4.2.41e}$$

$$\text{s.t. } v_j \leq \min_{i\in[m]} \left\{\alpha\|\boldsymbol{\xi}_i - \boldsymbol{\zeta}_j\|^p - f(\boldsymbol{x}, \boldsymbol{\xi}_i)\right\}, \tag{4.2.41f}$$

$$= \sum_{j=1}^{n} q_j \min_{i\in[m]} \left\{\alpha\|\boldsymbol{\xi}_i - \boldsymbol{\zeta}_j\|^p - f(\boldsymbol{x}, \boldsymbol{\xi}_i)\right\}. \tag{4.2.41g}$$

Replacing (4.2.40b) by its equivalent reformulation (4.2.41g), we come to the following reformulation.

The inner maximization problem of (4.2.39a)–(4.2.39b) has the following dual reformulation:

$$\max_{\mathbb{P}\in\mathscr{P}(\mathscr{U})} \left\{\sum_{i=1}^{m} p_i f(\boldsymbol{x}, \boldsymbol{\xi}_i) \ : \ W_p(\mathbb{P}, \mathbb{Q}_0) \leq d\right\}$$

$$= \min_{\alpha\geq 0} \left\{d^p \cdot \alpha - \sum_{j=1}^{n} q_j \min_{i\in[m]} \left\{\alpha\|\boldsymbol{\xi}_i - \boldsymbol{\zeta}_j\|^p - f(\boldsymbol{x}, \boldsymbol{\xi}_i)\right\}\right\}. \tag{4.2.42a}$$

Therefore, when $\mathbb{P}$ and $\mathbb{Q}_0$ are discrete distributions, the DRO problem (4.2.38) has the following equivalent reformulation

$$\min_{\boldsymbol{x}\in X, \alpha\geq 0} \left\{d^p \cdot \alpha - \sum_{j=1}^{n} q_j \min_{i\in[m]} \left\{\alpha\|\boldsymbol{\xi}_i - \boldsymbol{\zeta}_j\|^p - f(\boldsymbol{x}, \boldsymbol{\xi}_i)\right\}\right\}. \tag{4.2.42b}$$

A very important generalization is when $\mathbb{Q}_0$ is finite, but $\mathbb{P}$ is not restricted to be finite. For example, $\mathbb{Q}_0$ may be an empirical distribution obtained from sampling the unknown continuous distribution $\mathbb{Q}$. Then, $\mathbb{Q}_0$ is naturally a discrete distribution, but it is desirable to include continuous distributions in the ambiguity set. The above derivation can be extended to this more general setting. We have the following reformulation.

Given a discrete distribution $\mathbb{Q}_0 = \sum_{j=1}^{n} q_j \delta_{\boldsymbol{\zeta}_j}$, for any $d > 0$ and $p \in [1, +\infty)$, the inner maximization problem in the DRO model (4.2.38) with the Wasserstein ambiguity set of $p$-th order

$$\sup_{\mathbb{P}\in\mathscr{P}(\mathscr{U})} \left\{\int_{\mathscr{U}} f(\boldsymbol{x}, \boldsymbol{\xi}) d\mathbb{P}(\boldsymbol{\xi}) \ : \ W_p(\mathbb{P}, \mathbb{Q}_0) \leq d\right\} \tag{4.2.43a}$$

(continued)

has the following strong dual reformulation

$$\inf_{\alpha \geq 0} \left\{ d^p \cdot \alpha - \sum_{j=1}^{n} q_j \inf_{\xi \in \mathscr{U}} \{\alpha \|\xi - \zeta_j\|^p - f(x, \xi)\} \right\}. \tag{4.2.43b}$$

Therefore, the overall DRO problem in this case has the equivalent reformulation

$$\inf_{x \in X, \alpha \geq 0} \left\{ d^p \cdot \alpha - \sum_{j=1}^{n} q_j \inf_{\xi \in \mathscr{U}} \{\alpha \|\xi - \zeta_j\|^p - f(x, \xi)\} \right\}. \tag{4.2.43c}$$

An even more general case is when $\mathbb{P}$ and $\mathbb{Q}_0$ are both continuous distributions. The space of the support of $\mathbb{P}$ and $\mathbb{Q}_0$ could also be generalized from a finite dimensional Euclidean space $\mathbb{R}^l$ to a very general type of topological space, called the Polish space, which is roughly speaking a nice metric space (or precisely, a completely metrizable topological space.) The norm used in the definition of Wasserstein distance is then replaced by a metric of the Polish space. The derivation of the dual is much more involved, however, the form of the dual is exactly the same as the above two special cases. We will just write down the dual reformulation for the general problem without proof. Interested readers can find more details in [13, 14].

Given $\mathbb{Q}_0 \in \mathscr{P}(\mathscr{U})$, $\mathscr{U} \subseteq \mathbb{R}^l$, and $f \in L^1(\mathbb{Q}_0)$, for any $d > 0$ and $p \in [1, +\infty)$, the inner maximization problem of DRO with the Wasserstein ambiguity set of $p$-th order

$$\sup_{\mathbb{P} \in \mathscr{P}(\mathscr{U})} \left\{ \int_{\mathscr{U}} f(x, \xi) d\mathbb{P}(\xi) \ : \ W_p(\mathbb{P}, \mathbb{Q}_0) \leq d \right\} \tag{4.2.44a}$$

has a strong dual

$$\inf_{\alpha \geq 0} \left\{ d^p \cdot \alpha - \int_{\mathscr{U}} \inf_{\xi \in \mathscr{U}} \{\alpha \|\xi - \zeta\|^p - f(x, \xi)\} d\mathbb{Q}_0(\zeta) \right\}. \tag{4.2.44b}$$

In this general setting, the DRO problem (4.2.38) has the following equivalent reformulation

(continued)

$$\inf_{x \in X, \alpha \geq 0} \left\{ d^p \cdot \alpha - \int_{\mathcal{U}} \inf_{\xi \in \mathcal{U}} \left\{ \alpha \|\xi - \zeta\|^p - f(x, \xi) \right\} d\mathbb{Q}_0(\zeta) \right\}. \tag{4.2.44c}$$

The three strong dual problems (4.2.42a), (4.2.43b), and (4.2.44b) can be written in the following common form

$$\min_{\alpha \geq 0} \Bigg\{ d^p \cdot \alpha + \underbrace{\mathbb{E}_{\mathbb{Q}_0}\left[ \max_{\xi \in \mathcal{U}} \left\{ f(x, \xi) - \alpha \|\xi - \zeta\|^p \right\} \right]}_{=: h(\alpha)} \Bigg\} = \min_{\alpha \geq 0} \left\{ d^p \cdot \alpha + h(\alpha) \right\}. \tag{4.2.45}$$

We can see that (4.2.45) is a one-dimensional optimization problem over the scalar variable $\alpha$. This is a remarkable fact, considering that the primal problem (4.2.44a) in the most general case involves an infinite dimensional space of probability measures. Furthermore, we can see that the function $h(\alpha)$ is a convex, nonincreasing function of $\alpha$. Moreover, since the sum $d^p \cdot \alpha + h(\alpha) \geq d^p \cdot \alpha + \mathbb{E}_{\mathbb{Q}_0}[f(x, \zeta)]$ by choosing $\xi = \zeta$ in the inner supremum, the sum $d^p \cdot \alpha + h(\alpha) \to +\infty$ as $\alpha \to +\infty$. So the infimum of (4.2.45) would occur at a finite $\alpha^*$, when $h(\alpha)$ is a proper convex function.

#### 4.2.3.4 Further Reformulation to Finite Convex Program

The next natural question is how to deal with the equivalent reformulations we have found in the previous subsection. In their current form, (4.2.43b) and (4.2.44b) both involve quite complicated nested optimization problems. We want to further reformulate them to a form that could be directly solved by an existing solver or is ready for numerical computation. We will focus on the case where $\mathbb{Q}_0$ is a discrete measure with a finite support. This is an important case, because in practice $\mathbb{Q}_0$ is usually an empirical distribution estimated from data. We also assume the order of the Wasserstein distance is one, i.e. $p = 1$. The case of $p > 1$ is in general more difficult. See some discussion in the end of Sect. 4.3.1.3. The case of $\mathbb{Q}_0$ being a general probability measure is more challenging to reformulate exactly. Notice that the inner minimization problem in (4.2.44b) involves an integration, which could be very challenging to evaluate when $\mathbb{Q}_0$ is a continuous probability measure in high dimension. In the next subsection, we will introduce a classic robust optimization that approximates the DRO models in this general case.

We always assume the support $\mathcal{U}$ is a compact convex set in $\mathbb{R}^l$ and moreover assume

$$f(\boldsymbol{x}, \boldsymbol{\xi}) = \max_{1 \le k \le K} f_k(\boldsymbol{x}, \boldsymbol{\xi}), \tag{4.2.46}$$

where $f_k(\boldsymbol{x}, \boldsymbol{\xi})$ is convex in $\boldsymbol{x}$ and concave in $\boldsymbol{\xi}$ and $K < \infty$. This is a critical assumption for the further reformulation of (4.2.43b). An important example of this setup is the two-stage distributionally robust linear program, where $f_k(\boldsymbol{x}, \boldsymbol{\xi})$ is a linear function in $\boldsymbol{x}, \boldsymbol{\xi}$. We will discuss two-stage DRO problems in details in Sect. 4.3.

Now we can start reformulating the inner maximization problem in (4.2.43b). We will use the concepts of dual norm, which we introduced in Chap. 2, conjugate function, and support function. To make the notation more clear, we will write $f(\boldsymbol{x}, \boldsymbol{\xi})$ as $f(\boldsymbol{\xi})$ and $f_k(\boldsymbol{x}, \boldsymbol{\xi})$ as $f_k(\boldsymbol{\xi})$. For each $j \in [n]$,

$$
\begin{aligned}
&\max_{\boldsymbol{\xi} \in \mathcal{U}} \left\{ f(\boldsymbol{\xi}) - \alpha \|\boldsymbol{\xi} - \boldsymbol{\zeta}_j\| \right\} \\
&= \max_{\boldsymbol{\xi} \in \mathcal{U}} \left\{ \max_{1 \le k \le K} f_k(\boldsymbol{\xi}) - \alpha \|\boldsymbol{\xi} - \boldsymbol{\zeta}_j\| \right\}, \\
&= \max_{1 \le k \le K} \left\{ \max_{\boldsymbol{\xi} \in \mathcal{U}} \left\{ f_k(\boldsymbol{\xi}) - \alpha \|\boldsymbol{\xi} - \boldsymbol{\zeta}_j\| \right\} \right\}, \\
&= \max_{1 \le k \le K} \left\{ \max_{\boldsymbol{\xi} \in \mathcal{U}} \left\{ f_k(\boldsymbol{\xi}) - \max_{\|\boldsymbol{w}\|_* \le \alpha} \boldsymbol{w}^\top (\boldsymbol{\xi} - \boldsymbol{\zeta}_j) \right\} \right\}, && \text{(4.2.47a)} \\
&= \max_{1 \le k \le K} \left\{ \max_{\boldsymbol{\xi} \in \mathcal{U}} \min_{\|\boldsymbol{w}\|_* \le \alpha} \left\{ f_k(\boldsymbol{\xi}) - \boldsymbol{w}^\top (\boldsymbol{\xi} - \boldsymbol{\zeta}_j) \right\} \right\}, \\
&= \max_{1 \le k \le K} \left\{ \min_{\|\boldsymbol{w}\|_* \le \alpha} \max_{\boldsymbol{\xi} \in \mathcal{U}} \left\{ f_k(\boldsymbol{\xi}) - \boldsymbol{w}^\top (\boldsymbol{\xi} - \boldsymbol{\zeta}_j) \right\} \right\}, && \text{(4.2.47b)} \\
&= \max_{1 \le k \le K} \left\{ \min_{\|\boldsymbol{w}\|_* \le \alpha} \max_{\boldsymbol{\xi} \in \mathbb{R}^l} \left\{ f_k(\boldsymbol{\xi}) - \boldsymbol{w}^\top (\boldsymbol{\xi} - \boldsymbol{\zeta}_j) - {}_{\mathcal{U}}(\boldsymbol{\xi}) \right\} \right\}, && \text{(4.2.47c)} \\
&= \max_{1 \le k \le K} \left\{ \min_{\|\boldsymbol{w}\|_* \le \alpha} \left\{ [-f_k + {}_{\mathcal{U}}]^*(\boldsymbol{w}) + \boldsymbol{w}^\top \boldsymbol{\zeta}_j \right\} \right\}, && \text{(4.2.47d)} \\
&= \max_{1 \le k \le K} \left\{ \min_{\|\boldsymbol{w}\|_* \le \alpha, \boldsymbol{v}} \left\{ [-f_k]^*(\boldsymbol{w} - \boldsymbol{v}) + \sigma_{\mathcal{U}}(\boldsymbol{v}) + \boldsymbol{w}^\top \boldsymbol{\zeta}_j \right\} \right\}. && \text{(4.2.47e)}
\end{aligned}
$$

In (4.2.47a), we use dual norm $\|\cdot\|_*$. In (4.2.47b), we use the standard min–max duality to swap the min and max, since the objective function is concave in $\boldsymbol{\xi}$ and convex in $\boldsymbol{w}$, and the feasible regions are convex compact. In (4.2.47c), we introduce the indicator function of the convex set $\mathcal{U}$, ${}_{\mathcal{U}}(\boldsymbol{\xi}) = 0$ if $\boldsymbol{\xi} \in \mathcal{U}$, $+\infty$ otherwise. Finally, in (4.2.47d), $[-f_k + {}_{\mathcal{U}}]^*$ is the conjugate function of $-f_k(\boldsymbol{x}, \boldsymbol{\xi}) + {}_{\mathcal{U}}(\boldsymbol{\xi})$ with respect to $\boldsymbol{\xi}$. Keep in mind that $[-f_k + {}_{\mathcal{U}}]^*(\boldsymbol{x}, \boldsymbol{w})$ is also a function of $\boldsymbol{x}$. The conjugate functions have closed form for many important cases. In the last equality (4.2.47e), we used the following fact

$$[-f_k + \mathscr{U}]^*(\boldsymbol{w}_{jk}) = \inf_{\boldsymbol{v}_{jk}} \big((-f_k)^*(\boldsymbol{w}_{jk} - \boldsymbol{v}_{jk}) + (\mathscr{U})^*(\boldsymbol{v}_{jk})\big)$$

and $(\mathscr{U})^*(\boldsymbol{v}_{jk}) = \max_{\boldsymbol{s}}\{\boldsymbol{v}_{jk}^\top \boldsymbol{s} - \mathscr{U}(\boldsymbol{s})\} = \max_{\boldsymbol{s}\in\mathscr{U}} \boldsymbol{v}_{jk}^\top \boldsymbol{s} =: \sigma_{\mathscr{U}}(\boldsymbol{v}_{jk})$, which is called the *support function* of $\mathscr{U}$ in convex analysis. Many convex sets have closed form for their support functions. We will see some examples below.

Now we can go back to further reformulate the overall DRO problem (4.2.43c). Here, we display $\boldsymbol{x}$ in $f$ and $f_k$.

$$
\begin{aligned}
&\min_{\boldsymbol{x}\in X, \alpha\geq 0} \left\{ d\cdot\alpha + \sum_{j=1}^{n} q_j \max_{\boldsymbol{\xi}\in\mathscr{U}} \left\{ f(\boldsymbol{x}, \boldsymbol{\xi}) - \alpha\|\boldsymbol{\xi} - \boldsymbol{\zeta}_j\| \right\} \right\} \\
= &\min_{\boldsymbol{x}\in X, \alpha\geq 0, \boldsymbol{z}} \{ d\cdot\alpha + \sum_{j=1}^{n} q_j z_j \} \\
&\quad \text{s.t. } \max_{\boldsymbol{\xi}\in\mathscr{U}} \left\{ f(\boldsymbol{x}, \boldsymbol{\xi}) - \alpha\|\boldsymbol{\xi} - \boldsymbol{\zeta}_j\| \right\} \leq z_j, \quad \forall j\in[n], \\
= &\min_{\boldsymbol{x}\in X, \alpha\geq 0, \boldsymbol{z}} \{ d\cdot\alpha + \sum_{j=1}^{n} q_j z_j \} \\
&\quad \text{s.t. } \max_{1\leq k\leq K} \left\{ \min_{\|\boldsymbol{w}\|_*\leq\alpha, \boldsymbol{v}} \{ [-f_k]^*(\boldsymbol{x}, \boldsymbol{w} - \boldsymbol{v}) + \sigma_{\mathscr{U}}(\boldsymbol{v}) + \boldsymbol{w}^\top \boldsymbol{\zeta}_j \} \right\} \leq z_j, \quad \forall j\in[n], \\
= &\min_{\boldsymbol{x}\in X, \alpha\geq 0, \boldsymbol{w}, \boldsymbol{v}, \boldsymbol{z}} \{ d\cdot\alpha + \sum_{j=1}^{n} q_j z_j \} \\
&\quad \text{s.t. } [-f_k]^*(\boldsymbol{x}, \boldsymbol{w}_{jk} - \boldsymbol{v}_{jk}) + \sigma_{\mathscr{U}}(\boldsymbol{v}_{jk}) + \boldsymbol{w}_{jk}^\top \boldsymbol{\zeta}_j \leq z_j, \quad \forall j\in[n],\ k\in[K], \\
&\qquad \|\boldsymbol{w}_{jk}\|_* \leq \alpha, \quad \forall j\in[n],\ k\in[K].
\end{aligned}
$$

If $[-f_k]^*$, $\sigma_{\mathscr{U}}$, and $\|\cdot\|_*$ can be expressed by convex conic constraints, then the above reformulation gives a convex conic optimization problem that may be solved by available solvers.

The above reformulation result is summarized below.

If the DRO model (4.2.38) has a Wasserstein ambiguity set of the first order with a discrete distribution $\mathbb{Q}_0 = \sum_{j=1}^{n} q_j \delta_{\boldsymbol{\zeta}_j}$, and the objective function $f(\boldsymbol{x}, \boldsymbol{\xi}) = \max_{1\leq k\leq K} f_k(\boldsymbol{x}, \boldsymbol{\xi})$ with each $f_k(\boldsymbol{x}, \boldsymbol{\xi})$ convex in $\boldsymbol{x}$ and concave in $\boldsymbol{\xi}$, then it can be equivalently reformulated as

(continued)

$$\min_{x\in X,\alpha\geq 0,w,v,z} \{d\cdot\alpha + \sum_{j=1}^{n} q_j z_j\} \tag{4.2.48}$$

$$\text{s.t. } [-f_k]^*(x, w_{jk} - v_{jk}) + \sigma_{\mathcal{U}}(v_{jk}) + w_{jk}^\top \zeta_j \leq z_j, \quad \forall j \in [n],\ k \in [K], \tag{4.2.49}$$

$$\|w_{jk}\|_* \leq \alpha, \quad \forall j \in [n],\ k \in [K]. \tag{4.2.50}$$

Let us apply the above result to an important special case: $f_k(x, \xi)$ is a linear function in $(x, \xi)$ defined as

$$f_k(x, \xi) = y_k^\top \xi + \ell_k(x), \quad \forall k \in [K], \tag{4.2.51}$$

where $\ell_k(x)$ is an affine function of $x$, and $\mathcal{U}$ is a polyhedron given by

$$\mathcal{U} = \left\{\xi \in \mathbb{R}^l : C\xi \leq d\right\}. \tag{4.2.52}$$

The conjugate function of $-f_k(x, \xi)$ with respect to $\xi$ can be calculated easily as

$$\begin{aligned}(-f_k)^*(x, w) &= \max_{\xi} \{w^\top \xi + f_k(x, \xi)\} \\ &= \max_{\xi} \{w^\top \xi + y_k^\top \xi\} + \ell_k(x) = \begin{cases} \ell_k(x) & \text{if } w = -y_k, \\ +\infty, & \text{otherwise.} \end{cases}\end{aligned} \tag{4.2.53}$$

The support function $\sigma_{\mathcal{U}}$ for the uncertainty set $\mathcal{U}$ can be dualized as

$$\sigma_{\mathcal{U}}(v) = \max_{\xi} \left\{v^\top \xi : C\xi \leq d\right\} = \min_{\kappa} \left\{d^\top \kappa : C^\top \kappa = v,\ \kappa \geq \mathbf{0}\right\}. \tag{4.2.54}$$

With all these preparations, we can state the reformulation for this special case (see Exercise 4.8.)

$$\min_{x\in X,\alpha\geq 0,w,v,z} \{d\cdot\alpha + \sum_{j=1}^{n} q_j z_j\} \tag{4.2.55a}$$

$$\text{s.t. } \ell_k(x) + d^\top \kappa_{jk} + w_{jk}^\top \zeta_j \leq z_j, \quad \forall j \in [n],\ k \in [K], \tag{4.2.55b}$$

$$w_{jk} - v_{jk} + y_k = \mathbf{0}, \quad \forall j \in [n],\ k \in [K], \tag{4.2.55c}$$

$$\boldsymbol{C}^\top \boldsymbol{\kappa}_{jk} = \boldsymbol{v}_{jk}, \quad \forall j \in [n],\ k \in [K], \tag{4.2.55d}$$

$$\|\boldsymbol{w}_{jk}\|_* \le \alpha, \quad \forall j \in [n],\ k \in [K], \tag{4.2.55e}$$

$$\boldsymbol{\kappa}_{jk} \ge \boldsymbol{0}, \quad \forall j \in [n],\ k \in [K]. \tag{4.2.55f}$$

#### 4.2.3.5 The Worst-Case Distribution and Relation to Robust Optimization

What is a worst-case distribution $\mathbb{P}^*$ in (4.2.44a), if there exists one? It turns out that a worst-case distribution $\mathbb{P}^*$ exists for the primal problem (4.2.44a) if and only if the dual problem (4.2.44b) achieves a finite minimum. When a worst-case distribution exists, it takes the form of a perturbation of $\mathbb{Q}_0$. Intuitively (omitting measure-theoretic justifications), we can see from (4.2.44b) that for each $\boldsymbol{\zeta}$, the inner minimization problem identifies some $\boldsymbol{\xi}(\boldsymbol{\zeta})$ as its minimizer. This is a mapping from $\boldsymbol{\zeta}$ to $\boldsymbol{\xi}(\boldsymbol{\zeta})$. Such a mapping transfers probability density from $\mathbb{Q}_0$ to $\mathbb{P}$. Since each $\boldsymbol{\zeta}$ may lead to multiple minimizers for the inner minimization problem, there may be multiple such mappings. It turns out that for (4.2.44a) the worst-case distribution $\mathbb{P}^*$ can be constructed as a convex combination of two transferred probability distributions formed by two such mappings.

The picture is more clear if we look at the case where $\mathbb{Q}_0$ is a discrete distribution as in the box (4.2.43a)–(4.2.43c). In this case, $\mathbb{Q}_0 = \sum_{j=1}^n q_j \delta_{\boldsymbol{\zeta}_j}$. Suppose the inner minimization problem

$$\inf_{\boldsymbol{\xi} \in \mathcal{U}} \left\{ \alpha \|\boldsymbol{\xi} - \boldsymbol{\zeta}_j\|^p - f(\boldsymbol{x}, \boldsymbol{\xi}) \right\} \tag{4.2.56}$$

has a unique optimal solution $\boldsymbol{\xi}_j^*$ for each $\boldsymbol{\zeta}_j$. Then, the worst-case distribution has the form $\mathbb{P}^* = \sum_{j=1}^n q_j \delta_{\boldsymbol{\xi}_j^*}$. In other words, the worst-case distribution is a discrete distribution with the same number of support points and the same probability masses as $\mathbb{Q}_0$. The locations of the support are in general different from those of $\mathbb{Q}_0$. This is in clear contrast to the result of $\phi$-divergence, where the worst-case distribution must be absolutely continuous with respect to $\mathbb{Q}_0$, i.e. its support is a subset of the support of $\mathbb{Q}_0$. If the inner minimization (4.2.56) may have multiple optimal solutions for some $\boldsymbol{\zeta}_j$, then $\mathbb{P}^*$ is supported on $n+1$ points as $\mathbb{P}^* = \sum_{j \in [n], j \neq j_0} q_j \delta_{\boldsymbol{\xi}_j^*} + p_0 q_{j_0} \delta_{\boldsymbol{\xi}_{j_0}^*} + (1-p_0) q_{j_0} \delta_{\boldsymbol{\xi}_{j_0 *}}$. Here $n-1$ support points are obtained as in the previous case with the full probability mass from the corresponding scenario of $\mathbb{Q}_0$, but for one scenario $j_0$, the probability mass $q_{j_0}$ is split to two scenarios $\boldsymbol{\xi}_{j_0}^*$ and $\boldsymbol{\xi}_{j_0 *}$, both of which are optimal solutions of (4.2.56) for $\boldsymbol{\zeta}_{j_0}$, and for some weight $p_0 \in [0, 1]$.

This characterization of the worst-case distribution in (4.2.43a) enables us to reformulate the DRO problem (4.2.38) as a classic robust optimization problem. In particular, we can construct the following robust optimization problem for (4.2.43a)

$$\max_{(\xi_1,\ldots,\xi_n)\in\mathscr{P}'_W(\mathbb{Q}_0,d)} \sum_{j=1}^{n} q_j f(\boldsymbol{x}, \boldsymbol{\xi}_j), \tag{4.2.57}$$

where the uncertainty set $\mathscr{P}'_W(\mathbb{Q}_0, d)$ is given by

$$\mathscr{P}'_W(\mathbb{Q}_0, d) = \left\{(\boldsymbol{\xi}_1, \ldots, \boldsymbol{\xi}_n) \; : \; \sum_{j=1}^{n} q_j \|\boldsymbol{\xi}_j - \boldsymbol{\zeta}_j\|^p \le d^p, \; \boldsymbol{\xi}_j \in \mathscr{U}, \; \forall j \in [n]\right\}. \tag{4.2.58}$$

This uncertainty set contains all probability distributions $\mathbb{P} = \sum_{j=1}^{n} q_j \boldsymbol{\xi}_j$ that satisfy the distance constraint from $\mathbb{Q}_0$, and the robust problem picks the worst-case distribution to maximize the expected cost. This connection between DRO and classic robust optimization revealed by (4.2.43a)–(4.2.58) is quite remarkable. The above robust optimization model and uncertainty set can be modified to handle the most general case where $\mathbb{Q}_0$ is a general distribution. In this situation, the robust optimization problem will provide an approximation to the DRO problem. For more details, we refer the reader to the excellent paper [13].

### 4.2.4 *Statistical Approaches for Determining the Size of Ambiguity Sets*

We introduce a very nice statistical point of view which provides a rigorous methodology for constructing many ambiguity sets that we have seen. The basic idea is the following. Suppose that all we have is data, which are iid random samples drawn from an unknown distribution $\mathbb{Q}$. We want to figure out what $\mathbb{Q}$ is, or more realistically, we want to find a set of distributions that cannot be distinguished from $\mathbb{Q}$ by our observation. How could we find these distributions? The answer comes from *hypothesis testing* or *goodness-to-fit test* [15]. Given a probability distribution $\mathbb{P}$ and a set of $N$ iid data $\{\widehat{\boldsymbol{\xi}^1}, \widehat{\boldsymbol{\xi}^2}, \ldots, \widehat{\boldsymbol{\xi}^N}\}$ drawn from $\mathbb{Q}$, we want to test the following null hypothesis

$$H_0 : \quad \{\widehat{\boldsymbol{\xi}^1}, \widehat{\boldsymbol{\xi}^2}, \ldots, \widehat{\boldsymbol{\xi}^N}\} \text{ were drawn from } \mathbb{P}, \tag{4.2.59}$$

against the alternative hypothesis

$$H_1 : \quad \{\widehat{\boldsymbol{\xi}^1}, \widehat{\boldsymbol{\xi}^2}, \ldots, \widehat{\boldsymbol{\xi}^N}\} \text{ were not drawn from } \mathbb{P}. \tag{4.2.60}$$

If the test rejects $H_0$, then $H_1$ is favored, showing that $\mathbb{P}$ is not a good fit to the data drawn from $\mathbb{Q}$, so we reject to use $\mathbb{P}$ to represent $\mathbb{Q}$. Otherwise, if the test does not reject $H_0$, then we say $\mathbb{P}$ passes the test. We collect such $\mathbb{P}$'s that pass the test in a set, which is our ambiguity set.

How do we carry out the goodness-of-fit test? The procedure is to first find a *test statistic*, denoted as $T^N(\widehat{\xi}^1, \widehat{\xi}^2, \ldots, \widehat{\xi}^N, \mathbb{P})$, which summarizes the data $\widehat{\xi}^1, \widehat{\xi}^2, \ldots, \widehat{\xi}^N$ and the hypothetical distribution $\mathbb{P}$ into a single real number, and then to compare it to a threshold $\rho$. In particular, the rule of the goodness-of-fit test is stated below.

If $T^N(\widehat{\xi}^1, \widehat{\xi}^2, \ldots, \widehat{\xi}^N, \mathbb{P}) > \rho$, $H_0$ is rejected. Otherwise, $H_0$ is not rejected and $\mathbb{P}$ passes the test. Therefore, the set of distributions that pass the goodness-of-fit test is given by

$$\mathscr{P}(\widehat{\xi}^1, \ldots, \widehat{\xi}^N, \rho) = \left\{ \mathbb{P} \in \mathscr{P}(\mathbb{R}^m) : T^N(\widehat{\xi}^1, \ldots, \widehat{\xi}^N, \mathbb{P}) \leq \rho \right\}, \tag{4.2.61}$$

which is called the *confidence region* of the test.

The threshold $\rho$ may also depend on the sample size $N$, the data, and $\mathbb{P}$. The goodness-of-fit test in the colored box provides a principled way to construct ambiguity sets using statistical inference. The confidence region (4.2.61) is what we are looking for, as it gives us a general form of *data-driven ambiguity sets*.

#### 4.2.4.1 $\phi$-Divergence Based Ambiguity Sets

The choice of $T^N$ and $\rho$ is critical. A widely used class of test statistics is given by $\phi$-divergence. It is defined as

$$T_\phi^N(\mathbb{Q}_N, \mathbb{P}) := \frac{2N}{\phi''(1)} D_\phi(\mathbb{Q}_N, \mathbb{P}), \tag{4.2.62}$$

where $\mathbb{Q}_N$ is obtained from the sampled data $(\widehat{\xi}^1, \widehat{\xi}^2, \ldots, \widehat{\xi}^N)$ as its empirical distribution $\mathbb{Q}_N = \frac{1}{N}\sum_{i=1}^N \delta_{\widehat{\xi}^i}$ and $D_\phi$ is the $\phi$-divergence introduced in (4.2.15) and we assume that $\phi(t)$ has second derivative and $\phi''(1) > 0$. This is satisfied by most of the $\phi$-divergence we studied in Sect. 4.2.2. Using (4.2.62), we come to the following $\phi$-divergence ambiguity set

$$\mathscr{P}_\phi'(\mathbb{Q}_N, d) = \left\{ \mathbb{P} \in \mathscr{P}(\mathbb{R}^m) : T_\phi^N(\mathbb{Q}_N, \mathbb{P}) \leq \rho \right\} \tag{4.2.63}$$

$$= \left\{ \mathbb{P} \in \mathscr{P}(\mathbb{R}^m) : \frac{2N}{\phi''(1)} D_\phi(\mathbb{Q}_N, \mathbb{P}) \le \rho \right\} \tag{4.2.64}$$

$$= \left\{ \mathbb{P} \in \mathscr{P}(\mathbb{R}^m) : D_\phi(\mathbb{Q}_N, \mathbb{P}) \le d := \frac{\phi''(1)}{2N}\rho \right\}. \tag{4.2.65}$$

What kind of statistical property does this ambiguity set (4.2.65) have in the large data regime? Remember, as the data $\widehat{\xi}^1, \ldots, \widehat{\xi}^N$ are randomly sampled, the test statistic $T_\phi^N(\mathbb{Q}_N, \mathbb{P})$ is a random variable and its distribution changes with the size of the data $N$. It would be very desirable that the distribution of $T_\phi^N(\mathbb{Q}_N, \mathbb{P})$ can be characterized when $N$ is large. If we know this asymptotic distribution of $T_\phi^N(\mathbb{Q}_N, \mathbb{P})$, we can calculate the probability that the goodness-of-fit test wrongly rejects the null hypothesis, i.e. $\delta := \mathbb{P}(T_\phi^N(\mathbb{Q}_N, \mathbb{P}) > \rho \mid H_0)$. This probability is called the *significance level* of the test, which usually is a small number like 0.05. For the family of $\phi$-divergence test statistics (4.2.62), we can exactly achieve this with the help of the following classic result from statistical inference [16].

Under the null hypothesis $H_0$ in (4.2.59), the $\phi$-divergence test statistic $T_\phi^N(\mathbb{Q}_N, \mathbb{P})$ converges in distribution to a $\chi^2$ distributed random variable with $m - 1$ degrees of freedom as $N \to +\infty$, where $m$ is the number of points in the support of the distributions $\mathbb{P}$ and $\mathbb{Q}_N$.

Using this asymptotic distribution of $T_\phi^N(\mathbb{Q}_N, \mathbb{P})$, we can determine the threshold $\rho$ for the ambiguity set from the significance level $\delta$. Indeed, if we set $\rho = \chi^2_{m-1,1-\delta}$, which is the $100(1-\delta)\%$-percentile of the $\chi^2$ distribution, then the ambiguity set $\mathscr{P}'_\phi(\mathbb{Q}_N, d)$ is a $(1-\delta)$ confidence region of the true distribution $\mathbb{Q}$. That is, under the null hypothesis $H_0$, when the number of samples $N$ is sufficiently large, the probability $\mathbb{P}(T_\phi^N(\mathbb{Q}_N, \mathbb{P}) \le \rho \mid H_0) \ge 1 - \delta$. Notice that for a fixed $\rho = \chi^2_{m-1,1-\delta}$, this probability does not depend on $\phi$. In other words, no matter which $\phi$-divergence we choose, as long as it satisfies the regularity condition that $\phi(x)$ is twice continuously differentiable and $\phi''(1) > 0$, then the corresponding ambiguity set (4.2.63) has the same significance level for the goodness-of-fit test as any other $\phi$-divergence ambiguity set that satisfies the regularity condition and has the same $\rho$, when $N$ is sufficiently large. The reason behind this is that the above asymptotic convergence of the $\phi$-divergence test statistic only depends on the first-order Taylor expansion of $\phi(t)$. Of course, when the sample size $N$ is not large enough, then the statistical properties of different ambiguity sets may be different. The idea of using hypothesis tests to construct $\phi$-divergence ambiguity sets is first proposed in [11, Section 3.2]. Also see [11, Section 6.1] and [16] for some discussion on the choice of $\phi$ using high-order asymptotics.

The alert reader would notice that in $\mathscr{P}'_{\phi}(\mathbb{Q}_N, d)$, the constraint is $D_{\phi}(\mathbb{Q}_N, \mathbb{P}) \leq d$, but in the original ambiguity set $\mathscr{P}_{\phi}(\mathbb{Q}_N, d)$ defined in (4.2.19), we have $D_{\phi}(\mathbb{P}, \mathbb{Q}_N) \leq d$, that is, the $\mathbb{Q}_N, \mathbb{P}$ are swapped. In fact, the same convergence result mentioned about also holds for $T_{\phi}^{N}(\mathbb{P}, \mathbb{Q}_N) := \frac{2N}{\phi''(1)} D_{\phi}(\mathbb{P}, \mathbb{Q}_N)$, i.e. the convergence of one test statistic implies the other. Therefore, we can construct $\mathscr{P}_{\phi}(\mathbb{Q}_N, d)$ as a confidence region with the same asymptotic significant level as $\mathscr{P}'_{\phi}(\mathbb{Q}_N, d)$.

#### 4.2.4.2 Wasserstein-Distance Based Ambiguity Sets

The Wasserstein distance can also be used as a test statistic in the goodness-of-fit test (4.2.59)–(4.2.60). In particular, we introduce the following test statistic $T_p(\mathbb{Q}_N, \mathbb{P})$ using Wasserstein distance of the $p$-th order for $p \geq 1$ as

$$T_{W_p}(\mathbb{Q}_N, \mathbb{P}) = W_p^p(\mathbb{Q}_N, \mathbb{P}). \tag{4.2.66}$$

A fundamental question that we want to ask about $T_p(\mathbb{Q}_N, \mathbb{P})$ is how fast it converges to zero as the number of samples $N$ becomes large, if $\mathbb{P}$ is the true distribution that iid samples are drawn from. Assuming the true distribution $\mathbb{P}$ has a *light tail*, i.e. there exists an exponent $\alpha > p$ and $\gamma > 0$ such that

$$\mathscr{E}_{\alpha,\gamma} := \mathbb{E}_{\mathbb{P}}\left[e^{\gamma \|\xi\|^{\alpha}}\right] = \int_{\mathscr{U}} e^{\gamma \|\xi\|^{\alpha}} d\mathbb{P}(\xi) < +\infty. \tag{4.2.67}$$

Also assume that the dimension $m$ of the support $\mathscr{U}$ is at least 2. Then, the following concentration inequality holds for all $N \geq 1$,

$$\mathbb{P}(T_{W_p}(\mathbb{Q}_N, \mathbb{P}) \geq \rho) \leq \begin{cases} c_1 e^{-c_2 N \rho^{m/p}} & \text{if } \rho \leq 1, \\ c_1 e^{-c_2 N \rho^{\alpha/p}} & \text{if } \rho > 1, \end{cases} \tag{4.2.68}$$

where $c_1, c_2$ are positive constants only dependent on the order $p$, the dimension $m$ of the support $\mathscr{U}$, the exponent $\alpha$, and $\mathscr{E}_{\alpha,\gamma}$. This concentration inequality (4.2.68) is derived in [17] and is first utilized in [18] to derive finite sample guarantees for Wasserstein distance based ambiguity sets. In particular, given a significance level $\delta \in (0, 1)$, the smallest radius $\rho$ of the Wasserstein ball such that it contains $\mathbb{P}$ with confidence $1 - \delta$ can be calculated using (4.2.68) as

$$\rho = \begin{cases} \left(\frac{1}{c_2 N} \log\left(\frac{c_1}{\delta}\right)\right)^{\frac{p}{m}} & \text{if } N \geq \frac{1}{c_2} \log\left(\frac{c_1}{\delta}\right), \\ \left(\frac{1}{c_2 N} \log\left(\frac{c_1}{\delta}\right)\right)^{\frac{p}{\alpha}} & \text{if } N < \frac{1}{c_2} \log\left(\frac{c_1}{\delta}\right). \end{cases} \tag{4.2.69}$$

To summarize, statistical hypothesis testing (4.2.59)–(4.2.61) provides a principled way to motivate and construct ambiguity sets. It is also proposed to construct data-driven uncertainty sets for standard robust optimization problems. See [19] for a unifying exposition and construction of a multitude of uncertainty sets. See [20] for using linear regression and $t$-test to calibrate an uncertainty set in portfolio optimization, and [21] for using Pearson's $\chi^2$-test for constructing ambiguity sets in an inventory problem.

## 4.3 Adaptive Distributionally Robust Optimization

Now we turn our attention to adaptive robust optimization in the distributionally robust setting. Recall that a two-stage robust linear program can be written as

$$\min_{\boldsymbol{x}_0 \in X_0, \boldsymbol{x}(\cdot) \in X(\boldsymbol{x}_0)} \max_{\boldsymbol{\xi} \in \mathscr{U}} \left\{ \boldsymbol{c}^\top \boldsymbol{x}_0 + \boldsymbol{g}^\top \boldsymbol{x}(\boldsymbol{\xi}) \right\}, \tag{4.3.1}$$

where $\boldsymbol{x}_0$ is the first-stage decision and $\boldsymbol{x}(\boldsymbol{\xi})$ is the second-stage policy as a function of the uncertainty $\boldsymbol{\xi}$ in the uncertainty set $\mathscr{U}$. Here, the uncertainty set $\mathscr{U}$ is deterministic. By contrast, a two-stage stochastic linear optimization model has the form

$$\min_{\boldsymbol{x}_0 \in X_0} \left\{ \boldsymbol{c}^\top \boldsymbol{x}_0 + \mathbb{E}_{\mathbb{Q}}\left[ V(\boldsymbol{x}_0, \boldsymbol{\xi}) \right] \right\}, \tag{4.3.2}$$

which minimizes the sum of the first-stage cost $\boldsymbol{c}^\top \boldsymbol{x}$ and the second-stage expected cost $\mathbb{E}_{\mathbb{Q}}\left[ V(\boldsymbol{x}_0, \boldsymbol{\xi}) \right]$, where $\mathbb{Q}$ is the probability distribution of the random parameter $\boldsymbol{\xi}$ and $V(\boldsymbol{x}_0, \boldsymbol{\xi})$ is the optimal cost-to-go function defined by the second-stage problem

$$\begin{aligned} V(\boldsymbol{x}_0, \boldsymbol{\xi}) = \min_{\boldsymbol{x} \in X(\boldsymbol{x}_0, \boldsymbol{\xi})} \boldsymbol{g}^\top \boldsymbol{x} &= \min_{\boldsymbol{x}} \left\{ \boldsymbol{g}^\top \boldsymbol{x} \ : \ \boldsymbol{B}\boldsymbol{x} \geq \boldsymbol{\xi} - \boldsymbol{A}\boldsymbol{x}_0 \right\} \\ &= \max_{\boldsymbol{y}} \left\{ \boldsymbol{y}^\top (\boldsymbol{\xi} - \boldsymbol{A}\boldsymbol{x}_0) : \boldsymbol{B}^\top \boldsymbol{y} = \boldsymbol{g}, \ \boldsymbol{y} \geq \boldsymbol{0} \right\}, \end{aligned} \tag{4.3.3a}$$

where we assume that $X(\boldsymbol{x}_0, \boldsymbol{\xi})$ is a nonempty polytope with $\boldsymbol{x}_0$ and $\boldsymbol{\xi}$ on the right-hand side of the defining constraints. By a standard duality argument, $V(\boldsymbol{x}_0, \boldsymbol{\xi})$ is a convex piecewise linear function in $(\boldsymbol{x}_0, \boldsymbol{\xi})$.

It is straightforward to generalize the above two-stage robust and stochastic programs to a two-stage distributionally robust linear program as

$$\min_{\boldsymbol{x}_0 \in X_0} \left\{ \boldsymbol{c}^\top \boldsymbol{x}_0 + \max_{\mathbb{P} \in \mathscr{P}} \mathbb{E}_{\mathbb{P}}\left[ V(\boldsymbol{x}_0, \boldsymbol{\xi}) \right] \right\}, \tag{4.3.4}$$

which minimizes the sum of the first-stage cost and the worst-case expected cost of the optimal cost-to-go function with respect to an ambiguity set of probability distributions $\mathscr{P}$ of the probability distributions $\mathbb{P}$ of the uncertain parameter $\boldsymbol{\xi}$. If we compare (4.3.4) with the general DRO problem (4.1.3) in the introduction of this chapter, we will see that the two-stage DRO is a special case of (4.1.3) as $\min_{\boldsymbol{x}_0 \in X_0} \max_{\mathbb{P} \in \mathscr{P}} \mathbb{E}_{\mathbb{P}}[f(\boldsymbol{x}_0, \boldsymbol{\xi})]$, where the objective function is defined as

$$f(\boldsymbol{x}_0, \boldsymbol{\xi}) = \boldsymbol{c}^\top \boldsymbol{x}_0 + V(\boldsymbol{x}_0, \boldsymbol{\xi}). \tag{4.3.5}$$

Therefore, the equivalent reformulations of static DRO that we discussed in the previous section can be applied to the two-stage DRO. We will demonstrate this for the moment-based, $\phi$-divergence based, and Wasserstein based ambiguity sets.

## *4.3.1 Two-Stage DRO and Reformulations*

### 4.3.1.1 Two-Stage DRO with Moment-Based Ambiguity Sets

Let us take the cross-moment ambiguity set $\mathscr{P}(\mathscr{U}, \boldsymbol{\mu}_0, \boldsymbol{\Sigma}_0, \gamma)$ (4.2.8) as an example. The cost-to-go function is given by $V(\boldsymbol{x}_0, \boldsymbol{\xi}) = \max_{1 \le k \le K}\{\boldsymbol{y}_k^\top(\boldsymbol{\xi} - \boldsymbol{A}\boldsymbol{x}_0)\}$, where $\boldsymbol{y}_k$ are the extreme points of the dual polytope in (4.3.3a). The reformulation of the static DRO with this ambiguity set (4.2.12) can be adapted to the two-stage setting as follows.

$$\min_{\boldsymbol{x}_0 \in X_0} \left\{ \boldsymbol{c}^\top \boldsymbol{x}_0 + \max_{\mathbb{P} \in \mathscr{P}(\mathscr{U}, \boldsymbol{\mu}_0, \boldsymbol{\Sigma}_0, \gamma)} \mathbb{E}_{\mathbb{P}}\big[V(\boldsymbol{x}_0, \boldsymbol{\xi})\big] \right\} \tag{4.3.6a}$$

$$= \min_{\boldsymbol{x}_0, \lambda, \boldsymbol{\beta}, \boldsymbol{Q} \succeq \boldsymbol{0}} \quad \lambda + \boldsymbol{\xi}_0^\top \boldsymbol{\beta} + \gamma \boldsymbol{\Sigma}_0 \bullet \boldsymbol{Q} \tag{4.3.6b}$$

$$\text{s.t.} \quad \boldsymbol{c}^\top \boldsymbol{x}_0 + V(\boldsymbol{x}_0, \boldsymbol{\xi}) - \lambda - \boldsymbol{\xi}^\top \boldsymbol{\beta} - (\boldsymbol{\xi} - \boldsymbol{\xi}_0)^\top \boldsymbol{Q}(\boldsymbol{\xi} - \boldsymbol{\xi}_0) \le 0, \quad \forall \boldsymbol{\xi} \in \mathscr{U}, \tag{4.3.6c}$$

$$= \min_{\boldsymbol{x}_0, \lambda, \boldsymbol{\beta}, \boldsymbol{Q} \succeq \boldsymbol{0}} \quad \lambda + \boldsymbol{\xi}_0^\top \boldsymbol{\beta} + \gamma \boldsymbol{\Sigma}_0 \bullet \boldsymbol{Q} \tag{4.3.6d}$$

$$\text{s.t.} \quad (\boldsymbol{\beta} - \boldsymbol{y}_k)^\top \boldsymbol{\xi}_0 - \alpha_k - \eta_k + \boldsymbol{y}_k^\top \boldsymbol{A}\boldsymbol{x}_0 + \lambda \ge 0, \quad \forall k \in [K], \tag{4.3.6e}$$

$$\begin{bmatrix} \eta_k & (\boldsymbol{\beta} - \boldsymbol{y}_k)^\top/2 \\ (\boldsymbol{\beta} - \boldsymbol{y}_k)/2 & \boldsymbol{Q} + \alpha_k \boldsymbol{\Lambda}_k \end{bmatrix} \succeq \boldsymbol{0}, \quad \forall k \in [K], \tag{4.3.6f}$$

$$\alpha_k \ge 0, \eta_k \ge 0, \boldsymbol{\Lambda}_k \succeq \boldsymbol{0}, \quad \forall k \in [K], \tag{4.3.6g}$$

$$\boldsymbol{x}_0 \in X_0, \tag{4.3.6h}$$

which is an SDP problem. However, note that the reformulation needs all the linear pieces of $V(\boldsymbol{x}_0, \boldsymbol{\xi})$, which may be many. See Exercise 4.9 for a question on computation.

#### 4.3.1.2 Two-Stage DRO with $\phi$-Divergence Based Ambiguity Sets

Now let us look at the situation with $\phi$-divergence based ambiguity sets. The equivalent reformulation (4.2.28) has the term $\alpha \cdot \phi^*((f(\boldsymbol{x}, \boldsymbol{\xi}) - \lambda)/\alpha)$. We can show that this term is jointly convex in $(\boldsymbol{x}, \lambda, \alpha)$ if $f(\boldsymbol{x}, \boldsymbol{\xi}) - \lambda$ is convex in $(\boldsymbol{x}, \lambda)$ (so in particular $f(\boldsymbol{x}, \boldsymbol{\xi})$ is convex in $\boldsymbol{x}$ for any $\boldsymbol{\xi}$.) To see this, we can work on the more general case $h(\boldsymbol{x}, \alpha) = \alpha \cdot \phi^*(g(\boldsymbol{x})/\alpha)$ by absorbing $\lambda$ into $\boldsymbol{x}$. Here $g(\boldsymbol{x})$ is convex in $\boldsymbol{x}$. Then, by the definition of the conjugate function $(\alpha\phi)^*$, c.f. (4.2.25), we have

$$h(\boldsymbol{x}, \alpha) = \sup_{t \geq 0} \left\{ g(\boldsymbol{x}) \cdot t - \alpha\phi(t) \right\}, \tag{4.3.7}$$

where $g(\boldsymbol{x}) \cdot t - \alpha\phi(t)$ is a convex function in $\boldsymbol{x}$, $\alpha$ for each nonnegative $t$, therefore, $h(\boldsymbol{x}, \alpha)$, which is the pointwise supremum over $t$, is also a convex function in $(\boldsymbol{x}, \alpha)$.

This argument shows us that we can directly apply the equivalent reformulation result (4.2.28) obtained for static DRO with $\phi$-divergence sets of discrete distributions to the two-stage DRO case.

A two-stage distributionally robust linear program (4.3.4) as

$$v_1 = \min_{\boldsymbol{x}_0 \in X_0} \left\{ \boldsymbol{c}^\top \boldsymbol{x}_0 + \max_{\mathbb{P} \in \mathscr{P}_\phi(\mathbb{Q}_0, d)} \mathbb{E}_{\mathbb{P}}\left[ V(\boldsymbol{x}_0, \boldsymbol{\xi}) \right] \right\}, \tag{4.3.8}$$

where $\mathscr{P}_\phi(\mathbb{Q}_0, d)$ is the $\phi$-divergence ambiguity set defined in (4.2.19) with a discrete probability measure $\mathbb{Q}_0$, is equivalent to the following deterministic convex optimization problem

$$v_2 = \min_{\boldsymbol{x}_0 \in X_0, \lambda, \alpha \geq 0} \left\{ \lambda + d \cdot \alpha + \alpha \sum_{i=1}^{m} q_i \phi^* \left( \frac{\boldsymbol{c}^\top \boldsymbol{x}_0 + V(\boldsymbol{x}_0, \boldsymbol{\xi}_i) - \lambda}{\alpha} \right) \right\}, \tag{4.3.9}$$

in the sense that they have the same optimal objective cost, i.e. $v_1 = v_2$, and the same optimal solution in $\boldsymbol{x}_0$.

Problem (4.3.9) can be further reformulated if we have a closed form of the conjugate $\phi^*$. Let us take the KL divergence as an example. Recall that for KL divergence, $\phi^*_{KL}(s) = e^s - 1$. Problem (4.3.9) has the following explicit form

$$\min_{\boldsymbol{x}_0 \in X_0, \lambda, \alpha \geq 0} \left\{ \lambda + (d - 1) \cdot \alpha + \sum_{i=1}^{m} q_i \alpha \exp\left( \frac{\boldsymbol{c}^\top \boldsymbol{x}_0 + V(\boldsymbol{x}_0, \boldsymbol{\xi}_i) - \lambda}{\alpha} \right) \right\}$$

$$
\begin{aligned}
&= \min_{x_0 \in X_0, \lambda, \alpha \geq 0, z} \left\{ \lambda + (d-1)\cdot\alpha + \sum_{i=1}^{m} q_i z_i \right\} \\
&\quad \text{s.t.} \quad \alpha \exp\left( \frac{c^\top x_0 + V(x_0, \xi_i) - \lambda}{\alpha} \right) \leq z_i, \quad \forall i \in [m], \\
&= \min_{x_0 \in X_0, \lambda, \alpha \geq 0, z} \left\{ \lambda + (d-1)\cdot\alpha + \sum_{i=1}^{m} q_i z_i \right\} \\
&\quad \text{s.t.} \quad c^\top x_0 + V(x_0, \xi_i) - \lambda - \alpha \log(z_i/\alpha) \leq 0, \quad \forall i \in [m], \\
&= \min_{x_0 \in X_0, \lambda, \alpha \geq 0, z} \left\{ \lambda + (d-1)\cdot\alpha + \sum_{i=1}^{m} q_i z_i \right\} \\
&\quad \text{s.t.} \quad c^\top x_0 + \min_{x} \left\{ g^\top x \ : \ Bx \geq \xi - Ax_0 \right\} - \lambda - \alpha \log(z_i/\alpha) \leq 0, \quad \forall i \in [m], \\
&= \min_{x_0 \in X_0, \lambda, \alpha \geq 0, z} \left\{ \lambda + (d-1)\cdot\alpha + \sum_{i=1}^{m} q_i z_i \right\} \\
&\quad \text{s.t.} \quad c^\top x_0 + g^\top x^i - \lambda - \alpha \log(z_i/\alpha) \leq 0, \quad \forall i \in [m], \\
&\quad\quad\quad Bx^i \geq \xi - Ax_0, \quad \forall i \in [m].
\end{aligned}
$$

All the $\phi$-divergence in Table 4.1 can be reformulated as convex programs using the same technique (see Exercise 4.10.) Note that the number of constraints are linear in the number of samples. Compare it to the reformulation with moment-based ambiguity sets (4.3.6), where the number of constraints is linear in the number of extreme points of the dual polyhedron of the primal second-stage constraints.

#### 4.3.1.3 Two-Stage DRO with Wasserstein Ambiguity Sets

A two-stage distributionally robust optimization problem with the Wasserstein ambiguity set is given below

$$
\min_{x_0 \in X_0} \left\{ c^\top x_0 + \max_{\mathbb{P} \in \mathscr{P}_W(\mathbb{Q}_0, d)} \mathbb{E}_{\mathbb{P}}\big[V(x_0, \xi)\big] \right\}, \tag{4.3.10}
$$

where the Wasserstein ambiguity set $\mathscr{P}_W(\mathbb{Q}_0, d)$ is assumed to have order 1, i.e. $p = 1$ and the norm is $\ell_1$-norm. And $\mathbb{Q}_0$ is assumed to be a discrete distribution with a finite support, i.e. $\mathbb{Q}_0 = \sum_{j=1}^{n} q_j \delta_{\zeta_j}$. The support set $\mathscr{U}$ of the distribution $\mathbb{P}$ is assumed to be a polyhedron as defined in (4.2.52). This DRO problem (4.3.10) can be reformulated by directly adapting the reformulation of static DRO developed in (4.2.43b). In particular, we have

$$\min_{x_0 \in X_0, \alpha \geq 0} \left\{ d \cdot \alpha - \sum_{j=1}^{n} q_j \min_{\xi \in \mathscr{U}} \left\{ \alpha \|\xi - \zeta_j\|_1 - c^\top x_0 - V(x_0, \xi) \right\} \right\}. \tag{4.3.11}$$

Observe that the cost-to-to function $V(x_0, \xi)$ is a convex piecewise linear function in $(x_0, \xi)$ as shown in (4.3.3a). So we can write

$$V(x_0, \xi) = \max_{1 \leq k \leq K} y_k^\top (\xi - A x_0). \tag{4.3.12}$$

Combining with the assumption that $\mathscr{U}$ is a polyhedron, we can further reformulate (4.3.11) by applying the static DRO reformulation (4.2.55).

$$\min_{x \in X, \alpha \geq 0, w, v, z} \quad d \cdot \alpha + \sum_{j=1}^{n} q_j z_j \tag{4.3.13a}$$

$$\text{s.t.} \quad - y_k^\top A x_0 + d^\top \kappa_{jk} + w_{jk}^\top \zeta_j \leq z_j, \quad \forall j \in [n],\ k \in [K], \tag{4.3.13b}$$

$$w_{jk} - v_{jk} + y_k = \mathbf{0}, \quad \forall j \in [n],\ k \in [K], \tag{4.3.13c}$$

$$C^\top \kappa_{jk} = v_{jk}, \quad \forall j \in [n],\ k \in [K], \tag{4.3.13d}$$

$$\|w_{jk}\|_\infty \leq \alpha, \quad \forall j \in [n],\ k \in [K], \tag{4.3.13e}$$

$$\kappa_{jk} \geq \mathbf{0}, \quad \forall j \in [n],\ k \in [K]. \tag{4.3.13f}$$

To summarize this subsection, some remarks are ready.

1. We have shown that the two-stage distributionally robust linear programs (DRLP), where the second-stage problem has uncertainty only in the right-hand-side of the constraints, can be explicitly reformulated as convex or linear optimization problems for a wide range of ambiguity sets, e.g. cross-moment, $\phi$-divergence, and Wasserstein distance of order 1. In contrast, the classic two-stage robust linear optimization problems, which are in general NP-hard problems [22]. This is quite amazing, because DRO is a generalization of classic RO, but the generalization turns out to be easier to solve in cases when its classic version is hard.
2. When the order of the Wasserstein distance is more than 1, the above two-stage DRLP becomes NP-hard. A reduction from the norm maximization problem is used to demonstrate this hardness result in [23].
3. When the objective function of the second-stage problem is also affected by uncertainty, then it can be shown that the two-stage DRLP becomes NP-hard [23], even with the Wasserstein distance of order 1. However, if the Wasserstein distance has order 2, i.e. $p = 2$, then the two-stage DRLP with such a Wasserstein ball can be equivalently reformulated as a completely positive program, which itself is a convex optimization problem, but is well-known to be computationally

intractable. Semi-definite relaxations have been developed to approximate such problems.

## 4.4 Distributionally Robust Chance Constrained Programs

### 4.4.1 *Motivation*

Consider a linear inequality with uncertain parameter $\boldsymbol{\xi}$ in the coefficients and right-hand side as

$$\boldsymbol{a}(\boldsymbol{\xi})^\top \boldsymbol{x} \leq b(\boldsymbol{\xi}). \tag{4.4.1}$$

As we have learned, robust optimization treats $\boldsymbol{\xi}$ as a deterministic uncertain parameter living in an uncertainty set $\Xi$ and requires the decision $\boldsymbol{x}$ to satisfy (4.4.1) for *all* uncertain parameters $\boldsymbol{\xi} \in \Xi$ as

$$\boldsymbol{a}(\boldsymbol{\xi})^\top \boldsymbol{x} \leq b(\boldsymbol{\xi}), \quad \forall \boldsymbol{\xi} \in \Xi. \tag{4.4.2}$$

We can view (4.4.2) as a "hard" constraint that is enforced for all scenarios of $\boldsymbol{\xi}$ in $\Xi$. An alternative approach is to allow $\boldsymbol{x}$ to violate the constraint for some scenarios of $\boldsymbol{\xi}$, which can be viewed as a "soft" constraint. The degree of violation that can be tolerated is measured by some probability distribution on $\boldsymbol{\xi}$. In particular, we can formulate the following probabilistic constraint

$$\mathbb{P}\left(\boldsymbol{a}(\boldsymbol{\xi})^\top \boldsymbol{x} \leq b(\boldsymbol{\xi})\right) \geq 1 - \epsilon, \tag{4.4.3}$$

where $\boldsymbol{\xi}$ is treated as a random vector with a probability distribution $\mathbb{P}$ and $\epsilon$ is a small positive number close to 0, say 0.001. This probabilistic constraint (4.4.3) is called a *chance constraint* or a *probabilistic constraint*. It requires the decision $\boldsymbol{x}$ to satisfy the linear inequality (4.4.1) with probability $1 - \epsilon$, which is close to 1. Equivalently, the chance constraint (4.4.3) requires the probability of violating the linear inequality to be $\epsilon$. We call $\epsilon$ the *probability margin*. Chance constrained programs have a long history dating back to the 1950's [24].

**Illustrative Example 4.1** *Let us see a very simple example to get a feeling of chance constraints. Consider a scalar random variable $\xi$ with a uniform distribution on $[-1, 1]$ and a chance constraint*

$$\mathbb{P}\big(x \leq \xi\big) \geq 1 - \epsilon, \tag{4.4.4}$$

*where $0 \leq \epsilon \leq 1$. This chance constraint says that the variable $x$ should be less than or equal to $\xi$ with a high probability. Notice that the inequality in the chance constraint, namely $x \leq \xi$, involves the random variable $\xi$ only in the right-hand side* *of the linear inequality, not in the coefficients on the left-hand side. The probability term $\mathbb{P}(x \leq \xi)$ can be easily computed from the cumulative distribution function (CDF) of $\xi$ as*

$$\mathbb{P}(x \leq \xi) = \begin{cases} 1, & \text{if } x < -1, \\ \frac{1}{2}(1-x), & \text{if } -1 \leq x \leq 1, \\ 0, & \text{if } x > 1. \end{cases} \tag{4.4.5}$$

*Therefore, the feasible region defined by this chance constraint is $x \leq 2\epsilon - 1$. Note that the feasible region is an unbounded interval, which is a convex set.*

□

**Illustrative Example 4.2** *Here is a little bit more involved example. Consider the following chance constraint*

$$\mathbb{P}\big((1-x) + \xi x \leq 0\big) \geq 1 - \epsilon, \tag{4.4.6}$$

*where $\xi$ is a random variable uniformly distributed on $[\frac{1}{2}, \frac{3}{2}]$ and $0 \leq \epsilon \leq 1$. Note that a coefficient of the left-hand side of the linear inequality is random. The probability term can be computed as*

$$\mathbb{P}((1-x) + \xi x \leq 0) = \begin{cases} \mathbb{P}(\xi \leq \frac{x-1}{x}), & \text{if } x > 0, \\ \mathbb{P}(\xi \geq \frac{x-1}{x}), & \text{if } x < 0, \\ 0, & \text{if } x = 0. \end{cases}$$

*The CDF of the uniform random variable $\xi$ is given by*

$$\mathbb{P}(\xi \leq x) = \begin{cases} 0, & \text{if } x < \frac{1}{2}, \\ x - \frac{1}{2}, & \text{if } \frac{1}{2} \leq x \leq \frac{3}{2}, \\ 1, & \text{if } x > \frac{3}{2}. \end{cases}$$

*Using the CDF, the chance constraint $\mathbb{P}((1-x)+\xi x \leq 0) \geq 1-\epsilon$ can be rewritten as*

$$\begin{cases} \mathbb{P}(\xi \leq \frac{x-1}{x}) \geq 1-\epsilon, & \text{if } x > 0, \\ \mathbb{P}(\xi \geq \frac{x-1}{x}) \geq 1-\epsilon, & \text{if } x < 0, \\ 0 \geq 1-\epsilon, & \text{if } x = 0, \end{cases} \Leftrightarrow \begin{cases} \frac{x-1}{x} - \frac{1}{2} \geq 1-\epsilon, \; x > 0, \\ \frac{3}{2} - \frac{x-1}{x} \geq 1-\epsilon, \; x < 0, \\ \epsilon = 1, \; x = 0, \end{cases} \Leftrightarrow \begin{cases} (\epsilon - \frac{1}{2})x \geq 1, \; x > 0, \\ (\epsilon - \frac{1}{2})x \leq -1, \; x < 0, \\ \epsilon = 1, \; x = 0. \end{cases}$$

*From these, we can derive the feasible region of the chance constraint as*

$$\left\{x : \mathbb{P}((1-x)+\xi x \leq 0) \geq 1-\epsilon\right\} = \begin{cases} (-\infty, -\frac{2}{2\epsilon-1}] \cup [\frac{2}{2\epsilon-1}, +\infty), & \text{if } \frac{1}{2} < \epsilon < 1, \\ (-\infty, -2] \cup \{0\} \cup [2, +\infty), & \text{if } \epsilon = 1, \\ \emptyset, & \text{if } \epsilon \leq \frac{1}{2}. \end{cases} \tag{4.4.7}$$

□

From this example, we can see that the feasible region of a chance constraint can be nonconvex and not even connected. In fact, except for a few cases, chance constraints are highly nonconvex. The few exceptions, where chance constraints are convex, include when $\mathbb{P}$ is a normal distribution and more generally when $\mathbb{P}$ is a log-concave distribution [25, 26].

The nonconvexity of chance constraints makes them computationally challenging to solve. Moreover, as we discussed in the beginning of this chapter, it is usually difficult to obtain the true distribution $\mathbb{P}$ to characterize the uncertain parameter $\xi$. Even if we could estimate some empirical probability distribution $\hat{\mathbb{P}}$ for $\xi$, the solution may be very sensitive to the choice of $\hat{\mathbb{P}}$ and does not perform well when the distribution deviates from $\hat{\mathbb{P}}$. Therefore, analogous to the development of distributionally robust optimization, similar concerns and practical limitations of handling specific probability distributions lead to the generalization of chance constrained programs to *distributionally robust chance constrained programs* (DRCC). In particular, we will study the following DRCC in this section

$$\inf_{\mathbb{P}\in\mathscr{P}} \mathbb{P}(f(\boldsymbol{x},\boldsymbol{\xi}) \leq 0) \geq 1-\epsilon, \tag{4.4.8}$$

where $f(\boldsymbol{x},\boldsymbol{\xi})$ is a scalar function and $\mathscr{P}$ is an ambiguity set of probability measures.

In the rest of this section, we first study conditions on the ambiguity set $\mathscr{P}$ and the constraint $\boldsymbol{f}(\boldsymbol{x},\boldsymbol{\xi}) \leq 0$ under which the DRCC (4.4.8) can be exactly reformulated as a deterministic optimization problem, even as a convex optimization problem for some cases. Then, we turn to the situations where exact reformulation is impossible, but a systematic approach to construct inner convex approximations is developed.

### 4.4.2 Exact Reformulations of DRCC with Moment Ambiguity Sets

Recall the cross moment ambiguity set introduced in Sect. 4.2.1. It is reproduced below for reader's convenience.

$$\mathscr{P}(\boldsymbol{\mu}_0, \boldsymbol{\Sigma}_0, \gamma) = \Bigg\{\mathbb{P} \in \mathscr{M}_+(\mathbb{R}^l) : \mathbb{P}(\boldsymbol{\xi} \in \mathbb{R}^l) = 1, \tag{4.4.9a}$$

$$\mathbb{E}_{\mathbb{P}}[\boldsymbol{\xi}] = \boldsymbol{\mu}_0, \tag{4.4.9b}$$

$$\mathbb{E}_{\mathbb{P}}[(\boldsymbol{\xi} - \boldsymbol{\mu}_0)(\boldsymbol{\xi} - \boldsymbol{\mu}_0)^\top] \preceq \gamma \boldsymbol{\Sigma}_0\Bigg\}. \tag{4.4.9c}$$

In this ambiguity set, the common support of the distributions is the entire space $\mathbb{R}^l$, $\boldsymbol{\mu}_0$ and $\boldsymbol{\Sigma}_0$ are respectively the mean and covariance matrix of the nominal distribution, and parameter $\gamma$ controls the size of the ambiguity set.

#### 4.4.2.1 Equivalence Between DRCC and CVaR

In this subsection, we will show that the following distributionally robust chance constraint with the cross-moment ambiguity set

$$\inf_{\mathbb{P} \in \mathscr{P}(\boldsymbol{\mu}_0, \boldsymbol{\Sigma}_0, \gamma)} \mathbb{P}\left(f(\boldsymbol{x}, \boldsymbol{\xi}) \leq 0\right) \geq 1 - \epsilon \tag{4.4.10}$$

can be exactly reformulated as a deterministic convex optimization problem, when the function $f(\boldsymbol{x}, \boldsymbol{\xi})$ is any concave function of $\boldsymbol{\xi}$ or any (possibly non-concave) quadratic function of $\boldsymbol{\xi}$. Furthermore, the resulting convex optimization problem has a special structure, which is a very well-known coherent risk measure, the so-called *conditional value-at-risk* (CVaR). Later we will see that this link between distributionally robust optimization and risk measures is a fundamental one.

Let us first introduce CVaR. Given $\epsilon \in (0, 1)$, the CVaR of $f(\boldsymbol{x}, \boldsymbol{\xi})$ with respect to the random element $\boldsymbol{\xi}$ is defined as

$$\text{CVaR}_{1-\epsilon}^{\mathbb{P}}(f(\boldsymbol{x}, \boldsymbol{\xi})) = \inf_{\alpha \in \mathbb{R}} \left\{\alpha + \frac{1}{\epsilon}\mathbb{E}_{\mathbb{P}}\left[(f(\boldsymbol{x}, \boldsymbol{\xi}) - \alpha)^+\right]\right\}. \tag{4.4.11}$$

When the probability measure $\mathbb{P}$ has a density function, $\text{CVaR}_{\epsilon}^{\mathbb{P}}(f(\boldsymbol{x}, \boldsymbol{\xi}))$ is the conditional expectation $\mathbb{E}_{\mathbb{P}}[f(\boldsymbol{x}, \boldsymbol{\xi}) \| \ f(\boldsymbol{x}, \boldsymbol{\xi}) \geq V]$, where $V$ is the quantile such that $\mathbb{P}(f(\boldsymbol{x}, \boldsymbol{\xi}) \leq V) \geq 1 - \epsilon$. Therefore, CVaR gives a conservative approximation of the DRC. In particular,

$$\text{CVaR}_{1-\epsilon}^{\mathbb{P}}(f(\boldsymbol{x}, \boldsymbol{\xi})) \leq 0 \implies \mathbb{P}\left(f(\boldsymbol{x}, \boldsymbol{\xi}) \leq 0\right) \geq 1 - \epsilon.$$

The main result we want to show in this subsection is that the reverse implication is also true for two broad classes of (4.4.10). Namely, we have the following result.

If $f(\boldsymbol{x}, \boldsymbol{\xi})$ is a concave function in $\boldsymbol{\xi}$, or a (possibly non-concave) quadratic function in $\boldsymbol{\xi}$, we have the following equivalence relation

$$\sup_{\mathbb{P}\in\mathscr{P}} \text{CVaR}_{1-\epsilon}^{\mathbb{P}}(f(\boldsymbol{x}, \boldsymbol{\xi})) \le 0 \iff \inf_{\mathbb{P}\in\mathscr{P}} \mathbb{P}(f(\boldsymbol{x}, \boldsymbol{\xi}) \le 0) \ge 1-\epsilon, \tag{4.4.12}$$

where the ambiguity set $\mathscr{P}$ is the cross-moment set $\mathscr{P}(\boldsymbol{\mu}_0, \boldsymbol{\Sigma}_0, \gamma)$ defined in (4.4.9).

Before we prove this equivalence, let us first see what the CVaR constraint gives us. To save notation, in this subsection the ambiguity set $\mathscr{P}$ always stands for the cross-moment ambiguity set (4.4.9), unless specified otherwise.

$$\sup_{\mathbb{P}\in\mathscr{P}} \ \text{CVaR}_{1-\epsilon}^{\mathbb{P}}(f(\boldsymbol{x}, \boldsymbol{\xi})) \le 0 \tag{4.4.13}$$

$$\iff \sup_{\mathbb{P}\in\mathscr{P}} \ \inf_{\alpha\in\mathbb{R}} \left\{\alpha + \frac{1}{\epsilon}\mathbb{E}_{\mathbb{P}}\left[(f(\boldsymbol{x}, \boldsymbol{\xi}) - \alpha)^+\right]\right\} \le 0,$$

$$\iff \inf_{\alpha\in\mathbb{R}} \left\{\alpha + \frac{1}{\epsilon}\sup_{\mathbb{P}\in\mathscr{P}} \ \mathbb{E}_{\mathbb{P}}\left[(f(\boldsymbol{x}, \boldsymbol{\xi}) - \alpha)^+\right]\right\} \le 0. \tag{4.4.14}$$

In (4.4.14), we used strong duality to switch sup and inf, because the objective function is convex in $\alpha$ and concave in $\mathbb{P}$ and the Slater condition holds. To further reformulate the problem, recall that the inner supremum is already reformulated in Sect. 4.2.1, Eq. (4.2.10)–(4.2.11). So directly applying the earlier result, we get the following reformulation.

$$\sup_{\mathbb{P}\in\mathscr{P}} \mathbb{E}_{\mathbb{P}} \ \left[(f(\boldsymbol{x}, \boldsymbol{\xi}) - \alpha)^+\right]$$

$$\iff \inf_{\lambda, \boldsymbol{\beta}, \boldsymbol{Q}\succeq \boldsymbol{0}} \ \lambda + \boldsymbol{\mu}_0^\top \boldsymbol{\beta} + \boldsymbol{Q} \bullet (\gamma\boldsymbol{\Sigma}_0 + \boldsymbol{\mu}_0\boldsymbol{\mu}_0^\top) \tag{4.4.15a}$$

$$\text{s.t.} \ \ \lambda + \boldsymbol{\xi}^\top\boldsymbol{\beta} + \boldsymbol{\xi}^\top\boldsymbol{Q}\boldsymbol{\xi} \ge (f(\boldsymbol{x}, \boldsymbol{\xi}) - \alpha)^+, \quad \forall \boldsymbol{\xi} \in \mathbb{R}^l. \tag{4.4.15b}$$

Substituting (4.4.15a)–(4.4.15b) back to (4.4.14), we can remove the infimum operators due to the $\le 0$ inequality and get the following equivalent reformulation of the CVaR constraint (4.4.13).

$$
(4.4.13) \iff \begin{cases} \alpha + \frac{1}{\epsilon}\left(\lambda + \boldsymbol{\mu}_0^\top \boldsymbol{\beta} + \boldsymbol{Q} \bullet (\gamma \boldsymbol{\Sigma}_0 + \boldsymbol{\mu}_0\boldsymbol{\mu}_0^\top)\right) \le 0, \\ \lambda + \boldsymbol{\xi}^\top \boldsymbol{\beta} + \boldsymbol{\xi}^\top \boldsymbol{Q}\boldsymbol{\xi} \ge 0, \quad \forall \boldsymbol{\xi} \in \mathbb{R}^l, \\ \lambda + \boldsymbol{\xi}^\top \boldsymbol{\beta} + \boldsymbol{\xi}^\top \boldsymbol{Q}\boldsymbol{\xi} \ge f(\boldsymbol{x}, \boldsymbol{\xi}) - \alpha, \quad \forall \boldsymbol{\xi} \in \mathbb{R}^l, \\ \boldsymbol{Q} \succeq \boldsymbol{0}. \end{cases} \tag{4.4.16a}
$$

The second and third constraints come from writing out (4.4.15b) LHS $\ge \max(0, f(\boldsymbol{x}, \boldsymbol{\xi}) - \alpha)$ as two cases LHS $\ge 0$ and LHS $\ge f(\boldsymbol{x}, \boldsymbol{\xi}) - \alpha$.

The second and third constraints in (4.4.16a) are robust constraints and can be further reformulated as deterministic constraints for the two classes of $f(\boldsymbol{x}, \boldsymbol{\xi})$. We will do this reformulation later. Next, we want to show the important equivalence relation (4.4.12) by proving the implication CVaR $\Leftarrow$ DRC. We will achieve this through a sequence of reformulations of DRC (4.4.10) until we can turn it into (4.4.16a). We break down the derivation into small steps. We will note that the main technique is the repeated use of Lagrangian duality and a few simple observations. Here are the steps.

1. The first basic observation is that the probability of an event can be expressed as an expectation of a function. In particular, the probability of an event $C$ is equal to the expectation of an indicator function of the event. That is,

$$
\mathbb{P}(\boldsymbol{\xi} \in C) = \mathbb{E}_{\mathbb{P}}[\ \ (\boldsymbol{\xi} \in C)], \tag{4.4.17}
$$

where the indicator function $\ \ (\boldsymbol{\xi} \in C)$ is equal to 1, if $\boldsymbol{\xi} \in C$, and 0, otherwise. To use this observation, let us denote the event $f(\boldsymbol{x}, \boldsymbol{\xi}) \le 0$ as $C(\boldsymbol{x}, \boldsymbol{\xi})$, i.e. $C(\boldsymbol{x}, \boldsymbol{\xi}) = \{\boldsymbol{\xi} \in \mathbb{R}^l : f(\boldsymbol{x}, \boldsymbol{\xi}) \le 0\}$.
2. With this observation, the left-hand side of DRCC (4.4.10) can be written as

$$
\inf_{\mathbb{P} \in \mathscr{M}_+(\mathbb{R}^l)} \int_{\mathbb{R}^l} \ \ (C(\boldsymbol{x}, \boldsymbol{\xi})) \boldsymbol{d}\mathbb{P}(\boldsymbol{\xi}) \tag{4.4.18a}
$$

$$
\text{s.t.} \int_{\mathbb{R}^l} d\mathbb{P}(\boldsymbol{\xi}) = 1, \tag{4.4.18b}
$$

$$
\int_{\mathbb{R}^l} \boldsymbol{\xi} d\mathbb{P}(\boldsymbol{\xi}) = \boldsymbol{\mu}_0, \tag{4.4.18c}
$$

$$
\int_{\mathbb{R}^l} \boldsymbol{\xi}\boldsymbol{\xi}^\top d\mathbb{P}(\boldsymbol{\xi}) \preceq \gamma \boldsymbol{\Sigma}_0 + \boldsymbol{\mu}_0\boldsymbol{\mu}_0^\top. \tag{4.4.18d}
$$

This is an infinite dimensional linear optimization problem over measures $\mathbb{P} \in \mathscr{M}_+(\mathbb{R}^l)$. As we have seen in the previous sections, duality theory will come to our aid. Indeed, we can apply the same derivation as in (4.2.10)–(4.2.11) to formulate the following dual problem of (4.4.18).

$$
\sup_{\lambda, \boldsymbol{\beta}, \boldsymbol{Q}} \quad \lambda + \boldsymbol{\mu}_0^\top \boldsymbol{\beta} + \boldsymbol{Q} \bullet (\gamma \boldsymbol{\Sigma}_0 + \boldsymbol{\mu}_0\boldsymbol{\mu}_0^\top) \tag{4.4.19a}
$$

$$\text{s.t.} \quad \lambda + \boldsymbol{\xi}^\top \boldsymbol{\beta} + \boldsymbol{\xi}^\top \boldsymbol{Q}\boldsymbol{\xi} \le \quad (C(\boldsymbol{x}, \boldsymbol{\xi})), \quad \forall \boldsymbol{\xi} \in \mathbb{R}^l, \tag{4.4.19b}$$

$$\boldsymbol{Q} \preceq \boldsymbol{0}. \tag{4.4.19c}$$

Next, we will incorporate it into the chance constraint inequality and further manipulate it into the CVaR form.

3. Incorporating (4.4.19) to the chance constraint, we get

$$\sup_{\lambda, \boldsymbol{\beta}, \boldsymbol{Q} \preceq \boldsymbol{0}} \left\{ \lambda + \boldsymbol{\mu}_0^\top \boldsymbol{\beta} + \boldsymbol{Q} \bullet (\gamma \boldsymbol{\Sigma}_0 + \boldsymbol{\mu}_0 \boldsymbol{\mu}_0^\top) \right\} \ge 1 - \epsilon$$

$$\text{s.t.} \quad \lambda + \boldsymbol{\xi}^\top \boldsymbol{\beta} + \boldsymbol{\xi}^\top \boldsymbol{Q}\boldsymbol{\xi} \le \quad (C(\boldsymbol{x}, \boldsymbol{\xi})), \quad \forall \boldsymbol{\xi} \in \mathbb{R}^l,$$

$$\Longleftrightarrow 1 - \epsilon + \inf_{\lambda, \boldsymbol{\beta}, \boldsymbol{Q} \succeq \boldsymbol{0}} \left\{ \lambda + \boldsymbol{\mu}_0^\top \boldsymbol{\beta} + \boldsymbol{Q} \bullet (\gamma \boldsymbol{\Sigma}_0 + \boldsymbol{\mu}_0 \boldsymbol{\mu}_0^\top) \right\} \le 0 \tag{4.4.20a}$$

$$\text{s.t.} \quad \lambda + \boldsymbol{\xi}^\top \boldsymbol{\beta} + \boldsymbol{\xi}^\top \boldsymbol{Q}\boldsymbol{\xi} \ge - \quad (C(\boldsymbol{x}, \boldsymbol{\xi})), \quad \forall \boldsymbol{\xi} \in \mathbb{R}^l. \tag{4.4.20b}$$

Here we turn the supremum objective into an infimum problem in (4.4.20a) and redefine all variables by their negation, i.e. $\lambda \leftarrow -\lambda$, $\boldsymbol{\beta} \leftarrow -\boldsymbol{\beta}$, $\boldsymbol{Q} \leftarrow -\boldsymbol{Q}$ in the constraint (4.4.20b).

4. Now observe we can further redefine a new $\lambda$ variable as the old $\lambda + 1$. Then, the 1 in (4.4.20a) can be absorbed and the constraint is also changed as

$$-\epsilon + \inf_{\lambda, \boldsymbol{\beta}, \boldsymbol{Q} \succeq \boldsymbol{0}} \left\{ \lambda + \boldsymbol{\mu}_0^\top \boldsymbol{\beta} + \boldsymbol{Q} \bullet (\gamma \boldsymbol{\Sigma}_0 + \boldsymbol{\mu}_0 \boldsymbol{\mu}_0^\top) \right\} \le 0 \tag{4.4.21a}$$

$$\text{s.t.} \quad \lambda + \boldsymbol{\xi}^\top \boldsymbol{\beta} + \boldsymbol{\xi}^\top \boldsymbol{Q}\boldsymbol{\xi} \ge 1 - \quad (C(\boldsymbol{x}, \boldsymbol{\xi})), \quad \forall \boldsymbol{\xi} \in \mathbb{R}^l. \tag{4.4.21b}$$

5. Now constraint (4.4.21b) can be further written out as

$$\lambda + \boldsymbol{\xi}^\top \boldsymbol{\beta} + \boldsymbol{\xi}^\top \boldsymbol{Q}\boldsymbol{\xi} \ge 0, \quad \forall \boldsymbol{\xi} \in \mathbb{R}^l, \tag{4.4.22a}$$

$$\lambda + \boldsymbol{\xi}^\top \boldsymbol{\beta} + \boldsymbol{\xi}^\top \boldsymbol{Q}\boldsymbol{\xi} \ge 1, \quad \forall \boldsymbol{\xi} : f(\boldsymbol{x}, \boldsymbol{\xi}) \ge 0. \tag{4.4.22b}$$

The trick used in (4.4.22a) is that $1 - \quad (C(\boldsymbol{x}, \boldsymbol{\xi})) \ge 0$ for all $\boldsymbol{\xi} \in \mathbb{R}^l$.

6. It is easy to see that the robust constraint (4.4.22a) is equivalent to

$$\begin{bmatrix} 1 \\ \boldsymbol{\xi} \end{bmatrix}^\top \begin{bmatrix} \lambda & \frac{1}{2}\boldsymbol{\beta}^\top \\ \frac{1}{2}\boldsymbol{\beta} & \boldsymbol{Q} \end{bmatrix} \begin{bmatrix} 1 \\ \boldsymbol{\xi} \end{bmatrix} \ge 0, \quad \forall \boldsymbol{\xi} \in \mathbb{R}^l,$$

which, by the definition of semidefinite matrices, is equivalent to

$$\begin{bmatrix} \lambda & \frac{1}{2}\boldsymbol{\beta}^\top \\ \frac{1}{2}\boldsymbol{\beta} & \boldsymbol{Q} \end{bmatrix} \succeq \boldsymbol{0}. \tag{4.4.23}$$

7. The robust constraint (4.4.22b) can be written as

$$\inf_{\boldsymbol{\xi}: f(\boldsymbol{x},\boldsymbol{\xi})\geq 0} \left\{\lambda + \boldsymbol{\xi}^\top \boldsymbol{\beta} + \boldsymbol{\xi}^\top \boldsymbol{Q}\boldsymbol{\xi}\right\} \geq 1. \tag{4.4.24}$$

If $f(\boldsymbol{x}, \boldsymbol{\xi})$ is a concave function in $\boldsymbol{\xi}$, then the above problem is a convex optimization problem, since $\boldsymbol{Q} \succeq \mathbf{0}$ as constrained by (4.4.23). Thus, strong duality holds. If $f(\boldsymbol{x}, \boldsymbol{\xi})$ is a (possibly non-concave) quadratic function in $\boldsymbol{\xi}$, then the above problem is a quadratic program with one quadratic constraint. As we already discussed in Chap. 2, S-lemma applies and strong duality also holds in this case. Therefore, in either case, we can apply Lagrangian duality and get an exact reformulation of (4.4.22b) through (4.4.24) as

$$\sup_{1/\tau\geq 0} \inf_{\boldsymbol{\xi}} \left\{\lambda + \boldsymbol{\xi}^\top \boldsymbol{\beta} + \boldsymbol{\xi}^\top \boldsymbol{Q}\boldsymbol{\xi} - \frac{1}{\tau} f(\boldsymbol{x}, \boldsymbol{\xi})\right\} \geq 1$$

$$\Longleftrightarrow \exists\, \tau \geq 0,\ \lambda + \boldsymbol{\xi}^\top \boldsymbol{\beta} + \boldsymbol{\xi}^\top \boldsymbol{Q}\boldsymbol{\xi} \geq \frac{1}{\tau} f(\boldsymbol{x}, \boldsymbol{\xi}) + 1, \quad \forall \boldsymbol{\xi} \in \mathbb{R}^l, \tag{4.4.25}$$

$$\Longleftrightarrow \exists\, \tau \geq 0,\ \tau\lambda + \boldsymbol{\xi}^\top (\tau\boldsymbol{\beta}) + \boldsymbol{\xi}^\top (\tau \boldsymbol{Q})\boldsymbol{\xi} \geq f(\boldsymbol{x}, \boldsymbol{\xi}) + \tau, \quad \forall \boldsymbol{\xi} \in \mathbb{R}^l. \tag{4.4.26}$$

8. Multiplying $\tau/\epsilon$ on both sides of the objective (4.4.21a), we get

$$-\tau + \frac{1}{\epsilon} \inf_{\lambda, \boldsymbol{\beta}, \boldsymbol{Q}\succeq \mathbf{0}} \left\{\tau\lambda + \boldsymbol{\mu}_0^\top (\tau\boldsymbol{\beta}) + (\tau \boldsymbol{Q}) \bullet (\gamma \boldsymbol{\Sigma}_0 + \boldsymbol{\mu}_0\boldsymbol{\mu}_0^\top)\right\} \leq 0 \tag{4.4.27a}$$

$$\text{s.t. (4.4.22a), (4.4.26).}$$

Now we can redefine $\tau\lambda$ as the new variable $\lambda$, $\tau\boldsymbol{\beta}$ as the new $\boldsymbol{\beta}$, and $\tau \boldsymbol{Q}$ as the new $\boldsymbol{Q}$. We can also define a new variable $\alpha = -\tau$. Note that the infimum in (4.4.27a) can be removed as we have a $\leq$ inequality. Putting all this together, we come to

$$\begin{cases} \alpha + \frac{1}{\epsilon}\left(\lambda + \boldsymbol{\mu}_0^\top \boldsymbol{\beta} + \boldsymbol{Q} \bullet (\gamma \boldsymbol{\Sigma}_0 + \boldsymbol{\mu}_0\boldsymbol{\mu}_0^\top)\right) \leq 0 \\ \lambda + \boldsymbol{\xi}^\top \boldsymbol{\beta} + \boldsymbol{\xi}^\top \boldsymbol{Q}\boldsymbol{\xi} \geq 0, \quad \forall \boldsymbol{\xi} \in \mathbb{R}^l, \\ \lambda + \boldsymbol{\xi}^\top \boldsymbol{\beta} + \boldsymbol{\xi}^\top \boldsymbol{Q}\boldsymbol{\xi} \geq f(\boldsymbol{x}, \boldsymbol{\xi}) - \alpha, \quad \forall \boldsymbol{\xi} \in \mathbb{R}^l, \\ \boldsymbol{Q} \succeq \mathbf{0}. \end{cases} \tag{4.4.28}$$

As an exercise, show why we can remove the constraint $\tau \geq 0$ (see Exercise 4.11.) Comparing (4.4.28) and (4.4.16a), we can see they are clearly identical. This completes the derivation and shows the equivalence of CVaR and DRC in (4.4.12).

9. We can further simplify the notation in (4.4.28) by introducing the following matrix, which contains the first- and second-order moments of the nominal

distribution

$$\boldsymbol{\Omega}_0 := \begin{bmatrix} 1 & \boldsymbol{\mu}_0^\top \\ \boldsymbol{\mu}_0 & \gamma \boldsymbol{\Sigma}_0 + \boldsymbol{\mu}_0 \boldsymbol{\mu}_0^\top \end{bmatrix}, \tag{4.4.29}$$

a new matrix variable

$$\boldsymbol{M} := \begin{bmatrix} \lambda & \frac{1}{2}\boldsymbol{\beta}^\top \\ \frac{1}{2}\boldsymbol{\beta} & \boldsymbol{Q} \end{bmatrix}, \tag{4.4.30}$$

and a matrix of $\boldsymbol{\xi}$ as

$$\boldsymbol{\Lambda}(\boldsymbol{\xi}) := \begin{bmatrix} 1 & \boldsymbol{\xi}^\top \\ \boldsymbol{\xi} & \boldsymbol{\xi}\boldsymbol{\xi}^\top \end{bmatrix}. \tag{4.4.31}$$

Then the constraints in (4.4.28) can be rewritten in the new variable $\boldsymbol{M}$ as

$$\begin{cases} \alpha + \frac{1}{\epsilon}\boldsymbol{\Omega}_0 \bullet \boldsymbol{M} \le 0, \\ \boldsymbol{M} \succeq \boldsymbol{0}, \\ \boldsymbol{\Lambda}(\boldsymbol{\xi}) \bullet \boldsymbol{M} \ge f(\boldsymbol{x}, \boldsymbol{\xi}) - \alpha, \quad \forall \boldsymbol{\xi} \in \mathbb{R}^l. \end{cases} \tag{4.4.32}$$

Let us summarize this major result.

If $f(\boldsymbol{x}, \boldsymbol{\xi})$ is a concave function in $\boldsymbol{\xi}$, or a (possibly non-concave) quadratic function in $\boldsymbol{\xi}$, the DRCC has the following equivalent reformulation in $(\alpha, \boldsymbol{x}, \boldsymbol{M})$,

$$\inf_{\mathbb{P} \in \mathscr{P}} \mathbb{P}(f(\boldsymbol{x}, \boldsymbol{\xi}) \le 0) \ge 1 - \epsilon \iff \begin{cases} \alpha + \frac{1}{\epsilon}\boldsymbol{\Omega}_0 \bullet \boldsymbol{M} \le 0, \\ \boldsymbol{M} \succeq \boldsymbol{0}, \\ \boldsymbol{\Lambda}(\boldsymbol{\xi}) \bullet \boldsymbol{M} \ge f(\boldsymbol{x}, \boldsymbol{\xi}) - \alpha, \quad \forall \boldsymbol{\xi} \in \mathbb{R}^l, \end{cases} \tag{4.4.33}$$

where the ambiguity set $\mathscr{P}$ is the cross-moment set $\mathscr{P}(\boldsymbol{\mu}_0, \boldsymbol{\Sigma}_0, \gamma)$ defined in (4.4.9).

#### 4.4.2.2 Tractable Reformulations

The tractability of (4.4.33) depends on the third constraint, which is a robust constraint in itself. In the following, we consider some concrete examples, where the third constraint can be reformulated as a deterministic convex constraint.

**When $f(\boldsymbol{x}, \boldsymbol{\xi})$ Is a Bilinear Function**

Our first example assumes a bilinear function $f(\boldsymbol{x}, \boldsymbol{\xi}) = a(\boldsymbol{x}) + \boldsymbol{b}(\boldsymbol{x})^\top \boldsymbol{\xi}$, where $a(\boldsymbol{x})$ and $\boldsymbol{b}(\boldsymbol{x})$ are linear functions of $\boldsymbol{x}$. Clearly, $f(\boldsymbol{x}, \boldsymbol{\xi})$ is a concave (linear) function of $\boldsymbol{\xi}$. Then we have

$$
\begin{aligned}
& \boldsymbol{\Lambda}(\boldsymbol{\xi}) \bullet \boldsymbol{M} \geq a(\boldsymbol{x}) + \boldsymbol{b}(\boldsymbol{x})^\top \boldsymbol{\xi} - \alpha, \quad \forall \boldsymbol{\xi} \in \mathbb{R}^l, \\
\iff & \begin{bmatrix} 1 \\ \boldsymbol{\xi} \end{bmatrix}^\top \left( \boldsymbol{M} - \begin{bmatrix} a(\boldsymbol{x}) - \alpha & \frac{1}{2} b(\boldsymbol{x})^\top \\ \frac{1}{2} b(\boldsymbol{x}) & \boldsymbol{0} \end{bmatrix} \right) \begin{bmatrix} 1 \\ \boldsymbol{\xi} \end{bmatrix} \geq 0, \quad \forall \boldsymbol{\xi} \in \mathbb{R}^l, \\
\iff & \boldsymbol{M} \succeq \begin{bmatrix} a(\boldsymbol{x}) - \alpha & \frac{1}{2} b(\boldsymbol{x})^\top \\ \frac{1}{2} b(\boldsymbol{x}) & \boldsymbol{0} \end{bmatrix}.
\end{aligned}
$$

This result is summarized below.

The following DRCC with a bilinear function and the cross-moment ambiguity set (4.4.9c) can be equivalently reformulated as a set of SDP constraints in $(\boldsymbol{x}, \alpha, \boldsymbol{M})$.

$$
\inf_{\mathbb{P} \in \mathscr{P}} \mathbb{P}\left( a(\boldsymbol{x}) + \boldsymbol{b}(\boldsymbol{x})^\top \boldsymbol{\xi} \leq 0 \right) \geq 1 - \epsilon \iff \begin{cases} \alpha + \frac{1}{\epsilon} \boldsymbol{\Omega}_0 \bullet \boldsymbol{M} \leq 0, \\ \boldsymbol{M} \succeq \boldsymbol{0}, \\ \boldsymbol{M} \succeq \begin{bmatrix} a(\boldsymbol{x}) - \alpha & \frac{1}{2} b(\boldsymbol{x})^\top \\ \frac{1}{2} b(\boldsymbol{x}) & \boldsymbol{0} \end{bmatrix}. \end{cases} \tag{4.4.34}
$$

**When $f(\boldsymbol{x}, \boldsymbol{\xi})$ Is Quadratic in $\boldsymbol{\xi}$**

Suppose $f(\boldsymbol{x}, \boldsymbol{\xi}) = \boldsymbol{\xi}^\top \boldsymbol{A}(\boldsymbol{x}) \boldsymbol{\xi} + \boldsymbol{b}(\boldsymbol{x})^\top \boldsymbol{\xi} + a(\boldsymbol{x})$, where $a(\boldsymbol{x})$, $\boldsymbol{b}(\boldsymbol{x})$, and $\boldsymbol{A}(\boldsymbol{x})$ are linear in $\boldsymbol{x}$, and $\boldsymbol{A}(\boldsymbol{x})$ is a real symmetric matrix, not necessarily positive or negative semidefinite. Then $f(\boldsymbol{x}, \boldsymbol{\xi})$ is a possibly non-concave or nonconvex quadratic function of $\boldsymbol{\xi}$. The reformulation in this case is very similar to the linear case. We will leave the derivation in Exercise 4.12. Interested reader can also consult [5, Theorem 2.3].

The following DRCC with a quadratic function in $\boldsymbol{\xi}$ and linear in $\boldsymbol{x}$ and the cross-moment ambiguity set (4.4.9c) can be equivalently reformulated as a set of SDP constraints in $(\boldsymbol{x}, \alpha, \boldsymbol{M})$.

(continued)

$$\inf_{\mathbb{P}\in\mathscr{P}} \mathbb{P}\left(a(\boldsymbol{x}) + \boldsymbol{b}(\boldsymbol{x})^\top \boldsymbol{\xi} + \boldsymbol{\xi}^\top \boldsymbol{A}(\boldsymbol{x})\boldsymbol{\xi} \le 0\right) \ge 1-\epsilon \iff \begin{cases} \alpha + \frac{1}{\epsilon}\boldsymbol{\Omega}_0 \bullet \boldsymbol{M} \le 0, \\ \boldsymbol{M} \succeq \boldsymbol{0}, \\ \boldsymbol{M} \succeq \begin{bmatrix} a(\boldsymbol{x}) - \alpha & \frac{1}{2}b(\boldsymbol{x})^\top \\ \frac{1}{2}b(\boldsymbol{x}) & \boldsymbol{A}(\boldsymbol{x}) \end{bmatrix}. \end{cases} \tag{4.35}$$

### 4.4.3 Exact Reformulations of DRCC with $\phi$-Divergence Ambiguity Sets

Now let us turn to $\phi$-divergence ambiguity sets which are introduced in Sect. 4.2.2. In particular, we assume the ambiguity set $\mathbb{P}$ takes the following form

$$\mathscr{P}_\phi(\mathbb{Q}_0, d) = \left\{\mathbb{P} \in \mathbb{R}^m_+ : \mathbb{P}(\boldsymbol{\xi} \in \mathscr{U}) = 1,\ D_\phi(\mathbb{P}, \mathbb{Q}_0) \le d\right\}, \tag{4.4.36}$$

where $\mathbb{Q}_0 = (q_1, \ldots, q_m)$ is the nominal discrete distribution with $m$ support points in $\mathscr{U}$ and $d$ controls the size of the ambiguity set. The DRCC (4.4.8) can be written as

$$\begin{aligned} &\inf_{\mathbb{P}\in\mathscr{P}} \mathbb{P}\left(f(\boldsymbol{x}, \boldsymbol{\xi}) \le 0\right) \ge 1-\epsilon \\ \iff\ & 1-\epsilon \le \min_{\mathbb{P}} \sum_{i=1}^m p_i \cdot \quad (C(\boldsymbol{x}, \boldsymbol{\xi}_i)) \\ & \qquad \text{s.t.} \sum_{i=1}^m q_i \cdot \phi\left(\frac{p_i}{q_i}\right) \le d, \quad (\alpha) \\ & \qquad \sum_{i=1}^m p_i = 1, \qquad\qquad (\lambda) \\ & \qquad p_i \ge 0, \quad \forall i \in [m], \end{aligned}$$

where $C(\boldsymbol{x}, \boldsymbol{\xi})$ denotes the event $\{\boldsymbol{\xi} : f(\boldsymbol{x}, \boldsymbol{\xi}) \le 0\}$ and the indicator function $(C(\boldsymbol{x}, \boldsymbol{\xi}_i)) = 1$, if $\boldsymbol{\xi}_i \in C(\boldsymbol{x}, \boldsymbol{\xi}_i)$, and 0, otherwise.

The Lagrangian can be formulated with the dual variables $\alpha$, $\lambda$ as

$$L(\mathbb{P}, \alpha, \lambda) = \sum_{i=1}^{m} \Big( (C(\boldsymbol{x}, \boldsymbol{\xi}_i)) - \lambda\Big) \cdot p_i + \sum_{i=1}^{m} q_i \cdot \alpha\phi\left(\frac{p_i}{q_i}\right) + \lambda - \alpha d. \tag{4.4.37}$$

Now we can directly adopt the reformulation (4.2.26) in Sect. 4.2.2 by adjusting min and max. We have

$$\inf_{\mathbb{P}\in\mathscr{P}_\phi(\mathbb{Q}_0,d)} \mathbb{P}(f(\boldsymbol{x}, \boldsymbol{\xi}) \le \mathbf{0}) \ge 1-\epsilon, \tag{4.4.38}$$

$$\Longleftrightarrow \max_{\lambda,\alpha>0} \left\{\lambda - d\cdot\alpha - \alpha\sum_{i=1}^{m} q_i\phi^*\left(\frac{\lambda - C(\boldsymbol{x},\boldsymbol{\xi}_i)}{\alpha}\right)\right\} \ge 1-\epsilon, \tag{4.4.39}$$

$$\Longleftrightarrow \max_{\lambda,\alpha>0} \left\{\lambda - d\cdot\alpha - \alpha\sum_{i:\ (C(\boldsymbol{x},\boldsymbol{\xi}_i))=1} q_i\phi^*\left(\frac{\lambda-1}{\alpha}\right) - \alpha\sum_{i:\ (C(\boldsymbol{x},\boldsymbol{\xi}_i))=0} q_i\phi^*\left(\frac{\lambda}{\alpha}\right)\right\} \ge 1-\epsilon,$$

$$\Longleftrightarrow \max_{\lambda,\alpha>0} \left\{\lambda - d\cdot\alpha - \alpha\mathbb{Q}_0(C(\boldsymbol{x},\boldsymbol{\xi}))\phi^*\left(\frac{\lambda-1}{\alpha}\right) - \alpha(1-\mathbb{Q}_0(C(\boldsymbol{x},\boldsymbol{\xi})))\phi^*\left(\frac{\lambda}{\alpha}\right)\right\} \ge 1-\epsilon,$$

$$\Longleftrightarrow \text{there exist } \alpha>0,\ \lambda,$$

$$\text{s.t. } \lambda - \alpha\cdot d + \alpha\left[\phi^*\left(\frac{\lambda}{\alpha}\right) - \phi^*\left(\frac{\lambda-1}{\alpha}\right)\right]\mathbb{Q}_0(C(\boldsymbol{x},\boldsymbol{\xi})) - \alpha\phi^*\left(\frac{\lambda}{\alpha}\right) \ge 1-\epsilon, \tag{4.4.40}$$

$$\Longleftrightarrow \exists\alpha>0,\ (\lambda-1)/\alpha \le \overline{m},\ \lambda/\alpha \ge \underline{m}, \tag{4.4.41}$$

$$\text{s.t. } \mathbb{Q}_0(C(\boldsymbol{x},\boldsymbol{\xi})) \ge \frac{1-\epsilon-\lambda+\alpha\cdot d+\alpha\phi^*\left(\frac{\lambda}{\alpha}\right)}{\alpha\cdot\left[\phi^*\left(\frac{\lambda}{\alpha}\right) - \phi^*\left(\frac{\lambda-1}{\alpha}\right)\right]}, \tag{4.4.42}$$

$$\Longleftrightarrow \exists\alpha>0,\ (\lambda-1)/\alpha \le \overline{m},\ \lambda/\alpha \ge \underline{m},$$

$$\text{s.t. } \mathbb{Q}_0(C(\boldsymbol{x},\boldsymbol{\xi})) \ge 1 - \underbrace{\frac{\epsilon+(\lambda-1)-\alpha\cdot d-\alpha\phi^*\left(\frac{\lambda-1}{\alpha}\right)}{\alpha\cdot\left[\phi^*\left(\frac{\lambda}{\alpha}\right) - \phi^*\left(\frac{\lambda-1}{\alpha}\right)\right]}}_{=:\epsilon_\phi(\lambda,\alpha,d)}, \tag{4.4.43}$$

$$\Longleftrightarrow \mathbb{Q}_0(C(\boldsymbol{x},\boldsymbol{\xi})) \ge 1 - \underbrace{\sup_{\alpha>0,\ \lambda-\alpha\overline{m}\le 1\lambda-\alpha\underline{m}\ge 0} \epsilon_\phi(\lambda,\alpha,d)}_{=:\epsilon'_\phi(d)}, \tag{4.4.44}$$

where we introduce two parameters $\overline{m}$ and $\underline{m}$ in (4.4.41), which are defined as $\overline{m} = \inf\{x : \phi^*(x) = +\infty\}$ and $\underline{m} := \sup\{x : \phi^*(x) \text{ is constant on } (-\infty, x]\}$. With these definitions, we can see that $\phi^*(x)$ is a finite, strictly increasing function on $x \in [\underline{m}, \overline{m}]$ (see Exercise 4.5.) Therefore, we can divide the coefficient of $\mathbb{Q}_0(C(\boldsymbol{x},\boldsymbol{\xi}))$

and obtain (4.4.42). Moreover, we can prove that $\epsilon'_{\phi}(d) \leq \epsilon$ using the properties of $\phi^*$ (see Exercises 4.5 and 4.13.)

What we achieve in (4.4.44) is quite interesting. It says that the DRCC (4.4.38) with the $\phi$-divergence ambiguity set is equivalent to a standard chance constraint with the nominal distribution $\mathbb{Q}_0$ over a tightened probability margin $\epsilon'_{\phi}(d)$, i.e. $\mathbb{Q}_0(C(\boldsymbol{x}, \boldsymbol{\xi})) \geq 1 - \epsilon'_{\phi}(d) \geq 1 - \epsilon$. Let us summarize this nice result.

A DRCC with a $\phi$-divergence ambiguity set (4.4.36) and a discrete nominal probability measure $\mathbb{Q}_0$ can be equivalently reformulated as

$$\inf_{\mathbb{P} \in \mathscr{P}} \mathbb{P}(f(\boldsymbol{x}, \boldsymbol{\xi}) \leq 0) \geq 1 - \epsilon \iff \mathbb{Q}_0(C(\boldsymbol{x}, \boldsymbol{\xi})) \geq 1 - \epsilon'_{\phi}(d), \tag{4.4.45}$$

where the modified probability margin $\epsilon'_{\phi}(d)$ is defined in (4.4.43) and (4.4.44), and $\epsilon'_{\phi}(d) \leq \epsilon$.

We can further reformulate the right-hand side of (4.4.45) using the discrete nature of $\mathbb{Q}_0$ as

$$\sum_{i=1}^{m} q_i \cdot \quad (f(\boldsymbol{x}, \boldsymbol{\xi}_i) \leq 0) \geq 1 - \epsilon'_{\phi}(d). \tag{4.4.46}$$

The indicator function $\quad (f(\boldsymbol{x}, \boldsymbol{\xi}_i) \leq 0)$ can be reformulated using binary variables and big-M parameters if the feasible region of $f(\boldsymbol{x}, \boldsymbol{\xi}_i) \leq 0$ is a set that can be represented by mixed integer constraints. The above derivation of the equivalent reformulation can be generalized to $\phi$-divergence ambiguity sets with a probability measure $\mathbb{Q}_0$ that has a density function (see [10, Theorem 1].)

### *4.4.4 Exact Reformulations of DRCC with Wasserstein Ambiguity Sets*

Now we turn to DRCC with Wasserstein ambiguity sets. We first demonstrate that an individual linear chance constraint with discrete nominal distribution can be equivalently reformulation as a CVaR constraint. Then, we show that the resulting CVaR constraint can be further reformulated as a set of mixed integer linear constraints, which would be amenable for solution with an off-the-shelf integer programming solver.

#### 4.4.4.1 Exact Reformulation of an Individual DRCC as a CVaR Constraint

We start from a simple case, where (1) the probabilistic constraint involves a single linear constraint in the decision variable $\boldsymbol{x}$ with uncertainty in the coefficients and right-hand side, (2) the ambiguity set is based on the 1st order Wasserstein metric over probability measures supported on the entire $\mathbb{R}^l$, and (3) the nominal distribution $\mathbb{Q}_0 = (q_1, q_2, \dots, q_n)^\top$ is a discrete measure with a finite support $\{\boldsymbol{\xi}_1, \boldsymbol{\xi}_2, \dots, \boldsymbol{\xi}_n\}$, e.g. $\mathbb{Q}_0$ could be an empirical distribution with $q_j = 1/n$ for all $j$. In particular, consider the following problem

$$\inf_{\mathbb{P}\in\mathscr{P}_W(\mathbb{Q}_0,d)} \mathbb{P}\left(\boldsymbol{a}(\boldsymbol{x})^\top\boldsymbol{\xi} \le b(\boldsymbol{x})\right) \ge 1-\epsilon, \tag{4.4.47}$$

where the Wasserstein ambiguity set $\mathscr{P}_W(\mathbb{Q}_0, d)$ is defined as

$$\mathscr{P}_W(\mathbb{Q}_0, d) = \left\{\mathbb{P} \in \mathscr{P}_0(\mathbb{R}^l) : W_1(\mathbb{P}, \mathbb{Q}_0) \le d\right\} \text{ with } d > 0. \tag{4.4.48}$$

The Wasserstein distance $W_1(\mathbb{P}, \mathbb{Q}_0)$ is defined as in (4.2.34) with $p = 1$ and a norm $\|\cdot\|$ on $\mathbb{R}^l$, i.e. a first-order Wasserstein metric. The functions $\boldsymbol{a}(\boldsymbol{x})$ and $b(\boldsymbol{x})$ are affine functions of $\boldsymbol{x}$. As we have shown in Chap. 2, such a constraint $\boldsymbol{a}(\boldsymbol{x})^\top\boldsymbol{\xi} \le b(\boldsymbol{x})$ can model uncertainty in both coefficients and right-hand side of an uncertain linear constraint. For example, the following constraint

$$\sum_i (a_i^0 + \sum_j a_{ij}\xi_j)x_i \le b^0 + \sum_j b_j\xi_j \tag{4.4.49}$$

can be written in the form of $\boldsymbol{a}(\boldsymbol{x})^\top\boldsymbol{\xi} \le b(\boldsymbol{x})$. An important special case is when uncertainty only appears in the right-hand side of (4.4.49). In an exercise, the reader will show that this special case has a simpler reformulation than the general case.

In the following we want to show that the DRCC with the Wasserstein ball (4.4.47) is equivalent to a constraint involving conditional value at risk (CVaR). Recall that a DRCC with a cross-moment ambiguity set can be equivalently reformulated as a distributionally robust CVaR constraint as shown in (4.4.12). In contrast, the equivalent reformulation of (4.4.47) is a *deterministic* constraint on CVaR over the nominal distribution $\mathbb{Q}_0$, rather than a distributionally robust CVaR. In particular, we have

A DRCC (4.4.47) with a Wasserstein ambiguity set (4.4.48) can be equivalently reformulated as

(continued)

$$\inf_{\mathbb{P}\in\mathscr{P}_W(\mathbb{Q}_0,d)} \mathbb{P}\left(a(x)^\top \xi \le b(x)\right) \ge 1-\epsilon \iff \text{CVaR}_{1-\epsilon}^{\mathbb{Q}_0}(-f(x,\xi)) + \frac{d}{\epsilon} \le 0, \tag{4.4.50}$$

where $g(x,\xi)$ is defined as

$$g(x,\xi) = \begin{cases} \frac{\max\{b(x)-a(x)^\top\xi,0\}}{\|a(x)\|_*}, & \text{if } a(x) \ne 0, \\ \delta(x|b(x)<0), & \text{if } a(x) = 0, \end{cases} \tag{4.4.51}$$

and $\delta(\cdot|C)$ is the characteristic function of the set $C$, i.e. $\delta(x|C) = 0$ if $x \in C$, and $+\infty$, otherwise.

We show this nice result in the following steps.

1. The probability in the original DRCC (4.4.47) can be written as an expectation with an indicator function as

$$\begin{aligned} \inf_{\mathbb{P}\in\mathscr{P}_W(\mathbb{Q}_0,d)} \mathbb{P}\left(a(x)^\top\xi \le b(x)\right) \ge 1-\epsilon &\iff \inf_{\mathbb{P}\in\mathscr{P}_W(\mathbb{Q}_0,d)} \mathbb{E}_{\mathbb{P}}\left[ \ (a(x)^\top\xi \le b(x))\right] \ge 1-\epsilon, \\ &\iff \sup_{\mathbb{P}\in\mathscr{P}_W(\mathbb{Q}_0,d)} \mathbb{E}_{\mathbb{P}}\left[ \ (a(x)^\top\xi > b(x))\right] \le \epsilon. \end{aligned} \tag{4.4.52}$$

Now we can apply the exact reformulation (4.2.42b) of a distributionally robust constraint with a Wasserstein ball to (4.4.52), and get

$$(4.4.52) \iff \inf_{\alpha\ge 0}\left\{ d\alpha - \sum_{j=1}^{n} q_j \inf_{\xi\in\mathbb{R}^l}\left\{\alpha\|\xi-\xi_j\| - \ (a(x)^\top x > b(x))\right\}\right\} \le \epsilon. \tag{4.4.53}$$

2. We need to reformulate the inner infimum problem. Observe that, for each $j$, the infimum can be rewritten as the following

$$\inf_{\xi\in\mathbb{R}^l}\left\{\alpha\|\xi-\xi_j\| - \ (a(x)^\top x > b(x))\right\} = \min\left\{\inf_{\xi:a(x)^\top\xi > b(x)} \alpha\|\xi-\xi_j\| - 1, \inf_{\xi:a(x)^\top\xi\le b(x)} \alpha\|\xi-\xi_j\|\right\}, \tag{4.4.54}$$

$$= \min\left\{\inf_{\xi:a(x)^\top\xi > b(x)} \alpha\|\xi-\xi_j\| - 1,\ 0\right\}. \tag{4.4.55}$$

Note that the second equality (4.4.55) can be obtained by looking at two cases.

Case 1: If $a(x)^\top \xi_j \le b(x)$, then $\inf_{\xi: a(x)^\top \xi \le b(x)} \alpha \|\xi - \xi_j\| = 0$, that is, when $\xi_j$ is contained in the halfspace $a(x)^\top x \le b(x)$, the minimum distance from $\xi_j$ to the halfspace is zero. Hence, we get (4.4.55).

Case 2: If $a(x)^\top \xi_j > b(x)$, then $\inf_{\xi: a(x)^\top \xi > b(x)} \alpha \|\xi - \xi_j\| = 0$ for the same reason as in Case 1, and the second term, then the right-hand side of (4.4.54) is equal to $\min\{-1, \inf_{\xi: a(x)^\top \xi \le b(x)} \alpha \|\xi - \xi_j\|\} = \min\{-1, 0\} = \min\{\inf_{\xi: a(x)^\top \xi > b(x)} \alpha \|\xi - \xi_j\| - 1, 0\}$, since $\inf_{\xi: a(x)^\top \xi \le b(x)} \alpha \|\xi - \xi_j\| \ge 0$.

Therefore, for both cases, we get (4.4.55).

3. Now we only need to look at $\inf_{\xi: a(x)^\top \xi > b(x)} \|\xi - \xi_j\|$, which can be solved in the following closed form

$$g(x, \xi_j) := \inf_{\xi: a(x)^\top \xi > b(x)} \|\xi - \xi_j\| = \begin{cases} \frac{\max\{b(x) - a(x)^\top \xi_j, 0\}}{\|a(x)\|_*}, & \text{if } a(x) \ne 0, \\ \delta(x | b(x) < 0), & \text{if } a(x) = 0. \end{cases} \tag{4.4.56}$$

Note that $\|\cdot\|_*$ denotes the dual norm of $\|\cdot\|$. It is a good exercise to derive (4.4.56). See Exercise 4.14. Note that this gives the definition of the function $g(x, \xi_j)$ in (4.4.51).

4. Substituting $g(x, \xi)$ into (4.4.53), the DRCC (4.4.47) is equivalent to the following

$$\inf_{\alpha \ge 0} \left\{ d\alpha - \sum_{j=1}^n q_j \min\left\{\alpha g(x, \xi_j) - 1, 0\right\} \right\} \le \epsilon,$$

$$\iff \exists \alpha \ge 0,\ d\alpha - \sum_{j=1}^n q_j \min\left\{\alpha g(x, \xi_j) - 1, 0\right\} \le \epsilon,$$

$$\iff \exists \alpha > 0,\ d\alpha - \sum_{j=1}^n q_j \min\left\{\alpha g(x, \xi_j) - 1, 0\right\} \le \epsilon, \quad (\because \alpha \text{ cannot be zero})$$

$$\iff \exists \alpha > 0,\ d\alpha + \sum_{j=1}^n q_j \max\left\{-\alpha g(x, \xi_j) + 1, 0\right\} \le \epsilon,$$

$$\iff \exists \gamma < 0,\ -\frac{d}{\gamma} - \frac{1}{\gamma} \sum_{j=1}^n q_j \max\left\{-g(x, \xi_j) - \gamma, 0\right\} \le \epsilon, \quad (\text{let } \gamma = -1/\alpha)$$

$$\iff \exists \gamma \in \mathbb{R},\ \frac{d}{\epsilon} + \gamma + \frac{1}{\epsilon} \sum_{j=1}^n q_j \max\left\{-g(x, \xi_j) - \gamma, 0\right\} \le 0, \quad (\because \gamma < 0 \text{ automatically holds})$$

$$\iff \frac{d}{\epsilon} + \inf_{\gamma} \left\{ \gamma + \frac{1}{\epsilon} \sum_{j=1}^n q_j \max\left\{-g(x, \xi_j) - \gamma, 0\right\} \right\} \le 0,$$

$$\iff \frac{d}{\epsilon} + \mathrm{CVaR}_{1-\epsilon}^{\mathbb{Q}_0}(-g(x, \xi)) \le 0.$$

The last line is exactly the CVaR reformulation of DRCC in (4.4.50). This finishes the derivation.

Some remarks are in order.

1. The above result can be extended to joint chance constraints of the following form

$$\inf_{\mathbb{P}\in\mathscr{P}_W(\mathbb{Q}_0,d)} \mathbb{P}\left(\boldsymbol{a}(\boldsymbol{x})^\top\boldsymbol{\xi}_i \le b_i(\boldsymbol{x}),\ \forall i\in[I]\right) \ge 1-\epsilon, \tag{4.4.57}$$

where $I$ is a finite index set and $\mathbb{P}$ is the joint probability measure of $(\boldsymbol{\xi}_i)_{i\in[I]}$. The DRCC (4.4.57) can also be equivalently reformulated as a CVaR constraint of a similar form (4.4.50) for the individual chance constraint case. The derivation is also similar. Interested reader can refer to [27, Theorem 1] for a proof and for similar results in [28, 29, 30].
2. The CVaR reformulation (4.4.50) is not of much use for practical computation yet. We need to reformulate it explicitly to a mixed integer linear program, which we will show in the next subsection. But the CVaR reformulation is useful as a conceptual tool for developing inner and outer approximations of the DRCC, which we will demonstrate in the next section.

#### 4.4.4.2 Mixed Integer Representation

Let us write out the CVaR reformulation (4.4.50) again and view it as defining a feasible region $Z$ of $\boldsymbol{x}$,

$$\exists\gamma>0,\ d-\epsilon\gamma+\sum_{j=1}^{n} q_j \max\left\{-g(\boldsymbol{x},\boldsymbol{\xi}_j)+\gamma,0\right\}\le 0. \tag{4.4.58}$$

There are two cases:

- If $\boldsymbol{a}(\boldsymbol{x})=0$, then $g(\boldsymbol{x},\boldsymbol{\xi}_j)=\delta(\boldsymbol{x}|b(\boldsymbol{x})<0)$. If $b(\boldsymbol{x})<0$, then $g(\boldsymbol{x},\boldsymbol{\xi}_j)=0$, therefore, (4.4.58) becomes

$$\exists\,\gamma>0,\ d+(1-\epsilon)\gamma\le 0.$$

Since $d>0, \gamma>0, \epsilon\le 1$, this constraint is infeasible. If $b(\boldsymbol{x})\ge 0$, then $g(\boldsymbol{x},\boldsymbol{\xi}_j)=+\infty$. The constraint (4.4.58) becomes $\exists\,\gamma>0, d-\epsilon\gamma\le 0$, which is feasible. This discussion implies that the feasible region $Z$ contains the following set

$$Z_0 := \left\{\boldsymbol{x}\in\mathbb{R}^s : \boldsymbol{a}(\boldsymbol{x})=0, b(\boldsymbol{x})\ge 0\right\}. \tag{4.4.59}$$

- If $\boldsymbol{a}(\boldsymbol{x}) \neq 0$, then $g(\boldsymbol{x}, \boldsymbol{\xi}_j) = \max\{b(\boldsymbol{x}) - \boldsymbol{a}(\boldsymbol{x})^\top \boldsymbol{\xi}_j), 0\}/\|\boldsymbol{a}(\boldsymbol{x})\|_*$. So $\|\boldsymbol{a}(\boldsymbol{x})\|_* > 0$. Multiplying it to both sides of (4.4.58), we get

$$\begin{aligned} &\exists\, \gamma > 0,\ d\|\boldsymbol{a}(\boldsymbol{x})\|_* - \epsilon\gamma\|\boldsymbol{a}(\boldsymbol{x})\|_* \\ &\qquad + \sum_{j=1}^{n} q_j \max\left\{- \max\{b(\boldsymbol{x}) - \boldsymbol{a}(\boldsymbol{x})^\top \boldsymbol{\xi}_j, 0\} + \gamma\|\boldsymbol{a}(\boldsymbol{x})\|_*, 0\right\} \le 0, \end{aligned} \tag{4.4.60}$$

which is equivalent to the following reformulation (see Exercise 4.15,)

$$\begin{cases} dv - \epsilon\gamma + \sum_{j=1}^{n} q_j z_j \le 0, \\ z_j + \max\{b(\boldsymbol{x}) - \boldsymbol{a}(\boldsymbol{x})^\top \boldsymbol{\xi}_j, 0\} \ge \gamma, \\ \|\boldsymbol{a}(\boldsymbol{x})\|_* \le v, \\ z_j \ge 0, v \ge 0, \gamma > 0. \end{cases} \tag{4.4.61}$$

This defines another set $Z_1$ of $\boldsymbol{x}$ as

$$Z_1 := \left\{\boldsymbol{x} \in \mathbb{R}^s \ :\ \exists \gamma > 0,\ \text{s.t. (4.4.61) is satisfied}\right\}. \tag{4.4.62}$$

What we have shown so far is the following result.

The feasible region $Z$ of $\boldsymbol{x}$ defined by the CVaR constraint (4.4.50) or equivalently by the DRCC (4.4.47) is a disjunction of $Z_0$ and $Z_1$, i.e.

$$Z = Z_0 \cup Z_1,$$

where $Z_0$ is a polyhedron defined in (4.4.59) and $Z_1$ is a nonconvex set defined in (4.4.62).

The set $Z_0$ has simple structure (see Exercise 4.16.) However, $Z_1$ is not a convex set, due to the second constraint in (4.4.61), which is a nonconvex constraint. All the other constraints in (4.4.61) are clearly convex. The remaining task is to reformulate $Z_1$ using mixed integer linear constraints.

We only need to reformulate the second constraint $z_j + \max\{b(\boldsymbol{x}) - \boldsymbol{a}(\boldsymbol{x})^\top \boldsymbol{\xi}_j, 0\} \ge \gamma$, which is equivalent to $z_j + s_j \ge \gamma$, $s_j \ge 0$, and a disjunction

$$\text{either } s_j \le 0, \quad \text{or } s_j \le b(\boldsymbol{x}) - \boldsymbol{a}(\boldsymbol{x})^\top \boldsymbol{\xi}_j. \tag{4.4.63}$$

When $s_j$ and $s_j - b(\boldsymbol{x}) + \boldsymbol{a}(\boldsymbol{x})^\top \boldsymbol{\xi}_j$ are bounded, it is a standard exercise to reformulate (4.4.63) with a binary variable $y_j \in \{0, 1\}$ and a big $M_j$ parameter as

$$s_j \leq M_j y_j, \quad s_j \leq b(\boldsymbol{x}) - \boldsymbol{a}(\boldsymbol{x})^\top \boldsymbol{\xi}_j + M_j(1 - y_j), \quad y_j \in \{0, 1\}.$$

Putting everything together, we have the following mixed integer reformulation of $Z_1$.

When the following problem is bounded with a finite constant $M_j$

$$\max_{\boldsymbol{x} \in Z_1} \left| b(\boldsymbol{x}) - \boldsymbol{a}(\boldsymbol{x})^\top \boldsymbol{\xi} \right| = M_j,$$

the set $Z_1$ (4.4.62) is representable by the following mixed integer set

$$\begin{cases} d\nu - \epsilon\gamma + \sum_{j=1}^n q_j z_j \leq 0, \\ s_j \leq M_j y_j, \quad \forall j = 1, 2, \ldots, n, \\ s_j \leq b(\boldsymbol{x}) - \boldsymbol{a}(\boldsymbol{x})^\top \boldsymbol{\xi}_j + M_j(1 - y_j), \quad \forall j = 1, 2, \ldots, n, \\ \|\boldsymbol{a}(\boldsymbol{x})\|_* \leq \nu, \\ \nu \geq 0, \gamma > 0, \\ z_j \geq 0, \ y_j \in \{0, 1\}, \ \forall j = 1, 2, \ldots, n. \end{cases} \tag{4.4.64}$$

The above reformulation of $Z$ works for the general case when the uncertainty $\boldsymbol{\xi}$ is in both the coefficients and right-hand side of the linear constraint $\boldsymbol{a}(\boldsymbol{x})^\top \boldsymbol{\xi} \leq b(\boldsymbol{x})$. An important special case is when the uncertainty $\boldsymbol{\xi}$ is only in the right-hand side, i.e. $\boldsymbol{a}(\boldsymbol{x}) = \boldsymbol{a}$ is independent of $\boldsymbol{x}$. The reader is asked to derive the exact reformulation of the set $Z$ for this case in Exercise 4.17.

Interested readers can further consult [27] for more discussions on mixed integer representations of joint DRCC constraints, and for related results in [28, 30].

### 4.4.5 Theory of Safe Convex Approximations of DRCC

In this subsection, we describe in details a general theory of inner convex approximations of distributionally robust chance constraints. Such inner approximations are convex programs themselves and enjoy the computational tractability of convex optimization. The solution of an inner approximation is guaranteed to be a feasible suboptimal solution to the original DRCC, therefore, it is called a *safe* approximation.

We start from chance constraints over a fixed and known probability measure, and show that a simple idea of using generating functions to over-approximate indicator functions leads to a general way to construct inner approximations of chance constraints. Moreover, we show that the CVaR function naturally arises as an inner approximation to chance constraints. This establishes the link between chance constraints and the CVaR function, which has already manifested in our previous discussions of exact and approximation reformulations of DRCC with moment-based ambiguity sets and Wasserstein ambiguity sets. Furthermore, we show that a "best" choice of the generating function gives rise to the CVaR approximation, which justifies that the CVaR approximation is actually the tightest convex and safe approximation of chance constraints within the framework of generating function based approximation schemes.

Next, we introduce the well-known *Bernstein approximation*, which, instead of using the "best" generating function, relies on the exponential function. Such a choice stems from computational considerations that CVaR approximation may not be easily computable, while exponential generating functions directly leads to the so-called moment generating functions, which are readily available for many probability distributions.

Lastly, we extend the CVaR and Bernstein approximations to DRCC. In this process, we show that DRCC is naturally related to the notion of *risk measures*, which is a broad topic of its own right and has many applications in finance and actuarial science.

In all the following development, we focus on individual chance constraints to make the main ideas clear. The exposition is heavily based on the ideas from the foundational paper [31].

#### 4.4.5.1 Chance Constraints and CVaR Approximation

Consider the following scalar chance constraint

$$\mathbb{P}(f(\boldsymbol{x}, \boldsymbol{\xi}) > 0) \leq \epsilon, \tag{4.4.65}$$

where $f : X \times \mathcal{U} \to \mathbb{R}$ is a scalar function and $\boldsymbol{\xi}$ is a random vector with a known probability measure $\mathbb{P}$. For the simplicity of notation, we will introduce a random variable $Z := f(\boldsymbol{x}, \boldsymbol{\xi})$. The chance constraint becomes $\mathbb{P}(Z > 0) \leq \epsilon$. We want to find an inner approximation to the feasible region defined by this chance constraint. Here is the key idea.

**Safe Approximation with Generating Function**

We introduce a class of functions $\phi : \mathbb{R} \to \mathbb{R}$ with the following properties:

1. $\phi$ is a nonnegative, nondecreasing, convex function.
2. $\phi(z) > \phi(0) = 1$ for all $z > 0$.

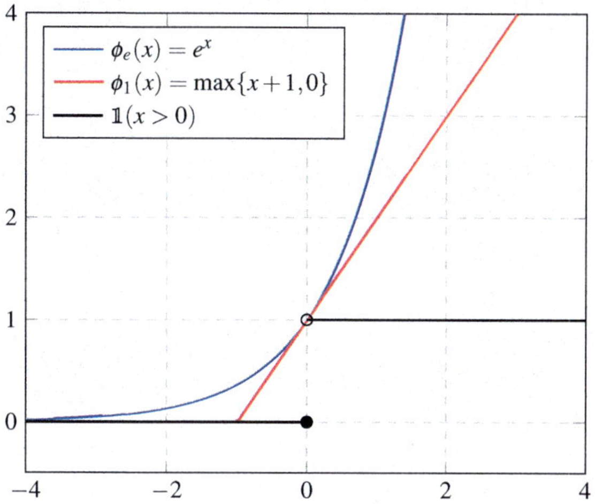


**Fig. 4.1** Illustration of $\phi_e = e^x$, $\phi_1 = \max\{x+1, 0\}$, and $\quad (x > 0)$

For example, the exponential function $\phi_e(z) := e^z$ satisfies these two properties. So does $\phi_1(z) := \max\{z+1, 0\}$. These two generating functions will play crucial roles in the following development. We call any real-valued function with the above two properties a *generating function*.

The purpose of introducing generating functions is clear from the following relations: For any $t > 0$, we have

$$\mathbb{P}(Z > 0) = \mathbb{P}(tZ > 0) = \mathbb{E}_{\mathbb{P}}[\quad (tZ > 0)] \leq \mathbb{E}_{\mathbb{P}}[\phi(tZ)], \tag{4.4.66}$$

where the $\leq$ inequality exactly follows from the two properties of a generating function $\phi$. In other words, a generating function $\phi(x)$ gives an over-approximation of the step function $\quad (x > 0)$. The relation between $\quad (x > 0)$ and the two special generating functions $\phi_e(x)$ and $\phi_1(x)$ is illustrated in Fig. 4.1.

Plugging $Z = f(\boldsymbol{x}, \boldsymbol{\xi})$ into (4.4.66) and changing $t$ to $t^{-1}$, we get

$$\mathbb{P}(f(\boldsymbol{x}, \boldsymbol{\xi}) > 0) \leq \mathbb{E}_{\mathbb{P}}[\phi(t^{-1} f(\boldsymbol{x}, \boldsymbol{\xi}))], \quad \text{for any } t > 0. \tag{4.4.67}$$

With this preparation, we have the following implication,

$$\exists\, t > 0,\ \ \underbrace{t\mathbb{E}_{\mathbb{P}}[\phi(t^{-1} f(\boldsymbol{x}, \boldsymbol{\xi}))]}_{=:\Psi(\boldsymbol{x}, t)} \leq t\epsilon \implies t\mathbb{P}(f(\boldsymbol{x}, \boldsymbol{\xi}) > 0) \leq t\epsilon$$
$$\iff \mathbb{P}(f(\boldsymbol{x}, \boldsymbol{\xi}) > 0) \leq \epsilon. \tag{4.4.68}$$

Observe that

$$\exists\, t > 0,\ \ \Psi(\boldsymbol{x}, t) - t\epsilon \leq 0 \iff \inf_{t>0} \{\Psi(\boldsymbol{x}, t) - t\epsilon\} \leq 0.$$

We come to the following safe approximation of the chance constraint

$$\inf_{t>0} \{\Psi(\boldsymbol{x}, t) - t\epsilon\} \leq 0 \quad \Longrightarrow \quad \mathbb{P}(f(\boldsymbol{x}, \boldsymbol{\xi}) > 0) \leq \epsilon, \tag{4.4.69}$$

because if $\boldsymbol{x}$ satisfies the inequality on the left-hand side of (4.4.69), then it must satisfy the chance constraint on the right-hand side. So the feasible region defined by the left-hand side inequality is an inner (i.e. safe) approximation of that of the chance constraint.

The key question is whether this safe approximation is a convex program. The answer is yes, if we have convexity in $f$. In particular, we have the following result.

If $f(\boldsymbol{x}, \boldsymbol{\xi})$ is a convex function of $\boldsymbol{x}$ for any given $\boldsymbol{\xi} \in \mathcal{U}$, and $\phi : \mathbb{R} \to \mathbb{R}$ is a generating function, then the function $\Psi(\boldsymbol{x}, t) := t\mathbb{E}_{\mathbb{P}}[\phi(t^{-1} f(\boldsymbol{x}, \boldsymbol{\xi}))]$ is a convex function in $(\boldsymbol{x}, t)$ for $t > 0$. Therefore,

$$\inf_{t>0} \{\Psi(\boldsymbol{x}, t) - t\epsilon\} \leq 0 \tag{4.4.70}$$

is a convex safe approximation of the scalar convex chance constraint (4.4.65).

It is a good exercise to verify that the function $\Psi(\boldsymbol{x}, t)$ is indeed a convex function (see Exercise 4.18.)

**CVaR Approximation Is Natural**

We want to show that CVaR is naturally involved in approximation of chance constraints. Let us recall the definition of CVaR below

$$\text{CVaR}_{1-\epsilon}^{\mathbb{P}}(Z) = \inf_{t \in \mathbb{R}} \left\{ t + \frac{1}{\epsilon} \mathbb{E}_{\mathbb{P}} \left[ \max\{Z - t, 0\} \right] \right\}. \tag{4.4.71}$$

A closely related measure of risk is the so-called *value-at-risk* (VaR) of a random variable $Z$, which is defined as

$$\text{VaR}_{1-\epsilon}^{\mathbb{P}}(Z) = \inf \{t \ : \ \mathbb{P}(Z \leq t) \geq 1 - \epsilon\}. \tag{4.4.72}$$

In words, $\text{VaR}_{1-\epsilon}^{\mathbb{P}}(Z)$ is the $(1-\epsilon)$-quantile of $Z$. Moreover, we can observe the following equivalence

$$\mathbb{P}(Z \leq 0) \geq 1 - \epsilon \quad \Longleftrightarrow \quad \text{VaR}_{1-\epsilon}^{\mathbb{P}}(Z) \leq 0. \tag{4.4.73}$$

So a VaR constraint is just another way to write a chance constraint.

The final observation is a known fact (see e.g. [32]) that $\mathrm{VaR}^{\mathbb{P}}_{1-\epsilon}(Z)$ is a minimizer of the right-hand side of CVaR (4.4.71), so that it always holds $\mathrm{CVaR}^{\mathbb{P}}_{1-\epsilon}(Z) \geq \mathrm{VaR}^{\mathbb{P}}_{1-\epsilon}(Z)$. This relation can also be seen from the fact that $\mathrm{CVaR}^{\mathbb{P}}_{1-\epsilon}(Z) = \mathbb{E}_{\mathbb{P}}[Z \mid Z \geq \mathrm{VaR}^{\mathbb{P}}_{1-\epsilon}(Z)]$, when $Z$ has a probability density function.

Combining this fact with (4.4.73), we see that CVaR provides a safe approximation of the chance constraint, i.e.

$$\mathrm{CVaR}^{\mathbb{P}}_{1-\epsilon}(Z) \leq 0 \quad \Longrightarrow \quad \mathbb{P}(Z \leq 0) \geq 1-\epsilon. \tag{4.4.74}$$

From the definition (4.4.71), we know that CVaR is a convex functional on $Z$. This shows that CVaR is a natural candidate for convex safe approximation of chance constraints.

In the following, we show that the CVaR approximation (4.4.74) also arises from the generating function based approximation scheme by choosing the generating function as $\phi_1(x) = \max\{x+1, 0\}$. In fact, it is the tightest among all such convex safe approximations of the chance constraint.

**CVaR Approximation Is the Best**

The quality of the safe approximation (4.4.70) depends on the choice of the generating $\phi(x)$. The relation (4.4.66) shows that the closer $\phi$ is to the step function $(x \geq 0)$, the better is the approximation. In Exercise 4.19, we argue that any generating function is lower bounded by some convex piecewise linear function of the form $\phi_a(x) = \max\{ax+1, 0\}$ for $a \geq 0$. Substituting $\phi_a$ into the safe approximation (4.4.70), we get

$$\inf_{t>0} \left\{ t\mathbb{E}_{\mathbb{P}}[\max\{at^{-1} f(\boldsymbol{x}, \boldsymbol{\xi}) + 1, 0\}] - t\epsilon \right\} \leq 0. \tag{4.4.75}$$

If $a = 0$, i.e. $\phi_0(x) \equiv 1$, then the above constraint becomes $\inf_{t>0} t(1-\epsilon) \leq 0$, which is trivially true, because $\epsilon \leq 1$. If $a > 0$, then we can redefine $t$ to be $t/a$. In this way, (4.4.75) is equivalent to the case of $\phi_1(x) = \max\{x+1, 0\}$ with $a = 1$ as

$$\inf_{t>0} \left\{ t\mathbb{E}_{\mathbb{P}}[\max\{t^{-1} f(\boldsymbol{x}, \boldsymbol{\xi}) + 1, 0\}] - t\epsilon \right\} \leq 0,$$

$$\Longleftrightarrow \inf_{t>0} \{-t\epsilon + \mathbb{E}_{\mathbb{P}}[\max\{f(\boldsymbol{x}, \boldsymbol{\xi}) + t, 0\}]\} \leq 0,$$

$$\Longleftrightarrow \inf_{t>0} \{-t\epsilon + \mathbb{E}_{\mathbb{P}}[\max\{f(\boldsymbol{x}, \boldsymbol{\xi}) + t, 0\}]\} \leq 0,$$

$$\Longleftrightarrow \inf_{t\in\mathbb{R}} \{-t\epsilon + \mathbb{E}_{\mathbb{P}}[\max\{f(\boldsymbol{x}, \boldsymbol{\xi}) + t, 0\}]\} \leq 0, \tag{4.4.76a}$$

$$\Longleftrightarrow \inf_{t\in\mathbb{R}} \left\{ t + \frac{1}{\epsilon}\mathbb{E}_{\mathbb{P}}[\max\{f(\boldsymbol{x}, \boldsymbol{\xi}) - t, 0\}] \right\} \leq 0. \tag{4.4.76b}$$

Why can we enlarge the region of $t$ from $t > 0$ to $t \in \mathbb{R}$ in (4.4.76a)? The reason is simple, because when $t < 0$, the function in the infimum is positive, so it does not introduce any extra constraint to the original problem with $t > 0$.

The reader would notice that (4.4.76b) is nothing but the following CVaR constraint

$$\mathrm{CVaR}_{1-\epsilon}^{\mathbb{P}}(f(\boldsymbol{x}, \boldsymbol{\xi})) \le 0. \tag{4.4.77}$$

Therefore, we have the following result on the optimality of the CVaR approximation of chance constraints.

Among all convex safe approximations of the chance constraint (4.4.65) given by generating functions, the *tightest* one is given by the CVaR approximation (4.4.77).

This result gives a theoretical justification for using CVaR approximation of chance constraints. However, in general, CVaR may be computationally difficult to evaluate as it may involve high-dimensional integration. In the next subsection, we introduce another generating function based approximation, which is easier to compute than CVaR. It is a trade-off between optimality and computability.

#### 4.4.5.2 Bernstein Approximation

In the following discussion, we assume the chance constraint (4.4.65) takes the following form

$$\mathbb{P}\left(f_0(\boldsymbol{x}) + \sum_{j=1}^{n} \xi_j f_j(\boldsymbol{x}) \le 0\right) \ge 1 - \epsilon. \tag{4.4.78}$$

Furthermore, we assume the random variables $\xi_1, \xi_2, \ldots, \xi_n$ are independent. Each $\xi_j$ has a probability measure $\mathbb{P}_j$, and the joint distribution $\mathbb{P}$ of $\{\xi_1, \ldots, \xi_n\}$ is given by the product $\mathbb{P} = \mathbb{P}_1 \times \mathbb{P}_2 \times \cdots \times \mathbb{P}_n$. We further assume each $\xi_j$ has a finite moment generating function, i.e. $M_j(t) = \mathbb{E}_{\mathbb{P}_j}[e^{t\xi_j}] < \infty$ for all $t > 0$.

Let us consider the exponential function $\phi_e(x) = e^x$ as the generating function. Applying the convex safe approximation scheme (4.4.70) developed in the preceding subsection with this choice of generating function, the chance constraint (4.4.78) is safe approximated by the following constraint for some $t > 0$ as

$$\mathbb{E}_{\mathbb{P}}\left[\phi_e\left(tf_0(\boldsymbol{x}) + \sum_{j=1}^{n} tf_j(\boldsymbol{x})\xi_j\right)\right] \le \epsilon,$$

$$\Longleftrightarrow \mathbb{E}_{\mathbb{P}}\left[\phi_e\left(tf_0(\boldsymbol{x})+\sum_{j=1}^{n} tf_j(\boldsymbol{x})\xi_j\right)\right] \leq \epsilon,$$

$$\Longleftrightarrow \mathbb{E}_{\mathbb{P}}\left[e^{tf_0(\boldsymbol{x})}\prod_{j=1}^{n} e^{tf_j(\boldsymbol{x})\xi_j}\right] \leq \epsilon,$$

$$\Longleftrightarrow e^{tf_0(x)}\cdot\prod_{j=1}^{n}\mathbb{E}_{\mathbb{P}_j}\left[e^{tf_j(\boldsymbol{x})\xi_j}\right] \leq \epsilon, \quad (\because \text{ independence}) \tag{4.4.79a}$$

$$\Longleftrightarrow tf_0(\boldsymbol{x})+\sum_{j=1}^{n}\ln\left(\mathbb{E}_{\mathbb{P}_j}\left[e^{tf_j(\boldsymbol{x})\xi_j}\right]\right) \leq \ln(\epsilon),$$

$$\Longleftrightarrow tf_0(\boldsymbol{x})+\sum_{j=1}^{n}\ln(M_j(tf_j(\boldsymbol{x})) \leq \ln(\epsilon).$$

The last constraint directly leads to the following important result.

Suppose the random variables $\xi_1, \xi_2, \ldots, \xi_n$ are independence with moment generating functions $M_j(t)$ for each $j = 1, 2, \ldots, n$, then the chance constraint (4.4.78) is inner approximated by the following convex constraint

$$\inf_{t>0}\left\{tf_0(\boldsymbol{x})+\sum_{j=1}^{n}\ln(M_j(tf_j(\boldsymbol{x}))\right\} \leq \ln(\epsilon), \tag{4.4.80}$$

which is called the *Bernstein approximation*.[1]

Furthermore, if the logarithmic moment generating function $\ln(M_j(t))$ is upper bounded by another function $\overline{\phi}_j(t)$ for each $j$, i.e. $\ln(M_j(t)) \leq \overline{\phi}_j(t)$, then the following constraint

$$\inf_{t>0}\left\{tf_0(\boldsymbol{x})+\sum_{j=1}^{n}\overline{\phi}_j(tf_j(\boldsymbol{x}))\right\} \leq \ln(\epsilon), \tag{4.4.81}$$

is also a convex safe approximation of the chance constraint.

[1] So who is Bernstein? A. Nemirovski and A. Shapiro named Bernstein approximation after the great Russian mathematician Sergei Natanovich Bernstein (1880–1968), who did many pioneering works in differential equations, probability theory, and approximation theory. Bernstein inequality

The benefit of using a further approximation $\overline{\phi}_j$ to replace $\ln(M_j(t))$ is that the resulting approximation (4.4.81), although maybe weaker than the Bernstein approximation (4.4.80), could be easier to compute. We will discuss some examples below.

**Illustrative Example 4.3** *As a simple example, consider a simple chance constraint* $\mathbb{P}(-2-x+\xi x \le 0) \ge 1-\epsilon$ *for a uniform distribution on* $[\frac{1}{2}, \frac{3}{2}]$. *In this case,* $f_0(x) = -2 - x$, $f_1(x) = x$, *and the random variable* $\xi$ *has a moment generating function* $M(t) = \mathbb{E}[e^{t\xi}] = \int_{1/2}^{3/2} e^{tx} dx = (e^{3t/2} - e^{t/2})/t$. *We can numerically evaluate the Bernstein approximation and compare it with the true feasible region of the chance constraint. See Exercise 4.20.*

□

**Illustrative Example 4.4** *As another example, consider independent Bernoulli random variables* $\xi_1, \ldots, \xi_n$ *taking values in* $\{-1, 1\}$. *Then, the moment generating functions take the form*

$$M_j(t) = \frac{e^t + e^{-t}}{2} = \cosh(t). \tag{4.4.82}$$

*The* $\cosh(t)$ *function may be inconvenient to deal with. However, by Taylor expansion of* $\ln(\cosh(t))$, *we can work out that* $\ln(\cosh(t)) \le t^2/2$ *for all* $t$, *i.e.* $\ln(M_j(t))$ *is upper bounded as follows,*

$$\ln(M_j(t)) \le \frac{1}{2}t^2, \quad \forall j = 1, 2, \ldots, n. \tag{4.4.83}$$

*Now, let us denote* $\overline{\phi}_j(t) := t^2/2$. *Suppose that we have a linear chance constraint as*

$$\mathbb{P}\left( \underbrace{(\boldsymbol{a}_0^\top \boldsymbol{x} - b_0)}_{f_0(\boldsymbol{x})} + \sum_{j=1}^n \underbrace{(\boldsymbol{a}_j^\top \boldsymbol{x} - b_j)}_{f_j(\boldsymbol{x})} \xi_j \le 0 \right) \ge 1 - \epsilon.$$

*Then, using the upper bound functions* $\overline{\phi}_j(t)$, *we obtain a safe approximation*

$$\inf_{t>0} \left\{ t f_0(\boldsymbol{x}) + \frac{1}{2} \sum_{j=1}^n f_j^2(\boldsymbol{x}) t^2 \right\} \le \ln(\epsilon), \tag{4.4.84}$$

*which actually can be solved in closed form as a second-order conic constraint*

---

in measure concentration is also named after him, which was the inspiration for Bernstein approximation. A simpler version of the Bernstein approximation was developed by Pinter [33].

$$\left(\sum_{j=1}^{n}(b_j - \boldsymbol{a}_j^\top \boldsymbol{x})^2\right)^{\frac{1}{2}} \leq \Omega \cdot (b_0 - \boldsymbol{a}_0^\top \boldsymbol{x}), \tag{4.4.85}$$

*where* $\Omega := \sqrt{\frac{1}{2\ln(\frac{1}{\epsilon})}}$.

*This second-order conic reformulation would surely remind the reader about Chap. 2 on static robust optimization. Indeed,* (4.4.85) *is the deterministic reformulation of the following robust constraint*

$$f_0(\boldsymbol{x}) + \sum_{j=1}^{n} f_j(\boldsymbol{x})\xi_j \leq 0, \quad \forall \boldsymbol{\xi} = (\xi_1, \ldots, \xi_n)^\top : \|\boldsymbol{\xi}\|_2 \leq \Omega. \tag{4.4.86}$$

*Is this connection to robust optimization a coincidence or a general phenomenon? In the next subsection we show that this remarkable connection is no coincidence.*

□

#### 4.4.5.3 Connections to Robust Optimization

Now we are going to show that the Bernstein approximation of chance constraints under the independence assumption is *equivalent* to a static robust optimization version of the chance constraint. In this way, we have gone a full circle from static robust optimization to chance constraints and back.

Let us assume $\ln(M_j(t)) \leq \overline{\phi}_j(t)$ for each random variable $\xi_j$ and all $\xi_j$'s are independent. We also assume that $\overline{\phi}_j(t)$ is a closed finite convex function. In this case, the conjugate function $\overline{\phi}_j^*(\zeta) := \sup_t\{\zeta t - \overline{\phi}_j(t)\}$ is also closed, finite, and convex, and $\overline{\phi}_j$ is equal to its bi-conjugate, i.e. $\overline{\phi}_j = \overline{\phi}_j^{**}$ (see e.g. [34, Chapter 12].)

Now we derive an equivalent robust optimization formulation of the safe convex approximation (4.4.81). To save notation, we let $z_0 := f_0(\boldsymbol{x})$, $z_j := f_j(\boldsymbol{x})$, and $z = (z_1, z_2, \ldots, z_n)^\top$.

$$\inf_{t>0}\left\{tz_0 + \sum_{j=1}^{n}\overline{\phi}_j(tz_j)\right\} \leq \ln(\epsilon),$$

$$\Leftrightarrow \quad \inf_{t>0}\left\{tz_0 + \sum_{j=1}^{n}\sup_{\zeta_j}\left\{\zeta_j(tz_j) - \overline{\phi}_j^*(\zeta_j)\right\}\right\} \leq \ln(\epsilon), \quad \text{(use bi-conjugacy of } \overline{\phi}_i) \tag{4.4.87a}$$

$$\Leftrightarrow \quad \inf_{t>0}\sup_{\boldsymbol{\zeta}}\left\{t\cdot(z_0 + \boldsymbol{\zeta}^\top z) - \sum_{j=1}^{n}\overline{\phi}_j^*(\zeta_j)\right\} \leq \ln(\epsilon), \quad (\boldsymbol{\zeta} = (\zeta_1, \ldots, \zeta_n)^\top) \tag{4.4.87b}$$

$$\Leftrightarrow \quad \sup_{\boldsymbol{\zeta}} \left\{ \inf_{t>0} \left\{ t \cdot (z_0 + \boldsymbol{\zeta}^\top \boldsymbol{z}) \right\} - \sum_{j=1}^{n} \overline{\phi}_j^*(\zeta_j) \right\} \leq \ln(\epsilon), \quad \text{(strong duality)} \tag{4.4.87c}$$

$$\Leftrightarrow \quad \sup_{\boldsymbol{\zeta}} \left\{ -\sum_{j=1}^{n} \overline{\phi}_j^*(\zeta_j) : z_0 + \boldsymbol{\zeta}^\top \boldsymbol{z} \geq 0 \right\} \leq \ln(\epsilon), \quad \text{(solve the inner inf problem)} \tag{4.4.87d}$$

$$\Leftrightarrow \quad \inf_{\boldsymbol{\xi}} \left\{ \sum_{j=1}^{n} \overline{\phi}_j^*(\zeta_j) : z_0 + \boldsymbol{\zeta}^\top \boldsymbol{z} \geq 0 \right\} \geq \ln(1/\epsilon), \quad \text{(multiply } -1 \text{ on both sides)} \tag{4.4.87e}$$

$$\Leftrightarrow \quad \sum_{j=1}^{n} \overline{\phi}_j^*(\zeta_j) \geq \ln(1/\epsilon), \quad \forall \boldsymbol{\zeta} : z_0 + \boldsymbol{\zeta}^\top \boldsymbol{z} \geq 0, \quad \text{(rewrite inf as a robust constraint)} \tag{4.4.87f}$$

$$\Leftrightarrow \quad \left( z_0 + \boldsymbol{\zeta}^\top \boldsymbol{z} \geq 0 \Rightarrow \sum_{j=1}^{n} \overline{\phi}_j^*(\zeta_j) \geq \ln(1/\epsilon) \right), \quad \text{(rewrite robust constr as an implication)} \tag{4.4.87g}$$

$$\Leftrightarrow \quad \left( \sum_{j=1}^{n} \overline{\phi}_j^*(\zeta_j) \leq \ln(1/\epsilon) \Rightarrow z_0 + \boldsymbol{\zeta}^\top \boldsymbol{z} \leq 0 \right), \quad \text{(contrapositive implication)} \tag{4.4.87h}$$

$$\Leftrightarrow \quad z_0 + \boldsymbol{\zeta}^\top \boldsymbol{z} \leq 0, \ \forall \boldsymbol{\zeta} : \sum_{j=1}^{n} \overline{\phi}_j^*(\zeta_j) \leq \ln(1/\epsilon). \quad \text{(rewrite the robust constraint)} \tag{4.4.87i}$$

Note that the inf-sup problem in (4.4.87b) is dualized by swapping the inf and sup to get the sup-inf problem in (4.4.87c). Since we assume $\overline{\phi}_j(t)$ is a closed and finite convex function, strong duality holds between this pair of primal and dual problem. The implication in (4.4.87h) is the contrapositive statement of (4.4.87g), plus we also invoked the semi-lower continuity of $\phi_i^*$. To summarize the above derivation, we have the following

**Connection to Robust Optimization:** Suppose random variables $\xi_1, \ldots, \xi_n$ are independent. Also suppose the logarithmic moment generating function of each $\xi_j$ has an upper bounding function that is closed finite and convex, i.e. $\ln(\mathbb{E}[e^{t\xi_j}]) \leq \overline{\phi}_j(t)$ for all $t \in \mathbb{R}$. The conjugate of $\overline{\phi}_j$ is denoted as $\overline{\phi}_j^*$. Then the scalar chance constraint

$$\mathbb{P}\left( f_0(\boldsymbol{x}) + \sum_{j=1}^{n} \xi_j f_j(\boldsymbol{x}) > 0 \right) \leq \epsilon$$

(continued)

has a safe convex approximation

$$\inf_{t>0}\left\{tf_0(\boldsymbol{x})(\boldsymbol{x})+\sum_{j=1}^{n}\overline{\phi}_j(tf_j(\boldsymbol{x}))\right\}\le \ln(\epsilon),$$

which is equivalent to the following static robust constraint

$$f_0(\boldsymbol{x})+\sum_{j=1}^{n}\zeta_j f_j(\boldsymbol{x})\le 0,\quad \forall\boldsymbol{\zeta}\in\mathcal{U}, \tag{4.4.88}$$

where the uncertainty set $\mathcal{U}$ is defined as

$$\mathcal{U}:=\left\{\boldsymbol{\zeta}\in\mathbb{R}^n:\sum_{j=1}^{n}\overline{\phi}_j^*(\zeta_j)\le \ln(1/\epsilon)\right\}. \tag{4.4.89}$$

#### 4.4.5.4 Generalizations to DRCC

We finally come to generalizing convex safe approximations of chance constraints to distributionally robust chance constraints. The preceding subsection develops essentially two types of convex safe approximations for chance constraints from the same technique based on generating functions, namely (1) the CVaR approximation, which is the tightest among all generating function based approximations, and (2) the Bernstein approximation (and its weaker version by upper bounding the logarithmic moment generating function), which works under the independence assumption. It turns out that both types of approximations can be generalized to DRCC. We discuss them in sequence.

**CVaR Approximation for DRCC**

Let us recall the CVaR approximation of a chance constraint with a fixed probability measure $\mathbb{P}$:

$$\text{CVaR}_{1-\epsilon}^{\mathbb{P}}(f(\boldsymbol{x},\boldsymbol{\xi}))\le 0 \implies \mathbb{P}(f(\boldsymbol{x},\boldsymbol{\xi})>0)\le\epsilon.$$

Now if we have a DRCC over an ambiguity set $\mathscr{P}$, i.e. $\sup_{\mathbb{P}\in\mathscr{P}}\mathbb{P}(f(\boldsymbol{x},\boldsymbol{\xi})>0)\le\epsilon$, then the CVaR approximation can be naturally generalized as

$$\sup_{\mathbb{P}\in\mathscr{P}}\text{CVaR}_{1-\epsilon}^{\mathbb{P}}(f(\boldsymbol{x},\boldsymbol{\xi}))\le 0 \implies \sup_{\mathbb{P}\in\mathscr{P}}\mathbb{P}(f(\boldsymbol{x},\boldsymbol{\xi})>0)\le\epsilon. \tag{4.4.90}$$

Let us write down the details for the above CVaR approximation, using (4.4.76b),

$$\sup_{\mathbb{P}\in\mathscr{P}} \inf_{t\in\mathbb{R}} \left\{ t + \frac{1}{\epsilon}\mathbb{E}_{\mathbb{P}}[\max\{f(\boldsymbol{x},\boldsymbol{\xi}) - t, 0\}] \right\} \le 0. \tag{4.4.91}$$

The next step involves the switching of sup and inf in (4.4.91). This essentially requires a strong duality result for an infinite dimensional optimization problem. We have the following theorem for this purpose (cf [35, Theorem 2.1] and discussion in [29]).

**Theorem 4.1** *Let $\mathscr{P}$ be a nonempty (not necessarily convex) set of probability measures on $(\mathscr{U}, B(\mathscr{U}))$, where $\mathscr{U} \subseteq \mathbb{R}^l$ and $B(\mathscr{U})$ is the Borel $\sigma$-algebra. Assume that $\mathscr{P}$ is weakly compact. Consider a function $f : \mathbb{R}^s \times \mathscr{U} \to \mathbb{R}$. Assume that there exists a convex subset $X$ of $\mathbb{R}^s$ such that for all $\boldsymbol{x} \in X$, the function $f(\boldsymbol{x}, \cdot)$ is measurable and integrable with respect to all $\mathbb{P} \in \mathscr{P}$, and $\sup_{\mathbb{P}\in\mathscr{P}} \mathbb{E}_{\mathbb{P}}[f(\boldsymbol{x}, \cdot)] < \infty$. Further assume that $f(\cdot, \boldsymbol{\xi})$ is convex on $X$ for all $\boldsymbol{\xi} \in \mathscr{U}$ and $f(\boldsymbol{x}, \cdot)$ is bounded and continuous on $\mathscr{U}$ for every $\boldsymbol{x} \in X$. Then $\inf_{\boldsymbol{x}\in X} \sup_{\mathbb{P}\in\mathscr{P}} \mathbb{E}_{\mathbb{P}}[f(\boldsymbol{x}, \boldsymbol{\xi})] = \sup_{\mathbb{P}\in\mathscr{P}} \inf_{\boldsymbol{x}\in X} \mathbb{E}_{\mathbb{P}}[f(\boldsymbol{x}, \boldsymbol{\xi})]$.*

Some assumptions in Theorem 4.1 can be further weakened. For example, the continuity assumption of $f(\boldsymbol{x}, \cdot)$ for every $\boldsymbol{x} \in X$ can be relaxed to be continuous in a neighborhood of a minimizer of the inf problem. However, the above version of the theorem suffices for our purpose.

If $f(\boldsymbol{x}, \boldsymbol{\xi})$ is a convex function in $\boldsymbol{x}$ for all $\boldsymbol{\xi} \in \mathscr{U}$ and is continuous and bounded in $\boldsymbol{\xi}$ for all $\boldsymbol{x}$, then the assumptions of Theorem 4.1 are satisfied. Thus, it holds that (4.4.91) is equivalent to the following problem

$$\inf_{t\in\mathbb{R}} \left\{ t + \frac{1}{\epsilon} \sup_{\mathbb{P}\in\mathscr{P}} \mathbb{E}_{\mathbb{P}}[\max\{f(\boldsymbol{x},\boldsymbol{\xi}) - t, 0\}] \right\} \le 0. \tag{4.4.92}$$

**CVaR Approximation of DRCC with Wasserstein Metric**

A nice property of the Wasserstein ambiguity set is that it is weakly compact. Therefore, the above strong duality result applies. In particular, we can apply the reformulation (4.4.92) to the DRCC problem (4.4.48) with a 1st order Wasserstein ambiguity set (4.4.47) and a finite discrete $\mathbb{Q}_0$ that we discussed in Sect. 4.4.4.1. Substituting $f(\boldsymbol{x}, \boldsymbol{\xi}) = \boldsymbol{a}(\boldsymbol{x})^\top \boldsymbol{\xi} - b(\boldsymbol{x})$ and $\mathscr{P} = \mathscr{P}_W(\mathbb{Q}_0, d)$ into (4.4.92), we get

$$\inf_{t\in\mathbb{R}} \left\{ t + \frac{1}{\epsilon} \sup_{\mathbb{P}\in\mathscr{P}_W(\mathbb{Q}_0,d)} \mathbb{E}_{\mathbb{P}}\left[\max\{\boldsymbol{a}(\boldsymbol{x})^\top \boldsymbol{\xi} - b(\boldsymbol{x}) - t, 0\}\right] \right\} \le 0. \tag{4.4.93}$$

Using the equivalent reformulation (4.2.43c) of the inner DRO maximization problem with a Wasserstein ambiguity set (see Sect. 4.2.3.3,) the CVaR approximation (4.4.93) is equivalent to the following constraint

$$\inf_{t\in\mathbb{R}}\left\{t\epsilon+\inf_{\alpha\geq 0}\left\{d\alpha-\sum_{j=1}^{n}q_j\inf_{\xi\in\mathcal{U}}\left\{\alpha\|\xi-\xi_j\|-\max\{a(x)^\top\xi-b(x)-t,0\}\right\}\right\}\right\}\leq 0,$$

wherein the two outer inf can be safely ignored as,

$$\exists\, t\in\mathbb{R},\ \alpha\geq 0,\ \text{s.t. } t\epsilon+d\alpha+\sum_{j=1}^{n}q_j\sup_{\xi\in\mathcal{U}}\left\{-\alpha\|\xi-\xi_j\|+\max\{a(x)^\top\xi-b(x)-t,0\}\right\}\leq 0,$$

which can be reformulated as

$$\begin{aligned}&\exists\, t\in\mathbb{R},\ \alpha\geq 0,\ \text{s.t. } t\epsilon+d\alpha\\ &+\sum_{j=1}^{n}q_js_j\leq 0,\ s_j\geq\sup_{\xi\in\mathcal{U}}\left\{-\alpha\|\xi-\xi_j\|+\max\{a(x)^\top\xi-b(x)-t,0\}\right\},\ \forall j=1,2,\ldots,n.\end{aligned}$$

We assume that the support $\mathcal{U}$ of the random variable $\xi$ is a polytope i.e. $\mathcal{U}=\{\xi\in\mathbb{R}^l: C\xi\leq h\}$. Then, for each $j=1,2,\ldots,n$, we have

$$\begin{aligned}s_j&\geq\sup_{\xi\in\mathcal{U}}\max\left\{a(x)^\top\xi-b(x)-t-\alpha\|\xi-\xi_j\|,-\alpha\|\xi-\xi_j\|\right\},\\ &=\max\left\{\sup_{\xi\in\mathcal{U}}\left\{a(x)^\top\xi-b(x)-t-\alpha\|\xi-\xi_j\|\right\},\sup_{\xi\in\mathcal{U}}\left\{-\alpha\|\xi-\xi_j\|\right\}\right\},\end{aligned}$$

where we are allowed to switch the sup and max. Equivalently, we get

$$s_j\geq -b(x)-t+\sup_{\xi\in\mathcal{U}}\left\{a(x)^\top\xi-\alpha\|\xi-\xi_j\|\right\},\quad s_j\geq\sup_{\xi\in\mathcal{U}}\left\{-\alpha\|\xi-\xi_j\|\right\}.\tag{4.4.94}$$

The first sup can be reformulated as

$$\begin{aligned}\sup_{\xi\in\mathcal{U}}\left\{a(x)^\top\xi-\alpha\|\xi-\xi_j\|\right\}&=\sup_{\xi\in\mathcal{U}}\left\{a(x)^\top\xi-\sup_{\|u_j\|_*\leq\alpha}u_j^\top(\xi-\xi_j)\right\},\\ &=\inf_{\|u_j\|_*\leq\alpha}\ \sup_{\xi:C\xi\leq h}\left\{a(x)^\top\xi-u_j^\top(\xi-\xi_j)\right\},\\ &=\inf_{\|u_j\|_*\leq\alpha}\ \inf_{\substack{C^\top\lambda_j=a(x)-u_j,\\ \lambda_j\geq 0}}\left\{u_j^\top\xi_j+h^\top\lambda_j\right\},\end{aligned}$$

where the second equality swaps the inf and sup by invoking strong duality, and the third equality uses the linear programming duality. With this reformulation, the first inequality on $s_j$ in (4.4.94) becomes equivalent to the following set of constraints,

$$s_j \geq -b(\boldsymbol{x}) - t + \boldsymbol{\xi}_j^\top \boldsymbol{u}_j + \boldsymbol{h}^\top \boldsymbol{\lambda}_j, \quad \|\boldsymbol{u}_j\|_* \leq \alpha, \quad \boldsymbol{C}^\top \boldsymbol{\lambda}_j = \boldsymbol{a}(\boldsymbol{x}) - \boldsymbol{u}_j, \quad \boldsymbol{\lambda}_j \geq \boldsymbol{0}. \tag{4.4.95}$$

Similarly, the second constraint on $s_j$ in (4.4.94) is equivalent to

$$s_j \geq \boldsymbol{\xi}_j^\top \boldsymbol{v}_j + \boldsymbol{h}^\top \boldsymbol{\mu}_j, \quad \|\boldsymbol{v}_j\|_* \leq \alpha, \quad \boldsymbol{C}^\top \boldsymbol{\mu}_j = -\boldsymbol{v}_j, \quad \boldsymbol{v}_j \geq \boldsymbol{0}. \tag{4.4.96}$$

Putting everything together, we get the following convex equivalent reformulation of the CVaR approximation (4.4.93) of DRCC over a Wasserstein ball,

$$t\epsilon + d\alpha + \sum_{j=1}^{n} q_j s_j \leq 0, \quad \alpha \geq \boldsymbol{0}, \quad (4.4.95),\ (4.4.96)\ \forall j = 1, 2, \ldots, n. \tag{4.4.97}$$

**Bernstein Approximation for DRCC**

We can also extend the Bernstein approximation to DRCC. In order to apply the Bernstein approximation, we need to assume the independence of the random variables. The derivation is similar to the above case for the Wasserstein ambiguity set, namely we need to switch the inf and sup by applying Theorem 4.1. Rather than writing down a general result, which is inevitably messy in notations, we work out a concrete example for illustration.

**Illustrative Example 4.5** *Consider a DRCC with a scalar linear constraint*

$$\mathbb{P}\Big( \underbrace{(\boldsymbol{a}_0^\top \boldsymbol{x} - b_0)}_{f_0(\boldsymbol{x})} + \sum_{j=1}^{n} \underbrace{(\boldsymbol{a}_j^\top \boldsymbol{x} - b_j)}_{f_j(\boldsymbol{x})} \xi_j \leq 0 \Big) \geq 1 - \epsilon, \qquad \forall \mathbb{P} \in \mathscr{P} := \mathscr{P}_1 \times \mathscr{P}_2 \times \cdots \times \mathscr{P}_n, \tag{4.4.98}$$

*where the random variables $\xi_j$ are independently distributed and the ambiguity set $\mathscr{P}_j$ for each probability measure $\mathbb{P}_j$ of $\xi_j$ is the set of probability measures with zero mean and supported on* $[-1, 1]$. *Using the Bernstein approximation* (4.4.81), *we have*

$$\sup_{\mathbb{P} \in \mathscr{P}} \inf_{t > 0} \left\{ t f_0(\boldsymbol{x}) + \sum_{j=1}^{n} \ln(M_j(t f_j(\boldsymbol{x}), \mathbb{P}_j)) \right\} \leq \ln(\epsilon) \quad \Longrightarrow \quad (4.4.98), \tag{4.4.99}$$

*where* $\ln(M_j(tf_j(\boldsymbol{x}), \mathbb{P}_j)) = \ln(\mathbb{E}_{\mathbb{P}_j}[e^t])$ *is the logarithmic moment generating function of* $\xi_j$ *when its probability measure is* $\mathbb{P}_j \in \mathscr{P}_j$.

*In our example, each* $\mathscr{P}_j$ *is a weakly compact set, therefore, their direct product* $\mathscr{P}$ *is also a weakly compact set. We can apply the strong duality result, Theorem 4.1, to swap sup and inf in* (4.4.98)*. With the help of the independence structure, we get*

$$\inf_{t>0}\left\{tf_0(\boldsymbol{x}) + \sum_{j=1}^{n} \sup_{\mathbb{P}_j\in\mathscr{P}_j} \ln(M_j(tf_j(\boldsymbol{x}), \mathbb{P}_j))\right\} \le \ln(\epsilon) \quad \Longrightarrow \quad (4.4.98). \tag{4.4.100}$$

*In order to further reformulate* (4.4.100)*, we need to figure out* $\sup_{\mathbb{P}_j\in\mathscr{P}_j} \ln(M_j(t, \mathbb{P}_j))$ *or an upper bound for it. Luckily, in this case, we can exploit the structure of* $\mathscr{P}_j$*, namely zero mean on* $[-1, 1]$*, and have the following exact solution,*

$$\sup_{\mathbb{P}_j\in\mathscr{P}_j} \ln(M_j(t, \mathbb{P}_j)) = \frac{e^t + e^{-t}}{2} = \cosh(t),$$

*and the maximum is achieved by the Bernoulli random variable on* $\{-1, 1\}$ *with zero mean. This reduces the problem to the chance constrained problem with independent Bernoulli random variables that we considered in Sect. 4.4.5.2. In particular, the Bernstein approximation to the DRCC problem* (4.4.98) *is exactly given by the second-order conic program* (4.4.85)*, reproduced below*

$$\left(\sum_{j=1}^{n}(b_j - \boldsymbol{a}_j^\top \boldsymbol{x})^2\right)^{\frac{1}{2}} \le \sqrt{\frac{1}{2\ln(1/\epsilon)}} \cdot (b_0 - \boldsymbol{a}_0^\top \boldsymbol{x}). \tag{4.4.101}$$

□

## 4.5 End-of-Chapter Exercises

**4.1** Show that if the support $\mathscr{U}$ of the probability measure is a finite set in (4.2.4), then (4.2.6c)–(4.2.6d) exactly recovers the dual linear program of (4.2.3).

**4.2** In (4.2.12) we derived a reformulation of a DRO problem with second-order moment information. Show that the SDP reformulation (4.2.12b)–(4.2.12d) is indeed an exact reformulation of the robust constraint (4.2.12a).

**4.3** Section 4.2.2.2 defines the KL divergence. Verify that $\phi_{KL}(t) = t\log(t) - t + 1, \quad t \ge 0$ is a convex function on $t \ge 0$.

**4.4** Derive the four properties of the KL divergence given in Sect. 4.2.2.2.

**4.5** Derive conjugate functions $\phi^*$ in Table 4.1. Show that (1) $\phi^*$ is a convex function. (2) $\phi^*$ is a nondecreasing function. (3) $\phi^*(x) \geq x$ for all $x \in \mathbb{R}$.

**4.6** Show that the composite function $(\alpha\phi)^*(f(\boldsymbol{x}, \boldsymbol{\xi}_i)-\lambda)$, defined in the equivalent reformulation of a DRO with a $\phi$-divergence set (Sect. 4.2.2.4), is indeed a convex function *jointly* in $(\boldsymbol{x}, \lambda, \alpha)$ for $\alpha \geq 0$.

**4.7** In the reformulation of DRO with Hellinger divergence (4.2.30), verify that $z_i + 2\alpha - l_i \geq 0$.

**4.8** Derive the reformulation (4.2.55) of the DRO problem with a first-order Wasserstein ambiguity set with an empirical distribution $\mathbb{Q}_0$ and a convex piecewise linear objective function $f(\boldsymbol{x}, \boldsymbol{\xi}) = \max_{1\leq k\leq K} \boldsymbol{y}_k^\top \boldsymbol{\xi} + \ell_k(\boldsymbol{x})$.

**4.9** The reformulation (4.3.6) of a two-stage DRO with a moment-based ambiguity set involves all the extreme points $\boldsymbol{y}_k$ of the dual polytope. If we do not have all the extreme points $\boldsymbol{y}_k$ explicitly, can you design an algorithm to solve the two-stage DRO problem?

**4.10** Derive deterministic reformulations (4.3.9) for two-stage DRO problems with $\phi$-divergence ambiguity sets for all the $\phi$-divergence in Table 4.1.

**4.11** Show that in (4.4.28), the constraint $\tau \geq 0$ can be ignored.

**4.12** Derive the exact reformulation (4.35) of the DRCC with a cross-moment ambiguity set and a quadratic constraint function.

**4.13** Show that the exact reformulation of the DRCC with $\phi$-divergence is equivalent to a nominal chance constraint over the empirical distribution $\mathbb{Q}_0$ and a tightened probability margin $\epsilon'_\phi(d)$, i.e. show that $\epsilon'_\phi(d) \leq \epsilon$ (reference (4.4.44).)

**4.14** Derive (4.4.56). Hint: Rewrite $\inf_{\boldsymbol{\xi}:\boldsymbol{a}(\boldsymbol{x})^\top\boldsymbol{\xi}>b(\boldsymbol{x})} \|\boldsymbol{\xi}-\boldsymbol{\xi}_j\|$ by using the definition of dual norm as

$$\inf_{\boldsymbol{\xi}:\boldsymbol{a}(\boldsymbol{x})^\top\boldsymbol{\xi}>b(\boldsymbol{x})} \|\boldsymbol{\xi}-\boldsymbol{\xi}_j\| = \inf_{\boldsymbol{\xi}:\boldsymbol{a}(\boldsymbol{x})^\top\boldsymbol{\xi}>b(\boldsymbol{x})} \sup_{\|\boldsymbol{z}\|_*\leq 1} \boldsymbol{z}^\top(\boldsymbol{\xi}-\boldsymbol{\xi}_j).$$

Use strong duality to switch inf and sup. Then, solve the inner infimum $\inf_{\boldsymbol{\xi}:\boldsymbol{a}(\boldsymbol{x})^\top\boldsymbol{\xi}>b(\boldsymbol{x})} \boldsymbol{z}^\top(\boldsymbol{\xi}-\boldsymbol{\xi}_j)$ by discussing two cases regarding whether $\boldsymbol{a}(\boldsymbol{x})^\top\boldsymbol{\xi} > b(\boldsymbol{x})$ or not.

**4.15** Show that (4.4.60) and (4.4.61) are equivalent. Hint: view $\gamma\|\boldsymbol{a}(\boldsymbol{x})\|_*$ in (4.4.60) as the new variable $\gamma$ in (4.4.61).

**4.16** Describe the structure of the set $Z_0$ defined in (4.4.59), when the uncertainty is (1) only in the coefficient, (2) only in the right-hand side, and (3) both.

**4.17** Derive the exact mixed integer reformulation of the DRCC constraint (4.4.47) for the special case where the uncertainty is only in the right-hand side, i.e. $\boldsymbol{a}(\boldsymbol{x})$ is a constant vector $\boldsymbol{a}$.

**4.18** Show that the function $F(\boldsymbol{x}, t) := \Psi(\boldsymbol{x}, t) - t\epsilon$ defined in (4.4.68) is a convex function in $(\boldsymbol{x}, t)$. Hint: It is well-known that if $f(x)$ is a convex function, then the perspective function $tf(x/t)$ is a convex function in $(x, t)$ for $t > 0$.

**4.19** Given a generating function $\phi : \mathbb{R} \to \mathbb{R}$, i.e. $\phi$ is a nonnegative, nondecreasing, convex function, $\phi(0) = 1$, and $\phi(x) > 1$ for $x > 1$. Let $a$ be a subgradient of $\phi$ at $x = 0$, i.e. $a \in \partial\phi(0)$. Show that $\phi(x) \geq \max\{ax + 1, 0\}$. Hint: Use the subgradient inequality $\phi(x) \geq \phi(x_0) + g(x - x_0)$ for $g \in \partial\phi(x_0)$.

**4.20** Consider a simple chance constraint $\mathbb{P}(a - x + \xi x \leq 0) \geq 1 - \epsilon$ for a uniform distribution on $[\frac{1}{2}, \frac{3}{2}]$. In this case, the random variable $\xi$ has a moment generating function $M(t) = \mathbb{E}[e^{t\xi}] = \int_{1/2}^{3/2} e^{tx} dx = (e^{3t/2} - e^{t/2})/t$. Compute the exact feasible region defined by the chance constraint with $a = -2$. Then, compute the feasible region defined by the Bernstein approximation. How big is the difference between the two feasible regions? Try other values of $a$, e.g. $a = 1$ as the example in (4.4.6). What do you find? Hint: Bernstein approximation may lead to an empty feasible region, which is still an inner approximation, albeit not a very useful one.

## References


1. Lin, G. D. (2017). Recent developments on the moment problem. *Journal of Statistical Distributions and Applications, 4*, 5. https://doi.org/10.1186/s40488-017-0059-2.
2. Shapiro, A. (2001). On Duality theory of conic linear problems. In M. A. Goberna & M. A. Lopez (Eds.) *Semi-Infinite Programming. Nonconvex Optimization and Its Applications* (vol. 57). Boston, MA: Springer.
3. Ekeland, I., & Temam, R. (1976). *Convex analysis and variational problems*. Amsterdam: North-Holland Publishing Company.
4. Schaefer, H. (1971). *Topological vector spaces*. Berlin: Springer.
5. Zymler, S., Kuhn, D., & Rustem, B. (2013). Distributionally robust joint chance constraints with second-order moment information. *Mathematical Programming, Series A, 137*, 167–198.
6. Delage, E., & Ye, Y. (2010). Distributionally robust optimization under moment uncertainty with application to data-driven problems. *Operations Research, 58*(3), 595–612.
7. El Ghaoui, L., Oks, M., & Oustry, F. (2003). Worst-case value-at-risk and robust portfolio optimization: A conic programming approach. *Operations Research, 51*(4), 543–556.
8. Wiesemann, W., Kuhn, D., & Sim, S. (2014). Distributionally robust convex optimization. *Operations Research, 62*(6), 1358–1376.
9. Kullback, S., & Leibler, R. A. (1951). On information and sufficiency. *The Annals of Mathematical Statistics, 22*(1), 79–86.
10. Jiang, R., & Guan, Y. (2016). Data-driven chance constrained stochastic program. *Mathematical Programming, Series A, 158*, 291–327.
11. Ben-Tal, A., den Hertog, D., De Waegenaere, A., Melenberg, B., & Rennen, G. (2013). Robust solutions of optimization problems affected by uncertain probabilities. *Management Science, 59*(2), 341–357.
12. Villani, C. (2009). *Optimal transport, old and new*. Grundlehren der mathematischen Wissenschaften Series (vol. 338). Berlin: Springer.
13. Gao, R., & Kleywegt, A. Distributionally robust stochastic optimization with Wasserstein distance. https://arxiv.org/abs/1604.02199.

14. Blanchet, J., & Murthy, K. (2019). Quantifying distributional model risk via optimal transport. *Mathematics of Operations Research, 44*(2), 565–600.
15. Lehmann, E. L., & Romano, J. P. (2005). *Testing statistical hypotheses.* Springer Texts in Statistics (3rd ed.)
16. Pardo, L. (2020). *Statistical inference based on divergence measures.* Boca Raton: Chapman & Hall/CRC.
17. Fournier, N., & Guillin, A. (2015). On the rate of convergence in Wasserstein distance of the empirical measure. *Probability Theory and Related Fields, 162*, 707–738.
18. Esfahani, P. M., & Kuhn, D. (2018). Data-driven distributionally robust optimization using the Wasserstein metric: performance guarantees and tractable reformulations. *Mathematical Programming Series A, 171*, 115–166.
19. Bertsimas, B., Gupta, V., & Kallus, N. (2017). Data-driven robust optimization. *Mathematical Programming Series A, 167*, 235–292.
20. Goldfarb, D., & Iyengar, G. (2003). Robust portfolio selection problems. *Mathematics of Operations Research, 28*(1), 1–38.
21. Klabjan, D., Simchi-Levi, D., & Song, M. (2013). Robust stochastic lot-sizing by means of histograms. *Production and Operations Management, 22*(3), 691–710.
22. Guslitser, E. (2002). Uncertainty-immunized solutions in linear programming. Unpublished Master's Thesis. Technion-Israel Institute of Technology, Haifa.
23. Hanasusanto, G., & Kuhn, D. (2018). Conic programming reformulations of two-stage distributionally robust linear programs over Wasserstein balls. *Operations Research, 66*(3), 849–869.
24. Charnes, A., Cooper, W. W., & Symonds, G. H. (1958). Cost horizons and certainty equivalents: an approach to stochastic programming of heating oil production. *Management Science, 4*, 236–263.
25. Prékopa, A. (1973). Contributions to the theory of stochastic programming. *Mathematical Programming, 4*, 202–221.
26. Birge, J. R., & Louveaux, F. (2011). *Introduction to stochastic programming* (2nd ed.) Berlin: Springer.
27. Xie, W. (2021). On distributionally robust chance constrained programs with Wasserstein distance. *Mathematical Programming Series A, 186*, 115–155. https://doi.org/10.1007/s10107-019-01445-5.
28. Chen, Z., Kuhn, D., & Wiesemann, W. (2018). Data-driven chance constrained programs over Wasserstein balls. arXiv:1809.00210v1.
29. Hota, A., Cherukuri, A., & Lygeros, J. (2018). Data-driven chance constrained optimization under Wasserstein ambiguity sets. https://arxiv.org/abs/1805.06729.
30. Ji, R., & Lejeune, M. A. (2021). Data-driven distributionally robust chance constrained optimization with Wasserstein metric. *Journal of Global Optimization, 79*, 779–811.
31. Nemirovski, A., & Shapiro, A. (2006). Convex approximations of chance constrained programs. *SIAM Journal on Optimization, 17*(4), 969–996.
32. Rockafellar, R. T., & Uryasev, S. P. (2000). Optimization of conditional value-at-risk. *Journal of Risk, 2*, 21–41.
33. Pinter, J. (1989). Deterministic approximations of probabilistic inequalities. *Operations Research, 33*, 219–239.
34. Rockafellar, R. T. (1970). *Convex analysis.* Princeton: Princeton University Press.
35. Shapiro, A., & Kleywegt, A. (2002). Minimax analysis of stochastic problems. *Optimization Methods and Software, 17*(3), 523–542.

# Chapter 5
# Hybrid Adaptive Robust Optimization Models

This chapter provides a detailed description of Adaptive Robust Optimization (ARO) models that involve uncertainties of different nature, specifically, long-term uncertainty, such as that pertaining to electricity demand growth from year to year, and short-term uncertainty, such as that pertaining to weather-dependent renewable production throughout the hours of a day. Short- and long-term uncertainty are described first. The Adaptive Robust Optimization Stochastic Optimization (ARSO) model introduced in Chap. 1 is then expanded and further analyzed. Next, solution techniques for such model are described. Finally, a realistic ARSO model for the expansion of the transmission network of an electric energy system is described and discussed.

## 5.1 Introduction

Uncertainty affects many parameters within a planning exercise, such as transmission expansion planning or generation expansion planning. Moreover, uncertainty has different natures and requires different modeling representations within an optimization model. In fact, to achieve adequate accuracy, the representation of a given uncertainty type should be tailored to its nature.

This chapter specifically addresses two families of uncertainties: short- and long-term, and uses tailored representations for them.

In turn, these tailored uncertainty representations are incorporated into decision-making ARO models, resulting in hybrid ARO models, specifically ARSO models.

 
X. A. Sun, A. J. Conejo, *Robust Optimization in Electric Energy Systems*,
International Series in Operations Research & Management Science 313,
https://doi.org/10.1007/978-3-030-85128-6_5

## 5.2 Long- and Short-Term Uncertainty

Within a general power system modeling context, long-term uncertainty includes:

1. Peak demand growth: that is, the change in peak demand at different locations from year to year throughout the power system.
2. Investment cost in transmission lines: transmission line investment costs are known at the beginning of the study horizon, but change along it.
3. Investment cost in generating units: as transmission line investment costs, generation unit investment costs are known at the beginning of the study horizon, but change along it.
4. Fuel costs: fuel costs are known at the beginning of the study horizon, but change along it.
5. Regulatory changes: The regulatory framework governing the considered power system may change throughout the study horizon.

Long-term uncertainty of the type described above is conveniently represented via robust sets, as discussed in Chap. 2. These robust sets are built generally using historical data spanning a number of years and should reflect, if appropriate, inter-temporal coupling.

Short-term uncertainty includes:

1. Demand variability throughout the hours of the day: The demand in each node changes throughout the hours of the day with a significant level of day-ahead unpredictability.
2. Output of weather-dependent generating units: The power output of solar and wind power units change with significant unpredictability throughout the hours of each day.
3. Equipment failures: Equipment, including lines, transformers and generating units may fail at any time throughout the day.

Short-term uncertainty of the type described above is conveniently represented via scenarios, as discussed in Chap. 2. Depending on the power system under study, a scenario may represent 1 h or 1 day/week with hourly steps. Daily/weekly representation is needed if inter-temporal constraints (due to ramping limits or storage operation) are relevant.

## 5.3 Formulation and Solution

Long-term uncertainty is appropriately represented within a robust modeling framework since long-term decisions are generally security-related and are difficult to change.

On the other hand, short-term uncertainty is conveniently represented via scenarios within a stochastic programming framework since short-term decisions generally involve limited risk and are easy to change.

Adaptive robust stochastic optimization (ARSO) models combine robust protection (long-term uncertainty) and stochastic modeling (short-term uncertainty). As introduced in Chap. 1, a generic ARSO problem has the form [1]:

$$\min_{\mathbf{x}\in\mathscr{X}} \quad \max_{\mathbf{u}\in\mathscr{U}} \quad \min_{\mathbf{y}\in\mathscr{Y}(\mathbf{x},\mathbf{u},\boldsymbol{\xi})} \quad \mathbb{E}_{\boldsymbol{\xi}} f(\mathbf{x},\mathbf{u},\mathbf{y},\boldsymbol{\xi}). \tag{5.3.1}$$

This problem involves three levels. The first level represents a *planning* strategy prior to the uncertainty realization and seeks to minimize the objective function. Decision variables are represented by vector $\mathbf{x} \in \mathscr{X}$. For the transmission expansion planning problem, decision variables at this level are the candidate transmission lines to be built.

The second level represents *long-term* uncertainty realization in the worst possible manner within an uncertainty set, and thus it seeks to maximize the objective function. The variables describing long-term uncertain parameters are represented by vector $\mathbf{u} \in \mathscr{U}$. For the transmission expansion planning problem, the uncertainty at this level includes the future peak load and the future available production capacity of both conventional and stochastic units.

The third level represents the mitigation actions by the operator once the long-term uncertainty realizes and involves a number of *short-term* uncertain operating conditions represented via scenarios by the parameter vector $\boldsymbol{\xi}$. Therefore, the third level seeks to minimize the objective function. Decision variables at this level are represented by vector $\mathbf{y} \in \mathscr{Y}(\mathbf{x},\mathbf{u},\boldsymbol{\xi})$. For the transmission expansion planning problem, the uncertainty at this level includes:

1. The operating conditions in terms of actual demand and renewable and conventional available production capacity within the hours of the day, and across the days of one year.
2. Equipment failures.

The overall objective function to be minimized is the expected value of the objective over the short-term uncertainty parameters in vector $\boldsymbol{\xi}$ under the worst long-term uncertainty realization $\mathbf{u}$ within the robust set $\mathscr{U}$.

We emphasize that ARSO problems involve both ex-ante protection (planning decisions) and ex-post adjustment (operation decisions tailored per scenario).

A more explicit model description is provided below.

$$\begin{array}{llll}
\min_{\mathbf{x}} & \max_{\mathbf{u}\in\mathscr{U}} & \min_{\mathbf{y}} & \mathbb{E}_{\boldsymbol{\xi}} f(\mathbf{x},\mathbf{u},\mathbf{y},\boldsymbol{\xi}) \\
 & & \text{s.t.} \ \mathbf{h}^{\mathrm{Y}}(\mathbf{x},\mathbf{u},\mathbf{y},\boldsymbol{\xi}) = \mathbf{0} & \\
 & & \qquad \mathbf{g}^{\mathrm{Y}}(\mathbf{x},\mathbf{u},\mathbf{y},\boldsymbol{\xi}) \le \mathbf{0} & \\
\text{s.t.} \ \mathbf{h}^{\mathrm{X}}(\mathbf{x}) = \mathbf{0} & & & \\
\qquad \mathbf{g}^{\mathrm{X}}(\mathbf{x}) \le \mathbf{0}. & & &
\end{array} \tag{5.3.2}$$

As analyzed in Chap. 3, the solution of problem (5.3.2) generally relies on three steps:

1. Recasting the third-level min problem as a convex problem with an analytical form for its dual. This way, the dual of the third-level problem is readily available. We note that since the third-level problem is a min problem, its dual is a max problem.
2. Merging the second-level problem, which is a max problem, and the dual of the third-level problem, which is a max problem as well, results in a merged single max problem.
3. Solving by decomposition the bi-level problem consisting of the first-level problem and the merged problem. Both dual and primal Benders' schemes can be implemented [2], but primal schemes are generally more efficient [3, 4].

## 5.4 Transmission Expansion Planning (TEP)

This section describes a two-stage ARSO model for transmission expansion planning. Investment decisions pertain solely to the building of new transmission lines. The long-term uncertainty considered includes: peak demand, available stochastic production capacity and available conventional production capacity, all in the target year. The short-term uncertainty includes: demand variability throughout the hours of the day and weather-dependent generating output throughout the hours of the day. Further detail on the considered model can be found in [1].

We first discuss a very simple illustrative example, then describe the proposed model, and finally analyze a case study.

**Illustrative Example 5.1 (Simple adaptive robust stochastic optimization example.)**

*A transmission expansion planner has the option of building just one of two alternatives transmission lines of capacity either* 2 *or* 4 *to connect electrical nodes 1 and 2 (see Fig. 5.1). The per unit building cost for the transmission lines is* 1.

*At node 1, a generator of unlimited capacity and per unit production cost of* 5 *is available, while in node 2 another generator of unlimited capacity and per unit production cost of 10 is available.*

*At the target year, the peak of the demand located at node 2 can take solely two values, either* 3 *or* 5.

*Whichever the realization of the peak demand (either* 3 *or* 5*), two operating conditions (scenarios) need to be considered: peak demand with probability (fraction of hours in a year)* $\frac{1}{4}$, *and* $\frac{1}{2}$ *peak demand with probability* $\frac{3}{4}$.

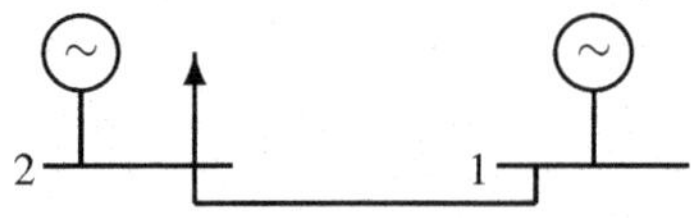


**Fig. 5.1** Simple ARSO model: Transmission expansion planning

*An ARSO model for the transmission planner to decide which transmission line to build is:*

$$\begin{aligned}
\min_{x\in\{2,4\}} \max_{d\in\{3,5\}} \min_{\substack{y_1^{(1)},\, y_2^{(1)}\geq 0\\ y_1^{(2)},\, y_2^{(2)}\geq 0}} \quad & z = 1\cdot x + \tfrac{1}{4}\left(5y_1^{(1)} + 10y_2^{(1)}\right) + \tfrac{3}{4}\left(5y_1^{(2)} + 10y_2^{(2)}\right)\\
\text{s.t.} \quad & y_1^{(1)} + y_2^{(1)} = 1\cdot d\\
& y_1^{(1)} \leq x\\
& y_1^{(2)} + y_2^{(2)} = \tfrac{1}{2}\cdot d\\
& y_1^{(2)} \leq x,
\end{aligned}$$

*where $x$ represents the capacity of the transmission line to be built, $d$ the unknown peak demand, $y_1^{(1)}$ and $y_2^{(1)}$, the production of the units at nodes 1 and 2, respectively, in scenario (1), i.e., if the demand is $d$, and $y_1^{(2)}$ and $y_2^{(2)}$, the production of the units at nodes 1 and 2, respectively, in scenario (2), i.e., if the demand is $\frac{1}{2}d$.*

*Given the small size and simplicity of this problem, it can be solved by enumeration. This is done below.*

1. *We first consider that the planner builds the line of capacity 2, i.e., $x = 2$. Then, the problem to be solved is:*

$$\begin{aligned}
\max_{d\in\{3,5\}} \min_{\substack{y_1^{(1)},\, y_2^{(1)}\geq 0\\ y_1^{(2)},\, y_2^{(2)}\geq 0}} \quad & z = 2 + \tfrac{1}{4}\left(5y_1^{(1)} + 10y_2^{(1)}\right) + \tfrac{3}{4}\left(5y_1^{(2)} + 10y_2^{(2)}\right)\\
\text{s.t.} \quad & y_1^{(1)} + y_2^{(1)} = 1\cdot d\\
& y_1^{(1)} \leq 2\\
& y_1^{(2)} + y_2^{(2)} = \tfrac{1}{2}\cdot d\\
& y_1^{(2)} \leq 2.
\end{aligned}$$

*To solve this problem we consider the two alternatives for the peak demand $d$,* 3 *and* 5.

*1.1. If the peak demand is $d = 3$, the problem to be solved becomes:*

$$\begin{aligned}
\min_{\substack{y_1^{(1)},\, y_2^{(1)}\geq 0\\ y_1^{(2)},\, y_2^{(2)}\geq 0}} \quad & z = 2 + \tfrac{1}{4}\left(5y_1^{(1)} + 10y_2^{(1)}\right) + \tfrac{3}{4}\left(5y_1^{(2)} + 10y_2^{(2)}\right)\\
\text{s.t.} \quad & y_1^{(1)} + y_2^{(1)} = 1\cdot 3\\
& y_1^{(1)} \leq 2\\
& y_1^{(2)} + y_2^{(2)} = \tfrac{1}{2}\cdot 3\\
& y_1^{(2)} \leq 2,
\end{aligned}$$

*whose solution is $y_1^{(1)} = 2$, $y_2^{(1)} = 1$, $y_1^{(2)} = \frac{3}{2}$, $y_2^{(2)} = 0$, and $z = 12.625$.*

*1.2. On the other hand, if the peak demand is $d = 5$, the problem to be solved becomes:*

$$\min_{\substack{y_1^{(1)},\, y_2^{(1)} \geq 0 \\ y_1^{(2)},\, y_2^{(2)} \geq 0}} \quad z = 2 + \tfrac{1}{4}\left(5y_1^{(1)} + 10y_2^{(1)}\right) + \tfrac{3}{4}\left(5y_1^{(2)} + 10y_2^{(2)}\right)$$

$$\text{s.t.} \quad \begin{aligned} & y_1^{(1)} + y_2^{(1)} = 1 \cdot 5 \\ & y_1^{(1)} \leq 2 \\ & y_1^{(2)} + y_2^{(2)} = \tfrac{1}{2} \cdot 5 \\ & y_1^{(2)} \leq 2, \end{aligned}$$

*whose solution is* $y_1^{(1)} = 2,\ y_2^{(1)} = 3,\ y_1^{(2)} = 2,\ y_2^{(2)} = \frac{1}{2}$, *and* $z = 23.25$.

*Considering the above results and the fact that maximum cost is pursued at this level (long-term uncertainty realization), the solution in case $x = 2$ is $d = 5$ and $z = 23.25$.*

2. *We then consider that the planner builds the line of capacity 4, i.e., $x = 4$. Then, the problem to be solved is:*

$$\max_{d \in \{3,5\}} \min_{\substack{y_1^{(1)},\, y_2^{(1)} \geq 0 \\ y_1^{(2)},\, y_2^{(2)} \geq 0}} \quad z = 4 + \tfrac{1}{4}\left(5y_1^{(1)} + 10y_2^{(1)}\right) + \tfrac{3}{4}\left((5y_1^{(2)} + 10y_2^{(2)}\right)$$

$$\text{s.t.} \quad \begin{aligned} & y_1^{(1)} + y_2^{(1)} = 1 \cdot d \\ & y_1^{(1)} \leq 4 \\ & y_1^{(2)} + y_2^{(2)} = \tfrac{1}{2} \cdot d \\ & y_1^{(2)} \leq 4. \end{aligned}$$

*To solve this problem we consider the two alternatives for the peak demand d, 3 and 5.*

*1.1. If the peak demand is $d = 3$, the problem to be solved becomes:*

$$\min_{\substack{y_1^{(1)},\, y_2^{(1)} \geq 0 \\ y_1^{(2)},\, y_2^{(2)} \geq 0}} \quad z = 4 + \tfrac{1}{4}\left(5y_1^{(1)} + 10y_2^{(1)}\right) + \tfrac{3}{4}\left((5y_1^{(2)} + 10y_2^{(2)}\right)$$

$$\text{s.t.} \quad \begin{aligned} & y_1^{(1)} + y_2^{(1)} = 1 \cdot 3 \\ & y_1^{(1)} \leq 4 \\ & y_1^{(2)} + y_2^{(2)} = \tfrac{1}{2} \cdot 3 \\ & y_1^{(2)} \leq 4, \end{aligned}$$

*whose solution is* $y_1^{(1)} = 3,\ y_2^{(1)} = 0,\ y_1^{(2)} = \frac{3}{2},\ y_2^{(2)} = 0$, *and* $z = 13.375$.

*1.2. On the other hand, if the peak demand is* $d = 5$*, the problem to be solved becomes:*

$$\min_{\substack{y_1^{(1)},\, y_2^{(1)} \geq 0 \\ y_1^{(2)},\, y_2^{(2)} \geq 0}} \quad z = 4 + \tfrac{1}{4}\left(5y_1^{(1)} + 10y_2^{(1)}\right) + \tfrac{3}{4}\left((5y_1^{(2)} + 10y_2^{(2)}\right))$$

$$\text{s.t.} \quad \begin{aligned} & y_1^{(1)} + y_2^{(1)} = 1 \cdot 5 \\ & y_1^{(1)} \leq 4 \\ & y_1^{(2)} + y_2^{(2)} = \tfrac{1}{2} \cdot 5 \\ & y_1^{(2)} \leq 4, \end{aligned}$$

*whose solution is* $y_1^{(1)} = 4$, $y_2^{(1)} = 1$, $y_1^{(2)} = \frac{5}{2}$, $y_2^{(2)} = 0$, *and* $z = 20.875$.

*Considering the above results and the fact that maximum cost is pursued at this level (uncertainty realization), the solution in case* $x = 4$ *is* $d = 5$ *and* $z = 20.875$.

*Finally, considering the two alternatives for investment* $x = 2$ *(*$z = 23.25$*) and* $x = 4$ *(*$z = 20.875$*), and that the planner seeks minimum cost, the solution is* $x = 4$, $d = 5$, $y_1^{(1)} = 4$, $y_2^{(1)} = 1$, $y_1^{(2)} = \frac{5}{2}$, $y_2^{(2)} = 0$ *and* $z = 20.875$.

*We conclude that the planner builds the larger transmission line (*$x = 4$*) to be protected against the high cost of the generator at node 2.*

□

We describe a general TEP model below, given first the notation and then the formulation. Then, a case study is analyzed.

### 5.4.1 Notation

The notation used is given below.

**Indices**

| | |
|---|---|
| $c$ | Conventional units. |
| $d$ | Demands. |
| $n$ | Nodes. |
| $s$ | Stochastic units. |
| $\ell$ | Transmission lines. |
| $r(\ell)$ | Receiving-end node of transmission line $\ell$. |
| $s(\ell)$ | Sending-end node of transmission line $\ell$. |
| $\omega$ | Operating scenarios. |

**Sets**

| | |
|---|---|
| $\Lambda_z^{\mathrm{C}}$ | Conventional units in geographical zone $z$. |

| | |
|---|---|
| $\Lambda_z^{\mathrm{D}}$ | Demands in zone $z$. |
| $\Lambda_z^{\mathrm{S}}$ | Stochastic units in zone $z$. |
| $\Lambda^{\mathrm{Z}}$ | All zones. |
| $\Omega^{\mathrm{C}}$ | All conventional units. |
| $\Omega_n^{\mathrm{C}}$ | Conventional units located at node $n$. |
| $\Omega^{\mathrm{D}}$ | All demands. |
| $\Omega_n^{\mathrm{D}}$ | Demands located at node $n$. |
| $\Omega^{\mathrm{G}}$ | All units. |
| $\Omega^{\mathrm{L}}$ | All transmission lines. |
| $\Omega^{\mathrm{L}^+}$ | Candidate transmission lines. |
| $\Omega^{\mathrm{N}}$ | All nodes. |
| $\Omega^{\mathrm{S}}$ | All stochastic units. |
| $\Omega_n^{\mathrm{S}}$ | Stochastic units located at node $n$. |
| $\Omega^{\mathrm{W}}$ | All scenarios. |

**First-Level Problem Constants**

| | |
|---|---|
| $I_\ell$ | Annualized investment cost of transmission line $\ell$ [$]. |
| $\Pi^{\mathrm{Invest}}$ | Investment budget for building new transmission lines [$]. |

**Second-Level Problem Constants**

| | |
|---|---|
| $\bar{D}_d^{\mathrm{exp}}$ | Expected level of future peak power for demand $d$ [MW]. |
| $\bar{D}_d^{\mathrm{max}}$ | Upper bound of future peak power for demand $d$ [MW]. |
| $\bar{P}_s^{\mathrm{S\,exp}}$ | Expected level of the future capacity of stochastic unit $s$ [MW]. |
| $\bar{P}_s^{\mathrm{S\,min}}$ | Lower bound for the future capacity of stochastic unit $s$ [MW]. |
| $\bar{P}_c^{\mathrm{C\,exp}}$ | Expected level of the future capacity of conventional unit $c$ [MW]. |
| $\bar{P}_c^{\mathrm{C\,min}}$ | Lower bound for future capacity of conventional unit $c$ [MW]. |
| $\Gamma_z^{\mathrm{S}}$ | Uncertainty budget parameter for stochastic units in zone $z$ [pu]. |
| $\Gamma_z^{\mathrm{C}}$ | Uncertainty budget parameter for conventional units in zone $z$ [pu]. |
| $\Gamma_z^{\mathrm{D}}$ | Uncertainty budget parameter for demands in zone $z$ [pu]. |

**Third-Level Problem Constants**

| | |
|---|---|
| $C_s^{\mathrm{S}}$ | Production cost of stochastic unit $s$ [$/MWh]. |
| $C_c^{\mathrm{C}}$ | Production cost of conventional unit $c$ [$/MWh]. |
| $C_d^{\mathrm{U}}$ | Cost of unserved energy for demand $d$ [$/MWh]. |
| $e_s^{\mathrm{S}\omega}$ | Coefficient associated with the production availability of stochastic unit $s$ in scenario $\omega$ [pu]. |
| $e_c^{\mathrm{C}\omega}$ | Coefficient associated with the production availability of conventional unit $c$ in scenario $\omega$ [pu]. |
| $e_d^{\mathrm{D}\omega}$ | Coefficient associated with the level of demand $d$ in scenario $\omega$ [pu]. |
| $\sigma^{\omega}$ | Weight of scenario $\omega$ [pu]. |

**Other Constants**

| | |
|---|---|
| $b_\ell$ | Susceptance of transmission line $\ell$ [S]. |
| $f_\ell^{\mathrm{max}}$ | Capacity of transmission line $\ell$ [MW]. |
| $\beta$ | Weighting parameter to make comparable investment and operation cost [hours]. |

**First-Level Problem Variables**

$x_\ell$ Binary variable that is equal to 1 if candidate line $\ell$ is built, and 0 otherwise.

**Second-Level Problem Variables**

$\bar{D}_d$ Future peak power load of demand $d$ [MW].

$\bar{P}_c^{\mathrm{C}}$ Future capacity of conventional unit $c$ [MW].

$\bar{P}_s^{\mathrm{S}}$ Future capacity of stochastic unit $s$ [MW].

**Third-Level Problem Variables**

$f_\ell^\omega$ Power flow through transmission line $\ell$ in scenario $\omega$ [MW].

$P_s^{\mathrm{S}\omega}$ Power generation of stochastic unit $s$ in scenario $\omega$ [MW].

$P_c^{\mathrm{C}\omega}$ Power generation of conventional unit $c$ in scenario $\omega$ [MW].

$P_d^{\mathrm{U}\omega}$ Unserved energy of demand $d$ in scenario $\omega$ [MW].

$\delta_n^\omega$ Voltage angle at node $n$ in scenario $\omega$ [radian].

## 5.4.2 Formulation

The TEP problem formulation is provided below.

$$\min_{\Xi_1} \quad \max_{\Xi_2} \quad \min_{\Xi_3} \tag{5.4.1a}$$

$$\sum_{x_\ell \in \Omega^{\mathrm{L}+}} I_\ell x_\ell + \sum_{\omega \in \Omega^{\mathrm{W}}} \beta \sigma^\omega \left( \sum_{s \in \Omega^{\mathrm{S}}} C_s^{\mathrm{S}} P_s^{\mathrm{S}\omega} + \sum_{c \in \Omega^{\mathrm{C}}} C_c^{\mathrm{C}} P_c^{\mathrm{C}\omega} + \sum_{d \in \Omega^{\mathrm{D}}} C_d^{\mathrm{U}} P_d^{\mathrm{U}\omega} \right) \tag{5.4.1b}$$

s.t.

$$\sum_{x_\ell \in \Omega^{\mathrm{L}+}} I_\ell x_\ell \leq \Pi^{\mathrm{Invest}} \tag{5.4.1c}$$

$$x_\ell \in \{0, 1\} : \forall x_\ell \in \Omega^{\mathrm{L}^+}; \qquad x_\ell = 1 : \forall x_\ell \in \Omega^{\mathrm{L}} \backslash \Omega^{\mathrm{L}^+} \tag{5.4.1d}$$

s.t.

$$\bar{P}_s^{\mathrm{S\,min}} \leq \bar{P}_s^{\mathrm{S}} \leq \bar{P}_s^{\mathrm{S\,exp}}, \forall s \in \Omega^{\mathrm{S}} \tag{5.4.1e}$$

$$\sum_{s \in \Lambda_z^{\mathrm{S}}} \frac{\bar{P}_s^{\mathrm{Sexp}} - \bar{P}_s^{\mathrm{S}}}{\bar{P}_s^{\mathrm{Sexp}} - \bar{P}_s^{\mathrm{S\,min}}} \leq \Gamma_z^{\mathrm{S}}, \forall z \in \Lambda^{\mathrm{Z}} \tag{5.4.1f}$$

$$\bar{P}_c^{\mathrm{C\,min}} \leq \bar{P}_c^{\mathrm{C}} \leq \bar{P}_c^{\mathrm{Cexp}}, \forall c \in \Omega^{\mathrm{C}} \tag{5.4.1g}$$

$$\sum_{c \in \Lambda_z^{\mathrm{C}}} \frac{\bar{P}_c^{\mathrm{Cexp}} - \bar{P}_c^{\mathrm{C}}}{\bar{P}_c^{\mathrm{Cexp}} - \bar{P}_c^{\mathrm{C\,min}}} \leq \Gamma_z^{\mathrm{C}}, \forall z \in \Lambda^{\mathrm{Z}} \tag{5.4.1h}$$

$$\bar{D}_d^{\text{exp}} \leq \bar{D}_d \leq \bar{D}_d^{\text{max}}, \forall d \in \Omega^{\text{D}} \tag{5.4.1i}$$

$$\sum_{d \in \Lambda_z^{\text{D}}} \frac{\bar{D}_d - \bar{D}_d^{\text{exp}}}{\bar{D}_d^{\text{max}} - \bar{D}_d^{\text{exp}}} \leq \Gamma_z^{\text{D}}, \forall z \in \Lambda^{\text{Z}} \tag{5.4.1j}$$

s.t.

$$\sum_{s \in \Omega_n^{\text{S}}} P_s^{\text{S}\omega} + \sum_{c \in \Omega_n^{\text{C}}} P_c^{\text{C}\omega} + \sum_{\ell | r(\ell) \in \Omega_n} f_\ell^\omega - \sum_{\ell | s(\ell) \in \Omega_n} f_\ell^\omega$$

$$= \sum_{d \in \Omega_n^{\text{D}}} e_d^{\text{D}\omega} \bar{D}_d - \sum_{d \in \Omega_n^{\text{D}}} P_d^{\text{U}\omega}, \forall n \in \Omega^{\text{N}}, \forall \omega \in \Omega^{\text{W}} \tag{5.4.1k}$$

$$f_\ell^\omega = x_\ell b_\ell \left( \delta_{s(\ell)}^\omega - \delta_{r(\ell)}^\omega \right), \forall \ell \in \Omega^{\text{L}}, \forall \omega \in \Omega^{\text{W}} \tag{5.4.1l}$$

$$- f_\ell^{\text{max}} \leq f_\ell^\omega \leq f_\ell^{\text{max}}, \forall \ell \in \Omega^{\text{L}}, \forall \omega \in \Omega^{\text{W}} \tag{5.4.1m}$$

$$0 \leq P_s^{\text{S}\omega} \leq e_s^{\text{S}\omega} \bar{P}_s^{\text{S}}, \forall s \in \Omega^{\text{S}}, \forall \omega \in \Omega^{\text{W}} \tag{5.4.1n}$$

$$0 \leq P_c^{\text{C}\omega} \leq e_c^{\text{C}\omega} \bar{P}_c^{\text{C}}, \forall c \in \Omega^{\text{C}}, \forall \omega \in \Omega^{\text{W}} \tag{5.4.1o}$$

$$0 \leq P_d^{\text{U}\omega} \leq e_d^{\text{D}\omega} \bar{D}_d, \forall d \in \Omega^{\text{D}}, \forall \omega \in \Omega^{\text{W}} \tag{5.4.1p}$$

$$- \pi \leq \delta_n^\omega \leq \pi, \forall n \in \Omega^{\text{N}} \backslash n = \text{reference}, \forall \omega \in \Omega^{\text{W}} \tag{5.4.1q}$$

$$\delta_m^\omega = 0, m = \text{reference}, \forall \omega \in \Omega^{\text{W}}, \tag{5.4.1r}$$

where

$$\Xi_1 = \left\{ x_\ell \in \Omega^{\text{L}^+} \right\}, \tag{5.4.2a}$$

$$\Xi_2 = \left\{ \bar{P}_s^{\text{S}}, \forall s \in \Omega^{\text{S}}; \bar{P}_c^{\text{C}}, \forall c \in \Omega^{\text{C}}; \bar{D}_d, \forall d \in \Omega^{\text{D}} \right\}, \tag{5.4.2b}$$

$$\Xi_3 = \left\{ P_s^{\text{S}\omega}, \forall s \in \Omega^{\text{S}}, P_c^{\text{C}\omega}, \forall c \in \Omega^{\text{C}}, P_d^{\text{U}\omega}, \forall d \in \Omega^{\text{D}}, \right. \tag{5.4.2c}$$

$$\left. f_\ell^\omega, \forall \ell \in \Omega^{\text{L}}, \delta_n^\omega, \forall n \in \Omega^{\text{N}}; \forall \omega \in \Omega^{\text{W}} \right\}. \tag{5.4.2d}$$

The objective function (5.4.1b) include two terms. The first one:

$$\sum_{x_\ell \in \Omega^{\text{L}^+}} I_\ell x_\ell$$

is the annualized investment cost in transmission lines. The second one:

$$\sum_{\omega \in \Omega^{\text{W}}} \beta \sigma^\omega \left( \sum_{s \in \Omega^{\text{S}}} C_s^{\text{S}} P_s^{\text{S}\omega} + \sum_{c \in \Omega^{\text{C}}} C_c^{\text{C}} P_c^{\text{C}\omega} + \sum_{d \in \Omega^{\text{D}}} C_d^{\text{U}} P_d^{\text{U}\omega} \right)$$

is the expected operation cost over different short-term uncertainty realizations (demand level, stochastic units' production availability and conventional units' production availability) over the worst realization of the long-term uncertainty (peak demand, installed stochastic capacity and installed conventional capacity).

Constraints (5.4.1c)–(5.4.1d) belong to the first-level problem. Constraint (5.4.1c) sets a bound on the investment budget. Constraints (5.4.1d) declare binary variables and binary constants to model the building of prospective transmission lines.

Constraints (5.4.1e)–(5.4.1j) belong to the second-level problem.

Constraints (5.4.1e)–(5.4.1f) define an uncertainty budget for the capacity available in the target year of stochastic units and set that budget to be below a given value per zone $z$. The uncertainty budget parameter $\Gamma_z^{\mathrm{S}}$ may vary within the interval $[0, |\Lambda_z^{\mathrm{S}}|]$. If $\Gamma_z^{\mathrm{S}} = 0$, there is no long-term uncertainty on stochastic capacity. If, on the other hand, $\Gamma_z^{\mathrm{S}} = |\Lambda_z^{\mathrm{S}}|$, there is maximum uncertainty on the stochastic capacity available in the target year. Intermediate values refer to intermediate uncertainty levels.

Similarly, constraints (5.4.1g)–(5.4.1h) define an uncertainty budget for the capacity available in the target year of conventional units and set that budget to be below a given value per zone $z$. The uncertainty budget parameter $\Gamma_z^{\mathrm{C}}$ may vary within the interval $[0, |\Lambda_z^{\mathrm{C}}|]$. If $\Gamma_z^{\mathrm{C}} = 0$, there is no uncertainty on conventional capacity. If, on the other hand, $\Gamma_z^{\mathrm{C}} = |\Lambda_z^{\mathrm{C}}|$, there is maximum uncertainty on the conventional capacity available in the target year. Intermediate values refer to intermediate uncertainty levels.

Constraints (5.4.1i)–(5.4.1j) define the uncertainty budget for the peak demand in the target year and set that budget to be below a given value per zone $z$. The uncertainty budget parameter $\Gamma_z^{\mathrm{D}}$ may vary within the interval $[0, |\Lambda_z^{\mathrm{D}}|]$. If $\Gamma_z^{\mathrm{D}} = 0$, there is no uncertainty on peak demand. If, on the other hand, $\Gamma_z^{\mathrm{D}} = |\Lambda_z^{\mathrm{D}}|$, there is maximum uncertainty on the peak demand in the target year. Intermediate values refer to intermediate uncertainty levels.

Constraints (5.4.1k)–(5.4.1r) belong to the third-level problem. Constraints (5.4.1k) enforce nodal power balance per node and scenario (short-term uncertainty). Constraints (5.4.1l) define line flows per line and scenario. Constraints (5.4.1m) bound flows per line and scenario. Constraints (5.4.1n) bound the production level of each stochastic unit in each scenario. Constraints (5.4.1o) bound the production level of each conventional unit in each scenario. Constraints (5.4.1p) bound the unserved demand per demand and scenario. Constraints (5.4.1q) bound voltage angles per node and scenario. Constraints (5.4.1r) set the reference node for each scenario.

Set (5.4.2a) includes the optimization variables of the first-level problem, while sets (5.4.2b) and (5.4.2d) include the optimization variables of the second- and third-level problems, respectively.

Problem (5.4.1) above includes the set of nonlinear constraints (5.4.1l):

$$f_\ell^\omega = x_\ell b_\ell (\delta_{s(\ell)}^\omega - \delta_{r(\ell)}^\omega), \forall \ell \in \Omega^{\mathrm{L}}, \forall \omega \in \Omega^{\mathrm{W}}$$

that highly complicates its solution.

However, this set of constraints together with the set (5.4.1m) below:

$$-f_\ell^{\max} \leq f_\ell^\omega \leq f_\ell^{\max}, \forall \ell \in \Omega^{\mathrm{L}}, \forall \omega \in \Omega^{\mathrm{W}}$$

are easily linearized as follows:

$$-(1-x_\ell)M \leq \frac{f_\ell^\omega}{b_\ell} - (\delta_{s(\ell)}^\omega - \delta_{r(\ell)}^\omega) \leq (1-x_\ell)M, \forall \ell \in \Omega^{\mathrm{L}}, \forall \omega \in \Omega^{\mathrm{W}} \tag{5.4.3a}$$

$$-x_\ell f_\ell^{\max} \leq f_\ell^\omega \leq x_\ell f_\ell^{\max}, \forall \ell \in \Omega^{\mathrm{L}}, \forall \omega \in \Omega^{\mathrm{W}}, \tag{5.4.3b}$$

where $M$ is a large enough positive constant [5].

## 5.5 TEP: Case Study

### *5.5.1 Introduction*

Consider the three-area power system depicted in Fig. 5.2. It contains a renewable production area (node 1) with minimum and expected future installed capacity of 140 and 200 MW, respectively, and a production cost equal to \$2/MWh; and a conventional production area (node 2) with minimum and expected future installed capacity of 80 and 100 MW, respectively, and a production cost equal to \$20/MWh.

Both production areas may serve a consumption area (node 3) whose expected and maximum demands are 64 and 80 MW, respectively. The unserved energy cost of this area is \$200/MWh.

Two prospective transmission lines may connect each generating area and the demand area, as illustrated in Fig. 5.2. Each of these lines has a susceptance of 100 S, and a capacity of 50 MW. The annualized investment cost of the prospective line connecting the renewable production and the demand areas (line 1) is \$2 million, while that of the line connecting the conventional production and the demand areas (line 2) is \$3 million. There is no investment budget limit.

Two operating scenarios with equal probability of occurrence ($\frac{1}{2}$) are considered to represent the future operation conditions in the target year. The first one involves 75% availability of renewable production, 100% availability of conventional pro-

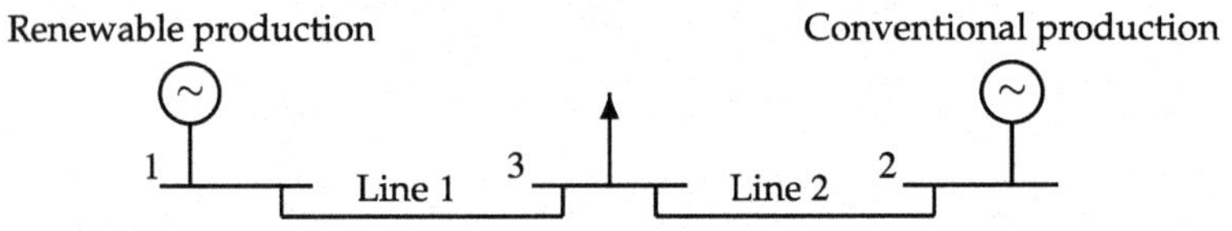


**Fig. 5.2** ARSO case study: Transmission expansion planning

duction and a 50% peak demand, while the second one involves the availability of 25% of renewable prosecution, 100% of conventional production and a 75% peak demand.

We formulate and solve below an ARSO model to determine the best transmission expansion plan.

### 5.5.2 *Formulation*

The formulation of the ARSO mode is provided below. Note that $\Gamma^{\text{S}}$, $\Gamma^{\text{C}}$ and $\Gamma^{\text{D}}$ are uncertainty budged parameters that are changed to achieve different solutions. A single zone is considered and thus these parameters are not indexed by the zone index $z$.

$$\min_{\{x_1,x_2\}} \quad \max_{\{\bar{P}^{\text{S}},\bar{P}^{\text{C}},\bar{D}\}} \quad \min_{\{P^{\text{S1}},P^{\text{C1}},P^{\text{U1}},f_1^1,f_2^1,\delta_1^1,\delta_2^1;P^{\text{S2}},P^{\text{C2}},P^{\text{U2}},f_1^2,f_2^2,\delta_1^2,\delta_2^2\}}$$

$$2\times 10^6 x_1 + 3\times 10^6 x_2 +$$

$$\frac{1}{2}8760\left(2P^{\text{S1}}+20P^{\text{C1}}+200P^{\text{U1}}\right)+\frac{1}{2}8760\left(2P^{\text{S2}}+20P^{\text{C2}}+200P^{\text{U2}}\right)$$

$$\text{s.t.}$$

$$x_1, x_2 \in \{0, 1\}$$

$$\text{s.t.}$$

$$140 \le \bar{P}^{\text{S}} \le 200, \qquad 200-\bar{P}^{\text{S}} \le 60\,\Gamma^{\text{S}}$$

$$80 \le \bar{P}^{\text{C}} \le 100, \qquad 100-\bar{P}^{\text{C}} \le 20\,\Gamma^{\text{C}}$$

$$64 \le \bar{D} \le 80, \qquad \bar{D}-64 \le 16\,\Gamma^{\text{D}}$$

$$\text{s.t.}$$

$$P^{\text{S1}} = f_1^1, \quad P^{\text{C1}} = f_2^1, \quad 0.5\bar{D} - P^{\text{U1}} = f_1^1 + f_2^1$$

$$f_1^1 = x_1 100\,\delta_1^1, \quad f_2^1 = x_2 100\,\delta_2^1$$

$$-50 \le f_1^1 \le 50, \quad -50 \le f_2^1 \le 50$$

$$0 \le P^{\text{S1}} \le 0.75\bar{P}^{\text{S}}, \quad 0 \le P^{\text{C1}} \le 1.0\bar{P}^{\text{C}}, \quad 0 \le P^{\text{U1}} \le 0.5\bar{D}$$

$$P^{\text{S2}} = f_1^2, \quad P^{\text{C2}} = f_2^2, \quad 0.75\bar{D} - P^{\text{U2}} = f_1^2 + f_2^2$$

$$f_1^2 = x_1 100\,\delta_1^2, \quad f_2^2 = x_2 100\,\delta_2^2$$

$$-50 \le f_1^2 \le 50, \quad -50 \le f_2^2 \le 50$$

$$0 \le P^{\text{S2}} \le 0.25\bar{P}^{\text{S}}, \quad 0 \le P^{\text{C2}} \le 1.0\bar{P}^{\text{C}}, \quad 0 \le P^{\text{U2}} \le 0.75\bar{D},$$

where $x_1$ and $x_2$ are the binary variables to represent the building of lines 1 and 2, respectively; $\bar{P}^{\mathrm{S}}$, $\bar{P}^{\mathrm{C}}$, $\bar{D}$ are the variables describing the long-term uncertainty pertaining to future stochastic capacity, future conventional capacity and future peak demand, respectively; $P^{\mathrm{S1}}$, $P^{\mathrm{C1}}$, $P^{\mathrm{U1}}$, $f_1^1, f_2^1, \delta_1^1, \delta_2^1$ are the operating variables pertaining to the first scenario, and $P^{\mathrm{S2}}$, $P^{\mathrm{C2}}$, $P^{\mathrm{U2}}$, $f_1^2, f_2^2, \delta_1^2, \delta_2^2$, the operating variables pertaining to the second scenario.

## 5.5.3 *Formulation Restructuring*

Solving the problem above cannot be done directly. It generally requires merging the second- and third-level problems and then decomposing the resulting bi-level problem using a Benders' type decomposition procedure [2, 3, 4]. This is detailed below. Note that this solution procedure follows the primal Benders generic algorithm described in Chap. 3.

### 5.5.3.1 Linearized Third-Level Problem

A linearized version of the third-level problem is provided below. Since the dual problem needs to be derived, the dual variable of each constraint is indicated following a colon in the corresponding constraint.

$$\min_{P^{\mathrm{S1}},P^{\mathrm{C1}},P^{\mathrm{U1}},f_1^1,f_2^1,\delta_1^1,\delta_2^1;P^{\mathrm{S2}},P^{\mathrm{C2}},P^{\mathrm{U2}},f_1^2,f_2^2,\delta_1^2,\delta_2^2}$$

$$2\times 10^6 x_1 + 3\times 10^6 x_2 +$$

$$\frac{1}{2}8760\left(2P^{\mathrm{S1}} + 20P^{\mathrm{C1}} + 200P^{\mathrm{U1}}\right) + \frac{1}{2}8760\left(2P^{\mathrm{S2}} + 20P^{\mathrm{C2}} + 200P^{\mathrm{U2}}\right)$$

s.t.

First scenario constraints:

$$P^{\mathrm{S1}} = f_1^1 : \alpha_1^1$$

$$P^{\mathrm{C1}} = f_2^1 : \alpha_2^1$$

$$0.5\bar{D} - P^{\mathrm{U1}} = f_1^1 + f_2^1 : \alpha_3^1$$

$$-(1-x_1)10^6 - (f_1^1/100 - \delta_1^1) \le 0 : \beta_{11}^{\min 1}$$

$$f_1^1/100 - \delta_1^1 \le (1-x_1)10^6 : \beta_{11}^{\max 1}$$

$$-x_1 50 - f_1^1 \le 0 : \beta_{12}^{\min 1}$$

$$f_1^1 \leq x_1 50 : \beta_{12}^{\max 1}$$

$$-(1 - x_2)10^6 - (f_2^1/100 - \delta_2^1) \leq 0 : \beta_{21}^{\min 1}$$

$$f_2^1/100 - \delta_2^1 \leq (1 - x_2)10^6 : \beta_{21}^{\max 1}$$

$$-x_2 50 - f_2^1 \leq 0 : \beta_{22}^{\min 1}$$

$$f_2^1 \leq x_2 50 : \beta_{22}^{\max 1}$$

$$-P^{S1} \leq 0 : \gamma_1^{\min 1}$$

$$P^{S1} \leq 0.75\bar{P}^{S} : \gamma_1^{\max 1}$$

$$-P^{C1} \leq 0 : \gamma_2^{\min 1}$$

$$P^{C1} \leq 1.0\bar{P}^{C} : \gamma_2^{\max 1}$$

$$-P^{U1} \leq 0 : \gamma_3^{\min 1}$$

$$P^{U1} \leq 0.5\bar{D} : \gamma_3^{\max 1}$$

Second scenario constraints:

$$P^{S2} = f_1^2 : \alpha_1^2$$

$$P^{C2} = f_2^2 : \alpha_2^2$$

$$0.75\bar{D} - P^{U2} = f_1^2 + f_2^2 : \alpha_3^2$$

$$-(1 - x_1)10^6 - (f_1^2/100 - \delta_1^2) \leq 0 : \beta_{11}^{\min 2}$$

$$f_1^2/100 - \delta_1^2 \leq (1 - x_1)10^6 : \beta_{11}^{\max 2}$$

$$-x_1 50 - f_1^2 \leq 0 : \beta_{12}^{\min 2}$$

$$f_1^2 \leq x_1 50 : \beta_{12}^{\max 2}$$

$$-(1 - x_2)10^6 - (f_2^2/100 - \delta_2^2) \leq 0 : \beta_{21}^{\min 2}$$

$$f_2^2/100 - \delta_2^2 \leq (1 - x_2)10^6 : \beta_{21}^{\max 2}$$

$$-x_2 50 - f_2^2 \leq 0 : \beta_{22}^{\min 2},$$

$$f_2^2 \leq x_2 50 : \beta_{22}^{\max 2},$$

$$-P^{S2} \leq 0 : \gamma_1^{\min 2}$$

$$P^{S2} \leq 0.25\bar{P}^{S} : \gamma_1^{\max 2}$$

$$-P^{C2} \leq 0 : \gamma_2^{\min 2}$$

$$P^{C2} \leq 1.0\bar{P}^{C} : \gamma_2^{\max 2}$$

$$- P^{U2} \leq 0 : \gamma_3^{\min 2}$$

$$P^{U2} \leq 0.75\bar{D} : \gamma_3^{\max 2}.$$

#### 5.5.3.2 Dual of the Third-Level Problem

We note that the third-level problem is linear in its optimization variables. The dual problem of this third-level problem is formulated below. Note that this is a maximization (not minimization) problem. For the sake of clarity, the corresponding primal variable is shown following a colon in each dual constraint.

$$\begin{aligned}
&\max_{\Xi} \\
&-\Big[(1-x_1)10^6\beta_{11}^{\max 1} + (1-x_1)10^6\beta_{11}^{\min 1} + x_1 50\beta_{12}^{\max 1} + x_1 50\beta_{12}^{\min 1} \\
&+(1-x_2)10^6\beta_{21}^{\max 1} + (1-x_2)10^6\beta_{21}^{\min 1} + x_2 50\beta_{22}^{\max 1} + x_2 50\beta_{22}^{\min 1} \\
&+0.75\bar{P}^{S}\gamma_1^{\max 1} + 1.0\bar{P}^{C}\gamma_2^{\max 1} + 0.5\bar{D}\gamma_3^{\max 1} - 0.5\bar{D}\alpha_3^1 \\
&+(1-x_1)10^6\beta_{11}^{\max 2} + (1-x_1)10^6\beta_{11}^{\min 2} + x_1 50\beta_{12}^{\max 2} + x_1 50\beta_{12}^{\min 2} \\
&+(1-x_2)10^6\beta_{21}^{\max 2} + (1-x_2)10^6\beta_{21}^{\min 2} + x_2 50\beta_{22}^{\max 2} + x_2 50\beta_{22}^{\min 2} \\
&+0.25\bar{P}^{S}\gamma_1^{\max 2} + 1.0\bar{P}^{C}\gamma_2^{\max 2} + 0.75\bar{D}\gamma_3^{\max 2} - 0.75\bar{D}\alpha_3^2\Big]
\end{aligned}$$

s.t.

First scenario dual constraints:

$$\frac{1}{2}8760 \times 2 + \alpha_1^1 + \gamma_1^{\max 1} - \gamma_1^{\min 1} = 0 : P^{S1}$$

$$\frac{1}{2}8760 \times 20 + \alpha_2^1 + \gamma_2^{\max 1} - \gamma_2^{\min 1} = 0 : P^{C1}$$

$$\frac{1}{2}8760 \times 200 - \alpha_3^1 + \gamma_3^{\max 1} - \gamma_3^{\min 1} = 0 : P^{U1}$$

$$- \alpha_1^1 - \alpha_3^1 - \beta_{11}^{\min 1}/100 + \beta_{11}^{\max 1}/100 - \beta_{12}^{\min 1} + \beta_{12}^{\max 1} = 0 : f_1^1$$

$$- \alpha_2^1 - \alpha_3^1 - \beta_{21}^{\min 1}/100 + \beta_{21}^{\max 1}/100 - \beta_{22}^{\min 1} + \beta_{22}^{\max 1} = 0 : f_2^1$$

$$\beta_{11}^{\min 1} - \beta_{11}^{\max 1} = 0 : \delta_1^1$$

$$\beta_{21}^{\min 1} - \beta_{21}^{\max 1} = 0 : \delta_2^1$$

Second scenario dual constraints:

$$\frac{1}{2}8760 \times 2 + \alpha_1^2 + \gamma_1^{\max 2} - \gamma_1^{\min 2} = 0 : P^{S2}$$

$$\frac{1}{2}8760 \times 20 + \alpha_2^2 + \gamma_2^{\max 2} - \gamma_2^{\min 2} = 0 : P^{C2}$$

$$\frac{1}{2}8760 \times 200 - \alpha_3^2 + \gamma_3^{\max 2} - \gamma_3^{\min 2} = 0 : P^{U2}$$

$$-\alpha_1^2 - \alpha_3^2 - \beta_{11}^{\min 2}/100 + \beta_{11}^{\max 2}/100 - \beta_{12}^{\min 2} + \beta_{12}^{\max 2} = 0 : f_1^2$$

$$-\alpha_2^2 - \alpha_3^2 - \beta_{21}^{\min 2}/100 + \beta_{21}^{\max 2}/100 - \beta_{22}^{\min 2} + \beta_{22}^{\max 2} = 0 : f_2^2$$

$$\beta_{11}^{\min 2} - \beta_{11}^{\max 2} = 0 : \delta_1^2$$

$$\beta_{21}^{\min 2} - \beta_{21}^{\max 2} = 0 : \delta_2^2,$$

where the optimization variable set is:

$$\Xi = \{\alpha_1^1, \alpha_2^1, \alpha_3^1, \beta_{11}^{\min 1}, \beta_{11}^{\max 1}, \beta_{12}^{\min 1}, \beta_{12}^{\max 1}, \beta_{21}^{\min 1}, \beta_{21}^{\max 1}, \beta_{22}^{\min 1}, \beta_{22}^{\max 1}, \gamma_1^{\min 1}, \gamma_1^{\max 1}, \gamma_2^{\min 1}, \gamma_2^{\max 1}, \gamma_3^{\min 1}, \gamma_3^{\max 1}\} \bigcup \{\alpha_1^2, \alpha_2^2, \alpha_3^2, \beta_{11}^{\min 2}, \beta_{11}^{\max 2}, \beta_{12}^{\min 2}, \beta_{12}^{\max 2}, \beta_{21}^{\min 2}, \beta_{21}^{\max 2}, \beta_{22}^{\min 2}, \beta_{22}^{\max 2}, \gamma_1^{\min 2}, \gamma_1^{\max 2}, \gamma_2^{\min 2}, \gamma_2^{\max 2}, \gamma_3^{\min 2}, \gamma_3^{\max 2}\}.$$

Additionally, it should be noted that:

1. Dual variables $\alpha_1^1$, $\alpha_2^1$, $\alpha_3^1$, $\alpha_1^2$, $\alpha_2^2$ and $\alpha_3^2$ are not restricted in sign.
2. Dual variables $\beta_{11}^{\min 1}$, $\beta_{12}^{\min 1}$, $\beta_{21}^{\min 1}$, $\beta_{22}^{\min 1}$, $\gamma_1^{\min 1}$, $\gamma_2^{\min 1}$, $\gamma_3^{\min 1}$, $\beta_{11}^{\min 2}$, $\beta_{12}^{\min 2}$, $\beta_{21}^{\min 2}$, $\beta_{22}^{\min 2}$, $\gamma_1^{\min 2}$, $\gamma_2^{\min 2}$, $\gamma_3^{\min 2}$, $\beta_{11}^{\max 1}$, $\beta_{12}^{\max 1}$, $\beta_{21}^{\max 1}$, $\beta_{22}^{\max 1}$, $\gamma_1^{\max 1}$, $\gamma_2^{\max 1}$, $\gamma_3^{\max 1}$, $\beta_{11}^{\max 2}$, $\beta_{12}^{\max 2}$, $\beta_{21}^{\max 2}$, $\beta_{22}^{\max 2}$, $\gamma_1^{\max 2}$, $\gamma_2^{\max 2}$ and $\gamma_3^{\max 2}$ are non-negative.

#### 5.5.3.3 Subproblem: Merged Second- and Third-Level Problem

Since both the second-level problem and the dual of the third-level problem are maximization problems, they can be merged into a single optimization problem. The subproblem resulting from merging the second- and third-level problems is provided below.

$$\max_{\Theta}$$

$$-\Big[(1-x_1)10^6\beta_{11}^{\max 1}+(1-x_1)10^6\beta_{11}^{\min 1}+x_1 50\beta_{12}^{\max 1}+x_1 50\beta_{12}^{\min 1}$$
$$+(1-x_2)10^6\beta_{21}^{\max 1}+(1-x_2)10^6\beta_{21}^{\min 1}+x_2 50\beta_{22}^{\max 1}+x_2 50\beta_{22}^{\min 1}$$
$$+0.75\bar{P}^{\mathrm{S}}\gamma_1^{\max 1}+1.0\bar{P}^{\mathrm{C}}\gamma_2^{\max 1}+0.5\bar{D}\gamma_3^{\max 1}-0.5\bar{D}\alpha_3^1$$
$$+(1-x_1)10^6\beta_{11}^{\max 2}+(1-x_1)10^6\beta_{11}^{\min 2}+x_1 50\beta_{12}^{\max 2}+x_1 50\beta_{12}^{\min 2}$$
$$+(1-x_2)10^6\beta_{21}^{\max 2}+(1-x_2)10^6\beta_{21}^{\min 2}+x_2 50\beta_{22}^{\max 2}+x_2 50\beta_{22}^{\min 2}$$
$$+0.25\bar{P}^{\mathrm{S}}\gamma_1^{\max 2}+1.0\bar{P}^{\mathrm{C}}\gamma_2^{\max 2}+0.75\bar{D}\gamma_3^{\max 2}-0.75\bar{D}\alpha_3^2\Big]$$

s.t.

Long-term uncertainty constraints (second-level problem):

$$140 \le \bar{P}^{\mathrm{S}} \le 200, \qquad 200-\bar{P}^{\mathrm{S}} \le 60\,\Gamma^{\mathrm{S}}$$
$$80 \le \bar{P}^{\mathrm{C}} \le 100, \qquad 100-\bar{P}^{\mathrm{C}} \le 20\,\Gamma^{\mathrm{C}}$$
$$64 \le \bar{D} \le 80, \qquad \bar{D}-64 \le 16\,\Gamma^{\mathrm{D}}$$

Fist scenario dual constraints:

$$\frac{1}{2}8760\times 2+\alpha_1^1+\gamma_1^{\max 1}-\gamma_1^{\min 1}=0$$
$$\frac{1}{2}8760\times 20+\alpha_2^1+\gamma_2^{\max 1}-\gamma_2^{\min 1}=0$$
$$\frac{1}{2}8760\times 200-\alpha_3^1+\gamma_3^{\max 1}-\gamma_3^{\min 1}=0$$
$$-\alpha_1^1-\alpha_3^1-\beta_{11}^{\min 1}/100+\beta_{11}^{\max 1}/100-\beta_{12}^{\min 1}+\beta_{12}^{\max 1}=0$$
$$-\alpha_2^1-\alpha_3^1-\beta_{21}^{\min 1}/100+\beta_{21}^{\max 1}/100-\beta_{22}^{\min 1}+\beta_{22}^{\max 1}=0$$
$$\beta_{11}^{\min 1}-\beta_{11}^{\max 1}=0$$
$$\beta_{21}^{\min 1}-\beta_{21}^{\max 1}=0$$

Second scenario dual constraints:

$$\frac{1}{2}8760\times 2+\alpha_1^2+\gamma_1^{\max 2}-\gamma_1^{\min 2}=0$$
$$\frac{1}{2}8760\times 20+\alpha_2^2+\gamma_2^{\max 2}-\gamma_2^{\min 2}=0$$

$$\frac{1}{2}8760 \times 200 - \alpha_3^2 + \gamma_3^{\max 2} - \gamma_3^{\min 2} = 0$$
$$- \alpha_1^2 - \alpha_3^2 - \beta_{11}^{\min 2}/100 + \beta_{11}^{\max 2}/100 - \beta_{12}^{\min 2} + \beta_{12}^{\max 2} = 0$$
$$- \alpha_2^2 - \alpha_3^2 - \beta_{21}^{\min 2}/100 + \beta_{21}^{\max 2}/100 - \beta_{22}^{\min 2} + \beta_{22}^{\max 2} = 0$$
$$\beta_{11}^{\min 2} - \beta_{11}^{\max 2} = 0$$
$$\beta_{21}^{\min 2} - \beta_{21}^{\max 2} = 0,$$

where the optimization variable set is:

$$\Theta = \{\bar{P}^{\mathrm{S}}, \bar{P}^{\mathrm{C}}, \bar{D}\} \bigcup \{\alpha_1^1, \alpha_2^1, \alpha_3^1, \beta_{11}^{\min 1}, \beta_{11}^{\max 1}, \beta_{12}^{\min 1}, \beta_{12}^{\max 1}, \beta_{21}^{\min 1}, \beta_{21}^{\max 1},$$
$$\beta_{22}^{\min 1}, \beta_{22}^{\max 1}, \gamma_1^{\min 1}, \gamma_1^{\max 1}, \gamma_2^{\min 1}, \gamma_2^{\max 1}, \gamma_3^{\min 1}, \gamma_3^{\max 1}\} \bigcup \{\alpha_1^2, \alpha_2^2, \alpha_3^2,$$
$$\beta_{11}^{\min 2}, \beta_{11}^{\max 2}, \beta_{12}^{\min 2}, \beta_{12}^{\max 2}, \beta_{21}^{\min 2}, \beta_{21}^{\max 2}, \beta_{22}^{\min 2}, \beta_{22}^{\max 2}, \gamma_1^{\min 2}, \gamma_1^{\max 2},$$
$$\gamma_2^{\min 2}, \gamma_2^{\max 2}, \gamma_3^{\min 2}, \gamma_3^{\max 2}\}.$$

Additionally, it should be noted that:

1. Dual variables $\alpha_1^1, \alpha_2^1, \alpha_3^1, \alpha_1^2, \alpha_2^2$ and $\alpha_3^2$ are not restricted in sign.
2. Dual variables $\beta_{11}^{\min 1}, \beta_{12}^{\min 1}, \beta_{21}^{\min 1}, \beta_{22}^{\min 1}, \gamma_1^{\min 1}, \gamma_2^{\min 1}, \gamma_3^{\min 1}, \beta_{11}^{\min 2}, \beta_{12}^{\min 2}, \beta_{21}^{\min 2}, \beta_{22}^{\min 2}, \gamma_1^{\min 2}, \gamma_2^{\min 2}, \gamma_3^{\min 2}, \beta_{11}^{\max 1}, \beta_{12}^{\max 1}, \beta_{21}^{\max 1}, \beta_{22}^{\max 1}, \gamma_1^{\max 1}, \gamma_2^{\max 1}, \gamma_3^{\max 1}, \beta_{11}^{\max 2}, \beta_{12}^{\max 2}, \beta_{21}^{\max 2}, \beta_{22}^{\max 2}, \gamma_1^{\max 2}, \gamma_2^{\max 2}$ and $\gamma_3^{\max 2}$ are non-negative.

Since the subproblem considers particular (fixed) values of the first-problem variables (investment decisions) and the overall objective is minimization, the optimal value of its objective function plus the corresponding investment cost constitutes an upper bound of the optimal value of the objective function of the original problem.

### 5.5.4 *Solution via Decomposition*

A Benders' type solution algorithm interchanging primal information is described below. Further details on this algorithm are provided in Chap. 3 and in [3] and [4].

The Benders' algorithm below, as applied to the simple example illustrated in Fig. 5.2, may seem inefficient. However, this is not generally the case if applied to large, realistic case studies.

#### 5.5.4.1 Master Problem

The original problem is solved considering the merged second- and third-level problem (stated in the previous section), which is henceforth referred to as the subproblem, and the master problem below.

This master problem is formulated for a generic iteration $\nu$, after having performed $k = 1, \ldots, \nu - 1$ iterations.

Input data for this master problem are the output variables of the subproblem indicated below for all the iterations already performed, i.e.:

$$\bar{P}^{S[k]}, \bar{P}^{C[k]}, \bar{D}^{[k]}, k = 0, 1, \ldots, \nu - 1.$$

The optimization variables of this master problem relevant to solve the following subproblem are:

$$x_1, x_2.$$

Note that the iteration number is denoted by the superscript $[k]$.

Considering the initial problem, the master problem is:

$$\min_{\substack{\{x_1, x_2, \eta\},\\ \{P^{S1[k]}, P^{C1[k]}, P^{U1[k]}, f_1^{1[k]}, f_2^{1[k]}, \delta_1^{1[k]}, \delta_2^{1[k]}; P^{S2[k]}, P^{C2[k]}, P^{U2[k]}, f_1^{2[k]}, f_2^{2[k]}, \delta_1^{2[k]}, \delta_2^{2[k]}, k = 1, \ldots, \nu\}}}$$

$$2 \times 10^6 x_1 + 3 \times 10^6 x_2 + \eta$$

s.t.

$$\eta \geq \frac{1}{2} 8760 \left(2P^{S1[k]} + 20P^{C1[k]} + 200P^{U1[k]}\right) +$$
$$\frac{1}{2} 8760 \left(2P^{S2[k]} + 20P^{C2[k]} + 200P^{U2[k]}\right), k = 1, \ldots, \nu$$

$$P^{S1[k]} = f_1^{1[k]}, P^{C1[k]} = f_2^{1[k]}, 0.5\bar{D}^{1[k-1]} - P^{U1[k]} = f_1^{1[k]} + f_2^{1[k]},$$
$$k = 1, \ldots, \nu$$

$$-(1 - x_1)10^6 - (f_1^{1[k]}/100 - \delta_1^{1[k]}) \leq 0, k = 1, \ldots, \nu$$

$$f_1^{1[k]}/100 - \delta_1^{1[k]} \leq (1 - x_1)10^6, k = 1, \ldots, \nu$$

$$-x_1 50 - f_1^{1[k]} \leq 0, k = 1, \ldots, \nu$$

$$f_1^{1[k]} \leq x_1 50, k = 1, \ldots, \nu$$

$$-(1 - x_2)10^6 - (f_2^{1[k]}/100 - \delta_2^{1[k]}) \leq 0, k = 1, \ldots, \nu$$

$$f_2^{1[k]}/100 - \delta_2^{1[k]} \leq (1 - x_2)10^6, k = 1, \ldots, \nu$$

$$- x_2 50 - f_2^{1[k]} \leq 0, k = 1, \ldots, \nu$$

$$f_2^{1[k]} \leq x_2 50, k = 1, \ldots, \nu$$

$$0 \leq P^{\mathrm{S1}[k]} \leq 0.75 \bar{P}^{\mathrm{S}[k-1]}, 0 \leq P^{\mathrm{C1}[k]} \leq 1.0 \bar{P}^{\mathrm{C}[k-1]}, 0 \leq P^{\mathrm{U1}[k]} \leq 0.5 \bar{D}^{[k-1]},$$
$$k = 1, \ldots, \nu$$

$$P^{\mathrm{S2}[k]} = f_1^{2[k]}, P^{\mathrm{C2}[k]} = f_2^{2[k]}, 0.75 \bar{D}^{[k-1]} - P^{\mathrm{U2}[k]} = f_1^{2[k]} + f_2^{2[k]},$$
$$k = 1, \ldots, \nu$$

$$- (1 - x_1) 10^6 - (f_1^{2[k]}/100 - \delta_1^{2[k]}) \leq 0, k = 1, \ldots, \nu$$

$$f_1^{2[k]}/100 - \delta_1^{2[k]} \leq (1 - x_1) 10^6, k = 1, \ldots, \nu$$

$$- x_1 50 - f_1^{2[k]} \leq 0, k = 1, \ldots, \nu$$

$$f_1^{2[k]} \leq x_1 50, k = 1, \ldots, \nu$$

$$- (1 - x_2) 10^6 - (f_2^{2[k]}/100 - \delta_2^{2[k]}) \leq 0, k = 1, \ldots, \nu$$

$$f_2^{2[k]}/100 - \delta_2^{2[k]} \leq (1 - x_2) 10^6, k = 1, \ldots, \nu$$

$$- x_2 50 - f_2^{2[k]} \leq 0, k = 1, \ldots, \nu$$

$$f_2^{2[k]} \leq x_2 50, k = 1, \ldots, \nu$$

$$0 \leq P^{\mathrm{S2}[k]} \leq 0.25 \bar{P}^{\mathrm{S}[k-1]}, 0 \leq P^{\mathrm{C2}[k]} \leq 1.0 \bar{P}^{\mathrm{C}[k-1]}, 0 \leq P^{\mathrm{U2}[k]} \leq 0.75 \bar{D}^{[k-1]},$$
$$k = 1, \ldots, \nu.$$

Since this master problem is a relaxation of the original problem, its objective function optimal value constitutes a lower bound of the optimal value of the objective function of the original problem.

#### 5.5.4.2 Algorithm

For given values of the uncertainty budget parameters $\Gamma^{\mathrm{S}}$, $\Gamma^{\mathrm{C}}$ and $\Gamma^{\mathrm{D}}$, the solution algorithm, illustrated in Fig. 5.3 proceeds as follows:

1. Set the iteration counter to $k = 1$ and guess initial values for the long-term uncertainty variables $\bar{P}^{\mathrm{S}}$, $\bar{P}^{\mathrm{C}}$ and $\bar{D}$, i.e., $\bar{P}^{\mathrm{S}[0]}$, $\bar{P}^{\mathrm{C}[0]}$ and $\bar{D}^{[0]}$.
2. Considering $\bar{P}^{\mathrm{S}[k-1]}$, $\bar{P}^{\mathrm{C}[k-1]}$ and $\bar{D}^{[k-1]}$, solve the master problem to obtain $x_1^{[k]}$ and $x_2^{[k]}$.
3. Considering $x_1^{[k]}$ and $x_2^{[k]}$, solve the subproblem to obtain $\bar{P}^{\mathrm{S}[k]}$, $\bar{P}^{\mathrm{C}[k]}$ and $\bar{D}^{[k]}$.
4. If the objective function values of (1) the previous master problem (lower bound) and (2) that of the subproblem plus the corresponding investment cost (upper bound) are close enough, stop; otherwise, set $k \leftarrow k + 1$ and continues in step 2.

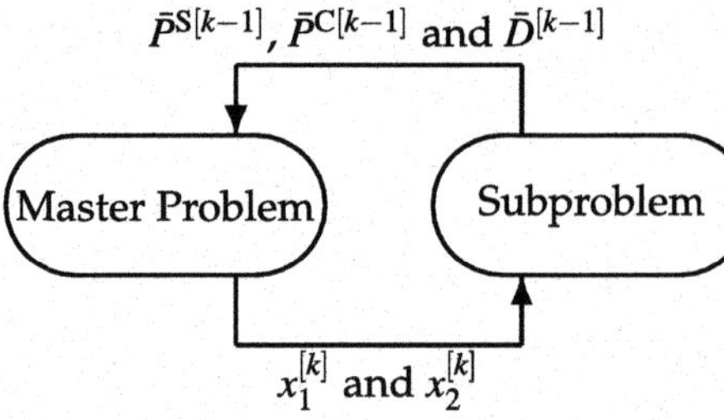


**Fig. 5.3** Simple ARSO model: Benders' algorithm

### 5.5.5 *Actual Solution*

We set $\Gamma^{\mathrm{S}} = 1$, $\Gamma^{\mathrm{C}} = 1$ and $\Gamma^{\mathrm{D}} = 1$ (maximum uncertainty budgets), and proceed with the decomposition procedure.

#### 5.5.5.1 First Master Problem

We guess initial values for the long-term uncertainty variables. These values are: $\bar{P}^{\mathrm{S}[0]} = 6$ MW, $\bar{P}^{\mathrm{C}[0]} = 2$ MW, and $\bar{D}^{[0]} = 2$ MW. Then, the first master problem is:

$$\min_{\substack{\{x_1 \in \{0,1\}, x_2 \in \{0,1\}, \eta \geq 0\},\\ \{P^{\mathrm{S1}[1]}, P^{\mathrm{C1}[1]}, P^{\mathrm{U1}[1]}, f_1^{1[1]}, f_2^{1[1]}, \delta_1^{1[1]}, \delta_2^{1[1]}; P^{\mathrm{S2}[1]}, P^{\mathrm{C2}[1]}, P^{\mathrm{U2}[1]}, f_1^{2[1]}, f_2^{2[1]}, \delta_1^{2[1]}, \delta_2^{2[1]}\}}}$$

$$2 \times 10^6 x_1 + 3 \times 10^6 x_2 + \eta$$

s.t.

$$\eta \geq \frac{1}{2} 8760 \left(2P^{\mathrm{S1}[1]} + 20P^{\mathrm{C1}[1]} + 200P^{\mathrm{U1}[1]}\right) +$$
$$\frac{1}{2} 8760 \left(2P^{\mathrm{S2}[1]} + 20P^{\mathrm{C2}[1]} + 200P^{\mathrm{U2}[1]}\right)$$

$$P^{\mathrm{S1}[1]} = f_1^{1[1]}, P^{\mathrm{C1}[1]} = f_2^{1[1]}, 0.5 \cdot 2 - P^{\mathrm{U1}[1]} = f_1^{1[1]} + f_2^{1[1]}$$

$$-(1 - x_1)10^6 - (f_1^{1[1]}/100 - \delta_1^{1[1]}) \leq 0, k = 1, \ldots, \nu$$

$$f_1^{1[1]}/100 - \delta_1^{1[1]} \leq (1 - x_1)10^6, k = 1, \ldots, \nu$$

$$-x_1 50 - f_1^{1[1]} \leq 0, k = 1, \ldots, \nu$$

$$f_1^{1[1]} \leq x_1 50, k = 1, \ldots, \nu$$

$$-(1 - x_2)10^6 - (f_2^{1[1]}/100 - \delta_2^{1[1]}) \leq 0, k = 1, \ldots, \nu$$

$$f_2^{1[1]}/100 - \delta_2^{1[1]} \leq (1 - x_2)10^6, k = 1, \ldots, \nu$$
$$- x_2 50 - f_2^{1[1]} \leq 0, k = 1, \ldots, \nu$$
$$f_2^{1[1]} \leq x_2 50, k = 1, \ldots, \nu$$
$$0 \leq P^{S1[1]} \leq 0.75 \cdot 6, 0 \leq P^{C1[1]} \leq 1.0 \cdot 2, 0 \leq P^{U1[1]} \leq 0.5 \cdot 2$$
$$P^{S2[1]} = f_1^{2[1]}, P^{C2[1]} = f_2^{2[1]}, 0.75 \cdot 2 - P^{U2[1]} = f_1^{2[1]} + f_2^{2[1]}$$
$$- (1 - x_1)10^6 - (f_1^{2[1]}/100 - \delta_1^{2[1]}) \leq 0, k = 1, \ldots, \nu$$
$$f_1^{2[1]}/100 - \delta_1^{2[1]} \leq (1 - x_1)10^6, k = 1, \ldots, \nu$$
$$- x_1 50 - f_1^{2[1]} \leq 0, k = 1, \ldots, \nu$$
$$f_1^{2[1]} \leq x_1 50, k = 1, \ldots, \nu$$
$$- (1 - x_2)10^6 - (f_2^{2[1]}/100 - \delta_2^{2[1]}) \leq 0, k = 1, \ldots, \nu$$
$$f_2^{2[1]}/100 - \delta_2^{2[1]} \leq (1 - x_2)10^6, k = 1, \ldots, \nu$$
$$- x_2 50 - f_2^{2[1]} \leq 0, k = 1, \ldots, \nu$$
$$f_2^{2[1]} \leq x_2 50, k = 1, \ldots, \nu$$
$$0 \leq P^{S2[1]} \leq 0.25 \cdot 6, 0 \leq P^{C2[1]} \leq 1.0 \cdot 2, 0 \leq P^{U2[1]} \leq 0.75 \cdot 2.$$

The solution of this master problem is:

$$x_1^{[1]} = 1, x_2^{[1]} = 0,$$

with an objective function value of \$2.0219 million.

Since the problem above is a relaxation of the original problem, the initial lower bound is \$2.0219 million.

A GAMS [6] code to solve this master problem is provided in Sect. 5.7 below.

#### 5.5.5.2 First Subproblem

The first subproblem (merged second- and third level problem) is

$$
\begin{aligned}
&\max_{\Theta} \\
&-\Big[50\beta_{12}^{\max 1} + 50\beta_{12}^{\min 1} \\
&\quad +10^6\beta_{21}^{\max 1} + 10^6\beta_{21}^{\min 1} + \\
&\quad +0.75\bar{P}^{S}\gamma_1^{\max 1} + 1.0\bar{P}^{C}\gamma_2^{\max 1} + 0.5\bar{D}\gamma_3^{\max 1} - 0.5\bar{D}\alpha_3^1 \\
&\quad +50\beta_{12}^{\max 2} + 50\beta_{12}^{\min 2} \\
&\quad +10^6\beta_{21}^{\max 2} + 10^6\beta_{21}^{\min 2} + \\
&\quad +0.25\bar{P}^{S}\gamma_1^{\max 2} + 1.0\bar{P}^{C}\gamma_2^{\max 2} + 0.75\bar{D}\gamma_3^{\max 2} - 0.75\bar{D}\alpha_3^2\Big]
\end{aligned}
$$

s.t.

Long-term uncertainty constraints:

$$
\begin{aligned}
&140 \le \bar{P}^{S} \le 200, \qquad 200 - \bar{P}^{S} \le 60 \\
&80 \le \bar{P}^{C} \le 100, \qquad 100 - \bar{P}^{C} \le 20 \\
&64 \le \bar{D} \le 80, \qquad \bar{D} - 64 \le 16
\end{aligned}
$$

First scenario dual constraints:

$$
\begin{aligned}
&\frac{1}{2}8760 \times 2 + \alpha_1^1 + \gamma_1^{\max 1} - \gamma_1^{\min 1} = 0 \\
&\frac{1}{2}8760 \times 20 + \alpha_2^1 + \gamma_2^{\max 1} - \gamma_2^{\min 1} = 0 \\
&\frac{1}{2}8760 \times 200 - \alpha_3^1 + \gamma_3^{\max 1} - \gamma_3^{\min 1} = 0 \\
&-\alpha_1^1 - \alpha_3^1 - \beta_{11}^{\min 1}/100 + \beta_{11}^{\max 1}/100 - \beta_{12}^{\min 1} + \beta_{12}^{\max 1} = 0 \\
&-\alpha_2^1 - \alpha_3^1 - \beta_{21}^{\min 1}/100 + \beta_{21}^{\max 1}/100 - \beta_{22}^{\min 1} + \beta_{22}^{\max 1} = 0 \\
&\beta_{11}^{\min 1} - \beta_{11}^{\max 1} = 0 \\
&\beta_{21}^{\min 1} - \beta_{21}^{\max 1} = 0
\end{aligned}
$$

Second scenario dual constraints:

$$
\begin{aligned}
&\frac{1}{2}8760 \times 2 + \alpha_1^2 + \gamma_1^{\max 2} - \gamma_1^{\min 2} = 0 \\
&\frac{1}{2}8760 \times 20 + \alpha_2^2 + \gamma_2^{\max 2} - \gamma_2^{\min 2} = 0
\end{aligned}
$$

$$
\begin{aligned}
&\frac{1}{2}8760 \times 200 - \alpha_3^2 + \gamma_3^{\max 2} - \gamma_3^{\min 2} = 0\\
&-\alpha_1^2 - \alpha_3^2 - \beta_{11}^{\min 2}/100 + \beta_{11}^{\max 2}/100 - \beta_{12}^{\min 2} + \beta_{12}^{\max 2} = 0\\
&-\alpha_2^2 - \alpha_3^2 - \beta_{21}^{\min 2}/100 + \beta_{21}^{\max 2}/100 - \beta_{22}^{\min 2} + \beta_{22}^{\max 2} = 0\\
&\beta_{11}^{\min 2} - \beta_{11}^{\max 2} = 0\\
&\beta_{21}^{\min 2} - \beta_{21}^{\max 2} = 0.
\end{aligned}
$$

Additionally:

1. Dual variables $\alpha_1^1, \alpha_2^1, \alpha_3^1, \alpha_1^2, \alpha_2^2$ and $\alpha_3^2$ are not restricted in sign.
2. Dual variables $\beta_{11}^{\min 1}, \beta_{12}^{\min 1}, \beta_{21}^{\min 1}, \beta_{22}^{\min 1}, \gamma_1^{\min 1}, \gamma_2^{\min 1}, \gamma_3^{\min 1}, \beta_{11}^{\min 2}, \beta_{12}^{\min 2}, \beta_{21}^{\min 2}, \beta_{22}^{\min 2}, \gamma_1^{\min 2}, \gamma_2^{\min 2}, \gamma_3^{\min 2}, \beta_{11}^{\max 1}, \beta_{12}^{\max 1}, \beta_{21}^{\max 1}, \beta_{22}^{\max 1}, \gamma_1^{\max 1}, \gamma_2^{\max 1}, \gamma_3^{\max 1}, \beta_{11}^{\max 2}, \beta_{12}^{\max 2}, \beta_{21}^{\max 2}, \beta_{22}^{\max 2}, \gamma_1^{\max 2}, \gamma_2^{\max 2}$ and $\gamma_3^{\max 2}$ are non-negative.

The solution of this subproblem is (dual variables not indicated for simplicity):

$$
\bar{P}^{\mathrm{S}[k]} = 140,\ \bar{P}^{\mathrm{C}[k]} = 80,\ \bar{D}^{[k]} = 80,
$$

with and objective function value of \$22.557 million.

The corresponding upper bound is obtained by adding to this objective function value the corresponding investment cost, i.e., \$22.557 + \$2.0 = \$24.557 million.

A GAMS [6] code to solve this subproblem is provided in Sect. 5.7 below.

#### 5.5.5.3 Second Master Problem

The second master problem is

$$
\min_{\substack{\{x_1 \in \{0,1\},\, x_2 \in \{0,1\},\, \eta \geq 0\},\\ \{P^{\mathrm{S1}[1]},\, P^{\mathrm{C1}[1]},\, P^{\mathrm{U1}[1]},\, f_1^{1[1]},\, f_2^{1[1]},\, \delta_1^{1[1]},\, \delta_2^{1[1]};\, P^{\mathrm{S2}[1]},\, P^{\mathrm{C2}[1]},\, P^{\mathrm{U2}[1]},\, f_1^{2[1]},\, f_2^{2[1]},\, \delta_1^{2[1]},\, \delta_2^{2[1]}\}\\ \{P^{\mathrm{S1}[2]},\, P^{\mathrm{C1}[2]},\, P^{\mathrm{U1}[2]},\, f_1^{1[2]},\, f_2^{1[2]},\, \delta_1^{1[2]},\, \delta_2^{1[2]};\, P^{\mathrm{S2}[2]},\, P^{\mathrm{C2}[2]},\, P^{\mathrm{U2}[2]},\, f_1^{2[2]},\, f_2^{2[2]},\, \delta_1^{2[2]},\, \delta_2^{2[2]}\}}}
$$

$$
2 \times 10^6 x_1 + 3 \times 10^6 x_2 + \eta
$$

s.t.

Fist cut constraints:

$$
\begin{aligned}
\eta \geq\ &\frac{1}{2}8760\left(2P^{\mathrm{S1}[1]} + 20P^{\mathrm{C1}[1]} + 200P^{\mathrm{U1}[1]}\right) + \\
&\frac{1}{2}8760\left(2P^{\mathrm{S2}[1]} + 20P^{\mathrm{C2}[1]} + 200P^{\mathrm{U2}[1]}\right)
\end{aligned}
$$

$$
P^{\mathrm{S1}[1]} = f_1^{1[1]},\ P^{\mathrm{C1}[1]} = f_2^{1[1]}, 0.5 \cdot 2 - P^{\mathrm{U1}[1]} = f_1^{1[1]} + f_2^{1[1]}
$$

$$- (1 - x_1)10^6 - (f_1^{1[1]}/100 - \delta_1^{1[1]}) \leq 0, k = 1, \ldots, \nu$$
$$f_1^{1[1]}/100 - \delta_1^{1[1]} \leq (1 - x_1)10^6, k = 1, \ldots, \nu$$
$$- x_1 50 - f_1^{1[1]} \leq 0, k = 1, \ldots, \nu$$
$$f_1^{1[1]} \leq x_1 50, k = 1, \ldots, \nu$$
$$- (1 - x_2)10^6 - (f_2^{1[1]}/100 - \delta_2^{1[1]}) \leq 0, k = 1, \ldots, \nu$$
$$f_2^{1[1]}/100 - \delta_2^{1[1]} \leq (1 - x_2)10^6, k = 1, \ldots, \nu$$
$$- x_2 50 - f_2^{1[1]} \leq 0, k = 1, \ldots, \nu$$
$$f_2^{1[1]} \leq x_2 50, k = 1, \ldots, \nu$$
$$0 \leq P^{\mathrm{S1}[1]} \leq 0.75 \cdot 6, 0 \leq P^{\mathrm{C1}[1]} \leq 1.0 \cdot 2, 0 \leq P^{\mathrm{U1}[1]} \leq 0.5 \cdot 2$$
$$P^{\mathrm{S2}[1]} = f_1^{2[1]}, P^{\mathrm{C2}[1]} = f_2^{2[1]}, 0.75 \cdot 2 - P^{\mathrm{U2}[1]} = f_1^{2[1]} + f_2^{2[1]}$$
$$- (1 - x_1)10^6 - (f_1^{2[1]}/100 - \delta_1^{2[1]}) \leq 0, k = 1, \ldots, \nu$$
$$f_1^{2[1]}/100 - \delta_1^{2[1]} \leq (1 - x_1)10^6, k = 1, \ldots, \nu$$
$$- x_1 50 - f_1^{2[1]} \leq 0, k = 1, \ldots, \nu$$
$$f_1^{2[1]} \leq x_1 50, k = 1, \ldots, \nu$$
$$- (1 - x_2)10^6 - (f_2^{2[1]}/100 - \delta_2^{2[1]}) \leq 0, k = 1, \ldots, \nu$$
$$f_2^{2[1]}/100 - \delta_2^{2[1]} \leq (1 - x_2)10^6, k = 1, \ldots, \nu$$
$$- x_2 50 - f_2^{2[1]} \leq 0, k = 1, \ldots, \nu$$
$$f_2^{2[1]} \leq x_2 50, k = 1, \ldots, \nu$$
$$0 \leq P^{\mathrm{S2}[1]} \leq 0.25 \cdot 6, 0 \leq P^{\mathrm{C2}[1]} \leq 1.0 \cdot 2, 0 \leq P^{\mathrm{U2}[1]} \leq 0.75 \cdot 2.$$

Second cut constraints:

$$\eta \geq \frac{1}{2} 8760 \left(2 P^{\mathrm{S1}[2]} + 20 P^{\mathrm{C1}[2]} + 200 P^{\mathrm{U1}[2]}\right) + \frac{1}{2} 8760 \left(2 P^{\mathrm{S2}[2]} + 20 P^{\mathrm{C2}[2]} + 200 P^{\mathrm{U2}[2]}\right)$$
$$P^{\mathrm{S1}[2]} = f_1^{1[2]}, P^{\mathrm{C1}[2]} = f_2^{1[2]}, 0.5 \cdot 80 - P^{\mathrm{U1}[2]} = f_1^{1[2]} + f_2^{1[2]}$$
$$- (1 - x_1)10^6 - (f_1^{1[2]}/100 - \delta_1^{1[2]}) \leq 0, k = 1, \ldots, \nu$$
$$f_1^{1[2]}/100 - \delta_1^{1[2]} \leq (1 - x_1)10^6, k = 1, \ldots, \nu$$

$$- x_1 50 - f_1^{1[2]} \leq 0, k = 1, \ldots, \nu$$

$$f_1^{1[2]} \leq x_1 50, k = 1, \ldots, \nu$$

$$- (1 - x_2)10^6 - (f_2^{1[2]}/100 - \delta_2^{1[2]}) \leq 0, k = 1, \ldots, \nu$$

$$f_2^{1[2]}/100 - \delta_2^{1[2]} \leq (1 - x_2)10^6, k = 1, \ldots, \nu$$

$$- x_2 50 - f_2^{1[2]} \leq 0, k = 1, \ldots, \nu$$

$$f_2^{1[2]} \leq x_2 50, k = 1, \ldots, \nu$$

$$0 \leq P^{\mathrm{S}1[2]} \leq 0.75 \cdot 140, 0 \leq P^{\mathrm{C}1[2]} \leq 1.0 \cdot 80, 0 \leq P^{\mathrm{U}1[2]} \leq 0.5 \cdot 80$$

$$P^{\mathrm{S}2[2]} = f_1^{2[2]}, P^{\mathrm{C}2[2]} = f_2^{2[2]}, 0.75 \cdot 80 - P^{\mathrm{U}2[2]} = f_1^{2[2]} + f_2^{2[2]}$$

$$- (1 - x_1)10^6 - (f_1^{2[2]}/100 - \delta_1^{2[2]}) \leq 0, k = 1, \ldots, \nu$$

$$f_1^{2[2]}/100 - \delta_1^{2[2]} \leq (1 - x_1)10^6, k = 1, \ldots, \nu$$

$$- x_1 50 - f_1^{2[2]} \leq 0, k = 1, \ldots, \nu$$

$$f_1^{2[2]} \leq x_1 50, k = 1, \ldots, \nu$$

$$- (1 - x_2)10^6 - (f_2^{2[2]}/100 - \delta_2^{2[2]}) \leq 0, k = 1, \ldots, \nu$$

$$f_2^{2[2]}/100 - \delta_2^{2[2]} \leq (1 - x_2)10^6, k = 1, \ldots, \nu$$

$$- x_2 50 - f_2^{2[2]} \leq 0, k = 1, \ldots, \nu$$

$$f_2^{2[2]} \leq x_2 50, k = 1, \ldots, \nu$$

$$0 \leq P^{\mathrm{S}2[2]} \leq 0.25 \cdot 140, 0 \leq P^{\mathrm{C}2[2]} \leq 1.0 \cdot 80, 0 \leq P^{\mathrm{U}2[2]} \leq 0.75 \cdot 80.$$

The solution of this second master problem is:

$$x_1^{[2]} = 1, x_2^{[2]} = 1,$$

with an objective function value of \$7.847 million.

The current lower bound is then \$7.847 million.

#### 5.5.5.4 Second Subproblem

The second subproblem (merged second- and third level problem) is

$$\max_{\Theta}$$

$$- \Big[ 50\beta_{12}^{\max 1} + 50\beta_{12}^{\min 1} + 50\beta_{22}^{\max 1} + 50\beta_{22}^{\min 1}$$

$$+0.75\bar{P}^{\mathrm{S}}\gamma_1^{\max 1} + 1.0\bar{P}^{\mathrm{C}}\gamma_2^{\max 1} + 0.5\bar{D}\gamma_3^{\max 1} - 0.5\bar{D}\alpha_3^1$$
$$+50\beta_{12}^{\max 2} + 50\beta_{12}^{\min 2} + 50\beta_{22}^{\max 2} + 50\beta_{22}^{\min 2}$$
$$\left. +0.25\bar{P}^{\mathrm{S}}\gamma_1^{\max 2} + 1.0\bar{P}^{\mathrm{C}}\gamma_2^{\max 2} + 0.75\bar{D}\gamma_3^{\max 2} - 0.75\bar{D}\alpha_3^2 \right]$$

s.t.

Long-term uncertainty constraints:

$$140 \le \bar{P}^{\mathrm{S}} \le 200, \qquad 200 - \bar{P}^{\mathrm{S}} \le 60$$
$$80 \le \bar{P}^{\mathrm{C}} \le 100, \qquad 100 - \bar{P}^{\mathrm{C}} \le 20$$
$$64 \le \bar{D} \le 80, \qquad \bar{D} - 64 \le 16$$

First scenario dual constraints:

$$\frac{1}{2}8760 \times 2 + \alpha_1^1 + \gamma_1^{\max 1} - \gamma_1^{\min 1} = 0$$
$$\frac{1}{2}8760 \times 20 + \alpha_2^1 + \gamma_2^{\max 1} - \gamma_2^{\min 1} = 0$$
$$\frac{1}{2}8760 \times 200 - \alpha_3^1 + \gamma_3^{\max 1} - \gamma_3^{\min 1} = 0$$
$$-\alpha_1^1 - \alpha_3^1 - \beta_{11}^{\min 1}/100 + \beta_{11}^{\max 1}/100 - \beta_{12}^{\min 1} + \beta_{12}^{\max 1} = 0$$
$$-\alpha_2^1 - \alpha_3^1 - \beta_{21}^{\min 1}/100 + \beta_{21}^{\max 1}/100 - \beta_{22}^{\min 1} + \beta_{22}^{\max 1} = 0$$
$$\beta_{11}^{\min 1} - \beta_{11}^{\max 1} = 0$$
$$\beta_{21}^{\min 1} - \beta_{21}^{\max 1} = 0$$

Second scenario dual constraints:

$$\frac{1}{2}8760 \times 2 + \alpha_1^2 + \gamma_1^{\max 2} - \gamma_1^{\min 2} = 0$$
$$\frac{1}{2}8760 \times 20 + \alpha_2^2 + \gamma_2^{\max 2} - \gamma_2^{\min 2} = 0$$
$$\frac{1}{2}8760 \times 200 - \alpha_3^2 + \gamma_3^{\max 2} - \gamma_3^{\min 2} = 0$$
$$-\alpha_1^2 - \alpha_3^2 - \beta_{11}^{\min 2}/100 + \beta_{11}^{\max 2}/100 - \beta_{12}^{\min 2} + \beta_{12}^{\max 2} = 0$$
$$-\alpha_2^2 - \alpha_3^2 - \beta_{21}^{\min 2}/100 + \beta_{21}^{\max 2}/100 - \beta_{22}^{\min 2} + \beta_{22}^{\max 2} = 0$$

$$\beta_{11}^{\min 2} - \beta_{11}^{\max 2} = 0$$

$$\beta_{21}^{\min 2} - \beta_{21}^{\max 2} = 0$$

Additionally:

1. Dual variables $\alpha_1^1$, $\alpha_2^1$, $\alpha_3^1$, $\alpha_1^2$, $\alpha_2^2$ and $\alpha_3^2$ are not restricted in sign.
2. Dual variables $\beta_{11}^{\min 1}$, $\beta_{12}^{\min 1}$, $\beta_{21}^{\min 1}$, $\beta_{22}^{\min 1}$, $\gamma_1^{\min 1}$, $\gamma_2^{\min 1}$, $\gamma_3^{\min 1}$, $\beta_{11}^{\min 2}$, $\beta_{12}^{\min 2}$, $\beta_{21}^{\min 2}$, $\beta_{22}^{\min 2}$, $\gamma_1^{\min 2}$, $\gamma_2^{\min 2}$, $\gamma_3^{\min 2}$, $\beta_{11}^{\max 1}$, $\beta_{12}^{\max 1}$, $\beta_{21}^{\max 1}$, $\beta_{22}^{\max 1}$, $\gamma_1^{\max 1}$, $\gamma_2^{\max 1}$, $\gamma_3^{\max 1}$, $\beta_{11}^{\max 2}$, $\beta_{12}^{\max 2}$, $\beta_{21}^{\max 2}$, $\beta_{22}^{\max 2}$, $\gamma_1^{\max 2}$, $\gamma_2^{\max 2}$ and $\gamma_3^{\max 2}$ are non-negative.

The solution of this subproblem is (dual variables are not indicated):

$$\bar{P}^{S[k]} = 140,\ \bar{P}^{C[k]} = 80,\ \bar{D}^{[k]} = 80,$$

with and objective function value of \$2.847 million.

The corresponding upper bound is obtained by adding to this objective function value the corresponding investment cost, i.e., \$2.847 + (\$2.0 + \$3.0) = \$7.847 million.

#### 5.5.5.5 Convergence Achieved

Since the objective function values of the master problem and the subproblem are identical, the solution has been reached. the best expansion strategy is:

$$x_1^* = 1, x_2^* = 1.$$

That is, building lines 1 and 2.

## 5.6 End-of-Chapter Exercises

**5.1** Expand the ARSO model in Illustrative Example 5.1 to consider a 3-node, 3-line network.

**5.2** Modify the ARSO model in Illustrative Example 5.1 to consider investment in both generation and transmission facilities.

**5.3** Modify the ARSO model in Illustrative Example 5.1 to consider solely investment in generation facilities.

**5.4** Modify the ARSO model in Sect. 5.5.1 to consider a 3-node, 3-line, non-radial network.

**5.5** Solve the model in Exercise 5.4 above following the methodology in Sect. 5.5.

## 5.7 Appendix: GAMS Code

An input GAMS [6] file to solve the first master problem of the TEP case study is provided below.

```
variables
z, f111, f211, d111, d211, f121, f221, d121, d221;
binary variables
x1, x2;
positive variables
eta, ps11, pc11, pu11, ps21, pc21, pu21;
parameter
M  /10000/;
equations of, c1,
s11,s12,s13,s141,s142,s151,s152,s16,s17,s18,s19,s110,s111,s112,
s21,s22,s23,s241,s242,s251,s252,s26,s27,s28,s29,s210,s211,s212;
*
of..    z =e= 2000000*x1+3000000*x2+eta;
c1..    eta =g= 0.5*8760*(2*ps11+20*pc11+200*pu11)+
                0.5*8760*(2*ps21+20*pc21+200*pu21);
s11..   ps11 =e= f111;
s12..   pc11 =e= f211;
s13..   0.5*2-pu11 =e= f111+f211;
*
s141..  -M*(1-x1) =l= f111 - 100*d111;
s142..  f111 - 100*d111 =l= M*(1-x1);
s151..  -M*(1-x2) =l= f211 - 100*d211;
s152..  f211 - 100*d211 =l= M*(1-x2);
s16..   -50*x1 =l= f111;
s17..   f111 =l= 50*x1;
s18..   -50*x2 =l= f211;
s19..   f211 =l= 50*x2;
s110..  ps11 =l= 0.75*6;
s111..  pc11 =l= 1.00*2;
s112..  pu11 =l= 0.50*2;
*
s21..   ps21 =e= f121;
s22..   pc21 =e= f221;
s23..   0.75*2-pu21 =e= f121+f221;
*
s241..  -M*(1-x1) =l= f121 - 100*d121;
s242..  f121 - 100*d121 =l= M*(1-x1);
s251..  -M*(1-x2) =l= f221 - 100*d221;
s252..  f221 - 100*d221 =l= M*(1-x2);
s26..   -50*x1 =l= f121;
s27..   f121 =l= 50*x1;
s28..   -50*x2 =l= f221;
s29..   f221 =l= 50*x2;
s210..  ps21 =l= 0.25*6;
s211..  pc21 =l= 1.00*2;
s212..  pu21 =l= 0.75*2;
*
model MP1 /all/;
solve MP1 using mip minimizing z;
```

Note that this GAMS code reproduces almost verbatim the mathematical formulation of the TEP master problem.

The part of the GAMS output file that provides the optimal solution is given below:

```
                              LOWER     LEVEL      UPPER    MARGINAL

---- VAR z                    -INF   2.0219E+6    +INF         .
---- VAR f111                 -INF       1.000    +INF         .
---- VAR f211                 -INF         .      +INF         .
---- VAR d111                 -INF       0.010    +INF         .
---- VAR d211                 -INF     100.000    +INF         .
---- VAR f121                 -INF       1.500    +INF         .
---- VAR f221                 -INF         .      +INF         .
---- VAR d121                 -INF       0.015    +INF         .
---- VAR d221                 -INF     100.000    +INF         .
---- VAR x1                     .        1.000    1.000 2.0000E+6
---- VAR x2                     .          .      1.000 -4.124E+7
---- VAR eta                    .    21900.000    +INF         .
---- VAR ps11                   .        1.000    +INF         .
---- VAR pc11                   .          .      +INF  87600.000
---- VAR pu11                   .          .      +INF  8.6724E+5
---- VAR ps21                   .        1.500    +INF         .
---- VAR pc21                   .          .      +INF  87600.000
---- VAR pu21                   .          .      +INF         .
```

Note that this output file is self-explanatory.

An input GAMS [6] file to solve the first subproblem of the TEP case study is provided below.

```
variables
* long-term uncertain variables
PS, PC, D,
* Dual variables equality constraints scenario 1
alpha_1_1, alpha_1_2, alpha_1_3,
* Dual variables equality constraints scenario 2
alpha_2_1, alpha_2_2, alpha_2_3,
* Objective function value
z;
positive variables
* Dual variables inequality constraints scenario 1
beta_max1_11,beta_min1_11,beta_max1_12,beta_min1_12,
beta_max1_21,beta_min1_21,beta_max1_22,beta_min1_22,
gamma_max1_1,gamma_min1_1,gamma_max1_2,gamma_min1_2,
gamma_max1_3,gamma_min1_3,
* Dual variables inequality constraints scenario 1
beta_max2_11,beta_min2_11,beta_max2_12,beta_min2_12,
beta_max2_21,beta_min2_21,beta_max2_22,beta_min2_22,
gamma_max2_1,gamma_min2_1,gamma_max2_2,gamma_min2_2,
gamma_max2_3,gamma_min2_3;
```

```
*
PS.up = 200; PS.lo = 140;
PC.up = 100; PC.lo = 80;
D.up  = 80;  D.lo  = 64;
equations
obj,ro1,ro2,ro3,
fs11,fs12,fs13,fs14,fs15,fs16,fs17,
fs21,fs22,fs23,fs24,fs25,fs26,fs27;
*
obj.. z =e= -(
   50*beta_max1_12+50*beta_min1_12+1000000*beta_max1_21+1000000*
       beta_min1_21
+ 0.75*PS*gamma_max1_1+PC*gamma_max1_2+0.5*D*gamma_max1_3-0.5*D*
    alpha_1_3
+ 50*beta_max2_12+50*beta_min2_12+1000000*beta_max2_21+1000000*
    beta_min2_21
+ 0.25*PS*gamma_max2_1+PC*gamma_max2_2+0.75*D*gamma_max2_3-0.75*D
    *alpha_2_3 );
*
ro1..  200 - PS =l= 60;
ro2..  100 - PC =l= 20;
ro3..  D - 64 =l= 16;
*
fs11.. 0.5*8760*2   +alpha_1_1+gamma_max1_1-gamma_min1_1 =e= 0;
fs12.. 0.5*8760*20  +alpha_1_2+gamma_max1_2-gamma_min1_2 =e= 0;
fs13.. 0.5*8760*200-alpha_1_3+gamma_max1_3-gamma_min1_3 =e= 0;
fs14.. - alpha_1_1-alpha_1_3-beta_min1_11/100+beta_max1_11/100
       - beta_min1_12+beta_max1_12 =e= 0;
fs15.. - alpha_1_2-alpha_1_3-beta_min1_21/100+beta_max1_21/100
       - beta_min1_22+beta_max1_22 =e= 0;
fs16.. beta_min1_11 - beta_max1_11 =e= 0;
fs17.. beta_min1_21 - beta_max1_21 =e= 0;
*
fs21.. 0.5*8760*2   + alpha_2_1+gamma_max2_1-gamma_min2_1 =e= 0;
fs22.. 0.5*8760*20  + alpha_2_2+gamma_max2_2-gamma_min2_2 =e= 0;
fs23.. 0.5*8760*200- alpha_2_3+gamma_max2_3-gamma_min2_3 =e= 0;
fs24.. - alpha_2_1-alpha_2_3-beta_min2_11/100+beta_max2_11/100
       - beta_min2_12+beta_max2_12 =e= 0;
fs25.. - alpha_2_2-alpha_2_3-beta_min2_21/100+beta_max2_21/100
       - beta_min2_22+beta_max2_22 =e= 0;
fs26.. beta_min2_11 - beta_max2_11 =e= 0;
fs27.. beta_min2_21 - beta_max2_21 =e= 0;
*
option nlp=conopt
model SP1 /all/;
solve SP1 using nlp maximizing z;
```

Note that this GAMS code reproduces almost verbatim the mathematical formulation of the TEP subproblem.

The part of the GAMS output file that provides the optimal solution is given below:

```
                              LOWER      LEVEL      UPPER     MARGINAL

---- VAR PS                 140.000    140.000    200.000 -2.168E+5
---- VAR PC                  80.000     80.000    100.000       EPS
---- VAR D                   64.000     80.000     80.000 6.6138E+5
---- VAR alpha_1_1            -INF   -8760.000     +INF          .
---- VAR alpha_1_2            -INF   -4.818E+4     +INF          .
---- VAR alpha_1_3            -INF    8760.000     +INF          .
---- VAR alpha_2_1            -INF   -8.760E+5     +INF          .
---- VAR alpha_2_2            -INF   -8.760E+4     +INF          .
---- VAR alpha_2_3            -INF   8.7600E+5     +INF          .
---- VAR z                    -INF   2.2557E+7     +INF          .
---- VAR beta_max1~             .          .       +INF        EPS
---- VAR beta_min1~             .          .       +INF          .
---- VAR beta_max1~             .          .       +INF     -10.000
---- VAR beta_min1~             .          .       +INF     -90.000
---- VAR beta_max1~             .          .       +INF   -1.000E+6
---- VAR beta_min1~             .          .       +INF   -1.000E+6
---- VAR beta_max1~             .          .       +INF        EPS
---- VAR beta_min1~             .    39420.000     +INF          .
---- VAR gamma_max~             .          .       +INF     -65.000
---- VAR gamma_min~             .          .       +INF     -40.000
---- VAR gamma_max~             .          .       +INF     -80.000
---- VAR gamma_min~             .    39420.000     +INF        EPS
---- VAR gamma_max~             .          .       +INF     -40.000
---- VAR gamma_min~             .    8.6724E+5     +INF          .
---- VAR beta_max2~             .          .       +INF        EPS
---- VAR beta_min2~             .          .       +INF          .
---- VAR beta_max2~             .          .       +INF     -15.000
---- VAR beta_min2~             .          .       +INF     -85.000
---- VAR beta_max2~             .          .       +INF   -1.000E+6
---- VAR beta_min2~             .          .       +INF   -1.000E+6
---- VAR beta_max2~             .    7.8840E+5     +INF          .
---- VAR beta_min2~             .          .       +INF        EPS
---- VAR gamma_max~             .    8.6724E+5     +INF          .
---- VAR gamma_min~             .          .       +INF     -35.000
---- VAR gamma_max~             .          .       +INF     -80.000
---- VAR gamma_min~             .          .       +INF        EPS
---- VAR gamma_max~             .          .       +INF     -35.000
---- VAR gamma_min~             .          .       +INF     -25.000
```

Note that this output file is self-explanatory.

## References

1. Zhang, X., & Conejo, A. J. (2018). Robust transmission expansion planning representing long- and short-term uncertainty. *IEEE Transactions on Power Systems*, *33*(2), 1329–1338.
2. Conejo, A. J., Castillo, E., Minguez, R., & Garcia-Bertrand, R. (2006). *Decomposition techniques in mathematical programming. engineering and science applications*. Springer.
3. Zeng, B., & Zhao, L. (2013). Solving two-stage robust optimization problems using a column-and-constraint generation method. *Operations Research Letters*, *41*(5), 457–461.
4. Bertsimas, D., Litvinov, E., Sun, X. A., Zhao, J., & Zheng, T. (2013). Adaptive robust optimization for the security constrained unit commitment problem. *IEEE Transactions on Power Systems* , **28**(1), 52–63.
5. Binato, S., Pereira, M. V. F., & Granville, S. (2001). A new Benders decomposition approach to solve power transmission network design problems. *IEEE Transactions on Power Systems*, *16*(2), 235–240.
6. GAMS Development Corporation. (2017). *GAMS – A user's guide*. http://www.gams.com

# Chapter 6
# Robust Optimization in Short-Term Power System Operations

## 6.1 Introduction

In this chapter, we study the applications of robust optimization in day-ahead and real-time operation of power systems with significant wind and solar generation. First, we introduce a two-stage robust optimization model for the unit commitment (UC) problem [1], which is one of the first robust optimization models proposed for power system operation [2, 3]. We show that the robust UC model can improve both the cost efficiency and the reliability of the real-time operation by preparing traditional generation resources against the rapid and uncertain fluctuations of renewable generation output. In [1], an efficient solution method is also introduced to solve the two-stage robust optimization model, which is later popularized as the constraint-and-column generation method [4]. A detailed discussion can be found in Chap. 3. Recently, such robust UC models and robust optimization methodology have been implemented in the US power markets for the scheduling of renewable generation, e.g. in the ISO New England [5].

Next, we extend this two-stage robust UC model to a multistage robust optimization model to account for the physical causal relation between observation and decision that need to be obeyed in a decision model under uncertainty [6]. We also introduce an approximation scheme using affine policy to improve computational tractability of the resulting multistage robust UC model.

After this, we go into real-time operation and study two key questions for robust economic dispatch models: 1) how to model temporal and spatial dynamics of wind and solar generation using uncertainty sets? 2) how to handle more complicated constraints that are critical for real-time operation such as AC optimal power flow (OPF) constraints? For the first question, we will propose the so-called *dynamic uncertainty sets* that explicitly model correlations of multiple wind and solar farms over multiple time periods [7, 8]. For the second question, we leverage the



X. A. Sun, A. J. Conejo, *Robust Optimization in Electric Energy Systems*, International Series in Operations Research & Management Science 313,
https://doi.org/10.1007/978-3-030-85128-6_6

recent development of strong convex relaxations of AC OPF in a two-stage robust optimization model [9].

## 6.2 Two-Stage Robust Unit Commitment

The unit commitment problem is a central decision making problem in the daily operation of a large-scale electricity system [10]. In a deregulated electricity market, the generation companies and load serving entities submit bids into the day-ahead market for the operation of the next day. The bids include various generation costs, demand level and prices, and physical parameters of the generation units such as the minimum up and down times, ramping rates, and the minimum and maximum economic output of generators. The Independent System Operator (ISO) collects all these information and formulates a social welfare maximization problem to find the optimal plan of generation commitment and dispatch schedule to meet the forecast demand in the next day (see [11] for a recent survey of the wholesale electricity market design in the U.S., [12] for a discussion of the electricity markets worldwide, and [13] for fundamental concepts of electricity market design.)

In the current U.S. electricity markets, the short-run price elasticity of electricity demand is still limited [14]. As a result, a fixed forecast demand level is usually used in the UC model and the objective becomes to minimize the total generation cost of meeting this forecast demand level. This is called a *deterministic* UC model, because the load level is deterministic. Here by load we mean the *net load* of forecast demand minus forecast renewable generation. Clearly, as the level of renewable generation increases in the power system, the impact of forecast error will increase. This is the motivation to use robust optimization to explicitly model renewable uncertainty.

Another important source of uncertainty comes from unexpected failures of generation units and transmission lines. These unexpected failures are called *contingencies* (see [15] for a broad discussion of power system security.) Losing a major generator or a transmission line could cause significant disturbance to the balance of supply and demand in the real-time market. Therefore, it is imperative to consider such uncertainties in the UC problem. To handle contingencies, the system operator would seek a UC decision that is feasible for any contingency of losing one generator or one transmission line in real time operation. This is known as the $N - 1$ rule. This in fact is a classic application of static robust optimization, where the uncertainty of losing any one equipment, a generator or a transmission line, is modeled by a simplex uncertainty set, and a static linear robust constraint over uncertainty in such a simplex is equivalent to enforcing deterministic linear constraints over every vertex of the simplex, which is exactly the $N - 1$ rule. This leads to the *security constrained* UC problem (SCUC).

In the following we first formulate a deterministic SCUC model and then describe the two-stage robust UC model to deal with net load uncertainty.

### 6.2.1 A Deterministic SCUC Model

A deterministic SCUC model is formulated below.

$$\min_{x,u,v,p,r} \quad \sum_{t\in\mathscr{T}}\sum_{i\in\mathscr{G}} \left(f_i^t(x_i^t, u_i^t, v_i^t) + c_i^t(p_i^t)\right) \tag{6.2.1a}$$

$$\text{s.t.} \quad x_i^{t-1} - x_i^t + u_i^t \geq 0, \quad \forall i \in \mathscr{G}, t \in \mathscr{T}, \tag{6.2.1b}$$

$$x_i^t - x_i^{t-1} + v_i^t \geq 0, \quad \forall i \in \mathscr{G}, t \in \mathscr{T}, \tag{6.2.1c}$$

$$x_i^t - x_i^{t-1} \leq x_i^\tau, \quad \forall \tau \in [t+1, \min\{t + \text{MinUp}_i - 1, T\}],\ t \in [2, T], i \in \mathscr{G}, \tag{6.2.1d}$$

$$x_i^{t-1} - x_i^t \leq 1 - x_i^\tau, \quad \forall \tau \in [t+1, \min\{t + \text{MinDw}_i - 1, T\}],\ t \in [2, T], i \in \mathscr{G} \tag{6.2.1e}$$

$$\sum_{i\in\mathscr{G}} p_i^t = \sum_{j\in CD} \bar{d}_j^t, \qquad \forall t \in \mathscr{T}, \tag{6.2.1f}$$

$$p_i^t - p_i^{t-1} \leq RU_i x_i^{t-1} + SU_i u_i^t, \quad \forall i \in \mathscr{G}, t \in \mathscr{T}, \tag{6.2.1g}$$

$$p_i^{t-1} - p_i^t \leq RD_i x_i^t + SD_i v_i^t, \quad \forall i \in \mathscr{G}, t \in \mathscr{T}, \tag{6.2.1h}$$

$$- f_{l,k}^{\max} \leq \boldsymbol{a}_{l,k}^\top(\boldsymbol{B}^p \boldsymbol{p}^t - \boldsymbol{B}^d \boldsymbol{d}^t) \leq f_{l,k}^{\max}, \quad \forall t \in \mathscr{T}, l \in \mathscr{C}_k, k \in \mathscr{L}, \tag{6.2.1i}$$

$$p_i^{\min} \leq p_i^t + \sum_{a\in\mathscr{A}} r_{i,a}^t \leq p_i^{\max}, \quad \forall i \in \mathscr{G}, t \in \mathscr{T}, \tag{6.2.1j}$$

$$p_i^{\min} x_i^t \leq p_i^t \leq p_i^{\max} x_i^t, \quad \forall i \in \mathscr{G}, t \in \mathscr{T}, \tag{6.2.1k}$$

$$\sum_{i\in\mathscr{G}, a\in\mathscr{A}_k} r_{i,a}^t \geq \bar{r}_k^t, \quad \forall t \in \mathscr{T}, k \in \mathscr{N}_r, \tag{6.2.1l}$$

$$\sum_{a\in\mathscr{A}_k} r_{i,a}^t \leq \bar{r}_{i,k}^t, \quad \forall i \in \mathscr{G}, t \in \mathscr{T}, k \in \mathscr{N}_r, \tag{6.2.1m}$$

$$x_i^t, u_i^t, v_i^t \in \{0, 1\}, \quad \forall i \in \mathscr{G}, t \in \mathscr{T}. \tag{6.2.1n}$$

The unit commitment includes binary decisions $x_i^t, u_i^t, v_i^t$, where $x_i^t = 1$ if generator $i$ is on at time $t$, and $x_i^t = 0$ otherwise; $u_i^t = 1$ if generator $i$ is turned on from the off state at time $t$; and $v_i^t = 1$ if generator $i$ is turned off at time $t$. The time horizon $\mathscr{T}$ usually includes hourly time intervals for 24 or 48 h. The dispatch decision $p_i^t$ is the generation level of generator $i$ at time $t$, where $\mathscr{G}$ is the set of generators. The reserve decision $\boldsymbol{r}_{i,a}^t$ is the amount of generation capacity of generator $i$ that is reserved for fast response type $a$ at time $t$.

In the objective function (6.2.1a), $f_i^t(x_i^t, u_i^t, v_i^t)$ is the fixed cost of generator $i$, which includes start-up and shut-down costs and no-load cost. The variable production cost is $c_i^t(p_i^t)$, which is usually approximated by a convex piecewise linear function of the real power output $p_i^t$. The forecast net load $\bar{d}_j^t$ is the demand minus renewable generation at bus $j$ time $t$.

Constraints (6.2.1b) and (6.2.1c) represent logic relations between on and off status and the turn-on and turn-off actions of a generator. For example, constraint (6.2.1b) states that generator $i$ is turned on at time $t$, i.e. $u_i^t = 1$, if it is on at time $t$ and off at time $t-1$, i.e. $x_i^t - x_i^{t-1} = 1$. Constraints (6.2.1d) and (6.2.1e) restrict the minimum up and down times for each generator. Constraint (6.2.1f) enforces system wide energy balance in each time period. Constraints (6.2.1g)–(6.2.1h) limit the rate of generation change over a single period, where $RU_i$ and $RD_i$ are limits for ramp-up and ramp-down rates when the generator is already running, and $SU_i$ and $SD_i$ respectively are ramping limits when generator $i$ is just starting up and shutting down. Constraint (6.2.1i) expresses the power flow in the transmission lines as a linear function of power production and load in the entire system, where the coefficients of the linear function, $\boldsymbol{a}_{l,k}$, are called the power shift factors of line $l$, and the index $k$ represents the $k$-th contingency, i.e., when the line $k$ is tripped, $\mathscr{C}_k$ is the set of remaining lines. $\boldsymbol{B}^p$ and $\boldsymbol{B}^d$ are the incidence matrices of generators and loads.

Equation (6.2.1j) constrains that the sum of the production output and the reserve should be within the upper and lower bounds for each generator. Equation (6.2.1k) is the coupled constraint indicating that only committed generators can be dispatched. Equation (6.2.1l) describes the requirement on how much reserve the system should have for reserve category $k \in \mathscr{N}_r$ at time $t$. Equation (6.2.1m) says that generator $i$ can provide at most $\bar{q}_{i,k}^t$ for reserve requirement $k$ at time $t$.

### 6.2.2 Two-Stage Robust UC Model

The UC decision, i.e. $\boldsymbol{x}, \boldsymbol{u}, \boldsymbol{v}$, is the critical decision that need to be made in the day before the real time operation. In other words, the decisions for which generators to turn on and off in each of the 24 h of the next day must be determined today, usually in the afternoon of the day before the real-time operation. This is due to the long minimum up and down times and slow ramping rates of some thermal and nuclear generators. Once the UC decision is fixed, it cannot be changed for most of the real-time operation in the next day. Sometimes, recommitment of generators in real time is allowed, however, recommitment is usually restricted to a small set of flexible generators.

In contrast to the UC decision, the generation level decisions $\boldsymbol{p}$ and the reserve level decisions $\boldsymbol{r}$ for the next day can be changed in real-time operation. This is due to the fact that the forecast load level used in the UC problem inevitably contains forecast errors. The net load in real-time operation will be different from this forecast. Then, generator and reserve need to be dispatched to meet the real-time load. For this purpose, a real-time electricity market is set up to dispatch generators to meet load in an hourly or even smaller time scale, such as every 15 min (see [16] for California ISO's 5 min and 15 min real-time markets.)

#### 6.2.2.1 Two-Stage Robust UC Model

The difference between the UC decision and the dispatch decision suggests a two-stage decision making structure as we introduced in Chap. 3, Sect. 3.2. In particular, we treat the UC decision, $\boldsymbol{x}, \boldsymbol{u}, \boldsymbol{v}$, as the first-stage decision, and the net load $\boldsymbol{d}$ in each of the next 24 h as the uncertainty that is observed after the UC decision is made, then the dispatch and reserve decision, $\boldsymbol{p}, \boldsymbol{r}$, are the second-stage decision that are made after observing the net load $\boldsymbol{d}$.

Now we can formulate the two-stage robust UC model as follows.

$$\min_{(\boldsymbol{x},\boldsymbol{u},\boldsymbol{v})\in X} \left\{ \sum_{t\in\mathscr{T}} \sum_{i\in\mathscr{G}} f_i^t(x_i^t, u_i^t, v_i^t) + \max_{\boldsymbol{d}\in\mathscr{D}} \min_{\boldsymbol{p}\in P(\boldsymbol{x},\boldsymbol{d})} \sum_{t\in\mathscr{T}} \sum_{i\in\mathscr{G}} c_i^t(p_i^t) \right\}, \tag{6.2.2a}$$

where the feasible region $X$ of the first-stage problem is defined by the deterministic UC constraints as

$$X = \left\{ (\boldsymbol{x}, \boldsymbol{u}, \boldsymbol{v}) \in \{0, 1\}^{3|\mathscr{G}||\mathscr{T}|} : (6.2.1\text{b}) - (6.2.1\text{e}), (6.2.1\text{n}) \right\}, \tag{6.2.2b}$$

and the feasible region $P(\boldsymbol{x}, \boldsymbol{d})$ of the second-stage real-time dispatch problem is defined as follows.

$$P(\boldsymbol{x}, \boldsymbol{d}) = \left\{ (\boldsymbol{p}, \boldsymbol{r}) \in \mathbb{R}^{2|\mathscr{G}||\mathscr{T}|} : (6.2.1\text{f}) - (6.2.1\text{m}) \right\}. \tag{6.2.2c}$$

We propose to use the following budgeted uncertainty set for the net load $\boldsymbol{d}$,

$$\mathscr{D} := \left\{ \boldsymbol{d} \in \mathbb{R}^{N_d \times T} : \sum_{t\in\mathscr{T}} \sum_{i\in\mathscr{N}_d} \frac{|d_i^t - \bar{d}_i^t|}{\hat{d}_i^t} \le \Delta, \right.$$
$$\left. \times \sum_{i\in\mathscr{N}_d} \frac{|d_i^t - \bar{d}_i^t|}{\hat{d}_i^t} \le \Delta^t, d_i^t \in \left[\bar{d}_i^t - \hat{d}_i^t, \bar{d}_i^t + \hat{d}_i^t\right], \forall i \in \mathscr{N}_d,\ t \in \mathscr{T} \right\}, \tag{6.2.2d}$$

where each net load $d_i^t$ lies in a confidence interval $[\bar{d}_i^t - \hat{d}_i^t, \bar{d}_i^t + \hat{d}_i^t]$ around the nominal value $\bar{d}_i^t$, the total variation from the nominal value of all net loads is upper bounded by $\Delta^t$ for each time $t$, and the total variation over both time and locations is upper bounded by $\Delta$.

### 6.2.3 Computational Experiments

This two-stage robust UC model (6.2.2a)–(6.2.2d) has linear constraints in both stages and also in the uncertainty set, while integer variables only appear in the first stage. These special structures enable the application of the column-and-constraint generation (CCG) algorithm introduced in [1, 4]. See detailed discussion in Chap. 3, Sect. 3.2. In the following, we apply this two-stage robust UC model to the ISO New England's day-ahead electricity market, which has the following system and market data.

The whole system has 312 generating units, 174 loads, and 2816 nodes. We select 4 representative transmission constraints that interconnect four major load zones in the ISO-NE's system. The market data is taken from a normal winter day of the ISO-NE's day-ahead energy market. In particular, we have 24 h data of generators' offer curves, reserve offers, expected nodal load, system reserve requirement (10 min spinning reserve, 10 min non-spinning reserve, and 30 min reserve), and various network parameters. The average total generation capacity per hour is 31,929 MW and the average forecasted load per hour is 16,232 MW.

We use the budgeted uncertainty set defined in (6.2.2d), in which $\bar{d}_j^t$ is the nominal load given in the data. We set the range of load variation to be $\hat{d}_j^t = 10\% \cdot \bar{d}_j^t$ for each load $j$ at time $t$. To simplify analysis, we assume the temporal uncertainty budget $\Delta$ to be large enough so that the uncertainty in different time periods are decoupled. The budget of uncertainty $\Delta^t$ is the main parameter for controlling the performance of the robust solution. In the following, we will show a proper way to choose $\Delta^t$ within this range that results in the best performance of the robust UC.

We compare the robust UC approach to the approach of adjustable reserve, which is used in the current practice in the ISO New England. The reserve approach solves the a deterministic UC problem presented in (6.2.1) with the forecast net load level and adjusts the reserve requirement. In particular, we model the reserve adjustment as follows,

$$q_{j,t} = q_{j,t}^0 + \frac{\Delta^t}{N_d} \sum_{i=1}^{N_d} \hat{d}_i^t,$$

where $q_{j,t}$ is the system reserve requirement of type $j$ at time $t$, composed of the basic reserve level $q_{j,t}^0$ and an adjustment part proportional to the total variation of load. Here, the uncertainty budget $\Delta^t$ also controls the level of conservatism of the reserve solution.

The computational experiments first obtain UC solutions by solving the reserve and the robust UC models respectively for different uncertainty budgets: $\Delta^t \in [0, N_d]$. Then, for each UC solution, we solve the dispatch problem repeatedly for two sets of 1000 randomly generated loads. One set of randomly sampled load follows a uniform distribution in the interval $[\bar{d}_j^t - \hat{d}_j^t, \bar{d}_j^t + \hat{d}_j^t]$ for each load $j$ at time $t$. The other set follows a normal distribution with mean $\bar{d}_j^t$ and standard deviation

$\hat{d}_j^t/1.44$, which results in an 85 percentile of load falling between $[\bar{d}_j^t - \hat{d}_j^t, \bar{d}_j^t + \hat{d}_j^t]$ (the load is truncated for nonnegative values). Notice that samples from both sets may fall outside of the budgeted uncertainty set, especially when the budget $\Delta^t$ is close to 0.

#### 6.2.3.1 Reduction of Average Cost and Budget Level

A central question is how to choose the level of budget in the uncertainty set (6.2.2d). Too high a budget level would lead to over-conservative solutions. A proper level of budget could lead to sufficient robustness and significant average cost reduction at the same time.

We observe that the robust UC approach performs the best when the budget $\Delta^t$ in the uncertainty set is set to be proportional $\sqrt{N_d}$, the square root of the number of uncertain resources. This phenomenon can be explained by the probability law, namely the central limit theorem. When a large number $N_d$ of random loads, independent as we assume, are aggregated, the volatility of the total load scales according to $\sqrt{N_d}$. Therefore, a proper level of uncertainty budget in the uncertainty set (6.2.2d) should be chosen as $\Delta^t \sim O(\sqrt{N_d})$.

Table 6.1 shows the comparison of the average dispatch cost and total cost (UC + dispatch) for two approaches, the robust UC (RobUC) approach and the reserve adjustment approach (ResAdj). The budget $\Delta^t$ takes values in $0.5\sqrt{N_d}$ to $3\sqrt{N_d}$, which is equivalent to $\Delta^t$ being in the range of $0.038N_d$ to $0.227N_d$, for $N_d = 174$ in our system. We can see that, in this range of the uncertainty budget, the RobUC has a rather high saving on average costs: the average dispatch cost saving from 1.86% or \$321.2k (at $\Delta^t = 1.5\sqrt{N_d}$) to 6.96% or \$1.27 million (at $\Delta^t = 0.5\sqrt{N_d}$), and the average total cost saving from 0.34% or \$64.1k (at $\Delta^t = 1.5\sqrt{N_d}$) to 5.48% or \$1.08 million (at $\Delta^t = 0.5\sqrt{N_d}$).

This demonstrates that, by choosing a proper level of uncertainty in the uncertainty set to control the conservativeness, the robust UC approach could achieve

**Table 6.1** The average dispatch costs and total costs of the Robust UC (RobUC) and Adjusted Reserve (ResAdj) for normally distributed load $\Delta^t/\sqrt{N_d} = 0.5, 1, \ldots, 3$ and $\hat{d}_j^t = 0.1\bar{d}_j^t$

| | RobUC | | ResAdj | |
|---|---|---|---|---|
| Budget $\Delta^t/\sqrt{N_d}$ | Dispatch cost (M\$) | Total cost (M\$) | Dispatch cost (M\$) | Total cost (M\$) |
| 0.5 | 16.9195 | 18.6050 | 18.1855 | 19.6837 |
| 1.0 | 16.9650 | 18.6688 | 17.4907 | 18.9942 |
| 1.5 | 16.9815 | 18.7365 | 17.3027 | 18.8006 |
| 2.0 | 17.0297 | 18.7937 | 17.7403 | 19.2415 |
| 2.5 | 17.0586 | 18.8366 | 17.6567 | 19.1618 |
| 3.0 | 17.0745 | 18.8526 | 18.0804 | 19.5889 |

significantly average cost savings from the reserve adjustment approach in the current practice.

#### 6.2.3.2 Reduction of Volatility and Penalty Costs

The robust UC approach can greatly reduce the volatility of the real-time dispatch costs and thus substantially improve the reliability of the dispatch solution against uncertain variation of renewable generation. Table 6.2 shows the standard deviation (std) of the dispatch costs of the two approaches, and their ratios (ResAdj/RobUC) for normally distributed load. We can see that the std for the reserve adjustment approach is almost an order of magnitude higher than that for the adaptive robust approach (8.15–14.48 times).

The significant reduction in the std of the dispatch cost is closely related to the significant reduction in the penalty cost. Table 6.2 shows the penalty costs of the two approaches. Recall that the dispatch cost is the sum of the production cost and penalty cost. The penalty cost occurs whenever there is a violation in the energy balance, reserve requirement, or transmission constraints. The system operator has to take expensive emergency actions such as dispatching fast-start units or load-shedding to maintain system reliability. All these add volatility to the dispatch costs.

As we observe, all three types of constraint violations (energy, reserve, and transmission) may occur for ResAdj solutions, indicating the potential ineffectiveness of a deterministic approach that only considers nominal load and system level reserves. In contrast, the RobUC approach commits resources by taking into consideration all possible load realizations in the uncertainty model. Furthermore, the robust

**Table 6.2** Standard deviation of the dispatch costs, the ratio, and penalty costs for normally distributed load

| | RobUC | | ResAdj | | | Ratio of std. |
|---|---|---|---|---|---|---|
| Budget $\Delta^t/N_d$ | Std. dispatch cost (k$) | Penalty cost (k$) | Std. dispatch cost (k$) | Penalty (k$) cost (k$) | Percent of dispatch cost | ResAdj/ RobUC |
| 0.0 | 1769.5107 | 2377.62 | 1769.5107 | 2377.6237 | 12.29% | 1 |
| 0.1 | 47.4900 | 0 | 687.5098 | 497.8243 | 2.85% | 14.48 |
| 0.2 | 46.3647 | 0 | 687.5098 | 272.4362 | 1.58% | 8.62 |
| 0.3 | 45.4248 | 0 | 377.7901 | 268.0298 | 1.55% | 8.32 |
| 0.4 | 44.2397 | 0 | 366.7359 | 252.3463 | 1.46% | 8.29 |
| 0.5 | 44.1075 | 0 | 377.1875 | 267.6559 | 1.55% | 8.55 |
| 0.6 | 43.9936 | 0 | 370.8673 | 259.7954 | 1.50% | 8.43 |
| 0.7 | 43.9263 | 0 | 377.0631 | 267.6559 | 1.54% | 8.58 |
| 0.8 | 43.9338 | 0 | 370.7203 | 259.7954 | 1.49% | 8.44 |
| 0.9 | 43.9023 | 0 | 357.9338 | 241.6133 | 1.39% | 8.15 |
| 1.0 | 43.9431 | 0 | 361.0376 | 247.4119 | 1.42% | 8.22 |

solutions remain feasible even when the load realization is outside of the uncertainty set (as the case for normally distributed load).

In conclusion, the low volatility of the dispatch cost and the zero penalty cost of the adaptive robust approach demonstrates its operational effectiveness in reducing costly emergency actions and improving system reliability.

## 6.3 Multistage Robust UC Model

A fundamental assumption in the two-stage robust UC model is that each hourly dispatch decision is made with the knowledge of the realization of the uncertain load in the entire scheduling horizon. This clearly violates *time causality* of the physical world, namely the dispatch decision at time $t$ can only depend on the realization of uncertainty before and up to time $t$, but not later than time $t$ in the future. Clearly, obeying causality will make the decision model more realistic. The question is whether obeying causality, also called *non-anticipativity*, would have any significant impact on the decisions of day-ahead and real-time operation of power systems.

The answer depends on the composition of power systems. If the generators have sufficient ramping capabilities to respond to the changes of net load, then a two-stage robust UC model may be sufficient. However, with the increasing penetration of renewable energy, power systems will be increasingly constrained by ramping capability to follow the net load fluctuations. In other words, the temporal coupling of decisions will become more significant. The following example illustrates the need for multistage robust UC models, when system ramping constraints are tight.

### 6.3.1 The Need for Multistage Robust UC Model

We present a simple example to illustrate that the UC solution from the two-stage robust UC model can lead to infeasibility in the real-time dispatch.

*Example 6.1* The system has 2 buses, $A$ and $B$, and two periods, so $T = 2$. See Fig. 6.1. Each bus has a conventional generator. The transmission line has a flow limit of 1 unit of power. The ramp rates of both generators are also 1 unit of power, i.e., $RU_A = RD_A = R_A = 1$, and $RU_B = RD_B = R_B = 1$. The initial generation levels of the two generators are at 12, i.e., $p_A^0 = p_B^0 = 12$ at $t = 0$.

The uncertainty sets for nodal net loads $(d_A^t, d_B^t)$ at $t = 1, 2$ are given as follows:

$$\mathscr{D}^1 = \left\{(d_A^1, d_B^1) = (12, 12)\right\}, \text{ and}$$

$$\mathscr{D}^2 = \left\{(d_A^2, d_B^2) : \ d_A^2 \in [10, 15], \ \ d_B^2 \in [10, 15], \ d_A^2 + d_B^2 = 25\right\}.$$

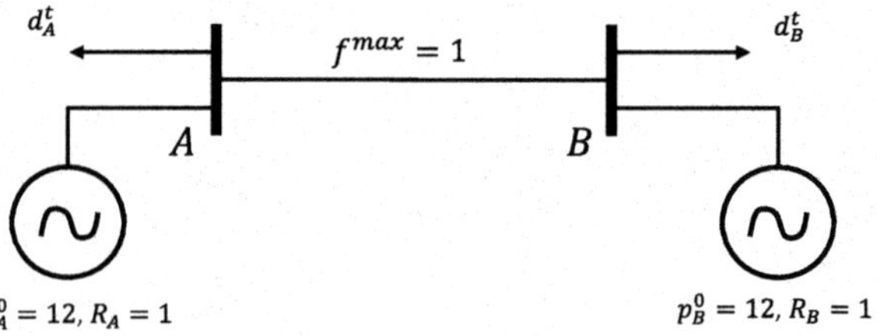


**Fig. 6.1** Simple two-bus system to illustrate the limitation of non-causal UC models

That is, the first period loads are deterministic with power level of 12 at each bus, and the net loads in the second period are uncertain, but the total net load is known to be 25. Denote $\mathscr{D} = \mathscr{D}_1 \times \mathscr{D}_2$.

*Claim* The two-stage robust UC model (6.2.2.1) is feasible for the system in Example 6.1.

In order to see Claim 6.3.1 is correct, consider $\boldsymbol{x}_{2S} = ((x_A^1, x_B^1), (x_A^2, x_B^2)) = ((1, 1), (1, 1))$. To prove that $\boldsymbol{x}_{2S}$ is feasible for the two-stage robust UC model, we construct a feasible dispatch policy. In particular, for any $\boldsymbol{d} = ((d_A^1, d_B^1), (d_A^2, d_B^2)) \in \mathscr{D}$, consider the following policy:

$$p_A^1(\boldsymbol{d}) = 12 + (2/5)(d_A^2 - 12.5), \quad p_B^1(\boldsymbol{d}) = 12 - (2/5)(d_A^2 - 12.5), \tag{6.3.1a}$$

$$p_A^2(\boldsymbol{d}) = 12.5 + (3/5)(d_A^2 - 12.5), \quad p_B^2(\boldsymbol{d}) = 12.5 - (3/5)(d_A^2 - 12.5). \tag{6.3.1b}$$

From (6.3.1), we can see that for $t = 1$, $p_A^1(\boldsymbol{d}) + p_B^1(\boldsymbol{d}) = 24$ for all $\boldsymbol{d} \in \mathscr{D}$, so energy balance is respected. By the definition of the uncertainty sets, we have $p_A^1(\boldsymbol{d}), p_B^1(\boldsymbol{d}) \in [11, 13]$ for all $\boldsymbol{d} \in \mathscr{D}$, so the ramping constraints from the initial states ($\boldsymbol{p}^0 = (12, 12)$) are respected. Furthermore, $p_A^1(\boldsymbol{d}) - d_A^1 = p_A^1(\boldsymbol{d}) - 12 \in [-1, 1]$ for all $\boldsymbol{d} \in \mathscr{D}$, so transmission constraints are respected. Similarly for $t = 2$, we have $p_A^2(\boldsymbol{d}) + p_B^2(\boldsymbol{d}) = 25$ for all $\boldsymbol{d} \in \mathscr{D}$, so energy balance is satisfied. Since $d_A^2 \in [10, 15]$, we can see that $p_A^2(\boldsymbol{d}) - p_A^1(\boldsymbol{d}) = 0.5 + (1/5)(d_A^2 - 12.5) \in [0, 1]$ and $p_B^2(\boldsymbol{d}) - p_B^1(\boldsymbol{d}) = 0.5 - (1/5)(d_A^2 - 12.5) \in [0, 1]$, hence ramping constraints are respected. Finally, $p_A^2(\boldsymbol{d}) - d_A^2 = 5 - (2/5)d_A^2 \in [-1, 1]$, so transmission constraints are respected. Therefore, $\boldsymbol{p}(\boldsymbol{d})$ given in (6.3.1) satisfies all constraints in (6.2.2.1), thus $\boldsymbol{x}_{2S}$ is feasible for the two-stage robust UC model.

Notice that the dispatch policy (6.3.1) is non-causal, because the dispatch decision at $t = 1$ depends on the uncertainty realization at $t = 2$. If this UC solution is implemented, the real-time dispatch under this UC solution can be infeasible, as shown in the following result.

*Claim* Let $\boldsymbol{x}_{2S}^*$ be the optimal UC solution of the two-stage robust UC model for Example 6.1. Under $\boldsymbol{x}_{2S}^*$, there does not exist any feasible dispatch policy that respects time causality, i.e. where $\boldsymbol{p}^1(\cdot)$ does not depend on $\boldsymbol{d}^2$.

Notice that $\boldsymbol{x}_{2S}^* = ((x_A^1, x_B^1), (x_A^2, x_B^2)) = ((1, 1), (1, 1))$ is the optimal solution of the two-stage robust UC for the system in Example 6.1, since keeping both generators online is the only candidate solution to satisfy net load. Now consider the real-time sequential operation under this commitment decision $\boldsymbol{x}_{2S}^*$, where the causal dispatch policy at $t$ can only depend on the information available up to $t$. We want to show that there does not exist any causal dispatch policy that can make the system feasible for all net load vectors in the uncertainty set. For this, we need to show that there is no $\boldsymbol{p}^1(\boldsymbol{d}^1)$ such that, for all $\boldsymbol{d}^2 \in \mathscr{D}^2$, there always exists a feasible $\boldsymbol{p}^2(\boldsymbol{d}^1, \boldsymbol{d}^2)$ at $t = 2$.

Since $\boldsymbol{d}^1$ is fixed at (12, 12), we write $\boldsymbol{p}^1(\boldsymbol{d}^1)$ as $\boldsymbol{p}^1 = (p_A^1, p_B^1)$ for brevity. Notice that due to the energy balance constraint, we must have $p_A^1 + p_B^1 = 24$, and due to the ramping capacity and transmission constraints, we must have $p_A^1, p_B^1 \in [11, 13]$. Suppose we choose $p_A^1 \leq 12$. Then take $\boldsymbol{d}^2 = (15, 10)$ from the uncertainty set $\mathscr{D}^2$. Due to ramping constraints, we must have $p_A^2 \leq 13$. However, it is impossible to satisfy energy balance at location $A$, because the transmission limit is 1. Similarly, if we choose $p_A^1 \geq 12$, the adversary can take $\boldsymbol{d}^2 = (10, 15) \in \mathscr{D}^2$, which leads to the impossibility of satisfying net load at location $B$. This means that no matter what $\boldsymbol{p}^1$ we choose to satisfy the constraints at $t = 1$, there always exists a $\boldsymbol{d}^2 \in \mathscr{D}^2$ so that the constraints at $t = 2$ cannot be satisfied.

### 6.3.2 Multistage Robust UC Model

The above example shows that when the system ramping capability to meet load is constrained, we need to consider multistage robust optimization models. For the UC problem, the commitment decision $\boldsymbol{x}$ is made several hours before the observations of uncertain net loads, and then the dispatch decisions are sequentially optimized in real time with observations of realized uncertainty up to the operating hour. To faithfully model this process, the dispatch decision $\boldsymbol{p}^t$ at time $t$ in the UC model should depend on the history of net load $\boldsymbol{d}^{[t]} \triangleq (\boldsymbol{d}^1, \ldots, \boldsymbol{d}^t)$. Based on this requirement, we formulate the following multistage adaptive robust UC model.

$$\min_{\boldsymbol{x},\boldsymbol{u},\boldsymbol{v},\boldsymbol{p}(\cdot)} \left\{ \sum_{t\in\mathscr{T}} \sum_{i\in\mathscr{G}} \left(G_i x_i^t + S_i u_i^t\right) + \max_{\boldsymbol{d}\in\mathscr{D}} \sum_{t\in\mathscr{T}} \sum_{i\in\mathscr{G}} C_i\, p_i^t(\boldsymbol{d}^{[t]}) \right\} \tag{6.3.2a}$$

s.t. Constraints (6.2.1b)–(6.2.1e), (6.2.1n) for $(\boldsymbol{x}, \boldsymbol{u}, \boldsymbol{v})$,

$$p_i^{\min} x_i^t \leq p_i^t(\boldsymbol{d}^{[t]}) \leq p_i^{\max} x_i^t, \qquad \forall \boldsymbol{d} \in \mathscr{D},\ i \in \mathscr{G},\ t \in \mathscr{T}, \tag{6.3.2b}$$

$$p_i^t(\boldsymbol{d}^{[t]}) - p_i^{t-1}(\boldsymbol{d}^{[t-1]}) \leq RU_i x_i^{t-1} + SU_i u_i^t, \quad \forall \boldsymbol{d} \in \mathscr{D},\ i \in \mathscr{G},\ t \in \mathscr{T}, \tag{6.3.2c}$$

$$p_i^t(\boldsymbol{d}^{[t]}) - p_i^{t-1}(\boldsymbol{d}^{[t-1]}) \geq -RD_i x_i^t - SD_i v_i^t, \quad \forall \boldsymbol{d} \in \mathscr{D},\ i \in \mathscr{G},\ t \in \mathscr{T}, \tag{6.3.2d}$$

$$-f_l^{\max} \leq \boldsymbol{a}_l^T(\boldsymbol{B}^p \boldsymbol{p}^t(\boldsymbol{d}^{[t]}) - \boldsymbol{B}^d \boldsymbol{d}^t) \leq f_l^{\max}, \quad \forall \boldsymbol{d} \in \mathscr{D},\ t \in \mathscr{T},\ l \in \mathscr{N}_l, \tag{6.3.2e}$$

$$\sum_{i \in \mathscr{N}_g} p_i^t(\boldsymbol{d}^{[t]}) = \sum_{j \in \mathscr{N}_d} d_j^t, \quad \forall \boldsymbol{d} \in \mathscr{D},\ t \in \mathscr{T}. \tag{6.3.2f}$$

The crucial feature of this formulation is that the generation of unit $i$ at time $t$, $p_i^t(\boldsymbol{d}^{[t]})$, is a function of net load uncertainty realized up to time $t$, thus respecting non-anticipativity. The binary UC decisions $\boldsymbol{x}, \boldsymbol{u}, \boldsymbol{v}$ are not adaptive to uncertainty, since they are decided in the first stage before observing any uncertainty. Constraints (6.3.2b)–(6.3.2f) enforce generation limits, ramping capacities, transmission line capacities, and energy balance, for any realization of $\boldsymbol{d} \in \mathscr{D}$. The uncertainty $\mathscr{D}$ is defined in (6.2.2d). We have omitted security constraints and reserve for the simplicity of exposition.

As we discussed in Chap. 3, the multistage robust UC problem (6.3.2) is an optimization problem with functional decisions $p_i^t(\boldsymbol{d}^{[t]})$ in an infinite dimensional space, which makes (6.3.2) computationally intractable. There are two ways to approximate the multistage robust UC: (1) the nested decomposition approach introduced in Chap. 3, Sect. 3.3.3; (2) the linear decision rule approach introduced in Chap. 3, Sect. 3.3.4. In the following, we will discuss in detail the linear decision rule approach, simplifications to make it computationally efficient, and a cutting plane method to solve large-scale multistage robust UC.

### 6.3.3 Affine Multistage Robust UC

A linear decision rule is applied to the dispatch decision $\boldsymbol{p}^t(\cdot)$ as

$$p_i^t(\boldsymbol{d}^{[t]}) = w_i^t + \sum_{j \in \mathscr{N}_d} \sum_{s \in [1:t]} W_{itjs} d_j^s, \tag{6.3.3}$$

where $[1:t] \triangleq \{1, \ldots, t\}$ and $(w_i^t, W_{itjs})$ are the coefficients of the affine policy. It is important to notice that the affine policy (6.3.3) automatically respects non-anticipativity. Using this affine dispatch policy, the multistage robust UC model has the following form

$$\min_{\boldsymbol{x},\boldsymbol{u},\boldsymbol{v},z,\boldsymbol{w},\boldsymbol{W}} \quad \sum_{t \in \mathscr{T}} \sum_{i \in \mathscr{G}} (G_i x_i^t + S_i u_i^t) + z \tag{6.3.4a}$$

s.t. Constraints (6.2.1b)-(6.2.1e), (6.2.1n) for $(\boldsymbol{x}, \boldsymbol{u}, \boldsymbol{v})$,

$$\sum_{t\in\mathcal{T}}\sum_{i\in\mathcal{G}} c_i\left(w_i^t + \sum_{j\in\mathcal{N}_d}\sum_{s\in[1:t]} W_{itjs}d_j^s\right) \le z, \qquad \forall \boldsymbol{d}\in\mathcal{D}, \tag{6.3.4b}$$

$$p_i^{min}x_i^t \le w_i^t + \sum_{j\in\mathcal{N}_d}\sum_{s\in[1:t]} W_{itjs}d_j^s \le p_i^{max}x_i^t, \qquad \forall \boldsymbol{d}\in\mathcal{D},\ i\in\mathcal{G},\ t\in\mathcal{T}, \tag{6.3.4c}$$

$$\left(w_i^t + \sum_{j\in\mathcal{N}_d}\sum_{s\in[1:t]} W_{itjs}d_j^s\right) - \left(w_i^{t-1} + \sum_{j\in\mathcal{N}_d}\sum_{s\in[1:t-1]} W_{i,t-1,js}d_j^s\right) \ge -RD_ix_i^t - SD_iv_i^t, \qquad \forall \boldsymbol{d}\in\mathcal{D},\ i\in\mathcal{G},\ t\in\mathcal{T}, \tag{6.3.4d}$$

$$\left(w_i^t + \sum_{j\in\mathcal{N}_d}\sum_{s\in[1:t]} W_{itjs}d_j^s\right) - \left(w_i^{t-1} + \sum_{j\in\mathcal{N}_d}\sum_{s\in[1:t-1]} W_{i,t-1,js}d_j^s\right) \le RU_ix_i^{t-1} + SU_iu_i^t \qquad \forall \boldsymbol{d}\in\mathcal{D},\ i\in\mathcal{G},\ t\in\mathcal{T}, \tag{6.3.4e}$$

$$-f_l^{max} \le \sum_m\sum_{i\in\mathcal{N}_g} a_{lm}B_{mi}^p\left(w_i^t + \sum_{j\in\mathcal{N}_d}\sum_{s\in[1:t]} W_{itjs}d_j^s\right) - \sum_m\sum_{j\in\mathcal{N}_d} a_{lm}B_{mj}^d d_j^t \le f_l^{max}, \qquad \forall \boldsymbol{d}\in\mathcal{D},\ t\in\mathcal{T},\ l\in\mathcal{N}_l, \tag{6.3.4f}$$

$$\sum_{i\in\mathcal{N}_g}\left(w_i^t + \sum_{j\in\mathcal{N}_d}\sum_{s\in[1:t]} W_{itjs}d_j^s\right) = \sum_{j\in\mathcal{N}_d} d_j^t \qquad \forall \boldsymbol{d}\in\mathcal{D}, t\in\mathcal{T}. \tag{6.3.4g}$$

We have created variable $z$ to denote the worst-case dispatch cost in constraint (6.3.4b). Constraints (6.3.4c)–(6.3.4g) correspond to (6.3.2b)–(6.3.2f), obtained by replacing $p_i^t(\boldsymbol{d}^{[t]})$ with the affine policy (6.3.3). Note that constraints (6.3.4b)–(6.3.4g) are robust constraints that should hold for all $\boldsymbol{d}\in\mathcal{D}$. We call (6.3.4) the affine multistage robust UC model.

To make the affine multistage robust UC model (6.3.4) a practical decision tool for the operation of large-scale power systems, we introduce further restrictions on the affine policy form. In particular, we consider affine policies with *simplified* structures by limiting the degrees of freedom in $W_{itjs}$. There are several ways to do this: we can restrict $\boldsymbol{p}^t(\cdot)$ to only depend on the most recently revealed information at time $t$, rather than on the whole history; we can partition time periods into peak-load, medium-load, and low-load periods and assume affine policies in each period have the same form; we can also partition the transmission network into zones and make generators' dispatch policies depend on the aggregated load in each zone. We use the following two very simple policies:

$$p_i^t(\boldsymbol{d}^{[t]}) = w_i^t + W_i\sum_{j\in\mathcal{N}_d} d_j^t \qquad \forall i\in\mathcal{N}_g, t\in\mathcal{T} \tag{6.3.5}$$

$$p_i^t(\boldsymbol{d}^{[t]}) = w_i^t + W_{it}\sum_{j\in\mathcal{N}_d} d_j^t \qquad \forall i\in\mathcal{N}_g, t\in\mathcal{T}. \tag{6.3.6}$$

We call (6.3.5) the $W_i$-policy, where the coefficients $W_i$ of the affine policy only depend on generators but not on time, and the dispatch level of each generator at time $t$ depends on the total load in the system at time $t$. Equation (6.3.6) presents a finer policy, which we call the $W_{it}$-policy, where the coefficients $W_{it}$ of the affine policy can change over time. It is instructive to calculate the numbers of decision variables and constraints for the various affine decision rules (see Exercise 6.3.) Surprisingly, it will be shown that these two very simplified affine policies are already quite powerful and produce close-to-optimal performance for the multistage robust UC model.

### 6.3.4 A Constraint Generation Algorithm and Speed-Ups

Since the constraints in the affine multistage robust UC model (6.3.4) have the form that the left-hand side is a linear function in $\boldsymbol{d}$ and the uncertainty set $\mathscr{D}$ is a polytope, each robust constraint is thus equivalent to an enumeration of the finitely many extreme points of the uncertainty set, in the following form:

$$\boldsymbol{c}^\top \boldsymbol{d} \leq h \qquad \forall \boldsymbol{d} \in \text{ext}(\mathscr{D}), \tag{6.3.7}$$

where $\text{ext}(\mathscr{D}) = \{d_1^*, \ldots, d_N^*\}$ is the set of extreme points of $\mathscr{D}$ (cf. Chap. 2). This applies to every robust inequality in the affine multistage robust UC model. Furthermore, the energy balance equality constraint (6.3.4g) in the affine multistage robust UC model can be reformulated using the full-dimensionality of the uncertainty sets as follows

$$W_i - \text{Policy:} \quad (6.3.4\text{g}) \iff \sum_{i \in \mathscr{N}_g} w_i^t = 0, \quad \sum_{i \in \mathscr{N}_g} W_i = 1 \qquad \forall t \in \mathscr{T}, \tag{6.3.8}$$

$$W_{it} - \text{Policy:} \quad (6.3.4\text{g}) \iff \sum_{i \in \mathscr{N}_g} w_i^t = 0, \quad \sum_{i \in \mathscr{N}_g} W_{it} = 1 \quad \forall t \in \mathscr{T}. \tag{6.3.9}$$

Then, we can reformulate the multistage affine robust UC model (6.3.4) in the following compact form:

$$\min_{y \in Y} \quad f(\boldsymbol{y}) \tag{6.3.10a}$$

$$\text{s.t.} \quad g_k(\boldsymbol{y}, \boldsymbol{d}) \leq 0 \qquad \forall \boldsymbol{d} \in \text{ext}(\mathscr{D}), \quad \forall k \in \{1, \ldots, K\}, \tag{6.3.10b}$$

where $\boldsymbol{y} = (\boldsymbol{x}, \boldsymbol{u}, \boldsymbol{v}, \boldsymbol{w}, \boldsymbol{W}, z)$ includes all decision variables in (6.3.4), the objective $f(\boldsymbol{y})$ represents (6.3.4a), and the set $Y$ in (6.3.10a) is defined by (6.2.1b)–(6.2.1e), (6.2.1n), and (6.3.8) or (6.3.9) according to the policy structure used. Constraints

(6.3.10b) represent (6.3.4b)–(6.3.4f), where $g_k(\boldsymbol{y}, \boldsymbol{d})$ is a bilinear function in $\boldsymbol{y}$ and $\boldsymbol{d}$, and $K = 1+2T(2N_g + N_l)$ in (6.3.10b) is the total number of robust constraints. This reminds us of the problem (3.3.30) in Chap. 3, Sect. 3.3.4. Algorithm 6 introduced there can be specialized to the following constraint generation algorithm.

**Algorithm 1** Constraint generation for multistage robust UC

```
Start with some initial D_k for all k ∈ {1, ..., K}
repeat
    y' ← optimal solution of the Master Problem (6.3.10).
    for k ∈ {1, ..., K} do
        d_k ← argmax_{d∈𝒟} g_k(y', d)
        If g_k(y', d_k) > 0 let D_k ← D_k ∪ {d_k}
    end for
until g_k(y', d_k) ≤ 0 for all k ∈ {1, ..., K}
output: y' is an optimal solution to (6.3.10)
```

#### 6.3.4.1 Algorithmic Speed-Ups

**Fast Separation Oracle**

The separation oracle in the constraint generation algorithm involves solving the problem

$$\max_{\boldsymbol{d}\in\mathscr{D}} g_k(\boldsymbol{y}, \boldsymbol{d}) \tag{6.3.11}$$

for each robust constraint $k$ in (6.3.4), in each iteration of the master problem. Thus, it is important to solve it efficiently. We can exploit two special structures of (6.3.11). First, as discussed above, $g_k(\boldsymbol{y}, \boldsymbol{d})$ is a linear function in $\boldsymbol{d}$ for any fixed $\boldsymbol{y}$. Second, the structure of the budgeted uncertainty set allows us to solve the separation problem (6.3.11) by a simple sorting procedure, as we show below.

Consider the separation problem $\max_{\boldsymbol{d}\in\mathscr{D}} \boldsymbol{c}^\top \boldsymbol{d}$, where the uncertainty set $\mathscr{D}$ defined in (6.2.2d) is separable over time, i.e. the uncertainty set $\mathscr{D} = \mathscr{D}^1 \times \cdot \mathscr{D}^T$. An optimal solution for this problem is given by $(d_j^s)^* = \overline{d}_j^s + \Gamma \hat{d}_j^s (u_j^s)^*$ for each $s \in \mathscr{T}$, where $(u_j^s)^*$ is obtained by the following procedure: let $\{|c^s_{\sigma(j)}\, \hat{d}^s_{\sigma(j)}|\}_{j\in\mathscr{N}_d}$ be a nonincreasing ordering of $\{|c_j^s\, \hat{d}_j^s|\}_{j\in\mathscr{N}_d}$, where $\sigma(\cdot)$ determines the indices of the non-increasing order, and $(u_j^s)^*$ is given as follows:

$$(u^s_{\sigma(j)})^* = \begin{cases} \operatorname{sign}(c^s_{\sigma(j)}) & \text{if } \sigma(j) \le \lfloor\sqrt{N_d}\rfloor, \\ (\sqrt{N_d} - \lfloor\sqrt{N_d}\rfloor)\cdot \operatorname{sign}(c^s_{\sigma(j)}) & \text{if } \sigma(j) = \lfloor\sqrt{N_d}\rfloor + 1, \\ 0 & \text{if } \sigma(j) \ge \lfloor\sqrt{N_d}\rfloor + 2, \end{cases}$$

where $\text{sign}(x) = 1$ if $x \geq 0$ and $-1$ otherwise.

**Complete Characterization for the $W_{it}$-Policy**
Recall that the $W_{it}$-policy is described as $p_i^t(\boldsymbol{d}) = w_i^t + W_{it} \sum_{j \in \mathcal{N}_d} d_j^t$. Under the $W_{it}$-policy or any simpler policy, and using the uncertainty set in (6.2.2d) where the budget constraint over time periods is redundant, i.e. the uncertainty set $\mathcal{D} = \mathcal{D}^1 \times \cdot \mathcal{D}^T$. Then, the following statements hold:

(i) The robust constraints on generation limits (6.3.4c) are equivalent to the ones with the uncertainty set $\mathcal{D}$ replaced by the finite set $\{\boldsymbol{d}^t_{min}, \boldsymbol{d}^t_{max}\}$, where $\boldsymbol{d}_{min}$ and $\boldsymbol{d}_{max}$ are defined as

$$\boldsymbol{d}^t_{max} \in \text{argmax}_{\boldsymbol{d} \in \mathcal{D}} \sum_{j \in \mathcal{N}_d} d_j^t \quad \forall t \in \mathcal{T}, \tag{6.3.12}$$

$$\boldsymbol{d}^t_{min} \in \text{argmin}_{\boldsymbol{d} \in \mathcal{D}} \sum_{j \in \mathcal{N}_d} d_j^t \quad \forall t \in \mathcal{T}. \tag{6.3.13}$$

(ii) The robust constraints on ramping limits (6.3.4d)–(6.3.4e) at time $t$ are equivalent to the ones with the uncertainty set $\mathcal{D}$ replaced by the finite set $\{\boldsymbol{d}_{min}, \boldsymbol{d}_{max}, \boldsymbol{d}_{minmax}(t), \boldsymbol{d}_{maxmin}(t)\}$, where $\boldsymbol{d}_{minmax}(t)$ and $\boldsymbol{d}_{maxmin}(t)$ are defined as

$$\boldsymbol{d}_{minmax}(t) = \left(\boldsymbol{d}^1_{min}, \ldots, \boldsymbol{d}^{t-1}_{min}, \boldsymbol{d}^t_{max}, \ldots, \boldsymbol{d}^T_{max}\right), \tag{6.3.14}$$

$$\boldsymbol{d}_{maxmin}(t) = \left(\boldsymbol{d}^1_{max}, \ldots, \boldsymbol{d}^{t-1}_{max}, \boldsymbol{d}^t_{min}, \ldots, \boldsymbol{d}^T_{min}\right), \tag{6.3.15}$$

This result implies that if we use the $W_{it}$-policy or any simpler policy such as the $W_i$-policy, the robust constraints corresponding to generation output limits and ramping capacities can be pre-computed before starting the constraint generation process. The only robust constraints left to deal with using constraint generation are the worst-case dispatch cost constraint (6.3.4b) and the transmission constraints (6.3.4f). This saves a tremendous amount of time checking feasibility and generating violated constraints. The overall convergence time of the constraint generation algorithm is significantly reduced.

### 6.3.5 Computational Experiments

We conduct extensive computational experiments on the IEEE 118-bus and the 2736-bus Polish systems (c.f. [29]). The major aspects of these instances are summarized in Table 6.3. In all cases, the UC problems involve a planning horizon of $T = 24$ h. Uncertain net loads are located at every node with electricity demand. The uncertainty sets are given below

**Table 6.3** Summary of test cases used

| Buses | 118 | 2736 |
|---|---|---|
| Units | 54 | 289 |
| Loads | 99 | 2011 |
| Lines | 186 | 100 |
| Total generation capacity (MW) | 7106 | 28,880 |
| Min total nominal net load (MW) | 3327 | 10,851 |
| Max total nominal net load (MW) | 4931 | 18,075 |

$$\mathscr{D} := \left\{ \boldsymbol{d} \in \mathbb{R}^{N_d \times T} : \sum_{i \in \mathcal{N}_d} \frac{|d_i^t - \bar{d}_i^t|}{\hat{d}_i^t} \leq \Delta\sqrt{N_d}, d_i^t \in [\bar{d}_i^t - \hat{d}_i^t, \bar{d}_i^t + \hat{d}_i^t], \forall i \in \mathcal{N}_d, \ t \in \mathscr{T} \right\}, \tag{6.3.16}$$

where we choose $\hat{d}_j^t = 0.1\overline{d}_j^t$ with various budget levels $\Gamma$, unless stated otherwise. All the experiments have been implemented using Python 2.7 in a PC laptop with an Intel Core i5 at 2.4 GHz and 4GB memory with CPLEX 12.5 as MIP and LP solver.

#### 6.3.5.1 Optimality Gap for Simplified Affine Policies

The two-stage robust UC formulation (6.2.2.1) is a relaxation of the multistage robust UC model (6.3.2) by ignoring non-anticipativity on dispatch decisions. Thus, the optimal objective value of the two-stage robust UC problem, denoted as $v_{2S}^*$, provides a *lower* bound to the optimal objective value of the multistage robust UC, denoted as $v_{MS}^*$. However, obtaining a globally optimal solution of the two-stage robust UC problem for large-scale power systems is still computationally challenging as we discussed in Chap. 3. To reduce computation time, we employ the heuristic used by Lorca and Sun [8], which generates a *lower* bound to $v_{2S}^*$, denoted as $\underline{v}_{2S}$. Furthermore, since the affine policy is an approximation to the optimal policy for the multistage robust UC problem, its optimal objective value, denoted as $v_{AFF}^*$, provides an *upper* bound to the optimal objective value of the multistage robust UC model. Because the MIP solver is terminated within a certain accuracy (e.g. with a 0.1% MIP gap), the solution at termination gives a further upper bound to $v_{AFF}^*$, denoted as $\overline{v}_{AFF}$. In summary, we have the following relations between objective values of different solutions: $\underline{v}_{2S} \leq v_{2S}^* \leq v_{MS}^* \leq v_{AFF}^* \leq \overline{v}_{AFF}$. Then, the optimality gap between $v_{AFF}^*$ and $v_{MS}^*$, i.e., $(v_{AFF}^* - v_{MS}^*)/v_{MS}^*$, is upper bounded as

$$0 \leq \frac{v_{AFF}^* - v_{MS}^*}{v_{MS}^*} \leq \frac{\overline{v}_{AFF} - \underline{v}_{2S}}{\underline{v}_{2S}} \triangleq \text{Guaranteed Optimality Gap}.$$

We call the upper bound to the optimality gap the *guaranteed optimality gap* of the affine multistage robust UC problem.

**Table 6.4** Guaranteed opt. gap under different policy structures ("inf" indicates infeasibility)

| Policy | $\Gamma = 0.25$ | $\Gamma = 0.5$ | $\Gamma = 1$ | $\Gamma = 1.5$ | $\Gamma = 2$ | $\Gamma = 3$ | $\Gamma = 4$ |
|---|---|---|---|---|---|---|---|
| *118-bus system* | | | | | | | |
| $W_i$ | 0.04% | 0.02% | 0.04% | 0.08% | 0.10% | 0.26% | 0.67% |
| $W_{it}$ | 0.04% | 0.02% | 0.03% | 0.07% | 0.07% | 0.17% | 0.35% |
| *2736-bus system* | | | | | | | |
| $W_i$ | 0.09% | 0.22% | 0.42% | 0.55% | 1.05% | inf | inf |
| $W_{it}$ | 0.07% | 0.11% | 0.25% | 0.35% | 0.53% | 0.94% | inf |

Table 6.4 presents the guaranteed optimality gaps of two simple affine policy structures for the 118-bus and 2736-bus systems with different values of the uncertainty set size parameter $\Gamma$.

From these results, we offer the following observations.

1. For each test system, the $W_{it}$-policy achieves a better guaranteed optimality gap than the $W_i$ policy, especially for larger uncertainty sets. For example, for the 2736-bus system with $\Gamma = 2$, the guaranteed optimality gap is improved from 1.05% of the $W_i$-policy to 0.53% by the $W_{it}$-policy. For smaller uncertainty sets, the $W_i$-policy has a more comparable performance to the $W_{it}$-policy.
2. The simple $W_{it}$-policy achieves surprisingly good performance in both test cases. The guaranteed optimality gap is at most 0.94% for all sizes of uncertainty sets in both test systems. Due to its strong performance and computational tractability, we will use the $W_{it}$-policy in all the following experiments.

#### 6.3.5.2 Worst-Case Performance Analysis

We will further study how much infeasibility can be caused in the real-time dispatch under the unit commitment solutions of the two-stage robust UC model vs the multistage robust UC model. For this purpose, the two-stage model is solved for different sizes of the uncertainty sets, then the obtained UC solutions are fed into the affine multistage robust model (6.3.4). That is, the UC decision in (6.3.4) is fixed at the two-stage UC solution, and the remaining affine multistage robust dispatch problem is solved. In this way, we can compare the worst-case operational costs (including penalty costs) of the real-time dispatch under the two-stage robust UC solutions against those obtained under the affine multistage robust UC solutions. It is important to carry out this type of worst-case performance study of the real-time dispatch under different UC solutions, because power system operations require extremely high reliability. Infeasibility in real-time operation has to be resolved by starting expensive fast-start units or shedding load, both of which bear significant economic consequences.

Table 6.5 presents the results. "Total Cost" is the worst-case dispatch cost plus penalty cost of the affine multistage robust dispatch model under a specific UC solution. "Penalty" is the total penalty cost associated with constraint violations in

**Table 6.5** Worst-case cost (US$) of multistage robust dispatch under the two-stage and multistage UC solutions. Multistage models use the $W_{it}$-policy

| | $\Gamma = 0.5$ | $\Gamma = 1$ | $\Gamma = 1.5$ | $\Gamma = 2$ | $\Gamma = 3$ |
|---|---|---|---|---|---|
| *118-bus system* | | | | | |
| Affine multistage UC solutions | | | | | |
| Total cost | 1,696,304 | 1,725,470 | 1,755,398 | 1,784,543 | 1,845,218 |
| Penalty | 0 | 0 | 0 | 0 | 0 |
| Two-stage UC solutions | | | | | |
| Total cost | 1,696,456 | 1,749,766 | 1,797,503 | 1,897,212 | 3,005,290 |
| Penalty | 0 | 52,501 | 55,268 | 196,101 | 1,229,300 |
| Rel diff. | 0.01% | 1.41% | 2.40% | 6.31% | 62.87% |
| *2736-bus system* | | | | | |
| Affine multistage UC solutions | | | | | |
| Total cost | 9,445,069 | 9,596,788 | 9,746,685 | 9,905,527 | 10,234,459 |
| Penalty | 0 | 0 | 0 | 0 | 0 |
| Two-stage UC solutions | | | | | |
| Total cost | 9,505,651 | 9,745,889 | 10,183,433 | 10,975,403 | 12,864,719 |
| Penalty | 96,313 | 224,952 | 591,661 | 1,165,324 | 2,703,522 |
| Rel diff. | 0.64% | 1.55% | 4.49% | 10.80% | 25.70% |

the dispatch model, where \$5000/MW is used as the unit penalty cost. "Rel Diff" is the relative difference between the total costs obtained by the multistage and two-stage UC solutions. We can make the following observations.

1. The multistage UC solutions do not cause any infeasibility in real-time operation for $\Gamma \leq 3$, whereas even though the two-stage UC model is feasible in itself for both 118-bus and 2736-bus systems, its UC solutions cause infeasibility to the multistage robust dispatch and incur quite significant penalties in the real-time operation.
2. The penalty costs and the total costs of the two-stage UC solutions increase as the size of the uncertainty set grows. For the 118-bus system, the two-stage model has 62.87% more total cost than the multistage model at $\Gamma = 3$, and the penalty cost is over \$1.2 M. For the 2736-bus system, the two-stage UC model incurs 25.70% more total cost than the multistage model at $\Gamma = 3$, and the absolute amount of penalty cost exceeds \$2.7 M.

These results further demonstrate the importance of non-anticipative constraints and the multistage robust UC model in power system operations.

#### 6.3.5.3 Average Performance

In this section, we study the average performance of different UC solutions and their impact on real-time dispatch. We develop a rolling-horizon simulation program to mimic the real time operation of the power system, where information about uncertain net load is revealed sequentially as time moves forward. In this program, we conduct Monte-Carlo simulations of different economic dispatch (ED) models that are suitable for the associated UC solution concepts. In particular, we propose a new robust ED model that exploits the affine policy obtained from the multistage robust UC model. For the two-stage robust UC and the deterministic UC solutions, we use a multi-period ("look-ahead") deterministic ED model in simulation, which has started to be adopted in some ISO markets, however, the most prevalent dispatch scheme in practice is still the single-period ED model ([17, Table 4], [18].)

**Efficient Robust Dispatch Model Leveraging Affine Policy**
Leveraging the multistage robust UC with affine policy, we introduce an efficient robust dispatch model. At each time $t$, the dispatch decision $\boldsymbol{p}^t$ is the first-stage decision, which satisfies all the dispatch constraints $\Omega_t(\boldsymbol{x}, \boldsymbol{d}^t, \boldsymbol{p}^{t-1})$ in the current period and will be implemented "right now" at time $t$. Furthermore, the efficient robust ED model also considers the next period's dispatch decision $\boldsymbol{p}^{t+1}$ and assumes that it takes the form of the affine policy with coefficients $(w_i^{t+1}, \boldsymbol{W}_i^{t+1})$ of time $t+1$ obtained from the day-ahead affine multistage robust UC model.

$$\min_{\boldsymbol{p}^t} \quad \sum_{i \in \mathcal{N}_g} C_i p_i^t \tag{6.3.17a}$$

$$\text{s.t.} \quad \boldsymbol{p}^t \in \Omega_t(\boldsymbol{x}, \boldsymbol{d}^t, \boldsymbol{p}^{t-1}) \tag{6.3.17b}$$

$$w_i^{t+1} + \boldsymbol{W}_i^{t+1}\boldsymbol{d}^{t+1} - p_i^t \geq -RD_i x_i^{t+1} - SD_i v_i^{t+1} \quad \forall \boldsymbol{d}^{t+1} \in \mathscr{D}^{t+1} \tag{6.3.17c}$$

$$w_i^{t+1} + \boldsymbol{W}_i^{t+1}\boldsymbol{d}^{t+1} - p_i^t \leq RU_i x_i^t + SU_i u_i^{t+1} \quad \forall \boldsymbol{d}^{t+1} \in \mathscr{D}^{t+1}. \tag{6.3.17d}$$

Here, $\Omega_t(\boldsymbol{x}, \boldsymbol{d}^t, \boldsymbol{p}^{t-1})$ includes all the dispatch related constraints in the deterministic UC model (6.2.1) at time $t$, with the observed values of the current period's net load vector $\boldsymbol{d}^t$ and the previous period's dispatch level $\boldsymbol{p}^{t-1}$. Constraints (6.3.17d) and (6.3.17c) enforce ramping limits between $\boldsymbol{p}^t$ and $\boldsymbol{p}^{t+1}$ for any realization of nodal net loads in the uncertainty set at time $t+1$. In this way, the proposed dispatch model coordinates the ramping capabilities in the two consecutive periods and hedges against unfavorable net load realizations in future periods.

**Results for the 2736-Bus System with Persistent Demand and Temporally Correlated Wind Data**
In the previous simulations, we sampled demand from specific distributions, first assuming temporal independence and then incorporating temporal correlations through an autoregressive model. However, in power systems with a high penetration of wind power, most of the uncertainty in net loads stems from the intermittency of wind power outputs, and we would like to study the performance of our approach under more realistic net load trajectories for such power systems. For this purpose,

we added 140 wind farms to the 2736-bus system, with each wind farm located at a different load bus, making use of one year of wind power output data from 140 locations of NREL's Western Wind Integration Dataset [19, 20]. The average hourly total wind power output is 1051 MW, which corresponds to 7.37% of average hourly total demand.

For each of these 24 h trajectories we also consider demand generated from a persistent model [21], which exhibits some simple temporal correlation. In particular, we sample the trajectory of demand at bus $j$ from the following autoregressive model:

$$\widetilde{d}_j^t = \mu_j^t + \sigma_j^t Z_j^t \quad \forall t \in \mathscr{T}$$

$$Z_j^t = \phi Z_j^{t-1} + \epsilon_j^t \quad \forall t \in \mathscr{T},$$

where the $\epsilon_j^t$'s are sampled independently from a normal distribution with an expected value of 0 and a standard deviation of $\sigma^\epsilon = \sqrt{1-\phi^2}$, and $Z_j^0$ is sampled from a normal distribution with an expected value of 0 and a standard deviation of 1. The value of $\sigma^\epsilon$ is selected so that the standard deviation of $Z_j^t$ is always 1. Further, $\sigma_j^t = 0.1\mu_j^t$. Given this, $\widetilde{d}_j^t$ has an expected value of $\mu_j^t$ and a standard deviation of $0.1\mu_j^t$, and the correlation between $\widetilde{d}_j^t$ and $\widetilde{d}_j^{t-1}$ is $\phi$. In the uncertainty set, we take $\overline{d}_j^t = \mu_j^t$ and $\hat{d}_j^t = \sigma_j^t = 0.1\mu_j^t$. The setting in previous sections corresponds to the case $\phi = 0$. In this section we use $\phi = 0.9$ denoting a strong temporal correlation in demand.

When building the uncertainty set for robust UC, we select $\overline{d}_j^t$ as the nominal value for net load at bus $j$ and time $t$, calculated as the expected demand minus the expected wind power output, and $\hat{d}_j^t$ as the standard deviation of net load, calculated as $\sqrt{\sigma_{demand,tj}^2 + \sigma_{wind,tj}^2}$, assuming independence between demand and wind power output.

Table 6.6 presents simulation performance results under the temporally correlated wind power data described above, and with demand sampled from the persistent model. The best average cost is still achieved at $\Gamma = 1$ for the multistage robust UC, at $\Gamma = 2$ for the two-stage robust UC, and at 30% reserve for the deterministic UC, with the multistage robust UC achieving a 1.23% and 24.52% reduction in average cost, with respect to the two-stage robust UC and deterministic UC, respectively. We can also observe that under $\Gamma = 3$ the multistage robust UC does not completely eliminate the penalty cost, but achieves a significant reduction as compared to the other models, with a penalty frequency average of 0.01% as compared to 2.07% for the two-stage robust UC under $\Gamma = 2$ and 15.03% for the deterministic UC under 30% reserve (which respectively achieve their minimum penalties). All of these experiments on a large-scale power system demonstrate that the multistage UC model together with the proposed robust ED approach can dominate the performance of the two-stage robust UC and the deterministic UC models with look-ahead ED in terms of both average cost and system reliability.

**Table 6.6** Simulation performance of the different models for the 2736-bus system with wind power and persistent demand

| $\Gamma$ | 0.25 | 0.5 | 1 | 1.5 | 2 | 3 |
|---|---|---|---|---|---|---|
| *Affine multistage robust UC with policy-enforcement robust ED* | | | | | | |
| Cost avg. ($) | 10,996,931 | 9,459,785 | 8,502,923 | 8,581,532 | 8,646,665 | 9,415,693 |
| Cost std. ($) | 3,665,301 | 2,007,317 | 490,457 | 466,999 | 424,801 | 458,865 |
| Penalty cost avg. ($) | 2,679,299 | 1,110,032 | 101,234 | 81,834 | 27,344 | 218 |
| Penalty freq avg. | 18.84% | 14.44% | 1.67% | 0.47% | 0.18% | 0.01% |
| *Two-stage robust UC with look-ahead ED* | | | | | | |
| Cost avg. ($) | 10,390,214 | 11,365,568 | 8,734,840 | 8,863,975 | 8,609,160 | 8,947,959 |
| Cost std. ($) | 1,831,279 | 1,059,427 | 620,301 | 802,441 | 522,881 | 793,447 |
| Penalty cost avg. ($) | 2,064,045 | 1,032,109 | 380,451 | 490,562 | 195,681 | 443,401 |
| Penalty freq avg. | 12.73% | 3.68% | 7.37% | 5.19% | 2.07% | 2.66% |
| Reserve | 2.5% | 5% | 10% | 15% | 20% | 30% |
| *Deterministic UC with reserve and look-ahead ED* | | | | | | |
| Cost avg. ($) | 13,186,705 | 14,272,477 | 13,110,030 | 13,617,194 | 11,879,817 | 11,248,546 |
| Cost std. ($) | 5,557,309 | 7,023,964 | 5,596,039 | 6,082,173 | 4,095,780 | 3,113,902 |
| Penalty cost avg. ($) | 4,905,635 | 6,003,861 | 4,827,766 | 5,334,746 | 3,578,986 | 2,912,186 |
| Penalty freq avg. | 30.45% | 29.94% | 33.00% | 32.43% | 23.61% | 15.03% |

## 6.4 Rolling-Horizon Robust Economic Dispatch with Dynamic Uncertainty Sets

In the previous sections, we discussed in details robust UC models for day-ahead planning. There is also a great amount of interest to improve the real-time economic dispatch in practice; in particular, as wind and solar generation increases rapidly, system operators need new tools to deal with the increasing uncertainty in the real-time operation. The existing robust UC and ED models have used similar types of uncertainty sets, which we call *static* uncertainty sets. It is important to consider uncertainty sets that could capture the highly dynamical and correlated variable resources such as wind and solar power.

### 6.4.1 Dynamic Uncertainty Sets

The budget uncertainty set that we have applied in the robust UC models has the following form

$$\mathscr{D}_t = \left\{ \boldsymbol{d}_t : \sum_{j \in \mathscr{N}^d} \frac{|d_{jt} - \overline{d}_{jt}|}{\hat{d}_{jt}} \le \Gamma^d \sqrt{N^d},\ d_{jt} \in [\overline{d}_{jt} - \hat{d}_{jt}, \overline{d}_{jt} + \hat{d}_{jt}],\ \forall\, j \in \mathscr{N}^d \right\}, \tag{6.4.1}$$

which we call a *static* uncertainty set, because the uncertainty at time $t$ is *independent* of those in earlier periods. That is, the dynamics of uncertainty evolution over time is not explicitly captured. In the budget uncertainty set (6.2.2d), we imposed a budget constraint over all time periods, which couples uncertainty between time periods and uncertain sources, however, similar to (6.4.1), it still does not directly characterize the temporal and spatial correlations of uncertainty; also, by coupling through the entire horizon, the realization of uncertainty breaks the time causality with past depending on the future realization. Another drawback of the static uncertainty sets (6.2.2d) or (6.4.1) is that uncertain sources of different nature are treated indistinguishably. For example, the uncertainty of wind power output should be treated differently from those of the conventional loads.

#### 6.4.1.1 Definition of Dynamic Uncertainty Sets

To explicitly model the temporal and spatial correlations of multiple uncertain sources over time and space, we propose the following general form of uncertainty sets, called **dynamic uncertainty sets**. For each time $t$,

$$\Xi_t(\boldsymbol{\xi}_{[1:t-1]}) = \left\{\boldsymbol{\xi}_t : \exists \boldsymbol{u}_{[t]} \text{ s.t. } f(\boldsymbol{\xi}_{[t]}, \boldsymbol{u}_{[t]}) \leq \mathbf{0}\right\}, \tag{6.4.2}$$

where $\boldsymbol{\xi}_{[t_1:t_2]} \triangleq (\boldsymbol{\xi}_{t_1}, \ldots, \boldsymbol{\xi}_{t_2})$ and $\boldsymbol{\xi}_{[t]} \triangleq \boldsymbol{\xi}_{[1:t]}$. In (6.4.2), the uncertainty vector $\boldsymbol{\xi}_t$ explicitly depends on uncertainty at stages before time $t$ and the $\boldsymbol{u}$'s are auxiliary variables. To be computationally tractable, $f(\boldsymbol{\xi}_{[t]}, \boldsymbol{u}_{[t]})$ is a vector of semidefinite representable convex functions that are used to characterize the dynamics of uncertainty evolution.

#### 6.4.1.2 Constructing Dynamic Uncertainty Sets for Wind Power

In this section, we present a specific method to construct a dynamic uncertainty set for wind power using linear functions for $f$. The key idea is to integrate time series models within dynamic uncertainty sets. We denote the wind speed vector of multiple wind farms at time $t$ as $\boldsymbol{r}_t = (r_{1t}, \ldots, r_{N^w t})$, where $r_{it}$ is the wind speed at wind farm $i$ and time $t$. Define the dynamic uncertainty set for *wind speed* $\boldsymbol{r}_t$ as:

$$\mathscr{R}_t(\boldsymbol{r}_{[t-L:t-1]}) = \Big\{\boldsymbol{r}_t : \exists \widetilde{\boldsymbol{r}}_{[t-L:t]},\ \boldsymbol{u}_t \quad \text{s.t.}$$

$$\boldsymbol{r}_\tau = \boldsymbol{g}_\tau + \widetilde{\boldsymbol{r}}_\tau, \quad \forall \tau = t-L, \ldots, t, \tag{6.4.3a}$$

$$\widetilde{\boldsymbol{r}}_t = \sum_{s=1}^{L} \boldsymbol{A}_s \widetilde{\boldsymbol{r}}_{t-s} + \boldsymbol{B}\boldsymbol{u}_t, \tag{6.4.3b}$$

$$\sum_{i \in \mathcal{N}^w} |u_{it}| \leq \Gamma^w \sqrt{N^w}, \tag{6.4.3c}$$

$$|u_{it}| \leq \Gamma^w, \qquad \forall i \in \mathcal{N}^w, \tag{6.4.3d}$$

$$\boldsymbol{r}_t \geq \boldsymbol{0}\Big\}, \tag{6.4.3e}$$

where vectors $\boldsymbol{r}_{t-L}, \ldots, \boldsymbol{r}_{t-1}$ are the realizations of wind speeds in periods $t - L, \ldots, t-1$. Equation (6.4.3a) decomposes wind speed vector $\boldsymbol{r}_\tau$ as the sum of a seasonal pattern $\boldsymbol{g}_\tau$, which is pre-estimated from wind data, and a residual component $\widetilde{\boldsymbol{r}}_\tau$ which is the deviation from $\boldsymbol{g}_\tau$. Equation (6.4.3b) is the key equation that represents a linear dynamic relationship involving the residual $\widetilde{\boldsymbol{r}}_t$ at time $t$, residuals realized in earlier periods $t-L$ to $t-1$, and an error term $\boldsymbol{u}_t$. The parameter $L$ sets the relevant time lags. In Eq. (6.4.3b), matrices $\boldsymbol{A}_s$'s capture the temporal correlation between $\boldsymbol{r}_t$ and $\boldsymbol{r}_{t-s}$, and $\boldsymbol{B}$ specifically captures the spatial relationship of wind speeds at adjacent wind farms at time $t$. Equation (6.4.3c)–(6.4.3d) describe a budgeted uncertainty set for the error term $\boldsymbol{u}_t$, where $\Gamma^w$ controls its size, and (6.4.3e) avoids negative wind speeds. $\mathcal{N}^w$ and $N^w$ denote the set and number of wind farms, respectively.

Using the above uncertainty sets (6.4.3) for wind speeds, we can further construct dynamic uncertainty sets for wind power through power curve approximations. In particular, we denote the *available wind power* of wind farm $i$ at time $t$ as $\overline{p}^w_{it}$. Given the wind speed $r_{it}$, $\overline{p}^w_{it}$ is described by the following constraints

$$\overline{p}^w_{it} \geq h^0_{ik} + h_{ik} r_{it} \quad \forall i \in \mathcal{N}^g,\ k = 1, \ldots, K, \tag{6.4.4}$$

where parameters $h^0_{ik}$, $h_{ik}$ are determined based on a convex piecewise linear approximation with $K$ pieces of the increasing part of the power curve at wind farm $i$ (in our experiments, we use the power curve of GE 1.5 MW wind turbine to approximate the aggregated output of a wind farm). Although (6.4.4) allows available wind power to exceed $\max_k\{h^0_{ik} + h_{ik} r_{it}\}$, the robust optimization model described below always ensures that the available wind power lies on the power curve including the plateau part for wind speed exceeding a cut-off value.

The dynamic uncertainty set of the available *wind power* $\overline{\boldsymbol{p}}^w_t$ is thus defined as

$$\overline{\mathcal{P}}^w_t(\boldsymbol{r}_{[t-L:t-1]}) = \Big\{\overline{\boldsymbol{p}}^w_t : \exists \boldsymbol{r}_t \in \mathcal{R}_t(\boldsymbol{r}_{[t-L:t-1]}) \text{ s.t. (6.4.4) is satisfied}\Big\}, \tag{6.4.5}$$

based on which we can define the uncertainty set for the trajectory of available wind power in time periods 2 through $T$, namely $\overline{\boldsymbol{p}}^w = (\overline{\boldsymbol{p}}^w_2, \ldots, \overline{\boldsymbol{p}}^w_T)$, as

$$\overline{\mathcal{P}}^w = \Big\{(\overline{\boldsymbol{p}}^w_2, \ldots, \overline{\boldsymbol{p}}^w_T) : \exists(\boldsymbol{r}_2, \ldots, \boldsymbol{r}_T) \text{ s.t. } \boldsymbol{r}_t \in \mathcal{R}_t(\boldsymbol{r}_{[t-L:t-1]}) \text{ and (6.4.4) for } t = 2, \ldots, T\Big\}. \tag{6.4.6}$$

### 6.4.2 A Rolling Horizon Robust Dispatch Model

Now we propose a two-stage robust optimization model for the multi-period economic dispatch (ED) problem. In particular, the ED problem with $T$ time periods is formulated in the following way. The first-stage of the robust ED model comprises the current time period $t = 1$, while the second-stage comprises future time periods $t = 2, \ldots, T$. In the first-stage, the decision maker observes the demand and the available wind power at the current time period, and determines the dispatch solution, which will be implemented right away for time $t = 1$. Given the first-stage decision, the second-stage of the robust ED model computes the worst-case dispatch cost for the remaining time periods in the dispatch horizon. The overall robust ED model minimizes the total cost of dispatch at the current time period and the worst-case dispatch cost over the future periods.

The two-stage robust multi-period ED model is formulated as follows,

$$\min_{\boldsymbol{x} \in \Omega_1^{det}} \left\{ \boldsymbol{c}^\top \boldsymbol{x} + \max_{\boldsymbol{d} \in \mathscr{D}, \overline{\boldsymbol{p}}^w \in \overline{\mathscr{P}}^w} \min_{\boldsymbol{y} \in \Omega(\boldsymbol{x}, \boldsymbol{d}, \overline{\boldsymbol{p}}^w)} \boldsymbol{b}^\top \boldsymbol{y} \right\}, \tag{6.4.7}$$

where $\boldsymbol{x} = (\boldsymbol{p}_1^g, \boldsymbol{p}_1^w)$ as the vector of first-stage dispatch decisions, composed of generation of thermal units $(\boldsymbol{p}_1^g)$ and wind farms $(\boldsymbol{p}_1^w)$. Note that we allow wind generation to be dispatchable. The uncertainty includes both conventional load $\boldsymbol{d} = (\boldsymbol{d}_2, \ldots, \boldsymbol{d}_T) \in \mathscr{D}$ described by (6.4.1) and the available wind power $\overline{\boldsymbol{p}}^w = (\overline{\boldsymbol{p}}_2^w, \ldots, \overline{\boldsymbol{p}}_T^w) \in \overline{\mathscr{P}}^w$ described by the dynamic uncertainty set (6.4.6). The second-stage decisions are dispatch solutions $\boldsymbol{y} = \left(\boldsymbol{p}_t^g, \boldsymbol{p}_t^w, \forall t = 2, \ldots, T\right)$.

The feasible region $\Omega_1^{det}$ of the first-stage decision variables corresponds to the constraints of a single-period dispatch problem, that is

$$\Omega_1^{det} = \Big\{ \boldsymbol{x} = (\boldsymbol{p}_1^g, \boldsymbol{p}_1^w) : \underline{p}_{i1}^g \le p_{i1}^g \le \overline{p}_{i1}^g \quad \forall i \in \mathscr{N}^g \tag{6.4.8a}$$

$$0 \le p_{i1}^w \le p_i^{w,max} \quad \forall i \in \mathscr{N}^w \tag{6.4.8b}$$

$$p_{i1}^w \le \overline{p}_{i1}^{w,det} \quad \forall i \in \mathscr{N}^w \tag{6.4.8c}$$

$$-RD_i^g \le p_{i1}^g - p_{i0}^g \le RU_i^g \quad \forall i \in \mathscr{N}^g \tag{6.4.8d}$$

$$-RD_i^w \le p_{i1}^w - p_{i0}^w \le RU_i^w \quad \forall i \in \mathscr{N}^w \tag{6.4.8e}$$

$$\left| \boldsymbol{a}_l^\top (\boldsymbol{B}^p \boldsymbol{p}_1^g + \boldsymbol{B}^w \boldsymbol{p}_1^w - \boldsymbol{B}^d \boldsymbol{d}_1^{det}) \right| \le f_l^{max} \; \forall l \in \mathscr{N}^l \tag{6.4.8f}$$

$$\sum_{i \in \mathscr{N}^g} p_{i1}^g + \sum_{i \in \mathscr{N}^w} p_{i1}^w = \sum_{j \in \mathscr{N}^d} d_{j1}^{det} \Big\}, \tag{6.4.8g}$$

where these constraints have the same form and meaning as those in the UC model (6.3.2), except that the UC decision is fixed and implicit now.

The constraints in the second-stage problem are parameterized by the first-stage decision variables and uncertain parameters realized in the uncertainty sets. The feasible region of the second-stage dispatch decision $\boldsymbol{y} = \left(\boldsymbol{p}_t^g, \boldsymbol{p}_t^w, \forall t = 2, \ldots, T\right)$ is defined as

$$\Omega(\boldsymbol{x}, \boldsymbol{d}, \overline{\boldsymbol{p}}^w) = \Bigg\{ \boldsymbol{y} : \text{ s.t. } \forall t = 2, \ldots, T$$

$$\underline{p}_{it}^g \le p_{it}^g \le \overline{p}_{it}^g \quad \forall i \in \mathcal{N}^g, \tag{6.4.9a}$$

$$0 \le p_{it}^w \le p_i^{w,max} \quad \forall i \in \mathcal{N}^w, \tag{6.4.9b}$$

$$p_{it}^w \le \overline{p}_{it}^w \quad \forall i \in \mathcal{N}^w, \tag{6.4.9c}$$

$$-RD_i^g \le p_{it}^g - p_{i,t-1}^g \le RU_i^g \quad \forall i \in \mathcal{N}^g, \tag{6.4.9d}$$

$$-RD_i^w \le p_{it}^w - p_{i,t-1}^w \le RU_i^w \quad \forall i \in \mathcal{N}^w, \tag{6.4.9e}$$

$$\left| \boldsymbol{a}_l^\top (\boldsymbol{B}^p \boldsymbol{p}_t^g + \boldsymbol{B}^w \boldsymbol{p}_t^w - \boldsymbol{B}^d \boldsymbol{d}_t) \right| \le f_l^{max} \; \forall l \in \mathcal{N}^l \tag{6.4.9f}$$

$$\sum_{i \in \mathcal{N}^g} p_{it}^g + \sum_{i \in \mathcal{N}^w} p_{it}^w = \sum_{j \in \mathcal{N}^d} d_{jt} \Bigg\}, \tag{6.4.9g}$$

where (6.4.9a)–(6.4.9g) are similar constraints as in (6.4.8), except that they are enforced for each time period $t = 2, \ldots, T$. Notice that (6.4.9b)–(6.4.9c) ensure that the dispatched wind generation is upper bounded by the minimum between the cut-off level $p_i^{w,max}$ and the available wind power $\overline{p}_{it}^w$. Also note that the first-stage dispatch decision is involved in constraints (6.4.9d)–(6.4.9e) to satisfy ramping constraints.

Note that there is a key difference between the two-stage structure of the proposed robust ED (6.4.7) and the existing two-stage robust UC models. In particular, the decision stages of (6.4.7) correspond to the actual time periods, so that the first-stage decision can be directly used in the dispatch at the current period, and the dispatch decisions in the second stage can be re-optimized in the following periods. In comparison, the two-stage robust UC models have UC decisions in the first stage and dispatch decisions in the second stage, both for the *entire horizon*. Moreover, the two-stage structure of the robust ED model makes it convenient to incorporate into the real-time dispatch procedure. In particular, the robust ED model can be implemented in a rolling horizon framework; the dynamic uncertainty sets can also be updated periodically when new information is available. The CCG algorithm in Chap. 3, Sect. 3.2. can be applied to solve this two-stage robust linear program.

### 6.4.3 Simulation Platform and Evaluation Metrics

In this Section, we describe the simulation platform and evaluation metrics for the proposed robust model. The motivation is to have a realistic simulation environment that integrates the dispatch optimization model with data analysis procedures which dynamically update the parameters in the optimization and uncertainty models. Figure 6.2 illustrates the simulation process.

The simulation process is implemented in a rolling horizon framework (Fig. 6.3). At each time period, the robust ED model is solved over a time window of $T$ time periods. The first-stage dispatch solution for the current time period is implemented, while the second-stage dispatch solutions for remaining periods are not materialized; the time horizon rolls forward by one time interval, where new realizations of demand and available wind power are observed, and dynamic uncertainty sets are periodically re-estimated and updated with the new observations. In order to focus the comparison on the ED policies, the simulation process uses a simplified UC schedule where all thermal generators are on all the time. In the future, we would like to extend the simulation framework to integrate UC decisions into the policy evaluation.

We compare different ED models by evaluating the average and standard deviation (std) of the production cost for every 10 min dispatch interval, which includes both generation cost and penalty cost resulting from the use of expensive fast-start units or load shedding.

### 6.4.4 Computational Experiments

We conduct extensive computational experiments on the simulation platform to compare the proposed robust ED model and dynamic uncertainty sets with existing

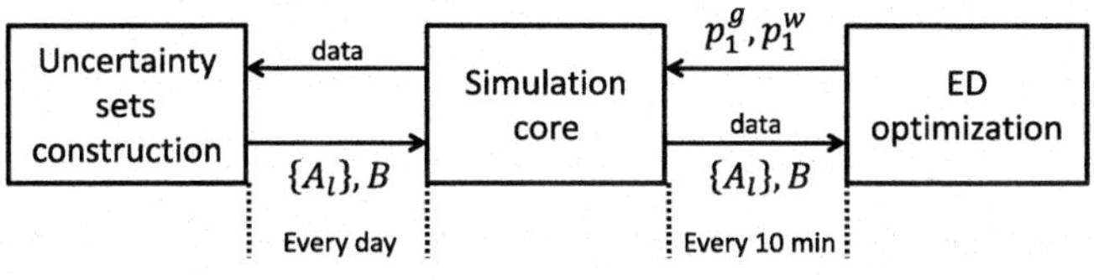


**Fig. 6.2** Simulation platform integrating ED optimization engine and data analysis tools for uncertainty model construction

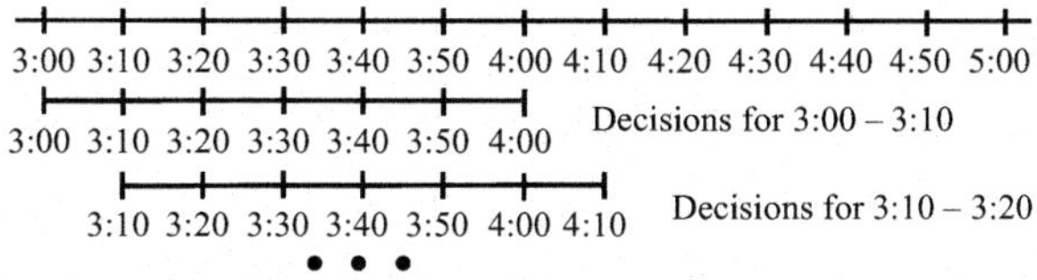


**Fig. 6.3** Concept of rolling horizon with 10 min time periods and $T = 6$

**Table 6.7** Thermal generators in 14-bus system

| Gen | Pmax (MW) | Pmin (MW) | Ramp (MW/10 min) | Cost ($/MWh) |
|---|---|---|---|---|
| 1 | 300 | 50 | 5 | 20 |
| 2 | 100 | 10 | 10 | 40 |
| 3 | 100 | 10 | 15 | 60 |

robust and deterministic dispatch models. The experiments are performed on the 14-bus and 118-bus IEEE test systems, both of which are modified to incorporate significant wind penetration. Table 6.7 summarizes $P_{\min}$, $P_{\max}$, 10 min ramping rates, and production costs of all three generators in the 14-bus system. The total generation capacity is 500 MW. The system has 20 transmission lines and 11 conventional loads. The daily system demand is between 132.6 MW and 319.1 MW with an average of 252.5 MW. The system has 4 wind farms, each with a capacity of 75 MW (equivalent of 50 units of GE 1.5 MW wind turbines). The total power output at each wind farm is approximated by a piecewise linear function of wind speed using the power curve data [22].

The wind speed data is obtained from [23] for four geographically adjacent locations with a 10 min data interval. The average wind speeds at the four wind farms are 4.8, 5.6, 5.1, 5.5 m/s, respectively. Using the power curve, the average total available wind power is 104.2 MW, equivalent to a 34.7% capacity factor, which is about 32.7% of peak demand and 20% of conventional generation capacity, representing a realistically high level of wind penetration. After removing stationary components, wind speeds at different sites present strong auto and cross correlation at several lags, which implies that the temporal and spatial dependencies are significant.

The proposed robust ED model has 9 time periods with a 10 min interval for each period (i.e. 1.5 h look ahead). The robust ED model is evaluated on the simulation platform in the rolling-horizon framework. In particular, it is solved every 10 min over 35 days, for which real wind data is used for all wind farms. On each of the 35 days, the simulation engine updates the parameters of the dynamic uncertainty sets (6.4.3) using the available wind data up to that day. The penalty cost is $C^+ = 6000$ \$/MWh for under-generation, and $C^- = 600$ \$/MWh for over-generation.

#### 6.4.4.1 Robust ED Versus Look-Ahead ED

In this section, we compare the proposed adaptive robust ED (Rob-ED) with the deterministic look-ahead dispatch (LA-ED). The robust ED model uses dynamic uncertainty sets (6.4.3) and (6.4.5) with 6 time lags i.e. $L = 6$. The parameter $\Gamma^w$ controls the size of the uncertainty sets. Notice that when $\Gamma^w = 0$, the uncertainty set contains only one path of the forecast wind speeds, the robust ED thus reduces to the LA-ED model.

**Table 6.8** Performance of robust and deterministic ED

| | LA-ED | Rob-ED | | | | |
|---|---|---|---|---|---|---|
| $\Gamma^w$ | 0.0 | 0.1 | 0.3 | 0.5 | 0.7 | 1.0 |
| Total cost avg. ($) | 771.1 | 758.5 | 734.0 | 716.0 | 718.2 | 742.2 |
| Total cost std. ($) | 1231 | 1172 | 1000 | 723 | 513 | 221 |
| Penalty avg. ($) | 88.2 | 77.1 | 54.2 | 30.6 | 15.8 | 2.4 |
| Penalty freq. (%) | 1.41 | 1.21 | 0.95 | 0.67 | 0.46 | 0.28 |

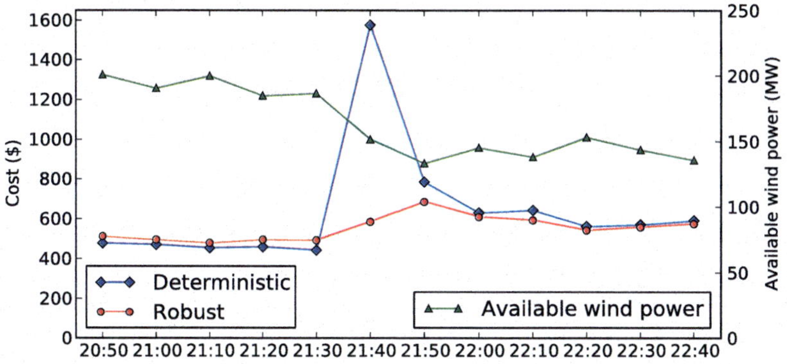


**Fig. 6.4** A snapshot of the product cost of LA-ED and Rob-ED with $\Gamma^w = 0.5$ when available wind power suddenly drops down

Table 6.8 shows the performance of the two models: Column 2 for LA-ED, and Columns 3 to 7 for Rob-ED with different $\Gamma^w$'s. The best average total cost of the Rob-ED model is achieved at $\Gamma^w = 0.5$, where the average cost of Rob-ED is 7.1% lower than that of LA-ED; at the same time, Rob-ED is able to reduce the standard deviation of the cost by 41.2%. We can also see that as $\Gamma^w$ increases to 1.0, the robust ED can reduce the std of cost by 82.1%, with the average cost reduced by 3.75%. The shortage event frequency of the robust ED model is decreased by up to 80.1% and the associated penalty cost is reduced by 97.3% at $\Gamma^w = 1.0$. The change in penalty costs also implies that Rob-ED incurrs less amount of constraint violation than LA-ED, when penalty occurs. The results show that the robust ED model is effective at improving economic efficiency and reducing risk associated with the dispatch solution, where the risk exactly comes from the highly uncertain wind power.

Figure 6.4 shows a typical snapshot from simulation. Available wind power starts a fast and large drop at 21:30 PM (green curve), the deterministic LA-ED runs short of ramping capacity and incurs a spike of penalty cost (blue curve), while the system under robust ED is much less affected by this sudden wind event (red curve). The example shows that when the system has significant wind penetration, properly balancing wind and thermal generation becomes very important for system reliability.

The insight is the following. The two-stage robust ED computes wind scenarios over the future periods that are the most detrimental to the system, and makes the optimal dispatch solution to prepare the system against these scenarios. The worst-case wind scenarios often correspond to scenarios with large wind variation between periods as shown in Fig. 6.4. The robust ED model hedges against the potential large swing of wind by increasing thermal generation and moderately curtailing some wind output. In this way, the system maintains enough ramping capability to deal with potential sudden loss of available wind power.

#### 6.4.4.2 Dynamic Uncertainty Sets Versus Static Uncertainty Sets

In this section, we compare adaptive robust ED equipped with dynamic uncertainty sets with the same robust ED model using static uncertainty sets. The goal is to study the benefits of dynamic uncertainty sets for modeling dynamic relations of wind power uncertainty across time stages and spatial locations.

We use dynamic uncertainty sets (6.4.3) with $L = 6$ as before (denoted as "DUS"), and construct two static uncertainty sets: one ignores the temporal correlation in (6.4.3) (denoted as "SUS1"), the other further ignores spatial correlations (denoted as "SUS2"). Note that both SUS1 and SUS2 are special cases of the dynamic uncertainty sets for $L = 0$, i.e. the uncertainty sets at different time intervals are independent of each other. To have a fair comparison, both in SUS1 and SUS2, $\boldsymbol{g}_t$ is improved after estimating $\boldsymbol{B}$ to force a persistent forecast of wind speeds for the nominal trajectory (improving the accuracy of the nominal trajectory considered).

Figure 6.5 plots the standard deviation of the cost per 10 min interval (x-axis) versus the average of this cost (y-axis) for DUS, SUS1 and SUS2 with different values of $\Gamma^w$. On each curve, the right most point corresponds to $\Gamma^w = 0$, i.e. the deterministic LA-ED model. As $\Gamma^w$ increases, both the average and std of the cost start to decrease, then after a certain apex value of $\Gamma^w$ around 0.4 to 0.5, the std keeps decreasing but the average cost starts to increase. This behavior endows a "U" shape for all three curves. Every point on the right half of the "U" shape for $\Gamma^w$ smaller than the apex value can be strictly improved in both average and std of cost by increasing $\Gamma^w$, while every point on the left half of the "U" shape cannot be strictly improved without trading off between average and std of the cost. In other words, on the right half of the curve, each point is dominated by the points to its left, whereas on the left half, no point is dominated by any other. Therefore, the left part of each curve shows the *Pareto frontier* of cost vs std performance of the associated robust ED model. The system should be operated on the Pareto frontier. This provides an informative guideline for choosing a proper $\Gamma^w$.

Comparing the Pareto frontiers of the three uncertainty sets in Fig. 6.5, we can see that the dynamic uncertainty set has the lowest Pareto frontier, which means that to retain a same level of average cost, the robust ED with dynamic uncertainty sets achieves the lowest std (i.e. the highest reliability); or, to maintain a same level of std (i.e. reliability), the robust ED with dynamic uncertainty sets incurs the lowest

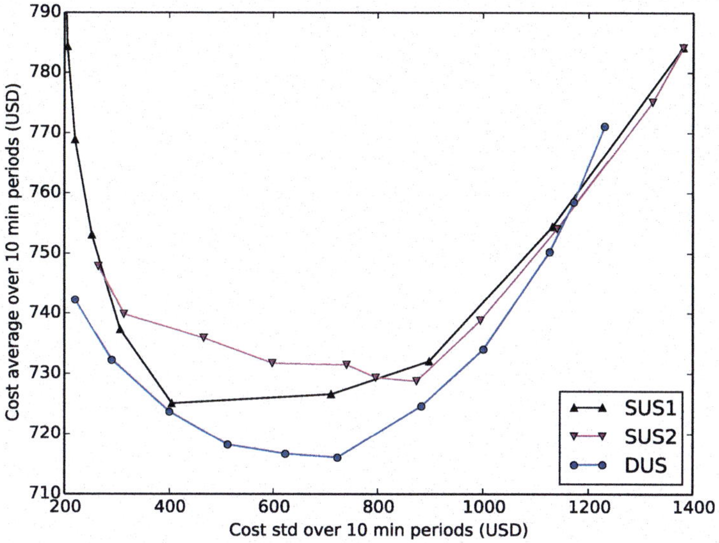


**Fig. 6.5** Cost std and cost average obtained for the policies determined by the different models with $\Gamma^w = 0.0, 0.1, \ldots, 1.0$

cost. That is, robust ED with DUS *dominates* robust ED with static uncertainty sets. Between the two static uncertainty sets, SUS1 (that considers spatial correlation) dominates SUS2, which has neither temporal nor spatial correlation.

#### 6.4.4.3 Impact of System Ramping Capacity

Now we study the relationship between system ramping capacity and the performance of robust ED models. The intuition is that higher ramping rates better prepare the system to deal with high variation of wind output. We want to see how much benefit the robust ED model provides under different system ramping capacities. Figure 6.6 summarizes the computational results for three scenarios: base case with no change in ramping rates, and −25% or +25% change on each generator's ramping rates.

We can see that the robust ED model saves the average cost by 7.1% in the base case (the same numbers as in Sect. 6.4.4.1) comparing with the look-ahead ED; the saving increases to 21.2% for the reduced ramping case; even for the system with 25% more ramping for every generator, the robust ED still demonstrates a 3.7% saving in average cost over LA-ED. This demonstrates the clear benefit of Rob-ED over a wide range of system ramping conditions.

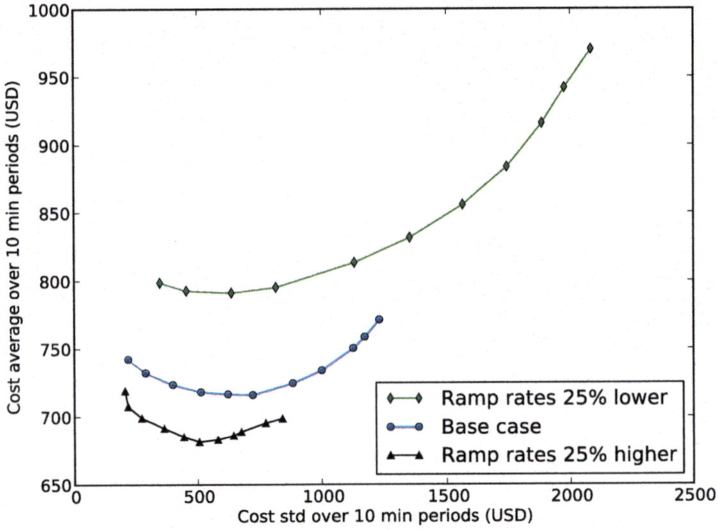


**Fig. 6.6** Cost std and cost average obtained for the Rob-ED with DUS for $\Gamma^w = 0.0, 0.1, \ldots, 1.0$, under modified ramping rates

#### 6.4.4.4 Tests on 118-Bus System

Extensive simulation is also conducted on the 118-bus system. The results for this larger system support similar conclusions as shown in the 14-bus system. The 118-bus system has 54 generators of total 7220 MW generation capacity and 273.2 MW/10 min system ramping capacity. There are 186 lines with flow limits ranging between 280 MW and 1000 MW, and 91 loads. Total electricity demand is between 2485.7 MW (3:30 am) and 5982.9 MW (8:20 pm) with an average of 4735.0 MW. There are 8 wind farms, each with a capacity $p^{w,max} = 750$ MW. The average total available wind power at any time is 1882.7 MW, equivalent to 31.5% of the peak demand. All the wind speeds used in simulation are real data collected from [23]. Each robust ED model can still be quickly solved in about 20 s in the laptop described before. For the simulation of 35-day rolling horizon with a 10 min interval, we use a computer cluster.

Table 6.9 shows the performance of the deterministic LA-ED and the Rob-ED with dynamic uncertainty sets of lags $L = 6$. From the table, we have the following observations:

(1) Rob-ED reduces the average cost by 43.4% ((15061 − 8528)/15061) at a properly chosen $\Gamma^w = 1.5$.
(2) Cost std is reduced by 87.7% at $\Gamma^w = 1.5$ and by 93.9% at $\Gamma^w = 2.0$.
(3) The average penalty cost is reduced by 98.4% or 60.7 times at $\Gamma^w = 1.5$ and is almost eliminated at $\Gamma^w = 2.0$. The frequency of penalty is 7.70% by LA-

**Table 6.9** Performance of LA-ED and Rob-ED for 118-bus system

| | LA-ED | Rob-ED | | | |
|---|---|---|---|---|---|
| $\Gamma^w$ | 0.0 | 0.5 | 1.0 | 1.5 | 2.0 |
| Cost avg. ($) | 15,061 | 12,193 | 8914 | 8528 | 9075 |
| Cost std. ($) | 38,138 | 30,903 | 14,671 | 4703 | 2325 |
| Penalty avg. ($) | 7775 | 4835 | 1214 | 126 | 1 |
| Penalty freq. (%) | 7.70 | 4.74 | 1.45 | 0.12 | 0.02 |
| Therm avg. (MW) | 2969 | 3007 | 3132 | 3399 | 3660 |
| Wind avg. (MW) | 1758 | 1723 | 1602 | 1336 | 1075 |

ED, and is reduced to 0.12% and 0.02% by Rob-ED at $\Gamma^w = 1.5$ and 2.0, respectively.

(4) Rob-ED dispatches more thermal and curtails more wind. On average, the thermal generation is up by 12.7% and 18.9%, and the wind generation is down by 24% and 38.9%, at $\Gamma^w = 1.5$ and 2.0, respectively. This is because that the robust ED dispatches the thermal generation with the anticipation of potential large drops of wind in the future. In this way, it could optimally balance thermal and wind generation in the system.

Comparing to the 14-bus system, the above results for the 118-bus system show a more significant benefit of the proposed Rob-ED model: the average operating cost is cut to almost half of the look-ahead ED, the cost variability is reduced by an order of magnitude, and the shortage events and penalty cost are almost eliminated. Table 6.9 also shows a Pareto frontier exists for the range of $\Gamma^w$ between 1.5 to 2.0.

## 6.5 Robust Economic Dispatch with AC Optimal Power Flow

The robust UC or robust ED models that we have discussed so far all rely on a crucial approximation, namely the DC approximation of power flows as in (6.2.1i), (6.3.2e), (6.3.4f), (6.4.8g), and (6.4.9g). Such an approximation ignores some key aspects of the physical reality of power systems. For example, in DC power flow models, the reactive power generation is completely ignored, the voltage magnitude at every bus is assumed to be constant and the same, and the difference of voltage angles across each transmission line is assumed to be small. In this section, we will consider the true AC power flow constraints which properly model the physics of power flow. First, let us describe a deterministic multi-period AC-OPF model.

### 6.5.1 Multi-Period AC-OPF Models and Convex Relaxations

Consider a multi-period AC-OPF problem (denoted simply as AC-OPF in this paper):

$$\min_{p^g, q^g, c, s, \theta} \quad \sum_{i \in \mathcal{G}} \sum_{t \in \mathcal{T}} C^g_{it}\, p^g_{it} \tag{6.5.1a}$$

$$\text{s.t.} \quad \underline{p}^g_{it} \le p^g_{it} \le \overline{p}^g_{it}, \quad \forall i \in \mathcal{G},\, t \in \mathcal{T}, \tag{6.5.1b}$$

$$\underline{q}^g_{it} \le q^g_{it} \le \overline{q}^g_{it}, \quad \forall i \in \mathcal{G},\, t \in \mathcal{T}, \tag{6.5.1c}$$

$$-RD_{it} \le p^g_{it} - p^g_{i,t-1} \le RU_{it}, \quad \forall i \in \mathcal{G},\, t \in \mathcal{T}, \tag{6.5.1d}$$

$$a^g_{im}\, p^g_{it} + b^g_{im}\, q^g_{it} \le h^g_{im}, \quad \forall i \in \mathcal{G},\, t \in \mathcal{T},\, m \in \mathcal{M}, \tag{6.5.1e}$$

$$\underline{V}_i^2 \le c_{iit} \le \overline{V}_i^2, \quad \forall i \in \mathcal{B},\, t \in \mathcal{T}, \tag{6.5.1f}$$

$$\sum_{k \in \mathcal{G}(i)} p^g_{kt} - p^d_{it} = G_{ii}\, c_{iit} + \sum_{j \in \delta(i)} \left(G_{ij}\, c_{ijt} - B_{ij}\, s_{ijt}\right), \ \forall i \in \mathcal{B}, t \in \mathcal{T}, \tag{6.5.1g}$$

$$\sum_{k \in \mathcal{G}(i)} q^g_{kt} - q^d_{it} = -B_{ii}\, c_{iit} - \sum_{j \in \delta(i)} \left(B_{ij}\, c_{ijt} + G_{ij}\, s_{ijt}\right), \ \forall i \in \mathcal{B}, t \in \mathcal{T}, \tag{6.5.1h}$$

$$\begin{aligned}(f^{max}_{ij})^2 \ge {} & \left(-G_{ij}\, c_{iit} + G_{ij}\, c_{ijt} - B_{ij}\, s_{ijt}\right)^2 \\ & + \left(B_{ij}\, c_{iit} - B_{ij}\, c_{ijt} - G_{ij}\, s_{ijt}\right)^2, \ \forall (i,j) \in \mathcal{L},\, t \in \mathcal{T},\end{aligned} \tag{6.5.1i}$$

$$c_{ijt} = c_{jit}, \quad s_{ijt} = -s_{jit}, \quad \forall (i,j) \in \mathcal{L},\, t \in \mathcal{T}, \tag{6.5.1j}$$

$$c^2_{ijt} + s^2_{ijt} = c_{iit}\, c_{jjt}, \quad \forall (i,j) \in \mathcal{L},\, t \in \mathcal{T}, \tag{6.5.1k}$$

$$\theta_{jt} - \theta_{it} = \arctan\left(s_{ijt}/c_{ijt}\right), \ \forall (i,j) \in \mathcal{L},\, t \in \mathcal{T}. \tag{6.5.1l}$$

Here, $\mathcal{B}, \mathcal{G}, \mathcal{L}, \mathcal{T}$ are the sets of buses, generators, transmission lines, and time periods, respectively. Decisions $p^g_{it}$ and $q^g_{it}$ are the active and reactive power output of generator $i$ at time $t$, respectively, and $\theta_{it}$ is the voltage angle at bus $i$, time $t$. The other decisions correspond to $c_{ijt} = |V_{it}||V_{jt}|\cos(\theta_{it} - \theta_{jt})$ and $s_{ijt} = -|V_{it}||V_{jt}|\sin(\theta_{it}-\theta_{jt})$, for buses $i, j$ at time $t$, where $|V_{it}|$ is the voltage magnitude at bus $i$, time $t$. For generator $i$ at time $t$, parameters $C^g_{it}$, $\underline{p}^g_{it}$, $\overline{p}^g_{it}$, $\underline{q}^g_{it}$, $\overline{q}^g_{it}$, $RD_{it}$, $RU_{it}$ correspond to the unit cost, lower and upper bounds of active power output, lower and upper bounds of reactive power output, and ramp-down and ramp-up capacities, respectively. Parameters $a^g_{im}$, $b^g_{im}$, $h^g_{im}$ determine a linear constraint for active and reactive power output at generator $i$. For bus $i$, parameters $\underline{V}_i$, $\overline{V}_i$ are the lower and upper bounds on voltage magnitude, respectively, $\mathcal{G}(i)$ is the set of generators at this bus, and $\delta(i)$ is the set of buses connected through a transmission line. For buses $i, j$, parameters $G_{ij}$ and $B_{ij}$ are the real and imaginary parts of the corresponding admittance matrix element, respectively, and $f_{ij}^{max}$ is the maximum apparent power flow allowed on line $(i, j)$.

In multi-period AC-OPF (6.5.1), objective (6.5.1a) represents total cost minimization. Constraints (6.5.1b)–(6.5.1c) impose active and reactive power output bounds; (6.5.1d) enforces ramping capacities; and (6.5.1e) represents a polyhedral model for reactive capability curve limitations. Constraints (6.5.1f) are voltage magnitude bounds; (6.5.1g)–(6.5.1h) are the power flow equations that determine active and reactive power balance; and (6.5.1i) represents transmission line power flow capacities. Constraints (6.5.1j)–(6.5.1l) are required relations between the $\boldsymbol{c}, \boldsymbol{s}, \boldsymbol{\theta}$ variables that guarantee the consistency of the formulation (see [24] for details on formulating AC-OPF using the $\boldsymbol{c}, \boldsymbol{s}$ variables).

We will consider two convex relaxations of (6.5.1), described below. First, the SOCP relaxation of AC-OPF (6.5.1) (denoted SOCP-OPF) (see [25, 26, 24]) is given by:

$$\min_{\boldsymbol{p}^g, \boldsymbol{q}^g, \boldsymbol{c}, \boldsymbol{s}} \quad \sum_{i \in \mathscr{G}} \sum_{t \in \mathscr{T}} C_{it}^g \, p_{it}^g \tag{6.5.2a}$$

$$\text{s.t.} \quad \text{Eqs. (6.5.1b)–(6.5.1j) hold} \tag{6.5.2b}$$

$$c_{ijt}^2 + s_{ijt}^2 \leq c_{iit} \, c_{jjt} \quad \forall (i, j) \in \mathscr{L}, t \in \mathscr{T}. \tag{6.5.2c}$$

The SOCP-OPF can be strengthened through several techniques to provide a stronger relaxation [24].

Second, the SDP relaxation (denoted SDP-OPF) (see [27, 24]) is given by:

$$\min_{\boldsymbol{p}^g, \boldsymbol{q}^g, \boldsymbol{c}, \boldsymbol{s}, \boldsymbol{X}} \quad \sum_{i \in \mathscr{G}} \sum_{t \in \mathscr{T}} C_{it}^g \, p_{it}^g \tag{6.5.3a}$$

$$\text{s.t.} \quad \text{Eqs. (6.5.1b)–(6.5.1i) hold} \tag{6.5.3b}$$

$$c_{ijt} = X_{ijt} + X_{i'j't} \quad \forall (i, j) \in \mathscr{L}, t \in \mathscr{T} \tag{6.5.3c}$$

$$s_{ijt} = X_{ij't} - X_{i'jt} \quad \forall (i, j) \in \mathscr{L}, t \in \mathscr{T} \tag{6.5.3d}$$

$$\boldsymbol{X}_t \succeq 0 \quad \forall t \in \mathscr{T}, \tag{6.5.3e}$$

where, $i' = i + |\mathscr{B}|$, $j' = j + |\mathscr{B}|$, and $\boldsymbol{X}_t$ is a symmetric positive-semidefinite $2|\mathscr{B}| \times 2|\mathscr{B}|$ matrix.

### 6.5.2 Robust AC-OPF

We can now describe the multi-period Robust AC-OPF model. Consider a time horizon encompassing time periods $\{0, \ldots, T\}$. We will assume that in this horizon, all parameters are exactly known at $t = 0$, while uncertain parameters in $t \in \{1, \ldots, T\}$ are uncertain. We formulate a robust optimization problem where the dispatch decision at $t = 0$ is selected in such a way that the cost of the current time period at $t = 0$ plus the worst-case cost over $t \in \{1, \ldots, T\}$ is minimized, where the worst-case cost is subject to uncertain parameters in some *uncertainty set*. The Robust AC-OPF problem is formulated as follows:

$$\min_{x \in X_{AC}} \left( c^\top x + \max_{\xi \in \Xi} \min_{y \in Y_{AC}(x,\xi)} b^\top y \right). \tag{6.5.4}$$

In this problem, $x = (p_0^g, q_0^g)$ and $X_{AC}$ represents all AC-OPF constraints (6.5.1b)-(6.5.11) at $t = 0$. Also, $\xi = (p^d, q^d, \overline{p}^r)$, and $\Xi = \mathscr{D} \times \overline{\mathscr{P}}^r$, where $\mathscr{D}$ is an uncertainty set for active ($p^d$) and reactive ($q^d$) load over $t \in \{1, \ldots, T\}$, and $\overline{\mathscr{P}}^r$ is an uncertainty set for available active power ($\overline{p}^r$) at all renewable units over $t \in \{1, \ldots, T\}$. Finally, $Y_{AC}(x, \xi)$ represents all AC-OPF constraints (6.5.1b)–(6.5.11) over $t \in \{1, \ldots, T\}$, under given dispatch decisions at $t = 0$ as well as given active and reactive loads and available active power at renewable units over $t \in \{1, \ldots, T\}$.

In all OPF models presented, we assume that there is a set $\mathscr{R}$ of renewable units such that $\mathscr{R} \subset \mathscr{G}$, with which the vector of available active power at all renewable units over $t \in \{1, \ldots, T\}$ is given by $\overline{p}^r = \left(\overline{p}_{it}^g : i \in \mathscr{R}, t \in \{1, \ldots, T\}\right)$. With this notation, we do not need to write separate equations for conventional generators and for wind and solar farms in the formulation of the problem.

Problem (6.5.4) is a two-stage adaptive robust optimization problem. We refer to $x$ as first-stage variables, since they are decided before uncertainty $\xi$ is revealed, and we refer to $y$ as second-stage variables, since they are decided after a specific realization of uncertain parameters is revealed, and can thus adapt to this realization. Also see [28] for discussion on two-stage adaptive robust optimization models.

### 6.5.3 Robust Conic-OPF Models

The Robust AC-OPF model (6.5.4) has complicated non-convex AC-OPF constraints in both the first and second stages. We want to find a computationally efficient way to approximately solve it. To do this, we replace the non-convex AC-OPF constraints by tractable relaxation or approximation models, such as the SOCP-, SDP- and DC-OPF. We construct three Robust *Conic*-OPF models, each of which uses a type of convex conic relaxation (or approximation) of the AC-OPF constraints. In particular, if problem (6.5.4) replaces AC-OPF constraints with the SOCP relaxation defined in (6.5.2), we obtain a Robust SOCP-OPF; if the AC-OPF constraints are replaced with the SDP relaxation defined in (6.5.3), we obtain a Robust SDP-OPF; and if these non-convex constraints are replaced with the DC-OPF, we obtain a Robust DC-OPF.

Using the framework of conic optimization, we can write the Robust SOCP-, SDP-, and DC-OPF models in the following unified form:

$$\min_{x \in X_M} \left( c^\top x + \max_{\xi \in \Xi} \min_{y \in Y_M(x,\xi)} b^\top y \right), \tag{6.5.5}$$

where $Y_M(x, \xi) = \{y : Ay \geq_K f + Gx + H\xi\}$, where $K$ is a closed, pointed, and self-dual cone with non-empty interior, and $X_M$ has an analogous representation. In particular, Robust SOCP-, SDP-, and DC-OPF has $K$ as the Lorentz cone (more precisely, a cross product of Lorentz cones), the SDP cone, and the non-negative orthant, respectively. To specifically denote each of these three cases in (6.5.5), we will write $M$ = SOCP, $M$ = SDP, and $M$ = DC, respectively.

### 6.5.4 Uncertainty Sets for Load and Renewables

We use the following *budget* uncertainty set for the active and reactive power of conventional load:

$$\mathscr{D} = \Big\{(p^d, q^d) : \sum_{i \in \mathscr{B}^d} \frac{|p_{it}^d - \tilde{p}_{it}^d|}{\hat{p}_{it}^d} \leq \Gamma \sqrt{|\mathscr{B}^d|} \tag{6.5.6a}$$

$$\sum_{i \in \mathscr{B}^d} \frac{|q_{it}^d - \tilde{q}_{it}^d|}{\hat{q}_{it}^d} \leq \Gamma \sqrt{|\mathscr{B}^d|} \tag{6.5.6b}$$

$$p_{it}^d \in [\tilde{p}_{it}^d - \Gamma \hat{p}_{it}^d, \tilde{p}_{it}^d + \Gamma \hat{p}_{it}^d] \ \forall i \in \mathscr{B}, t \in \mathscr{T} \tag{6.5.6c}$$

$$q_{it}^d \in [\tilde{q}_{it}^d - \Gamma \hat{q}_{it}^d, \tilde{q}_{it}^d + \Gamma \hat{q}_{it}^d] \ \forall i \in \mathscr{B}, t \in \mathscr{T} \Big\}, \tag{6.5.6d}$$

where $\mathscr{B}^d \subset \mathscr{B}$ is the set of load buses, $\tilde{p}_{it}^d$, $\tilde{q}_{it}^d$ are the nominal values for active and reactive load at bus $i$, time $t$, respectively, and $\hat{p}_{it}^d$, $\hat{q}_{it}^d$ are variability factors for active and reactive load, respectively (e.g. standard deviation from historic data). Parameter $\Gamma$ determines the size of the uncertainty set.

For wind and solar power, we consider the following dynamic uncertainty set, proposed in Sect. 6.4.1.2.

$$\overline{\mathscr{P}}^r = \Big\{\overline{p}^r = (\overline{p}_{it}^r)_{it} : \exists\, u,\, v \text{ s.t.} \tag{6.5.7a}$$

$$\overline{p}_{it}^r = f_{it} + g_{it} u_{it} \quad \forall i \in \mathscr{R},\ t \in \mathscr{T} \tag{6.5.7b}$$

$$\boldsymbol{u}_t = \sum_{l=1}^{L} \boldsymbol{A}^l \, \boldsymbol{u}_{t-l} + \boldsymbol{B} \, \boldsymbol{v}_t \quad \forall t \in \mathcal{T} \tag{6.5.7c}$$

$$\|\boldsymbol{v}_t\| \leq \Gamma \quad \forall t \in \mathcal{T} \tag{6.5.7d}$$

$$\sum_{t \in \mathcal{T}} \|\boldsymbol{v}_t\| \leq \rho \, \Gamma \, |\mathcal{T}| \tag{6.5.7e}$$

$$0 \leq \overline{p}^r_{it} \leq \overline{p}^{r,max}_{it} \quad \forall i \in \mathcal{R}, \, t \in \mathcal{T} \Big\}. \tag{6.5.7f}$$

Here, $\overline{p}^r_{it}$ is the available renewable real power at renewable unit $i$ at time $t$, parameters $f_{it}$ and $g_{it}$ are deterministic seasonality components, matrices $\boldsymbol{A}^l$ and $\boldsymbol{B}$ determine spatial and temporal correlations (of up to $L$ time periods), $\| \cdot \|$ is a norm, $\Gamma$ is an uncertainty set size parameter, $\rho$ determines a budget of uncertainty over time periods, and $\overline{p}^{r,max}_{it}$ is an upper bound on $\overline{p}^r_{it}$. Component $\boldsymbol{u}_t \in \mathbb{R}^{|\mathcal{R}|}$ can be seen as a residual uncertainty after seasonal components are filtered out, and $\boldsymbol{v}_t \in \mathbb{R}^{N_v}$ as a primitive uncertainty for which temporal and spatial correlations are further filtered out as well, where $N_v \in \{1, \ldots, |\mathcal{R}|\}$.

### 6.5.5 Computational Experiments

We focus on comparing the practical performance that the Robust AC-OPF can offer, using a simulation program that mimics the hour to hour operation of the power system under the true full AC-OPF power flow equations. The simulation consists of a rolling-horizon process, where Robust AC-OPF is repeatedly solved as time moves forward. The simulation starts by observing uncertain parameters at the first hour and solving the Robust AC-OPF under a horizon that spans from this hour (first-stage decision with known parameters) to 3 h ahead (second-stage decisions under uncertain parameters). Then, the decision for this first hour is implemented and we move on to observe the parameters at the second hour, solving now a Robust AC-OPF that spans this second hour (first-stage decision) and 3 h ahead (second-stage decisions). This process is repeated moving forward until the last simulated hour, after which we compute several cost and reliability performance metrics achieved by the implemented AC-OPF decisions. We consider a simulation horizon of 100 contiguous days (i.e. 2400 h). To simulate uncertain parameters, we use a normal distribution for active and reactive power demand at each node (assuming temporal and spatial independence), and a vector autoregressive process for wind and solar power as in [8] (that captures temporal and spatial correlations), for which we use data from NREL's Western Wind and Solar Integration Datasets [20] for parameter estimation. The average renewable penetration under these simulated trajectories is 21.6% for the 14-bus system and 18.8% for the 118-bus system.

**Table 6.10** Rolling-horizon simulation results under Robust AC-OPF

| $\Gamma$ | 0 | 0.5 | 1 | 1.5 | 2 | 2.5 |
|---|---|---|---|---|---|---|
| *14-bus system* | | | | | | |
| Cost avg. ($) | 9162 | 8123 | 7841 | 8116 | 8677 | 9405 |
| Cost std. ($) | 10,569 | 5700 | 2984 | 2625 | 2796 | 3056 |
| Penalty avg. ($) | 1642 | 540 | 78 | 6 | 0 | 0 |
| Penalty freq. | 4.88% | 2.29% | 0.50% | 0.04% | 0.00% | 0.00% |
| T Congestion | 4.97% | 4.66% | 4.31% | 3.78% | 2.71% | 1.71% |
| Ramp capacity | 57.51% | 60.72% | 66.50% | 74.73% | 84.71% | 92.09% |
| Renewable util | 99.98% | 99.93% | 99.75% | 99.00% | 96.85% | 91.45% |
| *118-bus system* | | | | | | |
| Cost avg. ($) | 181,625 | 155,358 | 149,778 | 153,822 | 163,126 | 181,540 |
| Cost std. ($) | 206,116 | 102,140 | 59,992 | 63,461 | 68,016 | 68,415 |
| Penalty avg. ($) | 37,032 | 9717 | 181 | 0 | 0 | 0 |
| Penalty freq. | 7.62% | 3.33% | 0.36% | 0.00% | 0.00% | 0.00% |
| T Congestion | 2.83% | 2.72% | 2.43% | 2.05% | 1.61% | 1.07% |
| Ramp capacity | 33.32% | 34.97% | 37.89% | 41.41% | 46.45% | 52.17% |
| Renewable util. | 99.99% | 99.99% | 99.99% | 99.99% | 99.98% | 99.95% |

The results from these simulations are summarized in Table 6.10, under several values for the uncertainty set size parameter $\Gamma$. In this Table, "Cost Avg" is the average hourly cost over the simulated horizon, "Cost Std" is the standard deviation of hourly cost, "Penalty Avg" is the average hourly penalty cost, "Penalty Freq" is the proportion of time periods where penalty occurred, "T Congestion" is the average transmission congestion, based on a metric corresponding to the proportion of transmission line capacities that have an utilization of 90% or more, "Ramp Capacity" is the average system-level ramp-up capacity as a proportion to the sum of all ramp-up rates, and "Renewable Util" is the average utilization of renewable power, corresponding to the proportion of dispatched renewable power with respect to its availability.

We can first observe that the tradeoff between economic effectiveness and system reliability can be controlled through the uncertainty set size parameter $\Gamma$. As $\Gamma$ increases we can see that: average costs tend first to decrease (until $\Gamma = 1$ for both systems) and then to increase, cost standard deviation decreases sharply first and then slowly increases, penalty costs and frequency decrease until being completely eliminated, transmission congestion decreases, ramping capacities increase, and renewable power can be slightly curtailed. These results show that the value of $\Gamma$ can be used to "tune" the conservativeness with which the power system is operated. A higher $\Gamma$ provides a more reliable operation, but potentially at a significant cost if $\Gamma$ is too large.

We can also observe that the Robust AC-OPF provides a tremendous advantage when compared to the Deterministic AC-OPF, which corresponds to the case with $\Gamma = 0$. For the 14-bus system the average cost savings can be up to 14.4% (with

$\Gamma = 1$) and cost standard deviation can be reduced up to 75.2% ($\Gamma = 1.5$), while for the 118-bus system the average cost savings can be up to 17.5% ($\Gamma = 1$) and cost standard deviation can be reduced up to 70.9% ($\Gamma = 1$). Also, for both systems a sufficiently large $\Gamma$ results in null penalty, while Deterministic AC-OPF presents a significant level of penalty.

In summary: (i) a convex relaxation of AC-OPF, such as SOCP-OPF, combined with the alternating direction method provides a good way for approximately solving the difficult max–min problem of finding a worst-case uncertainty realization; (ii) the Robust AC-OPF model can be efficiently solved in approximate form; and (iii) Robust AC-OPF provides an effective way to manage the uncertainty in active and reactive power demands, as well as in wind and solar power, offering an explicit way to control the desired conservativeness in the operation of the power system.

## 6.6 End-of-Chapter Exercises

**6.1** A fruitful exercise is to think about applying other uncertainty sets for the net load. For example, what if we use an ellipsoidal uncertainty set for the net load, which could approximate the notion of the covariance matrix of uncertain loads. How should we solve the resulting two-stage robust UC problem?

**6.2** Write down the dual linear program to the second-stage dispatch problem defined in (6.2.2a) and (6.2.2c). Argue that the extreme points of the feasible region of this dual LP do not depend on the first-stage decision $\boldsymbol{x}$ and the net load $\boldsymbol{d}$.

**6.3** Calculate the numbers of decision variables and constraints in the multistage robust UC model (6.3.4) for the full affine decision rule (6.3.3) and various simplified affine decision rules (6.3.5)–(6.3.6).

## References

1. Bertsimas, D., Litvinov, E., Sun, X. A., Zhao, J., & Zheng, T. (2013). Adaptive robust optimization for the security constrained unit commitment problem. *IEEE Transactions on Power Systems, 28*(1), 52–63.
2. Jiang, R., Wang, J., & Guan, Y. (2012). Robust unit commitment with wind power and pumped storage hydro. *IEEE Transactions on Power Systems, 27*(2), 800–810.
3. Zhao, L., & Zeng, B. (2012). Robust unit commitment problem with demand response and wind energy. *IEEE Power and Energy Society General Meeting*
4. Zeng, B., & Zhao, L. (2013). Solving two-stage robust optimization problems using a column-and-constraint generation method. *Operations Research Letters, 41*(5), 457–461.
5. ISO New England. Do Not Exceed Dispatch Project. https://www.iso-ne.com/participate/support/participant-readiness-outlook/do-not-exceed-dispatch.
6. Lorca, A., Sun, X. A., Litvinov, E., & Zheng, T. (2016). Multistage adaptive robust optimization for the unit commitment problem. *Operations Research, 64*(1), 32–51.

7. Lorca, A., & Sun, X. A. (2015). Adaptive robust optimization with dynamic uncertainty sets for multi-period economic dispatch under significant wind. *IEEE Transactions on Power Systems, 30*(4), 1702–1713.
8. Lorca, A., & Sun, X. A. (2017). Multistage robust unit commitment with dynamic uncertainty sets and energy storage. *IEEE Transactions on Power Systems, 32*(3), 1678–1688.
9. Lorca, A., & Sun, X. A. (2018). Adaptive robust multi-period AC optimal power flow. *IEEE Transactions on Power Systems, 33*(2), 1993–2003.
10. Anjos, M., & Conejo, A. (2017). Unit commitment in electric energy systems. *Foundations and Trends in Electric Energy Systems, 1*(4), 220–310.
11. Ela, E., & Helman, U. (2016). Wholesale electricity market design initiative in the United States: Survey and research needs. *Electric Power Research Institute Technical Update*
12. Cramton, P. (2017). Electricity market design. *Oxford Review of Economic Policy, 33*(4), 589–612.
13. Kirschen, D., & Strbac, G. (2018). *Fundamentals of power system economics*. Hoboken: John Wiley & Sons.
14. Burke, P. J., & Abayasekara, A. (2018). The price elasticity of electricity demand in the United States: a three-dimensional analysis. *The Energy Journal, 39*(2), 123–145.
15. Morison, K., Wang, L., & Kundur, P. (2004). Power system security assessment. *IEEE Power and Energy Magazine, 2*(5), 30–39.
16. CAISO. CAISO market processes and products. http://www.caiso.com/market/Pages/MarketProcesses.aspx.
17. Federal Energy Regulatory Commission (FERC) Operator initiated commitment in RTO and ISO markets. Price formation in organized wholesale electricity markets. Docket AD14-14-000, http://www.ferc.gov/legal/staff-reports/2014/AD14-14-operator-actions.pdf.
18. Navid, N., & Rosenwald, G. (2012). Market solutions for managing ramp flexibility with high penetration of renewable resource. *IEEE Transactions on Sustainable Energy 3*(4), 784–790.
19. National Renewable Energy Laboratory (NREL). Transmission grid integration—Western wind data set. http://www.nrel.gov/electricity/transmission/wind_integration_dataset.html.
20. Potter, C. W., Lew, D., McCaa, J., Cheng, S. Eichelberger, S., & Grimit, E. (2008). Creating the data set for the western wind and solar integration study (USA). *Wind Energy, 32*(4), 325–338.
21. Hamilton, J. D. (1994). *Time series analysis* (vol. 2). Princeton, NJ: Princeton University Press.
22. General Electric Company. GE Energy 1.5 MW Wind Turbine. https://www.ge.com/in/wind-energy/1.5-MW-wind-turbine.
23. RERL wind data. Center for energy efficiency and renewable energy, University of Massachusetts Amherst, http://www.ceere.org/rerl/publications/resource_data/index.html.
24. Kocuk, B., Dey, S., & Sun, X. A. (2016). Strong SOCP relaxations for the AC optimal power flow problem. *Operations Research, 64*(6), 1177–1565.
25. Gómez-Expósito, A., & Romero-Ramos, E. (1999). Reliable load flow technique for radial distribution networks. *IEEE Transactions on Power Systems, 14*(3), 1063–1069.
26. Jabr, R. A. (2008). Optimal power flow using an extended conic quadratic formulation. *IEEE Transactions on Power Systems, 23*(3), 1000–1008.
27. Bai, X., Wei, H., Fujisawa, K., & Wang, Y. (2008). Semidefinite programming for optimal power flow problems. *International Journal of Electrical Power & Energy Systems, 30*(6), 383–392.
28. Sun, X. A. (2017). Recent development on robust optimization in electric power systems operations. *Integration of Large Scale Renewable Energy into Bulk Power Systems: From Planning to Operation*, Springer International Publishing.
29. Zimmerman, R. D., Murillo-Sánchez, C. E., & Thomas, R. J. (2011). MATPOWER: Steady-state operation, planning and analysis tools for power systems research and education. *IEEE Transactions on Power Systems, 26*(1), 12–19.

# Chapter 7
# Medium-Term Planning Models

This chapter describes a number of medium-term power system planning problems amenable to be expressed and solved using Adaptive Robust Optimization (ARO) models. The considered problems are:

1. The preventive maintenance of the lines and/or transformers of a transmission or distribution network.
2. The procurement of primary fuel (e.g., natural gas) for an electricity producer.
3. The production scheduling of a hydroelectric producer.
4. The contracting strategy for selling energy of an electricity producer.
5. The procurement of electricity for a large consumer.

These problems are just representative examples. Many other medium-term planning problems in the power sector can be conveniently formulated as ARO models and solved efficiently.

## 7.1 Introduction

As discussed in the previous chapters, ARO models are particularly suited to identify decisions that protect an electric energy system against the most adverse uncertainty outcomes.

Wrong medium-term decisions generally entail highly undesirable short-term operating conditions. Therefore, deriving medium-term decisions that protect the power system against extreme uncertainty outcomes is most desirable.



X. A. Sun, A. J. Conejo, *Robust Optimization in Electric Energy Systems*,
International Series in Operations Research & Management Science 313,
https://doi.org/10.1007/978-3-030-85128-6_7

We consider in this chapter a number of medium-term decision making problems that are conveniently formulated and solved as ARO models. The decisions resulting from these models guarantee a high level of protection against extreme uncertainty outcomes. In this sense, these decisions are robust.

We illustrate the different problems considered by discussing very simple instances of them that retain their key modeling features, but avoid computational hurdles.

## 7.2 Grid Maintenance Scheduling

Preventive maintenance [1, 2] of lines and transformers in transmission and distribution grids is routinely carried out by network planners to minimize unexpected line or transformer failures that may result in operating conditions that are very expensive or entail unserved energy.

Nevertheless, after a preventive maintenance plan is identified and deployed, lines or transformers may fail, driving the system into operating conditions that are highly expensive or require load curtailment.

On the other hand, once a line/transformer failure occurs, the system operator strives to drive the system back to a secure operating condition that is as inexpensive as possible.

Therefore, regarding preventive maintenance scheduling the decision sequence for the network planner is as follows:

1. The network planner decides on preventive maintenance actions to minimize electricity supply cost, anticipating the realization of the worst line/transformer contingency and the subsequent reaction of the system operator to mitigate the impact of such contingency.
2. The contingency that, within the considered uncertainty set, leads to the maximum electricity supply cost realizes.
3. The system operator reacts to such contingency by introducing the required system adjustments (redispatching and load shedding) pursuing minimum electricity supply cost.

### *7.2.1 Simple Example*

We illustrate below how to use an ARO model to identify preventive maintenance decisions that are robust. For this, we use a very simple example.

Consider the two-line power system network depicted in Fig. 7.1. The capacity of both lines is 5 units. A demand of 6 units at the center node (node 3) is supplied by the two generating units at nodes 1 and 2, whose costs are \$2/unit and \$4/unit, respectively. The flows through the lines are denoted by $f_1$ (line 1 from node 1

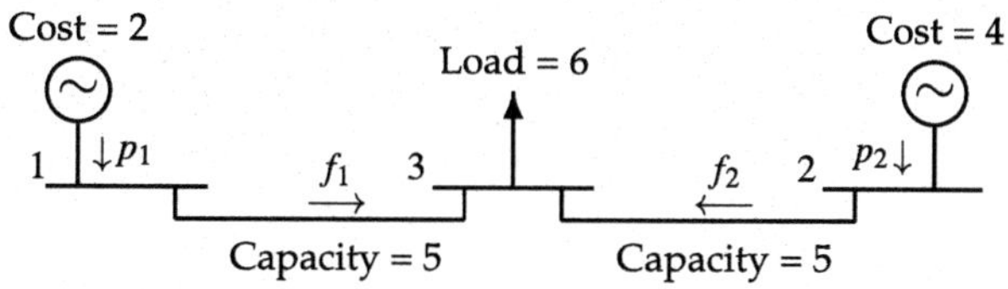


**Fig. 7.1** Line preventive maintainable example

to node 3) and $f_2$ (line 2 from node 2 to node 3), while the production of the generating units are denoted by $p_1$ (generating unit at node 1) and $p_2$ (generating unit at node 2).

The budget available for preventive maintenance allows for just a single maintenance intervention, out of two possible ones. Maintenance intervention 1 allows increasing the capacity of line 1 by 2 units, while maintenance intervention 2 allows increasing the capacity of line 2 by 3 units.

For the sake of simplicity, only two partial line-outages are considered. The first one reduces the capacity of line 1 in 4 units, while the second one reduces the capacity of line 2 in 3 units.

The ARO formulation below allows determining the best maintenance strategy that protects the system against the worst outage and results in minimum production cost once that contingency realizes. This formulation is as follows:

$$\min_{\substack{x_1,x_2\in\{0,1\}\\x_1+x_2=1}} \max_{\substack{u_1,u_2\in\{0,1\}\\u_1+u_2=1}} \min_{\substack{p_1,p_2\geq 0\\f_1,f_2\geq 0}} \quad z = 2p_1 + 4p_2$$
$$\text{s.t.} \quad \begin{aligned} & p_1 = f_1 \\ & p_2 = f_2 \\ & f_1 \leq 5 + 2x_1 - 4u_1 \\ & f_2 \leq 5 + 3x_2 - 3u_2 \\ & f_1 + f_2 = 6, \end{aligned} \tag{7.2.1}$$

where $x_1$ and $x_2$ are binary variables identifying the two preventive maintenance actions, and $u_1$ and $u_2$ are also binary variables identifying the occurrence of any of the two possible contingencies. The overall objective is minimum production cost. The third-level problem dispatches the generating units seeking minimum production cost. Its constraints include both power balance per node and transmission bounds per line. The second-level problem selects the worst contingency (leading to a maximum production cost) and the first-level problem selects the best maintenance intervention seeking minimum production cost.

We note that a general version of the problem above would be highly complex to solve as the third-level problem include binary decisions.

Given the simplicity of problem (7.2.1), its solution is straightforward. Since the cheapest generating unit is at node 1, the sending end of line 1, we select the preventive maintenance action that increases the capacity of line 1. That is, $x_1 = 1$ and thus $x_2 = 0$. On the other hand, the worst uncertainty realization entails the maximum reduction of the capacity of line 1, the line that allows transferring cheap energy. Thus, $u_1 = 1$ and $u_2 = 0$. The resulting single-level min problem is:

$$\begin{aligned}
\min_{\substack{p_1,p_2\geq 0\\ f_1,f_2\geq 0}} \quad & z = 2p_1 + 4p_2 \\
\text{s.t.} \quad & p_1 = f_1 \\
& p_2 = f_2 \\
& f_1 \leq 5 + 2 - 4 \\
& f_2 \leq 5 \\
& f_1 + f_2 = 6.
\end{aligned}$$

Solving this problem results in that the production of both generating units is 3 units and the production cost \$18.

### 7.2.2 General Formulation

Generally, the grid maintenance scheduling problem has the form:

$$\min_{\mathbf{x}\in\mathscr{X}} \quad \max_{\mathbf{u}\in\mathscr{U}} \quad \min_{\mathbf{y}\in\mathscr{Y}(\mathbf{x},\mathbf{u})} \quad f(\mathbf{x},\mathbf{y},\mathbf{u}).$$

This maintenance scheduling problem seeks to identify the best preventive maintenance strategy, anticipating the worst grid component failure, and assuming that the grid operator reacts to such contingency in the best possible manner, i.e., seeking minimum supply cost.

Variable $\mathbf{x} \in \mathscr{X}$ represents maintenance actions seeking to improve the status of the grid. Preventive maintenance actions generally reduce the probability of failure of the grid components preserving its transmission capacity.

Variable $\mathbf{u} \in \mathscr{U}$ represents grid component failures. Realistic uncertainty sets representing grid component outages and their evolution over time need to be considered.

Variable $\mathbf{y} \in \mathscr{Y}$ represents the system operator actions to supply the demand at minimum cost after the worst component failure (within an uncertainty set), which generally requires redispatching and eventually shedding load.

A rather generic but particular instance of the above formulation is:

$$\min_{\substack{x_1,\ldots,x_{n_L}\\ \in\{0,1\},\\ \sum_{\ell=1}^{n_L} x_\ell \le B^F}} \quad \max_{\substack{u_1,\ldots,u_{n_L}\\ \in\{0,1\},\\ \sum_{\ell=1}^{n_L} u_\ell \le B^U}} \quad \min_{\substack{p_{it}\ge 0,\forall i,\forall t\\ u_{it}\in\{0,1\},\forall i,\forall t}} \quad z = \sum_{t=1}^{n_T}\sum_{i=1}^{n_G} c_i(p_{it})$$

$$\text{s.t.} \quad u_{it}P_i^{\min} \le p_{it} \le u_{it}P_i^{\max}, \forall i, \forall t$$

$$\sum_{i\in\Omega_n^G} p_{it} - \sum_{j\in\Omega_n^D} D_{jt} - \sum_{\forall\ell|s(\ell)=n} B_\ell(\theta_{s(\ell)t} - \theta_{r(\ell)t}) + \sum_{\forall\ell|r(\ell)=n} B_\ell(\theta_{s(\ell)t} - \theta_{r(\ell)t}) = 0, \forall n, \forall t$$

$$|B_\ell(\theta_{s(\ell)t} - \theta_{s(\ell)t})| \le F_\ell^{\max} + K_\ell^M x_\ell - K_\ell^F u_\ell, \forall\ell, \forall t, \quad (7.2.2)$$

where the optimization variables are:

- $p_{it}$ is the production of unit $i$ ($i = 1, \ldots, n_G$) in time period $t$ ($t = 1, \ldots, n_T$).
- $u_\ell$ is a binary indicator to model the outage (or partial outage) of line $\ell$ ($\ell = 1, \ldots, n_L$). $u_\ell = 1$ if line $\ell$ fails and 0 otherwise.
- $x_\ell$ is a binary indicator pertaining to the maintenance of line $\ell$ ($\ell = 1, \ldots, n_L$). $x_\ell = 1$ if maintenance is performed in line $\ell$ and 0 otherwise.
- $u_{it}$ is a binary indicator providing the status of unit $i$ ($i = 1, \ldots, n_G$) in time period $t$ ($t = 1, \ldots, n_T$). $u_{it} = 1$ if unit $i$ is online in time period $t$ and 0 otherwise.
- $\theta_{r(\ell)t}$ is the angle of the receiving-end node of line $\ell$ ($\ell = 1, \ldots, n_L$).
- $\theta_{s(\ell)t}$ is the angle of the sending-end node of line $\ell$ ($\ell = 1, \ldots, n_L$).

The constants, sets and functions are:

- $B^F$ is the financial budget to carry out preventive maintenance interventions.
- $B^U$ is the uncertainty budget pertaining to line outages.
- $B_\ell$ is the susceptance of line $\ell$ ($\ell = 1, \ldots, n_L$).
- $c_i(\cdot)$ is the production cost (function) of unit $i$ ($i = 1, \ldots, n_G$).
- $D_{jt}$ is the load of demand $j$ in time period $t$ ($t = 1, \ldots, n_T$).
- $F_\ell^{\max}$ is the transmission capacity of line $\ell$ ($\ell = 1, \ldots, n_L$).
- $K_\ell^M$ is the transmission capacity increase as a result of performing preventive maintenance in line $\ell$ ($\ell = 1, \ldots, n_L$).

$K_\ell^{\mathrm{F}}$ is the transmission capacity reduction due to a failure (or partial failure) of line $\ell$ ($\ell = 1, \ldots, n_{\mathrm{L}}$).
$P_i^{\max}$ is the capacity of generating unit $i$ ($i = 1, \ldots, n_{\mathrm{G}}$).
$P_i^{\min}$ is the minimum power output of generating unit $i$ ($i = 1, \ldots, n_{\mathrm{G}}$).
$\Omega_n^{\mathrm{G}}$ is the set generating units located at node $n$.
$\Omega_n^{\mathrm{D}}$ is the set demands located at node $n$.

The third-level problem of tri-level problem (7.2.2) seeks to minimize the operating cost and includes three sets of constraints, namely, upper and lower production bounds on each generating unit in each time period, power balance at each node and each time period, and capacity limit of each line in each time period. The second-level problem seeks to maximize operating cost by selecting the worst line outage within a simple uncertainty set. The first-level problem seeks to minimize the operating cost by identifying the best preventive maintenance interventions complying with the maintenance budget.

The ARO problem (7.2.2) can be solved using the methodology described in Chap. 3.

We conclude indicating that preventive maintenance scheduling of both production [3] and transmission [1] facilities is most important for any power company.

Grid maintenance involves the preventive maintenance of both transmission and distribution assets and is generally carried out by different entities, as transmission and distribution facilities have generally different owners. Preventive maintenance of transmission facilities generally involves power lines and power transformers, while preventive maintenance of distribution systems involves substations, feeders and medium-to-low voltage transformers.

It is relevant to note that any preventive maintenance work should be carried out ensuring the security of the electric energy supply. This is particularly important in case of multiple ownership of both network and production facilities, as different owners may have conflicting objectives, which need to be coordinated to ensure high supply security.

## 7.3 Fuel Procurement

The fuel procurement problem [4, 5] is faced by any electricity producer that relies on a primary fuel to produce electricity. For instance, an electricity producer that owns a number of combined cycle gas turbines (CCGTs) needs to procure the natural gas used by these CCGTs to produce electricity.

Generally, primary fuel can be procured through long- or medium-term contracts and in the spot market (short-term). Procurement contracts are generally take-or-pay and thus the electricity producer seeks to procure just what it needs, not more than that. Spot (short-term) procurement is also possible, but generally at a much higher cost.

The key uncertainty faced by the considered electricity producer is the demand that it has to supply, which may be complex to predict within a medium-term planning horizon, of one to several months.

Within an ARO framework, the decision-making process of this electricity producer follows the three steps below:

1. The electricity producer decides on which medium-term contracts to sign to procure the primary fuel needed to run its generating units and serve its future electric demand. This producer seeks to minimize the cost of electricity supply.
2. The electric demand materializes in the worst possible manner within a given uncertainty set. That is, in such a manner that the cost of electricity supply is maximum.
3. On a daily basis, once the electricity demand is known with a certain level of accuracy, the producer proceeds to supply it using the primary fuel obtained via contracts and, if needed, by buying fuel in the spot market.

### *7.3.1 Simple Example*

We illustrate how to use an ARO model to address the fuel procurement problem using the very simple example depicted in Fig. 7.2.

The electricity producer in this example runs a single CCGT, and it can procure natural gas via a contract at \$2/unit and via the spot market at \$4/unit.

The available contract allows the producer to buy either 3 or 5 units of gas.

The electricity demand is uncertain and for simplicity we assume that it may take just two values, either 2 or 4 electricity units.

We assume also that the overall conversion efficiency from natural gas to electricity is 50%.

An ARO model for the electricity producer to decide which one of the two procurement contracts to sign is provided below.

$$\begin{aligned} \min_{x\in\{3,5\}} \quad \max_{d\in\{2,4\}} \quad \min_{y\geq 0} \quad & z = 2x + 4y \\ \text{s.t.} \quad & \tfrac{1}{2}(x+y) \geq d, \end{aligned} \tag{7.3.1}$$

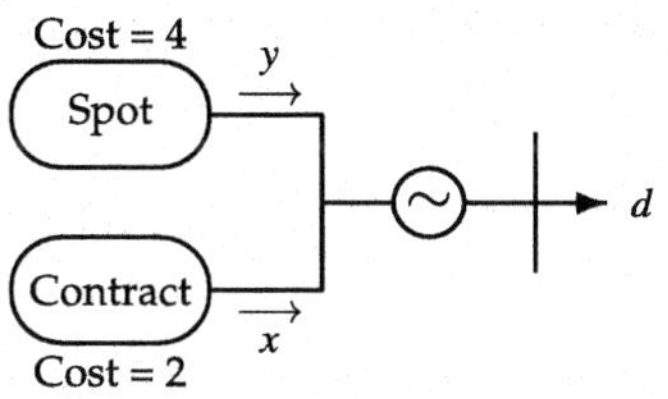


**Fig. 7.2** Fuel procurement example

where $x$ represents the gas contracting decision, $y$ represents the gas purchased in the pool, and $d$ represents the electric demand. The overall objective is minimum gas procurement cost, which is equivalent to minimum electricity supply cost. The third-level problem identifies the best pool purchases seeking minimum procurement cost. The second-level problem determines the worst electric demand realization (that results in maximum procurement cost). The first-level problem identifies the best contracting decisions seeking minimum procurement cost.

Given the simplicity of this problem, it can be solved by enumeration.

If the contract selected is the one involving 3 gas units and the demand realized in 2 electricity units, 1 gas unit needs to be bought in the spot market and the supply cost is \$10. If, on the hand, the demand realization is 4 electricity units, 5 gas units need to be bought in the spot market and the supply cost is \$26. We select the demand realization of 4 electricity units as it results in the highest electricity supply cost, \$26.

If, on the other hand, the contract selected is the one involving 5 gas units and the demand realization is 2 electricity units, 0 gas unit needs to be bought in the spot market and the supply cost is \$10. If, on the hand, the demand realization is 4 electricity units, 3 gas units need to be bought in the spot market and the supply cost is \$22. We select the demand realization of 4 electricity units as it results in the highest electricity supply cost, \$22.

Since the producer seeks to minimize its supply cost, it selects the 5-unit gas contract, which considering the worst demand realization (electricity demand of 4 units) entails a supply cost of \$22.

## 7.3.2 General Formulation

Generally, the fuel procurement problem has the form:

$$\min_{\mathbf{x}\in\mathscr{X}} \quad \max_{\mathbf{u}\in\mathscr{U}} \quad \min_{\mathbf{y}\in\mathscr{Y}(\mathbf{x},\mathbf{u})} \quad f(\mathbf{x},\mathbf{y},\mathbf{u}).$$

This procurement problem seeks to identify the best fuel contracting strategy, anticipating the worst electricity demand realization, and assuming that the electricity producer reacts in the pool to supply the worst electricity demand realization in the cheapest possible manner.

Variable $\mathbf{x}\in\mathscr{X}$ represents the different fuel procurement contracts that can be signed by the electricity producer.

Variable $\mathbf{u}\in\mathscr{U}$ represents the uncertain demand and gas pool prices. Appropriate uncertainty sets representing the future electricity demand and gas pool prices and their respective time evolutions over time need to be considered.

Variable $\mathbf{y}\in\mathscr{Y}$ represents the electricity producer actions to eventually buy fuel in the pool to supply the demand at minimum cost once the worst demand has realized.

A rather generic but particular instance of the above formulation is:

$$\min_{\substack{g_{i1}^{\mathrm{C}},\dots,g_{in_{\mathrm{T}}}^{\mathrm{C}}\geq 0\\ g_{i1}^{\mathrm{C}},\dots,g_{in_{\mathrm{T}}}^{\mathrm{C}}\in\Omega_i^{\mathrm{C}}\\ \forall i=1,\dots,n_{\mathrm{C}}}} \quad \max_{\substack{d_1,\dots,d_{n_{\mathrm{T}}}\in\Lambda^{\mathrm{D}}\\ c_1^{\mathrm{P}},\dots,c_{n_{\mathrm{T}}}^{\mathrm{P}}\in\Lambda^{\mathrm{P}}}} \quad \min_{g_1^{\mathrm{P}},\dots,g_{n_{\mathrm{T}}}^{\mathrm{P}}\geq 0} \quad z=\sum_{i=1}^{n_{\mathrm{C}}} c_i^{\mathrm{C}}\sum_{t=1}^{n_{\mathrm{T}}} g_{it}^{\mathrm{C}}+\sum_{t=1}^{n_{\mathrm{T}}} c_t^{\mathrm{P}} g_t^{\mathrm{P}}$$

$$\text{s.t.} \quad \eta\left(\sum_{i=1}^{n_{\mathrm{C}}} g_{it}^{\mathrm{C}}+g_t^{\mathrm{P}}\right)\geq d_t, \quad \forall t=1,\dots,n_{\mathrm{T}}, \tag{7.3.2}$$

where the optimization variables are:

$c_t^{\mathrm{P}}$ is the per unit cost of fuel bought in the pool in time period $t$ ($t = 1, \dots, n_{\mathrm{T}}$).
$d_t$ is the electricity demand in time period $t$ ($t = 1, \dots, n_{\mathrm{T}}$).
$g_{it}^{\mathrm{C}}$ is the quantity of fuel from contract $i$ ($i = 1, \dots, n_{\mathrm{C}}$) used in time period $t$ ($t = 1, \dots, n_{\mathrm{T}}$)
$g_t^{\mathrm{P}}$ is the quantity of fuel bought in the pool in time period $t$ ($t = 1, \dots, n_{\mathrm{T}}$).

The constants and sets are:

$c_i^{\mathrm{C}}$ (constant) is the per unit cost of fuel bought through contract $i$ ($i = 1, \dots, n_{\mathrm{C}}$).
$\eta$ (constant) conversion factor gas to electricity.
$\Lambda^{\mathrm{D}}$ is the uncertainty set pertaining to the demand.
$\Lambda^{\mathrm{P}}$ is the uncertainty set pertaining to the pool price.
$\Omega_i^{\mathrm{C}}$ is the set defining the contracting conditions of contract $i$ throughout all time periods.

The overall objective is minimum supply cost by using both fuel bought through contracts and in the pool. The third-level problem identifies fuel purchases in the pool seeking minimum supply cost. It is subject to the supply of the electricity demand per time period. The second-level problem selects the worst demand and pool-price realizations (those that result in maximum electricity supply cost). The first-level problem seeks to minimize the supply cost by selecting the most favorable contracts.

Problem (7.3.2) above is an ARO problem that can be solved using the solution techniques described in Chap. 3.

We conclude indicating that power plants that rely on fossil fuels need to ensure the procurement of such primary energy so that electricity can be produced uneventfully. This is particularly critical for natural gas-fired units, since the supply of natural gas is contingent to pipeline capacity availability [6], or the availability of natural gas from liquefied natural gas (LNG) facilities, which often depends on maritime shipments that might not be reliable.

Therefore, the adequate planning of fuel procurement is a critical problem faced by any electric energy producer that relies on fossil or nuclear fuels.

## 7.4 Medium-Term Hydro Scheduling

Hydroelectric producers [7] with load serving obligations are subject to two major uncertainties. On the one hand, water inflows to reservoirs are highly uncertain within a medium-term horizon that may span several months. On the other hand, the electricity demand to be served is also uncertain, but generally to a comparative lower degree.

Within this uncertain environment, hydroelectric producers establish an electricity production schedule well in advance of energy delivery, satisfying many requirements pertaining to the use of water for purposes other than electricity production, such as human consumption, ecological needs, or recreational ones [8].

Therefore, the decision-making process of a hydroelectric producer in the medium-term within an ARO framework follows the three steps below:

1. The hydroelectric producer schedules the electricity production of its hydro plants on a weekly basis throughout a several-month planning horizon, considering hydro, environmental, human-consumption, and other constraints. The producer seeks to minimize the cost of electricity supply.
2. The water inflow and electric demand materialize in the worst possible manner throughout the planning horizon. That is, in such a manner that the cost of electricity supply is maximum.
3. On a weekly basis, once the water inflow and the electricity demand are known with a sufficient level of accuracy, the producer proceeds to supply the electrical load using, if needed, alternative electricity sources. Additionally, the producer may incur in undesirable water spillage.

### *7.4.1 Simple Example*

The very simple example below illustrates how to use an ARO model to address the medium-term hydro-scheduling planning problem under uncertainty.

We consider a hydroelectric producer operating a hydroelectric system with a single reservoir and its associated hydro turbine, as depicted in Fig. 7.3. We consider a single planning period. The variable describing the uncertain water inflow to the reservoir is $h$ (water units), while the variable describing water spillage from the reservoir is $s$ (water units). We consider that the water inflow can only take two values, either 6 or 8. The variable describing the uncertain electricity demand is $d$ (electrical energy units). We consider that the electricity demand can only take two values, either 2 or 4.

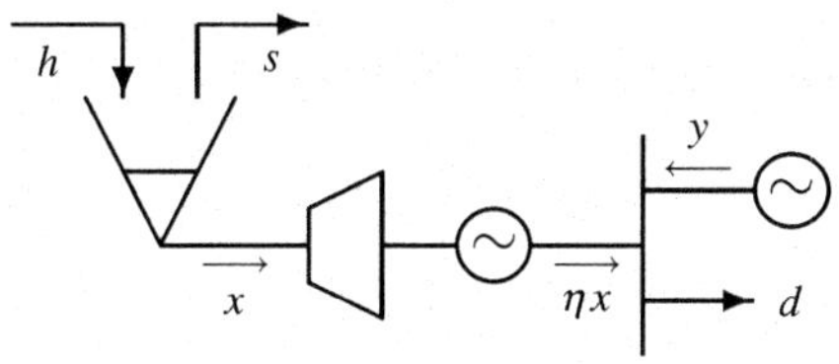


**Fig. 7.3** Hydro scheduling example

The potential energy of the water released from the reservoir is denoted by $x$ (potential energy units), and the considered conversion factor from potential energy to electrical energy is $\eta = \frac{1}{2}$. The energy bought from the alternative electricity source is denoted by $y$. See Fig. 7.3.

Since we assume that the reservoir content is bounded below and above by 1 and 4, respectively, and that its initial content in 2, the water balance must meet the double-sided constraint below:

$$1 \leq 2 + h - x - s \leq 4.$$

On the other hand, the electric energy balance requires:

$$\frac{1}{2}x + y = d.$$

The cost of buying electricity from the alternative source is \$10/unit and the cost of spilled water is assumed to be \$100/unit. The cost of hydroelectricity production is considered null.

The objective function of the ARO model includes two terms, namely, the cost of buying electricity from an alternative source $(10y)$ and the cost of water spillage $(100s)$.

Considering the above problem description, an ARO model for this very simple single-period hydro scheduling problem is:

$$\begin{aligned} \min_{x \geq 0} \ \max_{\substack{d \in \{2,4\} \\ h \in \{6,8\}}} \ \min_{y \geq 0} \quad & z = 10y + 100s \\ \text{s.t.} \quad & \tfrac{1}{2}x + y = d \\ & 1 \leq 2 + h - x - s \leq 4. \end{aligned} \tag{7.4.1}$$

The overall objective is minimum supply cost. The first level-problem decides on purchases from the alternative source seeking minimum cost. It is subject to water and electricity balances. The second-level problem selects the worst demand realization (that results in maximum supply cost) and the first-level problem establishes the best water release schedule seeking minimum supply cost.

Given the simplicity of this example, we solved it by inspection. The worst combination of hydro inflow and demand is $h = 6$ and $d = 4$, respectively, and since spillage is very costly, we set $s = 0$. The resulting single-level min problem is:

$$\begin{aligned} \min_{y \geq 0} \quad & z = 10y \\ \text{s.t.} \quad & \tfrac{1}{2}x + y = 4 \\ & 1 \leq 2 + 6 - x \leq 4, \end{aligned}$$

whose solution is $x = 7$ and $y = \frac{1}{2}$ with a worst-case supply cost of $z = 5$.

### 7.4.2 General Formulation

Generally, the medium-term hydroelectric scheduling problem has the form:

$$\min_{\mathbf{x} \in \mathscr{X}} \quad \max_{\mathbf{u} \in \mathscr{U}} \quad \min_{\mathbf{y} \in \mathscr{Y}(\mathbf{x}, \mathbf{u})} \quad f(\mathbf{x}, \mathbf{y}, \mathbf{u}).$$

This hydroelectric scheduling problem seeks to identify the best electricity production schedule, anticipating the worst inflow and demand realizations, and assuming that the electricity producer reacts under these worst realizations to supply the electricity demand at the minimum possible cost.

Variable $\mathbf{x} \in \mathscr{X}$ represents the scheduled hydro productions.

Variable $\mathbf{u} \in \mathscr{U}$ represents the uncertain water inflows, demands, and electricity purchase prices. Appropriate uncertainty sets representing future water inflows, electricity demands, and electricity purchase prices, and their evolution over time need to be considered.

Variable $\mathbf{y} \in \mathscr{Y}$ represents the electricity producer actions to supply the demand at minimum cost once the worst inflows and demands have realized, which may require using alternative electricity sources or spilling water.

A rather generic but particular instance of this problem is provided below:

$$\begin{aligned} \min_{x_1,\ldots,x_{n_\mathrm{T}} \geq 0} \quad \max_{\substack{d_1,\ldots,d_{n_\mathrm{T}} \in \Lambda^\mathrm{D} \\ h_1,\ldots,h_{n_\mathrm{T}} \in \Lambda^\mathrm{H} \\ c_1,\ldots,c_{n_\mathrm{T}} \in \Lambda^\mathrm{C}}} \quad \min_{y_1,\ldots,y_{n_\mathrm{T}} \geq 0} \quad & z = \sum_{t=1}^{n_\mathrm{T}} c_t \; y_t + M \; s_t \\ \text{s.t.} \quad & v^{\min} \leq v_{t-1} + h_t - x_t - s_t \leq v^{\max}, \\ & \quad \forall t = 1, \ldots, n_\mathrm{T} \\ & \eta x_t + y_t = d_t, \\ & \quad \forall t = 2, \ldots, n_\mathrm{T}, \end{aligned} \tag{7.4.2}$$

where the optimization variables are:

$c_t$ is the electricity purchase price in time period $t$ ($t = 1, \dots, n_T$).
$d_t$ is the electricity demand in time period $t$ ($t = 1, \dots, n_T$).
$h_t$ is the water inflow into the reservoir in time period $t$ ($t = 1, \dots, n_T$).
$s_t$ is the water spillage in time period $t$ ($t = 1, \dots, n_T$).
$v_t$ is water content of the reservoir in the beginning of time period $t$ ($t = 1, \dots, n_T$).
$x_t$ is the scheduled water discharge for electricity production in time period $t$ ($t = 1, \dots, n_T$).
$y_t$ is the electricity purchase in time period $t$ ($t = 1, \dots, n_T$).

The constants are:

$M$ is a large enough positive constant.
$v^{\max}$ is upper bound of the reservoir content.
$v^{\min}$ is lower bound of the reservoir content.
$\eta$ is the conversion factor from potential to electrical energy.
$v_1$ is the water content of the reservoir at the beginning of the study horizon.
$\Lambda^D$ is the uncertainty budget for the electrical demand.
$\Lambda^H$ is the uncertainty budget for water inflow into the reservoir.
$\Lambda^P$ is the uncertainty budget for electricity purchase prices.

The overall objective is to minimize the cost of supplying the electricity demand using hydro electricity and pool purchases.

The third-level problem decides on electricity pool purchases seeking minimum demand-supply cost. It is subject to two sets of constraints, namely, water balance and bounds of the reservoir in each time period, and electricity demand supply in each time period. The second-level problem selects the worst realizations of demand, water inflow, and electricity purchase price (that lead to maximum electricity supply cost). The first-level problem schedules water discharges per time period seeking minimum cost.

The ARO formulation (7.4.2) can be solved using the methodology described in Chap. 3.

We conclude indicating that seasonal hydro scheduling is most important in regions of the world that rely on hydroelectricity, e.g., the state of Washington, Brazil or Norway [7]. Seasonal scheduling, spanning several months, is followed by weekly and/or daily scheduling. The overall goal is to minimize the supply cost (case of the state of Washington) or to maximize the profit from selling electricity in the electricity market (case of Norway).

Give the high uncertainty of water inflows, hydroelectric scheduling is a critical task for hydroelectricity producers. ARO approaches for hydroelectric scheduling are most appropriate since they allow to minimize the need to use alternative electricity sources, which are comparatively very expensive, and the risk of water spillage, which is highly undesirable.

## 7.5 Selling Electricity via Contracts

Within an electricity market context [9], an electricity producer has generally the option of selling its production through contracts, which can be bilateral or standard from the futures market, spanning from weeks to months, or in the day-ahead pool, spanning one day on an hourly basis [10, 11].

Contract prices are stable, while pool prices are not (they are stochastic). Selling through a contract eliminate the uncertainty pertaining to the producer revenue since the contracting price is fixed. However, if the future average (over the contract duration) pool price is higher than the contracting price, the producer loses the opportunity of achieving a higher revenue if it signs the contract. If, on the other hand, the future average (over the contract duration) pool price is lower than the contracting price, the producer is better off by signing the contract.

Therefore, an electricity producer must find the best way to allocate its production to bilateral contracts (medium-term alternative) and the pool (short-term alternative), so that its profit is maximized and its risk of profit variability controlled.

If the producer is risk averse, it may consider an ARO approach to identify the best combination contracts/pool. Within such an ARO framework, the decision-making process for the electricity producer is as follows:

1. The electricity producer decides on which contracts to sign. It seeks to maximize its revenue from selling electricity.
2. Pool prices materialize in the worst possible manner (within an uncertainty set) throughout the contracting horizon. That is, in such a manner that the producer revenue is minimum.
3. On a daily basis, once the pool prices are known with a sufficient level of accuracy, the producer sells its remaining capacity in the pool seeking maximum profit.

### *7.5.1 Simple Example*

The very simple example below illustrates how to use an ARO model to address this medium-term contracting problem for an electricity producer.

We consider an electricity producer that may sell its production through a contract at $\lambda^{\mathrm{C}} = \$4/\text{unit}$. Alternatively, this producer may sell its electricity production in a 2-period pool, whose prices are $\lambda_1 \in \{1, 5\}$ and $\lambda_2 \in \{6, 8\}$. This is illustrated in Fig. 7.4. We exclude the price combination $\lambda_1 = 1$ and $\lambda_2 = 6$ from the four possible ones, as it is considered to be very unlikely.

The production sold through the contract is denoted by $p^{\mathrm{C}}$, while the productions sold in the pool are denoted by $p_1^{\mathrm{P}}$ and $p_2^{\mathrm{P}}$.

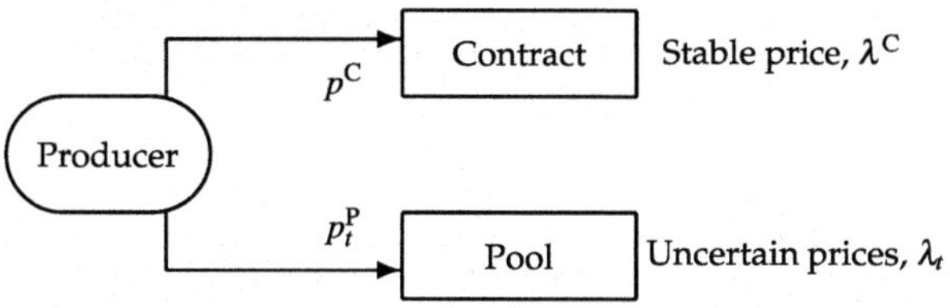


**Fig. 7.4** Contracting example for an electricity producer

The actual power output of the producer may vary between 10 and 20 units and its production cost is \$3.0/unit.

Finally, a policy affecting the producer requires that the energy sold through the contract is at least 25% of its capacity (20 units).

Considering the above problem description, an ARO model for this very simple contracting problem is provided below:

$$\max_{p^C \geq 0} \quad \min_{\substack{(\lambda_1,\lambda_2)\in \\ \{(1,8) \\ (5,6) \\ (5,8)\}}} \quad \max_{\substack{p_1^P \geq 0 \\ p_2^P \geq 0 \\ u_1 \in \{0,1\} \\ u_2 \in \{0,1\}}} \quad z = 2(4-3)p^C + (\lambda_1 - 3)p_1^P + (\lambda_2 - 3)p_2^P$$
$$\text{s.t.} \quad 10u_1 \leq p_1^P + p^C \leq 20u_1$$
$$10u_2 \leq p_2^P + p^C \leq 20u_2$$
$$p^C \geq \frac{1}{4}20. \tag{7.5.1}$$

The third-level problem represents the selling in the pool and is subject to the production bounds of the generating facility of the producer and the contracting policy. The second-level problem represents the pool price uncertainty, and the first-level one the contracting decision. The objective function includes the revenue from the contract, $2(4-3)p^C$, that spans the two periods (hence the factor 2), and the revenue from selling in the pool, $(\lambda_1 - 3)p_1^P + (\lambda_2 - 3)p_2^P$, that includes the two periods.

We note that a general version of the problem above would be highly complex to solve as the third-level problem include binary decisions. However, given the simplicity of this example, we proceed to solve it by enumeration.

Since from the producer perspective, price combination $(5, 8)$ is clearly superior to price combination $(1, 8)$, we consider solely the price combinations $(1, 8)$ and $(5, 6)$.

Specifically, the resulting single-level max problem for the price combination $(1, 8)$ is:

$$\max_{\substack{p^{\mathrm{C}}\geq 0\\ p_1^{\mathrm{P}}\geq 0\\ p_2^{\mathrm{P}}\geq 0\\ u_1\in\{0,1\}\\ u_2\in\{0,1\}}} \quad z = 2(4-3)p^{\mathrm{C}} + (1-3)p_1^{\mathrm{P}} + (8-3)p_2^{\mathrm{P}}$$

$$\text{s.t.} \quad 10u_1 \leq p_1^{\mathrm{P}} + p^{\mathrm{C}} \leq 20u_1$$

$$10u_2 \leq p_2^{\mathrm{P}} + p^{\mathrm{C}} \leq 20u_2$$

$$p^{\mathrm{C}} \geq \tfrac{1}{4}20.$$

We note that fixing the variables of the middle (second-level) problem to specific values allows merging the two max problems, the first- and the first-level ones. This is though a simplification that implicitly swaps problems in levels 2 and 3.

The problem above is a linear programming problem whose solution is $p^{\mathrm{C}} = 5$, $p_1^{\mathrm{P}} = 5$, $p_2^{\mathrm{P}} = 15$, with a profit of \$75.

The reader is encouraged to check the price combination (5, 6), which results in the solution $p^{\mathrm{C}} = 5$, $p_1^{\mathrm{P}} = 15$, $p_2^{\mathrm{P}} = 15$, with a profit of \$85.

Therefore the solution of the original problem is $\lambda_1 = 1$, $\lambda_2 = 8$, $p^{\mathrm{C}} = 5$, $p_1^{\mathrm{P}} = 5$, $p_2^{\mathrm{P}} = 15$, with a profit of \$75.

## 7.5.2 General Formulation

Generally, the medium-term contracting problem for a producer has the form:

$$\max_{\mathbf{x}\in\mathscr{X}} \quad \min_{\mathbf{u}\in\mathscr{U}} \quad \max_{\mathbf{y}\in\mathscr{Y}(\mathbf{x},\mathbf{u})} \quad f(\mathbf{x}, \mathbf{y}, \mathbf{u}).$$

This contracting problem identifies the best contracts to sign by an electricity producer seeking maximum profit, anticipating the worst pool price realizations (within an uncertainty set), and assuming that the producer subsequently reacts to such worst price realization by selling (or not) in the pool its remaining capacity to achieve maximum profit.

Variable $\mathbf{x} \in \mathscr{X}$ represents the quantities sold through contracts.

Variable $\mathbf{u} \in \mathscr{U}$ represents the uncertain pool prices. Appropriate uncertainty sets representing future pool prices and their evolution over time need to be considered.

Variable $\mathbf{y} \in \mathscr{Y}$ represents the quantities sold in the pool.

A particular but rather general instance of the above formulation is provided below:

$$
\max_{\substack{p^{\mathrm{C}}_{i1},\ldots,p^{\mathrm{C}}_{in_{\mathrm{C}}}\geq 0 \\ p^{\mathrm{C}}_{i1},\ldots,p^{\mathrm{C}}_{in_{\mathrm{C}}}\in\Omega^{\mathrm{C}}_i \\ \forall i=1,\ldots,n_{\mathrm{C}}}} \quad \min_{\lambda_1,\ldots,\lambda_{n_{\mathrm{T}}}\in\Lambda} \quad \max_{\substack{p^{\mathrm{P}}_1,\ldots,p^{\mathrm{P}}_{n_{\mathrm{T}}}\geq 0 \\ u_1,\ldots,u_{n_{\mathrm{T}}}\in\{0,1\}}} \quad z = \sum_{i=1}^{n_{\mathrm{C}}}\left[\sum_{t=1}^{n_{\mathrm{T}}} p^{\mathrm{C}}_{it}(\lambda^{\mathrm{C}}_i - c)\right] + \sum_{t=1}^{n_{\mathrm{T}}} p^{\mathrm{P}}_t(\lambda_t - c)
$$

$$
\text{s.t.} \quad u_t P^{\min} \leq \sum_{i=1}^{n_{\mathrm{C}}} p^{\mathrm{C}}_{it} + p^{\mathrm{P}}_t \leq u_t P^{\max} \quad \forall t = 1,\ldots,n_{\mathrm{T}} \tag{7.5.2}
$$

where the optimization variables are:

- $p^{\mathrm{C}}_{it}$ is the power sold through contract $i$ ($i = 1,\ldots,n_{\mathrm{C}}$) in time period $t$ ($\forall t = 1,\ldots,n_{\mathrm{T}}$).
- $p^{\mathrm{P}}_t$ is the power sold in the pool in time period $t$ ($\forall t = 1,\ldots,n_{\mathrm{T}}$).
- $u_t$ is a binary variable representing the status of the production facility in time period $t$ ($\forall t = 1,\ldots,n_{\mathrm{T}}$): 1 if on and 0 otherwise.
- $\lambda_t$ is the pool price in time period $t$ ($\forall t = 1,\ldots,n_{\mathrm{T}}$).

The constants and sets are:

- $c$ is the production cost of the producer.
- $P^{\max}$ is the capacity of the production facility of the producer.
- $P^{\min}$ is the minimum power output of the production facility of the producer.
- $\lambda^{\mathrm{C}}_i$ is the price to sell energy through contract $i$ ($i = 1,\ldots,n_{\mathrm{C}}$).
- $\Lambda$ is the uncertainty set of pool prices.

In the formulation above we consider that the producer owns a single production facility. We note that this assumption can be eliminated without complication.

The overall objective is maximum profit from selling electricity through contracts and in the pool. The third-level problem represents the selling of electric energy in the pool seeking maximum profit. It is subject to the lower and upper bounds of the production facility in each time period. The second-level problem seeks minimum profit by selecting the worst pool prices. The first-level problem seeks maximum profit by selecting the most profitable contracts.

The ARO problem (7.5.2) can be solved using the methodology described in Chap. 3.

We conclude indicating that selling through contracts [12, 10, 11] is an important alternative for electricity producers operating in an electricity market.

Contracts, which span weeks to months, stabilize the future revenues of the producer since contract prices are fixed, i.e., they function as risk-control mechanisms. On the other hand, selling in the pool involves a string of uncertain revenues since pool prices are stochastic. If the average (over the contract duration) pool price is higher than the contract price of a given contract, the electricity producer is better off on average by neglecting such contract, but if the average (over the contract duration) pool price is lower than the contract price, the electricity producer is better off on average by signing the contract.

Seeking maximum profit under a limited risk of profit variability, electricity producers may use ARO models to identify which are the best contracts to sign.

## 7.6 Consumer Electricity Procurement

Large consumers procure their electrical energy through long- or medium-term contracts (either bilateral, or standard from a futures market [9]), spanning from weeks to months, or in the pool on a daily basis [13, 14, 15].

Buying electricity via a bilateral contract freezes the risk of cost variability, but at the expense of losing the opportunity of buying from the pool if the average (over the contract duration) pool price is lower than the contracting price. On the other hand, if the average (over the contract duration) pool price turns out to be higher than the price of the contract, the consumer is protected against such high average pool price.

Given the pool price stochasticity, a large consumer must decide on the best combination of contracts and pool participation to procure its electric energy needs within a medium-term framework (ranging from weeks to months), at minimum cost and at an adequate level of risk of cost variability.

If an ARO framework is adopted, the decision-making process of the consumer is as follows:

1. The electricity consumer decides on which contracts to sign, seeking to minimize its cost from buying electricity.
2. Pool prices materialize in the worst possible manner (within an uncertainty set) throughout the contracting horizon. That is, in such a manner that the consumer cost is maximum.
3. On a daily basis, once the pool prices are known with a sufficient level of accuracy, the consumer buys its remaining electricity needs in the pool seeking minimum cost.

### *7.6.1 Simple Example*

The simple example below illustrates how to use an ARO model to decide on the right combination contract/pool by an electricity consumer.

We consider a consumer that has the option of signing a contract to buy electricity at \$5/unit during two time periods. Alternatively, this consumer may buy electricity in the pool during periods 1 and 2 at uncertain prices $\lambda_1 \in \{4, 5\}$ and $\lambda_2 \in \{6, 8\}$. This is illustrated in Fig. 7.5.

Statistical analysis of the price data shows that the combination $\lambda_1 = 5$ and $\lambda_2 = 8$ is impossible and thus, it can be neglected.

The demand to be supplied in periods 1 and 2 are 18 and 20, respectively.

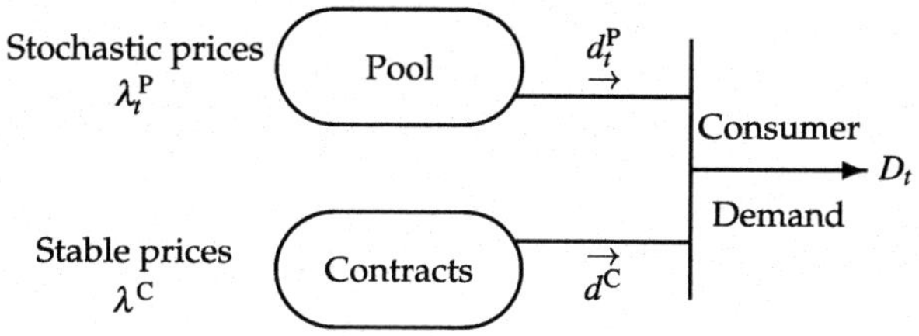


**Fig. 7.5** Electricity procurement for a large consumer

Considering the above problem description, an ARO model for this very simple electricity procurement problem is provided below:

$$\min_{d^{\mathrm{C}}\geq 0} \max_{\substack{(\lambda_1,\lambda_2)\in \\ \{(4,6)\\ (4,8)\\ (5,6)\}}} \min_{\substack{d_1^{\mathrm{P}}\geq 0\\ d_2^{\mathrm{P}}\geq 0}} \quad z = 2\cdot 5\cdot d^{\mathrm{C}} + \lambda_1 d_1^{\mathrm{P}} + \lambda_2 d_2^{\mathrm{P}} \tag{7.6.1}$$
$$\text{s.t.} \quad d^{\mathrm{C}} + d_1^{\mathrm{P}} = 18$$
$$d^{\mathrm{C}} + d_2^{\mathrm{P}} = 20,$$

where $d^{\mathrm{C}}$ is the demand procured through the contract (2 periods), $d_1^{\mathrm{P}}$ is the demand procured in the pool in period 1, and $d_2^{\mathrm{P}}$ is the demand procured in the pool in period 2. The objective function is the procurement cost, including contracting cost and pool purchase cost.

The third-level problem represents the electricity procurement in the pool and is subject to supplying the demand in the two considered periods. The second-level problem represents the pool price uncertainty, and the first-level one the contracting decision.

Since the problem above is very simple, it can be solved by enumeration. From the viewpoint of the worst price realization, since the price combination (4, 8) is superior to the price combination (4, 6), only price combinations (4, 8) and (5, 6) need to be considered. Using the price combination (4, 8), the problem above reduces to the single-level min problem below:

$$\min_{\substack{d_1^{\mathrm{P}}\geq 0\\ d_2^{\mathrm{P}}\geq 0\\ d^{\mathrm{C}}\geq 0}} \quad z = 10d^{\mathrm{C}} + 4d_1^{\mathrm{P}} + 8d_2^{\mathrm{P}}$$
$$\text{s.t.} \quad d^{\mathrm{C}} + d_1^{\mathrm{P}} = 18$$
$$d^{\mathrm{C}} + d_2^{\mathrm{P}} = 20,$$

whose solution is $d^{\mathrm{C}} = 18$, $d_1^{\mathrm{P}} = 0$ and $d_2^{\mathrm{P}} = 2$, with a procurement cost equal to \$196.

If the price combination is (5, 6), the solution is $d^{\mathrm{C}} = 18$, $d_1^{\mathrm{P}} = 0$ and $d_2^{\mathrm{P}} = 2$, with a procurement cost equal to \$192.

Therefore, the producer signs a contract for $d^{\mathrm{C}} = 18$ and is ready for the worst realization of pool prices that is $(\lambda_1, \lambda_2) = (4, 8)$.

### 7.6.2 *General Formulation*

Generally, the medium-term electricity procurement problem of a consumer has the form:

$$\min_{\mathbf{x}\in\mathscr{X}} \quad \max_{\mathbf{u}\in\mathscr{U}} \quad \min_{\mathbf{y}\in\mathscr{Y}(\mathbf{x},\mathbf{u})} \quad f(\mathbf{x}, \mathbf{y}, \mathbf{u}).$$

This procurement problem seeks to identify the best contracts to sign by an electricity consumer seeking minimum cost, anticipating the worst pool price realizations (within an uncertainty set), and assuming that the consumer subsequently reacts to such worst price realizations by buying (or not) in the pool its remaining demand to achieve minimum cost.

Variable $\mathbf{x} \in \mathscr{X}$ represents the quantities bought through contracts.

Variable $\mathbf{u} \in \mathscr{U}$ represents the uncertain pool prices. Appropriate uncertainty sets representing future pool prices and their evolution over time need to be considered.

Variable $\mathbf{y} \in \mathscr{Y}$ represents the quantities bought in the pool.

A rather general instance of this procurement problem can be formulated as:

$$\begin{aligned} \min_{\substack{d_{i1}^{\mathrm{C}},\dots,d_{in_{\mathrm{T}}}^{\mathrm{C}}\in\Omega_i^{\mathrm{C}} \\ \forall i=1,\dots,n_{\mathrm{C}}}} \quad \max_{\lambda_1,\dots,\lambda_{n_{\mathrm{T}}}\in\Lambda} \quad \min_{d_t^{\mathrm{P}}\geq 0} \quad & z = \sum_{i=1}^{n_{\mathrm{C}}} \lambda_i^{\mathrm{C}} \sum_{t=1}^{n_{\mathrm{T}}} d_{it}^{\mathrm{C}} + \sum_{t=1}^{n_{\mathrm{T}}} \lambda_t d_t^{\mathrm{P}} \\ \text{s.t.} \quad & \sum_{i=1}^{n_{\mathrm{C}}} d_{it}^{\mathrm{C}} + d_t^{\mathrm{P}} = D_t, \forall t, \end{aligned} \tag{7.6.2}$$

where the optimization variables are:

$d_{it}^{\mathrm{C}}$ is the quantity to be supplied by contract $i$ ($i = 1, \dots, n_{\mathrm{C}}$) in time period $t$ ($t = 1, \dots, n_{\mathrm{T}}$).
$d_t^{\mathrm{P}}$ is the quantity to be bought in the pool in time period $t$ ($t = 1, \dots, n_{\mathrm{T}}$).
$\lambda_t$ is the pool price in time period $t$ ($t = 1, \dots, n_{\mathrm{T}}$).

The constants and sets are:

$D_t$ is the demand to be supplied in time period $t$ ($t = 1, \dots, n_{\mathrm{T}}$).
$\lambda_i^{\mathrm{C}}$ is the price of contract $i$ ($i = 1, \dots, n_{\mathrm{C}}$).
$\Lambda$ is the uncertainty set for pool prices.
$\Omega_i^{\mathrm{C}}$ is the set defining the specific conditions of contract $i$ ($i = 1, \dots, n_{\mathrm{C}}$).

The overall objective is minimum electricity procurement cost by buying from contracts and in the pool. The third-level problem identifies the best purchases in the pool seeking minimum procurement cost. It is subject to demand supply per time period. The second-level problem selects the worst pool price realizations, which result in maximum procurement cost. The first-level problem establishes the best contracting decisions seeking minimum procurement cost.

Problem (7.6.2) above is an ARO problem that can be solved using the solution techniques described in Chap. 3.

We conclude indicating that the consumer procurement problem has a high industry significance and is a medium-term problem since contracting conditions can be changed on a monthly basis. Large consumers need to solve their electricity procurement problems on a regular basis. Finding an advantageous solution is critical for any consumer whose electricity cost is a large component of its total production cost, as it is the case of an aluminum producer or of an air liquifying one.

If regarding electricity cost variability, a consumer is risk averse, an ARO approach is most appropriate to address its electricity procurement problem.

## 7.7 Concluding Remarks

This chapter describes a number of medium-term decision-making problems under uncertainty that can be addressed using adaptive robust optimization models. These problems are:

1. The maintenance scheduling of transmission assets.
2. The primary fuel procurement for electricity producers.
3. The scheduling of hydroelectric plants.
4. The selling of electricity via contracts.
5. The procurement of electricity via contracts.

The description and analysis of these problems are carried out in this chapter emphasizing simplicity and clarity. Therefore, each of these problems is formulated retaining solely the key elements that make it amenable to be tackled via adaptive robust optimization.

Examples simple enough to be solved by inspection are used to illustrate these problems.

## 7.8 End-of-Chapter Exercises

**7.1** Extend the example in Sect. 7.2 to consider a 3-node 3-line power system.

**7.2** Extend the example in Sect. 7.3 to consider 2 contracts.

**7.3** Extend the example in Sect. 7.3 to consider that the electricity spot price is uncertain.

**7.4** Extend the example in Sect. 7.4 to consider 2 interconnected reservoirs.

**7.5** Extend the example in Sect. 7.5 to consider 2 contracts.

**7.6** Extend the example in Sect. 7.6 to consider 2 contracts.

## References

1. Pandzic, H., Conejo, A. J., Kuzle I., & Caro E. (2012). Yearly maintenance scheduling of transmission lines within a market environment. *IEEE Transactions on Power Systems, 27*(1), 407–415.
2. Dominelli, N., Rao, A., & Kundur, P. (2006). Life extension and condition assessment: Techniques for an aging utility infrastructure. *IEEE Power and Energy Magazine 4*(3), 24–35.
3. Yildirim, M., Gebraeel, N. Z., & Sun, X. A. (2017). Integrated predictive analytics and optimization for opportunistic maintenance and operations in wind farms. *IEEE Transactions on Power Systems, 32*(6), 4319–4328.
4. Fancher, R. B., Wilson, J. F., & Mueller, H. A. (1986). Fuel contracting under uncertainty. *IEEE Transactions on Power Systems, 1*(1), 26–32.
5. Babula, M., & Petak, K. (2014). The cold truth: Managing gas-electric integration: The ISO New England experience. *IEEE Power and Energy Magazine, 12*(6), 20–28.
6. Zhao, B., Conejo, A. J., & Sioshansi, R. (2017). Unit commitment under gas-supply uncertainty and gas-price variability. *IEEE Transactions on Power Systems, 32*(3), 2394–2405.
7. Rudnick, H., & Barroso, L. A. (2008). Water, water everywhere. *IEEE Power and Energy Magazine, 6*(4), 14–20.
8. Dashti, H., Conejo, A. J., Jiang, R., & Wang, J. (2016). Weekly two-stage robust generation scheduling for hydrothermal power systems. *IEEE Transactions on Power Systems, 31*(6), 4554–4564.
9. Conejo, A. J., Carrion, M., & Morales, J. M. (2010). *Decision making under uncertainty in electricity markets.* New York: Springer.
10. Conejo, A. J., Garcia-Bertrand, R., Carrion, M., Caballero, A., & de Andres, A. (2008). Optimal involvement in futures markets of a power producer. *IEEE Transactions on Power Systems, 23*(2), 703–711.
11. Garces, L. P., & Conejo, A. J. (2010). Weekly self-scheduling, forward contracting, and offering strategy for a producer. *IEEE Transactions on Power Systems, 25*(2), 657–666.
12. El Khatib, S., & Galiana, F. D. (2007). Negotiating Bilateral Contracts in Electricity Markets. *IEEE Transactions on Power Systems, 22*(2), 553–562.
13. Zare, K., Moghaddam, M. P., & Sheikh-El-Eslami, M. K. (2011). Risk-based electricity procurement for large consumers. *IEEE Transactions on Power Systems, 26*(4), 1826–1835.
14. Carrion, M., Philpott, A. B., Conejo, A. J., & Arroyo, J. M. (2007). A stochastic programming approach to electric energy procurement for large consumers. *IEEE Transactions on Power Systems, 22*(2), 744–754.
15. Gomez-Villalva, E., & Ramos, A. (2003). Optimal energy management of an industrial consumer in liberalized markets. *IEEE Transactions on Power Systems, 18*(2), 716–723.

# Chapter 8
# Long-Term Planning Models

This chapter describes four long-term power system planning problems that can be expressed and solved as Adaptive Robust Optimization (ARO) models. These four problems are:

1. Generation expansion planning.
2. Generation and transmission expansion planning.
3. Transmission expansion planning.
4. Long-term hydroelectric scheduling.

These problems are representative examples. Other long-term planning problems in the power sector can be conveniently formulated as ARO models and efficiently solved.

## 8.1 Introduction

Since long-term decisions generally entail lasting consequences and since such long-term decisions, once made, are difficult and costly to modify or reverse, such decisions should be made with utmost care. ARO provides a natural framework for such long-term decision making because ARO models provide flexible protection against the worst outcomes, not against average ones, and thus, lasting long-term decisions are made ensuring appropriate protection against *the worst*.

On the other hand, the outcome of an ARO model provides not just the *best robust solution*, but a portfolio of optimal robust solutions parameterized as a function of the uncertainty level, through an appropriate metric (uncertainty budget) representing such uncertainty level. This way, the decision maker has a number of choices as a function of his/her risk-aversion level.



X. A. Sun, A. J. Conejo, *Robust Optimization in Electric Energy Systems*,
International Series in Operations Research & Management Science 313,
https://doi.org/10.1007/978-3-030-85128-6_8

Moreover, these robust solutions can be assessed and ranked with respect to other criteria not explicitly represented in the ARO model due to the complexity or nature of these criteria.

## 8.2 Generation Expansion Planning

We note that generation expansion planning needs to be performed by electricity producers on a regular basis, and thus appropriate decision-making models to make such complex expansion decisions are required. Moreover, regulators often use such models to identify the best generation expansion plans from a social viewpoint. Therefore, such models are important for regulatory and policy analysts.

We note as well that generation expansion decisions are made under great uncertainty, and thus a precise modeling of the uncertain parameters involved is needed. ARO allows a detailed modeling of the uncertain parameters involved.

Recent relevant references pertaining to generation expansion planning using different modeling approaches include [1, 2, 3, 4, 5, 6].

In this section, we first describe a simple example of generation expansion planning considering uncertain solely the future demand. We then provide a general enough formulation of such problem.

### 8.2.1 *Simple Example*

Consider an insular power system whose energy demand is supplied by a rather expensive generating unit at the cost of \$20 per energy unit. This source is expensive, but has unlimited capacity. The future energy demand in this insular system is uncertain, but it may take solely two values, either 4 or 6 energy units. The system operator is considering installing a generating unit whose capacity can be either 5 or 7 power units. The operating cost of this unit is \$2 per energy unit, and its investment (building) cost \$4 per power unit. This simple system is illustrated in Fig. 8.1.

We formulate below a simple ARO model to make a robust decision on which capacity to select (either 5 or 7) for the generating unit to be built. Such a robust decision implies achieving the least total cost outcome under the worst uncertainty realization. The ARO model has the form:

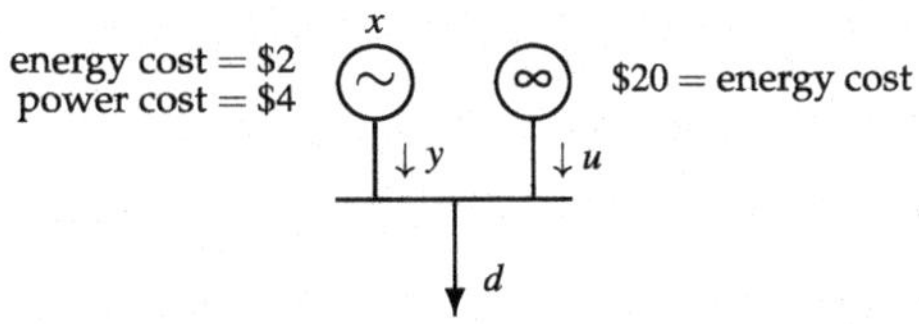


**Fig. 8.1** Generation expansion planning example

$$\begin{aligned}\min_{x\in\{5,7\}} \quad \max_{d\in\{4,6\}} \quad \min_{y\geq 0, u\geq 0} \quad & z = 4x + 2y + 20u \\ \text{s.t.} \quad & y + u = d \\ & 0 \leq y \leq x,\end{aligned} \tag{8.2.1}$$

where $x$ is the power capacity of the generating unit to be built, $y$ the power output of such generating unit, $u$ the power output of the existing (expensive) generating unit, and $d$ a variable representing the uncertain demand.

Considering a single time period of duration 1, the objective function of problem (8.2.1) above is the total cost, including both building and operation costs. The first-level subproblem decides on which generating capacity to build (to minimize investment plus operation costs), anticipating the worst demand realization (that results in maximum operation cost) as identified by the second-level subproblem, which in turn anticipates the best operating decision (that seeks minimum operation cost) at the third-level subproblem. The first constraint of the third-level subproblem enforces the energy balance, while the second one limits the production of the new unit.

Given the simplicity of this problem, it can be solve by enumeration. This is done below.

1. If the investment decision is $x = 5$, the demand may take two values, either $d = 4$ or $d = 6$. If the demand is 4, the minimum operation cost problem is:

$$\begin{aligned}\min_{y\geq 0, u\geq 0} \quad & z = 4 \cdot 5 + 2y + 20u \\ \text{s.t.} \quad & y + u = 4 \\ & y \leq 5,\end{aligned}$$

   whose solution is $y = 4$, $u = 0$ and $z = 28$.

   If, on the other hand, the demand is 6, the minimum operation cost problem is:

$$\begin{aligned}\min_{y\geq 0, u\geq 0} \quad & z = 4 \cdot 5 + 2y + 20u \\ \text{s.t.} \quad & y + u = 6 \\ & y \leq 5,\end{aligned}$$

   whose solution is $y = 5$, $u = 1$ and $z = 50$.

   Since the second level problem selects the demand that results in maximum cost, and given that the investment decision is $x = 5$, the optimal demand is $d = 6$ and the total cost $z = 50$.

2. If, on the other hand, the investment decision is $x = 7$, the demand may take two values as well, either $d = 4$ or $d = 6$. If the demand is 4, the minimum operation cost problem is:

$$\begin{aligned}
\min_{y\geq 0, u\geq 0} \quad & z = 4\cdot 7 + 2y + 20u \\
\text{s.t.} \quad & y + u = 4 \\
& y \leq 7,
\end{aligned}$$

whose solution is $y = 4$, $u = 0$ and $z = 36$.

If, on the other hand, the demand is 6, the minimum operation cost problem is:

$$\begin{aligned}
\min_{y\geq 0, u\geq 0} \quad & z = 4\cdot 7 + 2y + 20u \\
\text{s.t.} \quad & y + u = 6 \\
& y \leq 7,
\end{aligned}$$

whose solution is $y = 6$, $u = 0$ and $z = 40$.

Again, since the second level problem selects the demand that results in maximum cost, and given that the investment decision is $x = 7$, the optimal demand is $d = 6$ and the total cost $z = 40$.

Finally, since the planner pursues minimum cost and since investing $x = 5$ results in a worst cost of $z = 50$ and investing $x = 7$ results in a worst cost of $z = 40$, the optimal investment decision is $x^* = 7$ with a worst total cost of $z^* = 40$ under the worst demand realization $d^* = 6$.

### 8.2.2 General Formulation

A general enough ARO formulation of the generation expansion planning is provided below. For the sake of simplicity, a single-node model is considered and thus no network constraint is represented. Additionally, no weather-dependent uncertain production sources (e.g., wind- or solar-powered plants) are taken into account, and investment and operation cost are considered deterministic. Thus, the sole source of uncertainty is the future demand. The formulation is:

$$\begin{aligned}
\min_{g_i\in\Omega_i,\forall i} \quad \max_{d_{jt}\in\Delta_j,\forall j\,\forall t} \quad \min_{p_{it}\geq 0,\forall i\,\forall t} \quad & z = \sum_{i=1}^{n_\mathrm{G}} I_i g_i + \sum_{t=1}^{n_\mathrm{T}}\sum_{i=1}^{n_\mathrm{G}} O_i p_{it} \\
\text{s.t.} \quad & \sum_{i=1}^{n_\mathrm{G}} p_{it} = \sum_{j=1}^{n_\mathrm{D}} d_{jt}, \forall t \\
& p_{it} \leq g_i, \forall i\ \forall t,
\end{aligned} \tag{8.2.2}$$

where the optimization variables are:

$g_i$ is the capacity to be build of candidate generating unit $i$ (integer variable).
$d_{jt}$ is a variable representing the realization of uncertain demand $j$ in time period $t$.
$p_{it}$ is the power output of generating unit $i$ in time period $t$.

The constants, sets and numbers are:

$I_i$ is the annualized investment cost of candidate generating unit $i$.
$O_i$ is the operation cost of candidate generating unit $i$.
$\Omega_i$ is set of available capacities of candidate generating unit $i$.
$\Delta_j$ is a robust set representing the realization of demand $j$ throughout the study horizon, including uncertainty budget constraints.
$n_{\mathrm{G}}$ is the number of candidate generating units.
$n_{\mathrm{D}}$ is the number of demands.
$n_{\mathrm{T}}$ is the number of time periods that comprises the study horizon (e. g., $24 \times 365$).

The first-level subproblem of problem (8.2.2) selects the capacities of the generating units to be built pursuing minimum total (investment plus operation) cost. For the sake of simplicity, no existing generating capacity is considered. The second-level subproblem of this problem identifies the demand realizations throughout the study horizon that result in maximum operating cost. In turn, the third-level subproblem of problem (8.2.2) operates the generating units seeking minimum operation cost. Embedded in formulation (8.2.2) is the fact that first-level decisions anticipate second-level ones, which in turn anticipates third-level decisions. The first constraint of the third-level subproblem enforces energy supply per time period, while the second one sets power output bounds for all generating units and all time periods.

Problem (8.2.2) is an ARO model that can be solved using the methodology presented in Chap. 3.

## 8.3 Generation and Transmission Expansion Planning

Generation and transmission expansion planning models are not solely important in centrally operated systems, but in market-based systems as tools for the regulator to provide investment guidelines intended to promote social welfare.

Recent relevant generation and transmission expansion planning references include [7, 8, 9, 10, 11].

In this section and for the sake of illustration, we first describe a simple transmission expansion planning problem that can be recast as an ARO model. Then, we provide a rather general ARO model for this long-term decision-making problem under uncertainty.

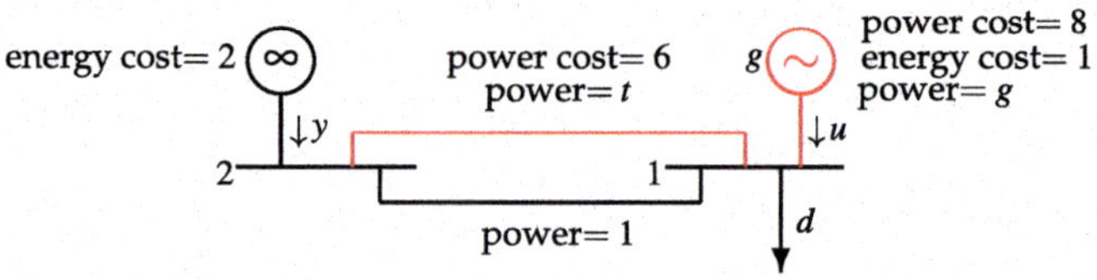


**Fig. 8.2** Generation and transmission expansion planning example

## 8.3.1 *Simple Example*

Consider the electric energy system depicted in Fig. 8.2. Initially, the electric demand at node 1 is supplied by a rather expensive production unit at node 2 through a single transmission line of capacity 1 power unit. The production cost of this unit that has unlimited capacity is \$2 per energy unit.

To face the future uncertain demand that can take solely two values, either 3 or 5, the system planner plans to build a new transmission line and a new production unit at node 1. The new transmission line increases the existing transmission capacity by either 1 or 2 power units. The building cost of this transmission line is \$6 per power unit. On the other hand, the capacity of the production unit to be built is either 2 or 4 and the building cost is \$8 per power unit. The production cost of this new generating unit is \$1 per energy unit.

The system planner needs to decide on the capacity of the transmission line (either 1 or 2) and on the capacity of the generating unit (either 2 or 4) to build so that the total cost (investment plus operation) is minimum under the worst demand realization.

An ARO model for the simple problem above is provided below:

$$\min_{\substack{g\in\{2,4\}\\ t\in\{1,2\}}} \max_{d\in\{3,5\}} \min_{y\geq 0, u\geq 0} \quad z = (8g + 6t) + 2y + 1u$$
$$\text{s.t.} \quad y + u = d \qquad (8.3.1)$$
$$u \leq g$$
$$y \leq 1 + t,$$

where $g$ is the capacity of the generation unit to be built, $t$ the capacity of the transmission line to be built, $d$ a variable representing the uncertain future demand, $y$ the power output of the new generation unit, and $u$ the power output of the existing (expensive) generation unit.

The objective function of problem (8.3.1) above is the total cost, including investment and operation costs. The first-level subproblem decides on the transmission capacity to add (either 1 or 2) and on the generating capacity to build (either 2 or 4) to minimize total cost, anticipating the worst demand realization (that entails maximum operation cost) as determined by the second-level subproblem, which in turn anticipates the best operator actions in the third-level subproblem to minimize operating cost. The constraints of the third-level subproblem include an energy supply equation, a generation output limit for the newly built unit and a transmission capacity limit.

Since problem (8.3.1) above is very simple, it can be solved by enumeration. Since both the transmission line and the generating unit have to be built, the investment alternatives are:

1. Transmission capacity to be built 1 and generation capacity to be built 2.
2. Transmission capacity to be built 1 and generation capacity to be built 4.
3. Transmission capacity to be built 2 and generation capacity to be built 2.
4. Transmission capacity to be built 2 and generation capacity to be built 4.

These four alternatives are considered below:

1. If the generation capacity to be built is $g = 2$ and the transmission capacity to be built is $t = 1$, two demand realizations are possible, either 3 or 5. If the demand realization is $d = 3$, the resulting operation problem is:

$$\begin{aligned} \min_{y \geq 0, u \geq 0} \quad & z = 8 \cdot 2 + 6 \cdot 1 + 2y + 1u \\ \text{s.t.} \quad & y + u = 3 \\ & u \leq 2 \\ & y \leq 2, \end{aligned}$$

whose solution is $y = 1$, $u = 2$ and $z = 22$.

If, on the other hand, the demand realization is $d = 5$, the resulting operation problem is:

$$\begin{aligned} \min_{y \geq 0, u \geq 0} \quad & z = 8 \cdot 2 + 6 \cdot 1 + 2y + 1u \\ \text{s.t.} \quad & y + u = 5 \\ & u \leq 2 \\ & y \leq 2, \end{aligned}$$

which is infeasible, and thus we assign to it a total cost $z = +\infty$.

Since the second-level problem identifies the demand that results in maximum cost, and since the investment decision is $t = 1$ and $g = 2$, the optimal cost is $z = +\infty$.

2. If the generation capacity to be built is $g = 4$ and the transmission capacity to be built is $t = 1$, two demand realizations are possible as well, either 3 or 5. If the demand realization is $d = 3$, the resulting operation problem is:

$$\begin{aligned} \min_{y\geq 0, u\geq 0} \quad & z = 8\cdot 4 + 6\cdot 1 + 2y + 1u \\ \text{s.t.} \quad & y + u = 3 \\ & u \leq 4 \\ & y \leq 2, \end{aligned}$$

whose solution is $y = 0$, $u = 3$ and $z = 41$.

If, on the other hand, the demand realization is $d = 5$, the resulting operation problem is:

$$\begin{aligned} \min_{y\geq 0, u\geq 0} \quad & z = 8\cdot 4 + 6\cdot 1 + 2y + 1u \\ \text{s.t.} \quad & y + u = 5 \\ & u \leq 4 \\ & y \leq 2, \end{aligned}$$

whose solution is $y = 1$, $u = 4$ and $z = 44$.

Since the second-level problem identifies the demand that results in maximum cost, and since the investment decision is $t = 1$ and $g = 4$, the optimal cost is $z = 44$.

3. If the generation capacity to be built is $g = 2$ and the transmission capacity to be built is $t = 2$, two demand realizations are possible as well, either 3 or 5. If the demand realization is $d = 3$, the resulting operation problem is:

$$\begin{aligned} \min_{y\geq 0, u\geq 0} \quad & z = 8\cdot 2 + 6\cdot 2 + 2y + 1u \\ \text{s.t.} \quad & y + u = 3 \\ & u \leq 2 \\ & y \leq 3, \end{aligned}$$

whose solution is $y = 1$, $u = 2$ and $z = 32$.

If, on the other hand, the demand realization is $d = 5$, the resulting operation problem is:

$$\begin{aligned} \min_{y\geq 0, u\geq 0} \quad & z = 8\cdot 2 + 6\cdot 2 + 2y + 1u \\ \text{s.t.} \quad & y + u = 5 \\ & u \leq 2 \\ & y \leq 3, \end{aligned}$$

whose solution is $y = 3$, $u = 2$ and $z = 36$.

Since the second-level problem identifies the demand that results in maximum cost, and since the investment decision is $t = 2$ and $g = 2$, the optimal cost is $z = 36$.

4. Finally, if the generation capacity to be built is $g = 4$ and the transmission capacity to be built is $t = 2$, two demand realizations are possible as well, either 3 or 5. If the demand realization is $d = 3$, the resulting operation problem is:

$$\begin{aligned}\min_{y\geq 0, u\geq 0} \quad & z = 8\cdot 4 + 6\cdot 2 + 2y + 1u \\ \text{s.t.} \quad & y + u = 3 \\ & u \leq 4 \\ & y \leq 3,\end{aligned}$$

whose solution is $y = 0$, $u = 3$ and $z = 47$.

If, on the other hand, the demand realization is $d = 5$, the resulting operation problem is:

$$\begin{aligned}\min_{y\geq 0, u\geq 0} \quad & z = 8\cdot 4 + 6\cdot 2 + 2y + 1u \\ \text{s.t.} \quad & y + u = 5 \\ & u \leq 4 \\ & y \leq 3,\end{aligned}$$

whose solution is $y = 1$, $u = 4$ and $z = 50$.

Since the second-level problem identifies the demand that results in maximum cost, and since the investment decision is $t = 2$ and $g = 4$, the optimal cost is $z = 50$.

Therefore, the four possible alternatives are:

1. Transmission capacity to be built 1 and generation capacity to be built 2, which result in a *worst* total cost of $\$\infty$.
2. Transmission capacity to be built 1 and generation capacity to be built 4, which result in a *worst* total cost of \$44.
3. Transmission capacity to be built 2 and generation capacity to be built 2, which result in a *worst* total cost of \$36.
4. Transmission capacity to be built 2 and generation capacity to be built 4, which result in a *worst* total cost of \$50.

Since the planner seeks minimum cost, the optimal solution is $t^* = 2$ and $g^* = 2$, which result in a total cost of $z^* = \$36$ for the worst demand $d^* = 5$.

### 8.3.2 General Formulation

A general enough ARO formulation of the generation and transmission expansion planning problem is provided below. Existing lines are considered, but no generating units.

$$\begin{aligned}
&\min_{\substack{g_i \in \Omega_i^{\mathrm{G}}, \forall i \\ x_\ell \in \{0,1\}, \forall \ell \in \Omega^{\mathrm{L}+} \\ x_\ell = 1, \forall \ell \notin \Omega^{\mathrm{L}+}}} \quad \max_{d_{jt} \in \Delta_j, \forall j\, \forall t} \quad \min_{\substack{p_{it} \geq 0, \forall i\, \forall t \\ f_{\ell t}, \forall \ell\, \forall t \\ \delta_{nt}, \forall n\, \forall t}} \quad z = \sum_{\forall \ell \in \Omega^{\mathrm{L}+}} I_\ell^{\mathrm{L}} x_\ell + \sum_{i=1}^{n_{\mathrm{G}}} I_i^{\mathrm{G}} g_i + \sum_{t=1}^{n_{\mathrm{T}}} \sum_{i=1}^{n_{\mathrm{G}}} O_i p_{it} \\
&\text{s.t.} \quad \sum_{i \in \Omega_n^{\mathrm{G}}} p_{it} - \sum_{j \in \Omega_n^{\mathrm{D}}} d_{jt} + \\
&\qquad \sum_{\ell | r(\ell) \in \Omega_n} f_{\ell t} - \sum_{\ell | s(\ell) \in \Omega_n} f_{\ell t} = 0, \forall n\, \forall t \\
&\qquad f_{\ell t} = x_\ell B_\ell (\delta_{s(\ell) t} - \delta_{r(\ell) t}), \forall \ell\, \forall t \\
&\qquad -f_\ell^{\max} \leq f_{\ell t} \leq f_\ell^{\max}, \forall \ell\, \forall t \\
&\qquad p_{it} \leq g_i, \forall i\, \forall t,
\end{aligned} \tag{8.3.2}$$

where the optimization variables are:

| | |
|---|---|
| $x_\ell$ | is a binary variable that is equal to 1 if candidate line $\ell$ is built and 0 otherwise. |
| $g_i$ | is the capacity to be build of candidate generating unit $i$ (integer variable). |
| $d_{jt}$ | is a variable representing the realization of demand $j$ in time period $t$. |
| $p_{it}$ | is the power output of generating unit $i$ in time period $t$. |
| $f_{\ell t}$ | is the power flow through line $\ell$ in time period $t$. |
| $\delta_{nt}$ | is the state variable (angle) of node $n$ in time period $t$. |

The constants, sets, numbers and selected indices are:

| | |
|---|---|
| $I_i^{\mathrm{G}}$ | is the annualized investment cost of candidate generating unit $i$. |
| $I_i^{\mathrm{L}}$ | is the annualized investment cost of candidate line $\ell$. |
| $O_i$ | is the operation cost of candidate generating unit $i$. |
| $B_\ell$ | is the susceptance of line $\ell$. |
| $f_\ell^{\max}$ | is the capacity of line $\ell$. |
| $\Omega_i^{\mathrm{G}}$ | is set of available capacities of candidate generating unit $i$. |
| $\Delta_j$ | is a robust set representing the realization of demand $j$ throughout the study horizon, including uncertainty-budget constraints. |
| $\Omega^{\mathrm{L}+}$ | is the set of candidate lines. |
| $\Omega_n^{\mathrm{G}}$ | is the set of generating units at node $n$. |
| $\Omega_n^{\mathrm{D}}$ | is the set of demands at node $n$. |
| $\Omega_n$ | is the set of nodes directly connected to $n$. |
| $n_{\mathrm{G}}$ | is the number of candidate generating units. |
| $n_{\mathrm{T}}$ | is the number of time periods that comprises the study horizon (e. g., $24 \times 365$). |
| $s(\ell)$ | is the sending-end node of line $\ell$. |
| $r(\ell)$ | is the receiving-end node of line $\ell$. |

The first-level subproblem of problem (8.3.2) selects the generating units and transmission lines to be built to minimize investment and operation costs, anticipating the worst demand realization throughout the planning horizon (that entails maximum operating cost) as determined by the second-level subproblem of problem (8.3.2), which in turn anticipates the best operator reaction pursuing minimum operating cost by solving the third-level subproblem of problem (8.3.2). The third-level subproblem includes the following constraints: power balance per node and time period, power flow evaluation per line and time period, power flow bounds per line and time period, and power output bound per generating unit and time period.

We conclude indicating that Problem (8.3.2) is an ARO model that can be solved using the methodology presented in Chap. 3.

## 8.4 Transmission Expansion Planning

Transmission expansion planning is important to ensure a non-binding transmission system that allows free trade of electrical energy.

Recent relevant transmission expansion planning references include [12, 13, 14, 15, 16, 17, 18].

We analyze first a simple motivating example that can be solved by inspection. Then, we provide a general enough formulation for the transmission expansion planning problem. We note that the formulation in this section complements that in Chap. 5.

### *8.4.1 Simple Example*

Consider the 3-node power system in Fig. 8.3. Lines 1, 2 and 3 connect nodes 1 and 2, 2 and 3 and 1 and 2, respectively. Each of these transmission lines has currently a capacity of 1 power unit and a susceptance of 1. The transmission planner has the option of expanding any of the existing transmission lines by 1 power unit. Expansion costs of lines 1, 2 and 3 are \$10, \$11 and \$12 per power unit, respectively. Additionally, a regulatory mandate requires the planner to build at least 2 new transmission lines.

The generating units at nodes 1 and 2 have capacities of 3 power units and production costs of \$1 and \$2 per energy unit, respectively. The planning horizon involves a single time period of 1 time unit. The future uncertain demand may take solely two values, 2.5 or 3.5 power units.

An ARO model for the simple transmission expansion planing problem above is provided below:

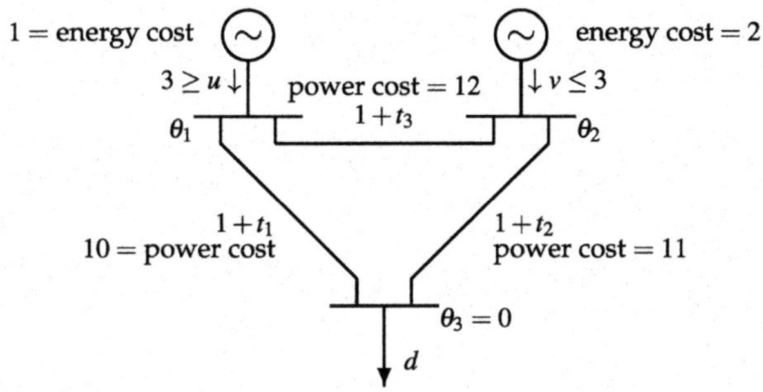


**Fig. 8.3** Transmission expansion planning example

$$\min_{\substack{t_1\in\{1,0\}\\ t_2\in\{1,0\}\\ t_3\in\{1,0\}\\ t_1+t_2+t_3\geq 2}} \; \max_{d\in\{2.5,3.5\}} \; \min_{\substack{0\leq u\leq 3\\ 0\leq v\leq 3\\ \theta_1,\theta_2}} \quad z = (10\,t_1 + 11\,t_2 + 12\,t_3) + 1u + 2v$$

$$\begin{aligned} \text{s.t.} \quad & u = \theta_1 + (\theta_1 - \theta_2) \\ & v = \theta_2 + (\theta_2 - \theta_1) \\ & d = \theta_1 + \theta_2 \\ & -1 - t_1 \leq \theta_1 \leq 1 + t_1 \\ & -1 - t_2 \leq \theta_2 \leq 1 + t_2 \\ & -1 - t_3 \leq \theta_1 - \theta_2 \leq 1 + t_3, \end{aligned} \tag{8.4.1}$$

where $t_1$, $t_2$ and $t_3$ are the capacity additions of lines 1, 2 and 3, respectively, $d$ a variable representing the uncertain future demand, $u$ the power output of the generation unit at node 1, $v$ the power output of the generation unit at node 2, and $\theta_1$ and $\theta_2$ the state variables (angles) of nodes 1 and 2, respectively.

The first-level subproblem of problem (8.4.1) decides on the transmission expansion to be carried out pursuing minimum total cost (that includes both building and operation costs) anticipating the worst demand realization (that results in maximum operation cost) as identified by the second-level subproblem, which in turn anticipates the operation of the 2 generating units seeking minimum operation cost at the third-level subproblem of problem (8.4.1). The third-level subproblem constraints include three energy balance equalities, one per node, and six transmission capacity limits, two per line.

Given the simplicity of this problem, it can be solved by enumeration. Since the planner needs to expand at least 2 lines, 4 alternatives are possible:

1. Expanding lines 1 and 2.
2. Expanding lines 1 and 3.
3. Expanding lines 2 and 3.
4. Expanding lines 1, 2 and 3.

These cases are analyzed below:

1. If lines 1 and 2 are built, the demand may take 2 values, either 2.5 or 3.5. If the demand is $d = 2.5$, the operation problem to be solved is:

$$\begin{aligned} \min_{\substack{0\le u\le 3\\ 0\le v\le 3\\ \theta_1,\theta_2}} \quad & z = (10\cdot 1 + 11\cdot 1) + 1u + 2v \\ \text{s.t.} \quad & u = \theta_1 + (\theta_1 - \theta_2) \\ & v = \theta_2 + (\theta_2 - \theta_1) \\ & 2.5 = \theta_1 + \theta_2 \\ & -2 \le \theta_1 \le 2 \\ & -2 \le \theta_2 \le 2 \\ & -1 \le \theta_1 - \theta_2 \le 1, \end{aligned}$$

whose solution is $u = 2.5$, $v = 0$, $\theta_1 = 1.667$, $\theta_2 = 0.833$, with and objective function value $z = 23.5$.

If, on the other hand, the demand is $d = 3.5$, the operation problem to be solved is:

$$\begin{aligned} \min_{\substack{0\le u\le 3\\ 0\le v\le 3\\ \theta_1,\theta_2}} \quad & z = (10\cdot 1 + 11\cdot 1) + 1u + 2v \\ \text{s.t.} \quad & u = \theta_1 + (\theta_1 - \theta_2) \\ & v = \theta_2 + (\theta_2 - \theta_1) \\ & 3.5 = \theta_1 + \theta_2 \\ & -2 \le \theta_1 \le 2 \\ & -2 \le \theta_2 \le 2 \\ & -1 \le \theta_1 - \theta_2 \le 2, \end{aligned}$$

whose solution is $u = 2.5$, $v = 1$, $\theta_1 = 2$, $\theta_2 = 1.5$, with and objective function value $z = 25.5$.

Since the second-level problem selects the demand level seeking maximum cost, if the investment consists of expanding lines 1 and 2, the optimal objective function is $z = 25.5$ corresponding to a demand $d = 3.5$.

2. If lines 1 and 3 are built, the demand may take 2 values, either 2.5 or 3.5. If the demand is $d = 2.5$, the operation problem to be solved is:

$$
\begin{aligned}
\min_{\substack{0 \le u \le 3 \\ 0 \le v \le 3 \\ \theta_1, \theta_2}} \quad & z = (10 \cdot 1 + 12 \cdot 1) + 1u + 2v \\
\text{s.t.} \quad & u = \theta_1 + (\theta_1 - \theta_2) \\
& v = \theta_2 + (\theta_2 - \theta_1) \\
& 2.5 = \theta_1 + \theta_2 \\
& -2 \le \theta_1 \le 2 \\
& -1 \le \theta_2 \le 1 \\
& -2 \le \theta_1 - \theta_2 \le 2,
\end{aligned}
$$

whose solution is $u = 2.5$, $v = 0$, $\theta_1 = 1.667$, $\theta_2 = 0.833$, with and objective function value $z = 24.5$.

If, on the other hand, the demand is $d = 3.5$, the operation problem to be solved is:

$$
\begin{aligned}
\min_{\substack{0 \le u \le 3 \\ 0 \le v \le 3 \\ \theta_1, \theta_2}} \quad & z = (10 \cdot 1 + 12 \cdot 1) + 1u + 2v \\
\text{s.t.} \quad & u = \theta_1 + (\theta_1 - \theta_2) \\
& v = \theta_2 + (\theta_2 - \theta_1) \\
& 3.5 = \theta_1 + \theta_2 \\
& -2 \le \theta_1 \le 2 \\
& -1 \le \theta_2 \le 1 \\
& -2 \le \theta_1 - \theta_2 \le 2,
\end{aligned}
$$

which is infeasible. We assign an objective function value of $z = +\infty$.

Since the second-level problem selects the demand level seeking maximum cost, if the investment consists of expanding lines 1 and 3, the optimal objective function is $z = +\infty$ corresponding to a demand $d = 3.5$.

3. If lines 2 and 3 are built, the demand may take 2 values, either 2.5 or 3.5. If the demand is $d = 2.5$, the operation problem to be solved is:

$$
\begin{aligned}
\min_{\substack{0 \le u \le 3 \\ 0 \le v \le 3 \\ \theta_1, \theta_2}} \quad & z = (11 \cdot 1 + 12 \cdot 1) + 1u + 2v \\
\text{s.t.} \quad & u = \theta_1 + (\theta_1 - \theta_2) \\
& v = \theta_2 + (\theta_2 - \theta_1) \\
& 2.5 = \theta_1 + \theta_2 \\
& -1 \le \theta_1 \le 1 \\
& -2 \le \theta_2 \le 2 \\
& -2 \le \theta_1 - \theta_2 \le 2,
\end{aligned}
$$

whose solution is $u = 0.5$, $v = 2$, $\theta_1 = 1$, $\theta_2 = 1.5$, with and objective function value $z = 27.5$.

If, on the other hand, the demand is $d = 3.5$, the operation problem to be solved is:

$$\begin{aligned}
\min_{\substack{0 \le u \le 3 \\ 0 \le v \le 3 \\ \theta_1, \theta_2}} \quad & z = (11 \cdot 1 + 12 \cdot 1) + 1u + 2v \\
\text{s.t.} \quad & u = \theta_1 + (\theta_1 - \theta_2) \\
& v = \theta_2 + (\theta_2 - \theta_1) \\
& 3.5 = \theta_1 + \theta_2 \\
& -1 \le \theta_1 \le 1 \\
& -2 \le \theta_2 \le 2 \\
& -2 \le \theta_1 - \theta_2 \le 2,
\end{aligned}$$

which is infeasible. We assign an objective function value of $z = +\infty$.

Since the second-level problem selects the demand level seeking maximum cost, if the investment consists of expanding lines 2 and 3, the optimal objective function is $z = +\infty$ corresponding to a demand $d = 3.5$.

4. If lines 1, 2 and 3 are built, the demand may take 2 values, either 2.5 or 3.5. If the demand is $d = 2.5$, the operation problem to be solved is:

$$\begin{aligned}
\min_{\substack{0 \le u \le 3 \\ 0 \le v \le 3 \\ \theta_1, \theta_2}} \quad & z = (10 \cdot 1 + 11 \cdot 1 + 12 \cdot 1) + 1u + 2v \\
\text{s.t.} \quad & u = \theta_1 + (\theta_1 - \theta_2) \\
& v = \theta_2 + (\theta_2 - \theta_1) \\
& 2.5 = \theta_1 + \theta_2 \\
& -2 \le \theta_1 \le 2 \\
& -2 \le \theta_2 \le 2 \\
& -2 \le \theta_1 - \theta_2 \le 2,
\end{aligned}$$

whose solution is $u = 2.5$, $v = 0$, $\theta_1 = 1.667$, $\theta_2 = 0.833$, with and objective function value $z = 35.5$.

If, on the other hand, the demand is $d = 3.5$, the operation problem to be solved is:

$$\begin{aligned}
\min_{\substack{0\le u\le 3\\ 0\le v\le 3\\ \theta_1,\theta_2}} \quad & z = (10\cdot 1 + 11\cdot 1 + 12\cdot 1) + 1u + 2v\\
\text{s.t.} \quad & u = \theta_1 + (\theta_1 - \theta_2)\\
& v = \theta_2 + (\theta_2 - \theta_1)\\
& 3.5 = \theta_1 + \theta_2\\
& -2 \le \theta_1 \le 2\\
& -2 \le \theta_2 \le 2\\
& -2 \le \theta_1 - \theta_2 \le 2,
\end{aligned}$$

whose solution is $u = 2.5$, $v = 1$, $\theta_1 = 2$, $\theta_2 = 1.5$, with and objective function value $z = 37.5$.

Since the second-level problem selects the demand level seeking maximum cost, if the investment consists of expanding lines 2 and 3, the optimal objective function is $z = 37.5$ corresponding to a demand $d = 3.5$.

The alternatives are as follow:

1. If lines 1 and 2 are expanded, the total cost is $z = 25.5$.
2. If lines 1 and 3 are expanded, the total cost is $z = +\infty$.
3. If lines 2 and 3 are expanded, the total cost is $z = +\infty$.
4. If lines 1, 2 and 3 are expanded, the total cost is $z = 37.5$.

Since the planner seeks minimum total cost, the optimal solution consists of expanding lines 1 and 2 ($t_1^* = 1$, $t_2^* = 1$ and $t_3^* = 0$), which results in a total cost of $z^* = 25.5$ under a worst demand of $d^* = 3.5$.

### 8.4.2 General Formulation

A general enough ARO formulation of the transmission expansion planning problem is provided below.

$$\begin{aligned}
\min_{\substack{x_\ell\in\{0,1\},\forall\ell\in\Omega^{\mathrm{L+}}\\ x_\ell=1,\forall\ell\notin\Omega^{\mathrm{L+}}}} \quad \max_{d_{jt}\in\Delta_j,\forall j\ \forall t} \quad \min_{\substack{p_{it}\ge 0,\forall i\ \forall t\\ f_{\ell t},\forall\ell\ \forall t\\ \delta_{nt},\forall n\ \forall t}} \quad & z = \sum_{\forall\ell\in\Omega^{\mathrm{L+}}} I_\ell^{\mathrm{L}} x_\ell + \sum_{t=1}^{n_{\mathrm{T}}}\sum_{i=1}^{n_{\mathrm{G}}} O_i p_{it}\\
\text{s.t.} \quad & \sum_{i\in\Omega_n^{\mathrm{G}}} p_{it} - \sum_{j\in\Omega_n^{\mathrm{D}}} d_{jt} +\\
& \sum_{\ell|r(\ell)\in\Omega_n} f_{\ell t} - \sum_{\ell|s(\ell)\in\Omega_n} f_{\ell t} = 0,\ \forall n\ \forall t\\
& f_{\ell t} = x_\ell B_\ell(\delta_{s(\ell)t} - \delta_{r(\ell)t}),\ \forall\ell\ \forall t\\
& -f_\ell^{\max} \le f_{\ell t} \le f_\ell^{\max},\ \forall\ell\ \forall t\\
& p_{it} \le g_i,\ \forall i\ \forall t,
\end{aligned} \tag{8.4.2}$$

where the optimization variables are:

$x_\ell$ is a binary variable that is equal to 1 if candidate line $\ell$ is built and 0 otherwise.
$d_{jt}$ is a variable representing the realization of demand $j$ in time period $t$.
$p_{it}$ is the power output of generating unit $i$ in time period $t$.
$f_{\ell t}$ is the power flow through line $\ell$ in time period $t$.
$\delta_{nt}$ is the state variable (angle) of node $n$ in time period $t$.

The constants, sets, numbers and selected indices are:

$g_i$ is the capacity of generating unit $i$.
$I_i^{\mathrm{L}}$ is the annualized investment cost of candidate line $\ell$.
$O_i$ is the operation cost of candidate generating unit $i$.
$B_\ell$ is the susceptance of line $\ell$.
$f_\ell^{\max}$ is the capacity of line $\ell$.
$\Delta_j$ is a robust set representing the realization of demand $j$ throughout the study horizon.
$\Omega^{\mathrm{L+}}$ is the set of candidate lines.
$\Omega_n^{\mathrm{G}}$ is the set of generating units at node $n$.
$\Omega_n^{\mathrm{D}}$ is the set of demands at node $n$.
$\Omega_n$ is the set of nodes directly connected to $n$.
$n_{\mathrm{G}}$ is the number of generating units.
$n_{\mathrm{T}}$ is the number of time periods that comprises the study horizon (e. g., $24 \times 365$).
$s(\ell)$ is the sending-end node of line $\ell$.
$r(\ell)$ is the receiving-end node of line $\ell$.

The first-level subproblem of problem (8.4.2) selects the transmission lines to be built to minimize investment and operation costs, anticipating the worst demand realization throughout the planning horizon (that entails maximum operating cost) as determined by the second-level subproblem of problem (8.4.2), which in turn anticipates the best operator reaction pursuing minimum operating cost by solving the third-level subproblem of problem (8.4.2). The third-level subproblem includes the following constraints: power balance per node and time period, power flow evaluation per line and time period, power flow bounds per line and time period, and power output bound per generating unit and time period.

Problem (8.4.2) is an ARO model that can be solved using the methodology presented in Chap. 3.

## 8.5 Long-Term Hydroelectric Scheduling

Long-term hydro-thermal scheduling is most important for hydro-dominated system, such as the ones in the state of Washington, in Norway or in Brazil.

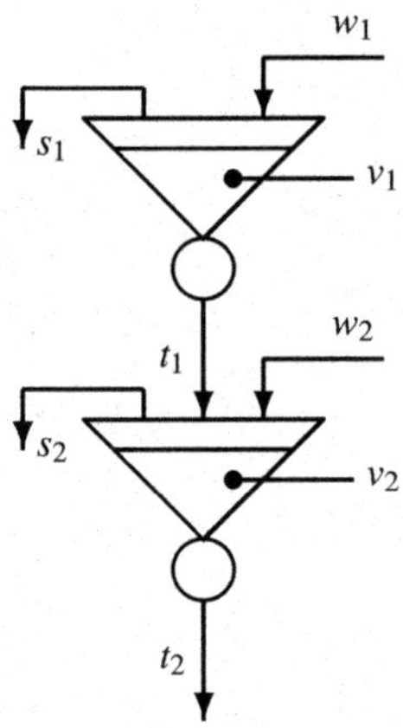


**Fig. 8.4** Long-term hydroelectric scheduling example

Recent relevant references on hydroelectric development include [19, 20, 21, 22, 23], and recent relevant long-term hydro-thermal scheduling references include [24, 25, 26, 27, 28].

We analyze first a simple example, followed by a general enough formulation.

### *8.5.1 Simple Example*

We consider the operator of the two interconnected hydro reservoirs in Fig. 8.4.

Under the worst inflow conditions, this operator needs to operate such hydro system to maximize the value of the total water content at the end of the single-period study horizon. The reservoirs are operated supplying the electric demand of the area around the reservoirs with the electricity produced by the power plants associated with these two reservoirs. The future value of water is \$20 per volume unit. On the other hand, spilling water has a cost to \$15 per volume unit.

Specifically, planning for the future the operator needs first to set initial contents for reservoirs 1 and 2. The cost per volume unit (current water value) of setting initial water contents for reservoirs 1 and 2 are, respectively, \$10 and \$12. On the other hand, regulatory constraints require the initial content of reservoir 1 to be 1 (no choice), and that of reservoir 2 to be either 1 or 4.

Subsequently, water inflows materialize in both reservoirs. These inflows to both reservoir are uncertain. They may take values 1 or 8 for reservoir 1, and 2 or 6 for reservoir 2.

In turn, the operator operates the hydro plants to supply the electric demand, while maximizing the water content value at the end of the single-period study horizon.

The electric demand to be supplied is 2, and the conversion ratio volume discharged to electric energy is $\frac{1}{2}$.

This long-term hydroelectric scheduling problem can be recast as an ARO model as follows:

$$
\begin{aligned}
\max_{\substack{x_1\in\{1\}\\ x_2\in\{1,4\}}} \ \min_{\substack{w_1\in\{1,8\}\\ w_2\in\{2,6\}}} \ \max_{\substack{v_1,t_1,s_1\geq 0\\ v_2,t_2,s_2\geq 0}} \quad & z = 20(v_1+v_2) - 15(s_1+s_2) - 10x_1 - 12x_2 \\
\text{s.t.} \quad & \tfrac{1}{2}t_1 + \tfrac{1}{2}t_2 = 2 \\
& x_1 + w_1 - t_1 - s_1 = v_1 \\
& x_2 + w_2 + t_1 - t_2 - s_2 = v_2 \\
& 1 \leq v_1 \leq 2 \\
& 1 \leq v_2 \leq 4,
\end{aligned}
\tag{8.5.1}
$$

where variables $x_1$ and $x_2$ are the initial contents of reservoirs 1 and 2, respectively, $w_1$ and $w_2$ are variables representing the water inflow to reservoirs 1 and 2, respectively, variables $v_1$ and $v_2$ are the volume contents of reservoirs 1 and 2, respectively, at the end of the study period, variables $t_1$ and $t_2$ are the volumes discharged by reservoir 1 and 2, respectively, during the study period, and variables $s_1$ and $s_2$ are the volumes spilled by reservoir 1 and 2, respectively, during the study period.

The objective function is the value of the water content at the end of the study period ($20(v_1+v_2)$) minus the cost of spilling water ($15(s_1+s_2)$) minus the cost of the initial reservoir contents ($10x_1 + 12x_2$).

The first-level subproblem of problem (8.5.1) sets the initial reservoir contents $x_1$ and $x_2$ seeking to maximize the objective function (water content value), anticipating the worst water inflow realization (materialized through variables $w_1$ and $w_2$) as determined by the second-level subproblem of problem (8.5.1) (which seeks to minimize the objective function), which in turn anticipates the best operator reaction (through variables $t_1$ and $t_2$) seeking to maximize the objective function as determined by the third-level subproblem of problem (8.5.1). The constraints of the third-level subproblem include an energy supply equality, two water balance equalities (for reservoirs 1 and 2), and four volume bounds, two per reservoir.

Since this example is very simple, it can be solved by enumeration. Eight alternative are possible:

1. Water contents of reservoir 1 and 2, 1 and 1, respectively; and water inflows to reservoirs 1 and 2, 1 and 2 respectively.
2. Water contents of reservoir 1 and 2, 1 and 1, respectively; and water inflows to reservoirs 1 and 2, 1 and 6 respectively.
3. Water contents of reservoir 1 and 2, 1 and 1, respectively; and water inflows to reservoirs 1 and 2, 8 and 2 respectively.
4. Water contents of reservoir 1 and 2, 1 and 1, respectively; and water inflows to reservoirs 1 and 2, 8 and 6 respectively.
5. Water contents of reservoir 1 and 2, 1 and 4, respectively; and water inflows to reservoirs 1 and 2, 1 and 2 respectively.

6. Water contents of reservoir 1 and 2, 1 and 4, respectively; and water inflows to reservoirs 1 and 2, 1 and 6 respectively.
7. Water contents of reservoir 1 and 2, 1 and 4, respectively; and water inflows to reservoirs 1 and 2, 8 and 2 respectively.
8. Water contents of reservoir 1 and 2, 1 and 4, respectively; and water inflows to reservoirs 1 and 2, 8 and 6 respectively.

The problem of alternative 1 is:

$$
\begin{aligned}
\min_{\substack{v_1,t_1,s_1\geq 0\\ v_2,t_2,s_2\geq 0}} \quad & z = 20(v_1+v_2) - 15(s_1+s_2) - 10\cdot 1 - 12\cdot 1\\
\text{s.t.} \quad & \tfrac{1}{2}t_1 + \tfrac{1}{2}t_2 = 2\\
& 1+1-t_1-s_1 = v_1\\
& 1+2+t_1-t_2-s_2 = v_2\\
& 1 \leq v_1 \leq 2\\
& 1 \leq v_2 \leq 4.
\end{aligned}
$$

The problem for the other seven alternatives can be similarly formulated. The solutions for all of them are provide in Table 8.1.

From Table 8.1 we observe the following:

1. If the planner (through the first-level subproblem) selects $x_1 = 1$ and $x_2 = 1$, the second-level subproblem identifies $w_1 = 8$ and $w_2 = 6$ as the uncertainty outcomes that minimize the objective function (future water value) through the third-level subproblem, resulting in a value of $z = 0.5$.
2. If, on the other hand, the planner selects (through the first-level subproblem) $x_1 = 1$ and $x_2 = 4$, the second-level subproblem identifies $w_1 = 8$ and $w_2 = 6$ as the uncertainty outcomes that minimize the objective function (future water value) through the third-level subproblem, resulting in a value of $z = -73$.

Since the planner ultimately pursues maximizing the objective function (future water value), it selects $x_1^* = 1$ and $x_2^* = 1$, which under the worst uncertainty outcome ($w_1^* = 8$ and $w_2^* = 6$) results in an objection function value of $z^* = 0.5$.

**Table 8.1** Hydro scheduling: Alternative problems

| # | 1 | 2 | 3 | 4 | 5 | 6 | 7 | 8 |
|---|---|---|---|---|---|---|---|---|
| $x_1$ | 1 | 1 | 1 | 1 | 1 | 1 | 1 | 1 |
| $x_2$ | 1 | 1 | 1 | 1 | 4 | 4 | 4 | 4 |
| $w_1$ | 1 | 1 | 8 | 8 | 1 | 1 | 8 | 8 |
| $w_2$ | 2 | 6 | 2 | 6 | 2 | 6 | 2 | 6 |
| $z$ | 18 | 88 | 30.5 | 0.5 | 42 | 32 | −28 | −73 |

### 8.5.2 General Formulation

A general enough ARO formulation of the long-term hydroelectric scheduling is provided below.

$$\begin{aligned}
\max_{x_i \in \Omega_i, \forall i} \quad \min_{w_{it} \in \Lambda_i, \forall i \; \forall t} \quad \max_{\substack{v_{it} \geq 0, \forall i \; \forall t \\ t_{it} \geq 0, \forall i \; \forall t \\ s_{it} \geq 0, \forall i \; \forall t}} \quad & z = C^{\mathrm{F}} \sum_{i=1}^{n_{\mathrm{R}}} v_{i,n_{\mathrm{T}}} - C^{\mathrm{S}} \sum_{i=1}^{n_{\mathrm{R}}} \sum_{t=1}^{n_{\mathrm{T}}} s_{i,t} - \sum_{i=1}^{n_{\mathrm{R}}} C_i^{\mathrm{I}} x_i \\
\text{s.t.} \quad & \sum_{i=1}^{n_{\mathrm{R}}} \rho_i t_{it} = d_t, \forall t \\
& v_{it} = v_{i,t-1} + w_{it} - t_{it} - s_{it} + \sum_{j \in \Delta_i} t_{jt}, \forall i \; \forall t \\
& v_i^{\min} \leq v_{it} \leq v_i^{\max}, \forall i \; \forall t \\
& t_i^{\min} \leq t_{it} \leq t_i^{\max}, \forall i \; \forall t,
\end{aligned} \tag{8.5.2}$$

where the optimization variables are:

- $x_i$ is the initial contents of reservoir $i$.
- $w_{it}$ is a variable representing the uncertain inflow to reservoir $i$ in time period $t$.
- $v_{it}$ is the volume of reservoir $i$ at the beginning of time period $t$.
- $t_{it}$ is the volume turbined from reservoir $i$ in time period $t$.
- $s_{it}$ is the volume spilled from reservoir $i$ in time period $t$.

The constants, sets, numbers and selected indices are:

- $C^{\mathrm{F}}$ is the future value of water.
- $C^{\mathrm{S}}$ is the cost penalty for water spilling.
- $C_i^{\mathrm{F}}$ is the current water value at reservoir $i$.
- $d_t$ is the electric demand in time period $t$.
- $\rho_i$ is the conversion ratio water volume to electrical energy of the electric power unit at reservoir $i$.
- $v_i^{\min}$ is the minimum content of reservoir $i$.
- $v_i^{\max}$ is the capacity of reservoir $i$.
- $t_i^{\min}$ is the minimum volume that can be turbined from reservoir $i$.
- $t_i^{\max}$ is the turbining capacity of reservoir $i$.
- $\Omega_i$ is the set of possible initial volume contents of reservoir $i$.
- $\Lambda_i$ is a robust set describing inflows to reservoir $i$ throughout the study horizon.
- $\Delta_i$ is the set of reservoirs directly upstream of reservoir $i$.
- $n_{\mathrm{R}}$ is the number of reservoirs.
- $n_{\mathrm{T}}$ is the number of time periods.

The first-level subproblem of problem (8.5.2) selects the initial reservoir levels to maximize the future water content value, anticipating the worst inflow realization throughout the planning horizon (that entails minimum future water content value) as determined by the second-level subproblem of problem (8.5.2), which in turn anticipates the best operator reaction pursuing maximum future water content value while supplying the electric demand by solving the third-level subproblem of problem (8.5.2). The constraints of the third-level subproblem include electric demand supply equality per time period, water balance equality per reservoir and time period, water content bounds per reservoir and time period, and turbining bounds per reservoir and time period.

Problem (8.5.2) is an ARO model that can be solved using the methodology presented in Chap. 3.

## 8.6 Concluding Remarks

This chapter describes four long-term decision-making problems under uncertainty that can be formulated and solved using adaptive robust optimization. These problems are:

1. Generation expansion planning.
2. Generation and transmission expansion planning.
3. Transmission expansion planning.
4. Hydroelectric scheduling.

Pursuing clarity and simplicity, each of these four problems is formulated retaining solely the key elements that make it amenable to be tackled via adaptive robust optimization.

Simple examples that can be solved by inspection are then used to illustrate these problems.

Complex instances of these formulation can be solved using the ARO algorithms comprehensively described in Chap. 3.

## 8.7 End-of-Chapter Exercises

**8.1** Reformulate and solve the generation expansion planning illustrative example in Sect. 8.2.1 to consider a 2-area power system with a binding transmission constraint between the two areas.

**8.2** Reformulate and solve the generation expansion planning illustrative example in Sect. 8.2.1 to consider a reduced number of representative time periods (e.g., 10), not $365 \times 24$. How should these representative time periods be selected?

**8.3** Reformulate and solve the generation and transmission expansion planning illustrative example in Sect. 8.3.1 to consider that generation units and/or transmission lines can be built.

**8.4** Reformulate and solve the transmission expansion planning illustrative example in Sect. 8.4.1 to consider 4 nodes and the possibility of reinforcing any number of lines.

**8.5** Reformulate and solve the hydroelectric scheduling illustrative example in Sect. 8.5.1 to consider three reservoirs, where reservoirs 1 and 2 are directly upstream of reservoir 3.

**8.6** Reformulate and solve the hydroelectric scheduling illustrative example in Sect. 8.5.1 to consider a time horizon involving 2 time periods, not just 1.

## References


1. Dehghan, S., Amjady, N., & Kazemi, A. (2014). Two-stage robust generation expansion planning: A mixed integer linear programming model. *IEEE Transactions on Power Systems*, *29*(2), 584–597.
2. Gil, E., Aravena, I., & Cardenas, R. (2015). Generation capacity expansion planning under hydro uncertainty using stochastic mixed integer programming and scenario reduction. *IEEE Transactions on Power Systems*, *30*(4), 1838–1847.
3. Hua, B., Baldick, R., & Wang, J. (2018). Representing operational flexibility in generation expansion planning through convex relaxation of unit commitment. *IEEE Transactions on Power Systems*, *33*(2), 2272–2281.
4. Jin, S., Botterud, A., & Ryan, S. M. (2014). Temporal versus stochastic granularity in thermal generation capacity planning with wind power. *IEEE Transactions on Power Systems*, *29*(5), 2033–2041.
5. Rashidaee, S. A., Amraee, T., & Fotuhi-Firuzabad, M. (2018). A linear model for dynamic generation expansion planning considering loss of load probability. *IEEE Transactions on Power Systems*, *33*(6), 6924–6934.
6. Zhan, Y., Zheng, Q. P., Wang, J., & Pinson, P. (2017). Generation expansion planning with large amounts of wind power via decision-dependent stochastic programming. *IEEE Transactions on Power Systems*, *32*(4), 3015–3026.
7. Zhang, X., & Conejo, A. J. (2018). Coordinated investment in transmission and storage systems representing long- and short-term uncertainty. *IEEE Transactions on Power Systems*, *33*(6), 7143–7151.
8. Baringo, L., & Baringo, A. (2018). A stochastic adaptive robust optimization approach for the generation and transmission expansion planning. *IEEE Transactions on Power Systems*, *33*(1), 792–802.
9. Li, J., et al. (2018). Robust coordinated transmission and generation expansion planning considering ramping requirements and construction periods. *IEEE Transactions on Power Systems*, *33*(1), 268–280.
10. Chen, B., & Wang, L. (2016). Robust transmission planning under uncertain generation investment and retirement. *IEEE Transactions on Power Systems*, *31*(6), 5144–5152.
11. Jabr, R. A. (2013). Robust transmission network expansion planning with uncertain renewable generation and loads. *IEEE Transactions on Power Systems*, *28*(4), 4558–4567.
12. Dehghan, S., Amjady, N., Conejo, A. J. (2018). A multistage robust transmission expansion planning model based on mixed binary linear decision rules—Part I. *IEEE Transactions on Power Systems*, *33*(5), 5341–5350.
13. Dehghan, S., Amjady, N., Conejo, A. J. (2018). A multistage robust transmission expansion planning model based on mixed-binary linear decision rules—Part II. *IEEE Transactions on Power Systems*, *33*(5), 5351–5364.

14. Zhang, X., & Conejo, A. J. (2018). Robust transmission expansion planning representing long- and short-term uncertainty. *IEEE Transactions on Power Systems*, *33*(2), 1329–1338.
15. Dehghan, S., Amjady, N., & Conejo, A. J. (2017). Adaptive robust transmission expansion planning using linear decision rules. *IEEE Transactions on Power Systems*, *32*(5), 4024–4034.
16. Chen, B., Wang, J., Wang, L., He, Y., & Wang, Z. (2014). Robust optimization for transmission expansion planning: minimax cost vs. minimax regret. *IEEE Transactions on Power Systems*, *29*(6), 3069–3077.
17. Yu, H., Chung, C. Y., & Wong, K. P. (2011). Robust transmission network expansion planning method with Taguchi's orthogonal array testing. *IEEE Transactions on Power Systems*, *26*(3), 1573–1580.
18. Oliveira, G. C., Binato, S., & Pereira, M. V. F. (2007). Value-based transmission expansion planning of hydrothermal systems under uncertainty. *IEEE Transactions on Power Systems*, *22*(4), 1429–1435.
19. Moreno, R., Ferreira, R., Barroso, L., Rudnick, H., & Pereira, E. (2017). Facilitating the integration of renewables in Latin America: The role of hydropower generation and other energy storage technologies. *IEEE Power and Energy Magazine*, *15*(5), 68–80.
20. Fortin, P. (2008). Canadian clean. *IEEE Power and Energy Magazine*, *6*(4), 40–46.
21. Blyden, B. K., & Akiwumi, F. A. (2008). Unrealized potential in Africa. *IEEE Power and Energy Magazine*, *6*(4), 52–58.
22. Ciocci, L. C. (2008). Keeping water in the U.S. mix. *IEEE Power and Energy Magazine*, *6*(4), 36–39.
23. Fu, S., & Zhong, J. (2008). Hydropower in China. *IEEE Power and Energy Magazine*, *6*(4), 47–51.
24. Zhou, B., Geng, G., & Jiang, Q. (2016). Hydro-thermal-wind coordination in day-ahead unit commitment. *IEEE Transactions on Power Systems*, *31*(6), 4626–4637.
25. Chen, Y., Liu, F., Liu, B., Wei, W., & Mei, S. (2016). An efficient MILP approximation for the hydro-thermal unit commitment. *IEEE Transactions on Power Systems*, *31*(4), 3318–3319.
26. Martins, L. S. A., Azevedo, A. T., & Soares, S. (2014). Nonlinear medium-term hydro-thermal scheduling with transmission constraints. *IEEE Transactions on Power Systems*, *29*(4), 1623–1633.
27. Baslis, C. G., Papadakis, S. E., & Bakirtzis, A. G. (2009). Simulation of optimal medium-term hydro-thermal system operation by grid computing. *IEEE Transactions on Power Systems*, *24*(3), 1208–1217.
28. Li, T., & Shahidehpour, M. (2005). Price-based unit commitment: a case of Lagrangian relaxation versus mixed integer programming. *IEEE Transactions on Power Systems*, *20*(4), 2015–2025.

# Index





X. A. Sun, A. J. Conejo, *Robust Optimization in Electric Energy Systems*,
International Series in Operations Research & Management Science 313,
https://doi.org/10.1007/978-3-030-85128-6

Printed by Printforce, United Kingdom